# Victorian
# *Social Life*

## British social history 1815–1914

**Jane** *Jenkins*
with **Eric** *Evans*

Series Editor: *Ian Coulson*

JOHN MURRAY

## Other books in this series:

*The English Revolution* by Barry Coward and Chris Durston 0 7195 7221 5
*Hitler's Germany* by Jane Jenkins with Edgar Feuchtwanger   0 7195 8554 6

**N.B.** The source questions directly follow the sources they relate to, which enables students to undertake in-depth analysis of the sources. Each set of questions is separately numbered and can refer to one source or to several.

© Jane Jenkins with Eric Evans, 2002

First published in 2002
by John Murray (Publishers) Ltd
50 Albemarle Street
London W1S 4BD

Layouts by Black Dog Design
Artwork by Mike Humphries
Typeset in Gill Sans by Wearset Ltd, Boldon, Tyne and Wear
Printed and bound in Spain by Bookprint, S. L., Barcelona

A catalogue entry for this title is available from the British Library

ISBN 0 7195 7725 X

# Contents

## Photo credits

## List of maps

## List of diagrams (including tables)

## List of illustrations

**Source 2.53** From a series of drawings, 1842:
a) A young girl draws coal
b) Women and girls haul coal to the surface c) A trapper
**Source 2.57** *The Sweater's Furnace: or, the real 'Curse' of labour*, an etching by Linley Sambourne from *Punch*, 1888

**Source 3.6** *A Court For King Cholera*, a cartoon from *Punch*, 25 September 1852
**Source 3.27** *Sanatory Measures. Lord Morpeth Throwing Pearls Before Aldermen*, a cartoon from *Punch*, 1848
**Source 3.40** *Father Thames Introducing his Offspring to the Fair City of London*, a cartoon from *Punch*, July 1858

**Source 4.28** Portrait of Thomas Malthus

**Source 5.15** Sampson Kempthorne's 'Y' plan of a workhouse and an aerial view of the Andover workhouse
**Source 5.16** *Interior of an English workhouse under the New Poor Law Act*, 1837, Public Records Office
**Source 5.20** *Oliver Twist Asks for More*, a book illustration by George Cruikshank, 1838
**Source 5.25** *An Attack on the Workhouse at Stockport*, a drawing from *Illustrated London News*, August 1842
**Source 5.32** Cartoon on the Andover scandal, from the *Penny Satirist*, 6 September 1845
**Source 5.39** a) *A Quaker soup kitchen*, from the *Illustrated London News*, 1862
b) *Refuge for the Destitute*, from the *Illustrated London News*, 1843

**Source 5.51** A photograph of St Pancras Workhouse, London, 1895

**Page 193** David Lloyd George
**Source 6.4** *Rich Fare*, a cartoon from *Punch*, 28 April 1909
**Source 6.39** *Forced Fellowship*, a cartoon from *Punch*, 27 October 1909
**Source 6.51** *The New Year's Gift*, a cartoon from *Punch*, 6 January 1909

**Source 7.23** *A Physical Force Chartist Arming For The Fight*, a cartoon from *Punch Volume 15*, 1848
**Source 7.45** *The Chartist procession according to the signatures of the Petition*, a cartoon from *Punch Volume 14*, April 1848

**Source 8.31** a) *Needle Money* b) *Pin Money*, cartoons from *Punch*, 15 July 1849
**Source 8.47** *Polling Booth Companions in Disgrace*, from the Artists' Suffrage League
**Source 8.53** *A Suffragette's Home*, from the National League for Opposing Woman Suffrage, 1912
**Source 8.62** *The Modern Inquisition – Treatment of Political Prisoners under a Liberal Government*, from a WSPU poster

**Source 9.28** *Who shall educate? Or, Our babes in the wood*, a cartoon from *Punch*, 23 April 1853
**Source 9.43** *Obstructives*, an etching from *Punch*, 2 July 1870

# Advice on answering source-based questions

AS and Advanced level students are required to analyse, evaluate, interpret and use historical sources of different kinds appropriate to the period studied. Students' evidential skills will be tested by a question based on one or several sources, which will focus on comprehension, drawing out information relevant to a specific question, cross-referencing, evaluation, analysis and reaching judgements. The question strategy employed in this book provides opportunities to develop these skills.

A wide variety of sources are available for studying social conditions in Victorian England – the reports of various Children's Employment Commissions, reports by government-appointed inspectors, reports of Commissions of Enquiry, Acts of Parliament, speeches in Parliament, minutes of meetings, parish records, census records, trade directories, personal accounts, autobiographies, local newspapers, pamphlets, statistics, diaries, letters, contemporary cartoons, and novels with a social commentary, particularly those by Charles Dickens.

There are a number of questions to consider when studying a historical source:

- What type of source is it?
- Who produced it and why? Authorship is important because we need to know whether the person was in a position to give an informed opinion and what sort of bias/prejudice we might expect to find in the writer.
- Was the author present at the event described or does s/he have first-hand experience of the situation commented upon?
- When was it written?
- What was the aim or purpose of it?
- In what context was the source produced?
- What information does it contain?
- What historical questions might it help to answer?
- What can it *not* tell me?
- Are there any other supporting sources I would need to consult to make sense of this source?
- Is it biased or objective? Bias can be introduced through various means: obvious prejudice, loaded language, omission or selection of facts, or unwitting bias through not having all of the available information. A biased source is not necessarily unreliable; often a source biased in one direction may include material which can be used to argue against the author's case. People's opinions or feelings are often gained from a very biased point of view or propaganda. Consciously-biased sources will tend to omit or distort only those points that their authors recognise as sensitive, and once this is detected the source will become more reliable in some respects than in others. Historians can take account of bias by establishing whether the suggested facts fit in with other known facts. The historian needs to balance a large number of sources one against the other. Bias or prejudice of the author is an important element in the historian's attempt to establish the reliability of a source.
- What emotions, feelings or attitudes does it show?
- How reliable is the source? Reliability can be tested by considering issues of authorship, motivation, bias, obvious prejudice and the purpose for which the historian employs the source.
- How useful is the source for a historian?

Always read the source extracts slowly and carefully to make sure that you understand them. In examinations, each sub-question will carry a maximum mark. This will indicate how much you are expected to write and the amount of time you should devote to each sub-question. The number of marks builds up so that the last question usually carries the highest mark.

## Strategy for answering source-based questions

| Skill being tested | Approach to answering the question |
|---|---|
| **Understanding of the content of the source** 'What can you learn from this source about…?' This might lead you to a **contextual follow-up question** requiring you to 'Use your own knowledge to explain…' or to a **cross-referencing of sources**: 'To what extent do A and B agree about how to explain the significance of C?' | **Use your comprehension skills** to show an understanding of the meaning of a source or group of sources. When you are asked to compare two sources look for similarity and difference in content. You might be asked to draw conclusions based directly on what is written, which is a comprehension skill. Or you might be asked to work out or 'infer' an attitude or position. This will require you to read between the lines. |
| **Analysis of the significance of authorship of a source** – this is sometimes referred to as the 'provenance' of a source. 'Use your own knowledge to identify the author of Sources I and 4 and explain why he was important to the reform of the Old Poor Law.' | **Discuss the importance of the author** – was the author in an important or obscure position? Are the views expressed representative of others or entirely the author's own? A person's social/economic position might well be relevant, for example an aristocrat is not really in a position to give reliable information on working-class feelings. The importance of authorship is that it is relevant for assessing the value and limitations of a source to historians. Build up profiles of the authors of major texts, such as Engels, Chadwick and Dickens. |
| **Assessment of the significance of sources in terms of the attitude(s) revealed** 'Compare the value of Sources I and 2 to a historian enquiring into A's attitude to B.' | **Examine use of language, tone and argument**, which help to reveal the presence of bias and indicate attitudes. One of the clues to identifying bias is to decide whether the information has been selected to give a particular perspective, either through a deliberate intention to distort or an unconsciously expressed viewpoint, which is natural bias, or because of poor memory, or rumour. There is also bias by omission. Material might be omitted to avoid contradicting the writer's point of view or because the writer is being 'economical with the truth'. No deliberate falsehood is intended, but the writer has prejudged the conclusion s/he wishes the reader to draw. |
| **Assessment of the usefulness or reliability of a source** 'How reliable are Sources I and 2 as evidence about how the Poor Law worked before 1834?' | **Discuss the criteria for establishing reliability** – reliable for what purpose? How consistent? This can involve cross-referencing with other sources. People's opinions and feelings are often gained only from a very biased point of view or propaganda. Reliability is concerned with authenticity based on authorship, motivation, bias, and the purpose for which a historian uses the source. |

**Evaluation of the source for value, limitations, significance, and completeness, and in terms of how satisfactory it is.**
'Assess the value of Sources 3 and 4 to a historian studying the factory reform campaign in the years 1840–51.'

**Show a critical awareness of style, language and the presence of truths and/or falsehoods.** Questions that ask you to evaluate can mean a number of things: you might be asked to distinguish between fact, opinion and/or judgement (opinion is a view put forward without factual support, judgement has factual substance). Or, you might be asked to recognise deficiencies in the material as evidence.

**Value and limitation** are assessed in terms of authorship. Remember that the presence of bias does not mean a source does not have value or reliability. A biased source will tend to be inaccurate only on those points that the author recognises as sensitive. A source biased in one direction may still include material that is of value.

**The importance** of a source to historians is based on how it might be used by a historian. Is it vital or just a side issue? Is there more than 'meets the eye'?

Assessing the **completeness** of a source involves considering what is said and what has been left out.

Evaluating how **satisfactory** a source is involves a consideration of questions left unanswered, gaps and/or inconsistencies.

**Synthesise information in the sources as well as applying your own knowledge.**

**Ability to arrive at a judgement**
'Using the information contained in Sources 2 and 3 and your own knowledge, how far do you agree with the claim that "in the period 1830–1914 governments adopted an increasingly informed and understanding attitude towards the causes of poverty"?'

## Some guidelines for establishing reliability, bias and value in different types of source

| State or government records | Newspapers | Letters/diaries | Cartoons and posters |
|---|---|---|---|
| • Are the sources censored?<br>• Are they for public view?<br>• Are they arguing a predetermined political viewpoint? | • Is the newspaper censored?<br>• Does the editor hold a particular political viewpoint?<br>• Are facts or opinions given? | • Why were the letters or diaries written? Were they intended for public consumption?<br>• Letters often contain information not provided elsewhere.<br>• Attitudes of the writer can be identified.<br>• Diaries can reveal attitudes and character insights, a way of life, important events, and people.<br>• Diaries of politicians should be treated with care because they are usually intended for publication so run the risk of distortion/bias. | • Do they give a particular point of view?<br>• Are they intended to influence people?<br>• What attitudes do they show?<br>• Are they propaganda? |

# Preface

## Historians' assessments of British society in the nineteenth century

**by Eric Evans**

### A historian's journey

In a way I have lived with the Victorians for most of my life. Like many British historians from my era, however, I came to them first as an undergraduate through studying their political leaders, particularly Peel, Gladstone and Disraeli. At that stage my historical study, like that of many of my contemporaries, was concerned with a very narrow social stratum. It was dominated by the story of rulers, monarchs, barons, constitutions and, latterly, elections. I knew much less about the societies over which the rulers presided.

When I began to do my own historical research I changed universities and I also quickly changed perspectives. My research supervisor, Edward Thompson, was one of the great social historians of the twentieth century. His interest was in the *relationships of power*. How did people acquire power over others and, more important to him, what did they do with that power? His powerful figures were not necessarily national rulers. They might be large landowners who saw themselves as the natural, hereditary leaders of rural society, or they might be factory owners in the early Industrial Revolution, concerned with the business of making profits. For Thompson, the key thing was the relationship between the powerful and the powerless. He believed that in the late eighteenth and early nineteenth centuries this relationship was increasingly dominated by class.

His most influential, and probably his greatest, book, *The Making of the English Working Class*, was first published in 1963. It is about the struggles for power between the articulate, and increasingly angry, working classes and their masters – factory owners, landowners or the British state itself.

Thompson was a Marxist historian, and interested in class relationships. However, he utterly rejected simplified and rigid notions of class conflict held by those Marxists who said that the all-important determining factor was people's relationship to 'the means of production'. For these Marxists, the aristocracy (whose income largely came from the rent which they obtained from those who worked their land), the middle class (whose income largely came from making profits) and the working class (who had no property of their own but were forced to make their living by selling their labour to an employer) were locked in inevitable struggle. Thompson rejected this 'economic' model of social relationships. He denied that class was a static thing. 'The working class', he said, 'did not rise like the sun at an appointed time. It was present at its own making.'

### 'History from below'

Thompson's book was one of the formative influences on my professional life. He gave me an insight into what became known as 'history from below'. It was an immense privilege to work with him, partly for the invigorating insights he provided, but also because he loved argument and debate and actively encouraged his students to disagree with him. Through working with Thompson, I gained the best possible practical experience of how historical ideas and interpretations are generated and of how to develop the confidence to express my own ideas. He advocated a process of study, reflection and then active debate with others (who are also encouraged to be sceptical) so that original positions are refined to become both more subtle and more persuasive.

Thompson's reputation, which was created almost overnight with the appearance of his big book, encouraged other scholars and research students to work with him. Together, they created an invigorating intellectual climate which determined the direction of my own career, and my own research, which has concentrated on British political and social history of the eighteenth and nineteenth centuries.

Some of the debates which I and my Warwick history students discovered together in the mid-1960s seem distinctly dated now. Far fewer historians would nowadays accept, at least without severe qualification, that class was the dominant organising social category in the early nineteenth century. We are now much more sensitive to the multiple identities which we share. Thus, class identity might dominate in some contexts and at some times. But equally, regional identity, workplace culture and – perhaps most important of all – gender might claim pride of place at other times. Thompson's book, however, rightly retains a central place on reading lists. Recent historiography has hardly seen the English working class 'unmade'.

## The central paradox

My engagement with these and other issues made me increasingly curious about the development of British society in the late eighteenth and nineteenth centuries. I became interested in what many have seen as a central paradox. Why was it that Britain, a country committed to policies of free trade and low taxation, developed from the 1830s new and significant forms of state intervention and central bureaucracies to administer factory legislation; a radically reformed poor law; and public health policy? This was the focus of my early research (E. J. Evans (ed.), *Social Policy, c.1830–1914* (Routledge and Kegan Paul, 1978)). Since then I have never strayed far from these issues which integrate the social and political histories of the period.

# Interpretations of the Victorians

What words and images do people link with the word 'Victorian'? On the positive side, the following are likely: 'industry', 'progress', 'Empire', 'moral', 'earnest', 'serious-minded', 'duty' and 'religious'.

## Industrial progress and success

For much of the Victorian period, Britain was the world's leading power. As the first country to experience an industrial revolution its manufactured goods were cheaper than those of its rivals. Its innovators were admired around the world. Victorian railway engineers laid iron rails in four continents, thus helping to produce a huge revolution in communications and opportunities for economic growth. Their feats were eagerly copied worldwide.

One of the greatest engineers of the period, William George Armstrong (1810–1900), made a massive fortune out of hydraulic engineering at his Elswick works on the banks of the River Tyne in Newcastle. He used part of this fortune to create in the 1880s a massive modern mansion some fifty kilometres away in the spectacular Northumberland countryside. Working with the Scottish architect Richard Norman Shaw (1831–1912), he designed 'Cragside' to reflect all of the benefits of modern technology. Here was found the new-fangled electric lighting powered by a Siemens dynamo-electric generator. Victorian material progress enabled a successful businessman like Armstrong to enjoy the life and status of a country gentleman. His story was spectacular but it was not atypical.

## The Empire

The Victorians created the largest empire the world had ever seen. By the 1860s, it covered 9.5 million square miles and included almost 150 million people, the vast majority of them living in India, a sub-continent over which Britain had been extending its control for two centuries. After frantic activity in the last quarter of the nineteenth century another 2 million square miles were added – mostly in Africa – and when Queen Victoria's grandson, George V, came to the throne in 1910, he was ruling over 410 million people. Truly, Britain's was the Empire on which the sun never set.

For many it was also the ultimate symbol of Victorian progress. The British Prime Minister, Benjamin Disraeli, had created a new title for Victoria in 1876: 'Empress of India'. It was one of the most inspired examples of image-making or, as we might now call it, 'spin'. Victoria had been an unpopular monarch in the 1860s and 1870s, inclined to spend indulgent amounts of time at her Scottish estate of Balmoral, and neglecting her public duties as she maintained a quite spectacularly long period of mourning for the death of her beloved Prince Albert. Now she could be marketed as the Queen-Empress, the symbol of a successful, self-confident and expanding nation. The golden and diamond jubilees of 1887 and 1897 became excuses for huge pageants and processions. For those less inclined to celebrate – and they were in a small minority – they were occasions of mawkishly indulgent and uncritical self-congratulation.

For 'imperialists', the Empire was not primarily about land-grabbing or an arrogant act of insensitive accumulation that trampled and exploited people whose lands were now declared 'British'. This negative image of empire is one which became fashionable in the second half of the twentieth century, as most of the old imperial territories, not just of Britain but of France, Germany, Portugal and Belgium, gained their independence. Many in the old colonial nations nowadays are inclined to apologise for their imperial past. This is an attitude which would have staggered those who lived through the period. For many of them, good government of a large empire was a high moral duty. The British, as the world's most advanced nation, should show that they intended to use those much-trumpeted virtues of morality, duty and self-reliance to make the world (or at least those large parts of it over which they now ruled) a better place.

## Self-help

There was a strong feeling that earnestness and attention to duty would bring success. Since industrial Britain was a land of new opportunities and much new wealth, in theory at least, opportunities were limitless. The other side of the coin was obvious: if people did not succeed, then their failures must be explained by personal, or family, shortcomings. Perhaps fittingly, Samuel Smiles, a Scottish writer much influenced by the power of education and self-discipline, made a fortune by encapsulating key articles of Victorian faith in two major works entitled *Self-Help* (1859) and *Thrift* (1875).

● **SOURCE 1**

From Samuel Smiles, *Self-Help*, 1859.

*'Heaven helps those who helps themselves' is a well-tried maxim, embodying . . . the results of vast human experience. The spirit of self-help is the root of all genuine growth in the individual and, exhibited in the lives of the many, it constitutes the true source of national vigour and strength. Help from without is often enfeebling in its effects, but help from within invariably invigorates. Whatever is done for men of classes, to a certain extent takes away the stimulus and necessity of doing for themselves . . .*

*National progress is the sum of individual industry, energy and uprightness, as national decay is of individual idleness, selfishness and vice . . . The highest patriotism and philanthropy consists, not so much in altering laws and modifying institutions, as in helping and stimulating men to elevate and improve themselves by their own free and independent individual action.*

## Social problems

7

There is another interpretation of the Victorian era. Words people might typically associate with the downside of Victorian Britain include 'dirt', 'disease', 'smoke', 'dark', 'grimy', 'hypocrisy', 'inequality' and 'exploitation'.

It is worth mentioning at the outset that contemporaries were far from insensitive to the enormous social problems surrounding them. Victorians both worried and wondered at the paradox that creating wealth in the world's most advanced towns and cities seemed to necessitate desperate living conditions for the large numbers who were drawn to them by the prospect of work. In 1835 the French historian and politician Alexis de Tocqueville visited Manchester – the centre of the cotton trade, which was the first industry to be revolutionised by machinery and factory production. Source 2 is his description of the town in mid-summer.

● **SOURCE 2**

A. de Tocqueville, *Voyage en Angleterre et en Irlande*, 2 July 1835.

*It is from the midst of this putrid sewer that the greatest river of human industry springs up and carries fertility to the whole world. From this foul drain pure gold flows forth. Here it is that humanity achieves for itself both perfection and brutalisation, that civilisation produces its wonders, and that civilised man becomes again almost a savage.*

From the 1830s, medical men led the way in pointing out not only the connection between dirt and disease, but also how these affected the habits of the people. The debate launched by Dr James P. Kay (see Chapter 3) would be repeatedly argued well into the twentieth century. The poor would breed much faster than the respectable propertied classes and probably faster than the nation could grow the food to keep them alive. This breeding would produce 'poor-quality' humanity. They would eat up the nation's resources, driving even the 'better quality' down and creating a pauper sub-class which would drain away all the wealth of the nation.

The Victorians increasingly saw society as being divided into 'respectables' (the majority) and 'roughs' (the dangerous minority). This was no crude division of class. Working men, for example, could be in either category. It was more about behaviour, attitudes and values.

Those who could not (or, as many Victorians said, would not) 'get on' by hard work, thrift and sturdy self-reliance, tended to be stigmatised as 'the dangerous classes' – people without regular work and lacking the will or the incentive to make the Victorian economic miracle work for them. In popular imagination, at least, they ignored the law, bred too fast and challenged respectability at every point. They drifted threateningly on the fringes of society. Tackling crime was a high priority. Following the establishment of metropolitan and county police forces in 1829 and 1839, the number of police increased rapidly. In the forty years from 1851 to 1891 (and further stimulated by a borough police act in 1859), police numbers almost trebled and the number of indictable offences almost halved (V. A. C. Gatrell, 'The Decline of Theft and Violence in Victorian and Edwardian England', in V. A. C. Gatrell, B. Lenman and G. Parker (eds), *Crime and Law: the Social History of Crime in Western Europe since 1500* (Cambridge University Press, 1980), pp. 282–3).

The outward self-confidence of the industrial, imperial world power was only skin deep and the ambivalence of many contemporary assessments is easy to understand. So too is the Victorians' ambivalence over how to tackle social problems. Free trade and low government taxation were considered essential. How could such policies, which were designed (with apparent success) to increase wealth, be reconciled with the need to intervene to limit the worst effects of unrestrained capitalism? This was a central paradox for the Victorians and remains one for historians seeking to understand them.

Preface

# Historical debates 1: the factory question

There are many more specific areas of study which have interested historians. I am going to look briefly at two of the most common to give a flavour of the debates.

The factory reform movement is a key element in any study of social conditions in nineteenth-century Britain. Historians have studied the stages by which effective (that is, government-inspected) factory reform came about and then spread. It has long been known that the factory reform campaign was no simple struggle between 'good' humanitarian reformers and 'bad' factory owners who wished to see no limits to their power to 'manage', or exploit, their workforce. After all, some of the most important factory campaigners, like Sir Robert Peel, whose son became prime minister, were factory owners themselves. They knew that a healthy workforce working reasonable hours was more likely to be both stable and more profitable for them (see, for example, E. J. Evans, *The Forging of the Modern State: Early Industrial Britain, 1783–1870* (3rd edn, Longman Pearson, 2001), pp. 239–42). However, historians have recently been trying to understand what factory reform meant both for the campaigners and for those who allegedly benefited from government protection after 1833. Some important and surprising conclusions have emerged.

One recent study has attacked the easy use of the term 'Tory humanitarians' to describe a group of factory reformers motivated by the desire to attack industrial capitalism and to assert the pre-eminence of the landowners. Some, like Richard Oastler, were indeed Tories committed to the Church of England and the monarchy. They were fervent opponents of extending the vote to working people. Oastler attacked both the Whigs and their allies in the commercial classes and produced a memorable series of attacks on the new Poor Law of 1834 (see Chapter 5) in the journal he largely wrote from prison, the *Fleet Papers*. But not all humanitarian reformers were Tories. One of the most significant of them, John Fielden of Todmorden, denied being a Tory at all and instead asserted that 'every man of sane mind, of twenty-one years of age, and untainted by crime, should have a voice in the choice of those who are to make the laws under which he is to be governed'.

● **SOURCE 3**

From S. A. Weaver, *John Fielden and the Politics of Popular Radicalism, 1832–1847*, 1987.

*This simple, democratic principle underlay his every radical involvement. He thought of the Ten Hours Act [see Chapter 2] in terms less of paternal benevolence than political obligation. Poor relief, a short working day – all these were to Fielden wholly inseparable from the issue of political citizenry. They were devices necessary to protect the interests of the disenfranchised. We need not, then, rely on . . . such elaborate or ambiguous concepts as Tory Radicalism to explain the confluence of the Chartist and Ten Hours movements. There was one popular movement during the early Victorian period, based on a simple belief in the political rights of labour, and corresponding more nearly to the popular radicalism of John Fielden than to the Tory Radicalism of Richard Oastler.*

Recent interpretations emphasise the activities of political radicals whose key aim was to greatly increase the number of voters beyond the restricted, propertied franchise settled by the so-called 'Great Reform Act' of 1832. Most were democrats in the sense that, like Fielden, they wanted the vote for all adult males who were neither criminals nor insane.

Though they do not deny their importance, historians have recently given rather less attention to the work of aristocratic humanitarians like Anthony Ashley Cooper, Seventh Earl of Shaftesbury. Following the advice of E. P. Thompson (see page 4) who urged historians to look at the ways in which the classes shaped their own making, and looking in detail at specific local conditions, they have stressed the importance of pressure from below. Factory reform movements are seen as being at least as much about active participation in the political process by workers as they were about well-intentioned members of the upper classes securing change for them. Equally important, historians are now much more concerned to know how factory legislation actually worked (once it was passed) rather than why it was passed.

# Historical debates 2: new ways of looking at Chartism

Of all the key areas of study covered by this book, Chartism has received the largest amount of scholarly attention in recent years. Chapter 7 extensively summarises what has been described as the most impressive movement of working people in the nineteenth century. Earlier discussions of Chartism tended to concentrate on its origins, objectives, leadership and its threat to the authorities. Stress was also placed on alleged divisions between 'moral force' and 'physical force' Chartists.

Some of these issues continue to interest historians. The origins of Chartism clearly lie in a reaction to what political radicals tended to see as the betrayal of the Great Reform Act. Put very crudely, the Reform Act confirmed that the country's rulers intended the vote to be seen as a privilege to be enjoyed exclusively by property owners. As Henry 'Orator' Hunt forcefully put it, 'There are seven millions of men in the United Kingdom who are rendered so many outlaws by the Reform Bill … they are to all intents and purposes so many political slaves' (quoted in E. J. Evans, *Chartism* (Longman Pearson, 2000), p. 31). Recent research has confirmed the view that the origins of Chartism were political, a view strengthened by an examination of the People's Charter itself. All six of its famous 'points' were political. There was no call, for example, for higher wages, welfare legislation or a Ten Hours Bill (see Chapter 2).

However, it cannot be denied that Chartism sprang to life during a period of economic depression. Some historians, notably Norman Gash (see Source 7.61, page 265), have used this to argue that the 'contemporary importance' of Chartism related directly to the severe economic depression that affected the industrial areas of Britain in the late 1830s and 1840s. People who see Chartism as primarily an economic movement often quote Joseph Rayner Stephens' statement that 'This question of Universal Suffrage was a knife and fork question after all; this was a bread and cheese question.' They might also reasonably ask why, if Chartism were an inevitable reaction to the 'betrayal' of 1832, it took five or six years for this betrayal to find united expression in the People's Charter.

Few historians would now support those parts of Gash's analysis that stress the economic dimension. It is, of course, perfectly true that mass political movements were only possible during periods of economic downswing. Most people will offer hearty support to a political movement only when they are in real want. However, it is possible to see Chartism as the culmination of a much more longer-term political agitation. Chartist leaders used the same forms of language in their speeches and their newspaper articles as had been used for more than half a century. Those outside the political system needed to band together to assert their freedoms and to challenge the authority of a government which, so they argued, perpetually ignored the interests of the people. This so-called 'artisan radical tradition' (because it was most powerfully supported by literate, skilled craftsmen who had a strong sense of identity) had long declared the government both corrupt and incapable of representing the people's interests. It was no accident that the forum for debating ideas for political change was the so-called 'National Convention'. That Convention claimed a legitimacy with ordinary people which a parliament elected by small numbers and controlled by the great landed interests could never match. The Chartists pictured their movement as a struggle by 'the people', with a strong sense of their historic freedoms, against their systematic suppression by 'Old Corruption'.

One reason for the delay in unfurling the People's Charter was the need to regroup after an important defeat in 1832. Another was that opposition to the introduction of the new Poor Law (see Chapter 5) provided a new rallying cry. The Poor Law Amendment Act was intended to make it more difficult for fit adults to claim poor relief and to act as an incentive for ordinary people to go out in search of work. Its working-class opponents saw it as one more example of hostility by the propertied classes to the interests of ordinary people. They noted that large majorities in both the leading political parties in Westminster had supported the law. In some industrial areas, notably Yorkshire's West Riding, outrage at the impact of the new law fed directly into the emergence of Chartism.

It is, of course, possible to characterise this opposition as economically motivated. However, the solutions proposed were very clearly political. William Cobbett, the veteran radical who had died in 1835, and J. R. Stephens were in agreement that *political* solutions must be found. If working men had the vote, so the argument ran, they would abandon all unjust laws. As Stephens put it in a much less often quoted part of his speech in 1838: 'If any man asked him what he meant by Universal Suffrage, he would answer that every working man in the land had a right to have a good coat to his back.' His whole point was that political struggle was necessary before economic improvements could be won. A parliament representative of the people would not tax ordinary people and would deal with the huge inequalities of wealth that the industrial revolution had served only to increase.

Chartism has been reinterpreted in other ways, too. First, there was the fashion of studying the movement in its local dimension. This was begun by Asa Briggs, whose *Chartist Studies*, published in 1959, aimed to relate Chartist objectives to local circumstances. Most historians in the 1980s and 1990s saw this as presenting far too fragmented a picture. Although local circumstances might be important in explaining the tactics employed in particular places, Chartist leaders were all certain that they were part of an important *national* movement of working people.

Second, less attention is now paid to leadership squabbles in explaining the alleged weaknesses of Chartism. In particular, the reputation of Feargus O'Connor has undergone a substantially more favourable re-evaluation. Early historians of the Chartist movement, particularly R. C. Gammage in his *History of the Chartist Movement* (1854) and Mark Hovell in *The Chartist Movement* (1918), denounced O'Connor as a violent rabble rouser. In their view he inflamed people with unrealistic visions and hare-brained schemes like the Land Plan, which aimed at returning Chartists to the land almost as peasant proprietors. Source 4 shows how he has been rehabilitated.

● **SOURCE 4**

D. Thompson, *The Chartists: Popular Politics in the Industrial Revolution*, 1984.

*Remove [O'Connor] and his newspaper [Northern Star] from the picture and the [Chartist] movement fragments, localises and loses its continuity . . . No other leader, or would-be leader, in these years had the energy, ability, physique or charisma of Feargus O'Connor. For good or ill, he was the main inspiration and guiding force of the movement.*

Some historical debates run fairly rapidly into the sands. The protagonists on both sides choose evidence which fits their case and talk across, rather than directly to, their opponents. Both sides might be right, but, because they have defined their terms to suit their own argument, they end up being right about different things.

However, attempts to reconstruct Chartism in the last two decades have confirmed its importance as a movement. There is beginning to be agreement, also, about a distinctive, Chartist culture which retained its power to inspire later generations of political leaders, long after the movement itself had died down. In that, very important, sense, Chartism did not fail. Although it did not achieve its famous 'six points' it provided both a focus and a context for later political movements. The history of the trade union movement and even of the early Labour party cannot be properly understood without understanding the contribution made by Chartism to the growing self-confidence of working people that they had both a voice and a message which needed to be heard. In terms of values, attitudes and beliefs, the ideas of Chartism proved immensely resilient.

Finally, the Chartist movement provides the historian with an object lesson in why it is necessary to come to the evidence with both political and social perspectives. This book will tell you much about British society in the nineteenth century. It will also give you a wide variety of evidence from which you can make up your own minds about some of the main controversies and debates with which historians engage. Your understanding will remain partial, however, unless you recognise that so much of the evidence you are examining needs to be seen in the context of the power structures that operated in nineteenth-century British society.

# 1

# What were the main changes in British society, 1815–1914?

● SOURCE 1.1

From Poor Law Report, 1909.

Performance of the economy – depression and boom, 1830–79.

**1830**
Culmination of distress (international). High social tension.

**1832**
Depression. High social tension.

**1833**
Extreme distress. High social tension.

**1834**
Revival. Low social tension.

**1835**
Prosperity (depression of agriculture). Low social tension.

**1837**
Reaction. High social tension.

**1838**
Distress. High social tension.

**1839**
Universal distress. High social tension.

**1842**
The lowest ebb. High social tension.

**1843**
Revival. Low social tension.

**1844**
Prosperity. Low social tension.

**1845**
Prosperity and speculation. Virtually no social tension.

**1846**
Potato famine. Low social tension.

**1847**
Crisis and depression. High social tension.

**1848**
Distress. High social tension.

**1849**
Revival. Some social tension.

**1850**
Revival. Low social tension.

**1851**
Prosperity

**1852**
Prosperity

**1853**
Pause

**1854**
Depression

**1855**
Distress

**1856**
Distress

**1857**
Distress and commercial collapse.

**1858**

Revival

**1859**

Prosperity

**1860**

Prosperity

**1861**

Cotton famine with the drying-up of imports from the southern states of America as a result of the Civil War, 1860–65.

**1862**

Distress

**1864**

Revival

**1865**

Wild speculation.

**1866**

Crash

**1867**

Depression

**1870**

Revival

**1871**

General prosperity.

**1872**

Economy grows by leaps and bounds.

**1873**

Never more prosperous.

**1874**

Highest point of prosperity.

**1875**

Declining prosperity.

**1876**

Depression

**1878**

Distress

**1879**

Culmination of distress.

# Introduction

There has been some debate over the use of the word 'Victorian' to describe the nineteenth century in Britain. 'Victorian' is used to mean different things, referring sometimes to a number of beliefs based on respectability, dedication to public service and a high level of self-discipline, and sometimes to the extreme social disruption that was typical of the earlier years of the Queen's reign. On the other hand, it has also been used to refer to the make-up of a social system that was typical of the period after 1850, the era of 'high Victorianism'. Most modern historians now accept that the word 'Victorian' best describes the kind of society and economic structure that formed the basis of British life after 1850.

Whichever view is taken, there is little doubt that the period from 1830 onwards saw a sweeping criticism of the old forms of government. A new class of men committed to business emerged. They challenged the dominant position occupied by those who held political power and privilege as a result of their possession of land.

Forces for change had been gathering for some years prior to 1830, with the demand for reform of Parliament. It was, however, at this time that the democratic principle, the claim that political power should be under the control of all men, irrespective of wealth or status, became an objective of political leaders. This development was accompanied by the growth of new thinking on the role of the state. Political reformers emerged who campaigned for the state to intervene and protect the people. Reformers wanted the state to accept greater responsibility for the welfare of individuals. Some of these issues will be discussed in greater detail in later chapters. The purpose of this chapter is to present you with the general economic and social context, to help you to understand and appreciate the economic and social movements of the nineteenth century.

# *1* How and why did population change in Britain between 1815 and 1914?

The first attempt at calculating population on a national scale did not take place until 1801. Public opinion had become aware that towns and new suburbs had grown since the 1740s and concern was expressed that such growth was too rapid for the supply of food to keep pace. The census gave information not only on size but also on distribution and economic activity of the population. It indicated that nearly four-fifths of the 9.2 million people lived in rural areas although there had been a growth in the population of the Midlands and the north as a result of the rise of the cotton, coal and iron industries. Britain remained a predominantly rural society until the second half of the century. After 1851 it became increasingly urban, so that by 1881 the division was 20 per cent rural to 80 per cent urban. Most of the developing towns were located on or near the coalfields of the north and west, since steam was the main motive power of industry. The other large towns were ports: London, Bristol and Liverpool. The industrial towns grew quickly because of high birth-rates and migration from the poor agricultural areas. Some were entirely new, such as Etruria, a pottery town in Staffordshire, or Crewe and Swindon, which developed at the junctions of the new railway network from the 1830s onwards, or Middlesbrough and Barrow, which developed as a result of the growth of the iron industry. Others grew from villages to vast towns, as in the case of Birmingham.

## What were the patterns in the growth of population?

Until the government passed an act requiring people to register births and deaths in 1837, birth- and death-rates could only be compiled from the baptism and burial totals recorded in parish registers of the Anglican Church. This meant that it was not until the census of 1841 that reasonably accurate estimates of population size became possible. This has led to some controversy amongst those who have attempted to explain the rise in population in the first half of the nineteenth century, with debate over whether it was due to an increase in births, or a fall in deaths or both.

● **SOURCE 1.2**

From N. Tranter, *Population since the Industrial Revolution*, 1973.

Growth in the population of England and Wales according to a) size and b) percentage, 1801–1911. (The first national census was carried out in 1801 and every ten years thereafter.)

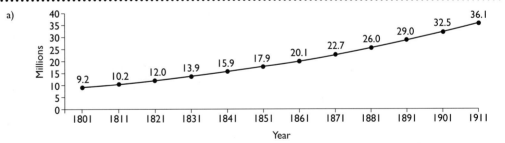

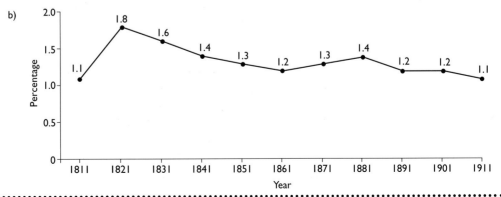

---

1 Using Source 1.2, comment on the overall trend in population growth between 1815 and 1911.

2 Identify the two periods that experienced the largest percentage growth in population.

● **SOURCE 1.3**

From B. R. Mitchell and P. Deane, *Abstract of British Historical Statistics*, 1962, and N. Tranter, *Population since the Industrial Revolution*, 1973.

Changes in the factors affecting population growth:
a) births and deaths 1811–1915
b) migration 1841–1915.

No figures have been identified for 1821–30; no reliable figures for migration are available before the 1841 census.

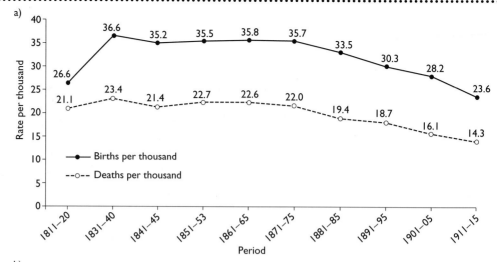

a)

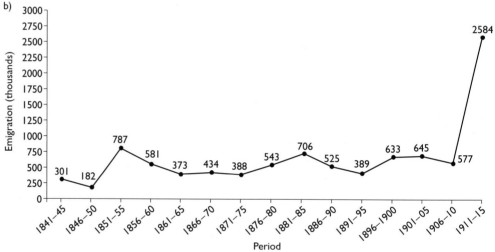

b)

Study the two graphs in Source 1.3.

1 Identify the highest peak in birth-rates in the period 1811–1915.

2 Identify the highest peak in death-rates in the period 1811–1915.

3 When did the birth-rate start to decline?

4 When did the death-rate start to decline?

5 What part was played by changes in
   a) birth-rate
   b) death-rate
   c) migration
   in influencing population growth?

● **SOURCE 1.4**

From B. R. Mitchell and P. Deane, *Abstract of British Historical Statistics*, 1962.

Changes in the proportion of the population married by age and sex, 1871–1911.

| Census | Ages 20–24 | | Ages 25–34 | | Ages 45–54 | |
|---|---|---|---|---|---|---|
| | M | F | M | F | M | F |
| 1871 | 23.3 | 34.8 | 68.4 | 71.1 | 90.3 | 87.9 |
| 1881 | 22.3 | 33.5 | 68.3 | 70.7 | 90.4 | 88.1 |
| 1891 | 19.5 | 29.9 | 65.7 | 67.4 | 90.0 | 87.6 |
| 1901 | 17.4 | 27.4 | 64.1 | 66.0 | 89.0 | 86.6 |
| 1911 | 14.3 | 24.3 | 61.4 | 64.5 | 87.8 | 84.2 |

1 Study Source 1.4. What changes took place in the proportion of women marrying in the reproductive age groups 20–34 years between 1871 and 1911?

15

How and why did population change in Britain between 1815 and 1914?

## SOURCE 1.5

From the Registrar General's Statistical Review, 1961.

Changes in family size, 1861–1914.

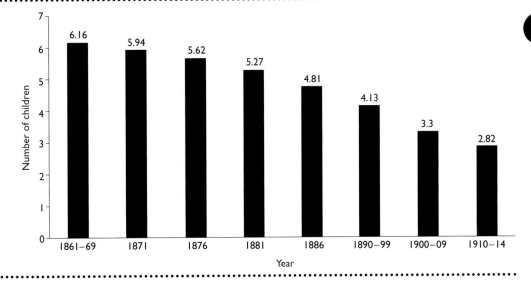

1 Using Source 1.5, comment on the overall trend in the average size of the family.

# Why did population growth take off?

## SOURCE 1.6

From N. Tranter, *Population since the Industrial Revolution*, 1973, in which the author assesses the present state of the debate on reasons for changes in population in the period 1780–1850.

**fertility**
number of births per year per thousand women in the child-bearing age groups.

**mortality**
number of deaths per year, per thousand of the population

. . . *it would appear that the 'take off' in rates of English population growth between 1780 and 1850 was primarily the result of the following factors: the existence of an age structure which had developed out of the 'bulge generation' created around the middle of the eighteenth century, and which was particularly suited to relatively high marriage and birth-rates and low death-rates; the vast increase in the demand for adult and child labour which encouraged earlier marriage and higher rates of marital FERTILITY by raising the average level of money (though not real) incomes; the adoption of inoculation and vaccination against smallpox which reduced the number of smallpox deaths and contributed to a decline in general rates of MORTALITY and finally the spread of the provincial hospital movement and of the use of drugs like mercury, iron and cinchona in medical treatment which also contributed to population increase through the contribution they made to falling mortality. On this evidence, therefore, the early English 'population revolution' was a response to both rising fertility and falling mortality.*

*The other oft quoted explanations for the 'take off' in the pace of English population growth between 1780 and 1850 do not stand up to close scrutiny. Before the middle of the nineteenth century high rates of population increase were not due to any positive rise in the level of real wages or in the standards of public health, personal hygiene and nutrition. The Industrial, Agricultural and Transport Revolutions of the late eighteenth and early nineteenth centuries had not yet proved of much benefit to the great mass of England's labour population. Neither is there any real support for the view that the Speenhamland system of poor relief (based on the number of children in the family) contributed to the increase in rates of population growth in those areas where it was widely applied.*

1 According to Source 1.6, what were the 'oft quoted explanations for the "take off" in the pace of English population growth between 1780 and 1850'?

2 Why do they 'not stand up to close scrutiny'?

3 What, according to Tranter, were the reasons for the 'take-off' in population growth before 1850?

# What were the main trends in birth- and death-rates?

● SOURCE 1.7

From N. Tranter, *Population since the Industrial Revolution*, 1973, in which the author comments on the main trends in birth- and death-rates.

| Changes in the percentage of adults in the working population (15–64 years) | |
|---|---|
| 1851 | 59.8% |
| 1891 | 60.1% |
| 1911 | 63.9% |

### (a) Changes in birth rates

. . . marked fertility differentials . . . already existed between the marriages of the principal social classes of England and Wales during the three or four decades before 1880. For at least one social group in which reproduction rates were relatively low in the mid-nineteenth century, the British peerage, the long-run decline in fertility had begun as early as the opening of the century, though it did accelerate during the 1880s. What we do not yet know is whether the same early decline in fertility was common to all those upper- and middle-class groups whose reproductive patterns were already below average by 1880. This remains to be tested. In the meantime, while allowing that for England and Wales as a whole the fall in fertility only began from the 1880s, we must also recognise the probability that in certain social classes it had begun rather earlier. Once under way after 1880, the pace at which the level of fertility declined varied greatly from one social group to another. Before the outbreak of the First World War it was most pronounced among families in the upper, middle, retired and private income sections of the population, somewhat less dramatic among those of skilled, semi-skilled and textile workers, and least obvious of all within the social classes represented by unskilled industrial workers, miners, and agricultural labourers. In other words, during the initial phase of the transition to lower fertility, the socio-occupational differentials in rates of fertility that already existed actually widened.

### (b) Changes in death rates

Crude death rates changed little in England and Wales during the three decades between 1841 and 1870. Thereafter . . . they fell continuously and fairly regularly. Significantly, however, the long-term decline in mortality since the late nineteenth century has proceeded much more slowly than that of fertility.

The use of crude death rates to illustrate mortality trends tends to obscure important differences in the onset of the fall in mortality by age-group. Mortality rates in the age-groups between 5 and 34 years began their continuous decline from at least as early as the middle of the 1840s, and accelerated from the late 1860s and 1870s. Those in the age-group 35–44 years began to fall from the mid-1870s; those for the ages between 45 and 74 years only from the middle of the 1890s. Infant death rates (that is, the number of deaths between the ages of 0 and 1 year per thousand live births) remained unchanged from 1841 to 1870, then fell slightly during the 1870s and 1880s, rose sharply in the last decade of the century and only began their long-term decline from the period 1901–10.

### (c) Changes in average expectation of life

The overall result of this complex pattern of declining mortality rates was a steady improvement in the average expectation of life. Males and females born between 1838 and 1854 could expect to live on average 39.9 and 41.9 years respectively. For those born in the period 1901–12 average life expectancy at birth had risen to 51.5 and 55.4 years . . .

### (d) Infant mortality

The use of death rates to illustrate changes in mortality also tends to hide the existence of substantial variations in the rate of mortality between the different social classes . . . noticeable were the social class differentials that existed in infant mortality. According to data available from the 1911 census, with the exception of agricultural labourers and textile workers (the former abnormally low and the latter abnormally high infant death rates), there was a close relationship between socio-occupational class variations in the levels of fertility and infant mortality. Social groups with relatively low rates of fertility had lower than average rates of infant mortality (and vice versa).

17

How and why did population change in Britain between 1815 and 1914?

1 According to Source 1.7, what role was played by social class and occupation in changes in
   a) fertility and family size
   b) infant mortality?

2 What was the effect of age in determining the 'onset of the fall in mortality'?

3 What effect did the fall in mortality have on average life expectancy?

4 What effect did the fall in mortality have on the age distribution of the population?

You should now have a clear understanding of the pattern of change in population growth. Historians have argued about whether changes in birth-rates or changes in death-rates were more crucial in causing population to grow. Study Sources 1.2–1.5.

5 'The growth in population during the course of the nineteenth century was due to a fall in death-rate rather than a rise in birth-rate.' To what extent does the statistical evidence support this claim?

## What changes took place in the distribution of population?

The growth in population was not uniform throughout the country. Initially the increase took place in the countryside where the majority of people lived. Between 1751 and 1831 rural areas saw an 88 per cent growth in numbers whereas urban areas grew by 129 per cent. In 1801 the counties of Suffolk and Warwickshire both had a population of 210,000 people. By 1871, Suffolk's population had grown by 66 per cent to 350,000; Warwickshire's by 300 per cent to 634,000. Suffolk remained largely agricultural, but Warwickshire had become industrial.

Growth was achieved partly by migration but also because there was a higher rate of fertility in the towns. Agricultural output expanded to meet the rising demand for food, but employment opportunities did not grow at the same pace as population. The growing surplus of labour contributed to low wages and rising poverty in the countryside, encouraging people to migrate to the towns. Initially such migration was over short distances as workers 'hopped' from town to town. Long-distance migration developed with the coming of the railways from the 1840s onwards.

Study Source 1.8 on page 18.

1 Which areas were most densely populated in 1701?

2 In which areas did population grow most rapidly between 1701 and 1801?

3 In which area had there been a relative decline?

4 Which areas attracted Irish immigrants?

5 Identify the four main movements of population shown in the map for 1801.

6 To what extent had changes occurred in the distribution of population by 1901 compared with 1801?

## ● SOURCE 1.8

From J. A. Morris, *The Growth of Industrial Britain, 1700 to the present day*, 1971.

Changes in the distribution of population, 1701–1901.

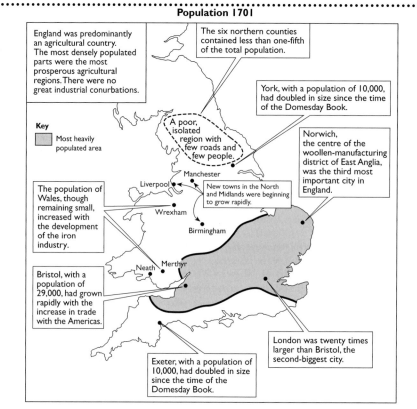

**Population 1701**

England was predominantly an agricultural country. The most densely populated parts were the most prosperous agricultural regions. There were no great industrial conurbations.

The six northern counties contained less than one-fifth of the total population.

York, with a population of 10,000, had doubled in size since the time of the Domesday Book.

Norwich, the centre of the woollen-manufacturing district of East Anglia, was the third most important city in England.

**Key**
▨ Most heavily populated area

A poor, isolated region with few roads and few people.

The population of Wales, though remaining small, increased with the development of the iron industry.

New towns in the North and Midlands were beginning to grow rapidly.

Bristol, with a population of 29,000, had grown rapidly with the increase in trade with the Americas.

London was twenty times larger than Bristol, the second-biggest city.

Exeter, with a population of 10,000, had doubled in size since the time of the Domesday Book.

*Cities labelled: Manchester, Liverpool, Wrexham, Birmingham, Neath, Merthyr*

**Population 1801**

Nearly four-fifths of the population still lived in rural areas. Apart from Irish and Scottish migrants there was little long-distance migration. The developing industries drew in workers from the surrounding countryside.

**Key**
▨ Most heavily populated areas
● Towns or cities with populations of 10–20,000
▲ Towns or cities with populations of 21–50,000
■ Towns or cities with populations of 51–100,000
→ Direction of migration

Scottish migrants

Little change in density of population in these agricultural counties.

South Wales coalfield developed late.

Irish migrants moving to South Lancashire and London

Irish migrants

Growing population along the south coast.

London's population was 864,000 – one-tenth of the entire population.

*Cities labelled: Newcastle, York, Hull, Leeds, Manchester, Sheffield, Liverpool, Leicester, Birmingham, Norwich, Bristol, Reading, Portsmouth, Dover*

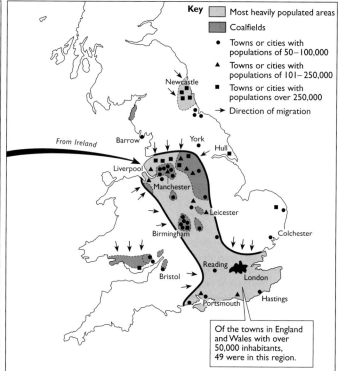

**Population 1901**

**Key**
▨ Most heavily populated areas
▨ Coalfields
● Towns or cities with populations of 50–100,000
▲ Towns or cities with populations of 101–250,000
■ Towns or cities with populations over 250,000
→ Direction of migration

From Ireland

Of the towns in England and Wales with over 50,000 inhabitants, 49 were in this region.

*Cities labelled: Newcastle, Barrow, York, Hull, Liverpool, Manchester, Leicester, Birmingham, Colchester, Bristol, Reading, London, Portsmouth, Hastings*

---

Study Sources 1.9 and 1.10.

1  What changes had taken place in industry, power and transport in the period 1800–50?

2  To what extent do Fischer and Smith differ over the importance they place on change?

3  How do you explain this difference in focus?

4  Compare Source 1.8 with Sources 1.9 and 1.10. What part was played by the developments described in Sources 1.9 and 1.10 in influencing changes in the distribution of population between 1801 and 1901?

19

How and why did population change in Britain between 1815 and 1914?

● SOURCE 1.9

From Johann Conrad Fischer, *Diary*, 1851, in which a foreign visitor comments on the pace and scale of change in the period 1800 to 1881.

*I visited England for the first time 52 years ago . . . to judge how far and how completely . . . industrial activity had developed as against that which the Continent could show; and I must confess that the verdict fell entirely in favour of England . . . Yet nothing very new could be observed there at that period . . . the same things were to be found elsewhere though not so good . . . Twenty years later . . . I found great new developments. Spinning mills, foundries, potteries . . . steel and file factories, the plating works of Birmingham and Sheffield, the spinning and weaving mills of Manchester and the cloth manufacture of Leeds had acquired a size and perfection of which there can be no conception without actually seeing them . . . Twelve or thirteen years later . . . the scale of everything and especially the expansion of London had increased yet more . . . The already extensive steam navigation, the general installation of gas lighting, Perkin's steam-driven shuttles, Brunel's great tunnel . . . besides much else of the greater interest . . . remain in my mind . . . as an ever fascinating picture.*

● SOURCE 1.10

From Reverend Sydney Smith, *Collected Works*, 1839, in which he comments on the 'modern changes' in his lifetime.

*It is of some importance at which period a man is born. A young man alive at this period hardly knows to what improvements of human life he has been introduced; and I would like to bring before his notice the following . . . changes which have taken place since I first began to breathe . . . Gas was unknown; I groped about the streets of London in all but the utter darkness of a twinkling oil lamp under the protection of watchmen . . . and exposed to every species of depredation and insult. I have been nine hours in sailing from Dover to Calais before the invention of steam. It took me nine hours to go from Taunton to Bath before the invention of steam-roads and I now go in six hours from Taunton to London! In going from Taunton to Bath I suffered between 10,000 and 12,000 contusions before stone-breaking Macadam was born. I can walk by the assistance of the police without molestation; or if tired get into a cheap and active cab . . . and whatever miseries I suffered I had no post to whisk my complaints for a single penny to the remotest corners of the empire.*

● SOURCE 1.11

From *Factory Commission, Supplementary Report*, 1834, in which a Bolton handloom-weaver gives evidence of the migration of workers to the spinning mills of Lancashire.

**operative class**
factory workers

**husbandmen**
farm labourers

'When power spinning came in, did it throw the hand spinners out of employ?' – 'No; spinners were very scarce then: families had to come in from different places and learn to spin, and whole families together were sent for by masters.' 'You have been a witness of the OPERATIVE CLASS in these parts; you have seen it grow from nothing into a great body in the space of a few years: how was it recruited? Of what was it composed? What were the spinners taken from?' – 'A good many from the agricultural parts; a many from Wales; a many from Ireland and from Scotland. People left other occupations and came to spinning for the sake of the high wages. I recollect shoemakers leaving their employ and learning to spin; I recollect tailors; I recollect colliers; but a great many more HUSBANDMEN left their employ to learn to spin; very few weavers at that time left their employ to learn to spin, but as the weavers could put their children into mills at an earlier age than they could put them to looms, they threw them into mills as soon as possible, and many of the weavers' children stopped in mills and learnt to spin; but during the last twelve years weavers have put almost all their children into mills since hand-loom weaving has got so bad.' 'Do you ever hear of people leaving other occupations now to learn to spin?' – 'No; the masters don't take men from other occupations now.' 'How long is it since that influx of grown-up men into the spinning branch began to cease?' – 'It did not break off at a time, but I should say it had ceased for fifteen or twenty years.'

● SOURCE 1.12

From A. K. Cairncross, *Home and Foreign Investment 1870–1913*, 1953.

Net gain (+) and loss (−) by migration in England, 1841–1911 (in thousands).

| Year | London | Other towns | Mining districts | Rural areas | Net external migration |
|---|---|---|---|---|---|
| 1841–51 | +274 | +386 | +82 | −443 | +294 |
| 1851–61 | +244 | +272 | +103 | −743 | −122 |
| 1861–71 | +262 | +271 | +91 | −683 | −60 |
| 1871–81 | +307 | +297 | +84 | −837 | −148 |
| 1881–91 | +169 | −31 | +90 | −845 | −617 |
| 1891–01 | +226 | +294 | +85 | −660 | −54 |
| 1901–11 | −232 | −89 | +114 | −295 | −502 |

● SOURCE 1.13

Statistics compiled by the author.

Percentage changes in the urban/rural distribution of the population, 1700–1911.

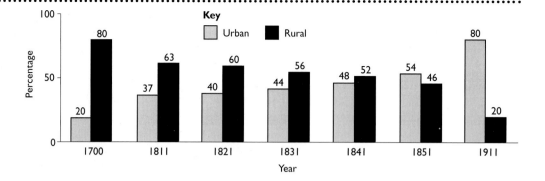

Study Sources 1.11–1.13.

1  Identify the period that witnessed the peak in the movement of people into the towns.

2  Identify the period that witnessed the peak in migration of people from rural areas.

3  Identify the period that witnessed the peak in emigration.

4  When did the majority of people become town dwellers?

5  What was the source of labour recruited to the spinning mills of Lancashire?

6  Why were people attracted to the spinning mills?

7  What was the attitude of weavers to the new spinning mills?

# Why did people decide to emigrate?

● SOURCE 1.14

From Schools Council History 13–16 Project – *Britain 1815–1851*, 1977.

Destination of emigrants from the UK, 1821–51.

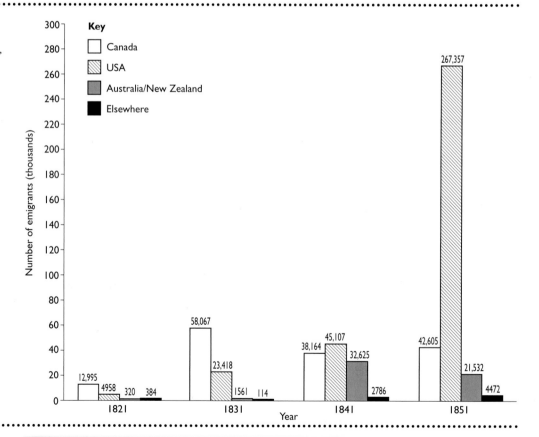

Study Source 1.14.

1  Which country attracted most immigrants in the period 1821–31?

2  Which country had become most popular by 1841?

3  Which country consistently attracted immigrants in the period 1821 to 1851?

4  Which country or countries experienced a decline in popularity amongst emigrants?

21

How and why did population change in Britain between 1815 and 1914?

## ● SOURCE 1.15

Here and There, or, Emigration, a remedy, a cartoon from *Punch*, 15 July 1848.

HERE AND THERE;
Or, Emigration a Remedy.

## ● SOURCE 1.16

From the *First Report of the Select Committee on Emigration from the United Kingdom*, 1826, in which the government encourages emigration.

**parochial rate**
money paid by certain householders in a local area.

**unappropriated**
without (European) owners

**subsisting**
providing enough food, etc., for people to live on.

*That there are extensive districts in Ireland, and districts in England and Scotland, where the population is at the present moment redundant; in other words, where there exists a very considerable number of able-bodied and active labourers, beyond that number to which any existing demand for labour can afford employment. That the effect of this redundancy is . . . to deteriorate the general conditions of the labouring classes . . . That in England, this redundant population has been in part supported by a PAROCHIAL RATE. That in the British Colonies in North America . . . at the Cape of Good Hope, and in New South Wales, and Van Diemen's Land, there are tracts of UNAPPROPRIATED land of the most fertile quality, capable of receiving and SUBSISTING any proportion of the redundant population of this country, for whose conveyance thither, means could be found at any time, present or future.*

Study Sources 1.14 to 1.16.

1   Compare Source 1.1 on pages 11–12, with Source 1.14 and the *Punch* cartoon, Source 1.15. To what extent was people's decision to emigrate influenced by the state of the economy?

2   What economic incentives are identified in Sources 1.15 and 1.16 that would have particular appeal to a would-be emigrant, and which particular group of people would be most likely to respond to these incentives?

3   What evidence is there in Source 1.16 that the government and property owners had their own motives for encouraging emigration?

## ● SOURCE 1.17

From H. A. Innis and A. R. Lower (eds), *Select Documents in Canadian Economic History 1783–1855*, 1933, in which a contemporary observer comments on the emigrants drawn to North America.

*As to the classes to which British America offers inducements to emigrate much will depend upon individual characters . . . The settlers who thrive soonest are men of steady habits accustomed to labour. Practical farmers possessing from £200 to £600 may purchase in any of the Colonies farms with from twenty to thirty acres . . . Joiners, stonemasons, saddlers, shoemakers, tailors, blacksmiths, cart, mill and wheelwrights and (in the seaports) coopers always find employment. Brewers may succeed . . . Butchers generally do well. For spinners, weavers or those engaged in manufactures there is not the smallest encouragement. Young men of education, clerks in mercantile houses or shopmen need not expect the least encouragement unless previously engaged by the merchants or shopkeepers in America. Many young men however by persevering minds and industrious habits have baffled every obstacle and finally succeeded in establishing themselves in trade. Many of the richest merchants in the Colonies were of this description.*

Study Sources 1.16 and 1.17.

1   What personal qualities were considered desirable for would-be emigrants?

2   What skills were in greatest demand for emigrants to North America?

3   How do you explain the limited demand for textile workers and clerks?

● SOURCE 1.18

From *Incentive for Female Migrants*, 1833, detailing the special incentives offered to single women who were in high demand by the 1830s.

In 1835 the government introduced a free bounty of £20 to young married mechanics and agricultural labourers who wanted to emigrate to Australia.

*Young women wanted*
## NOTICE TO YOUNG WOMEN

*Desirous of bettering their conditions by an emigration to New South Wales.*

*In New South Wales and Van Diemen's Land there are very few women compared with the whole number of people, so that it is impossible to get women enough as Female Servants or for other Female Employments. The consequence is, that desirable situations, with good wages, are easily obtained by Females in those countries; but the passage is so long that few can pay the experience of it without help. There is now, however, the following favourable opportunity of going to New South Wales.*

*The Committee has been formed in London for the purpose of facilitating emigration, which intends to send out a ship in the course of the Spring, expressly for the conveyance of Female Emigrants, under an experienced and respectable Man and his Wife, who have been engaged as Superintendents. The parties who go in that vessel must be Unmarried Women or Widows; must be between the ages of 18 and 30; and must be of good health and character. They must also be able to pay £6 towards the expense of their passage. The remainder of the expense will be paid by the [Committee]. Every arrangement will be made for the comfort of the Emigrants during the voyage; they will also be taken care of on their first landing in the Colonies; and they will find there . . . a list of the different situations to be obtained.*

---

Study Source 1.18.

1  Why were women in high demand as emigrants?

2  Which particular groups of women were in high demand?

3  How was the cost of emigration met?

4  What specific help was provided to encourage women to emigrate?

# 2  How did people earn their living?

Between 1800 and 1850 there were many changes in industry, which some historians term the 'Industrial Revolution'. There is some dispute as to the meaning of the term 'revolution'. W. W. Rostow (*The Stages of Economic Growth: A Non-Communist Manifesto*, Cambridge, 1960) argued that between 1780 and 1800 a sudden dramatic 'take-off' took place in the rate of growth of the economy, led by cotton and followed by coal and iron. Other historians, such as Professor Crafts (*British Economic Growth During the Industrial Revolution*, Clarendon Press, Oxford, 1985), have challenged Rostow's views, emphasising the gradualness of change. Crafts accepts that growth took place between 1700 and 1830 but he stresses the continuity of such changes. Historians who challenge the concept of a revolution claim that changes had started as early as the 1760s (or earlier) and were not fully worked out until the 1820s.

But, whenever changes may be said to have begun and whether or not there was a revolution, there is no doubt that the England of 1730 differed significantly from the England of 1830 onwards. There was a long-term decline in the relative proportion of the national income coming from primary production (agriculture, fishing and forestry) and a rise in the return from manufacturing, trade and transport. Furthermore, trade and services grew more rapidly than manufacturing. Ports and towns developed rapidly in the north, Midlands and South Wales as a result of changes in the organisation and location of iron, coal and textile production, especially cotton and woollen textiles. New machines were invented, requiring new sources of power: first water, and then steam, which made possible faster production of articles at a cheaper price.

These changes were reflected in the occupational redistribution of the population. The typical working man ceased to live in the country and work on the land with his wife and children. However, although agriculture lost its dominance in the economy, land and its ownership remained the main source of social and political prestige and influence.

# What changes took place in the structure of the economy between 1700 and 1860?

## ● SOURCE 1.19

From N. F. R. Crafts, 'The Industrial Revolution: Economic Growth in Britain, 1700–1860', 1986.

Estimates of economic growth during given periods between 1700 and 1860.

| Period | Industrial output (per cent) | Whole economy (per cent) |
|---|---|---|
| 1700–60 | 0.7 | 0.7 |
| 1760–80 | 1.5 | 0.7 |
| 1780–1801 | 2.1 | 1.3 |
| 1801–31 | 3.0 | 2.0 |
| 1831–60 | 3.3 | 2.5 |

1 When, according to Source 1.19, was the rate of growth in the economy at its greatest?

2 To what extent do Craft's figures support Rostow's claim of a 'take-off' in the economy between 1780 and 1800?

## What was the importance of the textile industries?

The textile industries, especially cotton, have been seen as the mainspring of the transformations that occurred throughout the economy. At the time of the 1851 census about 2.75 million people, or 10 per cent of the total population and 21.4 per cent of the occupied population, were working in the textiles and dress industries. Between 10 per cent and 15 per cent of these were under the age of fifteen years, though this percentage was to drop as a result of legislation to prevent the employment of children. By 1871 the numbers of people working in the textile industries had fallen to 2.6 million or 17.7 per cent of the occupied population.

## ● SOURCE 1.20

From P. Deane and W. A. Cole, *British Economic Growth 1688–1959*, 1969.

Net output of the principal textile industries, 1770–1870 (£ millions).

There was a cotton famine between 1860 and 1865 when imports of raw cotton from the southern states of America fell as a result of the Civil War.

| Year | Cotton | Woollens | Linen | Silk | Total | Total as percentage of National Income |
|---|---|---|---|---|---|---|
| 1770 | 0.6 | 7.0 | 3.4 | 1.0 | 12.0 | 9.0 |
| 1805 | 10.5 | 12.8 | 7.6 | 2.0 | 32.9 | 10.0 |
| 1821 | 17.5 | 16.6 | 12.5 | 3.0 | 49.6 | 14.0 |
| 1836 | 21.8 | 16.7 | 8.4 | 6.5 | 53.4 | 11.0 |
| 1845 | 24.3 | 21.1 | 8.4 | 6.5 | 60.3 | 11.0 |
| 1850 | 21.1 | 20.3 | 8.7 | 7.0 | 57.1 | 10.0 |
| 1855 | 26.2 | 20.2 | 9.0 | 8.0 | 63.4 | 10.0 |
| 1860 | 33.0 | 21.2 | 9.4 | 9.0 | 72.6 | 10.0 |
| 1865 | 30.1 | 25.0 | 13.5 | 9.0 | 77.6 | 9.0 |
| 1870 | 38.8 | 25.4 | 12.3 | 8.0 | 84.5 | 9.0 |

1 When, according to Source 1.20, does the textile industry appear to have grown fastest in terms of its total output in £ millions?

2 How does the growth of the textile industry suggest that the point of 'take-off' of industrial change varied within industries?

3 When did the rate of growth in the textile industry slow down in terms of its total output in £ millions?

# What was the pattern of growth in the coal industry between 1816 and 1913?

● SOURCE 1.21

From P. Deane and W. A. Cole, *British Economic Growth 1688–1959*, 1969.

Estimated output of the coal industry, 1800–50 (million tons)

Where no figures appear for workers the number is too small to be recorded or is unavailable.

| Year | Output (in million tons) | Value at pithead (£m) | Number of workers (millions) |
|---|---|---|---|
| 1816 | 15.9 | 5.2 | – |
| 1820 | 17.4 | 5.7 | – |
| 1825 | 21.9 | 6.9 | – |
| 1830 | 22.4 | 6.9 | – |
| 1835 | 27.7 | 8.8 | – |
| 1840 | 33.7 | 9.2 | 0.2 |
| 1845 | 45.9 | 10.3 | – |
| 1850 | 49.4 | 16.1 | 0.4 |
| 1860 | 80.0 | 20.0 | – |
| 1870 | 110.4 | 27.6 | 0.6 |
| 1880 | 146.8 | 62.4 | 0.6 |
| 1890 | 181.6 | 75.0 | 0.8 |
| 1900 | 225.2 | 121.7 | 0.9 |
| 1913 | 287.4 | 146.0 | 1.2 |

1 From the information in Source 1.21, when does the coal industry appear to have grown fastest in terms of total output?

2 How does the growth of the coal industry suggest that the point of 'take-off' of industrial change varied between industries?

3 When did the rate of growth in the coal industry slow down?

## When did the iron industry 'take off'?

During the first half of the nineteenth century the growth of the iron industry was associated with a substantial growth in the home market for iron and steel goods, but there was a significant shift in the early 1850s to greater dependence on the export trade. By 1871 blast furnaces, iron mills and foundries absorbed 25 per cent of the steam power while the earnings of ironworkers were relatively high and unemployment was low.

● SOURCE 1.22

a) From R. M. Reeve, *The Industrial Revolution 1750–1850*, 1971.
b) From P. Deane and W. A. Cole, *British Economic Growth 1688–1959*, 1969.

Estimated output of pig iron, 1796–1874 (thousand tons) and percentage share of iron industry in national income, 1805–71.

Britain was at war with France between 1793 and 1815.

| Year | (a) Output (in thousand tons) | Year | (b) % share of iron industry in national income |
|---|---|---|---|
| 1796 | 1,250 | 1805 | 5.9 |
| 1806 | 2,449 | 1818 | 3.4 |
| 1823 | 455 | 1821 | 3.6 |
| 1830 | 677 | 1831 | 3.6 |
| 1840 | 1,396 | 1841 | 3.8 |
| 1847 | 1,999 | 1851 | 6.2 |
| 1852 | 2,701 | 1861 | 7.6 |
| 1870–74 | 6,378 | 1871 | 11.6 |

Study Source 1.22.

1 What effect did the end of the war with France in 1815 have on
a) the market for iron products
b) the industry's contribution to national income?

2 When did the 'take-off' for the iron industry occur?

# What changes took place in the distribution of the workforce in various occupations?

Industrial workers of the early nineteenth century had to adapt to the totally new regime imposed by the factory, which required a significant change in attitudes and morals from those involved in farming. In particular, employment of children in factories or mines had to be accepted. Lives ceased to be governed by the changing course of the seasons but, instead, came under the control of the unchanging rhythm of the machine. Although the situation of the farm worker in earlier times can hardly be described as idyllic, the industrial worker of early Victorian Britain, with his wife and children, probably suffered a deterioration in living conditions and an increase in emotional stress. This made his acceptance of the working conditions in industry far less likely.

● **SOURCE 1.23**

From P. Deane and W. A. Cole, *British Economic Growth 1688–1959*, 1969.

a) Changes in the distribution of the labour force, 1811–1914 (as a percentage of the total occupied population).
b) Decline in the percentage of agricultural workers, 1811–1914.

a)

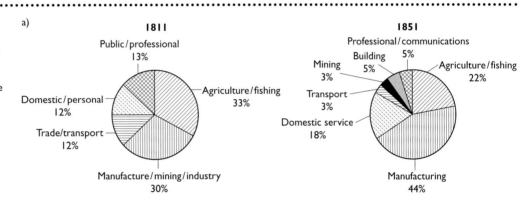
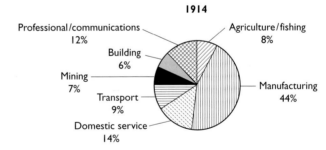

b)

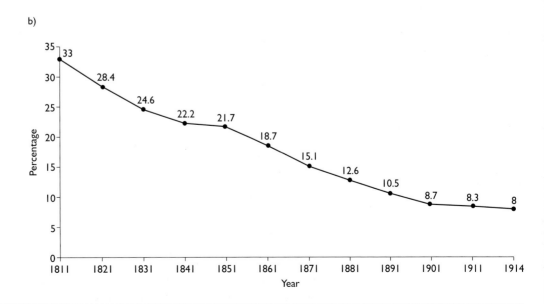

Study the pie charts and graph in Source 1.23.

1   What major changes took place in the distribution of the labour force between 1811 and 1914? In your answer comment on each of the following
    a)   When was agriculture at its peak in terms of the numbers employed?
    b)   When did agriculture cease to employ the major percentage of the labour force?
    c)   Which sector or sectors appeared to absorb the loss from agriculture?
    d)   Identify the sector that remained relatively stable in terms of the percentage of the labour force employed.
    e)   Identify the sector that was in decline by 1914 after a period of growth.
    f)   Which sector became dominant in the economy for the greater part of the nineteenth century?
    g)   When did the main shift of labour take place?

2   Using the evidence of the pie charts, identify which industries were on the rise and which were in decline. Record the changes that took place on your own copy of the following table.

|  | Change by 1851 compared with 1811 | Change by 1914 compared with 1851 |
|---|---|---|
| Industry on the rise |  |  |
| Industry in decline |  |  |

# 3   What was the social impact of changes in industry?

There is much debate among historians as to whether the economic changes brought about by the Industrial Revolution caused an increase or a decrease in living standards. Written evidence, whether in parliamentary reports or in other contemporary sources, suggests there was a widespread feeling that conditions generally were deteriorating. It is very hard to discover whether real wages – that is, the value of money wages in terms of the goods and services that they could buy – were rising or falling in the first half of the nineteenth century. One of the difficulties is that we lack an adequate national index of either wages or prices during this period. Moreover, it is clear, from the work that has been done, that major regional differences existed in both wage and price levels. Therefore, any attempt to identify a national trend in either before 1830 must be extremely weak.

On the other hand, the cost of living and the standard of living are two separate things. Although standard of living is a more vague concept, analysis suggests that the quality of life of the Victorian worker was becoming significantly worse before the 1850s. The breakdown of traditional values, and the loss of status and security, indicate a profound change in the way of life of the early Victorian worker, even though the statistical evidence is, at best, misleading and, often, unavailable. It has been estimated that, in the first half of the century, ten per cent of the population was in a permanent state of poverty. This created an underclass, deprived for most of their lives of the benefits industrialisation was supposed to bring. They were excluded from existing political processes. Furthermore, every major crisis left perhaps one-third of the working classes unemployed and dependent on charity and the poor laws. Although there was a fall in the cost of many important commodities, especially clothing, other products were far beyond the means of the mass of the labouring poor. It is probably true that rents tended to increase rather than fall in the first half of the nineteenth century, and it is very doubtful whether standards of diet improved.

The gainers from the changes in the organisation of industry were those who acquired the new skills required by the factory-machine age. They grasped the chance offered and rose, in some cases, even from artisan to employer. The casualties were those whose skills became obsolete, particularly the handloom-weavers and wool combers. Many of these resorted to machine breaking, or 'Luddism' as it became known, between 1811 and 1816. The unskilled, who were vulnerable to price rises and fluctuations in employment levels, also suffered. However, there were many workers who were unaffected by change because the domestic system (in which people worked in their own cottages – see page 41) continued, in some cases, until as late as the 1850s. All groups suffered during periods when there was a slump in the economy, as occurred in the years 1816, 1819, 1826–27, 1830–31, 1836–42 and 1846–47. People were driven to violent protests, as shown by the high number of riots that occurred during these years, threatening the entire fabric of society.

## What was the effect of power-driven machinery on the position of the handloom-weavers?

● SOURCE 1.24

From F. Crouzet, *The Victorian Economy*, 1981.

The impact of power-driven looms on the position of the handloom-weavers.

> The steam-driven power loom had not been invented in 1795.

| Year | Number of power looms | Number of handloom-weavers |
|------|----------------------|---------------------------|
| 1795 | – | 75,000 |
| 1813 | 2,400 | 212,000 |
| 1820 | 14,150 | 240,000 |
| 1829 | 55,500 | 225,000 |
| 1833 | 100,000 | 213,000 |
| 1835 | 109,000 | 188,000 |
| 1845 | 225,000 | 60,000 |
| 1850 | 250,000 | 43,000 |
| 1861 | 400,000 | 7,000 |

● SOURCE 1.25

From G. R. Porter, *The Progress of the Nation*, 1847.

Wages of a Bolton handloom-weaver, 1797–1830.

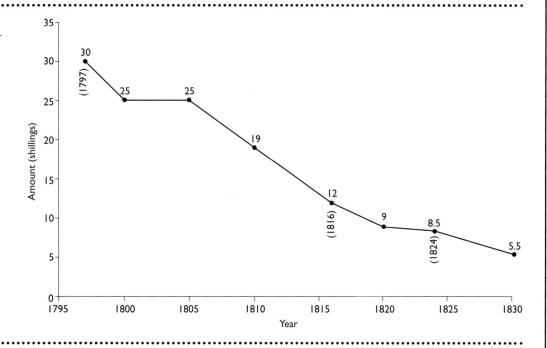

Study Sources 1.24 and 1.25. These relate to the handloom-weavers who were one of the victims of industrial change.

1  What was the initial impact of the introduction of spinning machines on the demand for handloom-weavers?

2  When did the demand for handloom-weavers peak?

3  What was the impact of these developments on the wages of weavers?

4  To what extent does the experience of the handloom-weavers support the claim that 'economic change often implies technological obsolescence'?

# What was the effect of the changes in industry on wages?

● **SOURCE 1.26**

From P. Deane and W. A. Cole, *British Economic Growth 1688–1959*, 1969.

Course of MONEY WAGES, 1800–60, and REAL WAGES where figures available.

**base year**
To make it possible to compare the statistics of one year with another, measurements are made against a base year to which the figure 100 is allocated.

**money wages**
is the amount paid in wages.

**real wages**
is the value of money wages in terms of the goods and services that can be bought.

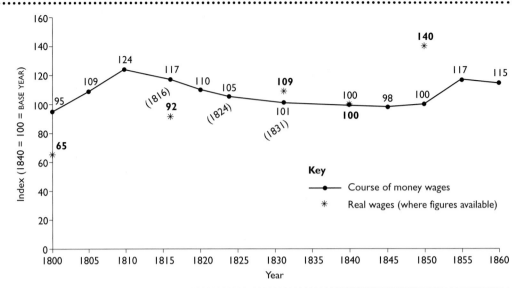

Study Source 1.26.

1 To what extent does the course of money wages suggest that there was no marked general change in living standards in the first half of the nineteenth century?

2 When did money wages reach a peak in the period 1800–60?

3 When did workers appear to have experienced an economic crisis?

4 What evidence is there in the course of money wages to support the view that the experience of the handloom-weavers was not representative of workers as a whole?

5 How useful is Source 1.26 in explaining why some contemporaries felt sure that living standards were falling during the period 1800–60 while others believed they were rising?

# What problems have historians faced in studying living standards?

● **SOURCE 1.27**

From N. Longmate, *Milestones in Working Class History*, 1975, in which the author discusses regional variations in wage rates.

Amounts are in shillings and pence (s.d.): 12d. = 1s. (5p); 20s. = £1 (100p).

*A survey of wages throughout the United Kingdom in 1810 and later years reveals some large regional variations with wages in Glasgow usually though not invariably from 1s. to 5s. lower than those paid in Manchester or Bolton. At the very top of the scale inevitably were the compositors on London morning newspapers earning £2. 8s. a week, an income which many a curate or governess would have envied. At the very bottom, equally inevitably, were labourers both urban and rural, earning in Manchester 15s. a week, in Glasgow 11s., with farm workers (except in a few particularly ill-paid counties) averaging 13s. a week. In between came tradesmen of varying degrees of skill: Carpenters: 25s. a week in Manchester, 18s. in Glasgow; Bricklayers: 22s. 6d. and 17s.; Masons: 22s. and 17s.; Tailors: 18s. 6d. in Manchester and unusually 6d. more in Glasgow; Shoemakers: 16s. and 15s. and – already a special case slipping down the earnings table – handloom-weavers 10s. 3d. in Manchester, 11s. 6d. in Glasgow. Another survey adds additional trades such as miners earning in Scotland 5s. a day and ironmoulders high up the table with 31s. a week. The earnings of the 'mule-spinners' using one of the earliest inventions to transform the cotton industry, Samuel Crompton's 'mule', which produced a finer and stronger thread than hand spinning, thus making possible the production of high-quality muslin, at 25s.–30s. a week showed clearly enough that machinery was by no means a threat to the livelihood of those who learned to master it. Engineers, a trade barely known twenty years earlier, already earned 28s. a week, another portent of changes still to come.*

*With the exception of the handloom-weavers most of these rates of pay altered little during the following twenty years apart from minor variations due to the state of trade. The pattern of occupations however changed markedly during this period. The cotton industry with only 162,000 employees in 1787 was by 1831 one of the two or three largest in the country with 833,000.*

1 From the evidence of Longmate's survey (Source 1.27), what reservations would you have about drawing conclusions on standards of living based on a general movement in money wages, as shown in Source 1.26?

2 Who were the 'labour aristocrats' in terms of rates of pay received?

3 What two important qualifying factors does Longmate produce at the end of the source extract?

## What main issues in the controversy over standards of living have historians debated?

● **SOURCE 1.28**

From P. A. M. Taylor, *The Industrial Revolution in Britain: Triumph or Disaster?*, 1958, in which the author identifies some of the difficulties faced in assessing standards of living.

*Controversy about working class living standards in the Industrial Revolution reflects in part uncertainties in the evidence. In part it reflects ideological opinion among modern writers . . . Within the limits of imperfect data . . . we know little of unemployment or underemployment. We know too little about working class consumption: did most workers really use the manufactured goods whose prices demonstrably fell, or even consume the meat and other foodstuffs about which historians argue? We know remarkably little about the distribution of national income; and some modern conclusions are of the order of 'it must have been', 'can we doubt that', or 'it is my guess'.*

1 According to Source 1.28, what are the key difficulties facing historians who attempt to analyse standards of living?

● **SOURCE 1.29**

From E. P. Thompson, *The Making of the English Working Class*, 1966, in which the author warns of the danger of confusing evidence relating to the *quality* of life with evidence concerned with *quantity*.

*From food we are led to homes, from homes to health, from health to family life, and thence to leisure, work discipline, education and play, intensity of labour, and so on. From standard of life we pass to way of life. But the two are not the same. The first is a measurement of quantities; the second a description (and sometimes an evaluation) of qualities. Where statistical evidence is appropriate to the first, we must rely largely upon 'literary evidence' as to the second. A major source of confusion arises from the drawing of conclusions to one from evidence appropriate only to the other. It is at times as if statisticians have been arguing: 'the indices reveal an increased per capita consumption of tea, sugar, meat and soap, therefore the working class was happier', while social historians have replied: 'the literary sources show that people were unhappy, therefore their standard of living must have deteriorated'.*

1 According to Source 1.29, what is meant by
   a) quality of life
   b) quantity of life?

2 What does Thompson regard as the main problems of reaching conclusions on standards of living?

3 What image of the condition of working people is revealed by the literary evidence?

● **SOURCE 1.30**

From R. M. Hartwell, 'The Standard of Living during the Industrial Revolution: A Discussion', 1963, in which the author criticises the pessimists' view of the negative effects of the Industrial Revolution on the labourers.

**cycles**
regular occurrences of events such as plague or famine

*Dr Hobsbawm twice claims that the eighteenth century is 'unknown' and that 'in the present state of our knowledge', comparisons with the nineteenth century 'must . . . still be left open'. Elsewhere, however, he still posits a golden age, and, in comparison with the earlier period, describes how the labouring poor of the Industrial Revolution felt an 'unquantifiable and spiritual sense of loss', and how 'the self confident, coherent, educated and cultured pre-industrial mechanics and domestic workers' declined and fell (in spite of agreeing also with Engels that the pre-industrial workers lived in 'ignorance and stagnation'). But the researches of Mrs M. D. George, Miss D. Marshall and the Webbs reveal a pre-industrial society that was static and sordid, with the labouring poor on subsistence wages and periodically decimated by CYCLES of plagues and famines. What Dr Hobsbawm has to prove is that living conditions in the eighteenth century were better than in the early nineteenth, not, as we all know, that conditions during the Industrial Revolution were bad. This debate on the dynamics of social change cannot be concluded here, but some specific social gains of this period might be mentioned to offset in the minds of more impressionable readers the pessimism of Dr Hobsbawm: (i) the increasing social and economic independence of women, (ii) the reduction in child labour, (iii) the growth of friendly societies, trade unions, savings banks, mechanics' institutes and cooperative societies, (iv) the growth of literacy (more of the population could read and write in 1850 than in 1800), and (v) the changing character of social disorder, which, as F. C. Mather recently demonstrated, was much less brutish and destructive in the 1840s than in the 1780s. The Marxist doctrine of social and economic evolution cannot be protected forever, even by Dr Hobsbawm, from that misfortune, long ago foreseen by Herbert Spencer, of being 'a deduction killed by a fact'. And in this case, the facts are legion.*

Study Source 1.30.

1 What did Hobsbawm claim to be the negative effects of the Industrial Revolution on labourers?

2 Why does Hartwell criticise Hobsbawm's argument?

3 What claims have other historians made about pre-industrial society?

4 What specific social gains does Hartwell identify to support his optimistic view of the Industrial Revolution?

## Is it possible to draw any conclusions about changes in standards of living?

● **SOURCE 1.31**

From P. Mathias, *The First Industrial Nation: Economic History of Britain 1700–1914*, 1969, in which the author questions whether it is possible to draw any conclusions about standards of living before 1850.

*Can one hope to draw conclusions about the changes in the standard of living between 1790 and 1850? There is no agreement now; there has been no agreement by contemporaries arguing ever since those days. Both sides agree that after 1850 the national income was expanding so fast that, even with wider gaps between rich and poor probably developing, the poor were benefiting from the expanding economy and industrialisation – again in those things that could be measured. The lack of a consensus means that one cannot yet speak with confidence of a single entity, 'the national economy', as far as the standard of living is concerned. The question is whether the handloom-weaver was more representative than the adult in the factories who maintained wages in the face of falling prices. Is the bad year 1842 more typical than the good year 1845? A lot of evidence both favourable and unfavourable depends on these two questions: which sector of the economy does it apply to and to which particular year?*

*But continuing debate today means that probably no marked general change took place, certainly no general movement towards deterioration, such as occurred between 1793 and 1815 from war inflation and high food prices and a shift in distribution of income away from wage-earners. This absence of drama in turn may be considered very dramatic given the increase in the population that had to be supported – from under 9 million to over 14 million in those 60 years after 1790.*

1 According to Source 1.31, to what extent is there agreement amongst historians on standards of living before 1850?

2 To what extent does the statistical evidence in Source 1.26 (page 28) support the claims in the final paragraph of Source 1.31 that there was no marked general change in living standards?

3 What is the value of Source 1.31 for an understanding of the complexities of the debate about living standards?

## ● SOURCE 1.32

From P. Deane and W. A. Cole, *British Economic Growth 1688–1959*, 1969.

Average real wages adjusted for unemployment, 1850–1906 (base year = 1850 = 100).

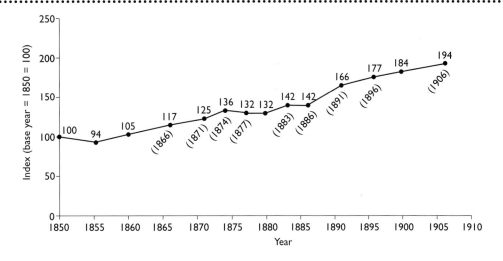

## ● SOURCE 1.33

From J. Burnett, *A History of the Cost of Living*, 1977, in which the author draws conclusions about changes in the cost of living between 1790 and 1900.

**Charles Booth and Seebohm Rowntree**
were researchers who carried out investigations among the urban poor in the late nineteenth century. (See Chapter 5 for more information on these investigations.)

*In total, then, the whole period from 1790 to 1900 saw an increase in the real earnings of the average worker of some 2½ times, and probably a doubling within the . . . period 1830–1900. Britain's productive resources had at last enabled her to realise a standard of life that was unique in time and in place . . . Because of this improvement, and because of the continuous upgrading of labour from less skilled to more skilled occupations, there can be little doubt that the worker had gained as much as other classes during the period of late Victorian prosperity . . . It was against this background of optimism that the revelations of poverty by CHARLES BOOTH AND SEEBOHM ROWNTREE came as such a disagreeable shock.*

*By the standards of the most rigorous measures available to them – a subsistence level defined by reference to the smallest amount of food necessary to support mere physical efficiency – they came to an almost precisely similar conclusion, that 30.7 per cent of the population of London and 27.8 per cent of the population of York were existing in poverty . . . In 1900 one half of all the children of the working classes still grew up in poverty, 1 in 6 babies died before reaching their first year, and 1 in 5 of the population would still look forward to the indignity of a pauper's funeral from the workhouse in which they would end their days.*

Study Sources 1.32 and 1.33.

1  What material progress was made in the period 1790–1900?

2  What percentage of workers, according to Booth and Rowntree, failed to make any gains?

3  In what ways did workers
   a) benefit
   b) suffer
   from industrialisation?

# 4 To what extent did the Industrial Revolution lead to class conflict?

During the first half of the nineteenth century, society was transformed. Eventually, a balanced social and economic order was created, which formed the basis of Victorian prosperity in the 1850s and beyond. But this was not immediately established and prior to 1850 there was social conflict and economic depression, as highlighted by the high level of social unrest. During the 1830s and 1840s revolutionary impulses seemed to be inherent in the nature of society. Significant sections of the labouring poor were alienated from the established order. This was partly due to the cyclical nature of economic development whereby alternate periods of boom and slump created large pockets of unemployment. When trade was poor, or on the 'downswing', resentment and bitterness built up. In the countryside, declining profits meant that the poorer land went out of cultivation and farmers tried to reduce their wage bills. In the towns, the situation was aggravated since there the poverty and misery appeared to be man-made. In the past when a failure of the harvest pushed up the price of food beyond the peasants' ability to pay, the peasant blamed the seasons; now, in the towns, the manufacturer was blamed since he was the agent responsible for hiring and firing, and for low wages.

The situation was not helped by the determination of the government to protect the rights of property and preserve the established social order, rather than remove distress and unemployment. There was, moreover, a rising middle class eager to take a share of political power from the landed aristocracy who dominated the political system. They were prepared to use violence, or the threat of violence. This situation led to the appearance of a 'class' struggle in the first three decades of the nineteenth century. However, the authorities were able to contain the new forces, by reforming the pattern of parliamentary representation and local government, giving the growing middle classes an enhanced political and social significance, and introducing a mass of legislation to improve conditions in town and factory.

## How frequent were the outbreaks of riot?

● **SOURCE 1.34**

Frequency of riot, 1812–50, based on evidence collated by the author.

| Year | State of the harvest | Incidence of riot |
|------|---------------------|-------------------|
| 1812 | Poor | • Machine-breaking (Luddism) by handloom-weavers, framework-knitters and wool combers in Nottingham, Lancashire, Yorkshire.<br>• Rise in crime in 18 out of 22 agricultural counties and 31 committals for arson, such as rick-burning. |
| 1816 | Poor | • Riots on the land – 33 committals for arson.<br>• Rise in crime in 18 out of 22 agricultural counties.<br>• Machine-breaking in Nottingham, Lancashire, Yorkshire.<br>• Political disturbances and rioting at Spa Fields, London. |
| 1817 | Poor | • Protest march by unemployed from Manchester to London (known as the March of the Blanketeers).<br>• Proposed demonstration by unemployed textile workers in Derbyshire and Huddersfield.<br>• Rise in crime in 21 out of 22 agricultural counties and 30 committals for arson. |
| 1818 | Poor | • Lancashire strikes. |
| 1819 | Poor | • Political disturbances at St Peter's Field, Manchester (the Peterloo massacre).<br>• Riots on the land in Norfolk.<br>• Rise in crime in 14 out of 22 agricultural counties and 22 committals for arson. |
| 1829 | Poor | • Agricultural counties: 37 committals for arson.<br>• Parliamentary Reform disturbances in towns of the Midlands and the North. |
| 1830 | Poor | • Agricultural counties: 45 committals for arson.<br>• Parliamentary Reform disturbances in towns of the Midlands and the North.<br>• Disturbances involving farm labourers. |

33

To what extent did the Industrial Revolution lead to class conflict?

| 1831 | Poor | • Agricultural counties: 102 committals for arson. <br> • Parliamentary Reform riots. |
|---|---|---|
| 1832 | Good | • Agricultural counties: 111 committals for arson. <br> • Parliamentary Reform riots. |
| 1833 | Good | • Agricultural counties: 64 committals for arson. <br> • Ten Hours Factory Reform campaign. |
| 1835 | Good | • Agricultural counties: 76 committals for arson. <br> • In Bircham, Norfolk, 800 men opposed attempts to introduce a new workhouse. |
| 1836 | Good | • Agricultural counties: 72 committals for arson. |
| 1837 | Good | • Agricultural counties: 42 committals for arson. <br> • Anti-Poor-Law riots in the Midlands and the North. |
| 1838 | Poor | • Agricultural counties: 39 committals for arson. |
| 1839 | Poor | • Agricultural counties: 37 committals for arson. <br> • CHARTIST uprisings in Newport and Birmingham. |
| 1840 | Poor | • Agricultural counties: 67 committals for arson. <br> • Chartist uprisings at Sheffield and Bradford. |
| 1841 | Poor | • Agricultural counties: 25 committals for arson. |
| 1842 | Good | • Agricultural counties: 48 committals for arson. <br> • Widespread Chartist-inspired strikes in the Midlands and the North. |
| 1843 | Good | • Agricultural counties: 44 committals for arson. <br> • Chartist-inspired riots in Wales, known as the Rebecca riots. |
| 1844 | Good | • Agricultural counties: 32 committals for arson. |
| 1845 | Good | • Agricultural counties: 90 committals for arson. |
| 1846 | Good | • Agricultural counties: 114 committals for arson. |
| 1847 | Poor | • Agricultural counties: 115 committals for arson. |
| 1848 | Poor | • Agricultural counties: 120 committals for arson. <br> • Revival of Chartism – Kennington Common meeting, London. <br> • Chartist riots in Bradford and East London. |
| 1849 | Good | • Agricultural counties: 206 committals for arson. |
| 1850 | Good | • Agricultural counties: 167 committals for arson. |

**Chartism**
appeared between 1838 and 1848. The movement drew its support from working people and was concerned with securing a number of parliamentary reforms. (See Chapter 7 for more information on the Chartists.)

● **SOURCE 1.35**

From J. Stevenson, *Popular Disturbances in England, 1700–1870*, 1979.

Number of committals for riotous offences per year by decade, 1839–68 (including riot and sedition).

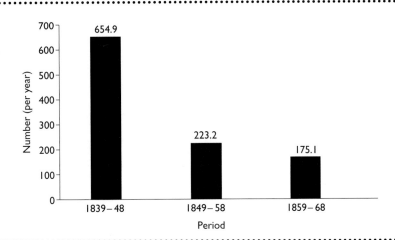

Study Sources 1.34 and 1.35.

1 Identify the period that saw the most incidents of riotous offences.

2 What link existed between the state of the economy and the outbreak of popular unrest in the period 1812–50?

3 What methods were used by each of the following groups to express their distress
   a) agricultural labourers
   b) traditional handicraft workers
   c) industrial workers?

# What views did contemporaries express on the relationship between the classes?

### ● SOURCE 1.36

*Capital and Labour*, a cartoon from *Punch* Volume 2, 1843.

CAPITAL AND LABOUR.

### ● SOURCE 1.37

From Friedrich Engels, *The Condition of the Working Class in England*, 1845, in which the author presents a 'socialist' viewpoint of the relationship between the classes.

*The middle class have more in common with every other nation in the world than with their own workers who live on their own doorsteps. The workers differ from the middle class in speech, in thoughts and ideas, in customs, morals, politics and religion.*

### ● SOURCE 1.38

From Benjamin Disraeli, *Sybil, or the Two Nations*, 1845, in which the author – who became Conservative Prime Minister in 1874 – comments on the existence of two nations.

*'Yes,' resumed the younger stranger after a moment's interval. 'Two nations; between whom there is no intercourse and no sympathy; who are as ignorant of each other's habits, thought and feelings as if they were dwellers in different zones, or inhabitants of different planets; who are formed by a different breeding, are fed by a different food, are ordered by different manners and are not governed by the same laws.'*
*'You speak of—' said Egremont hesitatingly.*
*'THE RICH AND THE POOR.'*

### ● SOURCE 1.39

From Elizabeth Gaskell, *North and South*, 1854, in which the writer comments on the relationship between the classes.

*I see two classes dependent on each other in every possible way, yet each evidently regarding the interests of the other as opposed to their own; I never lived in a place before where there were two sets of people always running each other down.*

---

Study Sources 1.36–1.39.

1  In what respects do the authors consider that the working class is different from the rest of society?

2  Why does Disraeli claim that two nations exist?

3  What is the message of the artist in the 1843 *Punch* cartoon (Source 1.36)?

4  What images does the artist adopt to convey his message?

5  Is it possible to tell whether the artist is sympathetic to a particular 'class'?

● **SOURCE 1.40**

From Joseph Arch, *The Life of Joseph Arch by himself*, 1898, in which he describes a Communion service in his parish church that he witnessed as a child.

---

**Joseph Arch (1826–1919)**
was a Warwickshire labourer who became a Nonconformist lay preacher and was the founder of the National Agricultural Labourers Trade Union in 1872. He later became an MP.

---

*I can also remember the time when the parson's wife used to sit in state in her pew in the chancel, and the poor women used to walk up the church and make a curtsey to her before taking the seats set apart for them. They were taught in this way that they had to pay homage and respect to those 'put in authority over them', and made to understand that they must 'honour the powers that be', as represented in the rector's wife. You may be pretty certain that many of these women did not relish the curtsey-scraping and other humiliations they had to put up with, but they were afraid to speak out. They had their families to think of, children to feed and clothe somehow; and when so many could not earn a living wage, but only a half-starving one, when very often a labouring man was out of work for weeks at a stretch, – why, the wives and mothers learned to take thankfully whatever was doled out to them at the parsonage or elsewhere, and drop the curtsey expected of them, without making a wry face. A smooth face and a smooth tongue was what their benefactors required of them, and they got both. My proud little spirit smarted and burned when I saw what happened at the Communion service. First, up walked the squire to the communion rails; the farmers went up next; then up went the tradesmen, the shopkeepers, the wheelwright, and the blacksmith; and then, the very last of all, went the poor agricultural labourers in their smock frocks. They walked up by themselves; nobody else knelt with them; it was as if they were unclean – and at that sight the iron entered straight into my poor little heart and remained fast embedded there. I said to myself, 'If that's what goes on – never for me!' I ran home and told my mother what I had seen, and I wanted to know why my father was not as good in the eyes of God as the squire, and why the poor should be forced to come up last of all to the table of the Lord. My mother gloried in my spirit.*

---

1 How, according to Source 1.40, was the class distinction within a rural community made evident?

2 How did the Anglican Church show its support of class distinctions in the village?

3 How does Arch show his resentment of such class distinctions?

4 In what ways were the agricultural workers kept subservient?

5 What was the response of rural labourers to situations like those described by Joseph Arch? (Refer back to Source 1.34 (pages 32–3) to answer this question.)

## Why did contemporaries fear riot?

● **SOURCE 1.41**

From J. Golby, 'Chartism and Public Order, Popular Politics', 1974, in which the historian comments on contemporaries' fears of Chartism.

*It must be remembered that at the time for many people Chartism aroused very real fears. To the middle and upper classes a Chartist rebellion was more than a remote possibility. The Home Office papers contain numerous reports to the Home Secretary from anxious magistrates and Lord Lieutenants passing on rumours of Chartist insurrections. Some of the reports are well founded, others have much less justification . . . Certainly it was the fear of mob violence that did much to shape the attitudes of the authorities and of sections of the general public to the grievances of the working classes. Nevertheless, it is important to take into account that, for a variety of reasons, fear was sometimes deliberately fostered by the authorities. There was a tendency to ascribe any industrial unrest or disturbances to the work of the Chartists and the more violent aspects of these disturbances were often emphasised in order to win the support of the uncommitted. By this means the authorities hoped to produce a united opposition against the rioters, or strikers, which would help prevent the disturbances . . . caused by Chartist agitators, [and] the authorities often succeeded in obscuring the very real grievances of the strikers.*

---

1 Why, according to Source 1.41, did Chartism arouse 'very real fears' among the middle and upper classes?

2 How justified were they in these fears?

3 What was the response of the authorities to the Chartists?

4 What were the motives of the authorities in dealing with Chartists?

# Conclusion

There is no doubt that workers in the period up to 1850 were faced with acute problems of unemployment, both short term as a result of trade cycles and long term as a result of technological change. Evidence of a discontented society was shown by the level of violent social protest. By the end of the 1840s wages had started to recover but convincing evidence of a rise in real wages did not appear until the 1860s. The years 1851–70 have been described by one historian as the age of 'equipoise', when there was a balance of interests. Restrictions had been removed on the import of foodstuffs; agriculture prospered and society became more settled. The mood of the period 1851–67 was very different from that of the period which preceded it. Nearly everyone appeared to prosper and there was a rise in the standard of living, though differentials remained. The aristocracy were not concerned with hard work, but with sport, hunting, fishing and shooting, and the town for them was the scene for leisure activities. Social attitudes were shaped by the landed classes.

From the evidence of the 1873 census on land ownership, sometimes referred to as the 'New Domesday Survey', four-fifths of the land was held by a small percentage of the population. The countryside was dotted with a large number of 'small' country houses, homes for the gentry, who had no European counterpart. Below the class of great landowners, farmers and industrialists benefited from Britain's advantage over rivals. The Great Exhibition of 1851 exemplified the glories of the age and the marvels of industry. Shopkeepers benefited from increased spending power, and local stores were developed, as were town centres and department stores in Liverpool and London. Shopping streets developed and the distribution system improved. The number of professional people was increasing, especially lawyers, but also clergy, registered medics, surveyors and engineers. They were rewarded through fees, stipends and honoraria, that is, their payment did not depend on whether anyone made a profit.

## A period of contrasts

It was also a period of contrasts. Provincial cities, led by reforming mayors such as Joseph Chamberlain in Birmingham, developed a sense of civic pride although people were socially segregated. The working class in Liverpool lived in cellars while the middle class had their suburbs on the edge of the town and were dependent on transport. Town life became more settled during the 1830s and 1840s when rail networks were built and timetables were drawn up.

Workers' lives were made up of long hours of work and limited holidays; Sundays were the exception, for the Sabbath was set apart for going to church or chapel. Middle-class women had too much leisure. They were discouraged from entering the professions and hard manual work was excluded. They played the piano, did embroidery and supervised work in the garden. There was a sharp contrast between overworked working men (and their wives) and over-leisured middle-class women.

The family developed as a key social institution and its size rose from 4.7 in 1851 to 6.2 by the end of the 1860s. The middle-class family could not survive without domestic servants and 'upstairs/downstairs' emphasised the great social divide. Housing conditions were poor for many people, and an inadequate water supply meant that it was difficult to keep clean. Food was often adulterated and regional and seasonal diets existed. Religion was a major preoccupation. There were different kinds of Christians: 'Church versus chapel'. Nonconformists had an austere lifestyle, while the Oxford movement in the Church of England emphasised ritual.

## Renewal of conflict

The last quarter of the nineteenth century, 1870–1901, saw a renewal of conflict with the demand for better protection for workers and the formation of working men's organisations. Consensus on the values of hard work, self-help and thrift broke down. This was also the period of the late-Victorian 'Great Depression' when agriculture and industry, challenged by foreign competitors, lost their dominance in world trade.

● **Summary task**

**Class discussion**
What are the uses and limitations of information about the cost of living and money wages as evidence for trends in living standards in the period 1800–50?

## Examples of examination-type questions

### A  AS questions

1  a) What main changes took place in the size and distribution of population?
   b) Why was there a rise in the urban population in nineteenth-century Britain?

### B  A2 questions

1  Account for the changing geographical distribution of population in England between 1800 and 1850.
2  What were the principal causes of the growth of urban population between 1800 and 1850?

● **Further reading**

S. G. Checkland, *The Rise of Industrial Society in England 1815–1885* (Longman, 1964); E. J. Evans, *The Forging of the Modern State: Early Industrial Britain, 1783–1870* (Addison, Wesley & Longman, 1993); G. Kitson Clark, *The Making of Victorian England* (Methuen, 1962); T. May, *An Economic and Social History of Britain, 1760–1990* (Addison, Wesley & Longman, 2nd edn, 1990); H. J. Perkins, *The Origins of Modern British Society* (Routledge, 1969); F. M. L. Thompson, *The Rise of Respectable Society: A Social History of Britain, 1830–1900* (Fontana, 1988)

# Did working conditions improve?

**1802**

Health and Morals of Apprentices Act bans the employment of pauper apprentices and night work in textile mills; day labour is limited to twelve hours. The act is ineffective due to the absence of both inspection and a system of penalties.

**1813**

Robert Owen's campaign to protect factory children leads to the setting up of a Select Committee chaired by Sir Robert Peel the Elder.

**1816**

House of Lords Committee is chaired by Lord Kenyon.

**1819**

Cotton Mills and Factories Act bans the employment of 'free' children under nine. It also restricts the hours worked by children aged nine to thirteen to 48 hours a week, and by young people aged thirteen to eighteen to 69 hours. There is no inspection, so the act is ineffective.

**1825**

Bill to reduce hours and stop night work fails.

**1832**

A Royal Commission is set up to enquire into the employment of children in textile mills.

**1833**

Factory Act (Althorpe's Act) bans the employment of children under nine and restricts the hours worked by children aged nine to thirteen to a maximum of 48 hours a week, with young persons aged thirteen to eighteen working a maximum of 69 hours a week. The act applies to all textile factories except silk mills. Government inspectors are appointed to implement and supervise the act.

**1838, 1839, 1841**

Ten Hour Bills are unsuccessful.

**1842**

Mines Act bans the employment of all children under ten and of women. Inspection of mines begins.

**1844**

Factory Act (Graham's Act) reduces the minimum working age in all textile factories to eight, and the hours that children are permitted to work are lowered to six per day, with half of their time to be spent in school. A maximum twelve-hour day is introduced for young persons aged thirteen to eighteen, and for women.

**1846**

Ten Hour Bill is rejected.

**1847**

Factory Act provides for a twelve-hour day for women and young persons, with two hours out of the twelve for meals. However, this does not mean that a ten-hour working day has in effect also been achieved for men. They cannot work without the help of children but the machinery is allowed to operate between 5.30 a.m. and 8.30 p.m. and children work in shifts, so the working day of men can still be much longer than that of women and children.

**1850**

Factory Act gives women and young persons the ten-hour day. Machinery operates between 6 a.m. and 6 p.m. but children aged nine to twelve may still work in shifts until the 1853 act.

## 1853

Factory Act lays down that children should carry out their work between 6 a.m. and 6 p.m. with one hour for meals. So, in effect, the ten-hour day for men is achieved, as they cannot work without the aid of the children, but this only applies in textile mills.

## 1863–67

Children's Employment Commission reports on bad conditions in the pottery, match- and lace-making industries.

## 1867

Factory and Workshop Regulation Act defines a workshop as a place employing five or more workers, including children, young persons and women employed in handicraft. The act bans the employment of children under eight, with half-time employment for those aged between eight and thirteen. A twelve-hour day for women and young persons brings workshops into line with the legislation already affecting the textile mills. Local authorities are made inspectors.

## 1871

Factory and Workshops Act provides for workshops to be inspected by factory inspectors.

## 1874

Factory Act raises the minimum working age from eight to ten, with half-time work for children up to the age of fourteen. Women and young persons are to work a maximum ten-hour day, as in the textile industry.

## 1878

Factory and Workshops Act redefines factories as establishments using mechanical power. Existing acts are improved and consolidated. This act extends the Factory Acts to all industries, although establishments employing men only are still not regulated.

## 1880

Employers' Liability Act makes employers liable for negligence by their workers.

## 1888–90

Select Committee of the House of Lords reports on the 'sweated trades', such as tailoring, boot-making, and cutlery-making.

## 1891

Sweated Trades Act attempts to protect women working very long hours in trades carried on in back rooms. Minimum working age of eleven is identified.

## 1895

Factory Act lays down that children under thirteen must work a maximum 30-hour week with no night work for under-fourteens. Docks, wharves, quays and laundries are brought under the Factory Acts. The Home Office is to make rules about places where only men are employed.

## 1897

Workmen's Compensation Act makes the employer responsible for accidents in some dangerous trades.

## 1901

Minimum working age is to be twelve.

## 1906

Workmen's Compensation Act makes employers liable for all accidents in all trades.

## 1906, 1913

Shops Act lays down 64 hours as the maximum hours for shop work and ends the system of living in.

## 1908

Industrial Compensation Act bans the use of white phosphorus to make matches and provides compensation for women suffering from 'phossy jaw'.

## 1909

Trades Board Act sets up wage boards to settle the rates of earnings and hours of work in four trades – lace-making, chain-making, paper-box-making and tailoring.

# Introduction

Changes in machinery and sources of power brought with them the factories, the 'dark satanic mills'. There is a tendency for historians to exaggerate the contrast between cottage industry and the later evils of the Industrial Revolution. Workers did not lead an idyllic life under the old domestic system. They might have been free to choose when they worked and to take a long weekend but they still had to work a twelve-hour day. The regulated day and loss of independence were the new elements introduced by the factory system. This system spread very slowly and proved to be very unpopular with workers. It became associated with all the ills of industrial society: low pay, long hours, dangerous conditions and the employment of a large number of children in a dirty environment. Families functioned as an economic unit as women and children joined the men in the workplace to supplement the family income.

Many workers united to seek an improvement in their living and working conditions, even though not all their problems could be solved by a reform of factory conditions. J. T. Ward has written that the factory reform movement 'underwent a long period of gestation. The evils which we have come to associate with the Factory age were present under the cottage system' (from J. T. Ward, 'The Factory Movement' in J. T. Ward (ed.), *Popular Movements c. 1830–1850*, Macmillan, 1970, page 56). Long hours, which affected adults and children, had been traditional in the textile industry. Eighteenth-century observers had considered this to be beneficial, particularly for the young; idleness was regarded as the cause of bad behaviour. Unhealthy working conditions were also characteristic of work in the cottage, with its small room filled with fluff and dirt. Children worked from a young age and parents could be harsh supervisors. The transition to the mill involved no significant change of principle. Child labour was not the creation of the Industrial Revolution; there was no golden age of rural bliss in pre-industrial society. Commenting on the implications of the Industrial Revolution, D. Fraser has stated that, 'as with so many other social problems, the industrial revolution concentrated and multiplied what had previously been diffuse and remote from public gaze' (from D. Fraser, *The Evolution of the British Welfare State*, Macmillan, 1973, page 11).

# 1 What were the main features of working conditions in the factories?

The first generation of factory workers undoubtedly experienced a fundamental change in their pattern of life with a loss of independence. They had to adjust to a new work pattern.

Study the two pictures in Source 2.1 opposite.

1 What images does the artist of picture a) use to idealise work in the cottage?

2 What images does the artist T. Onwyn use to stir the conscience of mid-Victorian England about factory conditions?

3 What are the main differences in the working conditions shown in the two sources?

4 What are
a) the values
b) the limitations
of contemporary illustrations to a historian studying the factory reform movement in the mid-Victorian period?

# What were the differences between working in a spinning mill and working in a cottage?

41

What were the main features of working conditions in the factories?

● **SOURCE 2.1**

Two views of women spinning:
a) Women spinning in the cottage;
b) *Children in a Cotton Factory*, a painting by T. Onwyn.
From *The Life and Adventures of Michael Armstrong, Factory Boy*, by Frances Trollope, 1840.

a)

SPINNING—REELING WITH THE CLOCK-REEL—BOILING YARN.

b)

## What were the main abuses affecting adults employed in the factories?

Working in factories involved harsh discipline. This was partly because the excessively long hours resulted in tired workers, so foremen were motivated as much by the need to keep children awake and alert as by a sense of cruelty. Beatings and fines were also used to discipline and train the workforce.

Initially, concern about working conditions in factories centred on children and the bad effect of factory work on their health and morals. At this time there was widespread support for Adam Smith's notion of *laissez-faire* – the idea that social and economic problems are best resolved by those directly involved, rather than by government – and many people felt that adult workers could look after themselves. Although the need to protect female workers eventually engaged the reformers' attention, men were never mentioned at all. The belief that the state should play only a minimal role in the affairs of industry helps to explain why the struggle for factory reform was so bitter and so prolonged.

● **SOURCE 2.2**

Adapted from Peter Gaskell, *The Manufacturing Population of England*, 1833, in which the author, who was a doctor and a campaigner for factory reform, describes the life of a domestic weaver in the eighteenth century.

*Down to 1800 the majority of artisans worked in their own houses and with their family. It may be termed the period of domestic manufacture . . . By all the processes being carried on under a man's roof, he retained his individual respectability; he was kept apart from associations that might injure his moral worth, while he generally earned wages which were sufficient not only to live comfortably upon, but which enabled him to rent a few acres of land . . . a secondary occupation . . . [working the land] filled up the vacant hours when he found it unnecessary to apply himself to his loom or spinning machine . . . gave him employment of a healthy nature, and raised him a step in the scale of society above the mere labourer.*

*The domestic manufacturers generally lived in the outskirts of the large towns . . . of simple habits and few wants . . . they rarely left their own house and lands. The yarn which they spun, and which was wanted by the weaver, was received or delivered . . . by agents who travelled for the wholesale houses . . . at weekly periods. Grey-haired men – fathers of large families – have thus lived through a long life, which has been devoted to spinning or weaving, and have never entered the precincts of town till driven, of late years, by the depression in their means of support, they have gone there, for the first time, when forced to migrate with their households in search of occupation at the steam looms.*

*The small farmer, spinner, or handloom-weaver, presented an orderly and respectable appearance . . . he worked 'by the rule of his strength and convenience'. They [his strength and convenience] were, however, sufficient to clothe and feed himself and family decently. And . . . to lay by a penny for an evil day, and to enjoy those amusements and bodily recreations . . . He was a respectable member of society; a good father, a good husband, and a good son . . . Amusements were exclusively sought in bodily exercise, the dance, the quoits, cricket, the chase, the numerous seasonal celebrations . . . an utter ignorance of printed books . . . seeking his stimulus in home-brewed ale; having for his support meat, . . . farm produce, meal or rye bread, eggs, cheese, milk, butter, etc.; the use of tea quite unknown . . . his children growing up under his immediate . . . control; no lengthened separation taking place until they married and became themselves heads of families; engaged in pursuits similar to his own, and in a subordinate capacity; and lastly, the same generation living age after age on the same spot, and under the same thatched roof.*

● **SOURCE 2.3**

From Dr James P. Kay, *The Moral and Physical Condition of the Working Classes Employed in the Cotton Manufacture of Manchester*, 1832, in which Kay describes the effects of working in factories and the standard of living enjoyed by workers employed in the factories of Manchester.

*Dr James P. Kay (1804–77)* was later knighted for his social work. On marriage he added his wife's maiden name, Shuttleworth, to his name. Early in his career he was secretary of the Board of Health in Manchester, where he carried out a number of surveys into the effects of factory work, including the risk of typhus or factory fever. He is best known for his work in extending the provision of state education (see page 312).

*Their means are too often consumed by vice and improvidence* they waste their money on drink (for example), with no thought for the future

*price* wages

*The population employed in the cotton factories rises at five o'clock, works . . . from six till eight o'clock, and returns home for half an hour . . . to breakfast. This meal generally consists of tea or coffee with a little bread. Oatmeal porridge is sometimes, but, of late, rarely used . . . The tea is almost always of a bad quality; little or no milk is added. The operatives return to the mills until twelve o'clock when an hour is allowed for dinner. Amongst those who obtain the lower rate of wages this meal generally consists of boiled potatoes. The mess of potatoes is put into one large dish and a few pieces of fried fat bacon are sometimes mingled with them, but seldom meat. Those who obtain better wages, or families whose total income is larger, add a greater proportion of meat to this meal, at least three times a week; but the quantity consumed by the labouring classes is not great. The family sits round the table and they all plunge their spoons into the dish with an animal eagerness . . . At the end of the hour they are all again employed in the mills, where they continue until seven o'clock or a later hour, when they generally again indulge in tea, often mingled with spirits accompanied by a little bread. The wages obtained by operatives are, in general, sufficient to provide them with the decent comforts of life; the average wages of all persons employed in the mills (young and old) being from nine to twelve shillings per week. THEIR MEANS ARE TOO OFTEN CONSUMED BY VICE AND IMPROVIDENCE. But the wages of certain classes are exceedingly meagre. The introduction of the power-looms . . . has . . . diminished the demand for certain kinds of labour and consequently their PRICE. The handloom-weavers still continue a very extensive class and though they work fourteen hours and upwards daily, earn only from five to seven shillings per week. Ill-fed, ill-clothed, half-starved and ignorant; weaving in close damp cellars or crowded workshops; it only remains that they should become, as is too frequently the case, demoralised and reckless . . .*

*. . . In Manchester . . . more than one-half of the inhabitants . . . require the assistance of public charity.*

● **SOURCE 2.4**

From William Cobbett, *Political Register*, 20 November 1824, Vol. II, in which he presents a case for government control of factories.

*William Cobbett (1762–1835)* was the self-taught son of a labourer from Farnham, Surrey. He served as a soldier before becoming the editor of a radical paper, the *Political Register*, which campaigned for reform of Parliament. In 1832 he became the Member of Parliament for Oldham.

*Some of these lords of the loom have in their employ thousands of miserable creatures. In the cotton-spinning work these creatures are kept, fourteen hours in each day, locked up, summer and winter, in a heat of from EIGHTY TO EIGHTY-FOUR DEGREES. The rules which they are subjected to are such as no negroes were ever subjected to . . . What, then, must be the situation of the poor creatures who are doomed to toil, day after day, for three hundred and thirteen days in the year, fourteen hours in each day, in an average heat of eighty-two degrees? Can any man, with a heart in his body, and a tongue in his head, refrain from cursing a system that produces such slavery and such cruelty?*

*Observe, too, that these poor creatures have no cool room to retreat to, not a moment to wipe off the sweat, and not a breath of air to come and interpose itself between them and infection. The door of the place wherein they work, is locked, except half an hour, at tea-time; the workpeople are not allowed to send for water to drink, in the hot factory; even the rain-water is locked up, by the master's order, otherwise they would be happy to drink; even if any spinner be found with his window open, he is to pay a fine of a shilling! Mr Martin of Galway has procured Acts of Parliament to be passed to prevent cruelty to animals. If horses or dogs were shut up in a place like this they would certainly be thought worthy of Mr Martin's attention. Not only is there not a breath of sweet air in these truly infernal scenes; but, for a large part of the time, there is the abominable and pernicious stink of the GAS to assist in the murderous effects of the heat. In addition to the heat and the gas; in addition to the noxious smell of the gas, mixed with the steam, there are the dust, and what is called the cotton-flyings or fur, which the unfortunate creatures have to inhale; and the fact is, the notorious fact is, that well-built men are rendered old and past labour at forty years of age, and that children are rendered decrepit and deformed, and thousands upon thousands of them slaughtered by consumptions, before they arrive at the age of sixteen. And are these establishments to boast of? If we were to admit the fact they compose an addition to the population of the country; if we were further to admit that they caused an addition to the pecuniary resources of the Government, ought not a government to be ashamed to derive resources from such means?*

**fines**
This list of fines quoted by Cobbett was typical of the severe code of discipline adopted by the new textile factories. In 1823 spinners on strike at the Tyldesley mill near Manchester published a similar list. Fines were deducted from wages. In 1823 the average wage was about £1 10s. (£1.50) at a time when the weekly expenditure for a family of five would be £1 6s. 5d. (£1.32), not including rent.

*If we wanted any proof of the abject slavery of these poor creatures, what proof do we want more than the following list of FINES?*

| | |
|---|---|
| *Any Spinner found with his window open:* | *1s.* |
| *Any Spinner found washing himself:* | *1s.* |
| *Any Spinner leaving his oilcan out of its place:* | *6d.* |
| *Any Spinner putting his gas out too soon:* | *1s.* |
| *Any Spinner spinning with his gas-light too long in the morning:* | *2s.* |
| *Any Spinner heard whistling:* | *1s.* |
| *Any Spinner being five minutes after the last bell rings:* | *2s.* |
| *Any Spinner being sick and cannot find another Spinner to give satisfaction must pay for steam, per day:* | *6d.* |

● **SOURCE 2.5**

From the *Report of Commissioners on the Employment of Children in Factories*, 1833, which describes a spinning mill in Kincardineshire.

**profligates**
immoral people

*It is dirty, unroofed, ill-ventilated, with machinery not boxed in, and passages so narrow that they could hardly be defined; it seemed more to be a receptacle of demons than the workhouse of industrious human beings. The appearance and language of the workers, both men and women, proved the state of demoralisation which exists here. The house of Gilchrist the mill-owner, presented a picture of filth and want of comfort of every kind, such as I have rarely seen elsewhere. It was painful to find in . . . the eating and sleeping room of such a nest of PROFLIGATES, two or three young females without a parent or relation in the neighbourhood to look after their conduct, or to make any attempt to rescue them.*

● **SOURCE 2.6**

From J. M. Ludlow and L. Jones, *Progress of the Working Class*, 1867, describing factory workers, the majority of whom were women and young people, in Manchester in 1832.

**wakes**
factory holidays

*What were the amusements of the masses, thus over-worked, ill-fed, ill-housed, – left for the most part uneducated? Large numbers of working people attended fairs and WAKES, at the latter of which jumping in sacks, climbing greased poles, grinning through horse collars for tobacco, hunting pigs with soaped tails, were the choicest diversions. An almost general immorality . . . prevailed amongst the women employed in factories, and generally throughout the lowest ranks of the working population. But drink was the mainspring of enjoyment. When Saturday evening came, indulgences began which continued till Sunday evening. Fiddles were to be heard on all sides, and limp-looking men and pale-faced women thronged the public-houses, and reeled and jigged until they were turned, drunk and riotous into the streets, at most unseasonable hours . . . In fact, sullen, silent work alternated with noisy, drunken riot; and Easter and Whitsun debauches, with an occasional outbreak during some favourite 'wakes', rounded the whole life of the factory worker.*

Supporting evidence in the accounts of other contemporaries indicates that Ludlow and Jones (Source 2.6) were not exaggerating. Their account shows that rural customs survived in the pastimes of the factory workers, despite the different social context of the town. Hard work, alternating with rowdy leisure, popular amusements and drinking were typical of a worker's lifestyle, especially among those employed in heavy manual work. It was this lifestyle which attracted the criticism of many of the middle classes and which gave rise to the Temperance Movement to stamp out drinking.

1 To what extent does Peter Gaskell (Source 2.2) present an idealised image of the working and family life of domestic weavers before the coming of the factories?

2 Compare Sources 2.3–2.6 with Source 2.2. What were the main effects of working in factories on the life of its workforce? Use your own copy of the following table to help you to organise your answer.

| Life of labourers | Pre-industrial society | Industrial society |
|---|---|---|
| Employment | | |
| Length of working day | | |
| Leisure and time off | | |
| Wages | | |
| Diet | | |
| Family relationships | | |
| Independence | | |

3 What physical and moral dangers did those who worked in factories face?

4 What were the main diseases associated with work in factories?

5 What did workers find most to complain about in their working conditions?

● **SOURCE 2.7**

From the evidence of R. Cookson, a hosier, before the Committee on the Woollen Manufacture of England, *Parliamentary Papers*, 1806, in which he describes the distaste of men for factory work.

*I found the utmost distaste on the part of the men, to any regular hours or regular habits . . . The men themselves were considerably dissatisfied, because they could not go in and out as they pleased, and have what holidays they pleased, and go on just as they had been used to do; and were subject, during after-hours, to the ill-natured observations of other workmen, to such an extent as completely to disgust them with the whole system.*

● **SOURCE 2.8**

From Andrew Ure, *The Philosophy of Manufactures*, 1835, in which a contemporary commentator describes male wage differentials according to age and by inference employers' preference for female workers.

*In the cotton factories of Lancashire, the wages of the males during the period when there is the greatest number of employed – from eleven to sixteen – are on the average 4s. 10¾d. [21p] a week; but in the next period of five years, from sixteen to twenty-one, the average rises to 10s. 2½d. [51p] a week; and of course the manufacturer will have as few at that price as he can. In the next period of five years, from twenty-one to twenty-six, the average weekly wages are 17s. 2½d [86p]. Here is a still stronger motive to discontinue employing males as far as it can practically be done. In the subsequent two periods the average rises still higher, to 20s. 4½d. [£1.02], and to 22s. 8½d. [£1.14] At such wages, only those men will be employed who are necessary to do work requiring great bodily strength, or great skill, in some art, craft, or mystery or persons employed in offices of trust and confidence.*

● SOURCE 2.9

From Nassau Senior, *Grounds and Objects of the Budget*, in which he describes the recruitment of labour for the factories, 1831–33.

**Nassau Senior (1790–1864)**
was a political economist and lawyer. He became Professor of Political Economy at Oxford University in 1825. He took an active part in national affairs and was a member of a number of commissions including that on the Poor Law in 1834. His work contributed to the growing influence of the policies of *laissez-faire* (see page 42) and *utilitarianism* (see page 139) which he promoted in a number of journals, such as the *Edinburgh Review* and the *Quarterly Review*.

*A girl of 18 can attend to a power-loom as well as a full-grown man; a child of 13 is more valuable as a piecer than an adult – its touch is more sensitive, and its sight is more acute. A factory lad of 18 who marries a factory girl of the same age, finds himself immediately richer; and although he may be pinched during some of the following years, yet as each child attains the age of 9 years it can earn more than its support; and the earnings of 3 children between the ages of 9 and 16 can, in prosperous times, support the whole family. It was under the influence of this enormous stimulus, with some assistance from immigration, that the population of our manufacturing districts increased during the thirty years that elapsed between 1801 and 1831 . . . at a rate equalled only in some portions of America.*

Study Sources 2.7–2.9.

1 Why were men reluctant to work in factories?

2 Why did factory owners prefer to appoint children and women rather than men to work in their factories?

● SOURCE 2.10

From B. R. Mitchell and P. Deane, *Abstract of British Historical Statistics*, 1962 (adapted).

Numbers employed in the cotton industry, 1806–62 (averages for decades).

| Year | Raw cotton consumption (in million lbs) | Numbers employed in factories | Hand-loom weavers |
|---|---|---|---|
| 1806–09 | – | 93,900 | 190,000 |
| 1810–19 | 934 | 112,400 | 218,000 |
| 1820–29 | 1,664 | 157,600 | 240,000 |
| 1830–39 | 3,208 | 219,000 | 192,400 |
| 1840–49 | 5,263 | 276,600 | 75,900 |
| 1850–59 | 7,963 | 369,400 | 28,300 |
| 1860–62 | 8,087 | 439,300 | 6,700 |

1 How do you explain the decrease in the number of hand-loom weavers between 1806 and 1862, as indicated in Source 2.10?

2 Why do you think the number of workers in the textile factories increased more rapidly after 1830?

3 How do you think the hand-loom weavers would react to the impact of industrialisation?

## What were the main abuses affecting children employed in the factories?

The apprenticeship system developed as a result of problems of recruitment. Agricultural communities were hostile and would not move voluntarily to work in the factories. Population growth led many manufacturers to employ pauper children from workhouses in southern Britain as 'slave' labour. They were not paid but were apprenticed until they reached the age of 21. There were many stories of children being overworked, harshly treated and underfed. The lives of such children varied enormously depending on mill owners. Some were sadists, but others were well meaning, such as David Dale and his better-known son-in-law, Robert Owen.

Robert Owen (1771–1858) is famous for his management of the New Lanark factories, the largest cotton-spinning mills in Europe, beside the Clyde in Scotland. He went there as a foreman and married David Dale's daughter. The mill employed several hundred pauper apprentices, who were properly clothed, housed and educated. It also provided a village near the mill and guaranteed constant employment. It pioneered better working conditions and shorter hours, combined with good housing and regular education for its workforce. Productivity increased and, initially, Dale but then, more famously, Owen became associated with an efficient and humanitarian approach to factory management.

Owen became a champion of factory reform, securing the 1819 Cotton Mills and Factories Act, although this proved ineffective. He subsequently became a leading figure in the trade union movement and in 1833 organised the first general trade union, the Grand National Consolidated Trades Union, which aroused the hostility of the government of the day. He also supported the Chartist movement for reform of Parliament but abandoned it after the violence of 1839 and 1842 (see Chapter 7).

47

What were the main features of working conditions in the factories?

● **SOURCE 2.11**

From an *Enquiry into the Causes of the Increase of the Poor*, 1738, in which the anonymous author describes abuses associated with the employment of pauper apprentices under the domestic system.

*A most unhappy practice prevails in most places to apprentice poor children; no matter to what master, provided he lives out of the parish; if the child serves the first forty days we are rid of him forever. The master may be a tiger in cruelty; he may beat, abuse, strip naked, starve, or do what he will to the poor innocent lad . . . I know a poor old weaver . . . who some time ago took a poor apprentice from another parish; he covenanted, as is usual, to teach him his trade, to provide and allow him meat, drink, apparel, etc., to save harmless and indemnify the parish whence he took him, and to give him two good suits of wearing apparel at the end of his apprenticeship . . . as soon as the money he had with the boy was spent [he] threw himself, apprentice and all, upon the parish.*

● **SOURCE 2.12**

From Robert Owen, *A New View of Society and Other Writings*, 1813, in which the author discusses the effects of the manufacturing system on workers.

*Not more than thirty years since, the poorest parents thought the age of fourteen sufficiently early for their children to commence regular labour: and they judged well; for by that period of their lives they had acquired by play and exercise in the open air the foundation of a sound robust constitution; and if they were not all initiated in book learning they had been taught the far more useful knowledge of domestic life which could not but be familiar to them at the age of fourteen and which as they grew up and became heads of families was of more value to them (as it taught them economy in the expenditure of their earnings) than one half of their wages under present circumstances . . .*

*Contrast this state of affairs with that of the lower orders of the present day . . . In the manufacturing districts it is common for parents to send their children of both sexes at seven or eight years of age in winter as well as summer at six o'clock in the morning, sometimes of course in the dark and occasionally amidst frost and snow, to enter the manufactories which are often heated to a high temperature and contain an atmosphere far from being the most favourable to human life and in which all those employed in them very frequently continue until twelve o'clock at noon when an hour is allowed for dinner, after which they return to remain in a majority of cases till eight o'clock at night . . .*

*The direct object of these observations is to effect the improvement and avert the danger. The only mode by which these objects can be accomplished is to obtain an Act of Parliament . . . To prevent children from being employed in mills of machinery until they shall be ten years old or that they shall not be employed more than six hours per day until they shall be twelve years old. Parents who have grown up in ignorance and bad habits and who consequently are in poverty may say, 'We cannot afford to maintain our children until they shall be twelve years of age without putting them into employment by which they may earn wages and we therefore object to that part of the plan which precludes us from sending them to manufactories until they shall be of that age.'*

● **SOURCE 2.13**

From the evidence of a visitor in 1796, published in *Gentleman's Magazine*, describing the model community established at New Lanark by David Dale and managed by Robert Owen.

*Four hundred children are entirely fed, clothed and instructed at the expense of this venerable philanthropist. The rest live with their parents in neat comfortable habitations, receiving wages for their labour. The health and happiness depicted on the countenance of these children show that the proprietor of the Lanark mills has remembered mercy in the midst of gain. The regulations here to preserve health of body and mind present a striking contrast to those of most large manufactories in this kingdom, the very hotbeds of contagion and disease. It is a truth that ought to be engraved in letters of gold, to the eternal honour of the founder of New Lanark that out of nearly three thousand children who have been at work in these mills throughout a period of twelve years, only fourteen have died, and not one has suffered criminal punishment.*

● **SOURCE 2.14**

From Robert Owen, *A New View of Society and Other Writings*, 1813, in which Owen describes conditions at New Lanark.

*The system of receiving apprentices from public charities was abolished; permanent settlers with large families were encouraged and comfortable houses built for their accommodation. The practice of employing children in the mills of six, seven and eight years of age was discontinued and their parents advised to allow them to acquire health and education until they were ten years old . . . The children were taught reading, writing and arithmetic during five years, that is, from five to ten in the village school without expense to their parents . . .*

*[The workers'] houses were rendered more comfortable, their streets were improved, the best provisions were purchased and sold to them at low rates . . . Fuel and clothes were obtained for them in the same manner . . . Those employed became industrious . . . temperate, healthy, faithful to their employers and kind to each other.*

Study Sources 2.11–2.14.

1   What was considered the ideal age for children to start work in the 1780s?

2   What changes in the employment of children had taken place by 1815?

3   How did parents justify the employment of child labour?

4   What are Robert Owen's main criticisms of child labour?

5   What does Owen regard to be the best method for solving the problems created by child labour?

Study Sources 2.13 and 2.14.

6   Why was the founder of New Lanark considered to be a model employer?

7   What were Owen's main arguments in favour of factory reform?

● **SOURCE 2.15**

From Robert Southey, *Espriella's Letters from England*, 1807, in which the author describes, through the eyes of an imaginary Spanish visitor, the lives of parish apprentices in the textile factories around Manchester.

*They come at five in the morning; we allow them half an hour for breakfast, and an hour for dinner; they leave work at six, and another set relieves them for the night; the wheels never stand still.' I was looking, while he spoke, at the unnatural dexterity with which the fingers of these little creatures were playing in the machinery, half giddy myself with the noise and the endless motion; and when he told me there was no rest in these walls, day or night, I thought that if Dante had peopled one of his hells with children, here was a scene worthy to have supplied him with new images of torment.*

Study Sources 2.11–2.15.

1   What was meant by the 'apprenticeship system'?

2   What was the main difference between pauper and 'free' apprentices?

3   What were the main features of the pauper apprenticeship system?

4   What were the advantages to
    a) the parish
    b) the employer
    of the apprenticeship system?

5   To what extent do Owen and Southey agree on the evils associated with the apprenticeship system?

● **SOURCE 2.16**

From S. Pollard, *The Genesis of Modern Management*, 1968.

Different methods used by firms to enforce discipline among factory children, 1833.

| Negative | Number of firms using this method | Positive | Number of firms using this method |
|---|---|---|---|
| Dismissal | 353 | Kindness | 2 |
| Threat of dismissal | 48 | Promotion or higher wages | 9 |
| Fines, deductions from wages | 101 | Reward or premium | 23 |
| Corporal punishment | 55 | | |
| Complaint to parents | 13 | | |
| Confined to mill | 2 | | |
| Degrading dress, badge | 3 | | |
| Total: | **575** | | **34** |

1 What methods, according to Source 2.16, did factory owners prefer in order to train their workforce to accept a regular work routine?

2 What were the least commonly used methods of
   a) punishments
   b) rewards?

3 What do you think would be the effect on relationships in the workplace of the management methods adopted?

# 2 Who were the main supporters of the factory reform movement?

Prior to 1830 there was not really a 'movement' in the sense of an organisation, but a gradual rise of protest from various independent individuals and groups who lacked direction and leadership. The factory reform movement in many respects can be said to have represented a 'strange agitation'. Most of its founders, parliamentary champions and foremost regional leaders were Tories and churchmen, the social group associated with factory ownership. They represented the gentry and the professions, and regarded agitation as improper whilst working men feared victimisation if they became involved. Even more unusual were the alliances made between old enemies from Tory and Radical ranks in the northern industrial towns. The movement encompassed a variety of opinions drawn from across normal party lines, as well as reflecting the views of leading social reformers. It included Tory paternalists and leading Benthamites who wanted unified control by central government. According to SAMUEL KYDD, the first historian of factory reform, 'It occupied many years of the lives of some self-sacrificing, strong-willed, determined and high-minded men, ultimately commanding an over-ruling share of public attention' (from J. T. Ward, 'The Factory Movement', in J. T. Ward (ed.), *Popular Movements c. 1830–1850*, Macmillan, 1970, page 54). This is certainly true in the case of Sir Robert Peel the Elder and Robert Owen (see page 47) who were responsible for the first two Factory Acts.

By the mid-1830s the factory reform movement was taking action on two fronts: in Parliament and outside. In Parliament the reformers were led successively by Sir John Cam Hobhouse, Michael Sadler, Lord Shaftesbury and John Fielden. The Whig Party took office in 1830, pledged to a policy of social reform which, if uninspired, contrasted with the approach of their Tory predecessors. The second line of action was outside of Parliament and it is here that a 'patchwork of opinion' existed over the scope and form of factory reform. Leadership was divided. Richard Oastler, an Evangelical Anglican, organised a moral and religious crusade against factory evils in the 1830s. Short-Time Committees, made up of Radical and Tory operatives and tradesmen, supported by Anglican clergy, Tory squires and Radicals, operated in Yorkshire, Lancashire and Scotland.

**Samuel Kydd**
was the secretary of the reformer Richard Oastler, and published the first history of the factory reform movement in 1857.

The complexity of the movement showed itself in the often-conflicting aims of the reformers; some wanted machinery stopped at certain times to ensure the enforcement of maximum working hours, but Oastler was not prepared to accept this. Some Lancashire workers were prepared to compromise on the ten-hour demand, but others regarded this as a weakening of policy.

● **SOURCE 2.17**

Adapted from J. T. Ward, *Popular Movements, c.1830–1850*, 1970, in which the author identifies the different social groups who campaigned for factory reform and their motives.

**Richard Oastler (1789–1861)**

was the son of a Leeds clothier. He was a Quaker with strong reforming beliefs. He became a prominent leader of the ten-hours factory reform movement and was greatly admired by many northern workers, despite being a 'Church and King Tory'.

**Michael Sadler**

was a Leeds linen merchant and a strong Evangelical churchman, with a humane, paternalist (fatherly) approach. He was leader of the factory reform campaign in Parliament and his efforts secured a Select Committee on Child Labour in 1832. He surrendered leadership to the Earl of Shaftesbury after he lost his seat in 1832.

**Short-Time Committees**

were first set up in the 1830s but became less effective in the 1840s. In Scotland the Short-Time Committee fell under middle-class control while in London the Quaker-dominated committee was described by Oastler as 'sterile and unfruitful'. Elsewhere, the Yorkshire, Leeds and Huddersfield committees fell under control of Radical workers. Manchester had trade-union backing whereas Blackburn was Tory-dominated. Such divisions weakened the movement from within in the 1840s when opposition was strengthened. This partly helps to explain why the reform struggle was so prolonged.

*a) Factory reform campaign pre-1830*

*At least four distinguishable groups participated in the varying strands of the initial, unorganised demand for legislative reform.*

*i) Old labour aristocracies, such as the East Midland framework-knitters, the Yorkshire woollen croppers and worsted-combers and the handloom-weavers, originally despised the new developments. But as technological innovations ruined both their prestige and their incomes, such men fought desperate rearguard actions against factory industry as a whole. Some indulged in Luddite machine wrecking; some battled through early trade unions; some participated in groups opposing child employment.*

*ii) Secondly, some courageous pioneers of social medicine drew attention to the harmful effects of factory labour on health. For instance, the celebrated John Aikin of Warrington wrote of 'children of very tender age . . . transported in crowds, as apprentices to masters resident many hundred miles distant, where they served unknown, unprotected, and forgotten' and were 'usually too long confined to work in close rooms, often during the whole night'. After periodic investigations of child-workers' health following a fever epidemic at Radcliffe Bridge in 1784, Thomas Perceval of Manchester organised a pioneer board of health in 1795 . . . a long succession of surgeons and doctors followed this lead which in fact announced the bulk of later reformers' policy and propaganda points.*

*iii) . . . A third group were Northern clergymen who were to play important roles in the successive factory campaigns . . . [they] . . . were predominantly Anglicans, . . . dissenters were, with a few exceptions, absent . . . OASTLER, the ever-active 'Church and King Tory', was 'a sincere member of the established, reformed, Protestant, national Episcopal Church'. He insisted in 1836 that throughout his campaign 'his only object had been to establish the principles of Christianity, the principles of the Church of England in these densely peopled districts . . . especially to show the working classes that their best interests were bound up in the well-working of the Church.'*

*The close connections between prominent nonconformists . . . and leading capitalist opponents of reform led reformers to indulge in considerable 'religious' controversy. Oastler never hid his contempt for dissenting opponents, ascribing their hostility to the influence of wealthy chapelgoers.*

*iv) A fourth group of reformers might be characterised as 'traditionalists'. Some were literary men . . . Robert Southey believed that the new progressive capitalists 'would care nothing for the honour and independence of England, provided their manufactories went on . . .'. He protested at 'a new sort of slave-trade' in workhouse children . . . MICHAEL SADLER, a Leeds and Belfast linen merchant . . . was angered by the new industrialism . . . Some landowners were influenced by 'class' hostility to the new rich middle class . . . but the industrial and agricultural interests were far from being solid interests and Tories, Whigs and Radicals were divided over industrial reform and free trade . . .*

*b) Factory reform movement after 1830 – SHORT-TIME COMMITTEES*

*. . . from 1831 [Oastler] demanded a ten-hour day . . . from the spring, workers' groups in Huddersfield, Leeds, Bradford and Keighley had formed 'Short-Time Committees' and in June a delegation of Huddersfield men prevailed upon Oastler to link his Tory paternalism with their Radical reformism. By the autumn Oastler was urging operatives to 'manage this cause themselves . . . [and] establish, instantly establish, committees in every manufacturing town and village, to collect information and publish facts' (Leeds Intelligencer, 24 November, 20 October, 1831). Thus began a new type of organisation. For over two decades a variable number of committees – generally composed of Radical and Tory operatives and tradesmen, supported and largely financed by Anglican clergymen, Tory country gentlemen, and Radical and Tory industrialists . . . spread across the textile districts of England and Scotland.*

51

Who were the main supporters of the factory reform movement?

**John Doherty, James Turner and Thomas Daniel** were Lancashire workers who organised the 'cotton' campaign and subsequently formed the cotton-spinners' union.

**Anthony Ashley, later the Earl of Shaftesbury** was the Tory MP for Dorset, an Evangelical Churchman, and one of the greatest humanitarians of the nineteenth century. He was responsible for reforms of factories (1833, 1844), mines (1842), agriculture, the treatment of destitute children, and public health.

### c) Leadership in the country

*The Lancashire reformers soon rallied again, under JOHN DOHERTY, JAMES TURNER and THOMAS DANIEL. Apart from mobilising local support and arranging Oastler's noisy winter campaign, the committees – almost invariably operating from pubs – organised a concerted campaign in support of the Ten Hours Bill movingly proposed by Sadler on 16 March 1832. Subsequently they selected witnesses for Sadler's controversial Select Committee and supported his unsuccessful candidature at Leeds in December. Throughout the early years of the Factory Movement Oastler acted as the pivot and central organiser. His speaking tours revealed a wide dramatic ability; he controlled the central funds, mainly his own savings and Wood's contributions; he unceasingly planned and argued and wrote; and he imparted the crusading tone to the Movement. 'God prosper your righteous cause!' he wrote to Daniel in 1832. 'Operatives,—This Cause is your own. Never desert it. Bend your thoughts always to it—publish the Horrors of the System—subscribe what you can, by what you can—and be assured God will prosper the right. Oppression has reigned long enough. Let the Nation see you have resolved your Sons and Daughters shall be free . . . Be united. Be firm. Be courteous and obedient to your Masters—but resolutely bent on using every means the Law provides, to remove Slavery from your helpless little ones. God bless you and the Holy cause.'*

*But a basically 'moral' approach never prevented heated persuasive outbursts. Oastler was angered by magisterial connivance at factory-owners' offences under the Factory Acts. . . . Oastler's home at Fixby Hall long remained the Movement's planning centre; but the organisation was gradually formalised.*

### d) Role of the Central Committee

*As the number of local committees grew, central committees were established to co-ordinate Yorkshire and Lancashire activities and to arrange periodic assemblies of delegates. Modelled to some extent on Methodist precedent, conference was to assume a managerial role; at least ostensibly it made the major policy decisions.*

### e) Leadership in Parliament

*After Sadler's defeat (1832), twenty delegates (with mandates from two Scottish, ten Lancashire, one Nottingham and eleven Yorkshire committees) assembled at Bradford in January 1833. This first conference authorised selection of a new parliamentary leader . . . the Evangelical Tory ASHLEY took over Sadler's Bill, but was compelled in April to accept investigation by a Royal Commission. Edwin Chadwick's Commissioners, influenced by Benthamite philosophy, inevitably aroused anger and apprehension in the North, and a Manchester conference planned a boycott campaign. Bitterly complaining of hostile demonstrations, Chadwick's colleagues nevertheless worked quickly to report in June . . .*

---

Study Source 2.17.

1 Identify the four main social groups who campaigned for early factory reform prior to 1830.

2 What were their main motives?

3 To what extent did the social composition of the movement change after 1830?

4 What was meant by the Short-Time Committees?

5 How did the formation of these committees transform the struggle for factory legislation?

6 What was the role of the Central Committee?

7 What methods were adopted by the campaigners to achieve reform?

8 To what extent would it be valid to describe the factory reform movement as a 'strange agitation'?

# 3 Who were the main opponents of factory reform?

In 1866 Shaftesbury, looking back on his reform campaign, declared that he 'had to break every political connection, to encounter a most formidable array of capitalists, millowners and men, who by natural impulse, hated all "humanity mongers". In the provinces, the anger and irritation of the opponents to the Ten Hours Bill were almost fearful ... It required, during many years, repeated journeys to Lancashire and Yorkshire, no end of public meetings in the large towns; visits, committees, innumerable hours, intolerable expense. In very few instances did any mill owner appear on the platform with me; in still fewer the ministers of any religious denomination. At first not one, except the Rev. Mr Bull of Bierley, near Bradford; and even to the last, very few, so cowed were they (or in themselves indifferent) by the overwhelming influence of the cotton lords.'

This hostile attitude predominated until 1860. Manufacturers and mill owners were concerned about the effect of the restriction of hours on output, fearing a reduction would result in loss of markets and profits. The 1844 Factory Bill, which had initially provided for the maximum ten-hour working day, was rejected by the then Prime Minister, Sir Robert Peel, on the grounds that the profits of industry were made in the last hour of the day. The spokesman for the manufacturers in the House of Commons was Wilson Patten, Tory MP for North Lancashire. However, not all manufacturers were opposed to factory reform, as the support of Sir Robert Peel the Elder, Robert Owen and John Fielden shows.

Politicians, who were *laissez-faire* supporters of a minimal government role, and classical economists, who were opposed to the principle of government intervention and regulation, opposed the Factory Acts; Nassau Senior, the Poor Law reformer (see page 46), condemned a Ten Hours Bill as 'utterly ruinous'. They placed emphasis on freedom of contract between master and man. However, while they tolerated and justified the overworking of men, they recognised the need to protect women and children. *Laissez-faire* politicians believed that women and children were not in a position to negotiate for their contracts fairly with employers in the way that was possible for men. They believed that 'at an age when children suffer injuries from the labour they undergo, they are not free agents, but are let out to hire, the wages they earn being received or appropriated by their parents or guardians'. The Factory Acts of 1833, 1844 and 1847 reflect these views of the position of men, women and children. Men were excluded from any protection by Factory Acts before 1850. The principle of freedom of contract between master and man was honoured, and only the hours of women and children were altered. In practice, however, these restrictions imposed a parallel limit on hours worked by adult males, since the factory population in the main consisted of women and children. According to A. J. Taylor, 'Though *laissez-faire* was unable to prevent the coming of factory reform, for 50 years it set significant limits to its scope' (*Laissez-faire and Government Intervention in the Nineteenth Century*, 1970, p. 54).

## What views did contemporaries express on the role of the state?

● **SOURCE 2.18**

From T. B. Macaulay, *Leeds Mercury*, 16 June 1832, in which he identifies for the Leeds electors the nature and function of government according to the *laissez-faire* philosophy of the classical economists.

*. . . The best government cannot act directly and suddenly and violently on the comforts of the people; it cannot rain down food into their houses; it cannot give them bread, meat and wine; these things they can only obtain by their own honest industry and to protect them in that honest industry and secure to them its fruits is the end of all honest government.*

*. . . The general rule – a rule more beneficial to the capitalist than to the labourer – is that contracts shall be free and that the state shall not interfere between the master and the workman. To this general rule there is an exception. Children cannot protect themselves and are therefore entitled to the protection of the public.*

● **SOURCE 2.19**

From the evidence of G. A. Lee of Manchester to the Select Committee on the State of Children Employed in Manufactories, 1816, in which a factory owner explains his reasons for opposing a reduction in hours.

*Questioner: 'How many persons do you employ in your factory?'*

*Lee: 'At present 937.'*

*Questioner: 'Will you state the numbers of each age?'*

*Lee: 'Under 10 years of age, 11; from 10 to 12, 121; from 12 to 14, 109; from 14 to 16, 101; above 16, 595.*

*Questioner: 'What is the least age among the eleven under ten years of age?'*

*Lee: 'There are none under 9 years of age.'*

*Questioner: 'Are all whom you employ free labourers?'*

*Lee: 'They are at full liberty to leave when they please.'*

*Questioner: 'What are their hours of work?'*

*Lee: 'From 6 in the morning till 8 in the evening, allowing 40 minutes for dinner and 20 minutes for coming in . . . 11 hours on Saturday, in all 76 hours per week . . .'*

*[After being questioned about the length of the working day and week Lee is asked if he would consider a reduction in hours for children.]*

*Questioner: 'The Committee is then to understand that unless any legislative provision takes place to compel you to diminish the hours of labour, you have no intention voluntarily to do so?'*

*Lee: 'I have no intention to alter the average hours of labour. If I could make them more regular I would.'*

---

Study Sources 2.18 and 2.19.

1  What does Macaulay believe to be the proper role of government?

2  What does Lee mean by 'free labourers'?

3  In what way does the evidence of Lee confirm Macaulay's claim that children were not free agents?

4  How does Lee's attitude contrast with that shown by reforming mill owners, such as Robert Owen and Sir Robert Peel the Elder?

---

● **SOURCE 2.20**

From J. R. McCulloch, *Edinburgh Review*, 1835, in which McCulloch, a supporter of *laissez-faire*, expresses his distrust of the findings of Sadler's Select Committee Report on Child Labour.

*Children . . . between the ages of nine and fourteen years are largely employed in factories. They have been described as stunted in their growth, and rendered decrepit and miserable for life, by the prolonged confinement, drudgery and ill treatment to which they are exposed. These representations of what has been called white slavery were embodied in Mr Sadler's famous Factory Report which, we believe, contains more false statements, and exaggerated and misleading representations, than any other document of the kind ever laid before the Legislature . . . Were children turned out of the factories . . . four-fifths of them would be thrown loose upon the streets, to acquire a taste for idleness, and to be early initiated in the vicious practices prevalent among the dregs of the populace in Manchester, Glasgow, Leeds and other great towns. Whatever may be the state of society in these towns, we hesitate not to say, it would have been ten times worse but for the factories. They have been the best and most important schools. Besides taking children out of harm's way, they have imbued them with regular, orderly and industrious habits.*

---

1  Why does McCulloch (Source 2.20) reject factory reform campaigners' claims that a factory act would benefit children's moral and physical welfare?

2  To what extent would Macaulay and Lee agree with McCulloch?

● **SOURCE 2.21**

From the second reading of Michael Sadler's Factory Bill, *Hansard*, 16 March 1832, in which Mr John Hope MP argues against factory regulation.

. . . He [Mr Hope] did not propose to enter into any discussion as to the propriety or impropriety of interference with free labour. He believed it was admitted on both sides of the House that such interference generally was unwarrantable. He was willing to admit that the labour of children must in some degree be considered of a compulsory nature; but he considered that those very circumstances which give such labour the character of compulsory carried also with them a remedy for the evil of which the hon. Member complained in the protection of their parents. He could not comprehend how it was possible by legislative enactments to supply the place of parental affections in behalf of the child . . . He doubted in the first place whether a case of necessity for parliamentary interference was fairly made out . . . It was material to look at the number of hours in which children were employed in other trades and manufactures. Children employed in the earthenware and porcelain manufactures worked from twelve to fifteen hours per day; file-cutters, nail-makers, forgers and colliers worked for twelve hours per day; those employed in the manufacture of hosiery and in lace manufactories worked for twelve, fourteen, and fifteen hours per day . . . He contended therefore that the children employed in cotton and other spinning factories were not subjected to greater labour than those employed in other manufactures to which no protection was to be afforded by this Bill. It was obvious that if they limited the hours of labour they would to nearly the same extent reduce the profits of the capital on which the labour was employed. Under these circumstances the manufacturers must either raise the price of the manufactured article or diminish the wages of their workmen; if they increased the price of the article the foreigner would enter into competition with them.

He was informed that the foreign cotton manufacturers and particularly the Americans trod closely upon the heels of our manufacturers. If the latter were obliged to raise the price of their articles the foreign markets would in a great measure be closed against them and the increased price would also decrease the demand in the home market.

1   To what extent does Hope (Source 2.21) support the claims of opponents that factory reform 'invaded the rights of the parents over the child'?

2   Why does he claim that factory reform would have a harmful effect on the competitiveness of manufacturing?

3   How valid is his claim that children in 'cotton and other spinning factories were not subjected to greater labour than those employed in other manufactures'?

4   What values and assumptions does Hope reveal in his arguments?

● **SOURCE 2.22**

From Nassau Senior, *Letters on the Factory Act*, 1837, to the President of the Board of Trade, in which the author, a prominent economist (see page 46), puts forward his reasons for opposing reform.

The exceeding easiness of cotton-factory labour renders long hours of work practicable. With the exception of the mule spinners . . . the work is merely that of watching the machinery, and piecing the threads that break. I have seen the girls who thus attend standing with their arms folded during the whole time that I stayed in the room – others sewing a handkerchief or sitting down . . . Under these circumstances, factories have always worked for very long hours. From thirteen to fifteen, or even sixteen, appear to be the usual hours per day abroad . . . Any plan therefore, which should reduce the present comparatively short hours, must either destroy profit, or reduce wages to the Irish standard, or raise the price of the commodity.

Under the present law, no mill in which persons under eighteen years of age are employed (and, therefore, scarcely any mill at all) can be worked more than eleven and a half hours a day, that is, twelve hours for five days in the week and nine on Saturday. Now, the following analysis will show that, in a mill so worked, the whole net profit is derived from the last hour. I will suppose a manufacturer to invest £100,000: £80,000 in his mill and machinery, and £20,000 in raw materials and wages. The annual return of that mill, supposing . . . gross profits to be fifteen per cent, ought to be goods worth £115,000 . . .

*Of this £115,000, each of the twenty-three half hours of work produces one twenty-third . . . £100,000 out of the £115,000 makes up for the deterioration of the mill and machinery. The remaining two 23rds, that is the last two of the twenty-three half hours of every day, produce the net profit of ten per cent. If, therefore, (prices remaining the same) the factory could be kept at work thirteen hours instead of eleven and a half . . . the net profit would be more than doubled. On the other hand, if the hours of working were reduced by one hour per day (prices remaining the same), net profit would be destroyed – if they were reduced by an hour and a half, even gross profit would be destroyed . . . there would be no fund to compensate the progressive deterioration of the fixed capital . . .*

1  How does Senior (Source 2.22) justify the long hours worked in the factories?

2  What are his main arguments against shortening the working day?

3  Study Sources 2.18–2.22 and summarise the main arguments adopted by opponents of the Ten Hours Bill in terms of the harmful effects of reform on each of the following
a) children
b) profits
c) wage levels
d) price of goods for consumers
e) foreign competition/markets
f) employment opportunities.

4  a) How convincing would these arguments have been to people at the time?
   b) How convincing do they seem today?

# 4 How successful was the factory reform movement?

The factory reform movement gathered its own momentum as its aims and tactics developed over time. Its scope grew not only in terms of the abuses tackled – first working hours, then safety – but also in the extension of its activities from the cotton-spinning mills to other branches of manufacturing. The centre of activity was inevitably rooted in the industrial cities, though reforms were ultimately achieved through parliamentary action. There was no single act of parliament that removed all factory abuses at one stroke. Legislation was extended over the period 1802–47, indicating that aims and effectiveness varied over time. Early reformers did not concern themselves with all the abuses created by the Industrial Revolution, but only with the evils arising from the employment of children, initially the use of paupers as apprentices. After that practice was banned by the 1802 act, the reformers turned their attention to the issue of 'free' child labour, which was tackled by the 1819 act. They did not criticise the employment of children in the light and easy labour of the cotton mill so long as it did not damage health or exclude moral training. The controversy was not about labour but about excessive labour and the education of children.

The development of an organised movement from the 1830s onwards meant that factory regulation assumed greater prominence. The issues on which reformers campaigned ranged from protection of 'young persons' and women and the introduction of a maximum ten-hour day, to improvements in working conditions and restrictions on the hours of the operation of machinery. However, no mention was made of wage levels or improvement in the working conditions of men.

# What progress was made before 1830?

● **SOURCE 2.23**

From a report on the large cotton factories by the Board of Health for Manchester, 1796, in John Aitkin, *A Description of the Country from thirty to forty miles around Manchester, 1795. Parliamentary Papers 1816.*

**fever**
typhus, which was often referred to simply as fever, or as factory or gaol fever.

**obviated**
removed

1 *It appears that the children and others who worked in the large cotton factories are peculiarly disposed to be affected by the contagion of* FEVER . . .
2 *The large factories are generally injurious to the constitution of those employed in them* . . .
3 *The untimely labour of the night, and the protracted labour of the day, with respect to children, not only tends to diminish future expectations as to the general sum of life and industry . . . but it too often gives encouragement to idleness, extravagance and wickedness in the parents* . . .
4 *It appears that the children employed in factories are debarred from all opportunities of education, and from moral or religious instruction.*
5 *From the excellent regulations which subsist in several cotton factories, it appears that many of these evils may, in a considerable degree, be* OBVIATED; *we are therefore warranted by experience, and are assured we shall have the support of the liberal owners of these factories, in proposing an application for Parliamentary aid (if other methods appear no likely to effect the purpose) to establish a general system of laws for the wise, humane and equal government of all such works.*

1 According to Source 2.23, what physical and moral dangers were faced by children who worked in factories?

2 What remedies are recommended by the report to remove these dangers?

The Manchester Board of Health was set up as a result of the efforts of Dr Thomas Perceval (1740–1804), who had dealt with an outbreak of factory fever in Manchester in 1784. Typhus epidemics in cotton factories continued unchecked and the call for regulation eventually persuaded Sir Robert Peel the Elder to introduce the Health and Morals of Apprentices Act, 1802. He had built up a large and very profitable cotton-spinning business from small beginnings as a calico (cotton cloth) printer. He had been one of the chief offenders in the abuse of child apprentices: his mills had been notorious for their scandals, and in 1784, and again in 1796, the magistrates had made complaints. Despite this record, he became a reformer, refusing to accept the argument of many contemporary mill owners that the victims of the factory system were really gainers by it. He explained his motives for sponsoring the 1802 act when the Select Committee on the State of Children employed in the Manufactories interviewed him in 1816.

● **SOURCE 2.24**

From Sir Robert Peel the Elder's evidence to the Select Committee on the State of Children Employed in the Manufactories, 1816, recording his motives for securing the Health and Morals of Apprentices Act, 1802.

*Having other pursuits, it was not often in my power to visit the factories, but whenever such visits were made, I was struck with the uniform appearance of bad health, and in many cases, stunted growth of the children; the hours of labour were regulated by the interest of the overseer, whose pay depending on the quantity of work done, he was often induced to make the poor children work excessive hours, and to stop their complaints by trifling bribes.*

1 What were the main evils of the apprenticeship system, as described by Peel in Source 2.24?

2 Why were his apprentices forced to work excessive hours?

The original 1802 bill was 'for the better preservation of the Health and Morals of Apprentices and others employed in cotton mills and cotton manufactories'; but attempts to extend the title to cover 'cotton and other mills, and cotton and other manufactories' failed. The act applied only to cotton and woollen mills. There were several debates on the bill, but attempts to extend its scope to include free-labour children were overturned by Peel. He thought that the bill, as it stood, 'would render the cotton trade as correct and moral as it was important'. He argued that if regulations were necessary for the free children, they should be made the subject of a different bill. He estimated that the 1802 act would apply to 20,000 parish apprentices.

● SOURCE 2.25

From the Health and Morals of Apprentices Act, 1802, summarising the main clauses of the act that attempted to remove the physical and moral abuses suffered by pauper apprentices.

*II . . . That all . . . rooms and apartments in or belonging to any such mill or factory shall twice at least in every year be well and sufficiently washed with quicklime and water over every part of the walls and ceiling thereof; and . . . provide a sufficient number of windows and openings in such rooms . . . to ensure a proper supply of fresh air . . .*

*III . . . That every . . . master or mistress shall constantly supply every apprentice . . . with two whole and complete suits of clothing . . . one complete suit being delivered to such apprentice once at least in every year.*

*IV . . . That no apprentice . . . shall be employed or compelled to work for more than 12 hours in any one day (between 6 a.m. and 9 p.m.), exclusive of the time that may be occupied . . . in eating the necessary meals.*

*VI . . . That every such apprentice shall be instructed, in some part of every working day, for the first 4 years at least of his or her apprenticeship . . . in the usual hours of work, in reading, writing and arithmetic or either [sic] of them, according to the age and abilities of such apprentice . . . in some room or place in such mill or factory to be set apart for the purpose.*

*IX . . . That the justices of the peace . . . shall . . . appoint two persons, not interested in or any way connected with, such mills or factories, to be visitors of such mills or factories . . . one of whom shall be a justice of the peace . . . and the other shall be a clergyman of the Established Church of England or Scotland . . . and the said Visitors shall have full power to enter into and inspect any such mill or factory . . . and shall report to quarter sessions.*

*XIII . . . That every master or mistress . . . who shall wilfully act contrary to or offend against any of the provisions of this Act, shall . . . forfeit and pay any sum not exceeding £5 and not less than 40s. . . . provided that all information for offences against this Act, shall be laid within one calendar month after the offence committed.*

The employment of parish apprentices in the cotton mills continued for some time after the 1802 act, though it gradually declined in importance. In 1815, a parliamentary committee reported unfavourably on the apprenticeship system.

● SOURCE 2.26

From the *Report of the Select Committee on Parish Apprentices*, 1815, commenting on continuing abuses affecting the apprenticeship system.

*Your Committee . . . cannot however avoid mentioning the very early age at which many of these children are bound apprentices. The evils of this system of these distant removals at all times severe and aggravating the miseries of poverty are yet felt more acutely . . . in the case of children of 6 or 7 years of age who are . . . in many cases prematurely subjected to a laborious employment frequently very injurious to their health; and generally highly so to their morals and from which they cannot be set free under a period of 14 or 15 years.*

*Without entering more at large into the enquiry Your Committee submit that enough has been shown to call the attention of the House to the practicability of finding employment for parish apprentices within a certain distance from their homes, without the necessity of having recourse to a practice so much at variance with humanity.*

Study Sources 2.25 and 2.26.

1 How did the 1802 act attempt to deal with the following abuses
   a) long hours
   b) the absence of moral, religious and general education
   c) insanitary conditions
   d) unprotected machinery?

2 What was the main weakness of the 1802 act in terms of regulation and inspection?

3 What main limitations to the 1802 act were identified in the 1815 Report of the Select Committee on Parish Apprentices?

## SOURCE 2.27

From the *Report of the Select Committee on Parish Apprentices*, 1815.

Fate of 2026 pauper apprentices from London, and some parishes in Middlesex and Surrey, 1802–11.

| Fate of pauper apprentices | Number |
| --- | --- |
| Now served under indenture | 644 |
| Served their time and in same employ | 108 |
| Served and settled elsewhere | 99 |
| Dead | 80 |
| Enlisted in Army or Navy | 86 |
| Sent back to friends | 57 |
| Transferred to tradesmen in different part of country | 246 |
| Incapable of service | 18 |
| In parish workhouse | 26 |
| Not traced for a variety of reasons, e.g. run away, not mentioned, not bound to person mentioned in the return | 662 |
| Total | 2026 |

I   Study Source 2.27.
   What was the significance of the findings of the 1815 Select Committee on Parish Apprentices on the fate of over 2000 apprentices protected by the 1802 act?

## SOURCE 2.28

A propaganda cartoon published to support Sir Robert Peel the Elder's campaign for the 1819 Factory Act, regulating the employment of 'free' apprentices.

English Factory Slaves. Pl.3 Their daily employment. —

Study Source 2.28.

1   In what ways does the cartoonist attempt to influence his audience on the issue of child labour?

2   How reliable is this source as a commentary on the effectiveness of the 1802 act?

3   Comment on the value and limitations of this cartoon to a historian studying the factory reform movement of the early nineteenth century.

The failure of the 1802 act to protect 'free' children led to a renewed campaign by Robert Owen, supported by Sir Robert Peel the Elder. In June 1815 a bill was drawn up to amend and extend the 1802 act, but it met with opposition and the issue was referred to a Select Committee in 1816. Evidence was collected from doctors, employers and supporters of child reform. Employers, apart from Peel and Owen, argued that interference by Parliament would ruin the country and benefit foreign competitors.

● SOURCE 2.29

From the evidence of Robert Owen to the Select Committee on the State of Children Employed in Manufactories, 1816, in which Owen describes his reforms at New Lanark and recommends a bill to control child employment.

*Questioner: 'At what age do you take children into your mills?'*
*Owen: 'At 10 and upwards.'*
*Questioner: 'What are your regular hours of labour per day, exclusive of meal times?'*
*Owen: '10 and three-quarter hours.'*
*Questioner: 'What time do you allow for meals?'*
*Owen: 'Three-quarters for dinner and one half hour for breakfast.'*
*Questioner: 'Then your full time of work per day is 12 hours?'*
*Owen: 'Yes.'*
*Questioner: 'Why do you not employ children at an earlier age?'*
*Owen: 'Because it would be injurious to the children and not beneficial to the proprietors . . . [When New Lanark was bought in 1799] . . . I found there five hundred children, who had been taken from poor houses, chiefly in Edinburgh, and these children were generally from the age of 5 and 6, to 7 and 8; they were taken so because Mr Dale could not, I learned afterwards . . . obtain them at all [except at that age].'*
*[Robert Owen then went on to recommend a starting age of twelve years and a working day of ten hours.]*
*Questioner: 'Do you think if such an arrangement was made in regard to the number of hours, the manufacturers would suffer any loss in consequence?'*
*Owen: 'My conviction is that no party would suffer.'*

1 What does Owen (Source 2.29) recommend as the starting age and length of working day for children?

2 How does Owen answer the criticisms of mill owners who argued that a reduction in hours would be harmful to industry?

● SOURCE 2.30

From the Factory Act, 1819, summarising the main clauses that attempted to regulate the employment of free children.

*I . . . That . . . no child shall be employed in any description of Work for the Spinning of COTTON Wool into Yarn, or in any Preparation of SUCH Wool, until he or she shall have attained the full Age of Nine Years.*
*II And be it further enacted, That no Person, being under the Age of Sixteen Years, shalt be employed in any description of Work whatsoever, in Spinning Cotton Wool into Yarn, or in the previous preparation of such Wool, or in the cleaning or repairing of any Mill, Manufactory, or Building, or any Millwork or Machinery therein, for more than Twelve Hours in any one Day, exclusive of the necessary time for Meals: such Twelve Hours to be between the hours of Five o'clock in the Morning and Nine o'clock in the evening.*
*III And be it further enacted, That there shall be allowed to every such Person, in the course of every Day, not less than Half an Hour for Breakfast, and not less than one full Hour for Dinner; such an Hour for Dinner to be between the Hours of Eleven o'clock in the Forenoon and Two o'clock in the Afternoon.*
*VII And be it further enacted, That every Master or Mistress of any such Cotton Mill, Manufactory, or Building, who shall wilfully act contrary to or offend against any of the Provisions of the above-recited Act, shalt for every such Offence forfeit and pay any Sum not exceeding Twenty Pounds nor less than Ten Pounds, at the Discretion of the Justices before whom such Offender shalt be convicted.*

1 Which branches of the textile industry were covered by the 1819 act (Source 2.30)?

2 What limitations were imposed on the employment of children and young persons?

3 How was the act to be enforced?

4 What penalties were introduced for those who broke the act?

5 How effective do you think the act would be?

● **SOURCE 2.31**

From the *Report on the Cotton Mills in the Parish of Bolton*, 1823, reporting on the effectiveness of the 1819 act.

*In all the above-mentioned mills there are no apprentices employed. In 15 mills out of 28 there is more or less number of children under 9 years of age employed, but the masters say this is contrary to their directions, as these children are engaged and paid by the journeymen spinners themselves. In the whole 28 mills there are only three that are stopped during breakfast. In all the others the workpeople eat their breakfasts as they work. All the mills are stopped during one hour at dinner. It does not appear that any of the mills have been whitewashed during the year but they generally promised to whitewash again before Christmas.*

*Only 14 out of 28 mills have the Act of Parliament or Regulations hung up, and there is not more than one copy in most of those that have it hung up, whereas it appears to us, the undersigned, there should be one affixed in every room. The average heat of the factories from the inspection that has taken place is from 60 degrees to 80 degrees of the thermometer. With two or three exceptions the hours of working are 12 per day, exclusive of meals. [In] Mill No. 2 the working hours are 12 and in No. 15, 13 hours, exclusive of such meals.*
*R. Fletcher and H. Richardson*
*Bolton, 1823.*

I   What conclusions can be drawn from Source 2.31 about the success of the 1819 act?

## What progress was made during the 1830s?

The development of an organised movement led to an extension of aims. Campaigners moved away from the issue of child labour to a range of other issues: a maximum ten-hour day, protection of children and women, improvement in working conditions, and protection of 'young persons'. Reformers in Lancashire wanted restrictions on the hours of operation of machinery because it would be easier to police than the working hours of different classes of labourers. The Short-Time Committees organised mass demonstrations, public meetings and petitions that mobilised public opinion, and also published pamphlets and employed staff to work as 'missionaries'. These activities had a limited effectiveness.

During 1832 evidence was collected by Michael Sadler's Select Committee on Child Labour. Witnesses were coached by supporters of reform who provided lots of information on deformities, accidents and ill health occurring as a result of long hours. Petitions were sent to Parliament in favour of the Ten Hours Bill but the movement received a setback in December 1832 when Sadler lost his parliamentary seat. Lord Shaftesbury took over the leadership and introduced a Ten Hours Bill. This led the Whig government of Lord Grey to refer the factory question to a Royal Commission. Its report became the basis of the 1833 Factory Act. The Short-Time Committees refused to co-operate with the Royal Commission because they believed that the enquiry would excuse the activities of the factory owners and prevent reform.

The reform movement's effectiveness was weakened by differences that emerged between the 'official' and 'unofficial' approaches to the factory question. The Ten Hours movement in Parliament was influenced by a humanitarian approach, which emphasised cruelties to children and aimed to regulate adult hours of work. Edwin Chadwick (see page 91), who influenced the official approach of the Royal Commission, took a more detached view. He believed that bad conditions represented both a waste of human resources and administrative inefficiency. He emphasised the need to improve sanitary conditions. His concern about long hours worked by children, which contributed to deformity and disease, stemmed from his dislike of the waste of human resources. Thus, the official view held by the Royal Commission was concerned with the weakness of body and lack of training for the mind, in contrast with the Ten Hours movement's concern with cruelties to children and long hours. But the most significant difference of opinion related to the issue of adult hours. The Commissioners refused to interfere with freedom of contract between master and man, and as a result of the influence of Chadwick the Ten Hours movement for adults was defeated in the 1830s. The 1833 Factory Act represented a failure for the campaigners in Parliament and beyond, and a victory for the 'official' view of the Royal Commission.

● **SOURCE 2.32**

From Richard Oastler's letter on 'Slavery in Yorkshire', published in the *Leeds Mercury*, 16 October 1830, in which he criticises the limitations of reform prior to 1830.

*Let the truth speak out . . . Thousands of our fellow-creatures and fellow-subjects, both female and male, the inhabitants of a Yorkshire town are at this very moment existing in a state of slavery more horrid than are the victims of that hellish system – Colonial Slavery. The very streets which receive the droppings of an Anti-Slavery Society are every morning wet by the tears of innocent victims at the accursed shrine of greed who are compelled, not by the cart whip of the negro slave driver, but by the dread of the equally appalling strap of the overlooker to hasten half dressed, but not half fed to those magazines of British infantile Slavery – the Worsted mills in the town and neighbourhood of Bradford. Thousands of little children both male and female . . . from seven to fourteen years are daily compelled to labour from six o'clock in the morning to seven in the evening with only . . . Britons blush while you read it . . . with only thirty minutes allowed for eating and recreation.*
*Richard Oastler,*
*Frixby Hall, near Huddersfield, 29 September 1830*

● **SOURCE 2.33**

From *Leeds Intelligencer*, 22 September 1831, announcing the campaign for a ten-hour day.

*Resolutions passed at a public meeting at Leeds*
1 *That the practice of working young children in mills and factories from twelve to sixteen hours a day, and in some instances thirty-five hours, with but very short intermission for meals, is greatly to be deplored, inasmuch as such a system has an exceedingly harmful effect on their constitutional vigour, health and morals.*
2 *That ten hours per day is as long a period for the juvenile population to labour as is consistent with the preservation of health, the allowance of necessary relaxation and rest, and the well-being of society at large, and that it is a stain on the character of Britain that her sons and daughters, in their infant days, should now be worked longer than the adult mechanic, agricultural labourer or negro slave.*

---

Study Sources 2.32 and 2.33.

1 What abuses in factory conditions had not been removed by the 1802 and 1819 acts?

2 To what extent had the campaign for factory reform extended its scope by 1831 (Source 2.33)?

3 How far do Sources 2.32 and 2.33 reflect a common argument in support of reform?

4 How does Oastler attempt to mould public opinion to accept government regulation and restriction?

5 How effective do you consider Oastler's language, argument and tone would be in persuading his middle-class audience to support his cause?

---

● **SOURCE 2.34**

From the *Report of Commissioners on the Employment of Children in Factories*, 1833, describing the treatment of children in factories prior to 1833.

*The children of the labouring classes stand in need of . . . legislative protection against the conspiracy insensibly formed between their masters and parents to tax them to a degree of toil beyond their strength . . . 'I am going 13 . . . the overlooker used to get a rope, put knots in it, and lick us with that . . . it was a good bit worse than the strap. I never told my mother but . . . when there were marks on me. She told me not to mind . . . she'd give me a halfpenny to go back again and be a good boy . . . When I ran away she . . . would have beat me if she could have catched me . . . I always paid my wage of 4s. a week to my mother . . . When I was 17 we went to night work. At first the hands thought of the money on Saturday night, but they got tired of it – they could not stand it: they would turn the hands off if they could not work over hours . . . I think there are many children here under 9: they stay from six in the morning to half past nine at night . . . If the children work only ten hours . . . it would be worse for their parents . . . they must get more wages . . .'*

. . .In one small factory sixteen workers of various ages were asked if they would prefer to work shorter hours. Answers were as follows:

| Response | Number | Age of person replying |
|---|---|---|
| Prefer shorter hours | 3 | ages 12; 22; 35 |
| Keep hours as they are | 11 | ages 9; 10; 11; 12 (two); 13 (two); 14 (two); 16 (two) |
| Don't know | 2 | ages 10; 16 |

. . . 'I rarely employ children under nine . . . we have many children from lace work in their homes, and find they improve in health: when they come from this domestic work they are almost as blind as bats, and their sight has improved here . . . The children play about . . . when the work is over. You should see them come out of the mill, as lively as larks. The adults could not do some of the work; also it is work which will not pay to employ adults at . . . When we want to work at night we always have plenty of volunteers . . . we frequently have more than we want. If the ten hours bill is passed the children would go to other trades . . . they would give in their ages different from what they are to get employment . . . the parents always tell the children to answer 'going ten' when they are asked their age.'

1  From the evidence of Source 2.34, what difficulties faced reformers who campaigned for state regulation of child employment?

2  a) Give examples of the ways in which parents connived at the abuse of children by their employers.
   b) Why were parents prepared to enter into a 'conspiracy . . . (with) masters . . . to tax children to a degree of toil beyond their strength'?

3  Why did children want to 'keep hours as they are'?

4  How reliable are the assertions and arguments given in evidence by an employer?

● SOURCE 2.35

From the *First Report of the Factory Commissioners*, 1833, describing the effects of prolonged labour on children's health.

**irremediable**
untreatable

*(i) Dangers arising from unprotected machinery*
One of the great evils to which people employed in factories are exposed is the danger of receiving serious and even fatal injury from the machinery. It does not seem possible by any precautions that are practicable to remove this danger altogether. There are factories in which everything is done that it seems practicable to do to reduce this danger to the least possible amount and with such success that no serious accident happens for years together . . . by the returns which we have received. However it appears that there are other factories and that these are by no means few in number nor confined to the smaller mills in which serious accidents are continually occurring and in which, notwithstanding, dangerous parts of the machinery are allowed to remain unfenced. The greater the carelessness of the owner in neglecting sufficiently to fence the machinery and the greater the number of accidents, the less their sympathy with the sufferers. In factories in which precaution is taken to prevent accidents care is taken of the workpeople when they do occur, and a desire is shown to make what compensations may be possible. But it appears in evidence that cases frequently occur in which the workpeople are abandoned from the moment that an accident occurs; their wages are stopped, no medical attendance is provided and whatever the extent of the injury no compensation is afforded.

*(ii) Effect of labour on children's health*
From the whole of the evidence laid before us, we find
**1st** That the children employed in all the principal branches of manufacture throughout the Kingdom work the same number of hours as the adults.
**2nd** That the effects of labour during such hours are, in a great number of cases:
– Permanent deterioration of the physical constitution;
– The production of disease often wholly IRREMEDIABLE;
– The partial or entire exclusion (by reason of excessive fatigue) from the means of obtaining adequate education and acquiring useful habits or of profiting by those means when afforded.

**3rd** *That at the age when children suffer these injuries from the labour they undergo, they are not free agents, but are let out to hire, the wages they earn being received and appropriated by their parents and guardians. We are therefore of opinion that a case is made out for the interference of the Legislature in behalf of the children employed in factories.*

**4th** *In regard to morals, we find that though the statements and depositions of the different witnesses that have been examined are to a considerable degree conflicting, yet there is no evidence to show that vice and immorality are more prevalent amongst these people, considered as a class, than amongst any other portion of the community in the same station, and with the same limited means of information . . . for any evil of this kind which may nevertheless exist, the proper remedy seems to be a more general and careful education of the young people.*

**5th** *In regard to the inquiry 'in what respect the laws made for the protection of such children have been found insufficient for such purpose', we find that in country situations the existing law is seldom or never attempted to be enforced, that in several principal manufacturing towns it is openly disregarded, that in others its operation is extremely partial and incomplete, and that even in Manchester, where the leading manufacturers felt an interest in carrying the act in to execution against evasions practised by the small mill-owners, the attempt to enforce its provisions through the agency of a committee of masters has for some time back been given up. On the whole we find the present law has been almost entirely inoperative.*

---

1  What criticisms are made in the Report (Source 2.35) about unfenced machinery?

2  What effect did prolonged labour have on children's health?

3  Why does the Report claim that children were not 'free agents'?

---

● **SOURCE 2.36**

Adapted from Factories Regulation Act, 1833, summarising the main clauses regulating the working hours of children.

The 1833 Factory Act also provided for children aged nine to thirteen to receive two hours of schooling per day.

*I . . . no person under eighteen years of age shall be allowed to work between half-past eight in the evening and half-past five in the morning, in any cotton, woollen, worsted, hemp, flax, tow, linen, or silk mill.*

*II . . . no person under the age of eighteen shall be employed in any such mill . . . more than twelve hours in . . . one day, nor more than sixty-nine hours in . . . one week.*

*VI . . . there shall be allowed in the course of the day not less than one and a half hours for meals . . .*

*VII . . . It shall not be lawful . . . to employ in any factory . . . as aforesaid, except in mills for the manufacture of silk, any child who shall not have completed his or her ninth year.*

*VIII . . . It shall not be lawful for any person to employ . . . in any factory as aforesaid for longer than forty-eight hours in one week, nor for longer than nine hours in one day, any child who shall not have completed his or her thirteenth year . . .*

*XVII . . . It shall be lawful for His Majesty to appoint four Inspectors of factories where . . . children and young persons under eighteen years of age [are] employed, empowered to enter any . . . mill, and any school . . . belonging thereto, at all times . . . by day or by night, when such . . . factories are at work. The Inspectors shall have power to make such rules as may be necessary for the execution of this act, binding on all persons subject to the provisions of this act; and are authorised to enforce the attendance at school of children employed in factories according to the provisions of this act.*

*Every child restricted to the performance of forty-eight hours of labour in any one week shall attend some school.*

---

1  What limitations did the 1833 act (Source 2.36) place on the employment of children?

2  Why is clause XVII so important?

3  How effective do you think this provision was in ensuring the enforcement of the act?

4  Why did the framers of the act limit the total number of hours worked in one week?

5  Assess the factors which were important in the achievement of factory legislation in the nineteenth century.

## The role of the factory inspectors

Inspectors were paid a very generous yearly salary of £1000, which attracted educated and able men. The four inspectors provided by the 1833 act were detached enough to hold a balance between master and worker and criticised each for their abuses. Below the inspectors were the superintendents who were paid £250 – later £350 – a year. Like the inspectors they did not receive travelling expenses, so there was a direct incentive to stay at home, and several who held the post proved to be unsatisfactory.

The inspectors, who each supervised a number of factories, had to report quarterly or half-yearly to Parliament. They had to meet periodically to co-ordinate their policies and issue a joint report, though until 1844 they had no central office. They tended to support each other against complaints from mill owners to the Home Office and Parliament, and petitions for their dismissal from the Short-Time Committees. They resorted to pamphlets, newspaper articles and the publication of official correspondence to fight their critics and to put pressure on their political superiors. Successive Home Secretaries tried to repress these independent activities, but eventually the inspectors came to be recognised as the experts on the administration of the factory laws. Their influence grew, to the point that the extension of government control over industrial conditions of employment came to depend largely on their advice.

## How did mill owners respond to the 1833 act?

The paperwork associated with inspection became a grievance. Time books and a register had to be kept, showing the hours the machinery was in operation and the hours worked by children. Children entering the mill had to bring a certificate showing that they were nine years of age and a weekly certificate signed by the teacher that they had attended school for at least twelve hours in the previous week. On reaching the age of thirteen they had to produce another certificate before they could start working a twelve-hour day. Age certificates were forged whilst medical certificates were signed by unqualified people. Often, inspectors would only accept certificates if doctors appointed for each group of factories had issued them. The problem was that the effectiveness of the 1833 act was undermined by the absence of any official registration of births, marriages and deaths before the introduction of compulsory registration in 1836 (effective from 1837).

The inspectors had no power to prosecute for physical cruelty whilst the education provision of two hours' schooling a day for children aged nine to thirteen was difficult to enforce. Some mill owners built good schools but many resented the cost of providing education that they argued was the responsibility of parents. Local day schools would not take children at irregular hours in filthy working clothes. In the last resort inspectors depended on the magistrates to punish offenders and so enforce the act, but the magistrates seized every opportunity to dismiss charges. Managers also devised early warning systems to signal the approach of the factory inspectors or superintendents and allow them to cover up abuses. Enforcement of the regulations was a slow and painful process, and the education of public opinion was essential for regulation to become effective. These loopholes in the 1833 act called for yet further legislation, which led eventually to the 1844 Factory Act.

## SOURCE 2.37

Adapted from the Report of Leonard Horner, an Inspector of Factories, 1837, in which he comments on progress made in the first four years of the 1833 act.

**Leonard Horner**
was an able man with varied experiences as a businessman, geologist and founder of the Edinburgh Mechanics' Institute. He eventually established his leadership over the other three inspectors.

*I see a decided change for the better within the last three months; for the strong dislike to the Act, which existed among a large number of the most respectable mill-owners, has greatly subsided. From what I have seen, and from the opinions I have heard expressed by them and their work people, there is evidently an increased conviction in the minds of both that an effective interference of the Legislature, for the protection of the children employed in factories, is necessary, and that it is a just principle. That there are still many [mill-owners] who appear to be indifferent to the health or moral state of the children they employ . . . is too clearly proved by the prosecutions . . . in my district in the last half-year . . . But that . . . cruelty and oppression are common or occur in greater proportion among mill-owners than other classes . . . may be most confidently denied. Indeed I know of no description of persons of whom so many instances may be brought forward of active generous efforts and large financial sacrifices to promote the welfare of the people they employ. To this I bear the most willing testimony from very ample opportunities of observation. I have often wished that those who so thoughtlessly believe and give currency to tales of miseries of the factory workers . . . would go to some of the mills to which I could send them . . . They would see how greatly they have been mistaken in their general condemnation . . . The statements as to the unhealthiness of factory employment are also exceedingly erroneous inasmuch as . . . a small part is unfairly held out as a representation of the general condition . . . One has only to see the workers in the woollen and worsted mills in the West Riding of Yorkshire . . . no collection of the working classes in other occupations in this country can possibly exhibit a larger proportion of well-fed, well-clothed, healthy and cheerful-looking people . . . The factory system . . . was defective in so far as young children laboured 12 hours a day . . . for no arrangement . . . could prevent the evils inherent in a system which deprived children of . . . air and exercise . . . and cut them off from all opportunity of being properly educated.*

1 Study Source 2.37. According to Leonard Horner, what changes had taken place in

a) the attitude of mill-owners
b) the conditions of workers

since the passing of the 1833 act?

## SOURCE 2.38

Adapted from the report of Leonard Horner, *Reports of Inspectors for Half-Year ending 31 December 1836.* Horner prosecuted for 504 offences and obtained 458 convictions within the first four months of his arrival in Lancashire. His figures must be treated with some caution because of the difficulty of proving that some age certificates were false.

Number of offences against the 1833 Factory Act brought in Lancashire, 1837.

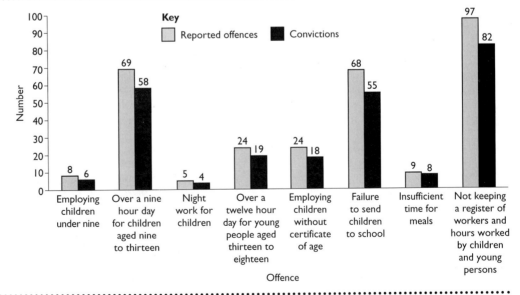

Study Source 2.38.

1 Which clauses of the 1833 act were most commonly ignored in Lancashire?

2 What evidence is there to indicate that the effectiveness of the 1833 act was undermined by an alliance of parents and employers?

3 To what extent does the evidence of Source 2.38 support the claims made by Horner in his 1837 report to Parliament (Source 2.37)?

# What progress did the Ten Hours movement make during the 1840s?

From 1834 the factory reform movement had a varied history. Oastler and the Short-Time Committees became involved in other working-class issues such as the reform of the Poor Law and parliamentary reform. Local differences developed in places such as Lancashire. This diversion of interest combined with internal divisions further prolonged the struggle. In the 1840s the pace of the campaign varied considerably with a failure to secure ten-hour working days in the bills of 1838, 1839 and 1841. Factory inspectors, men of the calibre of Leonard Horner, favoured further legislation to improve factory safety by fencing dangerous machinery after accounts of mutilations. They also pressed for an extension of control to silk and lace factories, and to calico printing and rope works, to which parents had moved their children from the mills. Here, the children worked between ten and fourteen hours a day to earn extra shillings. Protective legislation against the exhaustion of body and mind at work, public health measures, national education and various efforts to protect small children from neglect were introduced. Concern with the issue of female employment developed. The belief that the ideal woman was feminine, domesticated and economically dependent on a man was at the heart of government policies. From the beginning there was a contradiction between this view and the realities of many women's lives. The ideology supposed that working-class men earned sufficient money to provide for their female dependents. This was not the case. In the Lancashire cotton industry, women's contributions were crucial to the economic survival of the family. Government responded to the employment of women and children in factories by passing acts in 1844, 1847 and 1850 which limited the hours of work of women and children to a ten and a half hour day. The Mines Act of 1842 prohibited underground working for women. It was not until 1874 that a ten-hour day for women outside the textile mills was secured.

● **SOURCE 2.39**

From the Report of J. T. Howell, an Inspector of Factories, 1841, reporting on the serious accidents due to unfenced machinery in factories.

*On 23 November Mary Ann Lees aged 24, a married woman, the mother of one child, and in an advanced state of pregnancy, carried her husband's dinner to him in a room in Messrs T. & G. Marshall's mill (at Stockport) where he was employed as a dresser. She remained with him for a short time after the expiration of the dinner hour and having inadvertently approached too near an upright shaft . . . revolving with considerable rapidity, her shawl was caught by it. And she was consequently dragged against the shaft. From which she was with much difficulty released after her left arm had been torn completely off above the elbow joint, so as to render amputation necessary . . . This accident, I think, affords another strong proof of the necessity for legislative interference, since it is obvious that some mill owners will not take the precaution of fencing off dangerous machinery until compelled to do so by a stringent enactment.*

I   Study Source 2.39. How useful is this report for indicating the role played by the Factory Inspectorate in extending the scope of factory reform?

● **SOURCE 2.40**

From Mrs Anna Jameson, *Memoirs and Essays, Illustrative of Arts, Literature, Social Morals*, 1846, in which a middle-class feminist writer attacks the absence of education for working women.

*Those who have the choice, prefer the life of a factory girl to that of a household servant and they are not far wrong. They have comparative liberty, and work only at stated hours, but they thus acquire with habits of independence, habits of recklessness as regards others; impatience of all quiet, orderly obligations; selfishness, and every kind of unwomanly fault. The Commissioners thus sum up their view of the case.—'It appears that the education of the girls is even more neglected than that of the boys, that the vast majority of females are utterly ignorant; that it is impossible to overrate the evils which result from this deplorable ignorance.'*

*The unmarried girl, free, reckless, irresponsible, becomes in time the wife and the mother. What is the training that has fitted her for the working man's wife? By the labour of her hands she adds, perhaps, a third to his weekly wages, while, by her carelessness and ignorance of all household duties, she wastes one-half of their united means; or, by her insubordination and unwomanly habits, converts the home into a den of dirt, disquiet, misery. Even when well disposed, the disorderly habits of her childhood and youth leave her no chance but in a strength of character, and a combination of favourable influences, which are at least not common. 'The girls, removed from their home, or from the school to be employed in labour, are prevented from learning needlework, and from acquiring those habits of cleanliness, neatness and order, without which they cannot, when they grow up to womanhood, and have the charge of families of their own, economise their husband's earnings, or give their homes any degree of comfort; and this general want of the qualifications of a housewife in the women of this class, is stated by clergymen, teachers, medical men, employers and other witnesses, to be one great and universally prevailing cause of distress and crime among the working classes!'*

*Yes; here is the cause—but where is the remedy? If to exist, to procure a pittance of food and decent clothing, a young woman must toil incessantly at some handicraft from five years old and upwards, where and how is she to learn needlework, cookery, economy, cleanliness, and all 'the arts of home'? These things are not taught in Sunday-schools, nor in Dame-schools; and if they were, she has not time to learn them, nor opportunity to apply them, being learned;—she must toil in womanhood as in childhood and girlhood . . . What is the use of instituting a system of education if you continue a state of things in which that education is useless?—which renders it impossible for the woman to practise what the child has learned?—in which incessant labour is the sole condition of existence? The women of these classes have no home—can we wonder they have no morals?*

Study Source 2.40.

1  Why did women prefer to work as mill girls rather than in domestic service?

2  To what extent does Mrs Anna Jameson reflect contemporary views that the preferred social role of women was to be primarily concerned with the home?

3  What aspects of female education did reformers regard as most neglected?

4  What arguments are presented both for and against the employment of women?

5  To what extent does the evidence of Mrs Anna Jameson indicate an extension in the scope and issues raised in the campaign to reform the factories?

6  What value as historical evidence has the fact that Mrs Anna Jameson was a middle-class woman?

7  How far does this source illustrate the debate in some circles about whether or not working-class women should be educated?

● **SOURCE 2.41**

Adapted from the *Report of Commissioners on the Employment of Children in Factories*, 1833, discussing the issue of adult hours.

***Processions of children, and studied compositions presented by children***
a reference to the tactics used by campaigners for factory reform, who were accused of coaching children in their evidence to parliamentary committees.

*The most direct and undisputed consequence of the passing of the Ten Hours Bill would be the general limitation of the labour of adults within the same hours as those assigned to children and adolescents . . . Independently of the Objection which there appears to be in principle to any compulsory interference with the hours of adult labour, we find reason to anticipate very serious practical evils from imposing any such arbitrary restriction on the operations of so large a proportion of the manufacturing industry of the country . . . There is not one of the arguments which have been commonly urged by the friends of the Ten Hour Bill which affords an acceptable reason for extending the protection of the Legislature to the labour of adults . . . PROCESSIONS OF CHILDREN, AND STUDIED COMPOSITIONS PRESENTED BY CHILDREN, have been in all cases the machinery employed to divert public attention from the true state of the question.*

68

● SOURCE 2.42

From evidence presented to the Select Committee on Combinations of Workmen, 1837–38, reporting the outcome of Lord Ashley's interviews with Sheriff Alison, a magistrate, on the benefits of a ten-hour day.

*Lord Ashley [Shaftesbury]: Then you treat with contempt the argument often urged, that if the working classes had a little more time they would spend that time in an alehouse? Sheriff Alison: I think that if the working classes had more time a considerable portion of them would take to useful reading. In short, I think that the working classes are just like ourselves. In the House of Peers, or in the House of Commons, a certain portion of the Members are good men, who will read; a certain portion of them are indifferent characters, who will take to dissipation; and I think that the working classes are just the same.*

● SOURCE 2.43

From a Factory Inspectors' Report, 1843, in which the inspectors argue for restrictions on female labour.

*Twelve hours daily work is more than enough for anyone but however desirable it might be that excessive working should be prevented there are great difficulties in the way of legislative interference with the labour of adult men. The case however is very different regarding women: for not only are they much less free agents but they are physically incapable of bearing a continuance of work for the same length of time as men and a deterioration of their health is attended with far more injurious consequences to Society . . . the women being withdrawn from domestic duties . . . diminished comforts at home have the most corrupting influence upon the men.*

● SOURCE 2.44

From a speech by Lord Ashley in the House of Commons, 15 March 1844, introducing the Factory Bill, in which he argues for a curtailment of the hours worked by women.

*Female labour affects . . . all the arrangements and provisions of domestic economy – thrift and management are altogether impossible . . . Everything runs to waste; the house and children are deserted; the wife can do nothing for her husband and family; she can neither cook, wash, repair clothes, or take charge of the infants; all must be paid for out of her scanty earnings and after all most imperfectly done. Dirt, discomfort, ignorance, recklessness are the portion of such households because the men can discharge at home none of the especial duties that Providence has assigned to the females.*

● SOURCE 2.45

From Friedrich Engels, *The Condition of the Working Class in England*, 1845, in which the author, a prominent contemporary socialist, argues in favour of the Ten Hours Bill.

*There remains no doubt that, in a very short time, the Ten Hours Bill will really be adopted. The manufacturers are naturally all against it; they have used every honourable and dishonourable means against this dreaded measure, but with no other result than that of drawing down upon them the ever deepening hatred of the working men. The Bill will pass . . . The economic arguments of the manufacturers that a Ten Hours Bill would increase the cost of production and incapacitate the English producers for competition in foreign markets, and that wages must fall, are all half true; but they prove nothing . . . Naturally, if the Ten Hours Bill were a final measure, it must ruin England; but since it must inevitably bring with it other measures, it can only prove an advance.*

Study Sources 2.40–2.45.

1 To what extent do Sources 2.40, 2.43 and 2.44 agree on the effects of long hours on women?

2 In what ways, and to what extent, do the sources present similar evidence in favour of the Ten Hours Bill?

3 What similarities and what differences are there between the opinions shown in Sources 2.41 and 2.45 of the likely consequences of a Ten Hours Bill?

4 Assess the value of Sources 2.41–2.45 as evidence about attitudes to factory reform before the passing of the Ten Hours Bill.

5 To what extent do Sources 2.40–2.45 account for the success of Fielden's Ten Hours Bill in 1847?

● SOURCE 2.46

From Lord Ashley's introduction of the Ten Hours Bill, *Hansard*, 29 January 1846, in which Ashley highlights the limitations of the 1833 act.

*Among all the alterations that have been effected since the year 1833 I am sorry to perceive that nothing has been done for the benefit of young persons between the ages of thirteen and eighteen . . . now a very large portion of them are females and I think I may appeal to the House to say whether it is not cruel to take a young female on the very day on which she has passed the age of thirteen at the most tender period of her life and to demand of her precisely the same work in duration . . . which is demanded from ripe and vigorous manhood? . . .*

*How is it possible that they should learn the details of domestic life which constitute so powerfully to the morality of the rising generation . . . Sir, we must not shut out of our view the wide surface of society to be affected by our decision . . . it will be a fatal night whenever you decide adversely for you will have closed all hopes of moral and even of secular improvement to multitudes of the young and helpless. And will this not tend to widen the interval . . . that separates the rich from the poorer sort? . . . The overtoiled operatives both as children and adults are alone excluded from the common advantage; a few it is true of special genius may triumph over every opposing obstacle but the mass are abandoned to a state of things in which moral and intellectual culture, forethought and economy and the resources of independent action are far beyond their means . . . This surely is an unsound and fearful position; the contrast is seen, felt and resented . . . property and station become odious because they are founded on acquirements from which the multitudes are excluded by the prevailing system.*

● **SOURCE 2.47**

Adapted from Fielden's Ten Hours Act 1847, summarising the main clauses regulating the hours of children and women.

**John Fielden**
owned a cotton mill in Todmorden on the Lancashire–Yorkshire border. He was interested in reform, especially of factories, and took over leadership of the movement in the 1840s. He served as an MP from 1832 to 1847 and was largely responsible for the Ten Hours Act of 1847.

The 1847 act also increased the hours to be spent in school from two to three for children between the ages of nine and thirteen.

*Be it enacted . . . That . . . from the First Day of July One Thousand Eight Hundred and Forty-Seven no Person under the Age of Eighteen Years shall be employed in any such Mill or Factory, for more than Eleven Hours in any One Day, nor for more than sixty-three Hours in any One Week . . .*

*II And be it enacted. That from the First Day of May One Thousand Eight Hundred and Forty-Eight no Person under the Age of Eighteen Years shall be employed in any such Mill or Factory . . . for more than Ten Hours in any One Day nor more than Fifty-Eight Hours in any One Week.*

*III And be it enacted. That the Restrictions respectively by this Act imposed as regards the working of Persons under the Age of Eighteen Years shall extend to Females above the Age of Eighteen Years.*

Study Sources 2.46 and 2.47.

1  What limitation of the 1833 factory legislation does Ashley highlight in Source 2.46?

2  Why does he regard it as important that young adolescent girls should be protected by factory legislation?

3  What dangers for society does he foresee if factory legislation is not extended?

4  To what extent did the 1847 act represent a success for the reform movement?

5  What new group of workers in textile mills were included in the 1847 act?

6  What groups of workers in textile mills were excluded from the 1847 act?

7  To what extent were the terms of Fielden's act a disappointment for factory reform campaigners?

# 5 What progress had been made by 1850 in the reform of hours and working conditions?

The leaders of the Ten Hours movement were disappointed at the failure of the 1847 act to force down the hours of work for men as well as for women and children. Many employers worked women and children in relays and thus were able to work men for considerably longer than ten hours. It was to meet this difficulty that Ashley, now returned to the House of Commons, introduced a bill in 1850 to limit the hours during which a factory might open. He succeeded in getting it accepted but only at the cost of increasing the hours of work for women and young persons to ten and a half. At the time the act was passed he claimed that 'we have won the great object of all our labours – the Ten Hours Bill has become the law of the land; and we may hope, nay we believe, that we shall find in its happy results a full compensation for all our toils' (Letter to the Short-Time Committees, 1850). His fellow campaigners did not share his view. He lost much support among the working class, but the principle of a 'normal day' with a Saturday half-holiday was firmly established by the 1850 act. Factory Acts to further extend the protection of women and children continued to be passed in the second half of the nineteenth century (see timeline, pages 38–9).

● **SOURCE 2.48**

From P. Deane and W. A. Cole, *British Economic Growth 1688–1959*, 1969.

Growth of the cotton industry, 1829–96 (averages per three-year period).

| Period | Import of raw cotton (million lb) | Value of final product (£m) | Wages and salaries (£m) | Exports as percentage value of final product |
|---|---|---|---|---|
| 1829–31 | 249 | 32.1 | 10.7 | 56.4 |
| 1834–36 | 331 | 44.6 | 10.9 | 50.4 |
| 1844–46 | 560 | 46.7 | 10.6 | 55.4 |
| 1854–56 | 802 | 56.9 | 14.0 | 61.3 |
| 1864–66 | 771 | 43.1 | 17.8 | 64.0 |
| 1874–76 | 1274 | 66.0 | 26.7 | 70.1 |
| 1894–96 | 1558 | 55.4 | 32.7 | 78.6 |

Study Source 2.48.

1 To what extent does the statistical evidence rebut the claims of opponents of factory reform that it would have an adverse effect on
   a) productivity
   b) profits
   c) markets?

2 To what extent does the statistical evidence support the claim that workers benefited only from improvements in hours?

● **SOURCE 2.49**

Adapted from Factory Inspectors' Report, 1850, commenting on the effect of a Ten Hours Bill on the workers.

*I called in to see an old factory weaver. He was sitting with his youngest son and cutting the potatoes for sets. Both seemed at a loss, being new gardeners, but they were very glad to have an opportunity of learning. The old father said the Ten Hours Bill was a grand thing. He was learning to be a gardener, and would not like to have to give it up.*

*He had three daughters and two young women lodgers, very busy sewing and knitting, and all teaching one another.*

*I asked the old mother how she liked the Ten Hours Bill. She said, very well. She did not know how she must do if the girls worked any longer. They assisted her all they could, and were learning to do household work, and could read very nicely too.*

## SOURCE 2.50

From the Report by Leonard Horner, 1852, in which he comments on the prosperity of workers by 1852.

*I believe the workpeople were never so well off as they are at present; constant employment, good wages, cheap food and cheap clothing; many cheap, innocent and elevating amusements brought within their reach and thanks to the last Factory Act, the greater proportion of all the operatives in mills have at length time for some mental improvement, healthful recreation and enjoyment of their family and friends.*

Compare Sources 2.49 and 2.50 with Sources 2.41–2.44.

1  To what extent does the evidence support the claim of Ashley (Shaftesbury) that 'we have won the great object of all our labours' in terms of reforms to benefit
   a) female workers
   b) male workers?

2  What were the beneficial results for the workers that represented a 'full compensation for all our toils'?

## SOURCE 2.51

From G. H. Wood, 'The Statistics of Wages in the Nineteenth Century: The Cotton Industry', 1910.

Age and sex distribution of cotton workers in textile factories, 1835–1901, as a percentage of the total workers employed in cotton factories, compiled from factory inspectors' returns.

| Year | Children under 14 | Women and girls | Total women and children | Young males 14–18 | Adult males over 18 | Total males 14 and over |
|------|-------------------|-----------------|--------------------------|-------------------|---------------------|-------------------------|
| 1835 | 13.1 | 48.1 | 61.2 | 12.4 | 26.4 | 38.2 |
| 1850 | 4.5  | 55.5 | 60.0 | 11.2 | 28.8 | 40.0 |
| 1862 | 8.8  | 55.7 | 64.5 | 9.1  | 26.4 | 35.5 |
| 1874 | 13.9 | 53.7 | 67.6 | 8.3  | 24.1 | 32.4 |
| 1885 | 9.9  | 56.0 | 65.9 | 8.0  | 26.1 | 34.1 |
| 1895 | 5.8  | 58.8 | 64.6 | 7.8  | 27.6 | 35.4 |
| 1901 | 4.0  | 60.8 | 64.8 | 7.1  | 28.1 | 35.2 |
| 1907 | 3.2  | 60.6 | 63.8 | 7.9  | 28.3 | 36.2 |

Study Source 2.51.

1  What changes took place in the labour force in cotton textiles between 1850 and 1907 in terms of the employment of
   a) children under 14
   b) women
   c) men over 14?

2  How do you explain the sharp fall in the percentage of children employed by 1850 compared with 1835?

# 6 To what extent were working conditions in mines improved?

The only other industry to attract the attention of reformers was coal mining. By 1842 there were 2000 collieries stretching from Scotland to Somerset. The 1841 census listed 150,000 workers, of whom 5–6000 were female, and a significant number were children. The miners generally lived in isolated communities with limited access to towns or contact with other workers. Life revolved around the colliery with few alternative sources of employment being available. Young children followed their parents and were often trained by them for work in the mines. Miners had a sense of pride in their work and a culture based on customs and tradition. Adults and young children were better paid than factory workers, mainly because the work was dangerous and unpleasant. Mine explosions were frequent while the hard physical work in cramped conditions affected health. Coal dust caused 'black-spit' or lung disease and an early death.

# What was the composition of the workforce in coal-mining?

● **SOURCE 2.52**

From the *First Report of the Commission on the Employment of Women and Children in Mines and Collieries,* 1842.

Proportion of females, young persons and children to males in the labour force in coal-mining in 1842.

**Proportion of adult females, young persons and children to each 1000 males**

| District | Adult females | Young people aged 13–18 | | Children under 13 | |
|---|---|---|---|---|---|
| | | Male | Female | Male | Female |
| Yorkshire | 22 | 352 | 36 | 246 | 41 |
| Lancashire | 86 | 352 | 79 | 195 | 27 |
| Derbyshire | – | 240 | – | 167 | – |
| Leicestershire | – | 227 | – | 180 | – |
| S. Durham | – | 226 | – | 184 | – |
| Northumberland | – | 266 | – | 186 | – |
| Glamorgan | 19 | 239 | 19 | 157 | 12 |
| Pembrokeshire | 424 | 366 | 119 | 196 | 19 |
| Monmouthshire | – | 302 | – | 154 | – |

Study Source 2.52.

1 Identify the female-employing districts.

2 Identify the districts employing most children and young people.

3 Identify the main districts employing large numbers of females under eighteen.

4 To what extent would the use of child labour be a major issue in coal mining?

## What were the main abuses affecting employment in the coal industry?

Curtailment of the hours worked by children in the textile industry led some children to find employment in other unprotected industries. This in turn led reformers such as Lord Ashley to extend the reform campaign. In 1840 a Royal Commission was set up to investigate the conditions of children's employment in a range of industries. Four men headed the enquiry into mines while twenty sub-commissioners collected evidence. They shared the middle-class attitudes and values of campaigners for factory reform, believing that a woman's role was to be a wife and mother. Their disgust at the sight of women working in the mines led them to include such scenes in the reports.

● **SOURCE 2.53**

From a series of drawings accompanying the *First Report of the Commission on the Employment of Women and Children in Mines and Collieries,* 1842. Southwood Smith, one of the authors of the Report, suggested that drawings made on the spot would influence MPs. Opponents of reform found the images disgusting and obscene but defended the practices revealed in them.

a) A young girl draws coal. The report says, 'They buckle round their naked persons a broad leather strap, to which is attached a ring and about 4 feet of chain ending in a hook.'

a)

b) Women and girls haul coal to the surface.
c) A trapper.

b)

c)

● **SOURCE 2.54**

From *Parliamentary Papers*, 1842, describing the work of the young trappers, often boys, who sat all day in silence and darkness in a hole in the tunnel wall.

*The children that excite the greatest pity are those who stand behind the doors to open and shut them: they are called trappers who in the darkness, solitude and stillness as of night eke out a miserable existence for the smallest of wages. I can never forget the first unfortunate creature that I met with: it was a boy of about eight years old who looked at me as I passed with an expression the most abject and idiotic – like a thing, a creeping thing peculiar to the place. On approaching and speaking to him he shrank trembling and frightened into a corner.*

● **SOURCE 2.55**

From Children's Employment Commission, *Report on the Collieries and Iron Works in the East of Scotland*, 1842, describing the work of women and young girls who carried coal to the surface, up steep ladders in baskets strapped to their backs.

*Janet Cumming, 11 years old, bears coals. Works with father, has done so for two years. 'Father gangs [goes] at two in the morning; I gang with the women at five, and come up at five at night; work all night on Fridays, and come away at twelve in the day. I carry the large bits of coal from wall-face to the pit-bottom, and the small pieces called chows, in a creel: the weight is usually a hundredweight [50 kg] . . . it is some work to carry it; it takes three journeys to fill a tub of 4 cwt [200 kg] . . . The roof is very low: I have to bend my back and legs, and the water comes frequently up to the calves of my legs: I have no liking for the work; father makes me like it.'*

Study Sources 2.53–2.55.

1 What was the purpose of using illustrations in the *First Report of the Commission on the Employment of Women and Children in Mines and Collieries*?

2 What impact were they likely to have on their audience?

3 What types of work did women and young children do?

4 Why did mine owners employ children?

5 Why did mine workers allow their children to work in mines and collieries?

6 What were the dangers facing women and children who worked down the mines?

7 Who was likely to support and who to oppose the passage of the Mines Act of 1842?

## What were the main findings of the 1842 Report of the Royal Commission?

● **SOURCE 2.56**

From the *First Report of the Commission on the Employment of Women and Children in Mines and Collieries*, 1842, summarising the issues surrounding the employment of children and the dangers workers faced.

*(i) Issues surrounding child employment*

1 *That instances occur in which children are taken into these mines to work as early as four years of age, sometimes at five, and between five and six, not infrequently between six and seven, and often from seven to eight, while from eight to nine is the ordinary age at which employment in these mines commences.*

2 *That a very large proportion of the persons employed in carrying on the work of these mines is under thirteen years of age; and a still larger proportion between thirteen and eighteen.*

3 *That in several districts female children begin work in these mines at the same early ages as the males.*

7 *That the nature of the employment which is assigned to the youngest children . . . 'trapping', requires that they should be in the pit as soon as the work of the day commences . . . they should not leave the pit before the work of the day is at an end.*

8 *That although this employment scarcely deserves the name of labour, yet, as the children engaged in it are commonly excluded from light and are always without companions, it would, were it not for the passing and re-passing of the coal carriages, amount to solitary confinement of the worst order.*

10 *That at different ages, from six years old and upwards, the hard work of pushing and dragging the carriages of coal from the workings to the main ways or to the foot of the shaft begins . . . [it] requires the unremitting exertion of all the physical power which the young workers possess.*

*(ii) Moral dangers faced by women and young people*

11 *That, in the districts in which females are taken down into the coal mines, both sexes are employed together in precisely the same kind of labour, and work for the same number of hours; that the girls and boys, and the young men and young women, and even married women and women with child, commonly work almost naked, and the men, in many mines, quite naked; and that all classes of witnesses bear testimony to the demoralising influence of the employment of females underground.*

13 *That when the workpeople are in full employment, the regular hours of work for children and young persons are rarely less than eleven; more often they are twelve; in some districts they are thirteen; and in one district they are generally fourteen and upwards.*

14 *That in the great majority of these mines night-work is a part of the ordinary system of labour, . . . [this acts] most injuriously both on the physical and moral condition of the workpeople, and more especially on that of the children and young persons.*

17 *. . . the conduct of the adult colliers to the Children and Young Persons who assist them is harsh and cruel . . .*

### (iii) Physical dangers faced by miners

19 . . . That in all coalfields, accidents of a fearful nature are extremely frequent . . .

20 . . . That one of the most frequent causes of accidents in these mines is the want of superintendence by overlookers or otherwise to see to the security of machinery for letting down and bringing up the workpeople, the restriction of the number of persons who ascend or descend at a time, the state of the mine as to the quantity of noxious gas in it, the efficiency of the ventilation, the exactness with which the air-door keepers perform their duty, the places into which it is safe or unsafe to go with a naked lighted candle, and the security of the proppings to uphold the roof.

23 . . . That there are moreover two practices peculiar to a few districts which deserve the highest reprobation, namely,—first, the practice not unknown in some of the smaller mines in Yorkshire, and common in Lancashire, of employing ropes that are unsafe for letting down and drawing up the workpeople; and second, the practice, occasionally met with in Yorkshire, and common in Derbyshire and Lancashire, of employing boys at the steam engines for letting down and drawing up the workpeople.

26 . . . in the thin-seam mines, more especially, the limbs become crippled and the body distorted; and in general, the muscular powers give way, and the workpeople are incapable of following their occupation, at an earlier period of life than is common in other branches of industry.

27 . . . and each generation of this class of the population is commonly extinct soon after fifty.

---

1 Why were the Commissioners (Source 2.56) concerned about child employment down the mines?

2 What moral dangers threatened women who worked underground?

3 What were the main causes of accidents?

4 What image of the lifestyle of miners is presented in the Report?

5 What effect did work in the mines have on the health and life expectancy of miners?

The publication of the 1842 report with its vivid illustrations and descriptions shocked respectable middle-class society. Prior to the Report people had been ignorant of working conditions down the mines. The Marquis of Londonderry, who represented the owners of collieries in Durham and Northumberland, presented a petition to the House of Lords. It charged the Commissioners with putting questions in such a way as to suggest the answers and was particularly hostile to the illustrations, described as 'scandalous and obscene . . . more likely to excite the feelings than to increase careful judgement'. Despite this opposition Lord Ashley's bill was eventually passed. It banned the employment of women and girls and of boys under ten underground. It also prohibited boys under thirteen from operating the winding machinery that had caused many accidents. Inspectors were appointed to supervise the administration of the act although they were limited until 1850 in their ability to report on safety provisions.

# 7 Which other industries were affected by the extension of the Factory Acts in the late nineteenth century?

The vast majority of workers in 1851 were employed in workshops. These varied in size from the small family workshop in a cottage or backyard, such as those found in the nail-making, blacksmith and chain-making industries, to a larger 'shop' or garret requiring bench space, where bootmakers, glovers, seamstresses and dressmakers worked. Birmingham was the centre of many such workshops, specialising in brass goods, guns, buttons, jewellery and trinkets connected with the 'toy' trade. London was the site of many tailoring shops. Many women and young girls who found their employment opportunities curtailed by the Factory and Mines Acts moved into these unregulated areas of the economy. Even more numerous were the many out-trades carried on in the home, usually by married women and young children.

These workshops, often under the control of small employers, were out of the reach of the Factory Acts. They were also beyond the reach of the trade unions, which found this type of labour incapable of unionising. Employers were accused of exploiting, or 'sweating', their workforce, subjecting them to low pay, long hours and dirty, insanitary conditions. Also unregulated were larger workplaces such as ironworks, shipyards, rope-works, pottery works, quarries, glass works and brickyards. It was not until the late 1890s that public opinion became interested in the sweated trades, following a Board of Trade report. Earl Dunraven moved a motion in the House of Lords on 28 February 1888 for the establishment of a Select Committee on the Sweating System. Its Report in 1890 was not followed by legislation, although Sydney Buxton proposed an amendment of the Factory Acts to tackle part of the problem.

## What does 'sweating' mean and why did it occur?

● **SOURCE 2.57**

*The Sweater's Furnace: or, the real 'Curse' of labour*, an etching by Linley Sambourne and its accompanying text from *Punch*, 1888.

*All the circumstances of the trade, the hours of labour, the rate of remuneration, and the sanitary conditions under which the work is done are disgraceful . . . In the 'dens' of the Sweaters, as they are called, there is not the slightest attempt at decency . . . In the vast*

*majority of cases work is carried on under conditions in the highest degree filthy and unsanitary. In small rooms, not more than nine or ten feet square, heated by a coke fire for the presser's irons and at night lighted by flaring gas-jets, six, eight, ten and even a dozen workers may be crowded . . . The stench and foul vapour about the place are very bad . . . As regards hours of labour, earnings and sanitary surroundings, the conditions of these people is more deplorable than that of any body of working men in any portion of the civilised or uncivilised world.*

1  Is it possible to tell from the scenes shown in the etching (Source 2.57) and the comments made whether the illustrator was hostile to 'sweating'?

2  What images has the illustrator used to emphasise the abuses surrounding this type of work?

3  How reliable is this cartoon for a historian studying contemporary attitudes towards employment issues?

## ● SOURCE 2.58

From the *Fifth Report from the Select Committee of the House of Lords on the Sweating System, 1890,* which reported on the meaning, and causes of, 'sweating'.

---

**trade combinations**
trade unions

---

### (i) Definition of 'sweating'

*We are of opinion that, although we cannot assign an exact meaning to 'sweating', the evils known by that name are shown in the foregoing pages of the Report to be—*

1 *A rate of wages inadequate to the necessities of the workers or disproportionate to the work done.*

2 *Excessive hours of labour.*

3 *The insanitary state of the houses in which work is carried on. These evils can hardly be exaggerated.*

*The earnings of the lowest classes of workers are barely sufficient to sustain existence.*

*The hours of labour are such as to make the lives of the workers periods of almost ceaseless toil, hard and often unhealthy.*

*The sanitary conditions under which the work is conducted are not only injurious to the health of the persons employed, but are dangerous to the public, especially in the case of the trades concerned in making clothes, as infectious diseases are spread by the sale of garments made in rooms inhabited by persons suffering from small-pox and other diseases.*

### (ii) Causes of 'sweating'

1 *. . . we are told that the introduction of sub-contractors or middlemen is the cause of the misery. Undoubtedly, it appears to us that employers are regardless of the moral obligations which attach to capital when they take contracts to supply articles and know nothing of the condition of the workers by whom such articles are made, leaving to a sub-contractor the duty of selecting the workers and giving him by way of compensation a portion of the profit. But it seems to us that the middleman is the consequence, not the cause of the evil; the instrument, not the hand which gives motion to the instrument, which does the mischief. Moreover, the middleman is found to be absent in many cases in which the evils complained of abound.*

*Further, we think that undue stress has been laid on the injurious effect on wages caused by foreign immigration, inasmuch as we find that the evils complained of obtain in trades which do not appear to be affected by foreign immigration.*

*We are of opinion, however, that certain trades are, to some extent, affected by the presence of poor foreigners, for the most part Russian and Polish Jews. These Jews [are] thrifty and industrious, and they seldom or never come on the rates . . . live on . . . starvation wages . . . work for a number of hours almost incredible in length, and until of late they have not easily lent themselves to* TRADE COMBINATIONS.

*Machinery, by increasing the sub-division of labour, and consequently affording great opportunities for the introduction of unskilled labour, is also charged with being a cause of sweating. The answer to this charge seems to be, that in some of the larger clothing and other factories, in which labour is admitted to be carried on under favourable conditions to the workers, machinery, and sub-division of labour to the greatest possible extent, are found in every part of the factory. With more truth it may be said that the inefficiency of many of the lower classes of workers, early marriages, and the tendency of the residuum of the population in large towns to form a helpless community, together with a low standard of life and the excessive supply of unskilled labour, are the chief factors in producing sweating. Moreover, a large supply of cheap female labour is available in consequence of the fact that married women working at unskilled labour in their homes, in the intervals of attendance on their domestic duties and not wholly supporting themselves, can afford to work at what would be starvation wages to unmarried women. Such being the conditions of the labour market, abundant materials exist to supply an unscrupulous employer with workers helplessly dependent upon him.*

---

1 How does the Select Committee (Source 2.58) define 'sweating'?

2 What role was attributed to each of the following as a cause of 'sweating'
   a) middlemen
   b) immigrant labour
   c) 'inefficiency' of the lower classes of workers
   d) married women?

3 What difficulties faced any government attempt to remove the abuse of 'sweating'?

# What was the impact of 'sweating' on workers?

● **Source 2.59**

From Richard Mudie Smith, *Sweated Industries*, a *Daily News* handbook at the *Daily News* Exhibition, 1906, reporting a letter by an ex-machinist to the organising secretary of the National Anti-Sweating League formed in 1905. The League had held an exhibition of goods produced in the sweated trades in Queen's Hall, London. The *Daily News* had taken up the campaign.

*After paying for cotton and railway journey, I had 7s. per week on an average, sometimes less, and paid 5s. for rent: I worked from 6 a.m. in the morning until ten at night, only taking about one hour for my meals. While at warehouses I saw some had notices up that work kept longer than four days would not be paid full price . . . Work must be counted before taken away, or any deficiency must be paid for. A difficult matter to measure trimmings and count parts in a hurry, especially when you sometimes only had the floor to pack up on.*

*I had some flannelette shirts, lined, sent me at 1s. 9d. I could stand it no longer; took them to St Pancras Vestry; showed them to the lady Inspector, who sent me to the Working Women's League, who could do nothing unless the workers would strike.*

*Yours truly,*
*An Ex-machinist*

● **Source 2.60**

From *The Times*, 25 October 1906, reporting the Conference arranged by the National Anti-Sweating League, London.

*Sir Charles Dilke, MP, who took the chair, said, 'Even the roughest trades employing women and children in factories or large workshops have in them the remote possibility of organisation. Home industries in many cases have not even that bare chance. In these there is a misery which depresses both the workers and those who would help them . . . The home life of the home workers is often nothing at all, for the home becomes the grinding shop . . . The case of the children is still more deplorable than that of the feebler class of men and women. The absence of delimitation of hours is productive of evil in the child's more than in any other case. It is in this class of labour, utterly incapable of fixing a minimum wage for itself, that the evils of its absence stand revealed in its worst form.'*

Study Sources 2.59 and 2.60.

1  What was the attitude of employers towards their outworkers?

2  How did employers punish slow workers?

3  How would the system of punishment affect
   a) the sick
   b) the older workers?

4  Why, according to Source 2.60, were women and children worse off by working at home compared with their factory counterparts?

5  How far do the sources support the conclusion that in 1906 women's work was hard, low-skilled and poorly paid?

## What attempts were made to reform 'sweating'?

A Sweated Trades Act was passed in 1891. It attempted to identify a minimum working age of eleven and to protect women working very long hours in trades carried on in back rooms, but there were difficulties in enforcing these restrictions. Nothing was done to legislate against low wages because of the commitment to a free market, which held that wages should be determined by the laws of demand and supply. It was not until the twentieth century that the Liberals established a minimum wage for 200,000 workers in the box-making, tailoring and lace-making industries, as part of their welfare programme to remedy the causes of low wages (see Chapter 6).

By the last quarter of the nineteenth century the Factory Inspectorate had not only amassed years of experience in the regulation of factories, but had become a professional body well acquainted with both the social conditions and the technological life of the factory districts. It was concerned not only with the efficient use of existing labour power but also with the safeguarding of future labour. It became involved in issues concerning industrial health and hygiene and developed an expertise in the diseases associated with all kinds of industrial processes. Gradually the existing Factory Acts were extended to all industries, although establishments employing only men were still not regulated.

# 8 To what extent were working conditions in agriculture reformed?

In 1851 there were 1.25 million men and 144,000 women employed in farm work. Wives and children did regular fieldwork or, in the case of young girls, went into domestic service to supplement family income. Farm labourers did not attract the attention of reformers, since outdoor work was seen as healthy, unlike conditions in factories and mines. They worked long hours, especially at harvest time, and in East Anglia, where a 'gang' system operated, work was brutally hard. The gang workers were virtually the slaves of the gang master, especially the children. The evils of the gang system did not attract public attention until 1866 when the Children's Employment Commission reported on the conditions in agricultural gangs. The report led to the 1867 Agricultural Gangs Act, which banned the employment of children under eight on a public agricultural gang. Gangs had to be licensed and girls could not work alongside boys because of the risks of immorality. Private gangs that worked for one farmer, rather than being hired out to the best bidder, were excluded from the act. The act was not fully observed although gang work gradually died out as the Education Acts compelled children to attend school and casual labour became harder to find.

## What were the main abuses affecting workers employed on the land?

● **SOURCE 2.61**

From Edward Grey, *Cottage Life in a Hertfordshire Village*, in which Grey describes his experiences as a farmworker in north Hertfordshire in the late 1860s and 1870s.

. . . *hired farm hands, both boys and young men, had to rise at 4 o'clock to feed and water their horses, at some farms a bell was rung at that hour, and the horse-keeper boys have told me that if they were not quickly down the farmer would soon be after them. After tending to the horses, came breakfast, the head ploughman came along at 5 o'clock, and at 6 o'clock the men and their teams started off to the fields; they continued to plough until 12 o'clock with a break of half an hour at 10 o'clock for 'beaver'. By 2 o'clock each team was supposed to have ploughed an acre (ploughing an acre of land deemed a day's work). The horses would then be shut out from the plough, and they and the men get back to the farm, when the horses would be watered. Then came dinner, after which the horses would be cleaned and combed, stable littered, and the animals fed and made comfortable (or 'racked up' was the term used) for the night and the men's day's work ended; this was an ordinary day. At harvest and hay time the hours were much longer, the men working sometimes until 9 o'clock or past . . . The working hours of what one might call the general farm hands, were on most farms from 6 a.m. to 5 p.m. from the Monday until the Saturday night, the wages being 11s. to 13s. weekly. In the winter months shorter hours were worked, the wage during this shorter hour period sinking on some farms to 9s., or even less . . . There were no holidays other than Christmas Day, save that on Good Friday morning, when at a number of the nearby farms the men were allowed time off to attend the morning service at the Parish Church if they so wished, coming back to their work again in the afternoon; many of the older men availed themselves of the privilege.*

Study Source 2.61.

1 To what extent were the hours worked by agricultural labourers similar to those worked in factories?

2 Why were conditions for agricultural labourers particularly severe during the winter?

3 How did the problems of the rural labourer differ from those of labourers employed in factories?

# What abuses were associated with agricultural gangs?

**● SOURCE 2.62**

From N. Philip, *Victorian Village Life*, 1973, in which Samuel Peeling, a Norfolk labourer, gives evidence about his daughter's work in a gang to the Poor Law Commission in 1843.

*I have a daughter turned 11; has worked 2 years along with the gang. Pulling turnips is very back-breaking work; she's too young to pull turnips; she don't often pull 'em; the men pull and the girls set 'em up . . . I'm forced to let my daughter go else I'm very much against it. I earn nothing myself; she does not like it at all . . . she hears so much blackguard bad language; and she's never used to hearing that at home. She has complained of pain in her side very often; they drive them along—force them along—they make them work very hard.*

**● SOURCE 2.63**

From N. Philip, *Victorian Village Life*, 1973, in which Joseph Arch (see page 35) describes the Norfolk 'gang' system.

*There were private gangs and public ones; small ones and large ones; fixed ones and wandering ones. Sometimes the gang would consist of one man and three or four children working under him; they would go turnip singling and bean dropping. Sometimes there would be a mixed gang of men and women weeding and picking 'twitch'; some would consist of women only. The potato gangs would be among the largest . . . Such a gang would frequently number as many as seventy, and there would be a man walking up and down behind them superintending. Generally he was a rough bullying fellow, who could bluster and swear and threaten and knock the youngsters about and browbeat the women, but who was nothing of a workman himself.*

**● SOURCE 2.64**

From the *Sixth Report of the Children's Employment Commission*, 1867, describing conditions in agricultural gangs.

**depravity**
lust

*An organised agricultural gang consists of—*
*The gang master.*
*A number of*
*(a) Women          (b) Young persons of both sexes (those between 13 and 18)*
*(c) Children of both sexes from the age of 6 to 13.*
*The numbers in each public gang are from 10 or 12 to 20, 30, and 40; very rarely above 40. But the most common, because the most manageable number, is about 20 . . . the 'public gang-master' is an independent man, who engages the members of the gang, and contracts with the farmer to execute a certain kind and amount of agricultural work with his gang . . . The public gang-masters are usually described as men whom the farmers are not willing to have in their regular employ; men who belong to the class of 'catchwork labourers'; in most cases men of indolent and drinking habits, 'and in many cases men of notorious DEPRAVITY'; as a rule unfit for the office they undertake . . . Their influence is represented as very harmful to the moral principles and conduct of the children and young persons of both sexes under their management . . . The gang master is engaged with his gang more or less during the greatest part of the year, although continuous employment for young children seldom exceeds six months. The work varies . . . but consists principally in weeding corn and other crops, picking twitch . . . setting potatoes . . . spreading manure, topping and tailing mangolds and turnips, and other work of the like kind . . . His 'principal source of gain' is piece work, which seems essential to rendering his trade a profitable one . . . he makes his profit 'partly by pressing his gang to the utmost of their strength, and partly by a hasty and imperfect performance of his work' . . . the interest of the gang master leads him to keep the whole of his gang at full stretch while at their work, with the shortest possible intervals of interruption. When to this is added the length of the walk to and from their work, . . . this mode of employment must impose upon the young and the feeble a vast amount of fatigue, often to the point of entire exhaustion.*

Study Sources 2.62–2.64.

1   What was an agricultural gang?

2   To what extent was the role of the gang master similar to that of the factory overseer?

3   What were the abuses associated with the public gang master?

4   What physical and moral dangers faced children who worked in agricultural gangs?

5   To what extent did children who worked in agriculture experience the same dangers as those faced by child workers in industry?

6   What aspects of gang life would have most attracted the attention of reformers in the later nineteenth century?

# ● Summary task

**1 Individual activity**

The aim of this activity is to help you to evaluate

a) the social composition of the factory reform movement
b) progress in the reform of working conditions between 1815 and 1914.

Read through the timeline at the start of the chapter and the sources dealing with specific Acts of Parliament. Record the evidence, using your own copies of the following charts to organise your results.

**a) Social composition of the factory reform movement**

| Social group | Motives | Contribution |
|---|---|---|
| Old 'labour aristocracies' | | |
| 'Pioneers of social medicine' | | |
| Northern clergy | | |
| Traditionalists | | |
| Support inside Parliament | | |
| Support outside Parliament | | |

**b) Progress in the reform of working conditions 1815–1914**

| Acts | Industry covered | Terms | Effectiveness |
|---|---|---|---|
| 1802 | | | |
| 1819 | | | |
| 1825 | | | |
| 1833 | | | |
| 1842 | | | |
| 1844 | | | |
| 1847 | | | |
| 1850 | | | |
| 1853 | | | |
| 1867 | | | |
| 1871 | | | |
| 1874 | | | |
| 1878 | | | |
| 1880 | | | |
| 1891 | | | |
| 1895 | | | |
| 1897 | | | |
| 1901 | | | |
| 1906 | | | |

## 2 A2 essay-planning exercise

Write an essay answering the following question:

**How would you account for the extension of factory legislation between 1802 and 1847?**

This is a significance-type question that requires you to decide upon the relative importance of factors. You need to establish a line of argument and start each paragraph with a reason for the extension of issues covered by factory reform. It is a relatively straightforward question though you must avoid the danger of narrating the content of consecutive Factory Acts.

**Suggested plan:** You need to identify the contribution of each factor as the lead-in to each paragraph and then explain it using evidence to substantiate your point.

| Paragraph | Main factor explored | Developed content |
|---|---|---|
| Introduction | A comparison between the factory movement pre- and post-1830 | Absence of one all-embracing act dealing with all abuses, but a gradual extension of legislation over the period 1802–47 indicating that aims and effectiveness varied over time. Aims of the early reformers compared with later. |
| 2 | Attitude and activities of reformers | How these changed over time and the effect of this on the extension of the factory reform movement. |
| 3 | Leadership inside and outside of Parliament | How this affected the action and direction of the movement – a 'patchwork of opinion'. Scope and complexity of the movement manifested itself in the often conflicting aims of the reformers – effect of such divisions? |
| 4 | Impact of greater organisation and how this transformed the struggle | Limited effectiveness of activities – contribution of change in philosophy – debate on inclusion of women. |
| 5 | Extensions to overcome ineffectiveness of the various acts | Limitations and loopholes of successive acts in 1802, 1819, 1833 and 1844 which only became apparent when attempts were made to implement them – contribution of factory inspectors, men of the calibre of Leonard Horner, to the movement. |
| Conclusion | Issue of increasing government intervention | Parliament was required by the Industrial Revolution to intervene to protect the victims of technical progress – concern was not about labour but about excessive labour and the education of children – extension of legislation as the debate became extended. |

# Examples of examination-type questions

## A  AS questions

1  a) What were the main abuses affecting the employment of women and children in cotton textiles?
   b) What progress had been made by 1850 in the reform of hours, and of working conditions, in factories?

2  a) Who supported and who opposed factory reform?
   b) To what extent did the Factory Acts improve the working conditions of children under thirteen?

## B  A2 questions

1  Why did industrial workers in the years 1832–50 find so much to complain about in their working conditions?

2  Why has the factory reform movement been described as a 'strange agitation'?

3  Did the Factory Acts of the first half of the nineteenth century remedy the problems created by the mechanisation of the textile industries?

4  To what extent was the opposition of factory owners the major reason why it was difficult to improve conditions in the 1830s?

---

## ● Further reading

Working conditions and the Factory Acts are covered in a number of general social history textbooks: D. Fraser, *The Evolution of the British Welfare State*, chapters 1 and 5 (Macmillan, 1973); U. Henriques, *Before the Welfare State*, chapters 4, 5 and 12 (Longman, 1979); E. Hopkins, *A Social History of the English Working Classes 1815–1945*, chapters 1, 4, 7, 12 (Edward Arnold, 1979); J. T. Ward, *Popular Movements c. 1832–1850*, chapter 2 (Macmillan, 1970).

### Articles

U. Henriques, 'The Factory Acts and Their Enforcement', Historical Association pamphlet, 1971

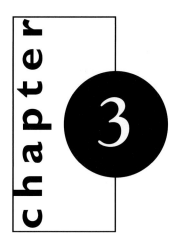

# chapter 3

# Did living conditions improve?

**1795–96**

Manchester Board of Health is set up following an outbreak of typhus in 1784.

**1831–32**

Cholera epidemic leads to establishment of temporary local boards of health.

**1832**

Dr James Kay publishes his investigation, *The Moral and Physical Condition of the Working Classes Employed in the Cotton Manufacture of Manchester*.

Cholera Act empowers local boards to finance anti-cholera provisions out of the poor rates.

**1834**

Poor Law Amendment Act provides for the appointment of Poor Law medical officers.

**1837**

Office of Registrar-General is set up to register births, marriages and deaths, a practice that was made compulsory by an act of 1836.

**1840**

*Report of the Select Committee on the Health of Towns* is published.

**1842**

*Report on the Sanitary Condition of the Labouring Population of Great Britain* by Edwin Chadwick is published.

**1844**

Health of Towns Association is set up.

**1845**

*Report of the Commission for Inquiring into the State of Large Towns and Populous Districts* is published.

**1847**

Liverpool appoints first medical officer of health.

**1848**

Public Health Act creates a General Board and local boards of health.

**1848–49**

Cholera epidemic breaks out.

**1851**

Common Lodging Houses Act provides the police with powers to inspect and, if necessary, close down lodging houses, some of which were no more than disreputable doss houses where the bed would be a bundle of straw.

Titus Salt begins building his model town, Saltaire, near Bradford.

## 1854

Edwin Chadwick is dismissed as first secretary to the Board of Health – established by the 1848 Public Health Act.

## 1858

Sir John Simon becomes Medical Officer of Health for the Privy Council. A surgeon and pathologist, he was responsible for a large number of reports on diseases and the effects on health of diet, housing and working conditions.

## 1862

Peabody Trust is set up by an American, George Peabody, to provide decent housing for London's poor.

## 1864

Octavia Hill, granddaughter of Southwood Smith, begins her work of raising money to buy working-class tenements and improve them.

## 1866

Sanitary Act provides local boards of health with uniform and universal powers to improve sanitation. Towns are compelled to appoint sanitary inspectors. The definition of 'nuisance' is broadened to include houses and nuisance removal authorities are obliged to act.

## 1868

Torrens Act entitles local authorities to clear insanitary houses.

## 1871

Local Government Board is created to oversee health policies of local councils.

## 1872

Public Health Act sets up sanitary authorities with obligatory powers including the appointment of a medical officer of health.

## 1875

Public Health Act codifies the provisions of 1872 in relation to the functions and duties of local authorities.

Artisans' Dwellings Act gives local authorities the right to buy up by compulsory purchase property condemned as insanitary by their medical officer and to improve or demolish it. The authorities could themselves rebuild on the cleared sites or let sites to private builders.

Fall of Sir John Simon.

## 1885

Report of the Royal Commission on the Housing of the Working Classes.

## 1888

Port Sunlight factory village is built by William Lever.

## 1890

Housing of the Working Classes Act lets local authorities demolish unfit housing and provide alternative accommodation.

## 1895

Bournville village is begun by the chocolate manufacturer George Cadbury in Birmingham.

## 1898

Garden Cities of Tomorrow is founded to promote the ideas of Ebeneezer Howard, who campaigns for overall town planning. It leads to the building of Letchworth Garden City.

## 1902

Midwives Act creates a Central Midwives Board to register trained midwives.

**1903**

Letchworth Garden City is founded.

**1904**

Devonshire Report on Physical Deterioration.
New Earswick is built by the chocolate manufacturer Joseph Rowntree for his workers in York.

**1907**

Medical inspection in schools is made compulsory.

**1909**

Housing and Town Planning Act gives local authorities the right to insist that any new town development is well laid out.

# Introduction

In pre-industrial England there were no obvious public health problems. But between 1801 and 1851 the population of Great Britain doubled. There was bad housing in rural areas as a result of the increase in population but it was in the rapidly expanding urban areas that the real public health problem developed. In the absence of a public transport system, houses and factories had to be located close together. Towns were ill equipped to cope with the phenomenal growth. In *The Evolution of the British Welfare State* (Macmillan, 1973, p. 51), D. Fraser states, 'It was the Industrial Revolution, accompanied by a massive shift in population from rural to urban areas, which created a public health problem.'

# 1 What were the main features of the growth of towns?

The rapid population growth posed enormous housing problems for urban communities. The main solution was to subdivide houses, with the cellar frequently being used. It was not unusual for a large family to be living in one room. Those with commercial interests in housing saw greater gains in overcrowding than in reconstruction and those who did embark on providing new housing did so as cheaply as possible. No initiative was used in any form of new construction. There was also the problem of finding suitable sites: it was impossible to build in areas of existing housing because of the need to rehouse the existing inhabitants. Nevertheless some areas were developed for workers' dwellings, as in the Hulme district of Manchester. Occasionally, co-operative building societies, sponsored by determined workers, struggled to create a housing estate, as in Birmingham or Sheffield. But, in general, as S. G. Checkland remarks, 'housing for the workers was a residual affair in all senses'. Large areas were set aside for the middle classes, where planning schemes were profitable. This low-density construction covered many acres, particularly on the edges of large towns. The lack of transport meant that workers' houses had to be close to factories; thus, the workers lived in the smoke and the middle classes beyond it.

# How rapidly did towns grow?

● **SOURCE 3.1**

From D. Fraser, *The Evolution of the British Welfare State*, 1973.

a) Population growth in British towns, 1801–61 (in thousands).
b) Percentage growth of population in British towns, 1801–61.

a)

| Town | 1801 | 1811 | 1821 | 1831 | 1841 | 1851 | 1861 |
|------|------|------|------|------|------|------|------|
| Birmingham | 71 | 83 | 102 | 144 | 183 | 233 | 296 |
| Glasgow | 77 | 101 | 147 | 202 | 275 | 345 | 420 |
| Leeds | 53 | 63 | 84 | 123 | 152 | 172 | 207 |
| Liverpool | 82 | 104 | 138 | 202 | 286 | 376 | 444 |
| Manchester | 75 | 89 | 126 | 182 | 235 | 303 | 339 |
| Salford | 14 | 19 | 26 | 41 | 53 | 64 | 102 |
| Sheffield | 46 | 53 | 65 | 92 | 111 | 135 | 185 |

b)

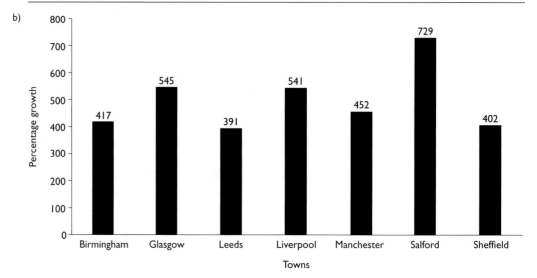

> **I** Study the table and graph in Source 3.1. Which towns saw the fastest growth in the early nineteenth century?

# What were the main features of housing in Manchester?

● **SOURCE 3.2**

From the *Report of the Select Committee on the Health of Towns*, 1840, in which the surgeon John Robertson describes conditions in Manchester by 1840.

**Manchester**
grew rapidly from a market town to a leading centre of the cotton industry. In 1840 it still did not have an elected town corporation with mayor and councillors but was governed by the lord of the manor of Mosley.

MANCHESTER *has no Building Act and hence with the exception of certain central streets over which the Police Act gives the Commissioners power each proprietor builds as he pleases. New cottages with or without cellars huddled together row behind row may be seen springing up in many parts but especially in the township of Manchester where the land is higher in price than the land for cottage sites in other townships is. With such proceedings as these authorities cannot interfere. A cottage row may be badly drained, the streets may be full of pits brimful of stagnant water, the receptacle of dead cats and dogs, yet no one may find fault. The number of cellar residences you have probably learned from the papers published by the Manchester Statistical Society is very great in all quarters of the town; and even in Hulme, a large portion of which consists of cottages recently erected, the same practice is continued. That it is an evil must be obvious on the slightest consideration, for how can a hole underground of from 12 to 15 feet square admit of ventilation so as to fit it for human habitation?*

*We have no authorised inspector of dwellings and streets. If an epidemic disease were to invade as happened in 1832 the authorities would probably order inspection as they did on that occasion but it would be merely by general permission not of right.*

*Manchester has no public park or other grounds where the population can walk and breathe the fresh air. New streets are rapidly extending in every direction and so great already is the expanse of the town that those who live in the more populous quarters can seldom hope to see the green face of nature.*

## SOURCE 3.3

From Friedrich Engels, *The Condition of the Working Class in England*, 1845, in which the author describes the growth of Manchester.

**Friedrich Engels (1820–95)**
was born in Germany and lived in Manchester in 1844–45, and again in 1850–70, as a respected businessman. He was co-author of the *Communist Manifesto*, 1848, in which he rejected the policy of *laissez-faire* and advocated its replacement by total state control.

**bourgeoisie**
the middle classes

*Manchester contains, at its heart, a rather extended commercial district, perhaps half a mile long and about as broad, and consisting almost wholly of offices and warehouses. With the exception of the commercial district Manchester proper and the surrounding districts are all unmixed working people's quarters, stretching like a girdle, averaging a mile and a half in breadth, around the commercial district. Outside, beyond this girdle, lives the upper and middle* BOURGEOISIE, *the middle bourgeoisie in regularly laid out streets in the vicinity of the working quarters, especially in Chorlton and the lower lying portions of Cheetham Hill; the upper bourgeoisie in remoter villas with gardens in Chorlton and Ardwick, or on the breezy heights of Cheetham Hill, Broughton and Pendleton, in free, wholesome country air, in fine, comfortable homes, passed once every half or quarter hour by omnibuses going into the city. And the finest part of the arrangement is this, that the members of this money aristocracy can take the shortest road through the middle of all the labouring districts to their places of business, without ever seeing that they are in the midst of the grimy misery that lurks to the right and the left.*

Study Sources 3.2 and 3.3.

1   Why, according to John Robertson (Source 3.2), was Manchester ill-equipped to deal with its rapid growth?

2   What were the consequences for Manchester of the absence of central control?

3   How did the growth of Manchester reflect the developing class structure in the towns?

## SOURCE 3.4

From the *Report on the Sanitary Condition of the Labouring Population*, 1842.

*On the early introduction of the cotton manufacture, the parties who entered into it were often men of limited capital, and anxious to invest the whole of it in mills and machinery. They were therefore too much absorbed with the doubtful success of their own affairs to look after the necessities of their workpeople.*

*Families were attracted from all parts for the benefit of employment, and obliged as a temporary resort to crowd together into such dwellings as the neighbourhood afforded: often two families into one house; others into cellars or very small dwellings. Eventually, as the works became established either the owner or some neighbour would probably see it advantageous to build a few cottages. These were often of the worst description; in such case the prevailing consideration was not how to promote the health and comfort of the occupants, but how many cottages could be built upon the smallest space of ground and at the least possible cost.*

1   What, according to Source 3.4, was the attitude of factory owners towards the provision of housing for their workers?

2   How was the demand for housing for factory workers met?

3   Study Sources 3.2–3.4. What criticisms of neglect could be directed against the builders of new towns?

4   Why were local authorities restricted in their ability to tackle living conditions in their towns?

# 2 Why did the growth of towns create a public health problem?

Houses were built without the sewerage, drainage and clean water supplies essential to healthy living conditions. Refuse was allowed to build up. Water, which was in short supply, often came from rivers that were open sewers. Workers were also faced with problems of disease, such as typhus, which first appeared in Manchester in 1785. Typhus became endemic, sometimes flaring up into more serious epidemics;

indeed, it was so common that it was simply referred to as 'fever'. As a virus carried by lice, it was closely associated with cramped, insanitary housing conditions and thus was almost exclusively a disease of the poor. Doctors were aware of it but little was done to control it.

The same was also true of tuberculosis or TB, which accounted for a third of all deaths in the first half of the nineteenth century. The smoky atmosphere and squalid housing, combined with the poor nutritional health of the urban workforce, provided the conditions in which TB could flourish. Other diseases included smallpox, and, more particularly from the 1830s onwards, cholera. The latter was carried in polluted water and affected all social groups. Such unhealthy conditions contributed to a low life expectancy, particularly in urban areas.

## What were the main features of living conditions in towns?

### ● SOURCE 3.5

From Friedrich Engels, *The Condition of the Working Class in England*, 1845.

#### (i) Birmingham

*In the older quarters of Birmingham there are many bad districts, filthy and neglected, full of stagnant pools and refuse. Courts are very numerous in the city, reaching 2,000 and containing the greater number of the working people of the city. These courts are usually narrow, muddy, badly ventilated [with little fresh air], ill drained, and lined with eight to 20 houses, which, by reason of having their rear walls in common, can usually be ventilated from one side only. In the background, within the court, there is usually an ash heap or something of the kind, the filth of which cannot be described. The newer courts, however, are more sensibly built and more decently kept, and even in the old ones the cottages are much less crowded than in Manchester and Liverpool.*

#### (ii) Liverpool

*Liverpool, with all its commerce, wealth and grandeur, yet treats its workers with barbarity. A full fifth of the population, more than 45,000 human beings, live in narrow, dark, damp, badly ventilated cellar dwellings, of which there are 7,862 in the city. Besides these cellar dwellings there are 2,270 courts, small spaces built up on all four sides and having but one entrance, a narrow, covered passage-way, the whole ordinarily very dirty and inhabited exclusively by proletarians.*

### ● SOURCE 3.6

*A Court for King Cholera*, a cartoon from *Punch*, 25 September 1852.

A COURT FOR KING CHOLERA.

Study Source 3.5 and the *Punch* cartoon in Source 3.6.

1  What is meant by a 'court'?

2  What public health hazards were likely to be found amongst the cellar population of Liverpool?

3  Why did the artist call his cartoon *A Court for King Cholera*?

4  What connection was the artist trying to make between cholera and the environment?

## What dangers did town dwellers face from disease?

● **SOURCE 3.7**

From Dr James P. Kay, *The Moral and Physical Condition of the Working Classes Employed in the Cotton Manufacture of Manchester*, 1832, in which the author presents an unpleasant picture of early nineteenth-century Manchester.

**noxious exhalations**
harmful fumes

*The state of the streets powerfully affects the health of their inhabitants. Sporadic cases of typhus chiefly appear in those which are narrow, ill-ventilated, unpaved, or which contain heaps of refuse, or stagnant pools. The confined air and NOXIOUS EXHALATIONS, which abound in such places, depress the health of the people, and on this account contagious diseases are also most rapidly propagated there . . . The houses, in such situations, are uncleanly, ill-provided with furniture; an air of discomfort if not of squalid and loathsome wretchedness pervades them, they are often dilapidated, badly drained, damp: and the habits of their tenants are gross. They are ill-fed, ill-clothed, and uneconomical, at once spendthrifts and destitute, denying themselves the comforts of life, in order that they may wallow in the unrestrained licence of animal appetite. An intimate connection subsists, among the poor, between the cleanliness of the street and that of the house and person. Uneconomical habits and dissipation are almost inseparably allied; and they are so frequently connected with uncleanliness, that we cannot consider their concomitance as altogether accidental . . . When the health is depressed by the concurrence of these causes, contagious diseases spread with a fatal malignancy among the population subjected to their influence. The records of the Fever Hospital of Manchester prove that typhus prevails almost exclusively in such situations.*

*. . . The evils affecting the working classes, so far from being the necessary results of the commercial system, furnish evidence of a disease which impairs its energies, if it does not threaten its vitality . . .*

*Want of cleanliness, of forethought, and economy, are found in almost invariable alliance with dissipation, reckless habits, and disease. The population gradually becomes physically less efficient as the producers of wealth, morally so from idleness, politically worthless as having few desires to satisfy, and noxious as dissipators of capital accumulated. Were such manners to prevail, the horrors of pauperism would accumulate. A debilitated race would be rapidly multiplied. Morality would afford no check to the increase of the population: crime and disease would be its only obstacles . . . A dense mass, impotent alike of great moral or physical efforts, would accumulate . . .*

Study Source 3.7.

1  What conditions encouraged the spread of typhus?

2  What connection does Dr Kay make between dirt and disease?

3  What moral judgements does he make of the responsibility of the working classes for their condition?

● **SOURCE 3.8**

From *Leeds Intelligencer*, 21 August 1841, in which a civil engineer describes the river Aire, which supplied many Leeds citizens with their drinking water.

*It is charged with the contents of about 200 water closets and similar places, a great number of common drains, the drainings from dung-hills, the Infirmary (dead leeches, poultices for patients, etc.), slaughter houses, chemical soap, gas, dung, dyehouses and manufactories, spent blue and black dye, pig manure, old urine wash, with all sorts of decomposed animal and vegetable substances from an extent of drainage . . . amounting to about 30,000,000 gallons per annum of the mass of filth with which the river is loaded.*

● **SOURCE 3.9**

From the *Report of the Leeds Board of Health*, 1833, by Dr Robert Baker, District Surgeon, describing the outbreak of cholera.

**cholera**

a highly infectious disease, which attacks the intestines and causes diarrhoea, sickness, cramp, fever and death within 36 hours. It was a new waterborne disease that spread rapidly. It attacked all classes, especially the poor. There were epidemics in 1831–32, 1846–49, 1853–54, 1855–56 and 1867. It forced the government to set up a Central Board of Health and the Cholera Act of 1832 empowered local boards to finance their anti-cholera provisions out of poor rates. Leeds set up its own local boards.

**miasmata**

means bad air or poison floating in the air. Doctors correctly linked disease with dirt but believed it was carried by the bad smell or poisonous miasma.

### (i) Outbreak of cholera in Leeds, 1832

On the 26th (May 1832) . . . the first case of . . . CHOLERA occurred in the Blue Bell Fold a small and dirty cul-de-sac containing about 20 houses inhabited by poor families . . . on the North side of the river in an angle between it and an offensive beck or streamlet which conveys the refuse water from numerous mills and dyehouses . . . the income of one family of eight persons . . . of whom four died in succession at the very start of the disease had not averaged more than twelve shillings per week for the four preceding months.

The disease . . . ran through the Blue Bell Fold, spread with considerable rapidity . . . became general in the beginning of July, was at its height in August and the Board of Health ceased to have reports from its district surgeons on 12th November.

. . . amidst a population of 76,000 persons . . . not more than 14 streets . . . have thorough common sewers.

. . . most of them are unsewered, undrained, unpaved, formed upon clayey soil and broken up by vehicles of every description, the only wonder is that diseases of this pestilential nature do not oftener and more fatally prevail . . . the disease has prevailed in those parts of the town where there is a deficiency often an entire want of sewerage, drainage and paving . . . in three parallel streets . . . occupied entirely by cottage dwellers with cellar dwellings . . . for a population . . . of 386 persons there are but two single privies.

From the privies in the Boot and Shoe yard which do not appear to have been thoroughly cleansed for the last thirty years 70 carts of manure were removed by order of the commissioners . . . In a town like Leeds where in so many parts it teems with human life and where the operatives are congregated together in small and narrow streets . . . little attention is paid by the owners of cottage property to their cleanliness and ventilation.

### (ii) Conditions that favoured the spread of cholera

With broken panes in every window frame, and filth and vermin in every nook. With the walls unwhite-washed for years, black with the smoke of foul chimneys, without water, with corded bed stocks for beds, and sacking for bed clothing, with floors unwashed from year to year, without out offices . . . while without, there are streets, elevated a foot sometimes two, above the level of the causeway, by the accumulation of years, and stagnant puddles here and there, with their foetid exhalations, causeways broken and dangerous, ash.

Places choked up with filth, and excrementitious deposits on all sides as a consequence, undrained, unpaved, unventilated, uncared for by any authority but the landlord, who weekly collects the miserable rents from his miserable tenants.

Can we wonder that such places are the hot beds of disease, or that it obtains, upon constitutions thus liberally disposed to receive it, and forms the mortality which Leeds exhibits. Adult life exposed to such MIASMATA, gives way. How much more then infant life, when ushered into, and attempted to be reared in, such obnoxious atmospheres. On the moral habits similar effects are produced. An inattention on the part of the local authorities to the state of the streets diminishes year by year the respectability of their occupiers. None dwell in such localities but those to whom nearness to employment is absolutely essential.

---

Study Sources 3.8 and 3.9.

1 What does Dr Baker imply about the causes of cholera?

2 What evidence does he cite to support his opinion?

3 How did the river Aire contribute to the problem of disease?

4 How did the Leeds Board of Health attempt to deal with the epidemic?

5 What had been the consequences for Leeds of a lack of proper local government control?

6 What effect did the dirty environment described by Dr Baker have on adult life in Leeds?

# 3 How serious were the threats to public health?

As the towns developed, a growing accumulation of local evidence indicated major public health problems. A multitude of overlapping authorities – paving trusts, commissioners of sewers and highway committees – were responsible for different areas that were causing concern but there was no central authority to decide upon and carry out improvements.

Private and charitable organisations did begin to address the problem – the Manchester Board of Health, for example, was established by Dr Thomas Perceval in 1795–96, following a major outbreak of typhus. However, no significant movement to improve public health existed until EDWIN CHADWICK became interested in the issue after 1835. He was motivated by the economic cost of disease, and saw that expenditure on poor relief (see Chapters 4 and 5) could be reduced if preventative action were taken to improve the environment. He began his campaign to have the removal of health hazards, or 'nuisances', made the responsibility of the Poor Law Commissioners. Three experts, Kay, Southwood Smith and Arnott, were appointed to collect evidence for a committee of enquiry set up in 1838. Chadwick also secured the appointment of Dr William Farr as the Registrar-General's Compiler of Abstracts for collecting statistics on deaths.

The outcome of these initiatives was Chadwick's famous *Report on the Sanitary Condition of the Labouring Population of Great Britian*, published in 1842. In his report, he stressed the relationship of insanitary housing, deficient sewerage and contaminated water supply to the incidence of disease and low life expectancy. Other notable reports published at around the same time were those of the Select Committee on the Health of Towns (1840) and the Commission for Inquiring into the State of Large Towns and Populous Districts (1844–45). Yet despite all the evidence, many well-to-do people refused to believe the details of these reports.

> **Edwin Chadwick (1800–1890)**
> trained as a lawyer before becoming a journalist and then secretary to the philosopher Jeremy Bentham. He worked as an investigator for the committees of enquiries into public health and the Poor Law. His main contributions to public service were as Secretary to the Poor Law Commission, 1834–46, and the Public Health Report, 1842, leading to the Public Health Act in 1848. He believed in Benthamism or Utilitarianism, which argued that public policies should be based on evidence and research.

## What was the effect of insanitary conditions on different classes?

● **SOURCE 3.10**

Adapted from Edwin Chadwick, *Report on the Sanitary Condition of the Labouring Population of Great Britain*, 1842, in which one of the researchers comments on the effects of insanitary conditions on different classes.

**erroneous**
wrong

*Mr Wood was asked:*

*'You have seen the following returns of the average ages of death among the different classes of people in Manchester and Rutland:*

| Average age of death | In Manchester | In Rutland(shire) |
|---|---|---|
| Professional persons and gentry and families | 38 | 52 |
| Tradesmen and their families | 20 | 41 |
| Mechanics, labourers and families | 17 | 38 |

*Are the different chances of life amongst each class of the population . . . conformable to what you would have anticipated from your examinations of the houses, and . . . of the inhabitants?'*

*'They are . . . That opinion is ERRONEOUS which ascribes greater . . . mortality to the children employed in factories than [to] children who remain in such homes as these towns afford to the labouring classes. Of all who are born of the labouring classes in Manchester, more than 57 per cent die before they attain 5 years of age; that is before they can be engaged in factory labour. At the period between 5 and 10 years of age the proportion of deaths which occur amongst the labouring classes [is] not so great as the proportion of deaths which occur amongst the children of the middle classes who are not so engaged; . . . [thus] the effect of employment is not shown to be injurious in any increase of the proportion who die.*

'But in Liverpool (which is a commercial and not a manufacturing town) when the condition of the dwellings are reported to be the worst – there the chances of life . . . [are] still lower than in Manchester, [or] Leeds. [In Liverpool], of the deaths which occurred amongst the labouring classes, . . . 62 per cent . . . [were] under 5 years of age. For Birmingham, where there are many insalubrious manufactories but where the drainage is comparatively good, the proportion of mortality was, in 1838, 1 in 40; whilst in Liverpool it was 1 in 31.'

● SOURCE 3.11

Adapted from Edwin Chadwick, *Report on the Sanitary Condition of the Labouring Population of Great Britain*, 1842.

Average age at death according to region and social class, during the period 1837–1840.

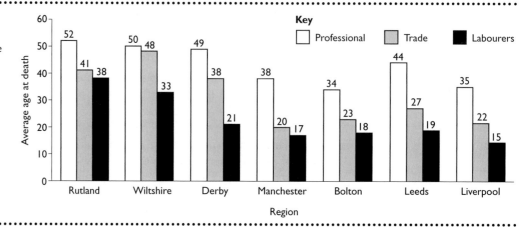

Study Sources 3.10 and 3.11.

1  Which social group had the longest life expectancy?

2  Which social group had the least life expectancy?

3  How did expectation of life in Manchester compare with that in Rutlandshire?

4  Can you suggest three reasons why the labourer in Rutlandshire had as high an expectation of life as the gentry in Manchester?

## How many people died from the different diseases?

● SOURCE 3.12

Adapted from Edwin Chadwick, *Report on the Sanitary Condition of the Labouring Population of Great Britain*, 1842.

Number of deaths nationally from contagious and respiratory diseases, 1838–39.

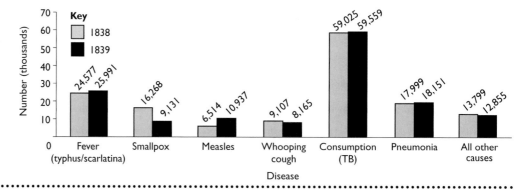

● SOURCE 3.13

Adapted from Edwin Chadwick, *Report on the Sanitary Condition of the Labouring Population of Great Britain*, 1842.

Comparison of the number of deaths from disease between rural and industrial counties, 1838.

| Disease | Rural | | Industrial |
| --- | --- | --- | --- |
| | Dorset | Rutland | Middlesex |
| Fever (typhus/scarlatina) | 137 | 11 | 4,422 |
| Smallpox | 255 | 2 | 3,359 |
| Measles | 80 | 0 | 487 |
| Whooping cough | 58 | 13 | 1,749 |
| Consumption (TB) | 571 | 64 | 6,220 |
| Pneumonia | 146 | 14 | 3,097 |
| All other causes | 106 | 8 | 2,334 |

Study Sources 3.10, 3.12 and 3.13.

1 What were the main causes of death in 1838–39?

2 What connection did Mr Wood find between housing conditions and the expectation of life in
   a) Manchester
   b) Liverpool?

3 What percentage of labourers' children died before the age of 5 in
   a) Manchester
   b) Liverpool?

4 At what age did they begin work in factories?

5 How did Mr Wood show that factory work was not injurious to health?

6 What, according to Mr Wood, was the main cause of the difference between the infant mortality rate for Birmingham and that for Liverpool?

Study Sources 3.2–3.13.

7 What appeared to be the most pressing problems concerning public health in the first half of the nineteenth century? In your answer comment on each of the following
   a) lack of planning controls
   b) absence of adequate clean water supplies, sewerage and drainage
   c) poor and inadequate housing
   d) diseases – both endemic and epidemic.

## What were the main findings of Chadwick's Royal Commission, 1840–42?

● **SOURCE 3.14**

From Edwin Chadwick, *Report on the Sanitary Condition of the Labouring Population of Great Britain*, 1842, in which he summarises the extent and operation of the evils which were the subject of his inquiry.

*After as careful an examination of the evidence collected as I have been enabled to make, I beg leave to recapitulate the chief conclusions . . .*

- *That the various forms of epidemic, and other disease caused, or aggravated, or propagated chiefly amongst the labouring classes by atmospheric impurities produced by decomposing animal and vegetable substances, by damp and filth, and close and overcrowded dwellings, prevail among the population in every part of the kingdom, whether dwelling in separate houses, in rural villages, in small towns, in the larger towns – as they have been found to prevail in the lowest districts of the metropolis.*

- *That such disease, wherever its attacks are frequent, is always found in connection with the physical circumstances above specified, and that where those circumstances are removed by drainage, proper cleansing, better ventilation, and other means of diminishing atmospheric impurity, the frequency and intensity of such disease is decreased; and where the removal of the noxious agencies appears to be complete, such disease almost entirely disappears.*

- *That high prosperity in respect to employment and wages, and various and abundant food, have afforded to the labouring classes no exemptions from attacks of epidemic disease, which have been as frequent and as fatal in periods of commercial and manufacturing prosperity as in any others.*

- *That the formation of all habits of cleanliness is obstructed by defective supplies of water.*

- *That the annual loss of life from filth and bad ventilation are greater than the loss from death or wounds in any wars in which the country has been engaged in modern times.*

- *That of the 43,000 cases of widowhood, and 112,000 cases of destitute orphanage relieved from the poor rates in England and Wales alone, it appears that the greatest proportion of deaths of the heads of families occurred from the above specified and other removable causes; that their ages were under 45 years; that is to say, 13 years below the natural probabilities of life as shown by the experience of the whole population of Sweden.*

- *That in the districts where the mortality is the greatest the births are not only sufficient to replace the numbers removed by death . . .*

- *That the younger population, bred up under noxious physical agencies, is inferior in physical organisation and general health to a population preserved from the presence of such agencies.*

**the population so exposed ... effects of education are more transient**
People brought up in the filth and pollution of the towns are of a poorer moral character and what they are taught makes little lasting impression on them.

**prevalence**
widespread existence

- That THE POPULATION SO EXPOSED IS LESS SUSCEPTIBLE OF MORAL INFLUENCES, AND THE EFFECTS OF EDUCATION ARE MORE TRANSIENT *than with a healthy population.*
- *That these adverse circumstances tend to produce an adult population short lived, improvident, reckless, and intemperate, and with habitual avidity for sensual gratifications.*
- *That these habits lead to the abandonment of all the conveniences and decencies of life, and especially lead to the overcrowding of homes, which is destructive to morality as well as the health of large classes of both sexes.*
- *That defective town cleansing fosters habits of the most abject degradation and tends to the demoralisation of large numbers of human beings, who subsist by means of what they find amidst the noxious filth accumulated in neglected streets and bye-places.*
- *That the expenses of local public works are in general unequally and unfairly assessed, oppressively and uneconomically collected, by separate collections, wastefully expended in separate and inefficient operations by unskilled and practically irresponsible officers.*
- *That the existing law for the protection of the public health and the constitutional machinery for reclaiming its execution, such as the Courts Leet, have fallen into disuse, and are in the state indicated by the* PREVALENCE *of the evils they were intended to prevent.*

1 What reasons does Chadwick give in Source 3.14 for the low life expectancy in towns?

2 Why were such early deaths not inevitable?

3 Why does Chadwick regard improvements in public health as a necessary precondition for reducing the financial burden of poor relief?

4 What effect does Chadwick think ill-health had on the character of the people?

5 Why, according to Chadwick, did central government have to take the initiative to provide public works?

## What were the main recommendations of the 1842 Report on the Sanitary Condition of the Labouring Population of Great Britain?

● **SOURCE 3.15**

From Edwin Chadwick, *Report on the Sanitary Condition of the Labouring Population of Great Britain*, 1842, in which he proposes improvements to sanitation in towns.

- *The primary and most important measures, and at the same time the most practicable, and within the recognised province of public administration, are drainage, the removal of all refuse [from] habitations, streets, and roads, and the improvement of the supplies of water.*
- *That the chief obstacles to the immediate removal of decomposing refuse of towns and habitations have been the expense and annoyance of the hand labour and cartage requisite for the purpose.*
- *That this expense may be reduced to one-twentieth or to one-thirtieth, or rendered inconsiderable, by the use of water and self-acting means of removal by improved and cheaper sewers and drains.*
- *That refuse when thus held in suspension in water may be most cheaply and innocuously conveyed to any distance out of towns, and also in the best form for productive use, and that the loss and injury by the pollution of natural streams may be avoided.*
- *That for all these purposes, as well as for domestic use, better supplies of water are absolutely necessary.*
- *That for successful and economical drainage the adoption of geological areas as the basis of operations is requisite.*
- *That appropriate scientific arrangements for public drainage would afford important facilities for private land-drainage, which is important for the health as well as sustenance of the labouring classes.*
- *That the expense of public drainage, of supplies of water laid on in houses, and of means of improved cleansing would be a financial gain, by diminishing the existing charges attendant on sickness and premature mortality.*

| levies |
| --- |
| taxes |

- *That for the protection of the labouring classes and of the ratepayers against inefficiency and waste in all new structural arrangements for the protection of the public health, and to ensure public confidence that the expenditure will be beneficial, securities should be taken that all new local public works are devised and conducted by responsible officers qualified by the possession of the science and skill of civil engineers.*
- *That the oppressiveness and injustices of LEVIES for the whole immediate outlay on such works upon persons who have only short interests in the benefits may be avoided by care in spreading the expense over periods coincident with the benefits.*
- *That by appropriate arrangements, 10 or 15 per cent on the ordinary outlay for drainage might be saved, which on an estimate of the expense of the necessary structural alterations of one-third only of the existing tenements would be a saving of one million and a half sterling, besides the reduction of the future expenses of management.*
- *That for the prevention of the disease occasioned by defective ventilation, and other causes of impurity in places of work and other places where large numbers are assembled, and for the general promotion of the means necessary to prevent disease, that it would be good economy to appoint a district medical officer independent of private practice, and with the securities of special qualifications and responsibilities, to initiate sanitary measures and reclaim the execution of the law.*
- *That by the combinations of all these arrangements, it is probable that, . . . an increase of 13 years at least, may be extended to the whole of the labouring classes . . .*
- *And that the removal of noxious physical circumstances, and the promotion of civic, household and personal cleanliness, are necessary to the improvement of the moral condition of the population; for that sound morality and refinement in manners and health are not long found co-existent with filthy habits amongst any class in the community.*

1 What recommendations does Chadwick make in Source 3.15 to ensure a proper policy of
   a) drainage
   b) sewerage, sanitation and water supply?

2 What administrative recommendations are made by Chadwick to ensure that experts would be put in charge of public health reforms?

3 Why does Chadwick argue that his proposals would save money?

4 What impact does Chadwick believe implementation of his reforms would have on the moral character of the people?

The Board of Poor Law Commissioners refused to publish Chadwick's Report because they feared it would upset the private water companies. Chadwick published it under his own name and it had a great impact on public opinion. Ten thousand free copies were distributed to politicians, journalists and MPs while a further twenty thousand were sold to the public. The Report showed that contemporaries were wrong to blame working-class people for bad housing and living conditions. The government was forced to act. It appointed a Royal Commission on the State of Large Towns and Populous Districts to investigate more fully the legislative and financial implications of Chadwick's proposals. The Commission was to suggest effective legislation and to establish 'the best means of promoting and securing the Public Health under the operation of the Laws and Regulations now in force, and the usages at present prevailing with regard to the drainage of lands, the erection, drainage and ventilation of buildings, and the supply of water in such towns and districts, whether for the purposes of health, or for the better protection of property from fire.'

The Commission was composed of experts who were organised by Chadwick. Questionnaires were sent to the 50 towns which had the highest annual death rates and the Commissioners studied for themselves the conditions in the most populous areas. Of 50 towns investigated, 42 had very bad drainage and 30 had a poor water supply. Only one town had reasonable drainage and six had good water supplies. Two reports were published in 1844 and 1845 but they did not produce enough public support to lead to legislation.

# 4 Who took the initiative to reform public health?

During the 1840s a number of important but local developments took place to secure a healthy environment. Towns such as Manchester and Liverpool took advantage of their newly incorporated status, acquired by the 1835 Municipal Corporation Act, to assume responsibility for draining, paving, sewerage and street cleaning under private Acts of Parliament. The first medical officers of health were appointed, also as a result of private acts. William Duncan became Medical Officer for Liverpool in 1847 and John Simon for London in 1848. Central government showed little interest. Chadwick embarked on a propaganda campaign of lectures, pamphlet distribution and publications to win public support for public health legislation. Health of Towns Bills were introduced in 1845 and 1847 but they were withdrawn for further consideration. Ignorance, apathy and the conservatism of vested interests in society proved to be powerful opponents.

## What were the main arguments in favour of reform?

● **SOURCE 3.16**

From D. Fraser, *The Evolution of the British Welfare State*, 1973, in which he quotes a letter written by Edwin Chadwick in 1838 complaining of the cost of sanitary neglect.

**poor rates**
money paid by certain householders in each parish to support those unable to work (see Chapter 4).

*In general all epidemics and all infectious diseases are attended with charges immediate and ultimate on the POOR RATES. Labourers are suddenly thrown by infectious disease into a state of destitution for which immediate relief must be given. In the case of death the widow and the children are thrown as paupers on the parish.*

*During the last two years the public has suffered severely from epidemics. In the course of the investigations of the claims for relief arising from the prevalent sickness, extensive and constantly acting physical causes of sickness and destitution have been disclosed. The amount of burthens thus produced is frequently so great as to render it good economy on the part of the administrators of the Poor Laws to incur the charges for preventing the evils where they are ascribable to physical causes.*

● **SOURCE 3.17**

From Dr Southwood Smith, Appendix C2 to the *Fifth Report of the Poor Law Commissioners*, 1839, in which the doctor comments on the link between fever and the rise in the cost of poor relief.

**Dr Southwood Smith**
was one of the three experts appointed to collect evidence for Chadwick's inquiry into the state of public health (see p. 91).

*There is no disease, which brings so much affliction into a poor man's family as fever. It most commonly attacks the heads of the family, those upon whose daily labour the subsistence of the family depends. Large sums of money must be expended year after year for the support of families afflicted with fever as long as those dreadful sources of fever which encompass the habitations of the poor are allowed to remain. While systematic efforts on a large scale have been made to widen the streets to remove obstructions to the circulation of free currents of air, to extend and perfect the drainage and sewerage, and to prevent the accumulation of putrefying vegetable and animal substances in places in which the wealthier class reside, nothing whatever has been done to improve the condition of the districts inhabited by the poor. These neglected places are out of view and are not thought of. The public meantime have suffered to a far greater extent than they are aware of from this appalling amount of wretchedness, sickness and mortality. Independently of the large amount of money which they have had to pay in the support of the sick they have suffered more seriously from the spread of fever to their own habitations and families.*

Study Sources 3.16 and 3.17.

1 What can be inferred from Chadwick's letter in Source 3.16 of his motives for supporting reform of public health?

2 In what ways do Chadwick and Southwood Smith argue that the problem of public health affects people other than the poor?

3 Comment on the usefulness of Southwood Smith's report for a historian studying public health improvements prior to state intervention in 1848.

● SOURCE 3.18

Adapted from Edwin Chadwick, *Report on the Sanitary Condition of the Labouring Population of Great Britain*, 1842, in which he expresses his fears for the preservation of society.

**metropolis**
London

*Whenever the adult population of a physically depressed district, such as Manchester, is brought out on any public occasion, the preponderance of youth in the crowd and the small proportion of aged, or even the middle-aged, amongst them is apt to strike those who have seen assemblies of the working population of more favourably situated districts.*

*In the METROPOLIS the experience is similar. The mobs from such districts as Bethnal Green are proportionately conspicuous for a deficiency of bodily strength.*

*The facts indicated will suffice to show the importance of moral and political considerations, namely, that a noxious physical environment depresses the health and bodily condition of the population, and hinders education and moral culture. In cutting short the duration of adult life among the working classes, it checks the growth of productive skill, social experience and steady moral habits in the community. Instead of a population that preserves instruction and is steadily progressive, it creates a population that is young, inexperienced, ignorant, credulous, irritable, passionate and dangerous, having a perpetual tendency to moral as well as physical deterioration.*

Study Source 3.18.

1 What evidence is there in Dr Southwood Smith's report (Source 3.17) to support Chadwick's reference to a 'noxious physical environment'?

2 What powerful arguments in support of public health reforms does Chadwick provide in Source 3.18?

3 What aspect of his argument was most likely to appeal to the well-to-do classes?

● SOURCE 3.19

From Edwin Chadwick, *Report on the Sanitary Condition of the Labouring Population of Great Britain*, 1842, in which he argues that services supplied by a municipal authority would be more cost-effective than those supplied by private companies.

**capitals**
investments

Chadwick used the example of Manchester to support his argument for public health reform. He believed in the need for strong local government with reasonable powers to improve sanitary provisions.

*In Manchester gas has for some years been supplied from works erected and conducted by a body appointed (under a local Act) by an elected committee of the ratepayers ... and the supplies of gas are of a better quality, and cheaper than those obtained from private companies in adjacent towns; improvements ... are more speedily adopted than in private associations, and the profits are reserved as a public fund ... Out of this fund a fine Town Hall has been erected, streets widened, and various large improvements made. The income now available for the further improvement of the town exceeds £10,000 per annum ... There are now in the same districts in [London] no less than three immense CAPITALS sunk in competition, – three sets of gas-pipes [in] the same streets, three sets of offices where one would suffice, comparatively high charges for gas to the consumers, and low dividends to the shareholders of the companies.*

*... A proposal was made in Manchester to obtain supplies of water for the town in the same manner as the supplies of gas, but the owners of the private pumps, who have the monopoly of the convenient springs, and exact double the charge for which even private companies are ready to convey supplies into the houses, made ... effectual opposition to the proposal, contending that the supplies of rain-water (which are sometimes absolutely black with the soot held in suspension), together with ... that from the springs was sufficient, and the proposal was defeated ... There appears to be no reason to doubt that the mode of supplying gas to the town of Manchester might be generally adopted in supplying water to the population.*

● SOURCE 3.20

From an article by W. A. Guy, 'The Sanitary Question', in *Fraser's Magazine*, Vol. XXXVI, 1847, in which the writer argues the advantages of central direction in public health.

**parochial system**
system of raising funds and carrying out works based on the parish (a small district centred on a church)

**parish vestry**
a group of local people who took responsibility for parish affairs, such as the provision of poor relief and maintenance of local roads

*The utter failure of the system of local self-government for sanitary purposes is notorious to all who have taken any pains to inquire into the subject. Even if the PAROCHIAL SYSTEM were perfect for all other purposes of administration it must necessarily fail when applied to some of the chief measures of sanitary improvement. Drainage, especially, which is of vast importance to health cannot be carried out by parishes. It presupposes an extensive area selected for that special object, surveyed and laid out with a scientific skill and judgement which few parishes have in their command and which popular election is extremely unlikely to ensure.*

*We look upon local self-government then, at least for sanitary purposes, whether the governing body be a PARISH VESTRY or a town council, as a popular delusion condemned by common sense and everyday experience. We are not advocates for the opposite system of centralisation as that term is generally understood but if we had to make our choice between the two systems we should prefer the most unpopular. We would rather trust to the central government than to the local authorities. The one is about as pure as the other but government nomination would secure a better class of officers than parish election.*

Study Sources 3.19 and 3.20.

1 What, according to Chadwick in Source 3.19, were the advantages of a municipal gas supply to
   a) the customer
   b) Manchester?

2 How did the example of London illustrate the disadvantages of private provision of services?

3 Why did Manchester not have a municipal water supply?

4 How could the example of Manchester be used as evidence for those who supported government intervention?

5 What weaknesses, according to Source 3.20, had emerged in the provision of a local system of sanitary provision by 1847?

6 Why does the writer of the article prefer central control?

7 To what extent would the writer of the article support Chadwick's arguments in Source 3.19?

Study Sources 3.16–3.20.

8 In what ways, and to what extent, do they indicate a similar concern for public health?

# What were the main arguments against reform?

● **SOURCE 3.21**

From *The Economist*, 1848, in which the principle of social reform is attacked as being out of place and misunderstood.

*Suffering and evil are nature's admonitions; they can not be got rid of, and impatient attempts of benevolence to banish them from the world by legislation, before benevolence has learned their object and their end, have always been productive of more evil than good.*

● **SOURCE 3.22**

From a report of the Parliamentary debate on Lord Morpeth's Bill, 1847, in which an opponent attacks the principle of central control.

*. . . new authority was proposed to be introduced totally foreign to every principle of the English Constitution . . . he [the opponent] regarded it as a departure from the free principles of the British Constitution and a gradual usurpation, behind the backs of the people, of the power which ought to belong to the representatives of the people and one step more towards the adoption of the continental system of centralisation.*

● **SOURCE 3.23**

From *The Times* report on the Commons debate on the second reading of the Public Health Bill, 22 February 1848.

*Mr Urquhart said he had an objection to the bill not to its intent and object, but to the establishment for the purposes of promoting the public health of an organisation, which he thought tended to increase the mode of foreign government which was known by the name of 'centralisation'. Mr Mackinnon . . . denied that this was a centralising bill. The Government merely reserved a superintending influence but the operating parts of the bill would be in the hands of the local authorities.*

● **SOURCE 3.24**

From an article in the *Leeds Mercury*, 1848, in which the writer accepts the necessity for good sewerage and pure water but opposes the loss of local rights.

*. . . we could not consent to purchase these blessings by a permanent infringement of the rights of municipal bodies and through them of the people at large.*

● **SOURCE 3.25**

From Chartist evidence to the General Board of Health Inquiry into the North Staffordshire Potteries District, *Parliamentary Papers*, 1851.

*Good sewerage may increase our personal comforts and conveniences but if it tends to deprive us still more of our now scanty living we fear the introduction of it . . .*

*The principal cause of nuisances in the township is a dereliction of duty on the part of owners of property in not constructing proper conveniences for the occupiers of their dwelling houses. And is the public at large to be taxed because these individuals fail to perform their duty?*

● **SOURCE 3.26**

From Thoresby Society, *Projected Leeds Waterworks*, in which the author cites the views of an unknown contemporary who defended the case of the property owners against the emerging collectivism of a municipal water supply.

*All they want is to expend other people's money and get popularity by letting what they may call poor have the water for nothing and also accommodating themselves and tenants at other people's expense. . . . I have 10,000 pounds worth of property and have been at considerable expense in getting water. My neighbour has the same, but no water, and his property will be considerably benefited by having water brought to it and mine can't possibly be benefited at all – is it just that I should be made to contribute a yearly sum towards furnishing his estate with water and increasing the value of his property 15 or 20 per cent which taxes me $1\frac{1}{4}$?*

● **SOURCE 3.27**

*Sanatory Measures. Lord Morpeth Throwing Pearls Before Aldermen,* a cartoon from *Punch*, 1848.

Study Sources 3.21–3.27.

1  Identify individuals and main groups who opposed state provision of public health works.

2  On what grounds might it be argued that social class influenced contemporary attitudes to sanitary reform?

3  With specific reference to sources, what administrative, political and financial issues arose from the attempts to improve public health?

4  What use would Source 3.27 be to a historian studying contemporary attitudes towards attempts to improve the health of towns?

5  How far does the evidence contained in these sources support the view that effective improvement of the nation's sanitary state would not be easily achieved?

6  Using Sources 3.16–3.27 and your own knowledge, identify the main features of the debate surrounding public health reform. Use a copy of the table below to organise your conclusions.

| Attitude towards reform | Identify individuals/ groups | Main details of argument | How effective do you consider their argument to be? |
|---|---|---|---|
| For | | | |
| Against | | | |

## What were the main provisions of the Public Health Act of 1848?

An attempt to introduce a Public Health Bill in 1847 was defeated owing to the opposition of MPs who became known as the 'Dirty Party'. The latter only withdrew their opposition when a cholera epidemic broke out in 1848, killing at least 130,000 people. Charles Dickens, commenting on public opinion in his weekly newspaper, *Household Words*, wrote in 1850 that, 'John Bull's heart is only reached through his pocket when in a state of alarm. Cry "Cholera!" and he bestirs himself. To cholera we owe the few sanitary measures now in force but that were passed by the House in its agonies of fright. The moment however, cholera bulletins ceased to be issued John buttoned up his pockets tighter than ever and Parliament was dumb regarding public health.'

● **SOURCE 3.28**

From K. Dawson and P. Wall, *Society and Industry in the Nineteenth Century, Vol. 6: Public Health and Housing,* 1970, summarising the main provisions of the Public Health Act of 1848.

This legislation was permissive – it gave local authorities the power to act if they chose. Except in the case of an unusually high death rate there was no question at this time of the government forcing local authorities to implement the act.

1  *There should be a permanent Board of Health, based in London. The three original members were Lord Morpeth, Lord Shaftesbury and Edwin Chadwick.*
2  *Local Boards of Health could be set up where either:*
   a) *10 per cent of the rate-payers petitioned for one, or:*
   b) *The death rate in a town exceeded 23 per 1000 per annum and the Government required a local board to be set up. The average death rate in the country was 21 per 1000 and the range was from 15 per 1000 to 30 per 1000, with some . . . areas reaching as high as 60 per 1000.*
3  *Local boards were permitted to appoint an Officer of Health, and an inspector of nuisances to be paid out of rates.*
4  *Local boards were empowered to enforce proper drainage, provide and maintain sewers, force the installation of privies, pave and cleanse streets, control offensive trades, inspect meat, inspect common lodging houses and control burial grounds.*

● **SOURCE 3.29**

From *Fraser's Magazine*, October 1848, commenting on the eventual success of the 'Clean Party' in securing the Public Health Act.

**'solitary sheaf'**
the Public Health Act

**somewhat thin in the ear and slightly damaged**
refers to the permissive element of the Act. A town could not be forced to set up a board of health if it did not wish to do so.

*The 'SOLITARY SHEAF' of the session of 1848—SOMEWHAT THIN IN THE EAR AND SLIGHTLY DAMAGED . . . has been safely garnered and is destined as we hope to furnish seed which shall bear fruit a hundred and a thousandfold . . . The spirit of the Act has clothed itself in the homely English proverb PREVENTION is better than CURE. This is the spirit which animates those material forms, the Model Lodging-House, the Bath and Washhouse, the Ragged School and all the mighty works of the New Philanthropy. Mr Chadwick . . . must not conceal from himself the unwelcome fact that in entering upon the responsible duties of the Central Board of which it is understood that he will be a paid member he will have to encounter a greater amount of suspicion and mistrust than has hitherto fallen to the share of any public man . . . It would be most unfortunate for the cause which Mr Chadwick is so capable of serving if acting under the stern compulsion of a theory . . . he should be tempted to counsel or commit an act of tyrannical injustice.*

Study Sources 3.28 and 3.29.

1  What evidence does *Fraser's Magazine* offer that the Public Health Act was passed only after strong opposition?

2  What powers were given to local boards of health by the 1848 act?

3  What were the main weaknesses of the act?

4  How might these weaknesses influence the effectiveness of the act in improving public health?

5  Why would *Fraser's Magazine* consider that Chadwick might 'have to encounter a greater amount of suspicion and mistrust than has hitherto fallen to the share of any public man'?

# 5 What progress was made in public health reform between 1848 and 1890?

The General Board of Health was set up for a five-year period only. Response to the 1848 act was slow. Often, local pressure was more concerned with reducing expenditure than with introducing improvements. Engineering posed a problem. In his 1842 report Chadwick had recommended waterborne disposal of sewage via glazed pipes but the men employed to solve the problem of supply and disposal were not competent to judge the merits of this system or any other. Technical disagreements often hampered well-meaning schemes while the physical size of the job of supplying large cities with water and disposing of sewage posed major engineering problems which could not be easily or quickly overcome. Such technical problems, along with arguments over 'who should pay' and ideological differences over the role of central government and its relationship with local self-government, meant that the 1848 act was a failure. Chadwick's personality was also a limiting factor on progress. He has been called the first 'public service expert' but his vanity, arrogance and impatience made him many influential enemies, including *The Times* newspaper. The latter's campaign against Chadwick fuelled public dislike. He was dismissed in 1854 and replaced by Sir John Simon, a surgeon and pathologist.

By 1854 only 182 local boards of health had been established, of which thirteen had established sewerage and water-supply systems. About 40 towns appointed officers of health but they were poorly paid and often temporary. Except where the death rate was higher than 23 per 1000, the General Board could not compel local health boards to pursue sanitary reforms. Its role was advisory and supervisory rather than authoritative; because of this, local commissions could still block progress. In 1858 the General Board was made obsolete by the terms of the Local Government Act, though local boards continued to be set up. The duties of the General Board were distributed between the Home Office, the Poor Law Office and the Privy Council. Chaos remained in regard to authorities, rates, and, worst of all, areas of responsibility.

## What did Chadwick and the General Board of Health achieve between 1848 and 1858?

101

What progress was made in public health reform between 1848 and 1890?

● SOURCE 3.30

From the *Report of the Board of Health*, July 1849, detailing the regulations issued to deal with the numerous local authorities that refused to surrender their powers to one authority.

*To the Guardian of the Poor named in the Schedules hereunto annexed: To the Councils and Governing Bodies, of Cities and Boroughs, Commissioners under local Acts, the Surveyors of Highways, their Deputies and Assistants, The Trustees, County Surveyors and others intrusted with the Care and Management of the Streets and Public Ways and Places within the said Unions and Parishes; the Owners and Occupiers of Houses, within the said Unions and Parishes; and to all to whom it may concern.*

*We, the General Board of Health, are authorised to issue such directions . . . as the . . . Board shall think fit for the prevention of . . . disease; these directions . . . shall extend to all parts or places in which the . . . Act shall . . . be in force.*

*We direct that all . . . bodies . . . intrusted with the care and management of the streets, and public ways and places, . . . shall . . . once in every twenty-four hours . . . cleanse all such of the streets, under their respective care and management, as by the medical officer of the guardians, shall be certified to be in a state dangerous to health.*

*Where any such streets to which any houses or tenements adjoin, which have not been intrusted by law to the care or management of any council, have been certified . . . to be in a state dangerous to health, we direct that every occupier of a house shall keep or cause to be kept sufficiently cleansed, at least once in every twenty-four hours such parts as adjoins the house or tenement occupied by him, by effectual washing or otherwise, and with the use of such fluids or substances as the medical officer of the guardians shall think necessary.*

*We do hereby authorise and require the guardians to superintend and see to the execution of the foregoing directions and where it shall appear that by want of the council, or by reason of poverty of the occupiers there may be any default in the cleansing of any street, we authorise the guardians to cause such street to be effectually cleansed and all nuisances removed . . .*

1  What does the report (Source 3.30) reveal of the multiplicity of different interest groups responsible for providing services?

2  What directions were issued in relation to streets to prevent disease?

3  What responsibilities were given to the medical officer of the guardians?

4  Who was responsible for seeing that the Board's regulations were carried out?

5  What objections might each of the following groups have to these regulations
   a)  property owners
   b)  local authorities
   c)  ratepayers?

### ● SOURCE 3.31

From the *Leeds Intelligencer*, 7 July 1838, criticising the local council for issuing a by-law on the regular whitewashing of slaughterhouses. Chadwick was blamed for such attempts to establish regulations for social control.

*The legislature has not yet given them the authority to dictate to tradesmen in what way they shall carry out their business, as how often they shall whitewash their buildings and if they are once permitted to usurp such an authority . . . such is the spirit of busy officious intermeddling . . . that no man's place of business or even private house would be safe . . .*

### ● SOURCE 3.32

From James Hole, *The Homes of the Working Classes*, 1866, in which the working-class housing reformer expresses his despair at the self-interest shown by democratic local self-government.

**despotism**
rule by a tyrant, with absolute power; here, a reference to authorities such as boards of health

**vagaries**
erratic or unreasonable behaviour

*When contemplating an ugly ill-built town where every little freeholder asserts his indefeasible rights as a Briton to do what he likes with his own; to inflict his own selfishness, ignorance and obstinacy upon his neighbours and on posterity for generations to come and where local self government means merely misgovernment we are apt to wish for a little wholesome DESPOTISM to curb such VAGARIES.*

### ● SOURCE 3.33

From *The Times*, July 1854, in which the editor joins the campaign to have Chadwick dismissed from the General Board of Health.

*We prefer to take our chance of cholera and the rest than be bullied into health. There is nothing a man so hates as being cleansed against his will, or having his floors swept, his walls whitewashed, his pet dung-heaps cleared away, or his thatch forced to give way to slate, all at the command of a sort of sanitary bombailiff (or interfering official). It is a fact that many have died of a good washing . . . The truth is, Mr Chadwick has very great powers, but it is not easy to say what they can be applied to. Perhaps a retiring pension, with nothing to do.*

### ● SOURCE 3.34

From a letter by Edwin Chadwick to Lord Ashley (later the Earl of Shaftesbury), April 1844, in which he comments on the reluctance of privately managed Improvement Commissions to surrender their public health services to the local council.

*Frequently, interested parties are seated at Boards of Guardians who are ready to stop anything which may lead to expenditure for the proper repair of the dwellings of the labouring classes.*

*Where measures of drainage are proposed and the works carried out by Commissioners of Sewers are found to be defective a cry is raised that nothing must be done for fear of offending the Commissioners.*

*. . . When additional supplies of water are called for . . . one cry raised is 'Oh the interest of the companies is too powerful to be touched.'*

### ● SOURCE 3.35

From a journal for engineers and officials, 1856, in which the writer assesses Chadwick's image amongst his contemporaries.

**impermeable**
water-tight

**necropolis**
a city of the dead

*Unquestioning, blind, passive obedience to the order, decree, bull or proclamation of the autocrat, pope, grand lama of sanitary reform, Edwin Chadwick, lawyer and commissioner . . . He was determined that the British world should be clean and live a century but on one condition only—that they consented to purchase real patent Chadwickian soap, the Chadwickian officially gathered soft water and the true IMPERMEABLE telescopic earthenware pipe and when they did die, were interred by his official undertakers in the Chadwickian NECROPOLIS!*

● **SOURCE 3.36**

From *The Economist*, 21 November 1846, in which the question is asked 'Who is to blame for the Condition of the People?'

*The state, because it assumes to provide for the welfare of the people . . . makes itself unwisely responsible for it. The . . . permanent effects of legislation . . . are so very complicated, and very often so much more important than the direct and temporary effects, that to make good laws seems a work fit rather for God than man. One of those . . . effects . . . is the general helplessness of the masses, which is sure to be induced by the state undertaking to provide for their welfare. They come to rely on it and take no care for themselves . . . We consider the mental degradation of the masses – the extinction amongst them of the spirit of enterprise and self reliance with the annihilation of the feeling of independence . . . which is everywhere the consequence of the perpetual interference of the State, to be one of the most disastrous . . . effects of the legislation which is intended to benefit the people.*

Study Sources 3.31–3.36.

1 Who opposed Chadwick's efforts to improve public health?

2 Why did Chadwick arouse 'a greater amount of suspicion and mistrust than has hitherto fallen to the share of any public man' (*Fraser's Magazine*, Source 3.29)? Refer, with supporting evidence from the sources, to the following issues
   a) the debate over who should pay
   b) defence of the rights of property owners
   c) defence of individual liberty
   d) suspicion of an extension of municipal power
   e) hostility to centralisation.

3 What evidence is offered in the sources that Chadwick was acting 'under the stern compulsion of a theory' (*Fraser's Magazine*, Source 3.29)?

● **SOURCE 3.37**

From an article, 'Sanitary Consolidation – Centralisation – Local Self-government', *Quarterly Review*, Vol. XXXVIII, 1850, defending the 1848 act and centralisation.

**the imperial power . . . over local affairs**
the central authority uses its officials to carry out orders that are against the wishes of the people

*(i) Criticism of pre-1848 system of local self-government*
*And first – to strike at once into the heart of the debate – let us meet the charge of 'Centralisation' or the alleged tendency of the new Sanitary system to supersede Local Self-government by the arbitrary rule of a Metropolitan Board. To reduce this question to its proper terms we must begin by laying down a well-marked preliminary distinction – that namely which exists between Local Self-government as it affects the mass of residents in any district and as it concerns the functionaries [officials] often corrupt and ignorant by whom they are rated and ruled. Obviously wherever district rates are squandered by jobbing or incompetent Local boards the corrective intervention of a Central power so far from diminishing may tend largely to increase the real self-governing power of the place as measured by the control of the population over the expenditure of their own funds.*

*(ii) Defence of Centralisation*
*Centralisation is in fact . . . legitimate provided that its action be based on valid public requirement, national or provincial. It is only when these limitations are disregarded, when in opposition to the public wish* THE IMPERIAL POWER EXERCISES BY ITS NOMINEES A DIRECT AND PERMANENT SWAY OVER LOCAL AFFAIRS *that Centralisation becomes excessive and offensive.*

*(iii) Relationship between Central and local government*
*These distinctions have been clearly kept in view by the framers of that admirable sanitary code the Public Health Act of 1848 . . . This masterly enactment while it places the general sanitary interests of the country under the care of a Metropolitan Board (the pretext of the anti-Centralisation cry) also recognises the principle of Local Self-government by the simultaneous institution of District boards elected by the ratepayers to whom they are consequently responsible. [They are] liable to central interference only in one of two cases: first on an appeal or petition (emanating from the district itself and signed by not less than one-tenth of the ratepayers); secondly on a duly certified district mortality exceeding the high annual rate of 23 in 1000. Even indeed when the regulating power of the Central authority is thus called forth either by . . . a suffering district or by a mortality prejudicial to society at large its operation is surrounded by official delays and restrictions designed to afford time for local deliberation and popular confirmation.*

1 What criticism is made in Source 3.37 of local self-government?

2 How will 'Centralisation' remove abuses in local government?

3 In what circumstances does the writer of the article consider 'Centralisation' to be legitimate?

4 How were the powers of central government controlled under the 1848 act?

5 To what extent did *Quarterly Review* counter the following objections to the 1848 act
   a) who should pay
   b) defence of the rights of property owners
   c) defence of individual liberty
   d) suspicion of an extension of municipal power
   e) hostility to centralisation?

## ● SOURCE 3.38

From the *Report of the Board of Health on its Work, 1848–54*, which comments on opposition to the Board of Health from local authorities, who were resentful of interference in local affairs by the government.

Other local interests, such as the water companies, objected to the boards of health taking over their work.

**promulgated**
spread about

### (i) Progress by 1854

*We have now to state that 284 towns have . . . petitioned in form for the application of the Act. Of these . . . the requisite forms and proceedings prescribed by the Act have been complied with in 182 . . . comprising altogether a total population . . . of upwards of two millions . . .*

### (iii) Opposition to the General Board

*. . . We are aware that, in the discharge of [our] duties . . . we have unavoidably interfered with powerful interests, which have the immediate means of making themselves heard by members of Government and by Parliament.*

*. . . we have been under the necessity of stating facts with relation to the inefficiency of former works, and their effects in aggravating existing evil. The scheme we proposed for [additional burial sites] endangered . . . cemetery companies and the entire body of trading undertakers.*

*. . . The report in condemnation of the present . . . supply of water to the good work of the Metropolis, necessarily excited the hostility of the existing water companies.*

*Accounts of particular stoppages of pipe sewers were PROMULGATED without any reference to the circumstances, which showed that they might have been expected to stop; without any notice of the large proportion executed . . . While the new works were in progress and approaching completion, an extraordinary epidemic which has prevailed in different parts of the country, in places where there are no new works whatsoever, attacked the higher class of houses in Croydon, those with old as well as those with new works. The disease was immediately ascribed to the operation of the new drainage works, although the first and most severe visitation of the epidemic was at the distance of upwards of three-quarters of a mile from the places where the works were going on.*

1 According to Source 3.38 what progress had the General Board of Health achieved by 1854?

2 Why did the creation of a General Board of Health, and local boards of health, not lead to immediate improvements in public health all over Britain?

3 What charges were brought against the General Board of Health by its enemies?

## ● SOURCE 3.39

From B. R. Mitchell and P. Deane, *Abstract of British Historical Statistics*, 1962, and N. Tranter, *Population since the Industrial Revolution*, 1973.

Movement in death-rate, 1811–75 (per thousand of the population).

No figures have been identified for 1821–30.

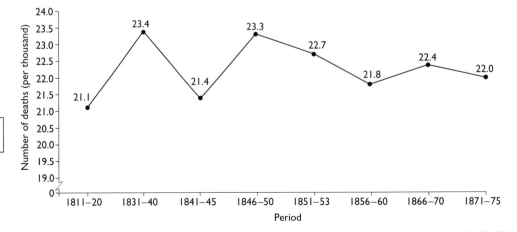

1   Using Source 3.39, identify the two periods of highest death-rate.

2   To what extent is it valid to claim that attempts to reduce deaths achieved no lasting success before 1875?

● SOURCE 3.40

*Father Thames Introducing his Offspring to the Fair City of London*, a cartoon from *Punch*, July 1858.

DIPHTHERIA.     SCROFULA.     CHOLERA.

FATHER THAMES INTRODUCING HIS OFFSPRING TO THE FAIR CITY OF LONDON.

1   What message is the illustrator of Source 3.40 trying to convey about progress in improving the supply of water to London?

2   In what ways does the illustrator show his attitude towards public health issues?

3   In what ways was the illustrator challenging the miasma theory of disease?

Study Sources 3.30–3.40.

4   Why was the Public Health Act of 1848 not more effective in achieving its objectives?

5   What were the main obstacles to the implementation of a public health policy?

## What did John Simon achieve between 1858 and 1875?

Progress between 1848 and 1875 appears to have been limited, judged by the number of laws passed extending the range of central control over public health matters. Despite all his ability, energy and drive, John Simon as Medical Officer of Health for the Privy Council could offer little central direction or control, his powers being restricted to sanctioning loans for major improvement schemes. He authorised investigations into the effect on health of diet, housing and working conditions, as part of the drive to combat disease. Acts were passed dealing with specific public health hazards – cemeteries, lodging houses, sewage and sanitation, adulteration of food, and contagious diseases. Simon campaigned for improvements to local sanitary measures and criticised local councillors for showing greater concern for cost-cutting than for improving conditions in working-class areas. The 1866 Sanitary Act, passed at the time of a cholera outbreak, marked a significant turning point in the history of public health. A Royal Sanitary Commission (1869–71) and the Local Government Board Act of 1871 followed. The latter established a new Local Government Board and a new government ministry that supervised most, though not all, of the activities of local government by consolidating the duties of the Poor Law Board, Privy Council and Home Office. The 1872 Public Health Act provided for the whole country to be covered by sanitary authorities with a compulsory basic staff, particularly medical officers of health.

● **SOURCE 3.41**

Excerpts from the Sanitary Act, 1866, summarising some of the clauses of the act that set up uniform and universal provision of sanitary powers, previously restricted to local boards of health under the 1848 act.

10. *If a Dwelling House . . . is without a drain . . . sufficient for effectual drainage, the Sewer Authority may by Notice require the Owner of such House within a reasonable Time . . . to make a sufficient drain emptying into any Sewer the Sewer Authority is entitled to use . . .*

19. *The Word 'Nuisances' . . . shall include,*
    i. *Any House . . . so overcrowded as to be dangerous or prejudicial to the Health of the Inmates.*
    ii. *Any Factory, Workshop or Workplace . . . not kept in a cleanly state, or not ventilated in such a Manner as to render harmless as far as practicable any Gases, Vapours, Dust, or other Impurities.*
    iii. *Any Fireplace or Furnace which does not as far as practicable consume the Smoke arising from the Combustible used.*

22. *If the Nuisance Authority shall be of opinion, upon the Certificate of any legally qualified Medical Practitioner, that the cleansing or disinfecting of any House . . . would tend to prevent or check infectious or contagious Disease, it shall . . . give Notice . . . requiring the Owner or Occupier . . . to cleanse and disinfect the same . . .*

35. *On Application of One of her Majesty's Principal Secretaries of State by the Nuisance Authority . . . the Secretary of State may . . . declare the following Enactment to be in force in the District of such Nuisance Authority . . .*
    i. *For fixing the Number of Persons who may occupy a House or Part of a House which is let in Lodgings or occupied by Members of more than One Family.*
    ii. *For the Registration of Houses thus let . . .*
    iii. *For the Inspection of such Houses and the keeping the Same in a cleanly and wholesome State.*
    iv. *For enforcing therein the Provision of Privy Accommodation . . . and the cleansing and Ventilation of the common Passages and Staircases.*
    v. *For the cleansing and lime whiting at stated Times of such Premises.*
    *The Nuisance Authority may provide for the Enforcement of the above Regulations by Penalties not exceeding Forty Shillings for any One Offence.*

1 What additions did the 1866 act (Source 3.41) make to the definition of a 'nuisance'?

2 How did it enlarge the powers of central government control over local government?

● **SOURCE 3.42**

From A. Briggs, *Victorian Cities*, 1968, quoting a description of Birmingham in the 1870s by a pastor of the Congregational Church, Robert William Dale.

**Joseph Chamberlain**
mayor of Birmingham in 1873–76, led the way in introducing municipal socialism.

*Towards the end of the 'sixties a few Birmingham men made the discovery that perhaps a strong and able Town Council might do almost as much to improve the conditions of life in the town as Parliament itself. I have called it a 'discovery' for it had all the freshness and charm of a discovery. One of its first effects was to invest the Council with a new attractiveness and dignity . . . Weaker and less effective members of the Corporation were gradually dropped and their places filled by men of quite a new type. The November Ward meetings assumed a new character. The speakers instead of discussing small questions of administration and economy dwelt with glowing enthusiasm on what a great and prosperous town like Birmingham might do for its people. They spoke of sweeping away streets in which it was not possible to live a healthy and decent life; of making the town cleaner, sweeter and brighter; of providing gardens and parks and a museum. They insisted that great monopolies like the gas and water supply should be in the hand of the corporation; that good water should be supplied without stint at the lowest possible prices; that the profits of the gas supply should relieve the pressure of the rates. Sometimes an adventurous orator would excite his audience by dwelling on the glories of Florence and of other cities of Italy in the Middle Ages and suggest that Birmingham too might become the home of a noble literature and art.*

1 According to Source 3.42 what benefits did Birmingham acquire as a result of the civic pride shown by its local council?

2 What aspects of the improvements represented early municipal socialism?

## What was the contribution of private individuals to improvements in public health?

There were a few philanthropists who tried to improve bad housing. Doctor Southwood Smith (see page 96) and some colleagues had campaigned in the 1840s to show the sense of rehousing, if only to avoid the costs of epidemics. Various societies were founded, such as Shaftesbury's Society for Improving the Conditions of the Working Classes, begun in 1844, and the Metropolitan Association for Improving the Dwellings of the Industrious Classes in 1845. Through the Improved Industrial Dwellings Company, Sir Sydney Waterlow showed that with sufficient middle-class money and effort, workers' housing could eventually profit. These private initiatives continued into the 1860s and 1870s with the work of Titus Salt, a Bradford manufacturer, who built a model town for his workers, and Octavia Hill, who pioneered improvement of working-class tenements in London. But the model dwelling house, which attempted to make housing conform to commercial criteria, with rents that covered costs, did little more than touch the problem.

● **SOURCE 3.43**

From Octavia Hill, *Homes of the London Poor*, 1875, in which the housing reformer and granddaughter of Southwood Smith describes her work of buying working-class tenements for improvement.

*As soon as I entered into possession, each family had an opportunity of doing better: those who would not pay, or who led clearly immoral lives, were ejected. The rooms they vacated were cleansed; the tenants who showed signs of improvement moved into them, and thus, in turn, an opportunity was obtained for having each room distempered and papered. The drains were put in order, a large slate cistern was fixed, the washhouse was cleared of its lumber, and thrown open on stated days to each tenant in turn. The roof, the plaster, the woodwork was repaired; the staircase walls were distempered; new grates were fixed; the layers of paper and rag (black with age) were torn from the windows, and glass was put in; out of 192 panes only eight were found unbroken. The yard and footpath were paved.*

*The rooms, as a rule, were re-let at the same prices at which they had been let before; but tenants with large families were counselled to take two rooms, and for these much less was charged than if let singly: this plan I continue to pursue. Incoming tenants are not allowed to take a decidedly insufficient quantity of room, and no sub-letting is permitted. The elder girls are employed three times a week in scrubbing the passages in the houses, for the cleaning of which the landlady is responsible. For this work they are paid, and by it they learn habits of cleanliness. It is, of course, within the authority of the landlady also to insist on cleanliness of washhouses, yards, staircases, and staircase-windows; and even to remonstrate concerning the rooms themselves if they are habitually dirty.*

*The financial result has been very satisfactory. Five per cent has been paid on all the capital invested. A fund for the repayment of capital is accumulating. A liberal allowance has been made for repairs. My tenants are mostly of a class far below that of mechanics. They are, indeed, of the very poor. And yet, although the gifts they have received have been next to nothing, none of the families who have passed under my care during the whole four years have continued in what is called 'distress', except such as have been unwilling to exert themselves. Those who will not exert the necessary self-control cannot avail themselves of the means of livelihood held out to them. But for those who are willing, some small assistance in the form of work has, from time to time, been provided – not much, but sufficient to keep them from want and despair.*

1 Explain Octavia Hill's attitude in Source 3.43 towards the people that she sought to help.

2 What improvements were carried out in the houses she acquired?

3 How did she try to tackle the problem of overcrowding?

4 In what ways did Hill insist that good business practice be observed?

● **SOURCE 3.44**

From an article by the Earl of Shaftesbury, in *Fortnightly Review*, 1883, in which the reformer warns of the 'mischief of State Aid'.

**domiciliary condition**
the living conditions; state of housing

*[There has been a] sudden manifestation of public feeling in regard to the* DOMICILIARY CONDITION *of large portions of the working classes in our cities and great towns. It is strange that this feeling has lain so long dormant, for the disclosure of this evil was made more than forty years ago, and ever since that date the efforts of individuals, companies and associations have been unremitting to proclaim the mischief, devise remedies, and, in some instances, to apply them . . . There is a loud cry, from many quarters, for the government . . . to undertake this mighty question and anyone who sets himself against such an opinion is likely to incur much rebuke and condemnation. Be it so. But if the state is to be summoned, not only to provide houses for the labouring classes, but also to supply such buildings at nominal rents, it will, while doing something on behalf of their physical condition, utterly destroy their moral energies. It will, in fact, be an official proclamation that, without any efforts of their own, certain portions of the people shall enter into the enjoyment of many good things, altogether at the expense of others. The State is bound, in such a case as this, to give every facility by law and enabling statutes; but the work . . . should proceed on voluntary effort.*

1  To what extent does Shaftesbury (Source 3.44) agree with Octavia Hill (Source 3.43) on the need for housing reform?

2  What is Shaftesbury's attitude towards
   a) the existing 'domiciliary condition of large portions of the working classes'
   b) the use of the Government to solve the 'mighty question' he was discussing?

3  What fears are voiced by the Earl of Shaftesbury about supplying 'dwellings at nominal rents'?

● **SOURCE 3.45**

From *The Times*, 1 December 1865, commenting on the need for a central authority to direct and control reforms.

*It would seem only reasonable that there should be some central authority to which the poor and their protectors may appeal against the greed of landlords, the despair of sanitary inspectors and the insensibility of vestries. At present everything depends on vestries and everything it must be added is neglected by them. It is more and more evident that some vigorous and efficient power must be placed in the hands of the Home Secretary . . . by which these inert bodies may be compelled to do their duty.*

1  What may be inferred both from the date and from the contents of Source 3.45 about the extent of the success of efforts to improve public health by the mid-1860s?

## What developments occurred in health and housing between 1875 and 1914?

It was not until the 1870s that the attitude changed from permitting local authorities to carry out public health works to the principle that the state or local authority should lay down and *enforce* regulations on such matters as water supply, drainage and sewerage, in order to safeguard the health of the community. Problems of health and housing were dealt with separately in two significant acts passed in 1875 – the Public Health Act and the Artisans' Dwelling Act. The latter empowered local authorities to require owners to keep their rented houses in good repair. It did not solve the problems of providing and improving working-class housing, owing to the compensation costs involved. The real turning point came in the 1890 Housing of the Working Classes Act, which made loans easier to obtain and ordered local authorities to demolish unfit housing and provide alternative accommodation. By 1900 towns were beginning to supply municipal gas and water services on efficient lines, and the true connection between filth and disease had been revealed through the research of Pasteur and Koch into the germ theory of disease.

● **SOURCE 3.46**

From *The Times*, 25 August 1875, reporting the details of Richard Cross's Public Health Act. This act laid down in clear terms the public health functions and duties of local authorities.

No less than 29 sanitary measures have been enacted since the Health of Towns Commission of 1846. In this uncodified state, these Acts naturally displayed much confusion, redundancy and apparent contradiction. They had been made at different times, by various hands, and with various objects. Some were permissive, some compulsory, some partly the one and partly the other. Each dealt with some special part of the subject, but none could be said to define its departments clearly and exhaustively.

Part 3, representing the main bulk of the Act, and occupying 131 clauses, consists of what are specially denominated sanitary provisions. It is divided into the heads of:

1  Sewerage and drainage;
2  privies, water-closets, etc;
3  scavenging and cleansing;
4  water supply;
5  regulation of cellar dwellings and lodging houses;
6  nuisances;
7  offensive trades;
8  unsound meat, etc;
9  infectious diseases and hospitals;
10  prevention of epidemic diseases;
11  mortuaries.

Each . . . includes . . . statutory regulations, together with the penalties by which they are severally to be enforced.

Part 4 is specially entitled 'Local Government Provisions' and contains, under several heads, the law upon such matters of Local Government as are only indirectly connected with the question of public health. Under this title we have—

1  Regulations with regard to highways and streets, including the power for widening, improving, paving, and lighting them;
2  public pleasure grounds, under which head stands, somewhat oddly, the power to provide urban districts with public clocks;
3  markets and slaughter houses;
4  police regulations.

---

1  According to Source 3.46, what were the weaknesses in the provision of public health that the 1875 act aimed to remedy?
2  To what extent did the 1875 act consolidate and codify existing practice?

---

● **SOURCE 3.47**

From the memoirs of Viscount Richard Cross, *A Political History 1868–1900*, privately published in 1903, in which the Home Secretary reviews the bill introduced in the House of Commons, 8 February 1875.

I take it as a starting point that it is not the duty of the Government to provide any class of citizen with any of the necessaries of life, and among the necessaries of life we must include that which is one of the chief necessaries – good and habitable dwellings . . . because if it did so, it would inevitably tend to make that class depend, not on themselves, but upon what was done for them elsewhere, and it would not be possible to teach a worse lesson than this – that 'If you do not take care of yourselves, the State will take care of you.'

Nor is it wise to encourage large bodies to provide the working classes with housing at greatly lower rents than the market value paid elsewhere. Admitting these two principles of action, there is another point of view from which we may look . . . No one will doubt the . . . right of the State to interfere in matters relating to sanitary laws . . . not to enable the working classes to have houses provided for them, but to take them out of that miserable condition in which they now find themselves—namely that, even if they want to have decent homes, they cannot get them.

The evil we have to grapple with . . . is the neglect of past . . . years. I would ask the political economist . . . to remember . . . that health is actually wealth. He must take into account the great waste of life even among those who reach manhood, the great waste of physical condition after infancy is passed, and the waste of stamina in the present generation and the future generation that will spring from it . . . If you consider that the death rate is about 22 per 1000 throughout the whole country – that in London it is 24 per 1000, and *that in Manchester it has been 30, in Liverpool during the last 10 years it has been 38, in Lancaster 30, and in Sunderland 37 per 1000 – there must be something wrong in these towns which makes the death rate so different. Then again see the marked difference between one part of a town and another . . . in Manchester . . . the death rate was in one district 67 per 1000 . . . if by our legislation we can prevent such a waste of life . . . it is our duty to interfere and . . . stop this waste. If we inquire what is the death rate among small and young children in particular parts of these towns, we shall arrive at the most terrible results. I have a Report of the Medical Officer of Health for Manchester which shows that in one particular district, out of a hundred deaths of persons of all ages, the deaths of children under five years reached the extraordinary rate of 49.7 . . . whether we can give the children of the working classes an equal chance of growing up to healthy manhood and womanhood. The causes of the present loss of life are not far to seek . . . it is not simply that houses are overcrowded, but districts are overcrowded . . .*

1 Why does Cross maintain in Source 3.47 that 'it is not the duty of the Government to provide any class of citizen with any of the necessaries of life'?

2 To what extent does Cross support the individualist views of those contemporaries who believed in the virtues of self-help?

3 What can be inferred from Cross's motives for introducing the bill of the success of attempts prior to the 1870s to improve public health?

4 What improvements does he hope will result from a policy of slum clearance?

● **SOURCE 3.48**

From the Act for Facilitating the Improvement of the Dwellings of the Working Classes in Large Towns, 1875, Part I, Clause 3 (commonly referred to as the Artisans' Dwellings Act), laying down the conditions necessary for intervention.

*Where an official representation as hereinafter mentioned is made to the local authority [in London and urban sanitary districts with over 25,000 population] that any houses, courts or alleys within a certain area under the jurisdiction of the local authority are unfit for human habitation or that diseases indicating a generally low condition of health amongst the population have been from time to time prevalent in a certain area within the jurisdiction of the local authority and that such prevalence may reasonably be attributed to the closeness, narrowness and bad arrangement or the bad condition of the streets and houses or groups of houses within such area . . . the local authority shall take such representation into their consideration and if satisfied of the truth thereof and of the sufficiency of their resources shall pass a resolution to the effect that such area is an unhealthy area and that an improvement scheme ought to be made in respect of such area and after passing such resolution they shall forthwith proceed to make a scheme for the improvement of such area.*

● **SOURCE 3.49**

From a report of the Charity Organisation Society, *Dwellings of the Poor*, 1881, assessing the operation of the act to the end of 1879.

*[In London] action is being taken regarding 1,402 houses. Areas comprising 945 houses and 6 acres have been sold and dealt with. There are, besides the Metropolis, 87 towns in England and Wales to which the Act is applicable. Out of these, one, Birmingham [is] dealing with an area of 93 acres, at an estimated cost of £1,310,000 . . . In 77 towns no steps whatever have been taken. In no provincial town have the transactions under the Act actually been completed.*

Study Sources 3.48 and 3.49.

1 In what ways was the Artisans' Dwellings Act a 'permissive' piece of legislation?

2 What impact did this permissive element have on the effectiveness of the act?

111

What progress was made in public health reform between 1848 and 1890?

## ● SOURCE 3.50

From the *Report of Birmingham City Improvement Committee*, 1882.

Fall in death-rates in slum-cleared areas of Birmingham, 1873–80.

The streets listed were part of the 40–50 acres of the most decayed parts of Birmingham redeveloped under the terms of the Artisans' Dwellings Act, 1875.

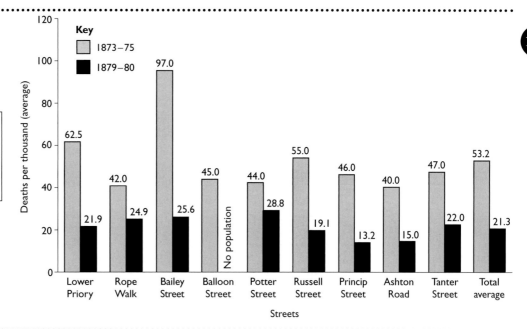

**Key**
- 1873–75
- 1879–80

Deaths per thousand (average)

| Street | 1873–75 | 1879–80 |
|---|---|---|
| Lower Priory | 62.5 | 21.9 |
| Rope Walk | 42.0 | 24.9 |
| Bailey Street | 97.0 | 25.6 |
| Balloon Street | 45.0 | No population |
| Potter Street | 44.0 | 28.8 |
| Russell Street | 55.0 | 19.1 |
| Princip Street | 46.0 | 13.2 |
| Ashton Road | 40.0 | 15.0 |
| Tanter Street | 47.0 | 22.0 |
| Total average | 53.2 | 21.3 |

Streets

---

1 What claims were made in Source 3.50 by the 1882 *Report of Birmingham City Improvement Committee*?

---

## ● SOURCE 3.51

From the *Report of the Royal Commission into the Housing Crisis*, 1884–85, summarising its main findings on the housing crisis.

**The Royal Commission**
had a number of influential members, including the Prince of Wales, the Marquis of Salisbury, leader of the Conservative Party, Archbishop Manning and former Home Secretary Richard Cross. It failed to recommend any decisive initiative.

**rookeries**
slum dwellings, tenements

*. . . Demolitions made by owners have for their main purpose the improvement of the value of the property . . . ROOKERIES are destroyed, greatly to the sanitary and social benefits of the neighbourhood but no kind of habitation for the poor has been substituted. This is the extreme instance of everything being sacrificed to the improvement of the property . . .*

*There are also the demolitions which take place under Mr Torren's and Sir Richard Cross's Acts. Such demolitions are undertaken in the interest of public health and welfare. The houses so removed are generally in a hopelessly bad condition, and the number thus pulled down is very small compared to the number which on every ground ought to be removed. Nevertheless a good deal of hardship is caused by this class of displacement. The overcrowded state of Spitalfields is attributed to a great measure of such clearances, and the rise of rent, which had doubled in the Mint district, is largely owing to demolitions of the same kind. Your Majesty's Commissioners are clearly of opinion that there has been a failure in administration rather than in legislation, although the latter is no doubt capable of improvement. What at the present time is specially required is some motive power, and probably there can be no stronger motive power than public opinion . . .*

*Evidence has been given showing that the inadequacy of the water supply in the poorer quarters of the metropolis and the great towns is the cause of much unhealthiness and misery in the dwellings of the working classes, and . . . [we] recommend that the water supply should, as a general rule, be in the hands of the local authority . . .*

*Your Majesty's Commissioners also recommend that it shall be declared by statute to be the duty of the local authority to put in force such powers as they are by law entrusted with, so as to ensure that no premises shall be allowed to exist in an insanitary state.*

---

1 Why, in the light of the findings of the Royal Commission of 1885 (Source 3.51), should the claims of the Birmingham Improvement Committee be viewed with some reservation?

2 Why, according to the report of the Royal Commission, had slum-clearance schemes not helped the poor?

3 Why, according to the Commission, had progress towards improvements in public health been limited?

# 6 What progress had been achieved by 1914?

By the end of the nineteenth century the negative approach associated with the supporters of a minimal government role or *laissez-faire* had given way to support for direct state interference. Despite the self-interest shown by some developers there had been some improvements in life expectancy amongst the poor, as shown by the 1901 census results. Overcrowding was lessening slightly, and even though there were still small epidemics, such as smallpox in the 1870s and cholera in 1893, the large epidemics had disappeared. It may be said that, considering the size of the problem, the Victorians had achieved an increasing amount of success.

● **SOURCE 3.52**

From B. R. Mitchell and P. Deane, *Abstract of British Historical Statistics*, 1962.

Movement in death-rate, 1846–1915 (per thousand of the population).

No figures have been identified for 1851–70.

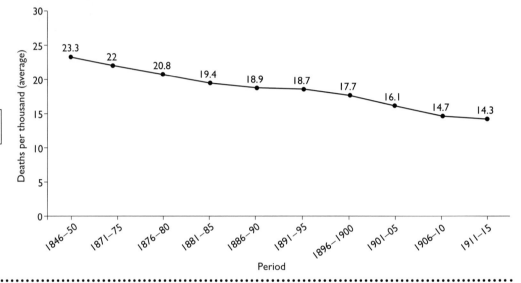

1 Using Source 3.52, identity and explain the trend in death-rate between 1846 and 1915.

2 Which period saw the most substantial fall?

● **SOURCE 3.53**

From E. Hobsbawm, *Industry and Empire*, 1969.

Movement in death-rate, 1838–1914 (per thousand of the adult and infant population).

No figures have been identified for the 1840s.

| Years | Average number of deaths per thousand population | | |
|---|---|---|---|
| | Male | Female | Live births, 0–1 years |
| 1838–42 | 22.9 | 21.2 | 150.0 |
| 1858–62 | 22.8 | 21.0 | 149.4 |
| 1868–72 | 23.5 | 20.9 | 155.8 |
| 1878–82 | 21.5 | 19.1 | 142.2 |
| 1888–92 | 20.2 | 17.9 | 145.6 |
| 1898–1902 | 18.6 | 16.4 | 152.2 |
| 1908–12 | 15.1 | 13.3 | 111.8 |
| 1914 | 15.0 | 13.1 | 105.0 |

1 Which group, according to Source 3.53, benefited most from the fall in death-rate – adult males, adult females or infants?

## ● Source 3.54

Adapted from T. McKeown, *The Modern Rise of Population*, 1976.

Percentage reduction in deaths from diseases by 1901, compared with 1848–54.

The number of deaths from bronchitis, pneumonia and influenza rose from 2239, between 1848 and 1854, to 2747 in 1901. Similarly, deaths from infections of the ear, larynx and pharynx rose from 75 to 100 in the same period.

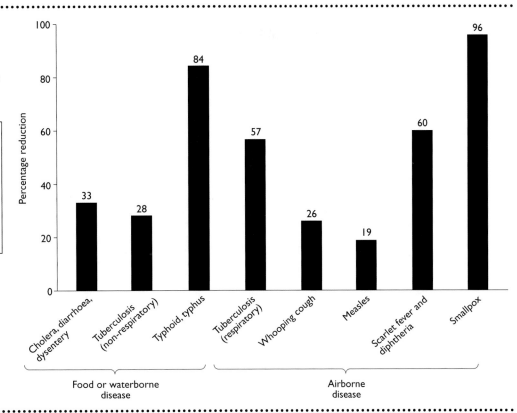

1 From the evidence provided by Source 3.54 what was the impact of improvements in public health on disease?

2 Which disease or group of diseases saw the biggest fall?

3 Study Sources 3.52–3.54. On the basis of the statistical evidence only, what conclusions can be drawn about the success of the public health movement?

## ● Summary task

1 Below are a number of questions that might be used for discussion or written answers as a way of testing your understanding of this chapter.

- What is meant by a 'nuisance'?
- Why did Chadwick claim in his 1842 report that it was necessary to improve the supplies of water?
- Who opposed Chadwick's report and for what reasons?
- What were the main weaknesses of the terms of the 1848 Public Health Act?
- How successful was Chadwick in achieving his aims for improvements to public health in the period 1842–54?
- Who was more successful in improving public health – Edwin Chadwick or John Simon?
- What improvements had been achieved in public health by 1914?

**2 An A2 essay-planning exercise**

Write an essay answering the following question:

**Account for the slowness and ineffectiveness of the public health movement to 1875.**

This question is a list-type question requiring you to give reasons for the slow progress of public health improvements. You need to establish a line of argument and start each paragraph with an obstacle. It is a relatively straightforward question but you must avoid the danger of narrating the content of consecutive public health acts.

**Suggested plan:** You need to identify an obstacle as the lead in to each paragraph and then explain it using evidence to substantiate your point. A suggested plan is provided on page 114.

| Paragraph | Main theme | Content |
|---|---|---|
| Intro | Scale of the problem | This paragraph should set the scene – assess <br><br>• the implications of population growth – pressure on housing – evils of slum housing <br>• the effects of a lack of planning and the lack of drainage, sewerage and water supply <br>• the role of improvement commissions – focus of their improvements <br>• the outcome – disease, most notably typhus, tuberculosis, cholera – death-rates. |
| 2 | Opposition of vested interests | Identify and explain the initiatives taken by various private vested interests <br><br>• lead taken by municipal initiatives encouraged by Local Improvement Acts – ineffective – administrative confusion and overlapping of functions of archaic authorities, e.g. Paving Trusts, Commissioners of Sewers, Highway Committees – run by private investors – concern with profit not a public service – London, for example, had 300 bodies operating under 250 local acts <br>• implications of opposition of private interests <br>• local government unable to cope with the increasing problems of growing towns – impact of industrial depression, especially 1837–42 – slow progress <br>• work of private companies in housing developments – large areas kept for the middle classes, where planning schemes were profitable <br>• contests at both local and national level between rival vested interests and in the debate about the role of the state/centralisation. |
| 3 | Political/Ideological | Explain the significance of each of the following themes to this issue <br><br>• hostility to Centralisation – support for *laissez-faire* – suspicion of the central officers who were viewed as impersonal, impartial and powerful administrators, able to enforce action and incur expenditure, over which there was no local control – outcome – weaknesses of 1848 Public Health Act <br>• 1835 Municipal Corporation Act – end of authority of the local lord of the manor – slow progress for thirteen years – new town councils failed to exercise their new powers and responsibilities to provide public amenities <br>• middle-class ratepayers not prepared to finance services for others through the rates when they had already made their own private provision – calls for economy paralysed any effort to improve <br>• political and local issues – suspicion of an extension of municipal power. |
| 4 | Rights – individual and property | Discuss the impact of and role played by each of the following <br><br>• Victorian values – self-help/individualism <br>• protection of property rights/resentment of regulations <br>• middle-class fear of enormous costs and reluctance to accept the burden <br>• apathy of many of the well-to-do in the face of such appalling evidence. |
| 5 | Technical problems | Describe the problems arising from <br><br>• medical ignorance – miasma theory of disease impeded search for effective solution – ignorance a powerful restraint on an effective solution to the evils of disease <br>• civil engineering in its infancy – principles of drainage, sewerage and water supply not fully mastered – schemes badly worked out and under-estimated, contractors late, poor workmanship <br>• scale of the task of supplying large cities with water and disposing of sewage. |
| 6 | Personality of Chadwick | Identify and explain <br><br>• public response to his views on reform <br>• relationship with others – opponents <br>• *The Times'* campaign. |
| 7 | Sanitation and Housing Acts | Describe and explain the contribution of the following to a more effective policy <br><br>• acceptance of a policy of state intervention <br>• 1866 Sanitation Act – a turning point – 1871 Local Government Board Act <br>• 1875 Acts – Artisans' Dwelling Act and Public Health Act <br>• Housing of the Working Classes Acts of 1890 and 1900. |
| Conclusion | Impact of the movement | • Achievements by 1875 – death-rate/civic pride <br>• But, limited progress – disease, deaths, poor housing. |

# Examples of examination-type questions

## A  AS questions

1  a) What were the obstacles to a successful public health policy in the years 1841–75?
   b) How successfully were those obstacles overcome by 1875?

2  a) What problems of public health had emerged by 1850?
   b) How far had progress been made in solving them by 1850?

3  a) Why did public health become a political issue in the years 1832–75?
   b) Why was the development of a public health policy so controversial?

## B  A2 questions

1  Was ignorance or indifference the greater obstacle to the improvement of public health in England in the years 1832–75?

2  Why was the Public Health Act of 1848 not more effective in achieving its objectives?

3  Was Edwin Chadwick more of a hindrance than a help to the public health movement in the years up to 1858?

---

## ● Further reading

The best detailed account of public health is: F. B. Smith, *The People's Health, 1830–1910* (Croom Helm, 1979); also A. Wohl, *Endangered Lives, Public Health in Victorian Britain* (Dent, 1990). Public health and housing are covered in a number of general textbooks: G. Kitson Clark, *The Making of Victorian England*, pp. 65–82 (Methuen, 1962); S. G. Checkland, *The Rise of Industrial Society in England 1815–1885*, pp. 18–35 and pp. 222–25 (Longman, 1964); D. Fraser, *The Evolution of the British Welfare State* (Macmillan, 1973); E. C. Midwinter, *Victorian Social Reform* (Seminar Studies in History, Longman, 1968); E. Hopkins, *A Social History of the English Working Class, 1818–1945*, chapter 2 (Edward Arnold, 1979); J. T. Ward, *Popular Movements c. 1832–1850*, pp. 183–98 (Macmillan, 1970); A. Briggs, *Victorian Cities* (Penguin, 1968); J. Burnett, *A Social History of Housing 1815–1985* (Methuen, 1978).

### Articles
C. Bradley, 'Titus Salt', *History Today*, May 1987
D. Fraser, 'Joseph Chamberlain and the Municipal Ideal', *History Today*, April 1987
A. S. Watts, 'Octavia Hill and the Influence of Dickens', *History Today*

# Did the old Poor Law fail the poor?

**1601**

43rd Elizabethan statute (act) sets up a system of poor relief based on the parish.

**1722**

Knatchbull's Act stops relief outside of the workhouse.

**1782**

Gilbert's Act allows parishes to join together to share the cost of the poor relief in their area, which can be given outside of the workhouse.

**1795**

The Speenhamland system is established to subsidise the wages of agricultural labourers from Poor Law funds.

**1798**

Thomas Malthus publishes his *First Essay on Population* in which he calls for an end to the system of poor relief.

The reformer Jeremy Bentham, who believed that institutions should be judged by their practical usefulness, publishes his *Pauper Management Improved* in which he calls for a centralised Poor Law based on 'Houses of Industry'.

**1817**

David Ricardo's *Principles of Political Economy and Taxation* adds to the demands for the end of the Poor Law.

**1819**

Sturges-Bourne Act provides for the setting up of specialised committees, called 'select vestries', to supervise the Poor Law.

**1824**

Select Committee on Labourers' Wages issues its report.

**1830**

Swing riots break out in the farming counties of southern England.

**1832**

A Royal Commission is set up to investigate the Poor Laws.

**1834**

Poor Law Amendment Act ends the different systems of poor relief, with the setting up of a central commission, the combination of parishes into unions and the establishment of the workhouse system.

## Introduction

The issues of poverty and poor relief illustrate many of the themes which make up the nineteenth century. The presence of large numbers of poor threatened society and property ownership and led to debates about the role of the state.

# 1 What were the causes of poverty in the early nineteenth century?

117

What were the causes of poverty in the early nineteenth century?

Data for the actual number of poor in pre-industrial England is rather rough because of the absence of reliable statistics. In 1700 the poverty problem was still predominantly an agricultural one, with 75 per cent of the poor living in villages, and this remained the situation until the end of the eighteenth century. It seems fairly certain that in the eighteenth century living standards did improve and wages rose. However, this improvement was not carried over into the industrial age and for most people life was hard in the first half of the nineteenth century. In years when the economy was depressed, particularly 1816–22, 1829–31 and 1836–42, many experienced a deterioration in their condition, reflected in the high level of unrest and rioting up to 1850. In the early nineteenth century there were many attempts to explain the causes of poverty, as the collection of sources below illustrates.

## What effect did changes in agriculture have on the condition of rural workers?

● **SOURCE 4.1**

From the evidence to the Lords Committee on the Poor Law, 1830, describing the effect of the decline of the practice of farm labourers living in with their employers.

*When I was a boy I used to visit a large farmhouse, where the farmer sat in a room with a door opening to the Servants Hall, and everything was carried from one table to the other. Now they will rarely permit a man to live in their houses and it is in consequence a total bargain and sale for money and all idea of affection is destroyed.*

● **SOURCE 4.2**

From William Cobbett, *Rural Rides*, 20 October 1825. In *Rural Rides*, an account of his travels, Cobbett defends the interests of labouring people, especially the poor in Southern England.

*Why do not farmers now feed and lodge their workpeople, as they did formerly? Because they cannot keep them upon so little as they give them in wages. This is the real cause of the change. There needs no more to prove that the lot of the working classes has become worse than it formerly was. This fact alone is quite sufficient to settle this point. All the world knows, that a number of people, boarded in the same house, and at the same table, can, with good food, be boarded much cheaper than those persons divided into twos, or fours, can be boarded. This is a well-known truth: therefore, if the farmer now shuts his pantry against his labourers, and pays them wholly in money, is it not clear, that he does it because he thereby gives them a living cheaper to him; that is to say, a worse living than formerly? Mind he has a house for them; a kitchen for them to sit in, bed rooms for them to sleep in, tables, and stools, and benches, of everlasting duration. All these he has; all these cost him nothing; and yet so much does he gain by pinching them in wages that he lets all these things remain as of no use, rather than feed labourers in the house. Judge, then, of the change that has taken place in the condition of these labourers! And, be astonished, if you can, at the pauperism and crimes that now disgrace this once happy and moral England.*

● **SOURCE 4.3**

From a Report of the Standing Committee on Poor Laws, 1830–41, in which T. L. Hodges, MP, speaks about the Weald of Kent.

*The wages that a servant received in a farmer's family bore no proportion to those he got out of it; he became dissatisfied with his situation; and the farmer, in consequence of the alteration of circumstances, and the high prices which prevailed during the French wars [1793–1815], got above his situation and was ready to part with all his men, whom he considered liabilities and annoyances to him; and thus, by mutual consent, the masters and labourers parted.*

Study Sources 4.1–4.3.

1  Why was there a decline in the old systems of employment in the village?

2  What effect were these changes likely to have on wage levels and security of employment for agricultural labourers?

● **SOURCE 4.4**

From Rev. D. Davies, *The Case of the Labourers in Husbandry*, 1795, in which he describes the impact of the practice of enlarging and enclosing farms.

**encloses/enclosure**
the fencing off of common land

***their resort is the parish***
they turn to the financial support provided by local parishes under the 1601 Poor Law

***hirelings***
day labourers, hired to do a particular task

The landowner, to render his income adequate to the increased expense of living, joins several small farms into one, raises the rent to the utmost, and avoids the expense of repairs. The rich farmer also ENCLOSES as many farms as he is able to stock; lives in more credit and comfort than he could otherwise do; and out of the profits of the several farms, makes an ample provision for one family. Thus thousands of families, which formerly gained an independent livelihood on those separate farms, have been gradually reduced to the class of day-labourers. But day-labourers are sometimes in want of work, and are sometimes unable to work; and in either case THEIR RESORT IS THE PARISH. It is a fact, that thousands of parishes have not now half the number of farmers that they had formerly. And in proportion as the number of farming families has decreased the number of poor families has increased.

. . . Formerly many of the lower sorts of people occupied tenements of their own with parcels of land about them, or they rented such of others. On these they raised for themselves a considerable part of their subsistence, without being obliged, as now, to buy all their wants at shops. And this kept members from coming to the parish. But since those small parcels of ground have been swallowed up in the enclosed farms, and the cottages themselves pulled down, the families which used to occupy them are crowded together in decayed farm houses, with hardly ground enough about them for a cabbage garden. They are thus reduced to be mere HIRELINGS; they are of course very liable to come to want. And not only the men occupying those tenements, but their wives and children too, could formerly, when they lacked work, employ themselves profitably at home. Now few of these are constantly employed, except in harvest so that almost the whole burden of providing for their families rests upon the men. Add to this, that the former occupiers of small farms and tenements, though poor themselves, gave away something in alms to their poorer neighbours; a resource which is now much diminished.

Thus an amazing number of people have been reduced from a comfortable state of partial independence to the precarious conditions of hirelings, who, when out of work, must immediately come to the parish. And the great plenty of working hands always to be had when wanted, having kept down the price of labour below its proper level, the consequence is universally felt in the increased number of dependent poor.

1 Why, according to Source 4.4, did enclosure increase the number of poor in the village?

2 What effect did the enclosure of land have upon the labourers' security of employment and wage levels?

● **SOURCE 4.5**

From Arthur Young, *An Inquiry into the Propriety of Applying WASTES to Better Maintenance and Support of the Poor*, 1801.

**Wastes**
common land in a village, not farmed for crops

Go to an alehouse kitchen of an old enclosed county, and there you will see the origin of poverty and poor rates. For whom are they to be sober? For whom are they to save? (Such are their questions.) For the parish? If I am diligent, shall I have leave to build a cottage? If I am sober, shall I have land for a cow? If I am frugal, shall I have half an acre of potatoes? You offer no motives; you have nothing but a parish officer and a workhouse! Bring me another pot. What is it to the poor man to be told that the Houses of Parliament are extremely tender of property, while the father of the family is forced to sell his cow and his land because the one is not competent to the other. Being deprived of the only motive to work [he] squanders the money, acquires bad habits, enlists for a soldier, and leaves the wife and children to the parish. If enclosures were beneficial to the poor, rates would not rise as in other parishes after an act to enclose. The poor in these parishes may say, and with truth, Parliament may be tender of property; all I know is, I had a cow, and an act of Parliament has taken it from me. And thousands may make this speech with truth.

1 To what extent does Arthur Young (Source 4.5) agree with the views expressed by the Rev. Davies in Source 4.4?

2 Why, in Young's opinion, had the character of the labouring class declined in enclosed villages?

119

What were the causes of poverty in the early nineteenth century?

## ● SOURCE 4.6

From William Cobbett, *Rural Rides*, 1830, in which he describes the effects on the agricultural family of the decline of cottage spinning and weaving with the coming of textile factories.

**lords of the loom**
the owners of the new textile factories

**raiment**
clothing

*The* LORDS OF THE LOOM *have taken from the land, in England, this part of its due; and hence one cause of the poverty, misery, and pauperism, the state of being dependent on public and private charity, that are becoming so frightful throughout the country . . . The country people lose part of their natural employment. The women and children, who ought to provide a great part of the* RAIMENT, *have nothing to do. The fields must have men and boys; but where there are men and boys there will be women and girls. The lords of the loom have now a set of real slaves, by the means of whom they take away a great part of employment of the countrywomen and girls, these must be kept by poor rates in whatever degree they lose employment through the lords of the loom. One would think that nothing could be much plainer than this; and yet you hear the* jolterheads *congratulating one another upon the increase of Manchester and such places!*

| **I** According to Source 4.6, how did industrialisation affect employment opportunities in the village? |
| --- |

## ● SOURCE 4.7

From *The Agricultural State of England*, 1816. This records East Anglian responses to a circular sent out by the Board of Agriculture in mid-1816, enquiring into the state of wages and employment.

*The State of the labouring poor is very deplorable and arises from the want of employment, which they are willing to seek, but the farmer cannot afford to furnish. The poor . . . they say never experienced such bad times. A parish in the next county (without any manufacture), consisting of 3,500 acres, has, at this time, 72 men besides boys, out of employment and upon the parish . . . the labouring poor are in as bad a situation as they were in the scarcity years. One third of them being out of employment, and their wages being reduced by more than another third and the price of every article of their consumption (bread excepted) being nearly equal the prices of the years 1811 and 1812.*

## ● SOURCE 4.8

From P. Deane and W. A. Cole, *British Economic Growth, 1688–1959*, 1962.

Decline in migration from south-eastern and eastern counties to London, 1751–1831.

Counties include Bedfordshire, Berkshire, Cambridgeshire, Essex, Hertfordshire, Hereford, Huntingdonshire, Lincolnshire, Norfolk, Oxon, Rutland, Suffolk, Sussex, and Wiltshire.

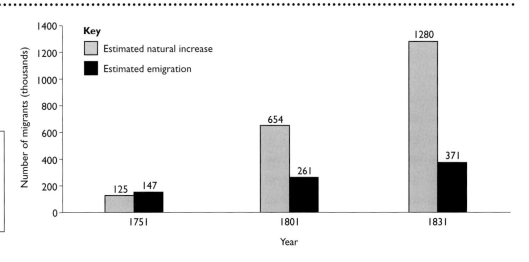

| Year | Population to the nearest thousand | Percentage of natural increase migrating |
| --- | --- | --- |
| 1751 | 1540 | 100 |
| 1801 | 2046 | 40 |
| 1831 | 2876 | 29 |

| **I** What conclusions can be drawn from Sources 4.7 and 4.8 about the main causes of poverty amongst agricultural labourers? |
| --- |

# What effect did the seasonal nature of work have on the condition of rural workers?

## ● SOURCE 4.9

From the *Report from the Commissioners on the Poor Laws, Report of Alfred Power*, Appendix A, Part 1, 1834, in which Power develops the PATERNALIST view of poverty as a natural condition, to be solved by those who have an obligation to care for the less fortunate members of society.

> **paternalist**
> governing in a paternal – fatherly, protective – way

*For a certain period of the year at least . . . there is for the whole County a surplus labouring population; as to the average degree of surplus (per parish) or the average extent of the period, it is impossible even to guess . . . the former varying from one to two hundred men, the latter from one week to eleven months, in different places.*

*Again, during another portion of the year, and this perhaps the greater portion, there is undoubtedly no surplus labour, the surface of the County sufficing at this period for the employment of the whole, if fairly distributed. Thirdly, during another very small portion of the year, namely one month of harvest, there is actually a deficiency; for, beside the labour on the spot, a great quantity of Irishmen, and labourers from the southern counties, are employed with advantage.*

I According to Source 4.9, what impact did the harvest have on the seasonal nature of employment within the village?

2 What argument is expressed by Alfred Power that indicates that he had a paternalist attitude towards the rights of the poor?

# What were the other causes of poverty?

## ● SOURCE 4.10

A letter from the overseers of Portsea to the overseers of St Peter's, Winchester, 16 May 1822, stating the case of John Taylor for relief.

Portsea Parish
May 16 1822
Gentl[emen],
*A very aged person by the name of John Taylor, who applied to you some time since who used to have 3s. [15p] per week, and on his appearing before you his relief was increased to 4s. [20p] per week, it appears that there is some difficulty in their obtaining the relief from Mr Woodman.*

*They are deserving people, the man is above 80, the woman 71, and a blind daughter I believe nearly 40. They are very poor but honest people, the old man is past labour and the woman is a little employed by some who has her services for the past 20 years, and although not capable of performing a day's work, yet they so respect the old woman, to give her a little employment. Mr Woodman has refused to pay them more than 3s. [15p] per week. I give you my word that they are every way deserving of your attention – if you choose we will pay them the 4s. [20p] per week, as it will be more convenient for them to receive it of us, and we shall apply for it once a year or every 6 months. Any further information I shall willingly give. Please to send me your answer.*
*I am*
*Mr Whillier*
*Vestry Clerk*
*[To] Overseers St Peter's*

I What other causes of poverty are revealed in Source 4.10, the case of John Taylor and his family?

2 What can be inferred from the letter of Mr Whillier's attitude towards the Taylor family?

# What factors affected the condition of industrial workers?

121

What were the causes of poverty in the early nineteenth century?

● **SOURCE 4.11**

From William Jackson to the Home Secretary, 1817.

**Combination Acts 1799/1800**
banned combinations or trade unions among workers as well as employers.

**you have legislated to keep up the price of corn**
refers to the Corn Laws (1815) which aimed to guarantee a market price of 80s. (£4) a quarter for corn.

*A statement of matters of fact, and things as they really are in this town [Leicester] and Neighbourhood. The Frame-Work Knitters in consequence of the reduction of their Wages are reduced to the lowest state of misery and wretchedness, and if the present system of giving low wages is persisted in, the whole of the common people must soon become paupers. One cause of this state of things is the COMBINATION ACT, which is unjust in its principles, and impolitic in its application. If this Act had never been enforced mechanics would in a great measure [have been able] to resist their employers in reducing their Wages . . . All ranks of People in this Town see and feel the evil of the present system of giving low Wages . . . It is not want of employment of which we complain but the lowness of our Wages, the hands out of work being comparatively few. YOU HAVE LEGISLATED TO KEEP UP THE PRICE OF CORN, and it is but just that you legislate to keep up the price of labour.*

I   What does William Jackson (Source 4.11) give as a cause of poverty among the frame-work knitters of Leicester?

● **SOURCE 4.12**

From Robert Owen, *A New View of Society and Other Writings*, 1813, in which he argues for an improvement in wages.

*The cause of poverty is the shortage of jobs at wages high enough to support the family of a working man. It is well known that over the past 50 years, Britain has increased its power to produce goods by great improvements in science and knowledge. The effect of these improvements should be to add to the wealth and happiness of the country, so that everyone benefits. What has really happened is that the working classes cannot obtain the comforts which their labour used to supply them with.*

I   To what extent does Robert Owen (Source 4.12) agree with the views expressed in Source 4.11 about the causes of poverty amongst industrial workers?

● **SOURCE 4.13**

From *Report of a Parliamentary Committee*, 1827, which comments on the effects on handloom-weavers and nail-makers of the introduction of machinery.

*An important change has taken place in industrial areas by the change from handloom to power-loom weaving. For some time the changes in the cotton trade meant that many workers who had lost their jobs as handloom-weavers were found jobs in the new factories. But soon there was a fall in demand for woven cloth and even cheaper ways of weaving were brought in. These two factors led to high unemployment and terrible poverty.*

● **SOURCE 4.14**

From *Letters from Leeds*, 18 January 1842, in which William Dodd, a former factory worker, records his experience of the impact of machinery on the workforce. Dodd was crippled in childhood by the strain of the work.

*As machinery became more general, wages went down and a number of men lost their jobs. The husband, finding that his earnings were not enough to make ends meet, had to send first the children, then his wife out to work in the factories. The women and children being made, with the help of machinery, to do the work of men, the men were cast off or their wages were reduced to a level with the women. We now find that men like the croppers, flax-dressers, wool-combers, handloom-weavers and calico printers are working [for] 6s. to 10s. [30p to 50p] per week, longer hours than they were working a few years ago for four times the amount. And the result of this? Widespread misery, poverty and destitution for the families of skilled men.*

Study Sources 4.11–4.14.

I   What were the long-term consequences for some groups of industrial workers of the introduction of machinery?

2   To what extent did town labourers experience the same problems of poverty as rural labourers?

● **SOURCE 4.15**

Compiled by the author from a selection of statistics.

Expenditure on poor relief, 1812–33, in relation to the state of the harvest and the incidence of riot.

| Year | State of the harvest | Incidence of riot | Total poor relief (£ million) | Approx. expenditure per head of population (s. d.) |
|---|---|---|---|---|
| 1812 | Poor | • Machine-breaking (Luddism) by handloom-weavers, framework-knitters and wool-combers in Nottingham, Lancashire, Yorkshire.<br>• Rise in crime in 18 of 22 agricultural counties and 31 committals for arson, such as rick-burning. | 6,676 | 8s. 11d. |
| 1813 | Good | • 18 committals for arson. | 6,295 | 11s. 10d. |
| 1814 | Good | • Decrease in crime in 18 out of 22 agricultural counties. | 5,419 | 10s. 0d. |
| 1815 | Good | • No significant riot of note. | 5,725 | 9s. 10d. |
| 1816 | Poor | • Riots on the land – 33 committals for arson.<br>• Rise in crime in 18 out of 22 agricultural counties.<br>• Machine-breaking in Nottingham, Lancashire, Yorkshire.<br>• Political disturbances and rioting at Spa Fields, London. | 6,911 | 12s. 4d. |
| 1817 | Poor | • Protest march by unemployed from Manchester to London (the March of the Blanketeers).<br>• Proposed demonstration by unemployed textile workers in Derbyshire and Huddersfield.<br>• Rise in crime in 21 out of 22 agricultural counties; 30 committals for arson. | 7,871 | 12s. 1d. |
| 1818 | Poor | • Lancashire strikes | 7,517 | 13s. 0d. |
| 1819 | Poor | • Political disturbances at St Peters Field, Manchester (Peterloo).<br>• Riots on the land in Norfolk.<br>• Rise in crime in 14 out of 22 agricultural counties, and 22 committals for arson. | 7,330 | 12s. 6d. |
| 1820 | Good | • Decrease in crime in 16 out of 22 agricultural counties.<br>• Failed attempt to blow up Cabinet (Cato Street Conspiracy). | 6,959 | 11s. 8d. |
| 1821 | Good | • Agricultural counties: 26 committals for arson. | 6,359 | 10s. 6d. |
| 1822 | Good | • Agricultural counties: 47 committals for arson. | 5,773 | 9s. 5d. |
| 1823 | Poor | • Agricultural counties: 28 committals for arson. | 5,737 | 9s. 2d. |
| 1824 | Poor | • Agricultural counties: 28 committals for arson. | 5,787 | 9s. 1d. |
| 1825 | Poor | • Agricultural counties: 22 committals for arson. | 5,929 | 9s. 2d. |
| 1828 | Poor | • Agricultural counties: 14 committals for arson. | 6,332 | 9s. 5d. |
| 1829 | Poor | • Agricultural counties: 37 committals for arson.<br>• Parliamentary reform disturbances in towns of the Midlands and the North. | 6,829 | 10s. 0d. |
| 1830 | Poor | • Agricultural counties: 45 committals for arson.<br>• Parliamentary reform disturbances in towns of the Midlands and the North.<br>• Disturbances involving farm labourers. | 6,799 | 9s. 10d. |
| 1831 | Poor | • Agricultural counties: 102 committals for arson.<br>• Parliamentary reform riots. | 7,037 | 10s. 1d. |
| 1832 | Good | • Agricultural counties: 111 committals for arson. | 6,791 | 9s. 7d. |
| 1833 | Good | • Agricultural counties: 64 committals for arson. | 6,317 | 8s. 10d. |

123

What were the causes of poverty in the early nineteenth century?

1   From the information in Source 4.15, what link existed between the state of the harvest and the outbreaks of popular unrest in the period 1812–33?

2   What methods were used by each of the following groups to express their distress
    a)  agricultural labourers
    b)  traditional handicraft workers
    c)  industrial workers?

3   What happened to the provision of poor relief in the period 1812–33?

4   Which year would you identify as the peak year in terms of distress for the labouring poor? Justify your answer on the basis of evidence contained in the table.

It is difficult to say exactly what wages could buy, because prices varied; but, as the above sources have indicated, life was particularly hard for those who earned low wages, worked in a declining traditional craft, or suffered from ill-health, disease or old age. People also suffered when there was bad weather, if the harvest failed, or if they worked in an industry that was dependent on trade, as well as suffering the more obvious problems arising from unemployment. These factors continued well into the nineteenth century and it was not until the 1860s that standards of living for the majority improved, although poverty was still present. It follows that, given the causes of poverty, those who made up the ranks of the poor were drawn from the able-bodied and their dependents, including young children, as well as from the old and the sick.

● **SOURCE 4.16**

From J. D. Marshall, *The Old Poor Law, 1795–1834*, 1968, Table 2, adapted by the author.

Composition of the pauper population by age showing the proportion of elderly, able-bodied and children to the total, 1802–03.

The counties selected used a system of supplementing wages, based on the price of either bread or flour, known as the Speenhamland system.

| County | Total number of paupers | Total number of elderly | Persons on relief outside (i) adults | Permanent workhouse (ii) children (age 0–15) |
|---|---|---|---|---|
| Sussex | 37,000 | 3,330 | 7,400 | 19,000 |
| Wiltshire | 42,100 | 5,052 | 12,500 | 16,900 |
| Berkshire | 22,600 | 2,938 | 5,300 | 7,500 |
| Buckinghamshire | 19,600 | 2,548 | 6,500 | 6,500 |
| Dorset | 15,900 | 3,180 | 5,800 | 4,600 |
| Huntingdonshire | 4,700 | 611 | 1,600 | 1,500 |
| Suffolk | 36,100 | 4,332 | 8,100 | 8,100 |
| Bedfordshire | 7,300 | 1,168 | 2,500 | 2,000 |
| **England/Wales** | **1,041,000** | **166,560** | **236,200** | **315,100** |

Study the statistics in Source 4.16.

1   Which age group formed the largest share of the total number of paupers for England and Wales in 1802–03?

2   Which counties in the agricultural south appear to have been problem counties in terms of the size and composition of their paupers?

3   To what extent did the agricultural counties in the south reflect the pauper problem for England and Wales as a whole?

● **SOURCE 4.17**

Compiled from *Abstract of Returns relative to the Expense and Maintenance of the Poor, 1802–1803.*

**Comparison of the composition of the pauper population between agricultural and industrial areas, 1802–03**

| Region | Total in receipt of relief (and as % of total population) | Non-able-bodied receiving relief | Able-bodied receiving relief | Able-bodied as % of total population relieved | Permanent workhouse residents as % of total population relieved |
|---|---|---|---|---|---|
| **Industrial/commercial** | | | | | |
| Lancashire | 46,200 (6.7) | 6,928 | 39,272 | 85.0 | 5.9 |
| London area | 63,173 (7.5) | 8,407 | 54,766 | 86.7 | 24.0 |
| Yorkshire, West Riding | 54,365 (9.3) | 9,867 | 44,498 | 81.9 | 4.7 |
| **Agricultural counties** | | | | | |
| Berkshire | 22,588 (20.0) | 2,872 | 19,716 | 87.3 | 5.2 |
| Sussex | 37,076 (22.6) | 3,231 | 33,845 | 91.3 | 10.3 |
| Wiltshire | 42,128 (22.1) | 5,219 | 36,909 | 87.6 | 3.8 |
| **Total: England and Wales** | 1,040,716 (11.4) | 166,829 | 873,887 | 84.0 | 8.0 |

Study Source 4.17.

1 Compare the percentage of paupers in industrial and commercial counties with that in agricultural counties.

2 On the basis of the composition of the pauper population, identify the most important causes of poverty in
   a) agricultural counties of the south
   b) industrial regions of the north.

If necessary refer back to the contemporary accounts of poverty in this section.

# 2 What different forms of poor relief were in operation by 1834?

Prior to 1834 measures to relieve the poor dated from acts passed in 1598 and 1601 which were designed to provide for emergency poor relief in times of acute distress and as a supplement to private charity schemes. The majority of the poor, apart from in the worst parishes of the agricultural south, were not permanently in receipt of relief. By the end of the eighteenth century, however, the pauper problem had not only become more complex and varied but had also grown in size. Illegitimacy was a growing problem while poor nutrition produced early ageing and sickness, as suggested by the statistical evidence of Source 4.17. The gradual loss of local crafts and alternative employments as a result of the industrial changes of the period added to the problems. Family ties and the difficulties of moving long distances faced by young families meant that few were prepared to migrate in search of work. Thus, the pauper problem was much more complex than contemporary accounts suggest.

## What main principles were set down by the 1601 Poor Law Act for the relief of the poor?

● **SOURCE 4.18**

Adapted by the author from the Elizabethan Poor Law, 1598, modified 1601.

*. . . The Churchwardens of every parish, and four substantial house-holders there . . . who shall be nominated yearly in Easter week, by two or more Justices of the Peace in the same county, . . . shall be called Overseers of the Poor.*

*I    The Overseers of the Poor, with the consent of two or more Justices of Peace, shall set to work the children of parents thought to be unable to keep and maintain their children. And also all such persons married or unmarried as having no means to . . . get their living. Also to raise weekly sums of money of every inhabitant and every occupier of lands in the said parish as they shall think fit. They shall buy a convenient stock of flax, hemp, wool, thread, iron, and other necessary ware and stuff to set the poor on work, and also competent sums of money for relief of the lame, impotent, old, blind, and such other among them being poor and not able to work, and also for the putting out of such children to be apprentices. Churchwardens, and Overseers . . . shall meet together at least once every month in the church of the said parish, upon the Sunday in the afternoon after divine service, there to consider some good course to be taken and some orders to be set down in the premises . . .*

*II    If the Justices of Peace recognise that the inhabitants of any parish are not able to levy among themselves sufficient sums of money to the Churchwardens and Overseers of the said poor parish for the purpose of providing relief . . . then the Justices of Peace at their general Quarter Sessions, . . . shall rate and assess . . . other parishes . . . as in their discretion . . .*

*IV    It shall be lawful for the said Churchwardens and Overseers by the assent of any two Justices of the Peace, to bind any such children to be apprentices where they shall see convenient, till such man-child shall come to the age of four and twenty years, and such woman-child to the age of one and twenty years;*

*V    Places of habitation [workhouses] may more be provided for such poor impotent people, at the general expense of the parish . . .*

*XII    All begging is forbidden . . . Justices of Peace for every county . . . shall rate every parish to such a weekly sum of money as they shall think convenient, . . . which sums so taxed shall be yearly assessed by the agreement of the parishioners . . . If any person shall refuse or neglect to pay any such portion of money so taxed, it shall be lawful for the said Churchwardens and Constables . . . to sell the goods of the party . . . or send such persons to prison, till he have paid the same.*

*XIII    Justices of the Peace at their general Quarter Sessions shall set down what competent sum of money shall be sent quarterly out of every county . . . to the upkeep of hospitals and almshouses.*

> **I**    What main principles were set down by the Elizabethan Poor Law (Source 4.18) for
> a)  administration of poor relief
> b)  financing of poor relief
> c)  provision of poor relief
> d)  measures for dealing with different categories of the poor?

## What different local measures were introduced to relieve the rising numbers of poor?

By the 1780s the old Poor Law of 1601 could not cope with the numbers seeking relief because of a number of factors, some of which were explored in section 1:

- a rise in population from the 3 million estimated by the end of the sixteenth century to 9.2 million at the time of the first census in 1801 and 13.9 million by 1831
- changes in the agricultural economy with the commercialisation of farming
- the decline of the domestic system and of agricultural crafts
- harvest failures, especially in the 1790s
- food shortages as a consequence of twenty years of war against France
- inflation, especially the rise in food prices, while wages lagged behind
- changes in people's attitudes whereby they ceased to regard poverty as the result of vice, idleness or laziness.

In this situation a number of new measures were introduced, at a local rather than national level, to deal with the rising numbers of poor, particularly as distress became widespread with the steep rise in the cost of living, a decline in the woollen industry and failure of the harvest. No two parishes had the same system, though there were generally four different methods of providing relief. One of these was the Speenhamland system of 1795. It was sympathetic, generous and well-meaning in that it recognised that there were real grievances and that people were 'casualties' of structural changes in the economy, made worse by war against France.

## ● SOURCE 4.19

From *Reading Mercury*, 11 May 1795, announcing the introduction of a wages supplement.

In May 1795, the Justices of the Peace of Berkshire met in the Pelican Inn at Speenhamland, near Newbury, to try to arrange some way of dealing with the acute distress in the county caused by the shortfall in wages compared with food prices. This system, known as the Speenhamland or allowance system, was sanctioned by an Act of Parliament, and between 1795 and 1833 spread to almost every county in England, although the scale varied.

*Resolved unanimously.*
*That the present state of the Poor does require further assistance than has been generally given them.*
*Resolved.*
*That they [the Magistrates] will, in their several divisions, make the following calculations and allowances for the relief of all poor and industrious men and their families, who to the satisfaction of the Justices of their Parish, shall endeavour (as far as they can) for their own support and maintenance.*
*That is to say,*
*When the Gallon Loaf of Second Flour, weighing 8lb. 11 ozs. [4 kilos] shall cost 1s. [5p]*
*Then every poor and industrious man shall have for his own support 3s. [15p] weekly, either produced by his own or his family's labour, or an allowance from the poor rates, and for the support of his wife and every other of his family, 1s. 6d. [7½p].*
*When the Gallon Loaf shall cost 1s. 4d. [6½p]*
*Then every poor and industrious man shall have 4s. [20p] weekly for his own, and 1s. 10d. [9p] for the support of every other of his family.*
*And so in proportion, as the price of bread rise or falls, [that is to say] 3d. [1p] to the man, and a 1d. [½p] to every other of the family, on every 1d. [½p] which the loaf rise above 1s. [5p].*

Study Source 4.19.

1 What were the two main factors affecting the amount of money each labourer received under this system of allowances?

2 What were the main changes in this allowance system from the provisions of the 1601 act (Source 4.18)?

## ● SOURCE 4.20

From *Select Committee on Labourers' Wages – Report VI*, 1824, recording the evidence of Rev. Phillip Hunt, a Bedford JP, on the operation of the Roundsman system.

**parochial settlement**
refers to the obligation of parishes to provide relief for those who had been born in the parish or who had lived there for a year and a day.

*Will you state exactly what the system that is called the SYSTEM OF ROUNDSMAN, is?*
*It is sending in rotation to each of the occupiers in the parish those unemployed labourers (who have a PAROCHIAL SETTLEMENT in the Parish) to work for such farmers, and to have their wages paid, in whole or in part, out of the poor rates.*
*When a part is to be paid by the farmer, is that sum fixed by the Parish?*
*Yes.*
*Are those men, called roundsmen, considered as good labourers?*
*Quite otherwise; they became roundsmen, perhaps, in consequence of their not being so well liked as the other labourers; and by being employed as roundsmen, they become still worse, by the lazy habits they thus acquire.*

**system of Roundsman**
the origins of the Roundsman system are obscure, but it had probably existed since the eighteenth century, and had been encouraged by statutes, such as Gilbert's Act of 1782. This imposed on the parish guardian the duty of finding work for the able-bodied unemployed, particularly in winter, when there was little to do on the farms.

Study Source 4.20.

1 How did the giving of poor relief operate under the Roundsman system?

2 In what form was relief granted?

3 According to Rev. Hunt what defects were there in this form of poor relief?

● **SOURCE 4.21**

From *Select Committee on Labourers' Wages – Report VI*, 1824, recording the evidence of Thomas Bowyer, a maltster and corn factor from Buckden, on the main features of the LABOUR RATE. By 1832, one in five parishes in the south used the labour rate.

**labour rate**
was seen by some people as a fairer method of adjusting the burden of agricultural unemployment. However, it was condemned for falling unfairly on the small farmer and tradesman who employed little or no labour, for confining labourers to their parish of settlement, and for destroying the distinction between pauperism and independence.

*A Plan to regulate the Employment of the Labouring Poor, as acted upon in the Parish of Oundle.*

*(Since the first edition of this little pamphlet was published in February last, experience has fully proved the usefulness of the plan proposed; and it is now adopting in most of the neighbouring villages, sanctioned with the approval of the Magistrates of the county.)*

*The Plan is as follows:*

*A separate rate for the above purpose, distinct from all other rates, is made upon the parish, which rate being regularly allowed and published as 'A Rate for the Relief of the Poor'. The payment of it, of course, may be legally enforced, in cases where any of the occupiers have neglected to employ a sufficient number of men and boys, at the wages fixed upon to excuse them from the rate.*

*The principle of the plan is this, that every occupier who is liable to be assessed, shall pay labourers' wages according to his assessment; leaving him the choice to whom to pay it, – either to the labourer himself if he chooses to employ one, or otherwise to the overseer, to whom ultimately the labourer must apply for support. It also gives the employer a proper control over his labourers, and it occasions a competition for the best hands, while, at the same time, it insures the best pay to those who best merit it, and stimulates others to try for the like advantages.*

---

Study Source 4.21 and compare it with Source 4.20.

1 In what way did the labour rate differ from the Roundsman system?

2 What was the main attraction to the farmer of this system of poor relief?

---

● **SOURCE 4.22**

From *Select Committee on the Employment or Relief of Able-Bodied Persons, Report IV*, 1828, recording the evidence of Henry Boyce who had been an overseer in the parish of Waldershare in Kent.

*In the parish of Ash, there is a regular meeting every Thursday, and the paupers are put up to auction.*

*What do they fetch? – That will depend on the character of the man; the best will fetch the full pay of twelve shillings per week.*

*Every Saturday? – Every Thursday, they are put up.*

*Are they all put up to auction, all the labourers? – Only those out of employment.*

*Does that include the whole number, or is there a considerable section that do not come to the auction? – There are a great number; those who go to the auction, the extent of their wages is twelve shillings a week; if a person bids eight or ten, it is made up by the poor rates.*

---

1 What insight does Source 4.22 offer into the desperate measures used by some parishes to find employment for the able-bodied poor?

---

## How did the industrial areas of the North and Midlands deal with their poor?

● **SOURCE 4.23**

From the *Report from the Commissioners on the Poor Laws, Report of J. D. Tweedy*, Appendix A, Part I, 1834, in which Tweedy, an assistant to the committee of enquiry into the working of the old Poor Law in the West Riding of Yorkshire, comments on the method of giving poor relief.

**composition**
parish funds collected for road maintenance

*In Tickhill the assistant overseer is also assistant surveyor of the highways, and the overseers are surveyors. There are 28 miles of highways, exclusive of six miles of turnpike-road which is under the direction of the turnpike-road surveyor; the men who are out of employ are therefore set to work, either in the quarries to get stone, or in breaking stones or in cleaning the road; and for this work they are paid out of the COMPOSITION, and if that be not sufficient, it is met out of the poor rate; for the last year the composition has been sufficient.*

*The work is let to the men generally, say 10d. [4p] a yard for getting and breaking limestone, and 4d. [1½p] a yard for walling stones that are thrown out;*

*If done by regular labourers, the rate of pay would be 1s. 3d. [6p] or 1s. 4d. [6½p] per yard; those who do not work by the piece are paid at from 1s. [5p] to 1s. 4d. [6½p] per day; a regular day labourer would earn 2s. 3d. [11p]; this plan, the overseers find, causes the able-bodied to seek for other work as soon as they can.*

1 What methods were adopted by the parishes described in Source 4.23 to deal with their poor?

2 How were labourers who applied for relief discriminated against compared with independent labourers?

3 What effect did this practice have on those thought to be work-shy?

● **SOURCE 4.24**

From Isaac Wiseman, *Norwich Mercury*, 7 March 1829, criticising the Norwich workhouse.

*In 1826, and for some years previous, the workhouse was in every part of it, a scene of filth, wretchedness and indecency which baffles all description, without regulations of any kind. Imagine, too, paupers who for weeks, months and years together, breakfasted, dined, and supped, without any order or regularity; who had neither knife, fork or plate; they were to be seen in groups with their hot puddings and meat in their hands, literally gnawing it. Imagine 600 persons indiscriminately lodged, crowded into rooms seldom or never ventilated, the beds and bedding swarming with vermin; single and married, old and young, all mixed without regard to decency. I say imagine this, and you will have a tolerable idea of the workhouse as it was.*

1 What criticisms are made in Source 4.24 against the Norwich workhouse?

2 What can be inferred from the article about the journalist's view of this form of poor relief?

3 Compare the experiences of the poor in Norwich with those in Winchester (Source 4.10). What different attitudes are shown by the parishes?

## How was the 1601 Poor Law changed prior to 1834?

● **SOURCE 4.25**

From Sturges-Bourne Act to amend the laws for the relief of the poor, 31 March 1819.

**Select vestry**
a small committee

*For the better and more effectual execution of the laws for the relief of the poor and for the amendment thereof*
*. . . it shall be lawful for the inhabitants of any parish . . . to establish a* SELECT VESTRY *for the concerns of the poor and to that end to elect householders or occupiers within such parish, not more than twenty or less than five, as shall be thought fit to be members of the select vestry;*
*. . . and every such select vestry is hereby empowered and required to examine into the state and condition of the poor of the parish, and to enquire into and determine upon the proper objects of relief, and the nature and amount of the relief to be given; and in each case shall take into consideration the character and conduct of the poor person to be relieved, and shall be at liberty to distinguish in the relief to be granted, between the deserving, and the idle, extravagant, or wicked poor;*
*. . . [the select vestry] shall inquire into and supervise the collection and administration of all money to be raised by the poor rates, and of all other funds and money raised or applied by the parish to the relief of the poor;*
*VII    And be it further enacted, that it shall be lawful for the inhabitants of any parish in vestry assembled, to . . . elect any persons to be assistant overseer or overseers of the poor of such parish, . . . and to fix such yearly salary for the execution of the said office as shall by such inhabitants in vestry be thought fit.*

1 In what way did the 1819 Sturges-Bourne Act (Source 4.25) attempt to make the administration of the old Poor Law more effective compared with the old system of unpaid amateurs?

2 What evidence is there to suggest that the introduction of select vestries would lead to a reduction in the cost of poor relief?

3 What distinctions were to be made in terms of those applying for poor relief?

4 What indications are there in this act that contemporary attitudes towards relief of the poor were becoming more harsh?

● **SOURCE 4.26**

From *Select Committee on the Employment or Relief of Able-Bodied Persons, Report IV*, 1828, recording the evidence of Lister Ellis.

In some parishes, the appointment of a select vestry led to the adoption of a stricter system with regard to outdoor relief (payment made to the poor, enabling them to live in their own homes, instead of relief given in the form of the workhouse). Such was the case in Liverpool, as described by Lister Ellis, a former overseer of the town and a member of the select vestry for two years.

*(i) A select vestry is introduced*
*When was the select vestry established?*
*In 1821 . . .*
*When did the select vestry adopt the . . . system of refusing relief, as the general rule to all applicants out of the workhouse?*
*Within six months of the first appointment of the select vestry.*

*(ii) A stricter relief system is introduced*
*What was the precise resolution adopted, by the select vestry operating in this charge at the end of 1821, as regarded the relief not to be given out of the walls of the workhouse?*

*(a) End of the practice of giving outdoor relief*
*No person was relieved with money who was able to labour, whatever the number of his family consisted of; but labour was offered to those who were able to work.*
*But money relief was absolutely and peremptorily refused?*
*Yes; and no sum was given nor is now given beyond 5s. [25p] per week, let their family be ever so numerous; with a family of five or six children, for instance.*
*Is that given out of the walls in any case?*

*(b) Special cases where outdoor relief is still granted*
*There are cases where it is given out of the walls; where there is no husband able to work.*

*(c) Setting the poor to work*
*At the same time this alteration of the rule with respect to relief took place did any new regulations of the workhouse also take place of a more strict kind?*
*They did.*
*What was the nature of those regulations?*
*There was several new branches of manufacture introduced; calicoes to a very considerable extent, that is, in the house; there was an establishment for the manufactory of pins, straw bonnets, shoes, for sale; exclusive of what the parish required for their own use; and in fact, ever since the establishment of the select vestry, no person has been in that house but who has been employed, and beneficially employed, up to the present period.*

*(d) Introduction of a stricter discipline*
*Was the discipline of the workhouse rendered more severe, when the intercourse with persons without the walls was cut off?*
*It was cut off altogether, with the exception of two days per week, when they are permitted to go out of the workhouse boundaries.*

*(e) Diet*
*Is the dietary of the workhouse of the humblest description consistent with the health of the persons within the walls?*
*I have the bill of fare for every day in the year.*
*Is it as humble as is consistent with the health of the parties?*
*In some cases more is given than is necessary, such as tea, sugar and butter, to persons above a certain age, whether they have been in the habit of using it or not; this is given by order of a general vestry, and extends to all persons above sixty years of age.*
*Then they are liberally treated?*
*Yes.*
*Generally speaking, is the dietary to able-bodied men within the walls as spare and humble as that of the labouring classes out of the workhouse?*
*I think it better, they get it much more comfortably from the way of cooking adopted.*

*(iii) Results of a stricter relief system*
*On the whole, is there a healthy fear of going into the workhouse among the labouring classes in Liverpool?*
*Not sufficiently so; there is generally a reluctance for it, but the moment they get acquainted with the sort of treatment they experience and the sort of labour imposed on them, there is no apparent dissatisfaction, although every person and child after a certain age is compelled to labour to a certain extent.*

*(iv) Criteria for relief outside of the workhouse*
*What is the description of persons who receive relief out of the workhouse?*
*They are principally the aged, the infirm and the blind.*
*Any able-bodied persons?*
*No able-bodied person whatever.*
*Did you not say that some able-bodied men were employed by the parish in breaking stones?*
*Yes, they are casual poor; they are paid for the labour they do.*
*Are they able, to a certain extent, to provide for their family by task work?*
*Yes, but it is a task work they dislike exceedingly; there is not one instance in fifty that a man remains at it for a month, he exerts himself, and contrives to procure employment.*
*The result of this change of system at Liverpool has been, that whereas in the year:*
*1821: 4,715 individuals were relieved at a cost of £36,013;*
*1827: 2,607 persons have been relieved at a cost of £19,395?*
*Since that period a vast increase of population has taken place?*
*Very great indeed.*

1   What evidence is provided in Source 4.26 that some areas, such as Liverpool, were prepared to adopt a stricter relief system?

2   What changes did the select vestry for Liverpool make in regard to the granting of relief for the able-bodied poor?

3   Did the Liverpool vestry regard itself as being unfair on the poor?

4   In what circumstances was the select vestry prepared to continue with the old system?

5   How successful were the changes?

Before we move on to examine criticism of the old Poor Law, it would be useful to sum up the main features of the old Poor Law by 1832.

- Poor relief was generally administered through the parish by unpaid, non-professional officials headed by an overseer or Justice of the Peace; some parishes, such as in Lancashire and Yorkshire, had started to reform their system with the appointment of select vestries and a paid overseer appointed annually.
- Money, raised by the parish poor rate on property, was limited, so an unusual burden, such as occurred in the bad years between 1815 and 1821, could be disastrous to the parish.
- Supporters of the old Poor Law argued that it was sympathetic and well meant. Every case was considered individually and paupers were helped according to their needs, as evidenced by the case of the treatment of the Taylor family (Source 4.10). The aged and ill were maintained and work was provided for the able-bodied.
- The old Poor Law created a vast but inefficient system of social welfare based on the close relationships of the village and adapted to meet the needs of an agricultural society. The method of providing relief varied between regions, reflecting the differences in the local economy due to trade, industry, and agriculture.
- Between 1795 and 1834 the system of poor relief was extensively adapted to a rapidly changing social and economic system. Growing unemployment and with it widespread distress and unrest meant that it was increasingly difficult to apply the Elizabethan principle of setting the poor to work. J. D. Marshall writes in his *History of the Old Poor Law 1795–1834* that 'Methods of relief out of the workhouse were an accepted and essential part of poor law practice and were a reaction to the increasing numbers of paupers in parishes in the 30 to 40 years before 1796. Most of these paupers were not able-bodied and offered too many problems for workhouses to deal with.'
- Parish officials opposed attempts to reform the system because they felt that they were being replaced.

You should now be in a position to evaluate the effectiveness or otherwise of the different systems of poor relief. Consider particularly

- the purpose of each act or system of relief
- the principles that lay behind them
- the differences between outdoor and indoor relief
- the effectiveness of the systems of relief
- the extent to which there was a national system of poor relief.

Record your findings in a table using the following headings:

| System | Purpose | Principles | Effectiveness | National or local? |
| --- | --- | --- | --- | --- |
|  |  |  |  |  |
|  |  |  |  |  |

# 3  Why was the old Poor Law criticised?

Few contemporaries were happy with the system of poor relief in early nineteenth-century Britain. It was criticised for being clumsy and inconsistent but the well-to-do had always justified providing poor relief with the argument that it would help to secure a stable society, remove discontent and so prevent riots. However, by the beginning of the nineteenth century there was a rising tide of protest against the Poor Law and a call for a more closely regulated and less attractive system of poor relief. A number of factors contributed to this increasingly hostile attitude.

## How was the cost of providing poor relief changing?

● **SOURCE 4.27**

Compiled by the author from a range of sources.

Approximate cost of poor relief, 1760–1832 (£ millions).

Population also rose from 9 to 14 million.

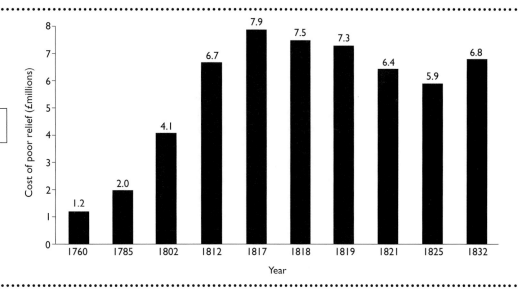

Study Source 4.27.

1  What was the overall trend of the cost of poor relief between 1760 and 1832?

2  In what year did the cost of poor relief peak prior to 1832?

Compare Source 4.27 with Source 4.15.

3  What was the connection between the state of the economy and the level of poor relief?

4  Which groups of workers would have been helped in the peak year of unemployment?

5  Which groups in society would have carried the burden of poor relief during the crisis?

6  Using your own knowledge drawn from your study of the preceding sources, to what extent would the various systems of poor relief in operation have been effective in solving the root causes of distress in the years covered by Source 4.27?

# Why did some contemporaries attack the system of giving relief outside of the workhouse?

● **SOURCE 4.28**

From Thomas Robert Malthus, *First Essay on Population*, 1798, in which the author criticises abuses arising out of the operation of the old Poor Law.

**Thomas Malthus (1766–1834)**
was Professor of History and Political Economy at the East Indian College at Haileybury from 1805 until his death. He is best known for his views on population growth. He believed that the Poor Law did not benefit the poor, but discouraged them from saving and made them careless of the future. His views strengthened the arguments of those who wanted greater control over the giving of poor relief. The word 'Malthusian' was a form of abuse directed against anyone who wanted to reform the old Poor Law.

### (i) Criticism of allowances on wages

*The Poor Laws of England tend to depress the general condition of the poor in these two ways.*

*Their first obvious tendency is to increase population without increasing the food for its support. A poor man may marry with little or no prospect of being able to support a family in independence. They may be said therefore in some measure to create the poor whom they maintain. As the resources of the country must, in consequence of the increased population, be distributed to every man in smaller proportions, it is evident that the labour of those who are not supported by parish assistance, will purchase a smaller quantity of provisions than before, and consequently, more of them must be driven to ask for support.*

*Secondly, the quantity of food used up in workhouses by a part of the society, that cannot in general be considered as the most valuable part, reduces the shares that would otherwise belong to more hardworking, and more worthy members; and thus in the same manner forces more to become dependent.*

### (ii) Demoralising effects of the old Poor Law

*Fortunately for England, a spirit of independence still remains among the peasantry. The Poor Laws are strongly calculated to destroy this spirit.*

### (iii) 'Dependent' poor as an enemy of the rest of the labouring population

*Hard as it may appear in individual instances, dependent poverty ought to be held disgraceful . . . If men are encouraged to marry from a prospect of parish provision, with little or no chance of maintaining their families in independence, they are not only unjustly tempted to bring unhappiness and dependence upon themselves and children; but they are tempted, without knowing it, to injure all in the same class with themselves. A labourer that marries without being able to support a family, may in some respects be considered as an enemy to all his fellow-labourers.*

*I feel no doubt whatever, that the parish laws of England have contributed to raise the price of food, and to lower the real price of labour. They have therefore contributed to impoverish that class of people whose only possession is their labour. It is also difficult to suppose that they have not powerfully contributed to generate that carelessness, and want of* saving observable among the poor, so contrary to the make-up frequently to be remarked among petty tradesmen and small farmers. The labouring poor, to use a vulgar expression, seem always to live from hand to mouth . . . they seldom think of the future. Even when they have an opportunity of saving they seldom exercise it; but all that is beyond their present necessities goes, generally speaking, to the alehouse. The Poor Laws of England may therefore be said to reduce both the power and the will to save, among the common people, and thus to weaken one of the strongest incentives to stop drinking and to work hard and consequently to find happiness.

It is a general complaint among master manufacturers, that high wages ruin all their workmen; but it is difficult to believe that these men would not save a part of their high wages for the future support of their families, instead of spending it in drunkenness and dissipation, if they did not rely on parish assistance for support in case of accidents . . . Men are encouraged to marry with little or no prospect of being able to maintain a family in independence.

The Poor Laws of England were undoubtedly introduced for the most considerate purpose; but there is great reason to think that they have not succeeded in their intention. They certainly lessen some cases of very severe distress which might otherwise occur; yet the state of the poor who are supported by parishes . . . is very far from being free from misery.

. . . if the Poor Laws had never existed, though there might have been a few more instances of very severe distress, yet that the combined . . . happiness among the common people would have been much greater than it is at present.

### (iv) A solution to the evils of the Poor Laws
If I was to propose a solution . . . it should be, in the first place, the total abolition of all the present parish laws. This would at any rate give liberty and freedom of action to the peasantry of England, which they can hardly be said to possess at present. They would then be able to settle without interruption, wherever there was a prospect of a greater plenty of work, and a higher price for labour. The market of labour would then be free.

Secondly, . . . encouragement to agriculture would tend to supply the market with an increasing quantity of healthy work, and at the same time, by increasing the production of the country, would raise the comparative price of labour, and improve the condition of the labourer. Being now in better circumstances, and seeing no prospect of parish assistance, he would be more able, as well as more inclined, to enter into organisations for providing against the sickness of himself or family.

Lastly, for cases of extreme distress, county workhouses might be established, supported by rates upon the whole kingdom, and free for persons of all counties. The food should be hard, and those that were able obliged to work. It would be desirable, that they should not be considered as comfortable institutions in all difficulties but merely as places where severe distress might be reduced.

A plan of this kind, the beginning of which, should be an abolition of all the present parish laws, seems to be the best calculated to increase the mass of happiness among the common people of England. To prevent the recurrence of misery is, alas! beyond the power of man.

Notwithstanding then, the establishment of the Poor Laws in England, I think it will be allowed, that considering the state of the lower classes altogether, both in the towns and in the country, the distresses which they suffer from the want of proper and sufficient food, from hard labour and unhealthy homes, must operate as a constant check to population.

1 Why, according to Malthus in Source 4.28, did the number of those claiming relief outside the workhouse increase after 1800?

2 What impact did this have on the poor rates?

3 Why, according to Malthus, did the Poor Laws of England tend to depress the general condition of the poor?

4 Why, according to Malthus, were the 'dependent' poor an enemy to the rest of the labouring population?

5 What solutions does Malthus recommend to what he sees as the evils of the old system of poor relief?

# Why were some contemporaries concerned with the effect of the Poor Law on the moral character of the poor?

● **SOURCE 4.29**

From Patrick Colquhoun, *A Treatise on Indigence*, 1806, in which he makes a distinction between poverty and indigence.

---

**Patrick Colquhoun (b. 1745)** spent his early career in commerce before moving to London. He became a magistrate in 1792 with a strong interest in local government. Unlike Malthus, he did not want an abolition of the Poor Law system but wanted it to be more centralised so that it could distinguish between poverty and indigence.

**poverty**
was the condition experienced by those who could work but did not. Poverty was avoidable by the labourer's efforts whereas indigence was not. It was fear of poverty that drove people to work.

**indigence**
was the condition of wanting to work but not being able to find paid employment or of earning wages too low to meet a labourer's needs.

---

POVERTY *is a most necessary ingredient in society, without which nations and communities could not exist in a state of civilisation. It is the lot of man. It is the source of wealth, since without poverty there would be no labour, no riches, no refinement, no comfort, and no benefit to those who may be possessed of wealth – inasmuch as without a large proportion of poverty surplus labour could never be made productive in obtaining either the conveniences or luxuries of life.*

INDIGENCE *therefore, and not poverty, is the evil. It is that condition in society that implies scarcity, misery and distress. It is the state of anyone that is destitute of the means of subsistence, and is unable to labour to obtain it to the extent nature requires. The natural source of subsistence is the labour of the individual; while that remains with him he is classified* poor: *when it fails in whole or in part he becomes* indigent.

*. . . But it may happen, and does sometimes happen in civil life, that a man may have ability to labour and cannot obtain it. He may have labour in his possession, without being able to dispose of it.*

*The great purpose, therefore, is to prop up poverty by practical arrangements at those critical periods when it is in danger of falling into indigence. The barrier between these two conditions in society is often slender, and the public interest requires that it should be narrowly guarded, since every individual who falls into indigence becomes a loss to the community, not only in the loss of productive labour, but also in an additional pressure on the community by the necessary support of the person and his family . . .*

---

1 Why does Colquhoun (Source 4.29) regard poverty as an essential part of society?

2 Why does he regard indigence as the 'evil' in society?

3 Why does he believe that it was in the public interest to provide measures to avoid indigence?

4 To what extent does Colquhoun agree with Malthus' views on the causes of poverty (Source 4.28)?

5 In what ways does Malthus' criticism of allowances on wages differ from the views expressed by Colquhoun?

6 Who was more sympathetic to the condition of the poor – Malthus or Colquhoun? Justify your answer with evidence drawn from the sources.

---

● **SOURCE 4.30**

From Rev. T. Thorp, *Individual Vice, Social Sin*, 1832, in which the author comments on the Church's attitude to poverty.

---

*For these things does my heart fail within me when I see in the poor, no marks of deference to the rich, in the ignorant none of submission to the wise, in the labourer none of attachment to his employer. When I hear no more . . . the sound of the shuttle in the cottage, nor the merry song in the fields; when I see boys lured to sin through the cheapness of drunkenness, and girls growing up to womanhood in ignorance of the simplest household cares; when I am told in a whisper, of evils of which Pauperism is the parent.*

---

1 What attitudes to the poor are shown by the Rev. Thorp in Source 4.30?

2 What reasons does the Rev. Thorp give for poverty amongst labourers?

3 To what extent does he agree with the views expressed by Malthus and Colquhoun?

● **SOURCE 4.31**

From *The Times*, 30 May 1816, commenting on the undermining of the moral character of the peasantry.

*Much of the disorderly conduct of the lower orders is doubtless owing to the habits generated by the existing system of the poor-laws . . .*

*. . . Without a fundamental change, it is clear that the moral character of that peasantry which has been described as 'its country's pride' must be entirely destroyed; and that even the present enormous burden of eight millions annually, which the poor-rates impose on the industry and capital of the country, must be rapidly increased.*

I   What is *The Times* referring to in Source 4.31 when it comments upon the 'disorderly conduct of the lower orders'? (Refer back to Source 4.15 for information.)

2   What criticism does *The Times* direct against the system of poor relief in 1816?

3   What connection is *The Times* making between the old Poor Law and the events of 1816?

● **SOURCE 4.32**

From the *Report from the Commissioners on the Poor Laws*, Appendix A, Part I, 1834, in which Henry Everett, who covered parts of East Anglia for the Royal Commission, comments upon reasons for the increase in poor rates.

*The great increase in the amount of the poor-rates of late years, I believe to be principally attributable to the shameful deterioration of the labouring classes, and to the utter want of that spirit of independence of others, and reliance upon his own exertions for his support, which formerly characterised an English peasantry. There are few persons to be found, amongst the labouring classes, who will struggle to maintain their families without parish help. The object with them is to get as much as possible from the parish; and a man whose average earnings during the year are fully sufficient to support his family, is frequently the person who receives the most in the shape of relief from the parish.*

I   According to Source 4.32, what was the reason for the rise in the amount of poor rates?

2   What does Henry Everett identify as the effects of poor relief on the moral character of the poor?

3   To what extent was there continuity between the comments of *The Times* in 1816 and those expressed by the Royal Commission in 1834?

● **SOURCE 4.33**

From S. G. Checkland and E. O. A. Checkland (eds), *The Poor Law Report of 1834*, 1974, in which Edwin Chadwick describes Cookham, a model parish which had imposed task work on the able-bodied at very low wages.

**dispauperised**
the ending of the allowance system and the return to the system of providing indoor relief inside a workhouse.

*I visited several of the residences of the labourers at their dinnertime, and I observed that in every instance meat formed part of the meal, which appeared to be ample, and was set forth in a very cleanly manner . . . I noticed some very trim hedges and ornaments in the gardens of the labourers, and it was stated to me that nothing of that sort had been seen in those places before the parishes had been DISPAUPERISED. Mr Knapp, the assistant overseer, stated that the labourers were no longer afraid of having a good garden with vegetables and fruit in it; they were no longer 'afraid of having a pig', and no longer 'afraid of being tidy'. Before the changes took place he had been in public-houses, and had seen paupers drunk there . . .*

I   What criticisms are made in Sources 4.32 and 4.33 of the unreformed old Poor Law?

2   Why had the labourers of Cookham been afraid of having a good garden, and a pig, and of being tidy under the unreformed Poor Law?

3   How might the evidence of Source 4.33 be used to support the claims made by *The Times* newspaper and Henry Everett (Sources 4.31 and 4.32)?

# 4 Which interest groups defended the old Poor Law?

Malthus and many contemporaries attacked the old Poor Law for creating the poor that it maintained. They believed that the allowance system encouraged laziness, drunkenness and early marriages with their attendant large families. They were influenced by the writings of economists such as David Ricardo, who developed the 'iron law of wages theory'. This was based on the idea that there was a fixed sum of money available for distribution. The more money that was used to raise the pay of labourers through allowances, the less was available for independent labourers. Contemporaries were worried that a subsidised Poor Law would lead to a crisis in the supply of capital for investment. However, not everyone criticised the old Poor Law, or regarded the allowance system as the cause of poverty and pauperism.

● **SOURCE 4.34**

From William Cobbett, *Two-Penny Trash*, Vol. 1, No. 6, December 1830, in which the radical journalist warns against those who wish to abolish the old Poor Law.

*. . . the labouring people of England, inherit, from their fathers, not any principle, not any doctrine, not any rule or maxim relative to this matter, but the habit of regarding parish relief as their right . . . These projectors [of poor law reform] ought to have known something of the habit of the people's mind in this respect. Every one of them looks upon it that he has a species of property in his parish they talk of losing their parish as a man talks of losing his estate . . . Now, men may talk, and do whatever else they please, as long as they please, they will never persuade the labourers of England, that a living out of the land is not their right in exchange for the labour which they yield or tender.*

I  How, according to Cobbett in Source 4.34, did the labouring people regard poor relief?

● **SOURCE 4.35**

From William Cobbett, *Political Register*, 14 December 1833, in which he attacks the ideas of thinkers like Malthus.

**Malthusian**
a term used to describe anyone who wanted to reform the old Poor Law.

**idlers**
probably refers to those able-bodied who were regarded as too lazy to work.

**parochial**
parish

**feelosofers**
'philosophers', a term used contemptuously by Cobbett to describe people such as Malthus.

*In the year 1821 I addressed a letter to Mr SCARLETT, upon the subject of his bringing in a bill, founded upon the MALTHUSIAN scheme. His declaration was, 'that the poor would consume the whole of the landed property, unless they were put a stop to.' I showed him that it was not the poor, but the IDLERS, who were consuming the property of the country; that the increase of the poor rates was only a proof of the reduction of the just payment for labour. The poor rates were, in fact, a debt contracted with the working people, who had been stripped of their little property by degrees. They were undergoing constant deductions from their wages, so as to render PAROCHIAL relief absolutely necessary to the maintenance of life; and that it was unjust, and monstrously unjust, to reproach the working people with the amount of the poor rates . . .*

*. . . But, now, suppose a township or a parish to contain a thousand working men, all working at something or another, either farmers, tradesmen, artisans, labourers, doctors, attorneys, or something, so as for them to be useful to one another, everyone yielding to the other his services, his goods or the use of his skill. Suppose that, all at once, God were to afflict this parish with the insane desire of having five idlers to every three and a half working men: and, further, to hurt this community with the willingness to consent to each of these idlers having three, four, or five times as much to live upon as every working man. Must not the working men become degraded and miserable wretches? Oh, no! say Brougham and his FEELOSOFERS; for the idlers would give employment to the working men; they would give them their money back again. Aye, but they must work for it and earn it back, after having earned it the first time to give it to them.*

I  What were the principal causes of poverty and pauperism, according to Cobbett (Source 4.35)?

2  Why is Cobbett so hostile towards those he described as 'idlers'?

3  Why does Cobbett regard the poor as victims of oppression?

● **SOURCE 4.36**

Adapted from the *Main Recommendations of the Poor Law Commissioners of 1834*, in which a Poor Law commissioner describes the treatment of a pauper family by a magistrate who took a paternalist attitude towards relief.

*A pauper named Sutton returned to the parish with his wife and child, having been away for some time, and applied for relief and clothes for himself and family. The overseers, suspecting that he possessed clothes, managed to get him and his wife out of the room, keeping his little girl in, and then asked the child where her Sunday frock was. She answered that it was locked up in a box at Cambridge with other things. Here the mother came in to call the girl out, but the overseers would not let her go, whereupon the father came in with a bludgeon, and seized the child by the arm. The overseers held her, but the father pulling her so as to hurt her, they let her go, and he took her out and beat her violently. He then returned, demanding relief, which they refused. He then abused them dreadfully, threatening to rip up one, burn the town etc., and behaved with such violence that they were compelled to have him handcuffed and his legs tied, and he was wheeled in a barrow to the magistrate, where they charged him with assault. The magistrate asked whether they could swear they were in bodily fear of Sutton, and they replying that they were not, he dismissed the charge and ordered Sutton relief.*

I   Why had the overseers in Source 4.36 refused Sutton relief?

2   In what way did Sutton show that he regarded receiving poor relief as his right?

3   Why didn't the magistrate regard the pauper Sutton as having committed a crime?

4   What use could those who were critical of the allowance system make of the Sutton case?

You should now be in a position to evaluate

a)  the arguments put forward by contemporaries for dealing with the problems of increasing pauperism. These could be summarised as
   • replace or amend the existing Poor Law          • maintain the existing Poor Law
   • remove the Poor Law
b)  the nature of nineteenth-century attitudes, including attitudes towards poverty
c)  the arguments used by different groups/individuals to support their views on poverty and poor relief.

Either individually or working in a group, choose one of the themes above and review the collection of documents in sections 3 and 4. You should then present your findings as

a)  a contribution to a class discussion, **or**
b)  a presentation to the rest of the group, **or**
c)  a report or essay recording your findings.

# 5 What was the role of the agricultural riots of 1830 in the eventual reform of the old Poor Law?

Those who defended the rights of the poor had very little effect on the politicians of the day. Most educated people accepted the idea that the poor laws 'create[d] the poor which they maintain[ed]', (from Schools Council History 13–16 Project, *Britain 1815–51*, Holmes McDougall, 1977, page 63) a view advocated by economists like David Ricardo (see page 136). Resentment at the increasing financial burden of poor relief stemmed from the burden it placed on property owners, who were required to pay the poor rates. This led to a harsher attitude and a desire to reduce the numbers seeking help. The philosopher Jeremy Bentham advocated stronger control by central government over the administration of the poor laws, a view that was becoming increasingly popular.

Events came to a climax in 1830. The newspaper *The Annual Register* reported that 'from the latter end of October [1830], the southern counties were kept in a state of great alarm. Stacks and farm buildings were set on fire during the night, and these atrocities extended into Cambridgeshire and the eastern counties. The peasantry, too, in many places, particularly in Hampshire, Wiltshire, Kent and Berkshire, assembled into tumultuous crowds, in order to obtain an increase in wages; destroyed mills, and other machinery and proceeded to other acts of outrageous violence.' These disturbances are sometimes known as the 'Swing' riots.

## ● SOURCE 4.37

From W. H. Hudson, *A Shepherd's Life*, 1910, in which the author records the grievances of agricultural labourers in Wiltshire in 1830.

*I can understand how it came about that these poor labourers, poor spiritless slaves as they had been made by long years of extremist poverty and systematic oppression, rose at last against their hard masters and smashed the agricultural machines, and burnt ricks and broke into houses to destroy and plunder their contents. It was a desperate, a mad adventure . . . but oppression had made them mad; the introduction of the threshing machines was but the last straw . . . It was not merely the fact that the wages of a strong man were only seven shillings a week at the outside, a sum barely sufficient to keep him and his family from starvation and rags (as a fact it was not enough, and but for a little poaching and stealing he could not have lived), but it was customary, especially on the small farms, to get rid of the men after the harvest and leave them to exist the best way they could during the bitter winter months. Thus every village, as a rule, had its dozen or twenty or more men thrown out each year . . . and besides these there were the aged and weaklings and the lads who had not yet got a place. The misery of these out-of-work labourers was extreme. They would go to the woods and gather faggots of dead wood, which they would try to sell in the villages; but there were few who could afford to buy them; and at night they would skulk about the fields to rob a swede or two to satisfy the cravings of hunger.*

> **1** What were the causes of the agricultural riots of 1830, according to W. H. Hudson in Source 4.37?

## ● SOURCE 4.38

From the *Main Recommendations of the Poor Law Commissioners of 1834*, which gives an interpretation of the causes of the 1830 riots.

*It appears from all our returns, especially from the replies to the rural queries, that in every district, the discontent of the labouring classes is proportioned to the money dispensed in poor rates, or in voluntary charities . . . The violence of most of the mobs seems to have arisen from an idea that all their hardships arose from the greed or fraud of those entrusted with the management of the fund provided for the poor. Whatever addition is made to allowances under these circumstances excites the expectation of still further allowances, increases the conception of the extent of the right, and ensures proportionate disappointment and hatred if that expectation is not fulfilled.*

> **1** What were the causes of the agricultural riots of 1830, according to Source 4.38?

## ● SOURCE 4.39

Compiled from Rural Question 53, *Report of the Royal Commission on the Poor Law*, Vol. XXXIV, 1834.

Causes of the 1830 Swing riots.

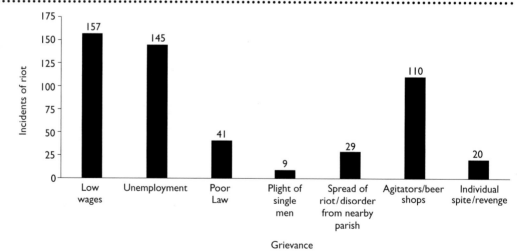

> **1** According to Source 4.39, what were the three most important causes of the riots (in order of importance)?
>
> **2** What were the two least important reasons?
>
> **3** How important was the sense of grievance over the Poor Law in the overall list of grievances?
>
> **4** What conclusions can be drawn from the evidence of Source 4.39 about the condition of labourers?
>
> **5** What effect was their condition likely to have on labourers' attitudes?
>
> **6** Were the Poor Law commissioners justified in their conclusions (Source 4.38) that the poor laws, particularly the allowance system, were to blame for the outbreak of the 1830 riots?

6 **What were the main achievements of the Poor Law Commission, 1832–34?**

139

What were the main achievements of the Poor Law Commission, 1832–34?

In February 1832 a Royal Commission was set up to investigate whether a change to the Poor Law was necessary and, if so, how this could be achieved. The actions of the government were motivated by a number of long- and short-term considerations:

- criticisms of the allowance system, which was seen as a direct encouragement to idleness
- a belief, which grew stronger in the 1820s, that poor relief was being mismanaged, making it expensive and inefficient
- concern over the financial burden of the poor rate, which peaked in the years 1817–19
- the depressed condition of agriculture, which increased the number of poor
- the threat to public order and property in the agricultural districts presented by the Swing riots of 1830.

**utilitarianism**
was a political philosophy associated with the writings of the philosopher and lawyer Jeremy Bentham (1748–1832). He judged institutions by their practical usefulness. Bentham believed that governments should be guided by the principle of maximising happiness and benefiting as many people as possible, to give the greatest happiness to the greatest number. This philosophy had most impact on social policy, especially in changes to the Poor Laws and in the proposals of Edwin Chadwick for public health. Utilitarians or Benthamites, as they are often referred to, believed that progress and policies should be based on evidence and research. The main flaw to this philosophy was that minorities could suffer as a result of serving the interests of the majority.

The governing classes felt that, despite costly poor relief, the poor had not been satisfied; the Poor Law was therefore considered a failure. Discontented people, gathered together in large numbers, seemed to be a threat to property and the established social order. It was felt that since a paternalistic system of relief had failed to cement labourers' loyalty, a harsher system of social control might be needed. The Swing riots dealt a deathblow to the old Poor Law and speeded up reform. The poor could not be left to starve, if only because this would drive them to commit further acts of desperation, so the sheer impracticality of total abolition meant that discussion was focused on options for reform.

The Commission had representatives from a number of interest groups: reformers, churchmen, political economists, such as Nassau Senior, and utilitarian Benthamites, in the person of Edwin Chadwick. The latter acted as secretary to the Commission and wrote the final report. This is seen as a statement for a Benthamite solution to the problem of poor relief. Benthamism or *UTILITARIANISM* judged everything in terms of its usefulness or its utility. If an institution did not work then it had either to be made to work or be abolished. Jeremy Bentham believed that people pursued pleasure and avoided pain. This meant that social policy had to be based on a system of reward or punishment. If people knew that their actions would be punished then they would avoid such actions in favour of those that would bring them advantages.

The Commission employed 26 assistant commissioners to collect evidence on the working of the allowance system, the Roundsman system and the poor rate administration in each district. Evidence was gathered through a questionnaire, with the commissioners additionally visiting roughly one-fifth of the existing Poor Law authorities. This evidence was combined selectively into the report of the Royal Commission in thirteen volumes of appendices. It was the first serious, systematic social investigation of modern times. However, judged by modern standards, the report itself has been criticised for its failure to analyse potentially valuable data on the condition of England and its system of poor relief. In the view of many historians, the commissioners had already decided the outcome of their investigations – namely that the old system was in need of reform.

# What criticisms did the Royal Commission make of the existing Poor Laws?

● SOURCE 4.40

Adapted from the *Main Recommendations of the Poor Law Commissioners of 1834*, in which the commissioners report on examples of what they regard as the evils of the old system.

### (i) An encouragement for children

*Four men were working together near a farmhouse; upon questioning them as to the wages they were earning, one among them who informed us that he was thirty years old and unmarried, complained much of the lowness of his wages, and added, without a question on the subject being put to him 'that if he was married and had a parcel of children, he should be better off as he should have either work given him by the parish or receive allowances for his children'.*

### (ii) An encouragement of idleness and vice in the workhouse

*But in by far the greater number of cases, it [the workhouse] is a large almshouse, in which the young are trained in idleness, ignorance and vice; the able-bodied maintained in sluggish indolence . . . and the whole body of inmates subsisted on food far exceeding in kind and amount, not merely the diet of the independent labourer, but that of the majority of the persons who contribute to their support.*

### (iii) A cause of bankruptcy of parishes

*. . . it appears that in this parish [Cholesbury, Buckinghamshire] the population, which has been almost stationary since 1801, has steadily climbed . . . the poor rates were only £10 10s. [£10.50] and only one person received poor relief . . . in 1832 . . . it was proceeding at the rate of £367 per year. Suddenly ceased in consequence at the impossibility to continue its collection.*

### (iv) An opportunity for employer abuse of the old Poor Law

*The employers of paupers are attached to a system which enables them [the employers] to dismiss and resume [the paupers'] labours to their daily or even hourly want of them, to reduce wages to a minimum of what will support an unmarried man and to throw upon others the payment of a part, frequently the greater part, and sometimes the whole of the wages actually received by their labourers.*

### (v) A discouragement to work

*. . . consider the case of the labourers with four children for the subsistence of which family, according to the Chelmsford scale, 11s. 6d. [57½p] is required. Of this sum the good labourer earns 10s. [50p], from the parish 1s. 6d. [7½p]. The man who does not work, and whom no one will employ, receives the whole from the parish.*

### (vi) A discouragement to save

*He [William Williams, an industrious labourer] told me [Mr Hickson, a manufacturer] at the time I was obliged to part with him: 'Whilst I have these things I shall get no work; I must part with all my savings; I must be reduced to a state of beggary before anyone will employ me.' I was compelled to part with him at Michaelmas; he has not yet got work, and he has no chance of getting any until he is a pauper, for until then, the paupers will be preferred to him. He cannot get work in his own parish, and he will not be allowed to get any in other parishes.*

### (vii) A discouragement to good personal habits

*[According to] Mr Issac Wilis, collector of the poor rates in the parish of St Mary-le-Bow, London . . . the independent labourer is comparatively clean in person, his wife and children are clean and the children go to school, the house in better order and more cleanly. Those who depend upon parish relief or on the benefactions, on the contrary, are dirty in their persons and slothful in their ways; the children are allowed to go about the streets in a vagrant condition.*

### (viii) A discouragement to care of the elderly and ill

*Those whose minds, say Messrs Wrottesley and Cameron, have been moulded by the operation of the Poor Laws, appear not to have the slightest scruple in asking to be paid for those domestic duties which the most brutal savages are in general willing to give free to their own family. 'Why should I tend my sick and aged parents when the parish is bound to do it or if I am to perform this service, why should I excuse the parish, which is bound to pay for it?'*

1  What criticisms does the Royal Commission make in Source 4.40 of the existing poor laws?

2  To what extent were the commissioners influenced in their conclusions by prevailing contemporary views on the evils of the old Poor Law?

141

# What recommendations were contained in the 1834 Report of the Royal Commission on the Poor Law?

● **SOURCE 4.41**

Adapted from the *Main Recommendations of the Poor Law Commissioners of 1834*, in which the commissioners argue for a harsher system of poor relief.

***alms-giving***
the giving of assistance or help

***sound and well-defined principle***
a reference to the principle of less eligibility, making the condition of the poor who are claiming relief inferior to that of the independent labourer

***eligible***
desirable

***indolence and vice***
laziness and immorality

*Principles of a sound system*
*The most pressing of the evils . . . are those connected with the relief of the Able-bodied. They are the evils, therefore, for which we shall first propose remedies.*

*If we believed the evils stated in the previous part of the Report . . . to be necessarily unintentional . . . we should not hesitate in recommending its entire abolition. But we do not believe these evils to be its necessary consequences. We believe that, under strict regulations, adequately enforced, such relief may be afforded safely, and even beneficially.*

*In all extensive communities, circumstances will occur in which an individual, by the failure of his means of subsistence, will be exposed to the danger of perishing. To refuse relief, . . . when it cannot be proved that the offender could have obtained subsistence by labour, is offensive to the common sentiments of mankind . . . In all extensive civilised communities, therefore, the occurrence of extreme necessity is prevented by ALMS-GIVING, by public institutions.*

*But in no part of Europe except England has it been thought fit that the provision, whether compulsory or voluntary, should be applied to more than the relief of indigence, the state of a person unable to labour, or unable to obtain, in return for his labour, the means of subsistence; it has never been deemed expedient that the provision should extend to the relief of poverty; that is the state of one, who, in order to obtain a mere subsistence, is forced to have to work.*

*From the evidence collected under this Commission, we are induced to believe that a compulsory provision for the relief of the indigent can be generally administered on a SOUND AND WELL-DEFINED PRINCIPLE; and that under the operation of this principle, the assurance [can be given] that no one need perish. It may be assumed, that in the administration of relief, the public is warranted in imposing conditions . . . The first and most essential of all conditions, a principle which we find universally admitted, . . . is, that his situation on the whole shall not be made really or apparently as ELIGIBLE as the situation of the independent labourer of the lowest class. Throughout the evidence it is shown, that in proportion as the condition of any pauper class is raised above the condition of independent labourers, the condition of the independent class is depressed; their work is reduced, their employment becomes unsteady, and its payment in wages is diminished. Such persons, therefore, are under the strongest inducements to quit the less eligible class of labourers, and enter the more eligible class of paupers. The opposite is the effect when the pauper class is placed in its proper position, below the condition of the independent labourer. Every penny bestowed, that tends to make the position of the pauper more eligible than that of the independent labourer, is a reward on INDOLENCE AND VICE. We have found that as the poor-rates are at present administered, they operate as rewards of this description, to the amount of several millions annually.*

*The standard, therefore, to which reference must be made in fixing the condition of those who are to be maintained by the public, is the condition of those who are maintained by their own labour . . .*

1  On what grounds do the commissioners in Source 4.41 argue against an abolition of the Poor Law?

2  What distinction do the commissioners make between indigence and poverty?

3  Why do the commissioners argue that the condition of the pauper should be 'less eligible' than that of the independent labourer?

4  How was the principle of 'less eligibility' meant to work?

5  How do the commissioners hope to improve the moral character of the poor by the application of the principle of less eligibility?

● **SOURCE 4.42**

Adapted from the *Main Recommendations of the Poor Law Commissioners of 1834*, in which the commissioners express concern for the effect of poverty on the moral character of labourers.

**improvident marriages**
marriages entered into with no thought for how the couple could support themselves and a family

**transported**
sent overseas to one of the colonies (e.g. Australia) as a punishment for crime

**felonies**
crimes

**industry**
willingness to work hard

**frugal habits**
efforts to save money and live within their means

*Effect of dispauperisation on morals*
. . . application of the principle of keeping the condition of the pauper inferior to that of the independent labourer . . . has stopped the increase of population, . . . In the Report from Cookham, it is stated, that 'some very striking consequences have resulted from the operation of the present system. In the eight years preceding, IMPROVIDENT MARRIAGES are less frequent.' In the Report from Swallowfield, it is stated that, 'the number of improvident marriages is fallen about one half.' In Bingham, the reduction in improvident marriages was about one-half; and yet in all these parishes, illegitimate births, instead of having been promoted by the decreasing of marriages, have been repressed still more effectually, and in the last, almost extinguished . . .

Whatever forces any class into sustained work must necessarily decrease crime; and we find that one characteristic of the dispauperised parishes is the comparative absence of crime. In Bingham, before the change of system took place, scarcely a night passed without mischief; and during the two years preceding 1818, seven men of the parish were TRANSPORTED for FELONIES; now there is scarcely any disorder in the place. In Uley and Southwell parishes crime has similarly ceased.

In almost every instance the content of the labourers increased with their work . . . We have seen that in every instance in which the able-bodied labourers have been made independent of partial relief, or of relief otherwise than in a well-regulated workhouse:

- their INDUSTRY has been restored and improved
- FRUGAL HABITS have been created or strengthened
- the permanent demand for their labour has increased
- their wages, so far from being depressed by the increased amount of labour in the market, have in general advanced
- the number of improvident and wretched marriages has declined
- their discontent has been lessened, and their moral and social condition in every way improved.

---

1 According to the commissioners in Source 4.42, what were the effects of dispauperisation on
  a) marriage rates
  b) crime levels
  c) the moral character of labourers
  d) demand for labour
  e) wages
  f) level of social unrest?

2 To what extent were the commissioners influenced by the views of Thomas Malthus in their accounts of the effects of dispauperisation?

---

● **SOURCE 4.43**

Adapted from the *Main Recommendations of the Poor Law Commissioners of 1834*, in which the commissioners recommend specific reforms.

*Proposed abolition of outdoor relief to the able-bodied*
The chief specific measures which we recommend for effecting these purposes are —
First, that except as to medical attendance, and subject to the exception respecting apprenticeship hereinafter stated, all relief whatever to able-bodied persons or to their families, otherwise than in well-regulated workhouses (i.e. places where they may be set to work according to the spirit and intention of the 43rd Elizabethan statute) shall be declared unlawful, and shall cease, . . . and that all relief afforded in respect of children under the age of 16 shall be considered as afforded to their parents . . .

*Need of central supervision*
. . . We recommend, therefore, the appointment of a Central Board to control the administration of the Poor Laws, with such Assistant Commissioners as may be found necessary; and that the Commissioners be empowered and directed to frame and enforce regulations for the government of workhouses, and as to the nature and amount of the relief to be given and the labour to be exacted in them, and that such regulations shall, as far as may be practicable, be uniform throughout the country . . .

## Segregation in workhouses

We suggest at least four classes are necessary:

1 Aged and really impotent;
2 Children;
3 Able-bodied females;
4 Able-bodied males.

Of whom we trust that the two latter will be the least numerous classes. Each class might thus receive appropriate treatment; the old might enjoy their pleasures without torment from the boisterous; the children might be educated, and the able-bodied subjected to labour and discipline as will ward off the indolent and vicious.

We recommend that:

The Central Board be empowered to cause any number of parishes to be incorporated for the purpose of workhouse management, and for providing new workhouses where necessary, to declare their workhouses to be the common workhouses of the incorporated district, and to assign to those workhouses separate classes of poor, each distinct parish paying to the support of the permanent workhouse establishment, and paying separately for the food and clothing of its own paupers.

## Further recommendations

We recommend, that the Central Board be empowered and required to take measures to:

- ensure a uniform system of accounts . . .
- appoint and pay permanent officers, and for the execution of works of public labour . . .
- state the general qualifications which shall be necessary to candidates for paid offices connected with the relief of the poor
- direct the PAROCHIAL CONSUMPTION to be supplied by tender and contract, and to provide that the competition be perfectly free . . .
- empower parishes to treat any relief afforded to the able-bodied, or to their families, and any expenditure in the workhouses, or otherwise incurred on their account, as a loan, and recoverable not only by the means given by the 29th Section of the 59th GEO. III. C. 12, but also by attachment of their subsequent wages, IN A MODE RESEMBLING THAT POINTED OUT IN THE 30TH, 31ST, AND 32ND, SECTIONS OF THAT ACT
- make such regulations as they shall think fit respecting the relief to be afforded by apprenticing children
- submit a Report annually, to one of Your Majesty's Principal Secretaries of State, containing an Account of their Proceedings; any further amendments which they may think it advisable to suggest;
- appoint and remove their Assistants and all their subordinate officers . . .

Every illegitimate child born after the passing of the Act, shall, until it attain the age of sixteen, follow its mother's settlement . . .

The mother of an illegitimate child born after the passing of the Act, [shall] be required to support it, and . . . any relief occasioned by the wants of the child [shall] be considered relief afforded to the parent . . . the same liability be extended to her husband . . .

The vestry of each parish [shall] be empowered to order the payment out of the rates raised for the relief of the poor, of the expenses of the emigration of any persons having settlements within such parish, who may be willing to emigrate; provided, that the expense of each emigration be raised and paid, within a period to be mentioned in the Act.

**parochial consumption**
provisions required for the workhouse

**59th Geo. III. C.12**
refers to Sturge Bourne's Act of 31 March 1819, to amend laws for the relief of the poor. The Act gave powers to those parishes that wanted to appoint small committees or select vestries of leading inhabitants to scrutinise the granting of poor relief. It also enabled them to appoint salaried assistant overseers to help the unpaid, part-time overseer with his increasing workload. The Act saved parishes, who wanted to improve their administration of poor relief, from seeking a private act of Parliament – a lengthy and expensive process.

**in a mode resembling . . . sections of that Act**
i.e. by setting the poor to work

143

What were the main achievements of the Poor Law Commission, 1832–34?

1   What did the Commission recommend in relation to relief of the poor (Source 4.43)?

2   To what extent would these recommendations disappoint the Malthusian critics of the old Poor Law?

3   What benefits can you infer that the commissioners believed would result from their recommendations in regard to future relief?

4   What did the commissioners claim to be the advantages of segregated workhouses?

5   What further recommendations were proposed which represented a return to strong central control?

6   What recommendations did the commissioners make to ensure a uniformity of approach in relation to the application of poor relief?

7   Do you think that the commissioners' recommendations would successfully solve the root problems of poverty? (Refer back to section 1 if necessary.)

8   To what extent did the Royal Commission report answer contemporary criticisms of the old Poor Law? Use a copy of the table below to organise your answer.

| Criticism | Royal Commission's recommendations |
|---|---|
| Allowance system's encouragement of idleness | |
| Mismanagement of poor relief at local level | |
| Financial burden – expensive and inefficient relief | |
| Harmful effect on moral character of poor | |
| Poverty as a crime | |

## ● Summary task

1   **A case study**
Below is a collection of sources, taken from the parish records of St Peter Chesil, Winchester, in the Hampshire Records Office, charting the experiences of the Taylor family over the twenty-year period 1816–36. Read the sources and then answer the questions that follow – these focus on an evaluation of the extent to which there was continuity between the old and new systems of poor relief.

*Extracts from table of overseers' expenditure*

*Weekly payments from 25th March 1816 to 25th March 1817*
*Thomas Bailey and Edward Godric*

|  | £ | s. | d. |
|---|---|---|---|
| *Taylor's family, Portsea* | 7 | 0 | 0 |

*Weekly payments from 25th March 1817 to 25th March 1818*

|  | £ | s. | d. |
|---|---|---|---|
| *Taylor's family, Portsea* | 7 | 0 | 0 |

**Disbursements paid by Mr Pyke** 1817

|  | £ | s. | d. |
|---|---|---|---|
| *July 25 Mr Bailey for Taylor Portsea to June 21st* | 3 | 10 | 0 |

£3 10s. 0d. = £3.50

*1822*
*Sir*
*I shall be very much obliged to you if you will be so good as to send me a TRIFELL of money as times is very bad with me at present I have had but one weeks work since I was with you*

*For Mr Churley*
*I remain your humble servant John Taylor*

**trifell**
John Taylor's mis-spelling of 'trifle', meaning an insignificant amount.

Portsea Parish
May 16 1822
*Gentl*
*A very aged person by the name of John Taylor, who applied to you some time since who used to have 3s. [15p] per week, and on his appearing before you his relief was increased to 4s. [20p] per week, it appears that there is some difficulty in their obtaining the relief from Mr Woodman.*

*They are deserving people, the man is above 80, the woman 71, and a blind daughter I believe nearly 40. They are very poor but honest people, the old man is past labour and the woman is a little employed by some who has her services for the past 20 years, and although not capable of performing a day's work, yet they so respect the old woman, to give her a little employment. Mr Woodman has refused to pay them more than 3s. [15p] a week. I give you my word that they are every way deserving of your attention – if you choose we will pay them the 4s. [20p] per week, as it will be more convenient for them to receive it of us, and we shall apply for it once a year or every 6 months. Any further information I shall willingly give. Please to send me your answer.*
*I am*
*Mr Whillier*
*Vestry clerk*
*[To] Overseers St Peter's*

Parish of Portsea
3rd March 1823
*Gentl*
*At foot, I hand you the amount paid by us to John Taylor his wife and blind daughter agreeably to your order which you will not fail to remit by the 25th as we balance our accounts at that period.*
*I am*
*Mr Whillier*
*Vestry Clerk*
*45 weeks to 25 Mar at 4s. £9.0.0*
*[To] Overseer Cheesehill*

Portsea Parish
Mar 24th 1823
*Sir*
*I have to acknowledge the receipt of £9 advance by us to J. Taylor, and at the same time I must beg to call your attention to the very distressed state they are now in. Taylor is above 80 years of age, his wife is above 70 and a blind daughter above 30. The old man a short time since was suddenly seized as to render it impossible to get him upstairs. A medical gentleman Dr Cooper was called in and he is recovered partially from that attack and the surgeon has ordered him nourishing food, which has in a manner been scantily supplied by the hand of charity, and the old woman who has been the* STAFF *of the family of late, is so* PALSIED *by her over exertion of work, as to render her employment very precarious, as she only gets employed by a few persons who she has worked for (some of above 25 years) and they employ her more for the respect they have for her and her extreme poverty than for the work she can perform. I should think that the old man cannot survive long and I think that it is impossible for them to struggle on without a further assistance. I should suggest 7s. [35p] per week during his illness. I assure you that I would not recommend the case unless it was urgent. If you wish I will send you the doctor's certificate or any other information you may wish. Your early answer will oblige.*
*Your most obliging humble servant*
*Mr Whillier*
*Vestry Clerk*
*[To] Mr Charles Lucas*

**staff**
the main support of her family

**palsied**
weak, almost helpless

### Printed bill sent to the overseers of St Peter's from Portsea

*The Churchwardens and Overseers of the Parish of St Peter, Cheesehill*
*To the Churchwardens and Overseers of the Parish of Portsea, in the County of Hants*

| Relief given to | From | To | No. of weeks | Per week | £ | s. | d. |
|---|---|---|---|---|---|---|---|
| Mr Taylor | 26 March 1828 | 25 March 1829 | 52 | 6s. [30p] | 15 | 12 | 0 |

*Gentlemen*
*As above I send your Account due to this parish, and request you will have the goodness to send an immediate Remittance, as we close our Accounts on the 25th March, next.*

*I am*
*Gentlemen,*
*Your Obedient Servant,*                          *March 26, 1829*
*Mr Whillier*                                      *The above came safe to hand*
*Vestry Clerk*                                     *Mr Whillier*

Portsea Parish
Mar 5 1829
*Memo – The widow Taylor is 79 years of age and so afflicted with the palsy that she cannot keep herself clean without assistance and her daughter is 35 years of age and blind – I have given them some assistance for a few weeks which is not charged to you, they are very worthy people but unless some addition is made to their relief it will be impossible for them to get on. I should not recommend them to your notice if their case was not bad.*
*Mr Whillier*

### Printed bills sent to the overseers of St Peter's from Portsea

*The Churchwardens and Overseers of the Parish of St Peter Cheesehill*
*To the Churchwardens and Overseers of the Parish of Portsea, in the County of Hants*

| Relief given to | From | To | No. of weeks | Per week | £ | s. | d. |
|---|---|---|---|---|---|---|---|
| Mr Taylor | 25 March 1829 | 25 March 1830 | 52 | 6s. | 15 | 12 | 0 |

*Gentlemen*
*As above I send your Account due to this parish, and request you will have the goodness to send an immediate Remittance, as we close our Accounts on the 25th March, next.*

*I am*
*Gentlemen,*
*Your Obedient Servant,*                          *March 26, 1830*
*Mr Whillier*                                      *The above came safe to hand*
*Vestry Clerk*                                     *Mr Whillier*

147

What were the main achievements of the Poor Law Commission, 1832–34?

*The Overseers of St Peter's Cheesehill*
*To Portsea Parish*

| | £ | s. | d. |
|---|---|---|---|
| *Relief advanced since Sept 20 1834 to March 25 1835* | | | |
| *Widow Taylor 26 weeks at 6s.* | 7 | 16 | 0 |
| *Carriage* | 0 | 1 | 0 |
| | 7 | 17 | 0 |

*Received the above by Mr Gardner March 16 1835*
*An early remittance will oblige*
*Mr Moorman, Vestry Clerk*

*The widow Taylor and her daughter lives in Chandos Street, Landport, Portsea*

⋯⋯⋯⋯⋯⋯⋯⋯⋯⋯⋯⋯⋯⋯⋯⋯⋯⋯⋯⋯⋯⋯⋯⋯⋯⋯⋯

*John Coles and William Hawkes, overseers in account with the Parish of St Peter's*
*Cheesehill from 25ᵗʰ March 1835 to 25ᵗʰ March 1836*

| | £ | s. | d. |
|---|---|---|---|
| *By relief to widow Taylor and daughter from 25ᵗʰ March to 29ᵗʰ September* | | | |
| *26 weeks at 3s each week* | 7 | 16 | 0 |
| *26ᵗʰ Sept By carriage of Taylor money* | 0 | 1 | 0 |

⋯⋯⋯⋯⋯⋯⋯⋯⋯⋯⋯⋯⋯⋯⋯⋯⋯⋯⋯⋯⋯⋯⋯⋯⋯⋯⋯

a) What does the history of the pauper family Taylor indicate about the working of the old Poor Law in respect of each of the following
   (i) the role of the parish overseer
   (ii) the different reasons for giving poor relief
   (iii) settlement laws (under which paupers could only claim relief from the parish of their birth)?
b) To what extent would critics of the old Poor Law quarrel with the relief given to the Taylor family?
c) Is it possible to tell whether Mr Whillier, the overseer for Portsea, was sympathetic to the condition of the Taylor family? Explain your answer fully, commenting on words, phrases, argument and tone.
d) How could
   (a) a critic
   (b) a defender
   of the old Poor Law make use of the Taylor case to support their arguments?
e) What continuities existed in the provision of poor relief for the Taylor family after 1834?

## 2 Local history investigation

The Poor Law provides excellent opportunities for examining a topic of national importance through a local study. This chapter has drawn on the experience of Hampshire and the evidence of the Taylor family over the twenty-year period 1816–36. Study of the operation of the Poor Law at local level provides opportunities for drawing comparisons to detect continuity and divergence from the national scene. The persistence of the allowance system after 1834 in the case of the Taylor family illustrates the relative failure of the framers of the 1834 act in achieving the principle of 'less eligibility', even though Winchester built a new workhouse on the model recommended by the 1834 act.

Much useful information can be obtained relating to workhouses and poor relief across the country. If you live in a northern industrial town you could compare the evidence of the predominantly rural Hampshire with your own locality, to draw out the influence of regional and economic differences on the operation of the Poor Law both before and after 1834. You might decide to concentrate on one aspect of the Poor Law, such as causes of poverty in your area, or a local or county workhouse, as the focus of your study. Much will depend on the availability of evidence. Useful sources of information can be found in local museums, libraries, or archive centres, not forgetting local history groups. Documents available could include parish records, workhouse admission and discharge registers, minutes of the parish vestries or workhouse Boards of Guardians, local newspapers (which may have advertisements for people to supply the workhouse, or photographs), workhouse architectural plans, trade directories, travellers' descriptions, Parliamentary reports, local town histories, and workhouse records.

# Examples of examination-type questions

## A  AS questions

1  a) What were the main causes of poverty in the early nineteenth century?
   b) How did different parishes attempt to deal with their poor?

2  a) What were the different forms of poor relief in operation by 1832?
   b) To what extent were contemporary criticisms of the old Poor Law justified?

3  a) Why did the cost of poor relief rise so dramatically between 1760 and 1832?
   b) What effect did this increase have on attitudes to the poor and poor relief?

4  a) What were the aims of the framers of the 1834 Poor Law Amendment Act?
   b) How did they attempt to achieve these aims?

5  a) What did the Poor Law Report mean by the principle of 'less eligibility'?
   b) How did the Poor Law commissioners propose to achieve this principle?

6  a) Why did the old Poor Law become a matter for concern by 1834?
   b) How far was the Poor Law Amendment Act an improvement upon the previous situation?

## B  A2 questions

1  'A flexible and humane system capable of adapting to new circumstances.' To what extent is this a valid comment on the Poor Law prior to 1834?

2  'Neither ramshackle nor disorganised, but reasonably successful' (E. C. Midwinter). To what extent is this a valid assessment of the operation of the Poor Law prior to 1834?

3  'A measure designed solely to cut costs.' How adequate a description is this of the aims of those who framed the Poor Law Amendment Act of 1834?

4  'Humane, diverse and lax.' To what extent is this an adequate description of the operation of the Poor Law prior to 1834?

5  To what extent would the framers of the Poor Law Amendment Act have been entitled to feel that they had improved on the situation existing before 1834?

---

### ● Further reading

D. Fraser, *The Evolution of the British Welfare State* (Macmillan, 1973); J. D. Marshall, *The Old Poor Law, 1795–1834* (Macmillan, 1968); G. Taylor, *The Problem of Poverty, 1660–1834* (Longman & Green, 1969)

**Articles**
A. Digby, 'The Poor Law in Nineteenth Century England', Historical Association pamphlet, 1982

chapter

# Did the new Poor Law achieve its aims between 1834 and 1905?

**1838**

Poor Relief Regulations allow the provision of relief as under the old system.

**1842**

The Outdoor Labour Test Order allows relief to able-bodied in return for task work.

**1843**

The Metropolitan Visiting and Relief Association is set up to provide local welfare.

**1844**

The Outdoor Relief Prohibitory Order bans outdoor relief to able-bodied men and women.
The first Retail Co-Operative Society is set up in Rochdale.

**1845**

The Andover scandal leads to a parliamentary inquiry in the following year which reveals mistreatment of paupers at the Andover workhouse.

**1847**

The Poor Law Board, under parliamentary control, replaces the Poor Law Commission.

**1849**

Henry Mayhew's report, *London Labour and the London Poor*, reveals that much poverty is due to an insufficiency of wages, challenging the idea that poverty is due to drunkenness or idleness.

**1852**

The third General Order, the Outdoor Relief Regulation Order, recognises that it is not possible to completely stop outdoor relief for the able-bodied.

**1858**

The Workhouse Visiting Society is formed to collect information on conditions and to press for improvements in the treatment of the sick or aged poor.

**1859**

Samuel Smiles' *Self-Help* outlines the philosophy underlying many Victorian attitudes to poverty and welfare.

**1865**

The Union Chargeability Act makes poor rates more equal between rich and poor areas.

**1867**

The Metropolitan Poor Act provides for the establishment of separate asylums for the sick and insane and dispensaries for outdoor medical relief.

## 1869

The Charity Organisation Society is set up to control the distribution of charity so that it encourages independence and self-help.

## 1870

The Local Government Board takes responsibility for the Poor Law and tries to restrict the availability of outdoor relief.

## 1886

Unemployment crisis; Chamberlain's Circular encourages local authorities to provide work schemes for the unemployed outside the Poor Law.

## 1889

Charles Booth's investigation into poverty in the East End of London, *Life and Labour of the People in London*, is published.

## 1901

Benjamin Seebohm Rowntree's investigation into poverty in York, *Poverty: A Study of Town Life*, is published.

## 1905–1909

The Royal Commission on the Poor Laws criticises the way poor relief is given but fails to agree on reform.

# 1 How successful was the introduction of the 1834 Poor Law Amendment Act?

Initially the framers of the 1834 act were entitled to feel that they had improved on the situation that had existed before 1834. They appeared to be successful because of the apparent ease with which the Amendment Act was passed (only 50 MPs voted against it), and the three commissioners were appointed at a salary of £2000 a year. They were Thomas Frankland Lewis, chairman, George Nicholls and John George Shaw-Lefevre. Edwin Chadwick, author of the 1834 report, who had hoped to be appointed a commissioner, was given the position of secretary at £1200 a year. Initially nine, but subsequently twenty-one, assistant commissioners were also recruited.

From its headquarters at Somerset House, the Poor Law Board quickly got down to its work of reorganising the administration of the Poor Law, beginning with the southern counties. Some months were spent in meeting with local people, making arrangements for the grouping of parishes into unions so that workhouses could be set up, setting the poor rates and establishing boards of guardians. Thus it was not until the spring of 1835 that the Poor Law unions were announced and regulations for giving relief were issued. The allowance system was banned for all able-bodied people, except in cases of sickness or accident.

Speedy progress was made in the south between 1834 and 1836, where the application of the act coincided with a revival in the local economy. The worst effects of the depression in agriculture wore off after 1836, with an improvement in the harvest and a growth of productivity in agriculture. There were also increased employment opportunities other than in agriculture as a result of the 'railway mania' which developed in the mid to later 1830s. In any case, the poverty problem in the south had always been seasonal rather than cyclical, in contrast with the north.

These three commissioners were subsequently increased to five: Thomas Frankland Lewis – a country gentleman; George Nicholls; John George Shaw-Lefevre; George Cornewall Lewis – son of T.F. Lewis; Edmund W. Head. See also source 5.10, page 156.

# How effective were the commissioners in applying the 1834 act in the south?

● **SOURCE 5.1**

From Nassau Senior to George Villiers, 1 December 1835, in which Senior (see page 46) comments on the effectiveness of the 1834 act in establishing central administration.

*Our domestic revolution is going on in the most peaceful and prosperous way. The Poor Law Act is covering England and Wales with a network of small aristocracies, in which the Guardians chosen by the occupiers and ratepayers are succeeding to the power and influence of the magistrates. By this time all Kent has been split into 21 Poor Law Unions, Sussex into certain others; in short, the old parochial authorities have been suspended in half the country already, and will be superseded in the rest by the end of next year. Fifteen Assistant Commissioners, with £1,000 a year to invigorate their exertions, are in constant motion to effect these operations, and ten more are to be added to them.*

> 1   What claims are made by Senior in Source 5.1 for the success of the Poor Law Commission in implementing the 1834 act?
>
> 2   How much reliance should the historian place on the statement of Senior that, 'Our domestic revolution is going on in the most peaceful and prosperous way'?

● **SOURCE 5.2**

From Edwin Chadwick to the Clerk of the Poor Law Guardians, St Luke Chelsea, 27 May 1843, in which Chadwick criticises the administration of the 1834 act in Chelsea.

*The Poor Law Commissioners regret to learn that their Assistant Commissioner, Mr Hall, on visiting the Chelsea workhouse, found it in a very unsatisfactory state. There was throughout a want of order, cleanliness, and ventilation, the heat in the female wards being excessive, in consequence of there being a number of unnecessarily large fires kept up . . .*

*Some of the paupers were in their own clothes, Article 7 of the workhouse rules having been, in this case, neglected.*

*Smoking was going on in several of the rooms, both bedrooms and day rooms. The Commissioners think the allowance of such a practice, particularly in the bedrooms, highly objectionable . . .*

*The Commissioners also learn that extra articles of food are freely admitted to be brought into the workhouse. Till Commissioners think it desirable that a dietary should be prescribed for the inmates of the workhouse . . . the practice of allowing provisions to be brought into the workhouse as presents, cannot, in the opinion of the Commissioners, fail to produce many Irregularities.*

> 1   What complaints does Edwin Chadwick make in Source 5.2 to the Clerk of the Poor Law Guardians about conditions in the St Luke Chelsea workhouse?
>
> 2   Why did the Poor Law Board regard the Board of Guardians at St Luke's as breaking the principle of less eligibility established by the 1834 act?
>
> 3   What may be inferred from Source 5.2 of the methods used by the Poor Law Commission to ensure central control and national uniformity?

● **SOURCE 5.3**

From T. M. Loveland, Clerk to the Board of Guardians, St Luke Chelsea, to the Poor Law Commissioners, 15 June 1843, in which he rejects the claims of and interference by the commissioners.

*The guardians . . . caused, on the receipt of your letter, a minute inspection of the house to be made, and have to state, that with the exception of the want of a little whitewashing, and that only here and there, . . . there is no want of order, cleanliness and ventilation in the Chelsea workhouse, as erroneously stated in your letter.*

*As to the charge of 'the heat in the female wards being excessive' . . . the guardians . . . find that there has been for some time past but one fire, and that only a moderate one, in the infirm wards.*

*As to some of the paupers wearing their own clothing, there are some who do; but they are of the elder class, and who have been allowed to wear their own clothes on account of their former respectability.*

*The guardians find [smoking] . . . is confined to five old infirm women, who smoke medicinally. Some old men also smoke, but which is allowed by the guardians.*

*As to 'extra articles of food' . . . these, the presents of friends, have been . . . permitted . . . but it is only to a trifling extent.*

1 What does the style and language of Mr Loveland's letter (Source 5.3) to the Poor Law commissioners imply about the relationship that existed between local Poor Law guardians and the central commissioners?

2 To what extent does Source 5.3 highlight the problems faced by the Poor Law Commission in achieving uniformity of approach?

3 How valid is it to claim that the cruelty of the new Poor Law lay more in its psychological impact than in its impact on people's physical condition?

## ● SOURCE 5.4

From *Operations of the Poor Law Amendment Act in the County of Sussex*, 1836, in which the auditor of the Uckfield Union in Sussex reports the beneficial effects of the new Poor Law.

> Sussex had been an area with a large number of paupers prior to the 1834 act.

*The annual average expenditure in the parishes forming this Union, for the years ending 1831–32, and 33, . . . produces £16,643 as the sum annually paid in parochial relief; this will show an average monthly expenditure of £1386, while a similar average on the Union expenditure, including the repairs and alterations to the workhouses, will be found not to exceed £550, being a difference of £836 per month, by which it will be seen a saving of £10,000 per annum will be ejected; and I will venture to assert, after having considered the question in all its bearings, that the sum [may be] looked on with reference to the ensuing year as a permanent reduction. But the mere saving of this sum is not the only nor yet the most important point of view in which the changes of the law should be regarded; the moral reformation effected, by checks given to vice, improvidence, and indolence, the stimulus offered to industry, and the means it has left in the hands of the rate-payers to reward that industry – have solved the question of surplus labour, by proving (in this Union at least) that where there exists a wish for employment, employment is to be found.*

*In the month of December, 1834, in the corresponding quarter of last year, upwards of 250 labourers were out of employment, and receiving relief for their families, although the state of the weather was not of such severity as at all to prevent the usual routine of a labourer's occupations.*

*In the quarter just past, at the end of a week's frost and when the snow had stopped most of the operations in agriculture, the greatest number of able-bodied men in the workhouses was 28 . . . as temporary shelter from the effects of circumstances over which they had no control, from a suspension of labour, not from want of employment.*

*The well-regulated system of employment, the boring detention, the discipline of our workhouses, and I trust a sincere desire to reform, has persuaded some who were unmarried to enlist as soldiers, and by thus entering the ranks in His Majesty's Services, they now form part of that body of men whose duty it is to support and maintain those laws and that peace which but a few months since they were among the foremost to outrage and disturb.*

*It is not from these circumstances alone that we have proofs of the beneficial operations of the bill; it may be sought for from other sources, not from the praise of its supporters, but in the complaints of its enemies, none of whom feel it more severely or complain more bitterly than the keepers of beer shops, and in short all that class of persons who were thriving on the improvidence and demoralisation of the labourer, but who now suffer from his reform.*

*The great mass of those individuals who were so noisy against the new enactments, on the ground of cruelty to the poor, are now silenced by the fact, that nearly two-thirds of the sum that they contributed, is left in their own hands, for their own distribution, according to their own discretion . . . [to be] dispensed as charity, to be received with gratitude, which was formerly claimed as a right, and exacted by intimidation.*

## ● SOURCE 5.5

From *Andover Workhouse Papers*, recording a letter that praises the effect of the new Poor Law on the character of the labourer by 1836.

> **sobriety**
> avoidance of alcohol

*Andover, May 2, 1836.*
*The result of my observations as to the moral effects of the new poor law system upon the general character of the labouring classes in this Union, is very satisfactory. The labourer has now to depend solely upon his own exertions and is thus obliged to exercise habits of foresight and frugality, and above all* SOBRIETY, *which under the old system was almost unknown. To prove the general improvement of morals, I will merely state that Beer houses have decreased; illicit connections and imprudent marriages have diminished.*

153

How successful was the introduction of the 1834 Poor Law Amendment Act?

1 What claims are made in Sources 5.4 and 5.5 that would have convinced the Poor Law commissioners that they had been successful in implementing the 1834 act? In your answer comment on each of the following
   a) expenditure on poor relief
   b) the character of the labouring poor.

2 What reasons are given for the changes reported upon by the auditor of the Uckfield Union in Source 5.4?

3 What evidence do the authors of Sources 5.4 and 5.5 quote to support their claims for the beneficial operation of the new Poor Law?

4 Why were those who had criticised the new Poor Law in Uckfield now 'silenced'?

## Did the commissioners meet any opposition in the south?

● SOURCE 5.6

From Poor Law Commission, *Second Annual Report*, 1836, in which W. J. Gilbert gives evidence of resistance to the introduction of the new Poor Law in Devon.

*Your orders and rules being calculated to lessen the resort to the beer-shop, and curtail the improper exercise of parish influence and parish funds, have here, as elsewhere, excited opposition amongst those parties who benefited by former abuses. The leaders of the opposition are to be found amongst the constant overseers (gentlemen accustomed to accept the office for £15 a year, and quit it with a well-furnished purse); the little shopkeeper, at whose house the poor were paid, and who received the amount for old debts and encouraged new, from which the pauper never got free; the beer-shop keeper, at whose house great part of the relief was spent; and the little farmer or the lime-kiln owner, whose influence at the vestry enabled him to pay one half of his labour from the parish funds, under the name of relief in aid of wages, or to speak correctly, relief in aid of vestrymen.*

*Wherever disturbances have taken place, they have been traced to the instigation of some or one of these parties. In the north of the county, where there were some disturbances, we found that the poor people were acting under the grossest deception.*

*There was not anything too horrible or absurd to be circulated and nothing too incredible for their belief. Few really understood the intended proceedings of the guardians, and the opposition was not against the execution of the law, but the falsehoods in circulation. As soon as the intentions of the law were understood, the most riotous submitted and received the alterations gladly. Amongst other ridiculous statements circulated, the peasantry fully believed that all the bread was poisoned, and that the only cause for giving it instead of money was the facility it afforded of destroying the paupers; that all the children beyond three in a family were to be killed; that all young children and women under 18 were to be spared; that if they touched the bread they would instantly drop down dead. I saw one poor person at North Molton look at a loaf with a strong expression of hunger, and when it was offered to her, put her hands behind her and shrink back in fear lest it should touch her. She acknowledged she had heard of a man who had dropped down dead the moment he touched the bread.*

*It was also believed that to touch the bread was like 'taking bounty', and the guardians would immediately seize them, kill their children, and imprison the parents.*

*Other stories to excite the small rate-payers were, that the chairman was to have £1200 a year, and all the guardians in proportion, and that £20,000 were to be immediately levied on the rate-payers for a workhouse.*

1 Which groups of people in the villages opposed the introduction of the new Poor Law?

2 What were their main motives for opposing its introduction?

3 How did they oppose the introduction of the new Poor Law?

4 How successful was their opposition?

5 To what extent would the Poor Law commissioners have been pleased with the contents of Mr Gilbert's report?

6 Compare Source 5.1 (page 151) with Source 5.6. To what extent does Gilbert's report throw doubt on the claims made in Source 5.1 that, 'Our domestic revolution is going on in the most peaceful and prosperous way'?

154

Did the new Poor Law achieve its aims between 1834 and 1905?

# Did the 1834 act achieve a reduction in the financial burden of poor relief?

## ● SOURCE 5.7

Adapted by the author from *Select Committee on Poor Law Returns*, 1828, and from Poor Law Commission, *Fourteenth Annual Report*, 1848.

Cost of poor relief, 1760–1853 (millions).

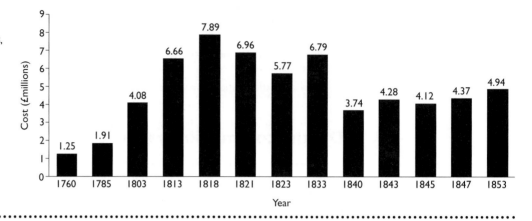

Study Source 5.7.

1 Which years saw a peak in the amount spent on poor relief?

2 What was the overall trend in the cost of poor relief after 1834?

3 On the basis of the statistical evidence in Source 5.7, to what extent would the Poor Law commissioners be justified in their claims to have
   a) reduced the burden of poor relief expenditure
   b) discouraged people from seeking relief after 1834?

# To what extent did specific local areas reflect the national picture?

## ● SOURCE 5.8

Adapted by the author from *Appendix to the Report from the Select Committee on the Andover Union*, 1846, and from the Poor Law Commission, *Fourteenth Annual Report*, 1848.

Comparison of the cost of a) poor relief expenditure for England and Wales 1840–45 with b) the expenditure of the Andover Union, 1837–45.

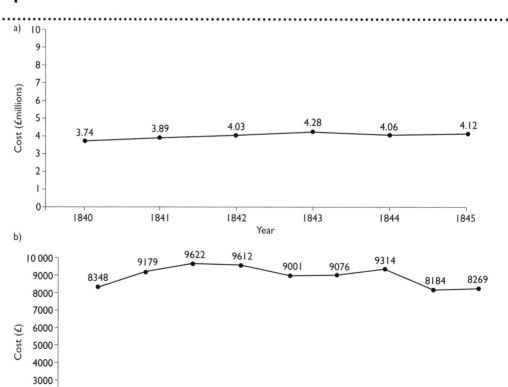

155

How successful was the introduction of the 1834 Poor Law Amendment Act?

The Andover Union was one of the most extreme examples of the strict implementation of the 1834 act (see page 171), particularly in relation to the establishment of a workhouse regime designed to achieve less eligibility.

1 According to Source 5.8, did the cost of poor relief for the Andover Union fall in the late 1830s?

2 What was happening to the cost of poor relief between 1840 and 1843 in the case of
  a) Andover
  b) England and Wales?

3 What was the overall trend in the period 1840–45 for
  a) Andover
  b) England and Wales?

4 Was there a significant saving in poor relief expenditure, as the Poor Law Commission claimed?

5 What relevance does a study of poor relief nationally have for a historian studying the experience of individual unions?

## Did the new Poor Law succeed in controlling the labouring poor?

● SOURCE 5.9

From *Returns, Criminal Offenders, Parliamentary Papers*, 1835.

Committals for rural 'protest' crimes in England and Wales, 1828–50.

| Year | Arson | Stealing sheep | Maiming cattle | Threatening letters |
|------|-------|----------------|----------------|---------------------|
| 1828 | 14 | 201 | 11 | 3 |
| 1829 | 37 | 237 | 3 | 4 |
| 1830 | 45 | 297 | 6 | 4 |
| 1831 | 102 | 253 | 19 | 62 |
| 1832 | 111 | 298 | 16 | 6 |
| 1833 | 64 | 266 | 33 | 12 |
| 1834 | 65 | 237 | 26 | 11 |
| 1835 | 76 | 221 | 34 | 15 |
| 1836 | 72 | 298 | 35 | 7 |
| 1837 | 42 | 371 | 42 | 3 |
| 1838 | 39 | 341 | 24 | 3 |
| 1839 | 37 | 324 | 25 | 4 |
| 1840 | 67 | 375 | 34 | 2 |
| 1841 | 25 | 339 | 28 | 1 |
| 1842 | 48 | 428 | 37 | 6 |
| 1843 | 94 | 403 | 34 | 15 |
| 1844 | 232 | 286 | 43 | 14 |
| 1845 | 90 | 215 | 28 | 6 |
| 1846 | 114 | 211 | 40 | 4 |
| 1847 | 115 | 283 | 25 | 7 |
| 1848 | 120 | 316 | 27 | 4 |
| 1849 | 206 | 358 | 42 | 4 |
| 1850 | 167 | 267 | 32 | 4 |

1 Comment on the trend in the incidence of rural 'protest' crime, shown in Source 5.9.

2 In what year did 'protest' crime reach a peak?

3 What forms of rural crime were most popular?

4 How might this popularity be explained?

5 What conclusions might contemporaries have reached about the link between the new Poor Law and the increase in rural crime?

6 How might the evidence of rural crime be used to argue that the new Poor Law failed to control the labouring poor and that its introduction was not 'going on in the most peaceful way' (as Nassau Senior had claimed in Source 5.1)?

# What methods were used to achieve 'less eligibility'?

● **SOURCE 5.10**

From *Appendix to the Report from the Select Committee on the Andover Union*, 1846, outlining the work to be carried out by the able-bodied poor.

**pounding of bones**
involved the crushing of animal bones to make fertiliser that was sold to local farmers. It was a smelly and unhealthy activity that was banned in the second half of the nineteenth century.

**picking oakum**
was a common task for men and women. It involved the unravelling of old, knotted and tarred ropes centimetre by centimetre so that the fibres could be reused.

*Ordered, by the Guardians of the Lymington Union [in Hampshire], at a meeting of the Board, held, this 23rd day of March 1844, that the master of the workhouse of the Lymington Union do set every adult person not suffering under any temporary or permanent infirmity of body, being an occasional poor person who shall be relieved in the said workhouse, in return for the food and lodging afforded to such person, to perform the following task of work (that is to say,) – POUNDING 28 LBS. OF BONES, or PICKING 2 LBS. OF OAKUM. Provided that no such person shall be detained against his or her will for the performance of such task of work for any exceeding four hours from the hour of breakfast, on the morning next after admission. And provided also that such amount of work shall not be required from any person to whose age, strength, and capacity it shall appear not to be suited.*
*Jos. Robins,*
*Clerk to the Guardians.*

*We, the Poor Law Commissioners, do consent to, and approve of, the above order of the Board of Guardians of the Lymington Union. Dated this 30th day of April 1844.*
*Geo. Nicholls.*
*G. C. Lewis.*
*Edmund W. Head.*

**Notice** – *Any such persons above who shall, while in such workhouse, refuse or neglect to perform such task of work suited to the age, strength, and capacity of such person, will be deemed an idle and disorderly person, and be liable to be imprisoned in the house of correction, with hard labour, for one calendar month.*

● **SOURCE 5.11**

From *Regulations Governing Life in the Southampton Workhouse*, 1841.

*Regulations governing workhouse life*

II   *That the Master read or cause to be read prayers every morning before breakfast, and every evening after Supper, out of some book the Minister shall appoint.*

III   *That the Master and Mistress, with as many as are not hindered by a just reason, do attend every Lord's day the public worship at the church.*

VI   *That the Master and Mistress rise themselves and cause all under their care, who are well, to rise by seven o'clock in the winter half year and at six in the summer half year.*

VII   *That the children's heads be combed every morning and the clothes of all the poor be kept clean and neat and be mended by the Mistress and women in the home at the appointment of the Master.*

VIII   *That all go to bed and all candles be carefully extinguished by eight o'clock in the winter half year and in the summer half year, that no candles at all be allowed and that all shall be in bed before nine.*

IX   *That they have their breakfast in the winter at eight and in the summer at seven in the morning, their dinner always at twelve and their supper at six in the winter and at seven in the summer and that the Master say Grace or make the boys say it by turns weekly.*

X   *That no waste be made of bread, beer or meat, but what is left be referred for another meal.*

XI   *That all the House be swept from top to bottom every morning and washed once a week and that all the women and girls above ten years of age do it, as the Master shall appoint.*

XII   *That they assist at baking, brewing and at meals, as he shall appoint.*

XIII   *That no person go out of the gate without leave of the Master or abroad or to work for any farmer without leave of an officer and that the same officer receive of the farmer what is due for their work.*

XIV   *That if any swear, lie or be guilty of any scandalous practice, they be punished accordingly.*

● SOURCE 5.12

From Poor Law Commission, *Seventh Annual Report*, 1841, which sets out the rules, regulations and discipline to be observed in workhouses.

*Workhouse (rules of conduct)*
*Any pauper who shall neglect to observe such of the regulations herein contained as are applicable to and binding on him:*

*Or who shall make any noise when silence is ordered to be kept;*
*Or shall use obscene or profane language;*
*Or shall by word or deed insult or revile any person;*
*Or shall threaten to strike or to assault any person;*
*Or shall not duly cleanse his person;*
*Or shall refuse or neglect to work, after having been required to do so;*
*Or shall pretend sickness;*
*Or shall play at cards or other games of chance;*
*Or shall enter or attempt to enter, without permission, the ward or yard appropriated to any class of paupers other than that to which he belongs;*
*Or shall misbehave in going to, at, or returning from public worship out of the workhouse, or at prayers in the workhouse;*
*Or shall return after the appointed time of absence, when allowed to quit the workhouse temporarily;*
*Or shall wilfully disobey any lawful order of any officer of the workhouse;*
*Shall be deemed DISORDERLY.*

*Any pauper who shall, within seven days, repeat any one or commit more than one of the offences specified in Article 34;*

*Or who shall by word or deed insult or revile the master or matron, or any other officer of the workhouse, or any of the Guardians;*
*Or shall wilfully disobey any lawful order of the master or matron after such order shall have been repeated;*
*Or shall unlawfully strike or otherwise unlawfully assault any person;*
*Or shall wilfully or mischievously damage or soil any property whatsoever belonging to the Guardians;*
*Or shall be drunk;*
*Or shall wilfully disturb the other inmates during prayers or divine worship;*
*Shall be deemed REFRACTORY.*

*It shall be lawful for the master of the workhouse . . . to punish any disorderly pauper by substituting, during a time not greater than forty-eight hours, for his or her dinner, as prescribed by the dietary, a meal consisting of eight ounces of bread, or one pound of cooked potatoes, and also by withholding from him during the same period, all butter, cheese, tea, sugar, or broth . . .*
    *And it shall be lawful for the Board of Guardians . . . to order any refractory pauper to be punished by confinement to a separate room, with or without an alteration of the diet . . . for . . . [no longer than] twenty-four hours . . .*

● SOURCE 5.13

From *Andover Workhouse Papers*, 1839, recording a letter suggesting that unmarried mothers be made to wear different clothes from the other women in the workhouse.

**ignominious dress**
clothing worn to show the woman is shamed and disgraced.

*Southampton, 17 March, 1839.*
*Gentlemen, The Minute of the Board on the subject of 'IGNOMINIOUS DRESS for unchaste women in Workhouses' appears to me of so much importance, that I would suggest whether it should not be sent to Every Union in my district. I am the more inclined to offer this advice as in many of the Unions a Yellow dress is provided for the Mothers of bastard children, but my memoranda do not enable me to name the Unions in which this arrangement exists. In none do I recollect to have heard objections.*

## ● SOURCE 5.14

Compiled by the author from *Poor Law Commission, Second Annual Report,* 1836, and from a *Bill of Fare for the House of Industry in the Isle of Wight,* 1804–06, summarising the contents of one of the six recommended diets.

### Comparison of a typical Tuesday diet in a post- and pre-1834 workhouse

|  | Post-1834 | Pre-1834 |
|---|---|---|
| Breakfast | 8 oz bread<br>$1\frac{1}{2}$ pints gruel | Unlimited thick broth<br>Bread |
| Dinner | 8 oz cooked meat<br>$\frac{3}{4}$ lb potatoes | Beer<br>Boiled pickled pork with vegetables |
| Supper | 6 oz bread<br>$1\frac{1}{2}$ oz cheese | No beer<br>Boiled rice sweetened with treacle |

## ● SOURCE 5.15

From A. Dickens, 'The Architect and the Workhouse', *Architectural Review,* 1976, showing a) Sampson Kempthorne's 'Y' plan of a workhouse for 300 paupers, adopted by the Winchester Union, and b) an aerial view of the ground floor and first floor of the Andover workhouse with its separate men's, women's and children's areas.

a)

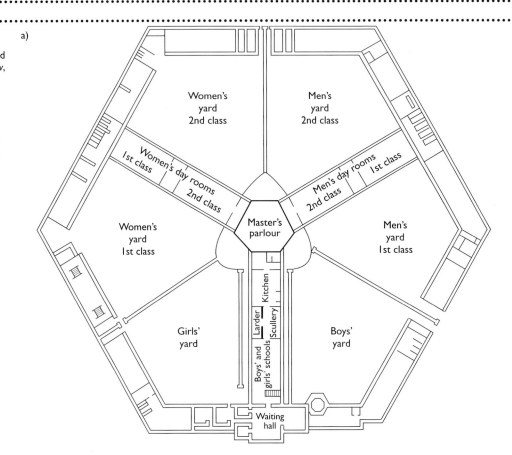

b)

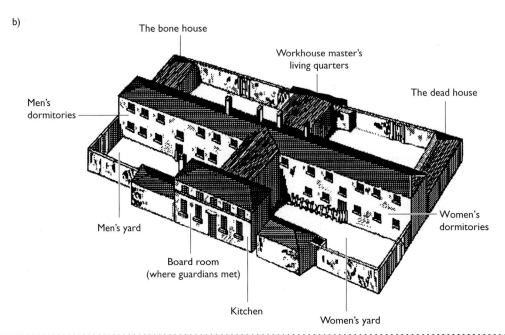

159

How successful was the introduction of the 1834 Poor Law Amendment Act?

Study Sources 5.10–5.15 which outline the standards set by the Poor Law commissioners in London to control workhouse life.

1 How did the Poor Law commissioners propose to make life in the workhouse 'less eligible' than the condition of the lowest independent labourer? In your answer comment on each of the following
    a) diet
    b) social control (rules/regulations)
    c) pauper uniform
    d) treatment of different classes of pauper
    e) work.

2 The Poor Law commissioners recognised that it was mental and emotional rather than material pain that would deter the labouring poor from applying for relief. Which aspects of life in the workhouse do you think those in need of relief would find most unacceptable?

3 How did the new workhouses achieve
    a) a climate of fear and hatred
    b) a loss of individuality
    c) a dull and exhausting routine?

4 Read again Sources 5.2 and 5.3 (page 151), the correspondence between Edwin Chadwick and Mr Loveland, the Clerk of the Poor Law Guardians, St Luke Chelsea, 1843. To what extent did the Chelsea Union depart from the standards set by the Poor Law commissioners, indicating that some unions adopted a more 'humane' approach to their inmates?

5 Refer again to the statistics in Source 5.7 (page 154). To what extent do the statistics imply that the commissioners had been successful in achieving the principle of 'less eligibility'?

## ● SOURCE 5.16

*Interior of an English workhouse under the new Poor Law Act*, 1837, Public Records Office.

Study the propaganda poster *Interior of an English workhouse under the new Poor Law Act,* 1837, and read the captions.

1   Is it possible to tell from the scenes shown in the poster and the comments made by the different inmates whether the illustrator was hostile to the new Poor Law?

2   What images has the illustrator used to emphasise the harshness of the less eligibility principle?

3   How reliable is this cartoon for a historian studying the workhouse system in this period?

4   To what extent were the critics of the Poor Law Amendment Act of 1834 justified in their description of the new workhouses as 'Bastilles' (prisons)?

# 2  Who opposed the Poor Law Amendment Act of 1834?

The new Poor Law aroused a great deal of opposition from the labouring poor and those who sympathised with them. Hostility to the new Poor Law united people of different social groups and political beliefs.

- Tory paternalists, who had a strong sense of duty to the lower order, were hostile because they saw the new Poor Law as a threat to their role in the old paternalist society. They saw the new law as bringing an end to parish responsibility for the poor and replacing it with an impersonal, bureaucratic system in which local authority would have to obey the orders of central government. They believed that society and the security of property rested on the principle that the wealthy looked after the poor and if that duty were no longer carried out, then the poor would rebel and anarchy would result.

- Radicals believed that the Poor Law was an attempt to reduce wages, a view reinforced by the efforts of the Poor Law Commission between 1835 and 1836 to move poor labourers from south-east England to Lancashire, Cheshire, and the West Riding of Yorkshire. The new Poor Law was seen as an attempt to place the whole of the labouring population at the mercy and disposal of the classes owning money and property.

- Many middle-class ratepayers, local Poor Law administrators, parish vestries and overseers, magistrates, clergymen and reformers sympathised with the condition of the poor and defended their right to relief under the allowance system. They were hostile to the threat of interference in local affairs by central government, which might result in the end of rights of local self-government. They believed that only local officials could distinguish between the deserving and the undeserving poor.

- Middle-class reformers believed the harshness of the act would push the poor to rebel and anarchy would result. They criticised the new Poor Law for its concentration on the problems of agricultural poverty. Trade depressions threw thousands out of work, and no workhouse could cope. They believed it was cheaper and more humane to continue with outdoor relief and that there was no need to break up homes. The new Poor Law seemed to override reform already begun in many areas, such as the select vestries or small committees of leading people that had been established to meet regularly and discuss relief policy. They initially believed that the Poor Law Commission intended to operate only in the south and east and would leave the well-administered low-rated northern parishes alone. Extension of the Commission's activities to the north infuriated a considerable number of influential people. There was a common belief that the commissioners wanted to get their clutches on the north as well as on the south to satisfy their eagerness for power.

- The labouring population viewed the 1834 act as the 'Poor Man's Robbery Bill' that took away their right to poor relief. They considered it unfair that relief was only allowed in a workhouse, since this would lead to harsh treatment and the break-up of family and home. The act was regarded as inhumane, while the boards of guardians were seen as strangers unwilling to be sympathetic or fair.

# Why did the north oppose implementation of the Poor Law Amendment Act from 1837?

Attempts to implement the 1834 act coincided with the onset of a serious depression that was to last until 1841. Unemployment and short-time working combined with rising prices to produce riots amongst industrial workers in the Lancashire cotton areas and the West Riding of Yorkshire. Attempts to apply the act highlighted the failure of the commissioners to investigate poverty in an urban and industrial environment. Unlike agriculture, where labourers suffered from seasonal underemployment, workers in the industrial Midlands and North experienced unemployment due to depressions in trade and changes in technology. Poor relief in the form of small payments had been used as a temporary measure.

● **SOURCE 5.17**

From Poor Law Commission, *Third Annual Report*, 1837, describing the consequences of unemployment in Nottingham.

*The greater part of the important manufacturing counties of Stafford, Nottingham and Leicester, was arranged in Unions before the close of the last parochial year, 23 March, 1837 . . . In these Unions the administration of relief by the Boards of Guardians had hardly been undertaken before the interruption of the American trade produced a cessation in the demand for labour . . . an opinion has prevailed with many persons, that the provisions of the Poor Law Amendment Act, though useful in the agricultural districts of the south and east of England [are] inapplicable in the populous manufacturing districts of the north . . . the new system was so imperfectly organised and established in the central manufacturing districts when the pressure of distress and difficulty arose . . . This Union, which consists of the three parishes constituting the town of Nottingham, and containing a population of 50,000, was formed in July, 1836 . . . the rule prohibiting outdoor relief to able-bodied male paupers was issued at once . . . in the early part of the spring the pressure of commercial distress and the suspension of employment caused the manufacturers to discharge a large proportion of their workmen . . .*

*We knew that the Union was very inadequately provided with workhouse accommodation. It was possessed of an old workhouse capable of containing about 520 persons . . . As the applications for relief increased . . . the Guardians took steps to increase the workhouse accommodation by occupying certain premises belonging to the parish as nurseries for children and as houses for old men, and finally by using a workhouse belonging to the parish of St Nicholas as a hospital for the sick. They were by these means enabled to provide room, for nearly 700 persons within their houses . . . it soon became evident that a necessity would speedily arise for relieving more persons than could be provided for within the walls of the workhouses. After full consideration we felt it to be our duty to assure the Guardians that the rule which prohibited them from giving relief to able-bodied male persons excepting in the workhouse should be suspended. At this stage of our proceedings it was determined by the principal inhabitants of the town to resort to a subscription for the purpose of relieving the unemployed operatives, this being considered a better mode of affording them support than by having recourse to the poor-rate. The kind feeling and praiseworthy generosity of the principal persons in the town and its neighbourhood succeeded in raising about £4,000 . . . it has not been the custom in Nottingham to give relief to able-bodied individuals when the usual amount of employment prevailed, and that the practice of resorting to outdoor labour as a medium of relief is adopted only when there is a pressure on the workhouse beyond what could conveniently be managed . . . the committee of management resolved to construct a road through some property belonging to the corporation . . . the persons employed were paid by the piece.*

● **SOURCE 5.18**

From E. J. Hobsbawm, 'The British Standard of Living, 1790–1850', *Economic History Review*, compiled from H. Ashworth, 'Statistics of the present depression of trade in Bolton', *Journal of the Statistical Society*, 1842.

Employment levels amongst different trades in Bolton, 1836 and 1842.

| Trade | Total employed in 1836 | Total employed whole- or short-time in 1842 | Percentage unemployed |
|---|---|---|---|
| Mills | 8,124 | 3,063 (whole-time) | 60 |
| Ironworkers | 2,110 | 1,325 (short-time) | 36 |
| Carpenters | 150 | 24 | 84 |
| Bricklayers | 120 | 16 | 87 |
| Stonemasons | 150 | 50 | 60 |
| Tailors | 500 | 250 | 50 |
| Shoemakers | 80 | 40 | 50 |

1 According to Source 5.17, what circumstances had led to the opinion 'that the provisions of the Poor Law Amendment Act [were] inapplicable in the populous manufacturing districts of the north'?

2 How does the evidence of Source 5.18 support the findings of the *Third Annual Report* of 1837 (Source 5.17)?

3 What measures were taken by the guardians of the Nottingham workhouse to deal with the situation within the restrictions laid down by the 1834 act?

4 How successful were they?

5 What evidence in the report indicates that the people of Nottingham were sympathetic to the plight of the unemployed operatives?

6 What form of relief did the guardians then introduce to deal with the able-bodied?

## What tactics were adopted by the anti-Poor-Law movement?

It was against this background of a crisis in the economy and society that agitation against the new Poor Law grew in the towns of Lancashire and the West Riding of Yorkshire. The anti-Poor-Law movement was well-organised and very effective. It temporarily absorbed the Ten Hours factory reform movement that had been active since 1830 and made use of its Short-Time Committees, which existed in most of the large towns of the North and Midlands. A meeting was organised at Bradford in March 1837 to organise a demonstration against the new Poor Law in the West Riding. The activities of the township committees were co-ordinated by the West Riding anti-Poor-Law committee, chaired by William Stocks, a Huddersfield yarn merchant. Resistance in south Lancashire, centred at Manchester, was led by R. J. Richardson, a Salford stationer and later a prominent Chartist. They sent out delegates to organise anti-Poor-Law committees in the factory towns of Lancashire and Cheshire. By 1838 there were 38 such committees. Methods employed included public meetings, a petition, great open-air demonstrations, support from newspapers – irrespective of party sympathy – and a policy of obstruction, so that new boards of guardians could not carry out their duties. People who were opposed to the Poor Law were elected to the boards whilst overseers refused to hand over the poor rates and ratepayers refused to pay poor rates. A policy of intimidation was adopted against guardians favourable to the new Poor Law and their property was destroyed. Riots that took place at Bradford in 1837 and at Todmorden and Dewsbury in 1838 were so serious that troops and squads of police were sent out from London.

● **SOURCE 5.19**

From Richard Oastler, *Damnation! Eternal Damnation to the Fiend-Begotten Coarser Food New Poor Law*, 1837, in which Oastler (see page 50) campaigns against the new Poor Law.

**Lucifer**
the chief rebel angel, Satan, who became known as the devil

**Belial**
a name for the devil or evil

CHRISTIAN READER.
Be not alarmed at the sound of the Title. I cannot bless that, which GOD and NATURE CURSE. The Bible being true, the Poor Law Amendment Act is false! The Bible containing the will of God, – this accursed Act of Parliament embodies the will of LUCIFER. It is the Sceptre of BELIAL, establishing its sway in the Land of Bibles!! DAMNATION; ETERNAL DAMNATION to the accursed Fiend!!

   . . . I tell you deliberately, if I have the misfortune to be reduced to poverty, that that man who dares to tear from me the wife whom God has joined to me, shall, if I have it in my power, received his death at my hand! If I am ever confined in one of those hellish Poor Law Bastilles, and my wife be torn from me, because I am poor, I will, if it be possible, burn the whole pile down to the ground. This will I do, if my case shall be thus tried, if I have the power, and every man who loved his wife, and who is unstained by crime, will if he can, do the same. – Further, I will not pay any tax imposed upon me, under this Act . . .
RICHARD OASTLER

> **I** In what ways, and how effectively, does Oastler (Source 5.19) make use of religion as a weapon in the campaign against the new Poor Law?

● **SOURCE 5.20**

a) Charles Dickens, *The Adventures of Oliver Twist*, first published in 1838, in which Dickens exposes the brutality of the Poor Law.

b) *Oliver Twist Asks For More*, George Cruikshank's famous illustration for Charles Dickens' novel, 1838.

**Charles Dickens (1812–70)**
began his literary career writing *Sketches* under the pen-name 'Boz' for the newspaper, the *Morning Chronicle*. He used his articles and novels to appeal to the conscience of the ruling classes and to persuade his middle-class audience to support campaigns for reform of political and social evils. Webster said of Dickens in 1842 that 'he had done more to improve the condition of the English poor than all the statesmen Great Britain has sent into Parliament. What other reformers hoped to do by legislation, he did by a supreme act of moral imagination'.

a) . . . 'Boy', said the gentleman in the high chair, 'listen to me. You know you're an orphan, I suppose? . . . Well! You have come here to be educated, and taught a useful trade . . . So you'll begin to pick oakum, tomorrow morning at six o'clock' . . .

   The members of this board were very [wise] men; . . . So, they established the rule, that all poor people should have the alternative . . . of being starved by a gradual process in the house, or by a quick one out of it. With this view, they contracted with the water-works to lay on an unlimited supply of water; and with a corn-factor to supply periodically small quantities of oatmeal; and issued three meals of thin gruel a day, with an onion twice a week, and half a roll on Sundays. They made a great many other wise and humane regulations, . . . kindly undertook to divorce poor married people . . . and, instead of compelling a man to support his family, as they had theretofore done, took his family away from him, and made him a bachelor!

   . . . the system . . . was rather expensive at first, in consequence of the increase in the undertaker's bill, and the necessity of taking in the clothes of all the paupers, which fluttered loosely on their wasted, shrunken forms, after a week or two's gruel. But the number of workhouse inmates got thin as well as the paupers; and the board were [happy].

   The room in which the boys were fed, was a large stone hall, with a copper at one end: out of which the master, dressed in an apron for the purpose, and assisted by one or two women, ladled the gruel at meal-times . . . each boy had one porringer, and no more – except on occasions of great public rejoicing, when he had two ounces and a quarter of bread besides. The bowls never wanted washing. The boys polished them with their spoons till they shone again . . . Oliver Twist and his companions suffered the tortures of slow starvation for three months . . .

   . . . Oliver remained a close prisoner in the dark and solitary room to which he had been consigned by the wisdom and mercy of the board . . . 'If the parish vould like him to learn a right pleasant trade, in a good 'spectable chimbley-sweepin' bisness,' said Mr Gamfield, 'I wants a 'prentis, and I am ready to take him.'

b)

George Cruikshank.

1    In what way does Dickens in Source 5.20 indicate his hostility to the new Poor Law?

2    Compare the language, style, tone and arguments of Sources 5.19 and 5.20. Which campaigner do you think would have been more effective in arousing support for the plight of the labouring poor and opposition to the new Poor Law? Justify your answer with reference to the sources.

## ● SOURCE 5.21

Adapted from the Chartist newspaper, the *Northern Star*, 10 March 1838, in which the owner and editor, Feargus O'Connor (see page 240), calls upon the people to resist the election of new guardians.

**Northern Star**
was a provincial, radical working-class newspaper established by Feargus O'Connor in November 1837. It had a weekly readership of 50,000 and was a severe critic of the 1834 Poor Law.

*Fellow Rate-payers,*
*The time has come for you to give a practical demonstration of your hatred to the new Starvation Law . . .*

*The 25th March is the day . . . for the election of new Guardians for the ensuing year; therefore it will depend on your exertions, whether you will allow men to be elected . . . who are the mere tools of the three Commissioners in carrying out their diabolical schemes for starving the poor, reducing the labourers' wages and robbing you the rate-payers of that salutary control you have hitherto exercised over your money and your township's affairs; or will you elect men of character and of humanity [who] . . . will prefer death itself, rather than sacrifice the rights of their neighbours and constituents at the bidding of three pensioned Lawyers residing in London, and living in princely splendour out of your hard-earned money . . .*

*First – We recommend the formation of local committees . . .*

*Ratepayers, do your duty and select none who are in the remotest degree favourable to the hellish Act. Remember that the law is cruel, illegal and unconstitutional . . . The real object of it is to lower wages and punish poverty as a crime. Remember also that children and parents are dying frequently in the same Bastille without seeing one another, or knowing of one another's fate.*

1    In Source 5.21, how does O'Connor propose that critics of the new Poor Law should show their opposition?

2    How effective do you consider the style and content of his article were likely to have been in mounting a successful campaign for 'the election of new Guardians'?

## ● SOURCE 5.22

From George Tinker, *The State of the Huddersfield Union*, in which he complains of the actions taken in June 1837 by some of the magistrates, who were *ex-officio* members of the board of guardians.

**the clerk**
was responsible for conducting the business of the union.

**individualised**
singled out; identified

**particularised**
singled out; picked on

**avocations**
work or pastimes

*At a meeting held on Monday 5 June, 1837 . . . the mob amounting to 6 or 8 thousand persons, led on by the notorious Oastler, broke open the gates of the workhouse and threatened to pull down the building if the Guardians did not immediately break up their meeting. It was with difficulty and by a very small majority that the meeting was adjourned to another place in the town, a motion having been made and strongly supported that it should be adjourned to the 1st Monday in April 1838. On the way to our second place of meeting, the guardians who were known to be favourable to the Law were repeatedly surrounded by the mob, and their lives threatened if they attempted to carry it into effect. The magistrate present, R. Battye, Esq. placed us under the merciful protection of Rchd. Oastler, and refused to read the Riot Act, notwithstanding that the heads of several of the constables had been broken and the windows of the room demolished with stones thrown by the mob. The opposition guardians during the meeting, regularly communicated its proceedings to the mob outside by haranguing them out at the windows and by writing. Only eleven out of thirty-nine guardians present voted for electing a* CLERK, *and those who had the manliness to do so were* INDIVIDUALISED *and the mob was promised that they should be afterwards acquainted with their names.*

*Being a sincere advocate of the Poor Law Amendment Act I am* PARTICULARISED *by the opposition guardians, put in bodily fear by the threats of the mob and prevented from following my usual* AVOCATIONS. *This, Gentlemen, you will perceive is the peculiar and dangerous situation in which some of the Guardians are placed – called upon by one portion of the Executive to administer a certain Act – refused the protection and support of another portion and subjected if honestly performing our duties to the violence of thousands of irritated persons who are under the command of One individual whose avowed object is, direct opposition to the established law of the country. I therefore most humbly request on behalf of myself and fellow Guardians your advice and protection.*
*I have the honour to be, Gentlemen,*
*Your Obedient Servant,*
*Geo. Tinker*
*Guardian for the Township of Hepworth, Scholes, nr. Huddersfield, June 8, 1837.*

207

What reforms were introduced to improve the welfare of the aged?

# 4 What reforms were introduced to improve the welfare of the aged?

The elderly were the largest group of poor. To many people it seemed unfair that old people who had worked hard all their lives should end their days in a workhouse because they were no longer able to support themselves. Old age pensions were first proposed by Joseph Chamberlain and were supported by social reformers such as Charles Booth, and by individual Liberals, although not by the party as a whole. A Royal Commission on the Aged Poor (1893–95) recognised the extent of the problem but no reforms materialised.

By 1908 there was broad agreement that some form of old age pension was necessary. Statistical investigations had proved the extent of poverty among old people and made it impossible for those opposed to reform to blame such poverty on moral weakness. The influence of 'New Liberalism' and the belief that the state should do more to address social problems were also important driving factors. Claims that the Liberals only took action on the issue after being defeated by Labour in by-elections held in 1907 are not supported by the evidence; plans were already being discussed before the by-election defeats.

There was, however, disagreement over how the pension should be funded. Some people, including Charles Booth, argued that it should be non-contributory – in other words, funded entirely by the government from taxation. Others argued that people should have to make contributions to a pension fund during their working life. They were concerned about the cost of the scheme, and also influenced by the nineteenth-century belief in the importance of self-help.

## Why was the provision of old age pensions a controversial issue?

● **SOURCE 6.26**

From Poor Law Board, *Twenty-Second Annual Report*, 1870, in which the President of the Poor Law Board, G. J. Goschen, restates the principles of the 1834 act.

**G. J. Goschen, President of the Poor Law Board**
was MP for the city of London and a leading Liberal. After 1880 he became increasingly suspicious of Radical influence in the party and broke with the Liberals over the question of Home Rule for Ireland in 1886. He then joined the Conservative Party and held office between 1886 and 1892 and from 1895 to 1902.

*One of the most recognised principles in our Poor Law is, that relief should be given only to the actually destitute, and not in aid of wages . . . In innumerable cases its application appears to be harsh . . . Still it is certain that no system could be more dangerous, both to the working classes and to the ratepayers, than to supplement insufficiency of wages by the expenditure of public money.*

*The fundamental doctrine of the English Poor Laws . . . is that relief is given not as a matter of charity but of legal obligation, and to extend this obligation beyond the class to which it now applies, namely, the actually destitute, to a further and much larger class, namely, those in receipt of insufficient wages, would be not only to increase to an unlimited extent the present enormous expenditure, but to allow the belief in a legal claim to public money in every emergency to supplant, in a further portion of the population, the full recognition of the necessity for self-reliance and thrift.*

1 In Source 6.26 what is meant by the principle 'that relief should be given only to the actually destitute, and not in aid of wages'?

2 What can be deduced from the report about mid-Victorian views on the virtues of self-help?

3 How might using public money 'to supplement insufficiency of wages' undermine those virtues?

● **SOURCE 6.27**

Adapted from George Lansbury, *My Life*, 1931, in which he describes conditions in the Poplar Workhouse, c.1900. Poplar was a dockside parish of East London.

**George Lansbury**

had become eligible to sit as a Poor Law guardian when the Local Government Act of 1894 allowed women and working men to become candidates for election to boards of guardians.

My first visit to the workhouse at Poplar was a memorable one. Going down the narrow lane, ringing the bell, waiting while an official with a not too pleasant face looked through a grating to see who was there, and hearing his unpleasant voice, made it easy for me to understand why the poor dreaded and hated these places, and made me in a flash realise how all these prison sort of surroundings were organised for the purpose of making self-respecting, decent people endure any suffering rather than enter. Everything possible was done to inflict moral and mental degradation – hostile officials, hard benches, huge books for entering one's name, history, etc., searching, being stripped and bathed in a communal tub, and the final crowning indignity of being dressed in clothes which had been worn by lots of other people.

Sick and aged, mentally deficient, lunatics, babies and children, able-bodied and tramps were all herded together in one huge range of buildings. Officers, both men and women, looked upon these people as a nuisance and treated them accordingly.

---

1  To what extent does the evidence of Source 6.27 support the view that, in 1900, pauperism was still treated as a moral defect?

2  To what extent did conditions at the Poplar Workhouse reflect the claim made in Source 6.26 that the 'application [of the Poor Law] appears to be harsh'?

3  How might the evidence of Sources 6.26 and 6.27 be used by critics of the treatment of the aged poor?

---

● **SOURCE 6.28**

From Mrs Barnett, *Canon Barnett*, 1919, Vol. II, in which her husband writes in support of old age pensions.

**Canon Barnett**

was the vicar of Whitechapel and founder of Toynbee Hall in the East End of London, 1880. University graduates worked there on education and welfare projects amongst the poor. It was also a base for Booth's researches.

We reached a . . . staircase, at the top of which lived a little old woman of eighty-three in an airy room with cheerful cross lights, with bird cages and flower-pots in the windows . . . Everything was beautifully tidy . . . the old lady was sitting down to a white cloth and a dinner of bread and dripping, with a beaming friendly face . . . She had been a widow for twenty years . . . It was a pleasure to see the old woman's thriftiness and cleverness; everything she touched seemed to go right, nor was she too old to attend upon the cobbler's sick wife upstairs. Wouldn't it be a pity to send that woman to the workhouse?

---

● **SOURCE 6.29**

From Charles Booth, *Pauperism and the Endowment of Old Age*, 1892, in which the author argues for the introduction of an old age pension.

Where out-relief is freely given there may not be very many poor who do not come more or less, sooner or later, upon the rates. But where out-relief is withheld, and especially in towns, we find numbers of people struggling on, working a little, begging a little, helped by their friends or helped by the Church . . . So hardly do they do this, so nearly do they sail to the rocks, that in the year of our inquiry at Stepney burial was provided for 76 individuals of whom very few had received anything when alive, or at any rate that year. Seventy-six such deaths must imply a very large population living on the same miserable terms, without having themselves provided for death, and without friends who care enough for them to bury them. Such people probably live in greater discomfort than those who frankly accept pauperism.

---

Study Sources 6.28 and 6.29.

1  What arguments are presented in the sources to support the case for an old age pension?

2  What would be the objection to solving the problem of old age by providing more extensive out-relief?

---

● **SOURCE 6.30**

From A. G. Gardner, *The Life of George Cadbury*, 1923, quoting a letter of 1899 by the famous Birmingham Quaker and chocolate manufacturer in favour of the introduction of old age pensions.

I have long felt that as a Christian nation we ought to make some effort to add to the comfort of the aged toilers of our country, of whom it is computed one third end their days as paupers; whereas if they had a pension by right they would no more be considered paupers than the generals, admirals, judges and ex-ministers of the Crown who draw their pensions. From the intimate connection we have had with working people for many years we knew that the workhouse was looked forward to with great dread by them.

209

What reforms were introduced to improve the welfare of the aged?

*I think old age pensions would promote thrift. It is now hopeless for a man earning 20s. [£1] to 25s. [£1.25p] per week if he does his duty to his family, to provide for the future, whereas if he was sure of 7s. [35p] per week there would be an inducement to add a trifle to it, either by joining a Friendly Society, by insurance or by savings.*

*I believe in the end it would not be costly, as such allowance would not be much greater than the maintenance paid under the present Poor Law, and the aged people would have the joy of remaining amid their accustomed surroundings, living possibly with sons or daughters without being a great burden to them.*

● **SOURCE 6.31**

From A. G. Gardner, *The Life of George Cadbury*, 1923, quoting a speech of 1908, in which Cadbury argues for a universal system of old age pensions.

*We want to see the whole scheme carried out – a shilling [5p] a day at sixty for every man and woman in England, from the Duke of Westminster downwards; only with this condition, that if the Duke wants his pension, he must go to the post office and get it. If we asked for too much at once, in all human possibility we should have got nothing. Now it is for us to work downwards in the scale of age. There is no work in England so hard as that of the wife of a working man earning 20s. [£1] a week. She can never put aside the money for old age pensions and yet she has earned it more than any man living.*

1 According to Sources 6.30 and 6.31, what are George Cadbury's motives for supporting a scheme of pension by right?

2 On what grounds does he believe that the granting of old age pensions would encourage thrift?

3 What does Cadbury regard as the benefits of such a scheme?

4 What were the arguments in favour of a universal pension for everyone?

## What were the Liberal proposals for an old age pension scheme?

● **SOURCE 6.32**

a) From *Hansard*, May 1908, reporting the original proposals for an old age pension.

b) From the Old Age Pensions Act, 1908.

**Herbert H. Asquith**
was Chancellor of the Exchequer from 1906 to 1908 and then became Prime Minister. He accepted the need for welfare reforms and a redistribution of wealth through taxation.

**£26 a year**
this proposal was later amended, replacing the fixed income level above which no pension would be paid with a sliding scale between incomes of £21 and £31.

**seventy**
was disappointingly high, since there were many people in their sixties who were no longer able to work.

**£13 a year**
this figure, equivalent to five shillings per week, was the same as the weekly Poor Law payment.

### a) Lloyd George's initial proposals

MR ASQUITH said . . . First, the income limit, apart from pension, should be fixed at £26 A YEAR, subject to reduction in the case of married couples living together from £52 to £39 a year . . . Secondly, we think that the age limit . . . at which a pension should accrue . . . should be fixed at SEVENTY. Thirdly, . . . the amount of the pension . . . should be £13 A YEAR and in the case of married couples living together £9 15s. per head. Fourthly, we think stringent conditions should be provided for forfeiture or suspension . . . We think that all persons should be disqualified who have within, say, five years of their application been convicted of serious crime or of such offences as desertion, habitual vagrancy, and so on . . .

### b) Revised proposals (Old Age Pensions Act)

The statutory conditions for the receipt of an old age pension by any person are—

1 The person must have attained the age of seventy.

2 The person must satisfy the pension authorities that for at least twenty years up to the date of the receipt of any sum on account of a pension he has been a British subject.

3 The person must satisfy the pension authorities that his yearly means as calculated under this Act do not exceed thirty-one pounds ten shillings.

A person shall be disqualified from receiving or continuing to receive an old age pension under this Act—

a) While he is in receipt of any poor relief (other than relief excepted under this provision), and,

b) If, before he becomes entitled to a pension, he has habitually failed to work according to his ability, opportunity, and need, for the maintenance or benefit of himself and those legally dependent upon him

c) While he is detained in an asylum

d) Where . . . convicted of any offence and ordered to be imprisoned without the option of a fine . . . he shall be disqualified . . . while he is in prison . . . and for a further period of ten years after the date on which he is released from prison.

1 To what extent were the Liberals' original proposals (Source 6.32) in accord with the recommendations made by George Cadbury in Sources 6.30 and 6.31?

2 Who was to be disqualified from receipt of an old age pension?

3 What were the cost implications of Asquith's proposals?

4 To what extent was the Old Age Pensions Act disappointingly limited?

● **SOURCE 6.33**

From Chancellor of the Exchequer David Lloyd George's speech introducing the old age pension legislation in the House of Commons, *Hansard*, 15 June 1908.

*I invite the supporters of old age pensions . . . to support the Government not merely on the general principle of the Bill, establishing at the expense of the State provision for old age, but also in the disqualifications which on the face of them may appear harsh and unjust . . . This is purely an experiment . . . We do not say that it deals with all the problems of unmerited destitution in this country. We do not even contend that it deals with the worst part of that problem. It might be held that many an old man dependent on the charity of the parish was better off than many a young man, broken down in health, or who cannot find a market for his labour. The provision which is made for the sick and the unemployed is grossly inadequate in this country . . . These problems of the sick, of the infirm, of the men who cannot find means of earning a livelihood are problems with which it is the business of the State to deal; they are problems which the State has neglected too long. In asking the House to give a Second Reading to this Bill, we ask them to sanction not merely its principle, but also its finance, having regard to the fact that we are anxious to utilise the resources of the State to make provision for undeserved poverty and destitution in all its branches.*

1 In what ways does Lloyd George's Commons speech (Source 6.33) support the view that ideas on the causes of poverty had changed since the mid-nineteenth century?

2 How does the role of the state as envisaged in Lloyd George's proposals differ from that suggested by G. J. Goschen (Source 6.26)?

3 What evidence is there in Lloyd George's speech to suggest that some MPs had more radical views than he had about how to combat poverty?

4 What kinds of measures to cope with the 'problems of the sick, of the infirm [and] of the men who cannot find means of earning a livelihood' were likely to have been supported by such MPs?

## Who opposed the introduction of an old age pension scheme?

● **SOURCE 6.34**

From *The Times*, 3 July 1908, in which C. H. T. Crosthwaite raises objections to an old age pension.

**doles**
portions

*Sir,*
*However the Ministers may attempt to hide it, we are in fact in the presence of the universal out-door relief scheme divested of the restraining provisions of the present Poor Law. How can any prudent thinking man contemplate such a situation without dismay? The strength of this kingdom, in all its past struggles, has been its great reserve of wealth and the sturdy independent character of its people. The measure that is being pushed through the House of Commons with haste and acclaim will destroy both sources. It will extort the wealth from possessors by unjust taxation . . . It will distribute it in small DOLES, the most wasteful of all forms of expenditure, and will sap the character of the people by teaching them to rely, not on their own exertions, but on the State.*
C. H. T. Crosthwaite

1 In Source 6.34 what does C. H. T. Crosthwaite mean by a 'universal out-door relief scheme'?

2 What do you think were Crosthwaite's motives for opposing old age pensions?

● **SOURCE 6.35**

From *The Times*, 2 July 1908, reporting a parliamentary debate in which the leader of the Conservative Party, Arthur Balfour, voiced his objection to the bureaucratic implications of an old age pension scheme.

**subvention**
government aid or subsidy

*Mr Balfour said . . . 'We ought not to throw the whole power over these seven and a half millions entirely into the hands of these very subordinate Civil Servants who are made practically the distributors of this gigantic national SUBVENTION according to their own views of justice and equity . . .'*

● **SOURCE 6.36**

From *The Times*, 4 July 1908, criticising the Liberal decision to introduce a non-contributory pension scheme.

*The Bill is still widely and justifiably regarded as a leap in the dark which has not been accorded the measure of free discussion which is pre-eminently desirable. By their adoption of the non-contributory basis, the Government are undoubtedly defying the experience of many human generations in which the maxim has held good that free doles undermine the character, while thrift and providence sustain it . . .*

1 What fears were expressed in Balfour's criticisms (Source 6.35)?

2 Why did *The Times* (Source 6.36) claim that the pensions bill was 'a leap in the dark'?

3 Using Sources 6.34–6.36, explain why some people opposed the introduction of an old age pension. In your answer comment on each of the following
   a) the moral character of the people
   b) the wealth of the country
   c) the role of the state.

## What was the constitutional crisis of 1909–11?

In order to pay for old age pensions and a renewed shipbuilding programme to meet a German naval threat, Lloyd George had to find new sources of revenue. The Liberals rejected any suggestion of ending free trade and reintroducing customs duties. The measures Lloyd George proposed have led to some debate of his motives. Were the Budget proposals deliberately made unreasonable to ensure they would be rejected? Did he use the 'People's Budget' to provoke a quarrel with the House of Lords so that he could reduce their powers, or did the crisis develop by accident? Or was he genuinely working for the benefit of the poor? Was Lloyd George a hero or a villain?

● **SOURCE 6.37**

From *Diaries of Charles Hobhouse*, Financial Secretary to the Treasury in 1909.

**Land Valuation clauses**
proposed a tax of twenty per cent on the amount by which land had risen in value and a halfpenny in the pound on the increased value of land on which minerals were mined. These land taxes required a survey of land ownership which opponents, particularly the Conservative landowners in the House of Lords, saw as being an invasion into an individual's property holdings.

*7 March*
*The Cabinet met very late. Lloyd George instead of working at the details of his Budget had gone off to Cannes to play golf. When he returned instead of sitting down to the Budget he began to 'collect ideas' by talking to journalists . . . The PM [Asquith] was not strong, he discussed McKenna's [who was at the Treasury] programme with him – accepted it en bloc, and then threw him over, but as the Admiralty stood together the Cabinet three days ago accepted four dreadnought battleships at once and four later if wanted. Haldane [Secretary of State for War] got his estimates by agreeing to help Lloyd George through the House with his LAND VALUATION CLAUSES. The whole Cabinet atmosphere has been upset by Churchill [President of the Board of Trade], before whose advent there was no electricity. Meanwhile . . . the Chancellor of the Exchequer insisted on drafting three different methods of Land Valuation, each more unworkable than the last.*
*31 October*
*. . . I asked Lloyd George what he really wanted, the Budget to pass, or be rejected, and suggested that the author of a successful financial scheme such as his was far more likely to go down to posterity than one who was Chancellor of the Exchequer merely, as others had been before him. He agreed but added that he might be remembered even better as one who had upset the hereditary House of Lords. I think he will now do all he can to make it impossible.*

● **SOURCE 6.38**

From Lloyd George's Budget speech, *Hansard*, 29 April 1909, in which he defends the case for increased taxation.

. . . *Unfortunately, I have to reckon not merely with an enormous increase in expenditure this year, but an inevitable expansion of some of the heaviest items in the course of the coming years. To what is the increase in expenditure due? It is well known that it must be placed to the credit of two items and practically two items alone. One is the Navy and the other is Old Age Pensions . . . The increased expenditure under both heads was substantially incurred with the unanimous assent of all political parties in this House.*

*. . . We are told that we ought not to have touched old age pensions – at least, not at the present moment, when heavy liabilities were in sight in connection with the defence of the country . . . But . . . we had no honourable alternative left. We simply honoured a cheque years ago in favour of the aged poor, which bore at its foot the signature of all the leaders of political parties in this country.*

*. . . next year the Treasury will have to find money for paying the whole cost of construction of four 'Dreadnoughts' during an unbroken period of twelve months. This, in addition to an eleven months' building on the two 'Dreadnoughts' which were laid down some time ago, will bring up the estimates of the year for construction to a figure which is considerably above even the increased estimate of this year . . .*

*Now I come to the consideration of the social problems which are urgently pressing for solution – problems affecting the lives of the people. The solution of all these questions involves finance . . . If we put off dealing with these social sores, are the evils which arise from them not likely to grow and to fester, until finally the loss which the country sustains will be infinitely greater than anything it would have to bear in the cost of an immediate remedy?*

*. . . This . . . is a War Budget. It is for raising, to wage implacable warfare against poverty and squalidness.*

---

Study Sources 6.37 and 6.38.

**1** How radical a measure was Lloyd George's 'People's Budget'? Consider the following aspects of the proposal
   a) the costs
   b) other pressures on the budget in 1909
   c) the funding of the Old Age Pensions Act.

**2** What proposals in Lloyd George's budget of 1909 most helped to hasten the Budget crisis?

**3** How does Lloyd George seek to put down any dissent over tax increases?

**4** What evidence is there in Source 6.37 that Lloyd George was motivated by considerations other than humanitarian concern in pursuing interventionist policies?

---

● **SOURCE 6.39**

*Forced Fellowship*, a cartoon from *Punch*, 27 October 1909, commenting on reactions to Lloyd George's taxation proposals in the People's Budget.

FORCED FELLOWSHIP
*Suspicious-looking party. "Any objection to my company, guv'nor? I'm agoin' your way"*
(aside) *"and further."*

1   How useful is the *Punch* cartoon (Source 6.39) to a historian as evidence of the public's view of the People's Budget?

213

What reforms were introduced to improve the welfare of the aged?

## ● SOURCE 6.40

From *The Times*, 8 May 1909, reporting a speech by the Leader of the Opposition, Arthur Balfour, in which he criticises the Budget at the Annual Demonstration of the Conservative Primrose League (see page 269) in the Royal Albert Hall.

| **the late Government** |
|---|
| refers to the Conservative government with Arthur Balfour as its Prime Minister. |

*The Chancellor of the Exchequer told us the other day that [the growth of expenditure] fell mainly under two heads – old age pensions and naval expenditure. Well, so it does in the main. What have we got to say about these two forms of expenditure? On the first I have to say what my friends and I have said consistently for many months past – namely, that while some form of – I will not say old age pensions merely, but some form of insurance against the inevitable accidents of life, be they old age or be they sickness – was of the first importance to the community, the subject itself was so difficult . . . it ought to have been taken in hand with every caution . . . with all the ardour of electioneers they rushed into the first hand-to-mouth scheme which they could find . . . And while they were putting on expenditure they were taking off taxes. [Shouts of 'Hear, hear'.] While they were priding themselves on giving the great masses of our fellow countrymen some new boon in the way of expenditure they were at the same time removing mainly from those very classes themselves some of the expenditure which might well have been used to achieve these great objects.*

*. . . how about the Navy? . . . THE LATE GOVERNMENT thought – and who, looking back, will say they thought wrongly? – that, on the whole, a programme of four Dreadnoughts a year at that time was enough, and not more than enough, to meet the needs of the country. No continuity is pursued by . . . the [present] Government . . . They dropped their construction . . . The Government . . . have set to work too late in the day, or very late in the day, to urge the contractors to increase their plant and to try and make up the arrears in shipbuilding which ought never to have existed. [Cheers.]*

1   What was Balfour's attitude towards the issue of old age pensions (Source 6.40)?

2   On what grounds did Balfour reject Lloyd George's reasons for tax increases?

## ● SOURCE 6.41

From David Lloyd George, *Better Times, Speeches*, 1910, in which he defends his proposals to tax landowners in a speech at Limehouse in east London.

*Now, all we say is this: 'In future you must pay one halfpenny in the pound on the real value of your land. In addition to that, if the value goes up, not owing to your efforts – if you spend money on improving it we will give you credit for it – but if it goes up owing to the industry and the energy of the people living in that locality, one-fifth of that increment shall in future be taken as a toll by the State.'*

*What is the landlord's increment? Who is the landlord? The landlord is a gentleman – I have not a word to say about him in his personal capacity – the landlord is a gentleman who does not earn his wealth. He does not even take the trouble to receive his wealth. He has a host of agents and clerks to receive it for him. He does not even take the trouble to spend his wealth. He has a host of people around him to do the actual spending for him. He never sees it until he comes to enjoy it. His sole function, his chief pride, is stately consumption of wealth produced by others.*

1   What evidence is there in Lloyd George's Limehouse speech (Source 6.41) to suggest that he was deliberately provoking a quarrel with the land-owning House of Lords?

2   To what extent does Balfour's criticism of the Budget proposals (Source 6.40) support the view that Lloyd George was stirring up class warfare?

## What role did the House of Lords play in the constitutional crisis?

The People's Budget included proposals for new taxes on land, as a means of raising money to pay for the old age pension. Lloyd George claimed that his budget was a declaration of war on poverty; the Conservatives saw it as an attack on property. The budget was passed by the House of Commons but in the House of Lords the Conservative majority was able to block it by 350 votes to 75. At that time the unelected, hereditary House of Lords did have the power to veto bills passed by the elected House of Commons, but its rejection of a money bill went against long parliamentary tradition. It meant that the government would have no revenue for the coming year and so provoked a constitutional crisis.

It was not immediately clear how the Liberals would respond. Asquith, the Prime Minister, was cautious but Lloyd George, encouraged by by-election results, believed that this was an opportunity to reduce the powers of the House of Lords. He accused the Lords of unconstitutional behaviour.

● **SOURCE 6.42**

From *The Times*, 10 October 1909, reporting the issues raised by the People's Budget.

*But the Lords may decree a revolution which the people will direct. If they begin, issues will be raised that they little dream of, questions will be asked . . . and answers will be demanded . . . The question will be asked 'Should 500 men, ordinary men chosen accidentally from among the unemployed, override the judgment . . . of millions of people who are engaged in the industry which makes the wealth of the country?'*

*Another [question] will be, who ordained that a few should have the land of Britain as a privilege; who made 10,000 people owners of the soil, and the rest of us trespassers in the land of our birth; who is it – who is responsible for the scheme of things whereby one man is engaged through life in grinding labour, to win a bare and precarious subsistence for himself, and when at the end of his days he claims at the hands of the community he served a poor pension of eightpence a day, he can only get it through a revolution; and another man who does not work receives . . . more than his neighbour receives in a whole year of toil? Where did . . . that law come from? . . . These are the questions that will be asked. The answers are charged with danger for the order of things the Peers represent . . .*

I   What evidence is there in *The Times* report (Source 6.42) that the debate over the Budget had taken on a significance that went beyond finance?

● **SOURCE 6.43**

From a speech by Lord Lansdowne in the House of Lords, *Hansard*, 22 November 1909, in which he argues that the peers should reject the 1909 Budget.

**Lord Lansdowne**
held the offices of Secretary of State for War and, in 1900, Foreign Secretary in a Conservative government.

*. . . a practice has grown up . . . of grouping together under one Bill a large number of measures dealing with different taxes . . . In all seriousness, my Lords, we have a right to know where this sort of thing is going to stop. If you can graft Licensing Bills and Land Valuation Bills and measures of that kind on to the Finance Bill, what is to prevent your grafting on it, let us say, a Home Rule Bill – setting up in Ireland an authority to collect and dispense all the taxes of the country?*

I   What arguments does Lord Lansdowne use in Source 6.43 to persuade the Lords to reject the 1909 Budget?

● **SOURCE 6.44**

From *The Times*, 30 November 1909, questioning the constitutional legality of the Liberal government's plans to curb the power of the Lords.

*There is no precedent for a Government avowedly pursuing the policy of destroying the power of the House of Lords to reject or amend any measure that a temporary majority in the Commons may be pleased to pass, whether that measure be desired or disliked by the country. But that, and nothing else, has been the declared policy of the present Government, and the Budget is merely the culmination of a design deliberately adopted and steadily pursued.*

I   In what ways does the writer of *The Times* article (Source 6.44) reveal his political sympathies?

2   How justified do you think *The Times* writer is in his claim that 'the Budget is merely the culmination of a design deliberately adopted and steadily pursued'?

● SOURCE 6.45

From Herbert H. Asquith in the House of Commons, 2 December 1909, in which the Prime Minister announces his intention to call an election for January 1910 on the issue of 'Peers v. People'.

*. . . I am not going to discuss in reference to this unprecedented act the merits of the Finance Bill with the House of Lords, but I think it is only fair and right, before I bring my case to a conclusion, that I should examine such justifications as have been put forward for the action which has been taken. In the first place I have seen it suggested . . . that this bill was not a finance bill at all, and that therefore the constitutional rule does not apply. That, of course, is one of the most absurd contentions . . . Here is a bill of nearly one hundred clauses, which imposed ten or eleven different sets of taxes. I will undertake to say there was not a single clause which was not relevant to its primary and governing purpose – namely, the raising of revenue.*

*. . . The House of Lords have deliberately chosen their ground. They have elected to set at nought in regard to finance the unwritten and time-honoured conventions of our Constitution. In so doing, whether they foresaw it or not, they have opened out a wider and more far-reaching issue. We have not provoked the challenge, but we welcome it. We believe that the first principles of representative government, as embodied in our slow and ordered but ever-broadening constitutional development, are at stake, and we ask the House of Commons by this Resolution today, as at the earliest possible moment we shall ask the constituencies of the country, to declare that the organ, the voice of the free people of this country, is to be found in the elective representative of the nation.*

---

1 How is *The Times'* claim that the Budget is merely the 'culmination of a design deliberately adopted and steadily pursued' (Source 6.44) disputed by Asquith in Source 6.45?

2 Why, in the circumstances of 1909, might Asquith be so anxious to insist that the 'primary and governing purpose' of the Budget had been 'the raising of revenue'?

3 How effective do you think the language and argument employed by Asquith would have been in winning support both from the supporters of the government and from its opponents?

4 How useful are Sources 6.42–6.45 as evidence of the bitterness of the debate?

## How did the electorate respond to the constitutional crisis?

Two months after the election of January 1910, Asquith announced his intention to proceed with the Budget and to bring in a Parliament Bill to reform the House of Lords. He proposed to abolish the Lords' authority over money bills and to restrict their right to delay other legislation to a maximum period of two years. Asquith made it plain that he would either ask the King to create a majority of Liberal peers to swamp the Conservative-dominated Upper House, or resign and let Balfour form a minority government. The House of Lords reluctantly passed the Budget but the attack on its powers was delayed by the death of King Edward VII in May 1910. The new King, George V, was in a difficult position. Asquith tried to break the deadlock with a round table conference with Opposition leaders, but rejected demands for a referendum and called another General Election in December 1910.

● SOURCE 6.46

From D. Butler and J. Freeman (eds), *British Political Facts 1900–1960,* 1963.

General Election results, 1900–10.

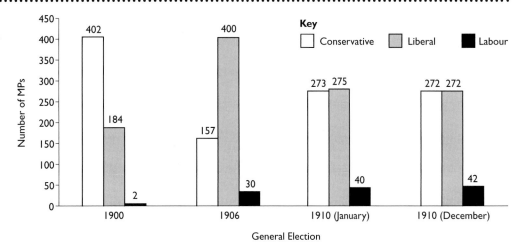

## To what extent did the constitutional crisis end in victory for the Liberals?

● **SOURCE 6.47**

From the Parliament Act, 1911, summarising the main clauses of the act with specific reference to money bills.

*And whereas it is intended to substitute for the House of Lords as it at present exists a Second Chamber constituted on a popular instead of hereditary basis, but such substitution cannot be immediately brought into operation:*

*And whereas provision will require hereafter to be made by Parliament in a measure effecting such substitution for limiting and defining the powers of the new Second Chamber, but it is expedient to make such provision as in this Act appears for restricting the existing powers of the House of Lords:*

*Be it therefore enacted . . .*

1  *If a Money Bill, having been passed by the House of Commons, and sent up to the House of Lords at least one month before the end of the session, is not passed by the House of Lords without amendment within one month after it is so sent up to that House, the Bill shall . . . be presented to His Majesty and become an Act of Parliament on the Royal Assent being signified, notwithstanding that the House of Lords have not consented to the Bill.*

   *A Money Bill means a Public Bill . . . [that] contains only provisions dealing with . . .regulation of taxation; the imposition for the payment of debt . . . supply . . . of public money; the raising or guarantee of any loan or the repayment thereof . . . the expressions 'taxation', 'public money', and 'loan' respectively do not include any taxation, money, or loan raised by local authorities or bodies for local purposes.*

   *There shall be endorsed on every Money Bill when it is sent up to the House of Lords and when it is presented to His Majesty for assent the certificate of the Speaker of the House of Commons signed by him that it is a Money Bill . . .*

2  *If any Public Bill (other than a Money Bill or a Bill containing any provision to extend the maximum duration of Parliament beyond five years) is passed by the House of Commons in three successive sessions (whether of the same Parliament or not), and, having been sent up to the House of Lords at least one month before the end of the session, is rejected by the House of Lords in each of those sessions, that Bill shall, on its rejection for the third time by the House of Lords, unless the House of Commons direct to the contrary, be presented to His Majesty and become an Act of Parliament on the Royal Assent being signified thereto, notwithstanding that the House of Lords have not consented to the Bill . . .*

# What was the impact of old age pensions on the elderly?

● **SOURCE 6.48**

From the *Norwich Mercury*, 9 January 1909, describing the first payment of old age pensions and its implications for the future.

---

**GPO**

General Post Office. Payment of the pension through the Post Office was intended to remove any association of the new scheme with the Poor Law.

---

*Friday was the beginning of a new era for the aged poor of this country, as on that date the first payment of Old Age pensions was made. In Norwich, at numbers of the district Post Offices there were old people waiting for the doors to open at 8 o'clock and by 9 o'clock the stream of callers was in full flow. As was necessarily to be expected the business done at the GPO was overwhelmingly larger than anywhere else. The first pensioner, an old man, made his call at 9.15. Close on his heels came an old lady. They produced their coupon books without a word, answered one or two routine questions, made their signature, pocketed their money and walked out. A small proportion of the applicants were unable to write their names.*

*It is evident that the incoming of pensions will have considerable effect upon the future of various charities in the nature of alms-houses and other foundations designed for the relief of old age. For example, the rule of the Great Hospital is that no one with an income of over £12 a year is eligible for admission . . . We believe the trustees have already come to a decision whereby the recipients of Old Age Pensions will be debarred in future.*

---

1 According to Source 6.48, to what extent was the introduction of pensions popular with the aged poor?

2 Why did the *Norwich Mercury* regard the coming of old age pensions as 'the beginning of a new era for the aged poor'?

---

● **SOURCE 6.49**

From *The Times*, 11 November 1911, describing the implications of old age pensions for the aged poor in workhouses.

---

After 31 December 1910, people who had been living in workhouses were no longer disqualified from drawing old age pensions, provided, of course, that they left the workhouse.

---

**The police court**

*At Marylebone Mr Plowden had before him a summons against a man in respect of his mother's maintenance. It was shown that the woman sometime since took her discharge from the Paddington workhouse to receive the Old Age pension. She had, however, now returned to the workhouse.*

*Mr Plowden expressed surprise at her being received back. Mr Bannister, the relieving officer, said that nearly all the old age pensioners had returned to the workhouse. They found it was more comfortable than being outside.*

*Mr Plowden said that as long as workhouses maintained their present standard of luxury no one would care about the old age pension. Once having tasted the luxury they would not give it up for 5s. a week.*

---

● **SOURCE 6.50**

From Flora Thompson, *Lark Rise to Candleford*, 1939, in which the author, who was a Post Office worker in an Oxfordshire village, describes the impact of old age pensions on the lives of independent aged poor.

---

*The Poor Law authorities allowed old people past work a small weekly sum as outdoor relief; but it was not sufficient to live upon, and, unless they had more than usually prosperous children to help support them, there came a time when the home had to be broken up. When, twenty years later, the Old Age Pensions began, life was transformed for such aged cottagers. They were suddenly rich. Independent for life! At first when they went to the post office to draw it, tears of gratitude would run down the cheeks of some, and they would say as they picked up their money, 'God bless that Lord George! (for they could not believe one so powerful and munificent could be a plain 'Mr') and God bless you, miss!' and there were flowers from their gardens and apples from their trees for the girl who merely handed them the money.*

● **SOURCE 6.51**

*The New Year's Gift*, a cartoon from *Punch*, 6 January 1909, commenting on the beginning of old age pensions.

THE NEW YEAR'S GIFT.

● **SOURCE 6.52**

Adapted from *The Times*, 18 October 1911, reporting on the Returns of Pauperism in London. It attributed the reduction in the number claiming relief mainly to the change allowing aged paupers to claim old age pensions.

Pauperism in London, 1908–11.

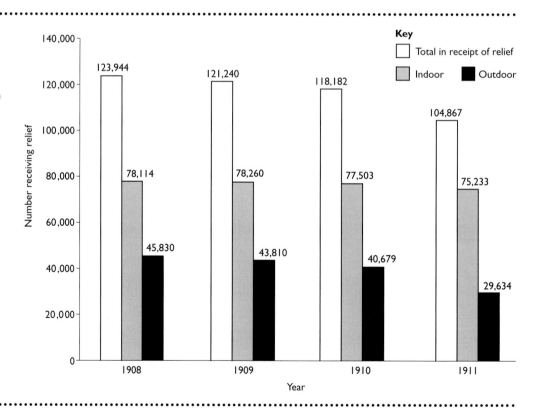

Key
☐ Total in receipt of relief
▨ Indoor   ■ Outdoor

1 Study Sources 6.48–6.52.

What were the effects of old age pensions upon

a) people in the workhouses
b) people receiving outdoor relief
c) the work of private charities
d) the attitude and values of the poor?

219

What reforms were introduced to improve the welfare of the aged?

● SOURCE 6.53

From R. Roberts, *The Classic Slum: Salford Life in the First Quarter of the Century*, 1971, in which the author, who grew up poor in the Salford area, criticises the limitations of the 1908 act.

*largesse*
large gifts, generosity

*Ever since the German Parliament in 1889 had passed the model 'law of insurance against old age and infirmity' there had been much talk, but no action, in England about making similar provisions for the aged. At last, in 1908, the Liberal government allocated £1,200,000 for the establishment of a non-contributory old-age pension scheme and an act was passed to become law on 1 January 1909. Pensions, however, would be withheld from those 'who had failed to work habitually according to their ability and need, and those who had failed to save money regularly'. Here was a means test with a vengeance. Paupers were not entitled to any pension.*

*There was to be no doling out of LARGESSE under the scheme. Pensions were graduated from 1s. to 5s. [5p to 25p] a week, provided the recipients had already an income of less than £31 a year. The combined weekly allowance for a married couple was fixed at 7s. 6d. [37½p] Nevertheless, even these small doles meant life itself for many among the elderly poor. Old folk, my mother said, spending their allowance at the shop, 'would bless the name of Lloyd George as if he were a saint from heaven'. The government met with much opposition to the introduction of a pension scheme from both the middle and working classes. Free gifts of money, many urged, would dishearten the thrifty who saved for their old age, and encourage the idle. Lord Rosebery, the great Liberal peer, had even greater misgivings: the provision of old age pensions, he thought, 'might deal a blow at the Empire which could be almost mortal'. Meanwhile our elderly paupers still went to the workhouse.*

1   According to Source 6.53, who were excluded from receiving a pension?

2   To what extent did nineteenth-century morality survive in the scheme?

3   What was the significance of the fact that it was a non-contributory scheme?

4   Why was there to be 'no doling out of largesse under the scheme'?

5   Why did old age pensions meet with 'much opposition ... from both the middle and working classes'?

Old age pensions were very popular. The government estimated that there would be 500,000 pensioners at a cost of £6.5 million but in fact there were 650,000 at £8 million in 1909, rising to just under 1 million people by 1915. As with child welfare, the Liberals' decision to provide a non-contributory scheme financed out of general taxation represented a new approach by the state to the relief of poverty. However, the provisions of the act were disappointingly limited for more radical reformers. Some aspects of relief of the aged under the Poor Law survived, although responsibility for financing relief passed from local to central government, from the rates to general taxes.

# 5 What reforms were introduced to improve the welfare of the able-bodied?

Legislation to help the working classes was driven by a complex range of influences. Popular pressure was an important factor in the introduction of unemployment insurance (1911), as was the need to divert the working class away from more extreme socialist solutions to their problems. The introduction of health insurance (1911) was driven by the need to improve people's health in the interests of national efficiency, as well as by concern for the welfare of the individual.

Statistical work by the Board of Trade and the example of welfare reform carried out in Germany led to the introduction of labour exchanges in 1909. Electoral links between the Liberals and the Labour party led in 1906 to the Workmen's Compensation Act and the Trade Disputes Act. The latter restored to trade unions their protection from being sued by employers for compensation after strike action, a protection they had lost as a result of a court ruling in 1900. The Trade Boards Act of 1909, which fixed minimum wages and maximum hours in a range of sweated trades, was the result of pressure from women's organisations, individual politicians and a newspaper-led public campaign.

# What problems did able-bodied workers face?

● **SOURCE 6.54**

From G. Haw, *From Workhouse to Westminster: the Life Story of Will Crooks*, 1907, in which Crooks describes the problems faced by casual labourers in the 1870s.

**Will Crooks**
was the first person born in a workhouse to rise to become one of the London pioneers of the Labour Party and eventually the MP for Woolwich, 1903–18.

**degenerates**
becomes of weaker moral character or physical condition

*I just went down to the riverside at Shadwell. No work was to be had there. Then I called at another place in Limehouse. No hands wanted. So I looked in at home and got two slices of bread in paper and walked eight miles to a cooper's yard in Tottenham. All in vain. I dragged myself back to Clerkenwell. Still no luck. Then I turned towards home in despair. By the time I reached Stepney I was dead beat, so I called at a friend's in Commercial Road for a little rest. They gave me some Irish stew and twopence to ride home. I managed to walk home and gave the twopence to my wife . . .*

*A man who is out of work for long nearly always DEGENERATES. For example, if a decent fellow falls out in October and fails to get a job say by March, he loses his anxiety to work. The exposure, the insufficient food, his half-starved condition, have such a deteriorating effect upon him that he becomes indifferent whether he gets work or not. He thus passes from the unemployed state to the unemployable state. It ought to be a duty of the nation to see that a man does not become degenerate.*

I   Why, according to Will Crooks in Source 6.54, was an unemployed man likely to degenerate?

● **SOURCE 6.55**

From Mrs Barnett, *Canon Barnett*, 1919, Vol. II, recording her husband's work in relieving distress in London during his period as vicar of Whitechapel, and his views on relief schemes available.

**1885**
*The report of the Committee which administered the [relief] fund in Whitechapel tells of how of 850 who were offered work, only 339 accepted the offer. The letter of the foreman is instructive. He says, 'The men were improvident, unsober and non-industrious. The lesson is enforced that although the poverty is great, so great that it may be said one-fifth of the inhabitants of Whitechapel have insufficient food and clothing, yet that this poverty, being due to weakness of mind and body, is out of the reach of such careless remedies as relief funds.'*

**1905**
*The winter of 1903–1904 began . . . without any adequate preparation and many of the things that ought to be done were impossible. The difficulty was met by relief doles in West Ham, and by the Central Committee for the Relief of the Unemployed. Within six weeks from its start there were Committees in each borough who were able to receive applications and visit applicants and put within their reach the sort of help or work they seemed to need . . . over 2,000 men were put to work and openings secured which gave occupation to some thousands more.*

*The work was ill-done and proved to be very costly. The men knew that it was made for them, and it seemed to them unfair that work should be required when the money had been given for their use. They knew that no one was concerned to dismiss them, so slack work became the order of the day, and men who started with a good will have confessed that the display of energy brought them into disrepute . . . once more an experiment in relief work has shown that it is not only costly, but demoralising. The recipients made no efforts to do themselves good, and on one gang the effect of an extra and unexpected day's work was to bring them drunk to the pay table.*

● **SOURCE 6.56**

From the *Norwich Mercury*, 23 December 1904, describing attempts to relieve distress during the harsh period 1904–05.

*It has been decided to give tickets of the value of sixpence each to all applicants who are considered worthy of relief. These tickets provide for the supply of the actual necessities of life and are negotiable with any tradesmen upon whom the holders like to call. The tickets will be distributed in the proportion of four for every adult and one each for every child. In deciding who are the proper recipients the Committee have had to take into account the collective earnings of each family . . . It is estimated that the number of tickets to be distributed will amount to three thousand . . .*

221

What reforms were introduced to improve the welfare of the able-bodied?

1  What, according to Source 6.55, was the cause of poverty amongst the poor of Whitechapel?

2  What were the main features of the relief provided for the unemployed?

3  What was the effect of the provision of relief on the unemployed of Whitechapel?

4  Why does Canon Barnett criticise the experiment in relief schemes in West Ham?

5  What measures were introduced in Norwich to relieve distress from unemployment (Source 6.56)?

## How did the Liberals attempt to deal with poverty caused by unemployment and sickness?

Before 1911 the vast majority of people had to rely on charity hospitals and dispensaries to treat them when they were sick and on the Poor Law to provide relief when they could not earn a living. Working-class pride revolted against such a situation, especially the Poor Law with its harsh and humiliating conditions. In 1909 the government introduced a system of labour exchanges, with the aim of directing surplus labour to places where it was needed and thereby reducing the number of unemployed. Lloyd George was also determined to introduce a national insurance scheme that would provide an income for people when they were sick or unemployed and he wanted the state to pay the full cost of it through taxation. However, his plans provoked great controversy. Opinion ranged from those who wanted no scheme to those who wanted a universal, free health service. A compromise measure had to be adopted. It was decided that the scheme would cover only men aged between 16 and 70, and earning less than £160 per year. The cost of insurance was to be divided between the state, the employer and the workman.

● SOURCE 6.57

From a speech made by Winston Churchill in the House of Commons, 19 May 1909, in which he argues the need for labour exchanges.

Earlier on in the speech he had argued that the idea was supported by both reports of the Royal Commission on the Poor Laws, 1909, by trade union leaders and by the Labour Party. Britain was copying the example set by European countries such as Germany.

*There are two general defects in the industrial position of this country, the lack of mobility of labour and the lack of information about all these questions of unemployment. For both defects the labour exchanges afford a remedy. Modern industry is national. Transport and communication knit the country together as no country has ever been knitted before. Labour alone has not profited by this improved organisation. The method by which labour obtains its market today is the old method, hawking labour about from place to place, and treating a job as a thing which places a man under an obligation when he has got it. The movement of labour when it is necessary should be effected with the least friction, the least suffering, the least loss of time and of status to the individual who is called upon by the force of economic conditions to move. The result of the policy will be to make it easy for him to move the moment the ordinary economic events arise which make movement necessary. Labour exchanges will not to any large extent create new employment. What they are going to do is to organise the existing labour by which we cannot help raising the general standard of economic life.*

*Labour exchanges are indispensable to any system of unemployment insurance, since it is not possible to make the distinction between the vagrant and the loafer on the one hand and the bona fide workman on the other, except in some elaborate and effective system of testing willingness to work such as is afforded by the system of labour exchanges. I shall tomorrow have an opportunity of asking the permission of the House to introduce this Bill, and we present it to the House as a piece of social machinery, nothing more and nothing less, the need of which has long been apparent, and the want of which has been widely and cruelly felt by large numbers of our fellow countrymen.*

1  What, according to Churchill in Source 6.57, are the two defects affecting the industrial position?

2  How did labourers find new employment before 1909?

3  What were the defects of this method?

4  What, according to Churchill, would be the benefits of labour exchanges?

5  Why were labour exchanges 'indispensable' to any system of unemployment insurance?

● SOURCE 6.58

From William Beveridge, *Unemployment: A Problem of Industry*, 1909, in which the author develops the new thinking on unemployment.

**William Beveridge**
had been a sub-warden at the Toynbee Hall settlement from 1903 to 1907, where he had been influenced by Charles Booth. In 1908 he joined the Board of Trade as a civil servant. He believed that unemployment was an inevitable result of the capitalist industrial system. He argued that there were bound to be periods of depression when no work was available, and believed that workers needed help to find work and financial support. He also believed that the state should create work in times of depression. These views became the basis of Liberal policy on unemployment.

**national ownership of the means of production**
nationalisation, or government control, of industries

*The de-casualisation of employment . . . may appeal to the Socialist as a part of that industrial organisation in regard to which . . . NATIONAL OWNERSHIP OF THE MEANS OF PRODUCTION is but a means to an end. It may appeal to the individualist, because by diminishing the chances of the labour market it gives more decisive influence to individual merit. The principle is clear – that every man who cannot be regularly employed by one firm should be engaged only from an Exchange . . . The practical application of the principle involves, no doubt, some system of public Labour Exchanges to cover the large amount of ground which will certainly not be covered in any other way . . . Casual employment is no local disease; it is found in all towns and to some extent in nearly all trades.*

*. . . De-casualisation is only a special form of labour market organisation. The under-employment of the dock labourer is paralleled by the constant leakage of employment and earnings affecting substantial minorities in nearly all occupations, skilled and unskilled alike. The problem . . . among the skilled men is not as a rule urgent, simply because the wages are as a rule high enough, particularly when spread out through unemployed benefits, to allow for an ample margin of idleness. The problem, however, differs only in degree, not in kind. The crowding of the labour market is common to the highest and the lowest ranks of industry, and in all ranks arises from the same central fact – the division of the total demand for labour in fluctuating proportions between different employers and different districts.*

*The concentration of demand at centres is required . . . to bring about the recruiting of trades in accordance with their real growth . . . and to give to employment in each occupation as a whole something of the continuity . . . Some measure of protection for those within a trade or district against the competition of those outside is an essential consequence of a system of Labour Exchanges. The aim of such a system is, . . . the enabling of men to go at once where they are wanted, but at the same time the discouraging of movement to places where men are not wanted.*

1  In Source 6.58, what is meant by a 'de-casualisation of employment'?

2  Why, according to Beveridge, were labour exchanges required?

3  What were the benefits of labour exchanges?

● SOURCE 6.59

From William Beveridge, *Unemployment: A Problem of Industry*, 1909, in which Beveridge develops his views on the importance of a state-provided insurance scheme against periods of unemployment.

*Insurance against unemployment . . . forms the second line of attack on the problem of unemployment. The Labour Exchange is required to reduce to a minimum the intervals between successive jobs. Insurance is required to tide over the intervals that will still remain. Insurance is needed to provide for . . . maintenance . . . while standing idle . . . No plan other than insurance, whether purely self-supporting or with assistance from other sources, is really adequate. The provision . . . must be far more flexible than anything to be achieved along the lines either of relief works or of elasticity in working hours. The provision required is one made in part by the individual himself; by simple grants of money . . . It cannot be made by the individual acting alone: unemployment may never come to him at all, but when it does come, may exceed all possibilities of private saving. The principle of insurance – which is simply that of spreading the wages in a trade so as to provide for the necessary margin of idleness in the trade – is therefore essential. It is at the same time adequate. The spreading of the burden of unemployment over all the men of the trade would make the burden tolerable in all but the most casual occupations. The premiums required for insurance in the principal unions are small relatively to the total wages – smaller indeed in most cases than the amounts added to those wages within recent years. There is no reason why the trade unions themselves should not extend the system of unemployed benefits. There is ample warrant in foreign example for giving State encouragement to such extension. There would, according to the opinion of those best qualified to judge – the authors of the German report already quoted – be no impossibility in the State's applying the principle of insurance to the risk of unemployment quite generally and comprehensively, once a test of unemployment had been made available.*

223

What reforms were introduced to improve the welfare of the able-bodied?

1  How would a system of insurance, as described in Source 6.59, supplement the work of labour exchanges?

2  How would insurance against unemployment benefit the able-bodied?

3  What do you think would be the limitations of an insurance scheme provided only by trade unions?

● **SOURCE 6.60**

From *Law Reports*, 1909, detailing some of the clauses from the Labour Exchanges Act, 1909.

**1**  *The Board of Trade may . . .*

*. . . establish and maintain, in such places as they think fit, labour exchanges.*

*. . . collect and furnish information as to employers requiring workpeople and workpeople seeking engagement or employment.*

*. . . authorise advances to be made by way of loan towards meeting the expenses of workpeople travelling to places where employment has been found for them through a labour exchange . . .*

**3**  *Labour Exchange means any office or place to be used for the purpose of collecting and furnishing information . . . respecting employers who desire to engage workpeople and workpeople who seek engagement or employment.*

1  What provisions did the 1909 Labour Exchanges Act (Source 6.60) make to help the unemployed find work?

● **SOURCE 6.61**

From Part II of the National Insurance Act, 1911, summarising the scheme for unemployment insurance introduced for those trades whose workers had been vulnerable to fluctuating levels of employment. The scheme covered 2.25 million workers.

*The scheme of insurance against unemployment which is contained in Part II of the National Insurance Act is to be administered by the Board of Trade . . . The object of the scheme is twofold.*

*In the first place provision is made for the payment of contribution by all employers and workpeople in the trades mentioned below, and for the payment of benefit to the workpeople when unemployed. This part of the scheme is compulsory. In the second place provision is made for the encouragement of voluntary insurance against unemployment by means of money grants from State funds to associations of persons, in all trades and occupations, which pay out-of-work benefits.*

**II  The Compulsory Insured Trades**

*On and after Monday, 15 July, 1912, all workpeople (whether men or women) over 16 years of age who are engaged wholly or mainly by way of manual labour in the following trades will be compulsorily insured against unemployment and have contributions towards the Unemployment Fund deducted from their wages:*

*1 Building . . .*
*2 Construction of Works . . .*
*3 Shipbuilding . . .*
*4 Mechanical Engineering . . .*
*5 Ironfounding . . .*
*6 Construction of vehicles . . .*
*7 Sawmilling . . .*

*Foremen other than manual workmen, clerks, indentured apprentices, and persons under 16 years of age are excluded.*

1  What did Part II of the National Insurance Act (Source 6.61) aim to achieve?

2  Which groups of workers were covered by the act?

3  Which groups were excluded from the act?

To what extent did the welfare reforms of 1900–14 change the lives of ordinary people?

224

Mortality rates had remained high amongst the working-class poor since many could not afford to insure themselves through friendly societies to cover the payment of medical bills.

*What is the explanation that only a portion of the working classes have made provision against sickness and unemployment? Because very few can afford to pay the premiums at a rate of 1s. 6d. [7½p] or 2s. [10p] per week at the very lowest. There are a multitude of the working classes who cannot spare that, because it involves the deprivation of children of the necessaries of life. Therefore the vast majority choose to insure against death alone. Those who can afford to take up two policies insure against death and sickness, and those who can afford to take up three insure against death, sickness and unemployment, but only in that order. Why not insure against all three? Their wages are too low to enable them to insure against all three. The second difficulty is that during a period of sickness or unemployment, when they are earning nothing, they cannot keep up the premiums, so, in circumstances over which they have no control, [they] abandon their policies. That is the reason why not one-half of the workmen have made any provision for sickness and not one-tenth for unemployment. There is a real need for some system which would aid the workmen over these difficulties. A system of national insurance which would invoke the aid of the State and of the employer to enable the workman to get over these difficulties and make provision for himself for sickness, and, as far as the most precarious trades are concerned, against unemployment.*

1 Why, according to Source 6.62, could only a portion of the working classes take out insurance policies?

2 In what order did working men take out insurance policies?

3 Why were they forced to abandon their policies?

4 Why was intervention by the state essential for any insurance scheme?

5 What do you think would be the cost implications of a state-provided scheme?

## Who opposed the introduction of a National Insurance Bill?

Part I of the National Insurance Bill provided for insured workers to receive free medical treatment from doctors who kept a register of such patients. Lloyd George wanted the medical insurance scheme to be administered by the friendly societies because of their experience, skill and organisation in providing private benefits to their insured members. This proposal was met with hostility by the medical profession.

*13 May*
*The Bill is a call to a great social duty, and we are confident that the medical profession will not be slow to respond and to lend every assistance that lies in its power to accomplish the desire of the nation 'to conquer the pestilence that walketh in darkness and the destruction that wasteth at noonday'.*

*20 May (a week later)*
*. . . reports from all over the country show that GPs are, to an extent never witnessed before, thoroughly roused and more than discontented that the measure, intended for the good of the working classes in the first place, should have been framed in a way which must inevitably inflict irreparable damage on the medical profession if the provisions affecting its interests do not undergo drastic amendment . . . [The profession] will, we believe, resist to the bitter end a scheme which will place it under the control of the friendly societies and at their mercy.*

● **SOURCE 6.64**

From W. J. Braithwaite, *Lloyd George's Ambulance Wagon: The Memoirs of William J. Braithwaite*, 1957, in which he explains the reasons for doctors' hostility to the private scheme of medical insurance operated by many friendly societies.

*I have interviewed a large number of doctors on the medical side of this scheme. They all agree in denouncing the present system of medical relief as organised by Friendly Societies. Doctors employed by these societies are paid an inclusive fee. This fee covers drugs and cheaper medical appliances. This fee is obviously insufficient and the medical profession are up in arms against it. I am assured that it has resulted in handing over this class of practice entirely to the more incompetent members of the profession, who shun the more costly drugs, however necessary they may be to effect a cure, and who habitually deceive their patients by plying them with water charged with pure colouring matter.*

Study Sources 6.63 and 6.64.

1  Why, according to the *British Medical Journal*, were doctors 'thoroughly roused and more than discontented'?

2  Why did doctors believe that administration of national insurance by the friendly societies would 'inevitably inflict irreparable damage on the medical profession'?

3  To what extent does the report of the *British Medical Journal* indicate that the doctors were not totally opposed to the idea of a national insurance scheme?

4  What abuses had developed under the scheme of medical insurance run by the friendly societies (Source 6.64)?

● **SOURCE 6.65**

From *The Times*, 12 June 1911, reporting on Lloyd George's 'Ambulance Wagon' speech at Birmingham.

**this bill**
the National Health Insurance scheme

*I never said THIS BILL was a final solution. I am not putting it forward as a complete remedy. It is one of a series. We are advancing on the road, but it is an essential part of the journey. I have been now some years in politics and I have had, I think, as large a share of contention and strife and warfare as any man in British politics today. This year, this Session, I have joined the Red Cross. I am in the ambulance corps. I am engaged to drive a wagon through the twistings and turnings and ruts of the Parliamentary road. There are men who tell me I have overloaded that wagon. I have taken three years to pack it carefully. I cannot spare a single parcel, for the suffering is very great. There are those who say my wagon is half empty. I say it is as much as I can carry. Now there are some who say I am in a great hurry. I am rather in a hurry, for I can hear the moanings of the wounded, and I want to carry relief to them in the alleys, the homes where they lie stricken, and I ask you, and through you, I ask the millions of good-hearted men and women who constitute the majority of the people of this land – I ask you to help me to set aside hindrances, to overcome obstacles, to avoid the pitfalls that beset my difficult path.*

1  How did Lloyd George respond to the critics of his health insurance proposals (Source 6.65)?

2  What encouragement did he give to those critics who wanted a more ambitious scheme?

● **SOURCE 6.66**

From *The Times*, 7 December 1911, reporting a statement by six disaffected members of the Labour Party (including Keir Hardie, Philip Snowden and George Lansbury), who objected to acceptance of a contributory scheme in 1911.

*We have opposed the Bill, first because of its contributory character. By exacting contributions from the workers to finance so-called schemes of social reforms, we are not only adopting a policy which can bring no real improvement, but we are continuing a practice which two generations of experience have proved to be ineffective and impractical. The contributory plan has been abandoned in our education system, in public health administration and in practically all our national services . . .; it is a discredited, irritating, unjust and wasteful method of financing a great national scheme . . . The method of compelling the employers to pay according to the amount of labour they employ instead of upon the profits they make is certain to fall as an additional burden upon the workpeople. It will encourage the displacement of labour by machinery; it will add to the cost of commodities . . . and it will be an excuse for resisting demands for the advances of wages. We object to the Bill, also, because it does not give relief to those who stand most in need of it and who are least able to help themselves. A contributory scheme can give conditional benefits only to those who contribute and a vast number of the poorer workers will never be able to fulfil the conditions laid down in this Bill.*

226

To what extent did the welfare reforms of 1900–14 change the lives of ordinary people?

● **SOURCE 6.67**

From a diary entry for 1 December 1912, *Beatrice Webb's Diaries, 1912–1914*, in which Beatrice Webb comments on her disappointment at the limitations of the National Insurance Act.

*The plain fact is that Lloyd George and the Radicals have out-trumped the Labour Party. They have taken up semi-socialist devices like compulsory insurance, which cannot be easily opposed even by the Conservative Party . . .*

*But we must make the best of the Insurance Act, and use to the full all its incidental advantages – it is something to have got the whole of the working population registered from the age of 16; it is a step forward to have some sort of machinery for paying out weekly pensions to sick and invalided without the stigma of pauperism, and the statistics of illness automatically collected will be of great value. The big fault of the Act is the creation of huge vested interests – the Industrial Insurance Companies' method of collection and the Panel system of medical attendance. These vested interests mean not only waste of public money and financial chaos . . . but wholesale demoralisation of character through the fraudulent withholding or the fraudulent getting of benefits . . .*

---

Study Sources 6.66 and 6.67, both reporting the reaction of some socialists to the 1911 insurance scheme.

1  What effect did the six disaffected Labour MPs believe the scheme would have on
   a) employers
   b) labour?

2  Why did they claim the scheme was limited?

3  What did Beatrice Webb regard as the beneficial elements of the Insurance Act?

4  What were her main criticisms?

5  How far did she agree with the six Labour MPs that the act did not serve the interests of the workers?

6  How would the Labour Party have preferred the insurance scheme to operate?

7  How do you explain the difference in attitudes shown in the two sources towards the insurance scheme?

---

● **SOURCE 6.68**

From an article, 'Some Reasons why the Public should Oppose the Insurance Act', 30 December 1911, by Sir James Barr, President of the British Medical Association, in the *British Medical Journal*. The author criticises the National Insurance Bill and its effect on the individual.

*The National Insurance Bill is a long step in the downward path towards socialism. It will tend to destroy individual effort, and increase that spirit of dependency which is ever to be found in degenerate races. This spoon-fed race will look more and more to a paternal government to feed and clothe it, and not require it to work more than a few hours daily. They will be further encouraged to multiply their breed at the expense of the healthy and intellectual members of the community.*

---

1  What view is advanced in Source 6.68 by Sir James Barr regarding a policy of state interference?

2  What are Barr's specific criticisms of the National Insurance Bill?

3  To what extent did debate of the National Insurance Bill indicate the survival of traditional nineteenth-century attitudes towards the individual and the role of the state?

4  Using the evidence of Sources 6.66–6.68, explain why the National Insurance Act of 1911 was such a controversial measure.

---

## What other measures did the Liberals introduce to protect workers?

The Workmen's Compensation Act of 1906 was the Liberal government's first important welfare legislation. There had been an earlier Compensation Act, which had made it compulsory for employers to compensate employees who were left incapable of earning a living as the result of an accident at work, but it had covered only a limited number of occupations. The 1906 act was more extensive. Other legislation included limits on working hours and a minimum wage.

● **SOURCE 6.69**

From *The Times*, 13 December 1906, reporting on the third reading of the Workmen's Compensation for Accidents and Industrial Diseases Bill.

*Mr Gladstone* (Home Secretary) moved the third reading; he said, 'Practically all classes of persons who are under contract of service, whether their employment is dangerous or safe, are included within the purview of the Bill . . . by this Bill an additional 6 million are made entitled to compensation for injuries sustained in their employment. I hope that great benefit will result from this enormous extension . . . hope that small employers will be aroused to a sense of the duty imposed upon them to insure against the liability to which they may be exposed . . .'

*Mr Gill* (Bolton) said, 'I support the third reading which now includes almost all classes of workers . . . I think too much has been made of the danger of encouraging malingerers . . . With other improvements the Government are to be congratulated upon the introduction of compensation for illness caused by diseases contracted in the course of employment. The diseases included in the schedule are few in number but I have confidence the Home Secretary will extend the list to cover all dangerous trades as evidence justifies his doing so.'

*Mr Money* (Paddington) said, 'Although the Bill has wisely included domestic servants, charwomen will be excluded. This is very unjust . . . Some of the most distressful cases of industrial disease do not come within the operation of the Bill.'

1 Explain the phrase 'danger of encouraging malingerers', as used in Source 6.69.

2 In what ways did the Liberal bill build on previous legislation?

3 How extensive was the bill?

4 What are Mr Money's criticisms of the limitations of the bill?

5 What were the implications for employers of the provisions of the bill?

● **SOURCE 6.70**

From the Trade Boards Act, 1909, identifying some of the provisions that established a minimum wage for 200,000 workers.

**Section 3**

A Trade Board for any trade shall consider . . . any matter referred to them, by a Secretary of State, the Board of Trade, or any other Government Department with reference to the industrial conditions of the trade.

**Section 4(1)**

Trade Boards shall fix minimum rates of wages for timework for their trades . . . and may also fix general minimum rates of wages for piecework for their trades . . .

**Section 5(2)**

Upon the expiration of six months from the date on which a Trade Board had given notice of any minimum time-rate or general minimum piece-rate fixed by them, the Board of Trade shall make an order . . . making that minimum rate obligatory in cases in which it is applicable on all persons employing labour and on all persons employed.

**Section 6(1)**

An employer . . . shall . . . pay wages to the person employed at not less than the minimum rate . . . and if he fails to do so shall be liable on summary conviction to a fine not exceeding £20 and to a fine not exceeding £5 for each day on which the offence is continued after conviction thereof.

**Schedule: Trades to which the Act applies**

1 Ready made and wholesale bespoke tailoring
2 The making of boxes of paper, cardboard, chip or similar material
3 Machine-made lace and net finishing and mending or darning . . .
4 Hammered and dollied or tommied chain-making.

1 What provisions were made by the Trade Boards Act (Source 6.70) to guarantee minimum wages?

2 What sanctions were provided for those employers who failed to pay a minimum wage?

3 What main trades were covered by the act?

4 To what extent did the 1909 act remedy the abuses associated with sweated labour? (Refer back to Chapter 2, pages 76–78 for more information.)

● SOURCE 6.71

From *The Times*, 7 July 1908, reporting on the debate in Parliament on the Eight Hours Bill to restrict working hours in the coal industry.

The coal industry was one of the earliest to number one million people in its workforce. It had close links with the formation of the Labour Party, and one of the first Labour MPs, Keir Hardie, was a Scottish miner.

*F. E. Smith* said, '. . . the Bill Labour members have pressed for during the last twenty years will . . . produce a shortage of coal causing insufferable inconvenience and possibly disastrous consequences to trade . . . a situation may be created under the eight hours system in which the economic interests of the miners will be opposed to the interests of the country at large . . .'

*Bonar Law* said, '. . . a small rise [in price] means much to every family and every working man in the country. The direct effect on the consumer will be that he will have to pay more for his coal and the indirect effect will be greater, for the price of coal is at the base of all our industries . . .'

*Churchill* (President of the Board of Trade) said, '. . . we believe that the well-being of the mining population, numbering some 900,000 persons, will be sensibly advanced in respect of health, industrial efficiency, habits of temperance, education, culture and the general habits of life . . . The general march of industrial democracy is not towards inadequate hours of work but towards sufficient hours of leisure . . .'

● SOURCE 6.72

From *Law Reports*, 1913, detailing the clauses of the Coal Industry Minimum Wages Act, 1912.

The 1912 act, though limited in scope, was significant for its shift away from the nineteenth-century *laissez-faire* attitude that the government did not intervene in setting wages.

1 (i)   It shall be an implied term of contract for the employment of a workman underground in a coal mine that the employer shall pay to that workman wages at not less than the minimum rate . . .

2 (i)   Minimum rates of wages and district rules for the purpose of this Act shall be settled separately for each district [there were 22 coal mining districts] . . . by a body of persons recognised by the Board of Trade as the joint district board.

(ii)   The Board of Trade may recognise as a joint district board . . . any body of persons which . . . in the opinion of the Board of Trade, fairly and adequately represents the workmen in coalmines in the district and the employers of those workmen, and the chairman of which is an independent person . . .

(iii)   The joint district board shall settle general minimum rates of wages and general district rules for their district . . .

Study Sources 6.71 and 6.72.

1   What were the main arguments for and against state control of hours and wages?

2   What machinery was set up for the fixing of wages?

# 6 How effective were Liberal social reforms, 1906–14?

● SOURCE 6.73

From Ministry of Health statistics, *Parliamentary Papers*, 1919.

Reduction of pauperism, for England and Wales compared with London, 1915–19.

| Year | Total population England and Wales (millions) | Total number of persons in England and Wales in receipt of poor relief (thousands) | Number per 1000 of total population in England and Wales in receipt of relief | Population of London (millions) | Number in receipt of relief in London (thousands) | Number per 1000 of London's population in receipt of relief |
|------|------|------|------|------|------|------|
| 1915 | 36.7 | 762 | 20.6 | 4.52 | 125 | 27.6 |
| 1916 | 37.3 | 685 | 18.4 | 4.54 | 108 | 23.7 |
| 1917 | 37.5 | 637 | 17.0 | 4.60 | 100 | 21.7 |
| 1918 | 37.6 | 587 | 15.6 | 4.49 | 91 | 20.3 |
| 1919 | 37.5 | 555 | 14.8 | 4.43 | 83 | 18.6 |

Study Source 6.73.

**1** To what extent do these statistics suggest that the Liberals had been successful in waging war against poverty?

**2** What reservations might historians have in accepting these figures in isolation?

● **SOURCE 6.74**

From R. C. Birch, *The Shaping of the Welfare State*, 1974, in which the author comments on the scope and scale of Liberal achievements.

---

**palliatives**
treatments that relieve symptoms rather than curing the disease

---

*The outbreak of war in 1914 found the welfare state in its infancy. The Poor Law was still the basis for the treatment of poverty, and unemployment benefits were low and limited in time. Treatment for ill-health, outside the Poor Law, was given to the worker and not to his family, and little was done for hospitals, specialist services or preventive medicine. In the wider sense of welfare, education was compulsory only up to the age of fourteen, and of the 200,000 pupils in secondary schools, only a quarter occupied free places; three million children, of whom many deserved better, were confined to primary education. Housing still lagged behind even basic necessity, and social reform of all kinds was still inhibited by the old laissez-faire suspicion of state intervention and still governed by the convenient permissive idea. PALLIATIVES, rather than radical programmes of reform, had been applied. Yet this kind of balance sheet tends to obscure real, if limited, achievement.*

● **SOURCE 6.75**

From D. Fraser, *The Evolution of the British Welfare State*, 1973, in which he assesses the significance of Liberal social reforms and their impact on the Poor Law.

*Lloyd George significantly pointed out, many of these [Liberal social policies] were actually provided for by the Poor Law, so that Liberal social policy was not just involved with extending state aid but [with] providing it on different, socially more acceptable terms. A person who was sick, hungry, unemployed or old could in fact turn to the Poor Law for help . . . [for the Liberals it was] . . . a deliberate act of policy to separate . . . newer provisions from the all-embracing but socially unacceptable scope of the Poor Law, and the Local Government Board was clearly right in anticipating that the ultimate result of such a policy was that the Poor Law would not so much be killed as die away through neglect. When all its functions were appropriated by other social institutions the Poor Law would fall apart. Whatever historical perspective is used, one cannot escape the conclusion that Liberal social policy before the First World War was at once at variance with the past and an anticipation of radical changes in the future. The work of continuing these developments was not performed by Liberal hands, for the greatest of all Liberal Governments turned out to be the last.*

**1** To what extent do Birch and Fraser (Sources 6.74 and 6.75) agree on Liberal achievements by 1914?

**2** What were the limitations of the social reforms in the period 1906 to 1914?

**3** How revolutionary was the Liberal social reform programme?

**4** What was the impact of Liberal reforms on the Poor Law?

**5** To what extent did the Liberals lay the foundations of the welfare state?

## ● Summary task

### 1 Group activity

As a class you are going to investigate the truth of the following claim

**'Reforms were introduced as a result of pressure from the Labour Party rather than flowing naturally out of Liberal philosophy.'**

This activity will help you to develop your key skills of research, analysis and evaluation. Divide the class into four groups representing
a) Defence counsel for the Liberal Party
b) Prosecution counsel for the Labour Party
c) Members of the jury
d) Court members.
Groups a)–c) need to read the sources relating to Liberal motives for sponsoring social reform and the details of the reform proposals. Each group will need to consider carefully possible reasons for Liberal fears of Labour and the need for reform in order to attract the loyalty of voters, as well as the extent to which the ideas of the Liberal collectivists were accepted by the rest of the party. Use the following table to record evidence to support your argument.

| Area | Policy | Motive/Influence? |
| --- | --- | --- |
| Child welfare | 1906<br>a) Free school meals<br>b) Free medical inspection | |
| Care of the elderly | 1908<br>Old age pensions | |
| Able-bodied and unemployment | 1909<br>Labour exchanges | |
| Insurance against ill-health and unemployment | 1911<br>National Insurance Act | |

The defence and prosecution teams must draw up their evidence and present their case to the jury and the court. There should be an opportunity for the jury and court to ask questions of the prosecution and defence teams. Before a vote is taken by secret ballot the jury/court should consider the following questions: Have you found it possible to arrive at a unanimous decision or is the jury divided? What is the view of the court? You might agree with the view of the contemporary Beatrice Webb who wrote, 'The plain fact is that Lloyd George and the Radicals have out-trumped the Labour Party. They have taken up semi-socialist devices like compulsory insurance, which cannot be easily opposed even by the Conservative Party...'

### 2 Individual activity

In this activity you need to evaluate whether the Liberal social reform record was 'disappointingly limited'.
a) Record the evidence using the following table to organise the results of your evaluation.

| Issue | Legislation | Terms of the act | Successful or disappointingly limited? |
| --- | --- | --- | --- |
| Child welfare | 1906<br>a) Free school meals<br>b) Free medical inspection | | |
| Care of the elderly | 1908 Old age pensions | | |
| Unemployment | 1909 Labour exchanges<br>1911 National Insurance Act (Part (II)) | | |
| Protection in the workplace | 1906 Workmen's Compensation Act<br>1908 Eight Hours Act – miners<br>1909 Trade Boards Act – 'sweated trades'<br>1912 Minimum Wages Act | | |
| Health | 1911 National Insurance Act (Part I) | | |

You will need to look back to Chapter 2 (pages 76–78) for Liberal reform of the sweated trades. You may also want to do further research on the reforms not covered in depth in this chapter, such as the 1910 Choice of Employment Act and the Shops Act of 1911.

b)  On the basis of your findings from the above activity, write an essay of about 2,000–2,500 words answering the following question

**To what extent is it valid to claim that the Liberal social reforms were disappointingly limited?**

**3  Group activity: assessment of Liberal reforms**

In groups use the evidence from this chapter to decide the extent to which each statement in the table below is true or false. Record your decisions in the appropriate column with a summary of supporting evidence.

| Assessment | True | False |
| --- | --- | --- |
| The Liberal governments were the architects of the welfare state | | |
| By 1914 most people, particularly the poor, were better off | | |
| The 1911 Parliament Act was a great step forward for democracy | | |

# Examples of examination-type questions

## A  AS questions

1  a) Why did the People's Budget cause such opposition in the House of Lords?
   b) To what extent was the outcome of the constitutional crisis of 1909–11 a success for the Liberal government?

## B  A2 questions

1  To what extent did Liberal social reforms mark a significant break with nineteenth-century attitudes towards the role of the state?

2  To what extent did Liberal social reforms mark a significant break with nineteenth-century attitudes towards poverty and the poor?

3  To what extent can Liberal social reforms be regarded as the beginnings of the welfare state?

## ● Further reading

Many of the books recommended in Chapter 5 cover the period 1900–14.
The following texts are specific to the Liberal period.

### Articles
P. Adelman, 'The Decline of the Liberal Party 1910–1931', *Modern History Review*, Vol. 1, Nos 1 and 2
S. Lemieux, 'A Rogue Result: Liberal Landslide 1906', *Modern History Review*, Vol. 4, No. 2
D. Tanner, 'New Liberalism and Government Reform 1906–1914', *Modern History Review*, Vol. 2, No. 2

### Fiction
Flora Thompson, *Lark Rise to Candleford* (OUP, 1939)

# chapter 7

# Who were the Chartists and why did they fail?

## 1832

Parliamentary Reform Act gives the vote to middle-class property owners and representation in Parliament to the new industrial towns of the North and Midlands.

## 1833

Factory Act bans the employment of children under nine in the spinning mills and reduces the hours worked by those between the ages of nine and eighteen.

Robert Owen forms his Grand National Consolidated Trades Union (GNCTU).

## 1834

Poor Law Amendment Act introduces the principle of 'less eligibility' and the workhouse test. Able-bodied poor can only receive relief in the workhouse.

Six farm labourers from the village of Tolpuddle in Dorset are tried and transported for the offence of administering unlawful oaths in an attempt to form a friendly Society of Agricultural Labourers as a section of the GNCTU. A public campaign is launched to secure the return of the Tolpuddle martyrs.

## 1835

Working Men's and Radical Associations are formed in Scotland and parts of the north of England.

## 1836

London Working Men's Association is formed.

## 1837–39

Economic distress and high social tension.

## 1837

Statement of the Six Points is issued by a joint committee of the London Working Men's Association and Radical MPs.

Various Radical Associations are formed to protest against the new Poor Law.

Birmingham Political Union declares its support for universal male suffrage.

Publication of the Chartist newspaper, the *Northern Star*, starts in Leeds.

## 1838

The People's Charter is published in London along with a National Petition.

First meeting of the Great Northern Union in Leeds.

Meeting at Birmingham launches a national campaign for the Charter.

Mass rallies and meetings are held.

## 1839

First National Convention of the Industrious Classes meets in London and then Birmingham.

Bull Ring riots in Birmingham in July.

Motion for consideration of the National Petition is defeated in the House of Commons by 235 to 46.

Outbreak of demonstrations and mass meetings.

Convention disperses.

Attempt at a rising in Newport, Monmouthshire, in November is defeated and leaders are executed.

Leading Chartists are arrested.

Three-day national holiday is staged with limited effect.

## 1840

Attempted uprisings at Sheffield and Bradford.

National Charter Association is founded in Manchester.

## 1841

William Lovett's National Association is founded.

Chartist support increases as a result of trade depression.

Sir Robert Peel and his Conservative Party win the General Election.

## 1842

Economy is at its lowest point. High social tension.

Complete Suffrage Union, a moderate, middle-class movement and a rival to the National Charter Association, is launched in Birmingham.

Second Chartist Convention meets in London.

Second Chartist Petition is presented in the Commons and defeated by 287 votes to 40.

Widespread outbreaks of strikes in the North and Midlands.

Chartists attempt to sabotage boilers – the Plug Plot.

Conference of trade delegates in Manchester calls for a strike in support of the Charter.

Conference convened by the Complete Suffrage Union in Birmingham breaks up when Chartist delegates carry a resolution in favour of the People's Charter. Attempts to unite the interests of middle-class and working-class supporters of radical reform follow.

## 1843

Trials of leading Chartists. Chartist Convention agrees to support Feargus O'Connor's Land Plan to buy land to resettle industrial workers.

## 1843–45

Period of prosperity and low social tension.

## 1845

Chartist Land Co-operative Society is approved by National Charter Association.

## 1846

Corn Laws are repealed.

## 1847

Ten Hours Factory Act is passed.

Economic crisis and depression. High social tension.

First Chartist land colony, O'Connorsville, is opened near Rickmansworth in Hertfordshire.

## 1848

Economic distress and high social tension.

Revolution in France leads to an end to the rule of King Louis Philippe.

Chartist Convention meets in London.

Kennington Common demonstration is held in London but the authorities prevent the Chartists from going in a large group to present their petition to Parliament.

Third Chartist petition is presented to Parliament and arouses ridicule because it contains fictitious signatures.

Riots in Bradford and east London.

Insurrectionary plotting, mainly in London and north-west.

## 1849

National Parliamentary and Financial Reform Association is founded to combine middle-class Radicals with moderate Chartists.

## 1850

National Reform League is founded by Bronterre O'Brien. Feargus O'Connor's leadership of Chartism weakens.

**1851**

Chartist Convention adopts extensive programme of social-democratic reform.

**1852**

George Julian Harney and Ernest Jones gain control of Chartism, but support drifts away as the economy becomes more prosperous.

**1858**

Last Chartist conference is held in London.

# Introduction

Industrial society with its increased size and greater concentration of young people in the towns placed enormous strains on resources and the machinery of government. The early towns were built too rapidly and before a sense of civic pride had developed, so that inadequate provision was made for housing, education and comforts such as parks and libraries. The crime rate rose and 'pure' crime, such as robbery, murder and violence, was supplemented by 'social' crime associated with bread riots and machine breaking. Sir James Graham, Home Secretary in Sir Robert Peel's Conservative Government of 1841 to 1846, spoke of the disturbances of the 1830s and the 1840s as 'a mad insurrection of the working classes'. This was a universally held attitude amongst the propertied classes prior to the 1850s. According to Graham, there was 'something inherent in an industrial society that predisposed men to riot'.

By the 1840s government was aware that something was wrong with the organisation of society and that government had a responsibility to remedy the situation. A more humanitarian approach was adopted. Home Secretaries, such as Sir James Graham, refused to continue to rely on the army, which had played the role of the police force of industrial England during the early years of the nineteenth century, to put down disturbances. A more constructive approach was adopted which combined remedies such as the removal of taxes on food and encouragement of education with the development of locally controlled police forces. However, the army remained in the background to deal with trouble in the last resort.

## Chartism

The high level of activity by labouring groups in the 1830s and 1840s, known as Chartism, has attracted a great deal of interest from historians. Perspectives on the movement have altered from time to time. In the early part of the twentieth century historians were concerned with whether the threat presented by the Chartists was that of a 'moral force' or a 'physical force'. From the 1960s attention shifted to the diversity of the movement, with the publication of F. C. Mather's pamphlet on *Chartism* (1965). *Chartist Studies*, edited by Asa Briggs (1959), stressed the variations in the character, strength and intensity of the movement in different regions, which make it difficult to generalise about Chartism. More recent work, such as that published in 1984 by Dorothy Thompson, *The Chartists*, has been concerned with the social composition and values of the Chartists and involves arguments about class.

# 1 When and why did Chartism appear?

Early historians of the Chartist movement, such as the French historian Dolleans (1913), viewed Chartism as 'a reaction of the working class against the Industrial Revolution, a process which had worsened the conditions of life of the common people'. More recent historians no longer wholly accept this early-twentieth-century definition. Even those historians who take a pessimistic view of the effects of industrialisation on living standards admit that the real wages of some workers, such as the mule spinners in the cotton mills, probably rose. The Chartist movement spanned the years 1838–48. It was preceded by the formation in 1836 of the London Working Men's Association and reached its height in 1838–39 although an impressive agitation was maintained until 1842. The movement then died away in the more prosperous years after 1848. It was the culmination of a decade of popular protest, an expression of the disappointment and disillusion felt at the failure of various reforms of the 1830s.

● **SOURCE 7.1**

From G. B. A. M. Finlayson, *England in the 1830s, Decade of Reform*, 1969, in which the author discusses the origins of Chartism.

**extend the franchise**
give more of the population the right to vote

*The makings of Chartism may be traced well before the 1830s (the political reforms embodied in the Charter were in circulation in the late eighteenth century) but in terms of the 1830s they were in existence before the final passage of the Reform Bill [in 1832]. There is a direct connection between the criticism of the bill in 1831 by the National Union of the Working Classes and the activities of the London Working Men's Association in 1836–37, for certain individuals, like Lovett and Hetherington, were active in both organisations . . . As early as 1833 Thomas Attwood expressed strong discontent with the Reform Act and in May of that year wrote . . . 'At a large meeting in Birmingham various speakers were critical of the failure of the government to* EXTEND THE FRANCHISE *and criticised it for "the great hostility shown to the interests of the working classes which exceeds that exhibited by the Tories".' The Birmingham Political Union it is true went out of existence with the passage of the Reform Act but it revived in 1837; and thereafter – with Attwood once again a moving spirit – joined forces with the London Working Men's Association to press for further parliamentary reform . . . disappointment with political reform formed a basis for later Chartist activity. This was however only one element in the discontent and frustration that came to be gathered up into Chartism. As has been seen the lesson of the thirties to working class radicals seemed to be that nothing could be expected from the Whig government or the reformed parliament except hostility to their interests. Opposition to further parliamentary reform, the Ten Hour Movement, the Trade Union movement and support of the Poor Law Amendment Act – these were simply manifestations of this basic hostility. And it merely emphasised the belief that nothing could be achieved without a change of rulers such as a radical reform along the lines of the Charter would achieve. Thus in 1837 'An Address to the Reformers on the Forthcoming Elections' issued by the London Working Men's Association traced 'most of our oppressive laws and institutions' to 'one common source – EXCLUSIVE LEGISLATION'.*

1 What did Chartism inherit from the radical movements of the 1830s?

2 What working-class grievances remained unresolved by 1837?

# 2 What was the link between Chartism and the economic and social changes of the time?

As we have seen in Chapter 1, there was a severe and protracted trade depression in the mid-1830s. For the industrial regions of the north 1837 was a particularly difficult year because the depression coincided with attempts to apply the new Poor Law, resulting in a short but very intense campaign against the Poor Law changes. The end of the railway boom in 1839, combined with the failure of the harvest in 1841–42, led to wide-scale emergencies. The reserves of working-class savings had been absorbed by the high food prices of previous years so that little was left. Small and weak businesses faced bankruptcy. Social distress was made worse by the inadequacy and misdirection of the Poor Law. These years, 1837–42, probably represented the worst social crisis of the nineteenth century. The recovery of 1842 was followed by a boom which peaked in 1845, followed by another short-lived collapse in 1847. Thereafter, rising prosperity in the 1850s, as a result of industrialisation and improvements in trade, meant that conditions and living standards gradually improved and were sustained. These social and economic changes are most important in understanding the complexity and history of the Chartist movement: its high level of activity in bad years and its ability to attract so many types of worker in different areas of the country. Against such a difficult background of unemployment, social distress and high unrest, trade unionism failed to protect the interests of those who were most vulnerable. Thomas Attwood, leader of the Chartists in Birmingham, declared that: 'Men do not generally act from abstract principles but from deep and unrewarded wrongs, injuries and sufferings.' It was the reduction of these sufferings with the rising tide of prosperity that led to the fading away of Chartism in the 1850s, rather than any particular action by the authorities to suppress the movement.

● **SOURCE 7.2**

From D. Reed, *Chartism in Manchester*, in which the author discusses the economic and social background to the agitation in 1837 to 1841.

Manchester had taken the lead in Radical activity to secure reform of Parliament in 1832. It had a working-class political tradition.

*The local Chartist agitation grew out of the almost unrelieved commercial depression that followed the collapse of the boom of 1836. Fifty thousand workers in the Manchester area alone were unemployed or on short time by June 1837. The worst sufferers were the handloom weavers. Even in good times they were now only just able to make a living; the power loom, introduced increasingly during the 1820s and 30s, had disastrously undercut their prices. As a result, by the mid-1830s large numbers of English handloom weavers seem to have given up their trade. But their places had been quickly taken by Irish immigrants who were flooding into the area. Over a hundred thousand Irish lived in Lancashire by 1841, some thirty-four thousand of them in Manchester. Their attachment to the decaying handloom trade meant that the greater part of them existed in a state of chronic distress. Most of the cases of pauperism at Manchester, whether settled or casual, were of Irish weavers, and 70 per cent of the juvenile offenders were the children of Irish parents.*

● **SOURCE 7.3**

From *Manchester Times*, 9 July 1842, reporting the impact of economic distress in Manchester.

*Any man passing through the district, and observing the condition of the people, will at once perceive the deep and ravaging distress that prevails, laying industry prostrate, desolating families, and spreading abroad discontent and misery where recently happiness and content were enjoyed. The picture that the manufacturing districts now present is absolutely frightful. Hungry and half-clothed men and women are stalking through the streets begging for bread.*

● **SOURCE 7.4**

From E. J. Hobsbawm, 'The British Standard of Living 1790–1850', *Economic History Review*, compiled from H. Ashworth, 'Statistics of the present depression of trade in Bolton', *Journal of the Statistical Society*, 1842.

Percentage of workers unemployed in Bolton in 1842.

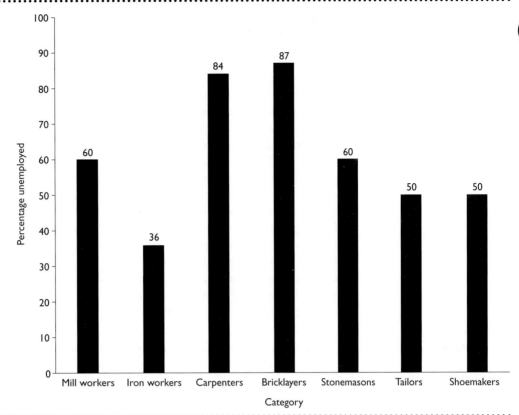

............................................................................................................................

● **SOURCE 7.5**

From the *Northern Star*, 29 September 1838, reporting a speech delivered by Joseph Rayner Stephens at the great Kersal Moor meeting, near Manchester, to elect delegates on 24 September 1838.

**Joseph Rayner Stephens**
was an independent Methodist minister and a fierce opponent of the new Poor Law and the factory masters. He was one of the most popular leaders in the north.

**Universal Suffrage**
by this the Chartists meant the right of all *men* to vote; later in the nineteenth century the suffragettes demanded votes for women.

*The principle of the resolution, therefore, which he had risen to speak to . . . was a principle that acknowledged the right of every man . . . to have his home . . . and his wife and children, as securely guaranteed to him as of any other man . . . This question of UNIVERSAL SUFFRAGE was a knife and fork question after all; this question was a bread and cheese question notwithstanding all that had been said against it; and if any man ask him what he meant by Universal Suffrage he would answer that every working man in the land had a right to have a good coat to his back, a comfortable abode in which to shelter himself and his family, a good dinner upon his table and no more work than was necessary for keeping him in health and as much wages for that work as would keep him in plenty and afford him the enjoyment of all the blessings of life which a reasonable man could desire. [Tremendous cheers.]*

............................................................................................................................

Study Sources 7.2–7.5.

1   What was the scale of the impact of the 1837 depression on workers in
    a)  Manchester
    b)  Bolton?

2   Which groups of workers were hardest hit in Manchester?

3   What difference was there between those worst affected by the 1837 crisis in Bolton and those worst affected in Manchester?

4   What did Joseph Rayner Stephens (Source 7.5) mean by 'a knife and fork question'?

5   To what extent did the level of unemployed workers in Bolton in 1842 support the claim made by Joseph Rayner Stephens that the 'question of Universal Suffrage was a knife and fork question'?

# 3 What did the Chartists hope to achieve?

Chartism derived its name from the People's Charter that was approved by the London Working Men's Association in 1836. The demands for parliamentary reform contained in the Charter owed much to the ideas of the eighteenth-century radical Thomas Paine. It represented the political creed of the movement and attracted support at a national level. The second Chartist aim was a broader regeneration of society to secure more freedom and more equality in legal, political and social rights. However, Chartism was complex and has been described as a 'snowball' of protest movements rather than a movement with a single aim. Coupled with the major demand for the Charter went a mixture of demands which varied from area to area, reflecting local views on how a regeneration of society could be achieved. Birmingham stressed taxation reform and improvement of the Poor Law system, Manchester wanted repeal of the Corn Laws, Manchester and Lancashire wanted factory reform, particularly the ten-hour day, whilst other areas were concerned with the issues of temperance and of education. In Wales and Leicestershire, Chartists wanted disestablishment of the Anglican Church, whilst in Leeds they demanded municipal and borough reform.

● **SOURCE 7.6**

From F. Peel, *The Rising of the Luddites, Chartists and Plugdrawers*, 1888, in which the author comments on the Chartist desire for political change to solve poor conditions.

*The settled conviction of the Chartists was that bad trade, dear living and all their misfortunes rose from bad laws, and that if only they could get votes and send men of their own to parliament they would so order matters that a reign of peace and plenty would at once be inaugurated.*

● **SOURCE 7.7**

From a petition from Birmingham, 1837.

The petition also directed special criticism against the new Poor Law because it made 'poverty as a crime' and brought 'punishment and degradation as well as misery upon the heads of the poor'.

*Your present petitioners feel compelled to declare that . . . Reform has most grievously disappointed the hopes and expectations of the country. After five years of patient trial your petitioners have no reason to believe that the wants and interests of the industrious classes are better understood or their rights and liberties better protected now than they were in the unreformed Parliament; and your petitioners are convinced that it is absolutely necessary to effect a further and much more extensive Reform of the Commons House of Parliament before the industrious classes can hope to enjoy any permanent relief and protection.*

> I   Why, according to Sources 7.6 and 7.7, did working-class leaders concentrate on political demands at a time of economic hardship?

● **SOURCE 7.8**

From F. C. Mather (ed.), *Chartism and Society: an Anthology of Documents*, 1980, summarising the six points of the People's Charter.

**the ballot**
at this time electors had to announce for whom they were voting, instead of casting a vote by secret ballot. This left voters open to intimidation.

1 A VOTE *for every man twenty-one years of age, of sound mind, and not undergoing punishment for crime.*
2 THE BALLOT – *To protect the elector in the exercise of his vote.*
3 NO PROPERTY QUALIFICATION *for Members of Parliament – thus enabling the constituencies to return the man of their choice, be he rich or poor.*
4 PAYMENT OF MEMBERS, *thus enabling an honest tradesman, working man, or other person, to serve a constituency, when taken from his business to attend to the interests of the Country.*
5 EQUAL CONSTITUENCIES, *securing the same amount of representation for the same number of electors, instead of allowing small constituencies to swamp the votes of large ones.*
6 ANNUAL PARLIAMENTS, *thus presenting the most effectual check to bribery and intimidation, since though a constituency might be bought once in seven years (even with the ballot), no purse could buy a constituency (under a system of universal suffrage) in each ensuing twelve-month; and since members, when elected for a year, would not be able to defy and betray their constituents as now.*

*Subjoined are the names of the gentlemen who embodied these principles into the document called the 'People's Charter' at an influential meeting held at the British Coffee House, London, on the 7th of June 1837:*

| | |
|---|---|
| Daniel O'Connell, Esq., MP | Mr Henry Hetherington |
| John Arthur Roebuck, Esq., MP | Mr John Cleave |
| John Temple Leader, Esq., MP | Mr James Watson |
| Charles Hindley, Esq., MP | Mr Richard Moore |
| Thomas Perronet Thompson, Esq., MP | Mr William Lovett |
| William Sharman Crawford Esq., MP | Mr Henry Vincent |

1 What did the Chartists hope to achieve by their demand for the six points of the Charter (Source 7.8)?

2 From your knowledge of the parliamentary system that existed at that time, how realistic do you think Chartist demands for parliamentary reform were?

● **SOURCE 7.9**

From William Lovett, *Life and Struggles of William Lovett*, 1876, in which the leader of the London Working Men's Association describes the drawing up of the aims and objectives of the Association in 1836.

**extirpation**
destruction

*The objects of the Association were the following:*

1 *To draw into one bond of unity the intelligent and influential portion of the working classes in town and country.*

2 *To seek by every legal means to place all classes of society in possession of their equal political and social rights.*

3 *To devise every possible means, and to use every exertion, to remove those cruel laws that prevent the free circulation of thought through the medium of a cheap and honest press.*

4 *To promote, by all available means, the education of the rising generation, and the* EXTIRPATION *of those systems which tend to future slavery.*

5 *To publish their views and sentiments in such form and manner as shall best serve to create a moral, reflecting, yet energetic public opinion; so as eventually to lead to a gradual improvement in the condition of the working classes, without violence or commotion . . .*

1 How, according to Source 7.9, did Lovett and his London Working Men's Association propose to achieve a regeneration of society?

● **SOURCE 7.10**

From James 'Bronterre' O'Brien's *National Reformer*, 7 January 1837, in which a Chartist leader gives his views on the aims of Chartism.

**James 'Bronterre' O'Brien (1805–64)**
was born in Ireland and trained as a lawyer. He was one of the most able of Chartist leaders, writing well-argued articles for the radical *Poor Man's Guardian* and Chartist *Northern Star*. At first a supporter of physical force (see pages 246–248), he later supported the call for socialism and the nationalisation of land to improve the conditions of workers.

*. . . the end I have in view is social equality for all and each [and] to obtain this we must first have political equality for each and all. To obtain political equality we must have a more extensive and effective organisation of the working classes and of that portion of the middle class which is immediately dependent on their custom than has hitherto been even though of, much less accomplished. It will therefore be an object of mine to promote such extensive and effective organisation and as the best means of promoting it, I will never cease to recommend and encourage among those classes knowledge and union; a full and accurate knowledge of their wrongs and of their rights; and a steady union of purpose to redress the one and obtain permanent enjoyment of the other.*

1 To what extent did O'Brien (Source 7.10) agree with Lovett (Source 7.9) on the means of achieving a regeneration of society?

2 To what extent does the evidence of Sources 7.1–7.10 support the claim that 'Chartism was not a creed but a blind revolt against hunger'?

# 4 Who were the Chartists?

## Leadership

The national and local leadership of the Chartist movement was seldom made up of working-class men but was often formed of sympathisers such as landowners, magistrates, doctors, parsons, merchants, small manufacturers and shopkeepers, as well as representatives of traditional trades such as shoemakers, tailors and printers. Many of its leaders were drawn from existing social and political movements, such as William Lovett in London, Thomas Attwood in Birmingham and Feargus O'Connor in Leeds. When Chartism declined after 1842, and certainly by 1851, its leaders returned to those other movements, often with their reputations enhanced and with greater experience in organising a political campaign.

● **SOURCE 7.11**

From William Lovett, *The Life and Struggles of William Lovett*, 1876, in which the leader of the London Working Men's Association reproduces his assessment, at the time, of the impact of Feargus O'Connor, a rival leader of Chartism.

---

**Feargus O'Connor (1794–1855)**

was one of the leaders of the Chartist movement. He was an Irishman and a lawyer and was elected MP for Nottingham in 1847. He campaigned for reform of Parliament, including giving the vote to all men. He possessed outstanding ability as a public speaker, with the power to sway the audience. Although he had a privileged background he could identify with the labouring people, particularly the factory operatives and domestic workers in the depressed industrial north of England, and won their devotion. A controversial figure, he was attacked for his support of physical force methods.

---

*I regard* FEARGUS O'CONNOR *as the chief agitator of our movement, a man who by his personal conduct joined to his malignant influence in the* Northern Star *has been the blight of democracy from the first moment he opened his mouth as its professed advocate. Not possessing a nature to appreciate intellectual exertions he began his career by ridiculing our 'moral force humbuggery' . . . By his great professions, by trickery and deceit, he got the aid of the working classes to establish an organ to declare their principles which he soon converted into an instrument for destroying everything intellectual and moral in our movement . . . the* Star [is] *a mere reflex of the nature of its master . . . By his constant appeals to the selfishness, vanity and mere animal propensities of man he succeeded in calling up a spirit of hate, intolerance and brute feeling previously unknown among Reformers . . . For myself I will have nothing to do with such a man . . . not only believing him to have done irreparable mischief to our cause but knowing him to be politically and morally dishonest; I believe he will still further injure every cause he may be connected with.*

---

1  In Source 7.11, what are Lovett's main criticisms of his rival?

2  What can be inferred from Lovett's attack on O'Connor about Lovett's motives?

3  What is the value of Lovett's comments to a historian assessing reasons for the failure of Chartism?

---

● **SOURCE 7.12**

From R. C. Gammage, *History of the Chartist Movement 1837–1854*, 1854, in which a minor Chartist describes the qualities of Feargus O'Connor and James 'Bronterre' O'Brien as Chartist leaders.

---

*(i) Feargus O'Connor*

*Upwards of six feet in height, stout and athletic, and in spite of his opinions invested with a sort of aristocratic bearing, the sight of his person was calculated to inspire the masses with a solemn awe . . . To assert that he possessed a mind solid and steady were to say too much, no man with an equal amount of intellect was ever more erratic. Had the solidity of his judgment been equal to his quickness of perception he would intellectually have been a great man, but this essential quality of greatness he lacked, hence his life presents a series of mistakes and contradictions . . . No man in the movement was so certain of popularity as O'Connor.*

*No man was so certain to lose it after its attainment. It was not till he proceeded to speak that the full extent of his influence was felt . . . Out of doors O'Connor was the almost universal idol, for the thunder of his voice would reach the ears of the most careless, and put to silence the most noisy of his audience . . . The effect was irresistible.*

### (ii) James 'Bronterre' O'Brien

*There was one man who wielded more of the real democratic mind than any other man in the movement; and who, with the single exception of O'Connor, was also more generally popular. Yet this man had been but little accustomed to the labours and honours of the platform. It was through the medium of the press that his influence had been principally felt. The name of the gentleman . . . was James Bronterre O'Brien . . . There was no man more fascinating . . . He was undoubtedly the man with the greatest breadth of mind. In the Chartist ranks he was universally known as the schoolmaster, a title bestowed on him by O'Connor. When reasoning a point he was deliberate to admiration . . . No other speaker was capable of rising to such a height, or of so impressing an audience with the strength and intensity of his feelings, while no orator could outrival him in action and flexibility of voice . . . No man could so easily mould reason, satire, or comment into one compact body . . . He always enjoyed, too, the happy ease of adapting himself to the comprehension of his audience . . . Three hours was about the usual time he occupied a meeting; but he sometimes spoke for four, and even five hours, riveting the attention of his audience to the close of his address.*

*A man who was possessed of such capabilities, was an orator of no ordinary power, and . . . he must have been a master, not only of words, but of ideas. He had but little sympathy with the class of landlords whom he looked upon as the hereditary enemies of society. But there was another class whom he regarded with greater dread – the great monied class – which had risen to immense importance, and whose power was on the increase . . . He contended then, that if those parties . . . were thus enabled to command a larger share of wealth, they could obtain it only at the expense of others, those others being the labouring class, who are the source of all the wealth produced.*

---

1 What, according to Gammage (Source 7.12), were the strengths of
   a) O'Connor
   b) O'Brien
   as leaders of Chartism?

2 To what extent do Lovett and Gammage agree on O'Connor's strengths and weaknesses as a leader?

3 Is it possible to identify whether Gammage had a favourable opinion of
   a) O'Connor
   b) O'Brien?

4 How reliable to a historian of Chartism is Gammage's personal account as a minor Chartist in the movement?

---

## ● SOURCE 7.13

From E. Royle, *Chartism*, 1980, in which the author assesses the qualities of leadership of prominent Chartists.

### (i) Feargus O'Connor

*Some degree of detachment, though, was a necessary characteristic of leadership, and this was the essence of O'Connor's appeal. His was the most important and significant leadership because he was able to combine elements of friendship and detachment, democracy and paternalism. He was both part of the movement and above it . . . The picture given of O'Connor's leadership by Gammage, most recently echoed in the study of Chartism by J. T. Ward, is unfavourable. In their view O'Connor was the man who took Chartism out of the hands of the thoughtful and moderate Lovett, and transformed it into the victim of his own megalomania. The talents of Lovett, O'Brien and, eventually, Harney were scorned by a man who could and would brook no opposition, who led the Chartists on to self-destruction by his bragging, his conceit and his inconsistency. The case is a powerful one. Yet there is also a more sympathetic view, for O'Connor has been very much the victim of a history written by other leaders, who were in no position to be impartial witnesses. It is true that O'Connor transformed Lovett's and Attwood's Chartism out of recognition, but this stands condemned only if one accepts that the strategy adopted by Lovett and Attwood would have succeeded*

. . . *What O'Connor did do is to link the various aspects of Chartism, and whilst dividing the leadership he united the movement . . . The fact remains that though O'Connor did drive out of Chartism all obvious rivals, yet none of them could really have replaced him. . . government by committee, which seems to have been the London Working Men's Association ideal, was totally unrealistic . . . Chartism therefore merges with O'Connorism despite the many protests against the trend, and Chartism was destined to be led by 'unquestionably the best-loved, as well as the most-hated, man in the Chartist movement'.*

### (ii) William Lovett
*Men like Lovett, who would be forever improving the working classes, were not typical of those classes, and it can be no surprise that Lovett failed to win the enduring sympathy of more than a tiny proportion of the people.*

### (iii) James 'Bronterre' O'Brien
. . . *[a] man whose powers of oratory were different but comparable to those of O'Connor, an experienced journalist with a radical reputation going back to the days when he had edited* Poor Man's Guardian, *and before the advent of Ernest Jones the advanced theorist of the Chartist movement, dubbed by O'Connor the 'schoolmaster of Chartism'. Unlike O'Connor, he was a clearsighted consistent strategist, opposed to premature action at the 1839 Convention, and yet essentially of the physical force party. Until he parted company with O'Connor, over the latter's support of Tory candidates at the 1841 general election, he was one of the best writers on the* Northern Star, *and his views earned a widespread respect. But in 1841 he became increasingly isolated. Opposed to O'Connor and not reconciled to the Lovett faction, he was left high and dry without a significant following in the movement. He gathered round him his disciples and continued to be admired for his intellectual powers . . .*

### (iv) George Julian Harney
*[Julian Harney] belonged to the younger generation of Radicals . . . he made his mark as a leader of London extremism in the later 1830s . . . convinced after 1839 that the time was not yet ripe for physical force, he became an O'Connorite in the 1840s and . . . editor of the* Northern Star . . . *Not till 1849 did the two men part company. He was no orator; he was an honest enthusiast with some journalistic talent . . .*

---

1  To what extent have historians agreed with contemporary commentators' assessments of O'Connor's leadership?

2  Why, according to Royle (Source 7.13), did Lovett lose control of the leadership of Chartism?

3  What factors divided the leadership of the Chartist movement?

## Rank and file members

A feature of Chartism which has been particularly stressed as indicating a new degree of working-class unity on a national scale is the movement's relative comprehensiveness in geographical and occupational terms. Membership of the movement was drawn almost entirely from the labouring groups of workers and its complexion varied considerably from one area to another. It was affected by the prevailing industrial pattern and by the underlying social and political tradition in each area.

● **SOURCE 7.14**

From F. C. Mather, *Chartism*, 1965, in which the author discusses the social composition of Chartism.

Britain in the 1830s and 1840s had a varied labour force because industrial development was still in its relatively early stages. New occupations had appeared but very many of the old still survived.

### (i) Attitude of domestic outworkers
*On balance, workers in the old, unrevolutionised handicrafts supported Chartism more faithfully than those engaged in modern large-scale industry. Certain of these crafts – handloom-weaving, frame-work knitting, wool-combing, nailmaking – had already entered upon a long and painful process of decline, with wages sinking nearly to starvation level. The men who worked in them were especially militant in Chartism and disposed to persevere in it when others had left it. When, in August 1839, the Convention called for a two- to three-day strike to devote the whole of that time to solemn processions and meetings, the response from the working classes was slight. It was greatest, however, in towns and areas having a substantial complement of outworkers – Barnsley and Nottingham, Bolton and Macclesfield,*

Loughborough and Shepshed, Manchester and the West Country clothing district . . . the distress of the declining handicraftsmen was partly the result of competition from power-driven machinery, but not entirely so. It was due also to hardships endemic in the unrevolutionised crafts themselves and heightened by the great population 'explosion' of the late eighteenth and early nineteenth centuries – overstocking of the labour market, heavy rents paid by stockingers for the hire of their frames and other forms of exploitation by middlemen. Moreover, when one considers the more highly paid sections of the labour force, one finds that again it was the long established crafts more than the newer ones engendered by the industrial revolution that supported Chartism.

### (ii) Attitude of factory workers

By contrast, the factory operatives were far less ardent . . . [with a] . . . distaste for anything like an appeal to physical force, . . . the handloom-weavers and block printers of Burnley urged the burning of mills in order to compel the hands employed in them to join in an insurrectionary movement. It is true that in times of bad trade, for example in 1838–39, the mill-hands adhered to the Chartist movement in considerable numbers, but they were easily disillusioned and fell back upon trade-union action when the cycle of boom and slump took an upward turn . . . In . . . 1842, the factory operatives . . . were among the most strenuous opponents of turning the movement into a strike for the People's Charter. They preferred to keep it harnessed to a demand for a restoration of the wages paid in 1840. Hardly less brief was the allegiance of the coalminers of Monmouthshire, who came into the Chartist Movement late, and, after imparting to it its most colourful episode, the Newport rising of November 1839, gradually moved out again.

### (iii) Attitude of craftsmen

The insignificance of the role of the engineering trades in the political movement has been perhaps overstressed. Glasgow Chartism owed much of its success to the leadership of a steam-engine maker named William Pattison, and the engineers of Manchester figured prominently in organising the strikes of August 1842 and harnessing them to a demand for the People's Charter. These, however, were not typical of their fellow craftsmen, whose outlook remained too narrowly sectional to permit them to become involved in a movement of the whole working class. By contrast, the traditional skills, those of the printers, shoemakers, cabinetmakers, tailors and coachbuilders, played a considerable part in Chartism in its earlier stages and contributed to a more limited extent afterwards. They formed the backbone of the London Working Men's Association, which originated the People's Charter in 1838, and were still active in the years 1840–42, when the conversion of local trade-union branches to Chartism was reported in the press. Thereafter, however, their participation waned. In Leicestershire, for example, after 1846, leadership in the Chartist agitation passed predominantly into the hands of the framework knitters, who had always constituted the rank and file of the movement; previously the leaders had been mainly self-educated artisans and small tradesmen or full-time lecturers from outside the district. The practitioners of these established skills constituted, together with the newly risen mechanics and engineers, an aristocracy of labour. They enjoyed a much higher standard of living than most working men. Some of them were self-employed persons rather than wage earners, and, as a group, they were linked socially with small shopkeepers and small-scale master manufacturers, who also engaged with them to some extent in Chartist activity. For the traditional handicraftsmen Chartism was not a reaction against the industrial revolution. Their crafts had been untouched, for the most part, by technological change and, by and large, they had managed to improve their living standards during industrialisation . . . their Chartism . . . [was due] to steady political conviction. It was one demonstration of a continuing intellectual tradition . . . a mature political awareness well in advance of the mass of the working class.

1  According to Source 7.14, what was the attitude of each of the following groups to Chartism
   a)  domestic outworkers
   b)  factory 'hands'
   c)  craftsmen?

2  What contribution did each of these three groups make to the development of Chartism?

FELLOW-COUNTRYMEN, – We call upon you to join us and help our fathers, husbands, and brothers, to free themselves and us from political, physical, and mental bondage, and urge the following reasons as an answer to our enemies and an inducement to our friends.

We have been told that the province of woman is her home, and that the field of politics should be left to men; this we deny; the nature of things renders it impossible, and the conduct of those who give the advice is at variance with the principles they assert. Is it not true that the interests of our fathers, husbands, and brothers, ought to be ours? If they are oppressed and impoverished, do we not share those evils with them? If so, ought we not to resent the infliction of those wrongs upon them? . . .

For years we have struggled to maintain our homes in comfort, such as our hearts told us should greet our husbands after their fatiguing labours. Year after year have passed away, and even now our wishes have no prospect of being realised, our husbands are over wrought, our houses half furnished, our families ill-fed, and our children uneducated – the fear of want hangs over our heads; the scorn of the rich is pointed towards us; the brand of slavery is on our kindred, and we feel the degradation. We are a despised caste; our oppressors are not content with despising our feelings, but demand the control of our thoughts and wants! – want's bitter bondage binds us to their feet, we are oppressed because we are poor.

Study Source 7.15.

1  How did female supporters of Chartism in the 1840s see their status and role in society?

2  What were the aims of female Chartists?

# 5 How did the regions respond to Chartism?

Broadly considered, Chartism appears . . . from the rising public opinion of the provinces, which, fostered by the growth of industry and the improvement in communications, began to snatch the leadership of English radicalism from London in the closing years of the eighteenth century. It was in the industrial provinces, more especially the North and North-east of England, the East Midlands and Scotland, that the movement displayed its greatest staying power.

More detailed analysis shows that Chartism was strongest in two kinds of place – in centres of decaying industry like Trowbridge, Carmarthen and the out-working villages of Lancashire and Leicestershire and in medium-sized industrial towns like Stockport, Bolton and Bradford, which were growing with amazing rapidity during the first half of the nineteenth century. Big cities like Manchester, Birmingham and Leeds were often well supplied with Chartists, but displayed less militancy than the adjacent industrial areas.

The movement was weak or non-existent in completely agricultural villages, those of Kent or Dorset, for example, in old market towns like Ripon or Bedford, and in new industrial centres with a mixed economy, like Glossop, St Helens and Crewe. The growth of some industries and the decline of others were complementary features of rapid industrialisation. We have enough evidence to link the Chartist movement with industrial decline; but the connection with industrial growth is less clear-cut. Given certain conditions Chartism did not attend the rise of modern industry. Its absence from some industrial towns is partly explained by the fact that these were later developers and, therefore, small. In a small town overcrowding was less pronounced than in a large one, and the community remained closely knit, thus preventing the emergence of serious fissures of class. Thus, in Glossop, the employers achieved remarkable success in maintaining contact with their workpeople through the churches and chapels and through the several reading rooms, literary institutes and sporting clubs which they and the local landowner helped to found. But Chartism also failed to take root in such towns because they were new. The totally new town did not have to carry over into the industrial age hordes of domestic weavers and framework knitters, relics of an older order which was then in decay. Unencumbered, too, by the urban arrangements of the past, it offered scope for rudimentary town planning supervised by landowners, manufacturers and railway companies. It is significant that the residents of Crewe loved to fling the taunt 'We have no slums in Crewe' at the inhabitants of historic Chester and Nantwich.

## ● SOURCE 7.17

From the *Northern Star*, 23 April 1842, naming the areas in Lancashire and Cheshire that contributed 10,000 signatures or more in support of the 1842 Petition.

Strength of support for the 1842 National Petition in Lancashire and Cheshire.

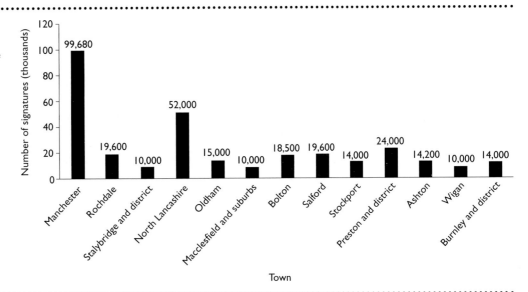

Study Sources 7.16 and 7.17.

1 What were the main centres of support for Chartism?

2 Where was Chartism weak or non-existent?

3 What was the link between Chartism and industrialisation?

## ● SOURCE 7.18

From *Hansard*, quoting from Thomas Attwood's presentation to Parliament in 1839 of the first Petition in support of the People's Charter.

Attwood was leader of the Birmingham Political Union. The Petition was rejected, as were the later Petitions of 1842 and 1848.

Mr T. Attwood said, in rising to present this very extraordinary and important petition . . . The petition originated in the town of Birmingham . . . and it was now presented to that House with 1,280,000 signatures, the result of not less than 500 meetings, which had been held in support of the principles contained in this petition. At each of those meetings there had been one universal anxious cry of distress – distress, he must say, long disregarded by that House . . . The men who signed the petition were honest and industrious – of sober and unblemished character – men who had always obeyed the laws. Gentlemen enjoying the wealth handed down to them by hereditary descent, whose wants were provided for by the estates to which they succeeded from their forefathers, could have no idea of the privations suffered by the working men of this country . . . They had seen no attempt to relieve their sufferings, whether they were handloom weavers, artisans, or agricultural labourers. They met with no support or even sympathy, from that House . . . Although he most cordially supported the petition . . . he washed his hands of any idea of any appeal to physical force; he repudiated all talk of arms – he wished for no arms but the will of the people, legally, fairly, and constitutionally expressed . . .

Having said so much, he should now read the prayer of the petition, which was to the following effect:

'That it might please their honourable House to take the petition into their most serious consideration, and to use their utmost endeavour to pass a law, granting to every man of lawful age, sound and uncontaminated by crime, the right of voting for Members to serve in Parliament; that they would cause a law also to be passed giving the right to vote by the ballot; that the duration of Parliaments might in no case be of greater duration than one year; that they would abolish all property qualifications, to entitle persons to sit in their honourable House; and that all Members elected to sit in Parliament, should be paid for their services.'

1   What evidence is there in Source 7.18 to indicate that there was widespread support for Chartism in 1839?

2   What main factor unified supporters of Chartism in 1839?

3   What methods to secure the Charter were recommended by Thomas Attwood, the leader of the Birmingham Political Union?

4   What evidence indicates that Chartists were divided on the issue of political action?

5   Why had the Chartists failed to meet with 'support or even sympathy' from the House of Commons?

# 6 How did the Chartists attempt to achieve their aims?

The Chartists employed a shrewd combination of activities. Within Parliament, reasoned pressure was exerted on MPs through three Petitions in 1839, 1842 and 1848, and through enquiries and submissions. Very little was achieved using Parliamentary pressure because the Chartists failed to produce working-class MPs to present their case directly. This meant that they had to rely on other methods to exert pressure from outside Parliament. There was disagreement among the Chartists over the form such pressure should take.

## Strategy advocated by Chartist leaders

● **SOURCE 7.19**

From *Parliamentary Representation*, in which William Lovett discusses physical force.

*The whole physical force agitation is harmful and injurious to the movement. Muskets are not what are wanted but education and schooling of the working people. Stephens and O'Connor are shattering the movement . . . Violent words do not slay the enemies but the friends of the movement. O'Connor wants to take everything by storm and to pass the Charter into law within a year. All this hurry and haste, this bluster and menace of armed opposition, can only lead to outbreaks and to the destruction of Chartism.*

1   Why, according to Lovett in Source 7.19, was physical force 'harmful and injurious to the movement'?

2   What strategy did Lovett support?

● **SOURCE 7.20**

From the *Northern Star*, 2 May 1840, reporting the aims of the Leeds Radical Universal Suffrage Association, formed after the decline of Chartism in the wake of the defeats of 1838–39.

*Inaugural meeting of Leeds Radical Universal Suffrage Association held in James Illingworth's public house, the White Horse Inn, in Vicar Lane:*
*The attainment of Universal Suffrage and the other main points of the Charter by the use of every moral and lawful means such as petitioning Parliament, procuring the return of Members of Parliament who will vote for Universal Suffrage and the other points of the Charter, publishing tracts, establishing reading rooms, holding public meetings for addresses and discussions, and giving public lectures on subjects connected with the politics of the country.*

1   What methods were advocated by those Chartists who supported the idea of moral force to achieve the vote for all men (Source 7.20)?

● **SOURCE 7.21**

From R. C. Gammage, *History of the Chartist Movement 1837–1854*, 1854, relating Feargus O'Connor's discussion of the use of physical force.

*He [O'Connor] had never counselled the people to use physical force because he felt that those who did were fools to their own cause; but at the same time those who decried it preserved their authority by physical force alone . . . He counselled them against all rioting, all civil war, but still in the hearing of the House of Commons he would say that rather than see the constitution violated while the people were in daily want, if no other man would do so, if the constitution was violated he would himself lead the people to death or glory . . . His desire was to try moral force as long as possible even to the fullest extent but he would always have them bear in mind that it is better to die freemen than to live slaves. Every conquest which was called honourable had been achieved by physical force but they did not want it because if all hands were pulling for Universal Suffrage they would soon pull down the stronghold of corruption. He hoped and trusted that out of the exercise of that judgement, which belonged exclusively to the working class, a union would arise, and from that union a moral power would be created, sufficient to establish the rights of the poor man, but if this failed, then let every man raise his arm in defence of that which his judgement told him was justice.*

Study Source 7.21.

1  What do you understand by the term 'physical force'?

2  In what ways did O'Connor and Lovett (Source 7.19) differ in their views on working-class tactics?

3  Under what circumstances did O'Connor support the use of force?

4  How does O'Connor justify the use of force?

● **SOURCE 7.22**

From the *Operative*, 10 February 1839, reporting Julian Harney's election speech in Derby in January 1839, in which he summed up the position of many Chartists in 1838–39 on the use of force.

**Julian Harney (1817–97)**
worked in the shop of another Chartist, Henry Hetherington. He was a leading Radical and editor of *Poor Man's Guide*. He urged the importance of physical force to gain real advantage for working men. He was a supporter of international socialism.

*What is it that we want? Not to destroy property and take life, but to preserve our own lives, and to protect our own property – namely our labour. We are for Peace, Law, Order; but if our oppressors shall break the peace – if our tyrants shall violate the law – if our despots shall trample upon order – then we will fall back upon the Constitution, and defend the few remaining of the blood-bought rights left us by our fathers. The Whigs shall never violate the constitution of this country . . . They charge us with being physical force men. I fling the charge back in the teeth of these insincere liberals. Let them call to mind their own words and deeds during the humbug reform agitation . . . Again I say, we are for peace, but we must have justice – we must have our rights speedily: peaceable if we can, forcibly if we must . . . Time was when every Englishman had a musket in his cottage, and along with it hung a fitch of bacon; now there is no fitch of bacon for there is no musket; let the musket be restored and the fitch of bacon will soon follow . . . You will get nothing from your tyrants but what you can take, and you can take nothing unless you are properly prepared to do so. In the words of a good man [Oastler], then, I say, 'Arm for peace, arm for liberty, arm for justice, arm for the rights of all and the tyrants will no longer laugh at your petitions.'*

1  In what circumstances did Harney (Source 7.22) argue that physical force was justifiable?

2  To what extent do Sources 7.19–7.22 indicate that the division between physical and moral force Chartism was not clear-cut?

● **SOURCE 7.23**

*A Physical Force Chartist Arming For The Fight*, a cartoon from *Punch* Volume 15, 1848.

## Tactics – events of 1839–40

Advocates of moral force, such as William Lovett, emphasised the use of political unions, public meetings, and lecturing tours around the country, which were led by respected middle-class Radicals and trade union delegates. Large processions and demonstrations were organised, especially in 1839, along with use of the press. Some Chartist newspapers, such as the *Northern Star*, which was launched in November 1837 and cost $4\frac{1}{2}$ d., had a national circulation, but there were also numerous local and regional papers. Social events and parties were held to raise funds and subscriptions, but these were not very successful.

Chartists who stressed more physical methods to intimidate government and the middle class organised strikes and a national rising. Chartist riots centred round the three Petitions that were presented to Parliament in 1839, 1842 and 1848, each launched at a time of great economic distress. For some historians an important measure of the development of working-class consciousness lies in the extent to which it became 'revolutionary'. Recent research has thrown new light on the 'physical force' aspect of Chartism. In Lancashire there were moves among Chartist supporters to distribute pikes and firearms in the belief that force would produce success. Had troops been employed, a general rising in the north-west might have resulted. A rebellion did occur in Wales at Newport in 1839. It involved 7000 people and showed that the mobilisation of large numbers of workers for revolutionary purposes was not impossible. It also showed what obstacles any such rising faced: only 30 soldiers were required to disperse the protesters.

● **SOURCE 7.24**

From Robert Lowery, *Passages in the Life of a Temperance Lecturer*, 1837, in which he describes the founding of the *Northern Star*.

*Seeing the want of a newspaper as an organ for the rising movement . . . [O'Connor established] the* Northern Star *. . . at the time he had no capital, and . . . the money of the shareholders was the only money ever invested in the paper. Fortunately for him it soon rose to a very large circulation, reaching at least some 60,000 a week, and during Frost's trial [see Source 7.33] he gave one week's profits to the defence fund. Thus the Star gave him and his party general influence, while the sayings and doings of his special favourites were regularly reported and praised . . .*

● **SOURCE 7.25**

From statistics from H. Martin, *Britain in the Nineteenth Century*, 1996.

Weekly sales of the *Northern Star*, 1838–50.

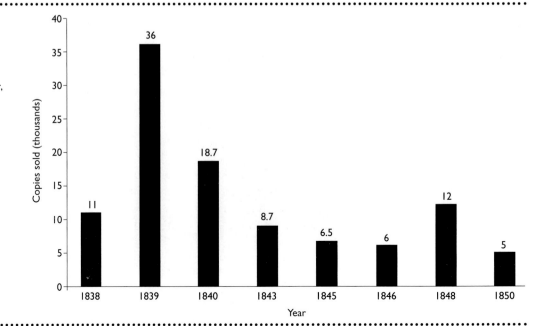

Study Sources 7.24 and 7.25.

**I** In what year did sales of the *Northern Star* peak?

**2** How do the circulation figures for the *Northern Star* reflect the fortunes of the Chartist movement?

**3** Why was the *Northern Star* so important to Feargus O'Connor?

● **SOURCE 7.26**

From General C. J. Napier to Colonel W. Napier, 3 June 1839, *Life and Opinions of General Sir Charles James Napier*, describing the threat presented by the Chartists at a second meeting at Kersal Moor in Manchester on 25 May 1839. The purpose of the meeting was to show support for measures to pressurise the government into accepting the first Chartist Petition.

*Our great meeting passed off quietly. There was a very general feeling amongst the respectables that we should come to blows; and a fervent hope that the soldiers would make an example. I adopted several tests to ascertain numbers and certainly including women and children there were under thirty thousand against the Chartist assertion that there were half a million. Mr Bingham [an intermediary used by Napier to communicate with the Chartists] told me that the presence of troops had prevented a row; that Doctor Taylor [an extreme physical force Chartist] came from Glasgow to lead them; that they consulted but decided we were too strong. The 10th Regiment having been suddenly brought up by railroad from Liverpool certainly upset their calculations of our strength.*

**I** According to Source 7.26, what was the scale of the threat to the authorities of the meeting held at Kersal Moor?

**2** What does the source reveal about the attitude of Sir Charles Napier as the general in charge of operations against the Chartists?

**3** What was the role played by the army in dealing with the Chartists?

**4** What insight does General Napier provide of reasons for the limited success of the Chartists?

The National Convention was a body of 53 elected Chartist representatives who met in London in 1839. Their main purpose was to organise the presentation of the Petition to Parliament. In May the Convention moved to Birmingham and workers began to hold meetings in the Bull-ring. In early July violence broke out between the authorities (who included members of the Birmingham Political Union) and the Chartists. Two of the Chartist leaders were arrested, provoking a protest from William Lovett, who was then arrested too. In July the Petition was presented to Parliament and rejected by 235 votes to 46. With its prestige undermined and many of its leaders under arrest, the Convention was adjourned indefinitely in August and dissolved in September by its remaining 23 members.

● **SOURCE 7.27**

From William Lovett, *Life and Struggles of William Lovett*, 1876, in which he recounts the circumstances leading to his arrest after the Birmingham riots of 4–6 July 1839.

**Bull-ring**
an open area of Birmingham where people met to discuss the day's events and newspapers were read aloud.

**ex-reform authorities**
the middle-class authorities in Birmingham who had supported the campaign for parliamentary reform in 1831–32 but were opposed to Chartism.

**seditious**
a threat to the state, or public order

*When, . . . the agitation for the People's Charter commenced, . . . the working classes began to hold their meetings . . . in the BULL-RING. But this of course was not to be endured by the EX-REFORM AUTHORITIES; what was once right and legal in themselves was denounced as SEDITIOUS and treasonable in the multitude. The poor . . . workers, however, could not perceive the distinction of the Birmingham authorities between the two political measures, but continued to meet as usual . . . At last the Governing powers of Birmingham . . . sent to London to their former friends and allies requesting them to send down a strong posse of the new police to assist them. They came down by rail, and were no sooner out of their vans than they were led on by the authorities, truncheon in hand, and commenced a furious attack upon the men, women and children who were assembled in the Bull-ring, listening peacefully to a person reading a newspaper. This proceeding, as may be supposed, greatly exasperated the people . . . The morning after this brutal attack, a number of the working classes of Birmingham called at the Convention Room . . . Feeling most strongly with them, that great injustice had been inflicted, I drew up and proposed to the Convention three resolutions [which condemned the actions of the authorities].*

● **SOURCE 7.28**

From the *Annual Register*, 1839, reporting the response of the authorities to the riots in Birmingham, 4–6 July 1839.

> **metropolis**
> London

*The borough magistrates, however, who had for some days been in constant communication with the Home Office, had by this time bespoken a picked body of sixty policemen from the* METROPOLIS. *The railway train delivered them at Birmingham that evening, and without even waiting for the cooperation of the military, they proceeded immediately to the scene of confusion. They began by directing the people to disperse, but when this injunction was seen to take no effect, the police filed off four abreast . . . the mob, who had been at first disconcerted by the impetuosity of the charge, when they beheld their flags, one of which bore a death's head, in the hands of the enemy, made a desperate return, recovered the contested banners, broke the poles up into short sticks, and after a fierce and indiscriminate combat in which several of the policemen, who were only armed with staves, were seriously hurt, and more than one man stabbed, the Chartists began at length to obtain the advantage.*

*Fortunately, however, at this juncture, the 4th dragoons arrived on the spot. Riding by concert up every avenue that led to the place, they completely enclosed the Bull-ring. The appearance of the military was the signal for the people to disperse, and the routed mob proceeded with the cavalry in close pursuit . . . [but] for a moment made a stand. But the tumult was eventually reduced, by midnight the streets were comparatively quiet, and the military, planting guard in the great square, retired to their barracks.*

---

Study Sources 7.27 and 7.28.

1   What did the Chartists hope to prove by their meetings at the Bull-ring?

2   How do you account for the difference in views between the Birmingham authorities and the Chartists?

---

● **SOURCE 7.29**

From the *Bolton Chronicle*, 17 August 1839, reporting serious and alarming riots in Bolton on Saturday, 17 August 1839.

> **sacred month . . . to three days**
> a reference to the month-long general strike which was planned to take place if Parliament rejected the first Petition. Lack of support led to the strike being reduced to just three days.
>
> **reading the Riot Act**
> reading the Riot Act to a crowd was a warning for it to disperse; troops could be brought in if the crowd refused to break up once the act had been read.

*In conformity with the orders of the* NATIONAL CONVENTION *the* SACRED MONTH WHICH WAS REDUCED BY SPECIAL LICENCE TO THREE DAYS *was commenced on Monday last. Great apprehension was expressed by inhabitants of the town that violence would be attempted. At the latter part of last week, therefore, about 1500 special constables were sworn in . . . It is not for us as reporters to express our opinions regarding the origin of such meetings nor do we wish to express our sentiments regarding the proper persons who should have been made responsible for the consequences. Whether incited by the Mayor or his friends is not for us to consider, whether the property of the town was placed in jeopardy by the men who had for years fostered the notions entertained by the Chartists is not for us to determine . . . The industrial operatives in this town took no share in the disturbances . . . A number of irritated ill-advised young men were the principal actors.*

MONDAY – *At ten o'clock the Chartists were asked to fall in, march four abreast and exhibit a second grand moral demonstration. The town was in great alarm. No arms were displayed by the Chartists but sufficient was indicated to manifest the hatred of the assembly. At this point the magistrates decided to arrest the three leaders. With knowledge that warrants were about to be issued the Chronicle strongly and earnestly urged the leaders to disperse the meeting. The meeting then broke up. The special constables then patrolled the streets but their services were not demanded.*

TUESDAY – *at 5 a.m. the Chartists assembled – about 300. Later the leaders and a Chartist delegate were arrested. The crowd attempted to rescue them; showers of stones were thrown [and] the commotion arrived at a tremendous pitch. The mayor and the magistrates consulted and determined upon* READING THE RIOT ACT. *The military comprising two companies of the 96th Foot was instantly called out. The appearance of the military as a defensive or if necessary offensive body discouraged the multitude. At eight o'clock information reached the office that disturbances had taken place on Bolton Moor.*

● **SOURCE 7.30**

From the *Observer*, 18 August 1839, describing attempts to achieve the National Holiday or 'sacred month'. It was hoped that the authorities would accept the Chartists' demands to avoid disruption.

*At Manchester on Monday at an early hour the Chartists proceeded to carry into execution their measures for enforcing the National Holiday by stopping the factories. They commenced by organising their forces, dividing them into four distinct bodies in order to visit the mills in the respective districts allotted them simultaneously at the hour of starting work. Before their progress was arrested by the police, they succeeded in their object at nearly twenty places. One of the parties walked in procession headed by a band of music.*

● **SOURCE 7.31**

From the *Observer*, 26 August 1839, reporting on activities in 1839.

*On Sunday evening a body of 6000 Chartists took possession of St Stephen's church. Near the close of the sermon, which was pointedly addressed to the Chartists, on the Reverend P. Booth quoting the words of St Paul, 'I have learned in whatever station of life therewith to be content', a number of the assembly called out, 'You get £200 a year; come and weave bombazines; put the gas out,' etc., etc., while some lifted up their sticks.*

● **SOURCE 7.32**

From *Report from J. Phillips*, 12 March 1839, in which a magistrate from Newport, Monmouthshire describes the activities of the local Chartist Society.

**missionaries**
i.e. Chartists

**insurrection**
rebellion

*There has existed in this town for some months a Chartist Society – some of the members whereof make circuits periodically into the neighbouring villages and mining districts to obtain signatures to the Chartist petition . . . The* MISSIONARIES *attend at public houses and beer shops . . . [and] expound to them the grievances under which they labour, tell them that half their earnings are taken from them in taxes, that these taxes are spent in supporting the rulers in idleness and profligacy – that their employers are tyrants who acquire wealth by their labour . . . I cannot say to what extent these appeals may influence the conduct of the working classes in this neighbourhood. I am loath to believe they will be hurried into actual* INSURRECTION *. . . I do not think that anything that has yet occurred need excite apprehension of immediate violence.*

● **SOURCE 7.33**

From *Annual Register*, 1840, reporting the evidence given by Edward Patton, a carpenter of Newport, at the trial of John Frost. Patton was an eyewitness to the events of the Newport rising of 4 November 1839.

**John Frost**
was a former mayor of Newport and a recently dismissed magistrate. He was chairman of the National Convention and led the march on the Westgate Hotel. He was arrested and sentenced to death but this was later commuted to transportation for life.

*The parcel of people I saw . . . were armed; they had guns, sticks, the sticks had iron points. I did not see many with guns. I saw of this body two hundred or three hundred. There were not many more. They were not very riotous. I had full view of those on Stowe Hill. I was a little bit alarmed but not particularly so . . . The body of the mob . . . asked for the prisoners who were taken before daylight . . . The first moment or two they asked for the prisoner Smith; then a rush was made. Then I heard firing and took to my heels. I cannot say whether the mob had guns, pikes or clubs. I cannot tell whether they were armed for the biggest part. I heard someone say in a very loud voice 'No, never' . . . I could not say where the firing began. No man could judge. You nor I could not tell. Saw no smoke outside. It is likely enough the firing began from the Westgate Inn . . .*

● SOURCE 7.34

From 'Reformator', *Charter*, 17 November 1839, in which the weekly paper of the London Working Men's Association reports on the events surrounding the Newport rising.

**Henry Vincent**
was a Chartist organiser in South Wales. Reports of his ill treatment after his arrest shocked Frost and angered the miners.

*At least eight thousand men, mostly miners (but also quarrymen and ironworkers) employed in the neighbourhood (which is very densely populated) were engaged in the attack upon the town of Newport and . . . many of them were armed. Their design seems to have been to wreak their vengeance upon the Newport magistrates for the prosecution of VINCENT and others now lying in Monmouth gaol and after securing the town to advance to Monmouth and liberate these prisoners. The ultimate design of the leaders . . . probably was to rear the standard of rebellion throughout Wales . . . until the people of England assured by successes should rise en masse for the same objects . . . Mr FROST, the late member of the Convention, led the rioters and he with others has been committed for high treason. On entering Newport the people marched straight to the Westgate Hotel where the magistrates with about 40 soldiers were assembled being fully informed of the intended outbreak. The Riot Act was read and the soldiers fired down with ease and security upon the people who had first broken and fired into the windows. The people in a few minutes found their position insupportable and retired to the outside of the town to concert a different plan of attack but ultimately returned home without attempting anything more. The soldiers did not leave their place of shelter to follow them. About thirty of the people are known to have been killed and several to have been wounded . . . The rioters did not disgrace themselves by any wanton destruction of property nor by plunder. The Chartists, as a body, are too well-informed to offer any countenance or encouragement to any such resorts to violence, for the attainment of their just rights.*

1   To what extent do the accounts of events in Newport in Sources 7.33 and 7.34 agree on the aim of Frost and his associates?

2   To what extent do the two accounts agree on the numbers involved and the sequence of events?

3   How far do the two accounts agree that there was an organised conspiracy with revolutionary aims behind the Newport rising of 1839?

4   Is it possible to determine whether the accounts are sympathetic to the Newport Chartists?

5   How do you account for the attitude shown by the authors of the two accounts?

● SOURCE 7.35

From a letter from the Home Office, 5 November 1839, to the Mayor of Newport, Monmouthshire, reporting on the restricted mobility of the forces of law and order before the coming of the railways.

**insurgents**
rebels

*I hasten to acknowledge receipt of a letter reporting the attack made upon the Town of Newport by a large body of Chartists and to inform you that I have lost no time in communicating with the military authorities and an arrangement has been made for the immediate march of eight companies of the 45th Regiment from Winchester. They will probably arrive at Bristol on the 10th and can of course if necessary cross by steamer to Newport the same evening. Two guns have also been ordered from Woolwich to Monmouth. They will proceed by railroad to Twyford from there by forced marches to Bristol. I regret much that there are no troops stationed at any nearer points but I think that the check which these INSURGENTS have received from the firmness of the inhabitants of Newport and the small body of troops stationed in the town together with the active measures taken by the Magistrates will have induced their dispersion for the time and the presence of the large force which will arrive in the course of a few days will be sufficient to maintain future peace.*

1   How useful is Source 7.35 as evidence of the means by which information on Chartist activities was acquired by the authorities?

2   What evidence does the Home Office letter provide of the problems faced by the authorities in dealing with the Chartist challenge?

3   To what extent did the Home Office view events in Newport as a serious challenge?

● SOURCE 7.36

From an eyewitness account of events in Newport by Barnabas Brough. Brough was a local brewer who was briefly detained by the Chartists in Newport. His account was written later and published as an anonymous pamphlet in 1847.

*Few . . . can have forgotten the insane attempt at insurrection made by the Chartists in Monmouthshire, at the latter part of the year 1839, when a body of misguided men, many thousands in number . . . were discomfited and totally dispersed by a small detachment of the 45th regiment, amounting to only twenty-eight men, at the Westgate Inn, at Newport.*

## ● SOURCE 7.37

From Thomas Dunning, *Reminiscences*, 1894, in which a former Radical recalls the response of the authorities to the Chartist protesters of 1839–40.

*The years 1839 and '40 were years of persecution and imprisonment for the poor Chartists, our Reform Government appearing to vie with their Tory predecessors in endeavouring most cruelly to crush out the agitation for universal suffrage, etc. . . . I have the names, etc., of 93 Chartists who were undergoing various terms of imprisonment at the end of 1840 including Frost, Williams and Jones and 17 others at Monmouth, at Chester 12 including William Benbow of Middlewich, Liverpool 32, including the Rev. W. V. Jackson, Bronterre O'Brien, J. R. Richardson and Christopher Doyle, York 23 nearly the whole of them for delivering seditious speeches. Dr P. M. McDouall and the Rev. J. R. Stephens were tried at the Chester Assizes held in August 1839 . . . The indictment in each case was misdemeanour, McDouall for having attended an unlawful meeting held at Hyde on the 22nd of April 1839 and with having used seditious and inflammatory language . . . McDouall was found guilty and sentenced to one year's imprisonment and was bound over to keep the peace for five years himself in £500 and two sureties of £200 each . . . During these trials the barristers' table was covered with arms of various kinds, Guns, Swords, pikes, etc., which had been found in the possession of the defendants offering on sale. This exhibition of arms in court it was believed was for the purpose of influencing the jury to convict . . . pickets of the Cheshire Yeomanry [were] on the lookout for the expected mob from Lancashire and Staffordshire coming to rescue the Chartist prisoners . . . In addition . . . a large number of special constables were sworn in to protect and assist the authorities in the event of a rescue of the political prisoners being attempted.*

---

1 According to Source 7.37, what charges did the authorities bring against Chartists arrested between 1839 and 1840?

2 How many Chartists were dealt with by the law courts?

3 According to Sources 7.36 and 7.37, what measures were applied by the law courts to deter future Chartists?

## ● SOURCE 7.38

From Lt Colonel Pringle Taylor, to the Mayor of Southampton, Sunday, 11 January 1840, *Letters Relative to the Chartists, 1839–1840*, commenting on the success of the authorities in dealing with the Chartists.

*A most influential Chartist Delegate from the North who was all for physical force and violent measures was led by one of our men through Birmingham and London to prove to him that all that organisation which existed previously in these towns was quite destroyed. The effects produced upon him and through him upon the other Delegates by the unexpected change in these places, the result of our action, led to such representations to the various leaders that their minds were paralysed and the intended general outbreak on New Year's Eve was postponed. To what period I have not yet learned. A spark would ignite the combustible materials and bring upon us all the horrors of a civil war.*

---

1 What reassurances was Lt Colonel Pringle Taylor trying to communicate in his letter to the Mayor of Southampton (Source 7.38)?

Study Sources 7.26–7.38 on Chartist activities in 1838–39.

1 Why did Chartism attract widespread support in 1839?

2 What did the Chartists identify as their rights?

3 How did the Chartists attempt to obtain their rights?

4 What sections of the population appear to have been obstacles to the spread of Chartism?

5 What were the motives of those who obstructed the Chartists?

6 To what extent did those who believed in physical force dominate Chartist activities in 1839?

7 To what extent did the events of 1839 suggest that the Chartists aimed at revolution?

8 What light do these sources throw on the effectiveness of measures taken by the authorities to meet the Chartist threats in 1839?

# Tactics – events of 1840–42

The failure of the Newport rising brought to a close a period of violent agitation. For a time the movement broke down, until high unemployment and real distress reappeared between 1840 and 1842 in the textile and metal industries. Under the influence of O'Connor from his prison cell in York, delegates at a conference in Manchester decided to reorganise the Chartist movement into the National Charter Association. It was managed by working men and claimed to represent 400 separate Chartist Societies all over the country, with members paying 1 d. a week subscription. Together with the *Northern Star*, the National Charter Association acted as the unifying force that the movement had lacked in its first period. Some Chartists, such as Lovett, who had been released from prison, campaigned for a 'new organisation' based on moral force. He argued that working men would have to gain acceptance for their demands by showing their moral worth through education, a strategy that was bitterly criticised by O'Connor.

In this second period the Chartists had to compete with the Anti-Corn-Law League for working-class support. It was decided to present a second petition of Chartist demands to Parliament. Even though the Petition secured $3\frac{1}{2}$ million signatures, it was rejected by Parliament in May 1842. The working class responded to this rejection by organising a series of strikes in the factory areas and attacks on magistrates' houses, known as the Plug Plot.

● **SOURCE 7.39**

From a newspaper article in *The Times*, 3 May 1842, commenting upon Chartist demands contained in the second Petition.

*. . . for the substance of their petition . . . It complains of a variety of particular grievances – some real and remediable by act of Parliament as the New Poor Law . . . the cruelties practised in the factories and the riots and corruption of elections; some of which are real enough . . . taxation and therein particularly the national debt; the contrast between the luxury of the rich and the poverty of the working classes; the existing restrictions on popular meetings, a police and a standing army . . . but the great and fundamental object of their attack is the present state of the representation. We are content with the . . . simple belief that the great question to be settled by the House of Commons . . . is not how the people shall be fully represented but how they shall be well governed; – that Governments do not rest their authority on the consent of the people but simply on their own established existence – that the powers that be have a claim upon our allegiance because they are – and that we have the benefits of their protection.*

1 What evidence is contained in the demands of the second Petition (Source 7.39) to indicate that the Chartists had extended the scope of their aims?

2 Is it possible to tell whether *The Times* was sympathetic to Chartism? Justify your answer with reference to the evidence of the article.

● **SOURCE 7.40**

From Thomas Cooper, *Life of Thomas Cooper, written by himself*, 1873, in which the Chartist leader provides an eyewitness account of the events in the Potteries on 15 August 1842.

**Thomas Cooper (1805–92)** was apprenticed as a shoemaker before he became a journalist and Chartist lecturer. He argued against physical force but was imprisoned in 1843 for urging workers to strike in support of the Charter.

**drew the plugs** stopped the boilers from working

*The 'Plug Plot' of 1842, as it is still called in Lancashire, began in reductions of wages by the Anti-Corn-Law manufacturers, who did not conceal their purpose of driving the people to desperation, in order to paralyse the Government. The people advanced at last, to a wild general strike, and DREW THE PLUGS so as to stop the works at the mills, and thus render labour impossible. Some wanted the men who spoke at the meetings held at the beginning of the strike to propose resolutions in favour of Corn Law Repeal; but they refused. The first meeting where the resolution was passed, 'that all labour should cease until the People's Charter became the law of the land', was held on the 7th of August, on Mottram Moor. In the course of a week, the resolution had passed in nearly all the great towns of Lancashire, and tens of thousands had held up their hands in favour of it . . . [Cooper was in Hanley, in the Potteries, on 15 August.] By six o'clock, thousands crowded into the large open space about the Crown Inn . . . Before I began, some of the men who were drunk, and who, it seems, had been in the riot at Longton came around and wanted to shake hands with me . . . I had heard there had been destruction of property that day, and I warned all who had participated in that act, that they were not the friends, but the enemies of freedom – ruin to themselves and others must attend this strike for the Charter, if they who pretended to be its advocates broke the law.*

. . . two pistols were fired off in the crowd. No policeman had I seen the whole day! And what had become of the soldiers I could not learn . . . the rioters were burning the houses of the Rev. Mr Aitken and Mr Parker, local magistrates, and the house of Mr Forrester, agent of Lord Granville [principal owner of the collieries in the Potteries] during the night . . . Next morning thousands were again in the streets of Hanley and began to pour into the other Pottery towns from the surrounding districts. A troop of Cavalry . . . entered the district and the daring colliers strove to unhorse the soldiers. Their commander reluctantly gave the order to fire; one man was killed at Burslem. The mob dispersed; but quiet was not restored until the day after . . . and scores apprehended and taken to prison. When I entered the railway carriage at Crewe, some who were going to the Convention recognised me . . . So soon as the City of Long Chimneys came in sight, and every chimney was beheld smokeless, Campbell's [Secretary of the National Charter Association] face changed, and with an oath he said, 'Not a single mill at work! something must come out of this, and something serious too!' . . . In the streets, there was unmistakable signs of alarm on the part of the authorities. Troops of cavalry were going up and down the principal thoroughfares, accompanied by pieces of artillery, drawn by horses.

In the evening, we held a meeting in the Reverend Mr Schofield's chapel, where O'Connor, the Executive, and a considerable number of delegates were present . . . There were nearly sixty delegates present; and as they rose, in quick succession, to describe the state of their districts, it was evident they were . . . filled with the desire of keeping the people from returning to their labour. They believed the time had come for trying, successfully, to paralyse the Government . . . the Executive and a few others all spoke in favour of the universal strike . . . The authorities of the land would try to quell it, but we must resist them. There was nothing now but a physical force struggle to be looked for.

● **SOURCE 7.41**

From John Mayhall, *Annals of Leeds, York and the Surrounding District*, 1865, in which a contemporary recalls the Plug Plot in Leeds 23 years after the event.

On the morning of the 17th [August 1842] the greatest excitement prevailed in Leeds from a report that a vast number of rioters were on the road from Bradford. The town of Leeds was well organised with troops and a large number of special constables had been sworn in . . . Meantime a large mob had assembled at Hunslet and commenced operations by turning out the hands at Messrs Petty's potteries; after which they went along Holbeck Moor to the mills in Holbeck. They forced in the boiler plug and summoned the hands out of the mill of Messrs E. and G. Tatham . . . They then proceeded to the mill of Messrs Titley, Tatham and Walker, Water Lane, which they were engaged in stopping when Prince George with the Lancers came up at full speed and formed in line in Camp Field. The Riot Act was read and two or three of the ring leaders were taken prisoners.

● **SOURCE 7.42**

From a report of the *Illustrated London News*, August 1842, commenting on the outbreak of strikes in and around Manchester.

The strikes affected 23 counties across Wales, Scotland and England. They were most severe and radical in the Midlands, Lancashire and the West Riding, involving workers in the pottery, mining and textile industries. Chartist leaders found that they were not in control of these activities.

We have to record the disastrous occurrence of a turn-out of manufacturing labourers in and about Manchester . . . It would appear that the sudden and turbulent display of congregated thousands leaving their daily employment – marching upon mills forcing willing and unwilling alike to join them and in a moment paralysing the whole activity of the natural enterprise of their neighbourhood – arose in the first instance from a reduction of wages in one quarter given almost without notice and taken by the men as the omen of a general intention on the part of the masters everywhere else. At once with a desperation of purpose they gathered in half-starved thousands resolved to withdraw from work unless they can have 'a fair day's pay for a fair day's labour'; and partly with riot, partly with abuse, partly with threat, plunged the sober population into fear and created anxieties natural to these troublous times from one end to the other of the land.

All the manufacturing districts have been up in arms; at Preston the insurgents were fired upon and some of them wounded mortally. At Stockport, where there are upwards of 20,000 persons out of employment who have no resources but those of plunder and beggary, a large body of rioters broke open and pillaged the workhouses of food and clothing and mobs robbed the provision shops. Troops, guards and artillery have been poured in upon the shocking scene of insurrection; and there seems to have been a spreading organisation of a most formidable and disciplined character. The fact that troops had been ordered to the disturbed *districts soon became publicly known and produced an intense feeling of alarm and excitement in the mind of individuals generally . . .*

*The more remarkable features of the proceedings at Stockport were the demand of money from mill-owners as well as shop-keepers and an attack on the New Union Workhouse . . . where the mob forced an entrance and immediately commenced to help themselves to bread and money. Information of this was conveyed to the authorities and they hastened to the spot with the constables and infantry and captured about forty of the rioters.*

● **SOURCE 7.43**

From *Parliamentary Papers*, 1850.

Total committals for riotous offences, 1838–48.

| Year | Riotously and feloniously demolishing buildings/machinery | Riot and sedition | Riot, breach of peace | High treason |
|------|-----|-----|-----|-----|
| 1838 | 9 | 231 | 592 | 0 |
| 1840 | 0 | 212 | 413 | 14 |
| 1841 | 7 | 5 | 553 | 0 |
| 1842 | 71 | 962 | 595 | 1 |
| 1843 | 60 | 60 | 543 | 0 |
| 1844 | 2 | 2 | 567 | 0 |
| 1845 | 0 | 0 | 363 | 0 |
| 1846 | 5 | 0 | 302 | 0 |
| 1847 | 13 | 0 | 373 | 0 |
| 1848 | 4 | 253 | 387 | 12 |

Study Sources 7.40–7.43.

1 Why were the events of August 1842 known as the 'Plug Plot'?

2 What were the immediate causes of the disturbances that broke out in
   a) Leeds
   b) Manchester?

3 Which groups of people were involved in each case?

4 What was the scale of the protests?

5 Why did the Stockport rioters make a particular point of attacking the workhouses?

6 According to Source 7.43, to what extent did Chartist forms of protest change in 1842 compared with
   a) 1838
   b) 1848?

7 Which year, according to the evidence of Source 7.43, represented the main Chartist threat to the authorities?

8 Who were the victims of the rioters?

9 By what means did the authorities try to maintain public order?

10 Was the system of law officers sufficient for a dispute of this scale?

11 What evidence is there in these sources to support each of the following descriptions of the events of August 1842
   a) 'rebellion of the belly'
   b) 'collective bargaining by riot'?

12 On what evidence does the report of the *Illustrated London News* (Source 7.42) claim that 'there seems to have been a spreading organisation of a most formidable and disciplined character'?

Representatives from all trades agreed to use the strike weapon to achieve the demands set out in the Charter. The General Council of the National Charter Association found itself with a strike that it had not planned or organised and only reluctantly endorsed it. Feargus O'Connor was lukewarm in his support, believing that mill-owners had ulterior motives in closing their mills so quickly.

The Chartist leadership was punished for the attempt to trigger a national strike, although O'Connor and 58 other Chartists were acquitted in the spring of 1843. The Conservative government of Sir Robert Peel, while determined to take firm action, was not prepared to create Chartist martyrs.

The renewed activity of 1842 was short-lived. The distressed workers in towns such as Bolton soon turned their attention to campaigning for repeal of the new Poor Law and for the ten-hour working day. Railway mania and the employment opportunities it offered, along with a return of workers' interest to trade union activity, led to a fading away of support for Chartism. O'Connor concentrated on his Land Plan, which was announced in 1845 and launched in the National Land Company of 1847, with shares at £1.30. Seventy thousand people paid total weekly subscriptions of £3,200, which made possible the purchase of five estates. The scheme lasted until 1851 when it was dissolved following a parliamentary Select Committee investigation into fraud.

## Tactics – events of 1848

Chartism revived in 1848, once again against a background of a winter of high flour prices, bad trade and an 'extreme prevalence' of influenza, bronchitis, pneumonia, typhus, measles and scarlatina. Smallpox was also widespread. Chartist activities, centred in London, occurred against the background of revolutions in Europe. A third Petition was circulated and plans were drawn up for a meeting at Kennington Common, London, on 10 April 1848. The meeting was to be followed by a mass march to Westminster, headed by O'Connor, who would present the third Petition to Parliament. The authorities took elaborate precautions to counter the Chartist threat – 150,000 special constables were enrolled – but the Chartist meeting was poorly attended, and rained off. O'Connor went in a cab to hand in the Petition. When it was examined, it was found to contain so many bogus signatures that it was laughed out of Parliament. The Charter was never revived. Although unrest continued throughout the spring and summer of 1848, the revolutionaries were only a small minority, and were led on by government spies. Support for Chartism drifted away as prosperity returned.

● **SOURCE 7.44**

From a letter from the Prime Minister, Lord John Russell, to Queen Victoria, 2 p.m., 10 April 1848, reporting the events at Kennington Common, 10 April 1848.

*Lord John Russell presents his humble duty to your Majesty, and has the honour to state that the Kennington Common Meeting has proved a complete failure. About 12,000 or 15,000 persons met in good order. Feargus O'Connor, upon arriving upon the ground in a car, was ordered by Mr Mayne, the Commissioner of Police, to come and speak to him. He immediately left the car and came, looking pale and frightened, to Mr Mayne. Upon being told that the meeting would not be prevented, but that no procession would be allowed to pass the bridges, he expressed the utmost thanks, and begged to shake Mr Mayne by the hand. He then addressed the crowd, advising them to disperse, and after rebuking them for their folly he went off in a cab to the Home Office, where he repeated to Sir George Grey, the Home Secretary, his thanks, his fears, and his assurances that the crowd should disperse quietly. Sir George Grey said he had done very rightly, but that the force at the bridges should not be diminished.*

*Mr F. O'Connor – 'Not a man should be taken away. The Government have been quite right. I told the Convention that if they had been the Government they never would have allowed such a meeting.'*

*The last account gave the numbers as about 5,000 rapidly dispersing. The mob was in good humour, and any mischief that now takes place will be the act of individuals; but it is to be hoped the preparations made will daunt those wicked but not brave men. The accounts from the country are good. Scotland is quiet. At Manchester, however, the Chartists are armed, and have bad designs. A quiet termination of the present ferment will greatly raise us in foreign countries. Lord John Russell trusts your Majesty has profited by the sea air.*

1　Comment on the image Lord John Russell presents of O'Connor's leadership in Source 7.44.

2　How serious a challenge to public order was the Chartist meeting at Kennington Common?

3　What precautions were taken by the government to prevent a disturbance in April 1848?

4　Did O'Connor betray the Chartist movement on 10 April 1848?

● **SOURCE 7.45**

*The Chartist procession according to the signatures of the Petition, a cartoon and its accompanying text from Punch Volume 14, April 1848. On examination of the signatures by a House of Commons committee, it appeared that Queen Victoria and seventeen Dukes of Wellington had signed.*

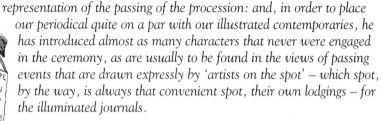

It is a very remarkable fact connected with the late Chartist Petition, that the parties who appear to have contributed the largest amount of signatures were not forthcoming to back the document on the day of its presentation. Our artist, in his beautiful simplicity following the pictorial practice of the present day, has drawn from his own imagination the exact representation of the passing of the procession: and, in order to place our periodical quite on a par with our illustrated contemporaries, he has introduced almost as many characters that never were engaged in the ceremony, as are usually to be found in the views of passing events that are drawn expressly by 'artists on the spot' – which spot, by the way, is always that convenient spot, their own lodgings – for the illuminated journals.

The Chartist Procession, with which we this day present our readers, is in accordance with the view we should be justified in taking of it, if the signatures to the Petition were bona fide, and comprised of the actual autographs of the illustrious personages whose names were found appended to the document in conjunction with those of the heroic Pugnoses, Flatnoses, and other great nasal organs of Chartist opinion that seemed desirous of being heard in favour of the six pints, or three quarts, as our friend Cuffey has ingeniously designated his favourite measures. Had the petition been anything but a hoax, Her Majesty would have been at an early hour wending her way towards Kennington Common with seventeen Dukes of Wellington at her side, and Sir R. Peel would have been conspicuous in the van that was bearing the monster document.

Perhaps, after all, the two Premiers – ex and present – have as much interest as the Cuffets, the Reynoldses, and the M'Graths in one.

● **SOURCE 7.46**

*From Benjamin Wilson, The Struggles of an Old Chartist, 1887, in which he recalls the events of 1848.*

In this year flour was very dear, reaching the price of 5s. per stone, whilst trade was also very bad. This was the time to make politicians, as the easiest way to get to an Englishman's brains is through his stomach. It was said by its enemies that Chartism was dead . . . and would never rise again, but they were doomed to disappointment. It was true that there had been no meetings or processions, nor had the agitation reached the height it attained in 1839, but it was going on. Amongst combers, handloom weavers and others, politics was the chief topic . . . We were only waiting for the time to come again. In 1848 it was said that the year was the year of agitations, of revolutions, and thousands of men fell on the field of battle fighting for the people's cause in Europe in this struggle. The French revolution of the 24th February gave the first impulse to this movement . . . A great many people in these districts were arming themselves with guns and pikes, and drilling on the moors. Bill Cockcroft, one of the leaders of the physical force party in Halifax, wished me to join the movement, I consented and purchased a gun, although I knew it to be a serious thing for a Chartist to have a gun or pike in his possession. I had several years practice in shooting, as the farmer for whom I worked supplied me with a gun, powder and shot for the purpose of shooting birds in summer. I saw Cockcroft who gave me instructions how to proceed until wanted, which did not occur as the scheme was abandoned . . . I have been a woollen weaver, a comber, a navvy on the railway, and a barer in the deiph [quarryman] that I claim to know some little of the state of the working classes. I well remember only a few years ago talking to a friend who told me he was moulding bullets in the cellar in 1848: he had a wife and five children dependent upon him, but was unable to get work, trade being so bad. Since then, however, under the blessings of free trade and by dint of perseverance he has succeeded in saving a considerable sum and is now living retired from business.

1 From the evidence of Source 7.46, to what extent was Chartism outside of London due to 'hunger politics'?

2 What influence did revolutions in Europe have on Chartist activities in 1848?

3 To what extent was the Chartism of 1848 different from its preceding outbreaks?

4 To what extent did Benjamin Wilson represent continuity with earlier Chartists?

5 Why, according to Wilson, did Chartism fail after 1848?

● **SOURCE 7.47**

From G. R. Porter, *The Progress of the Nation*, 1847.

Committals and convictions for indictable offences of riot, 1835–45.

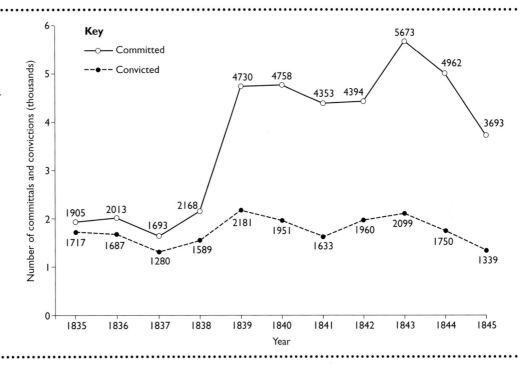

1 From the evidence of Source 7.47, what was happening to the level of riot in the Chartist period?

2 Which period of Chartist activity posed the greatest challenge to the forces of law and order?

● **SOURCE 7.48**

From *Parliamentary Papers*, 1835–70.

Committals for indictable riotous offences, 1837–49, as a percentage of all committals.

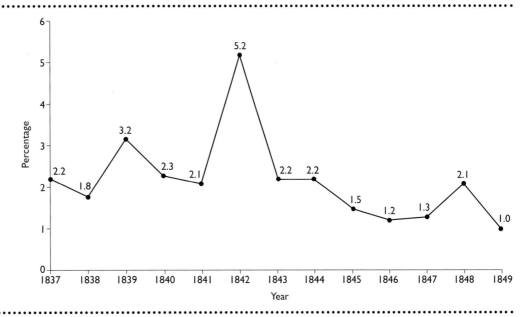

1 Using Source 7.48, identify the periods when committals for riotous offences as a percentage of all committals peaked.

2 What evidence is offered by the statistics that riot as a form of working-class protest was on the decline by 1849?

**How did the Chartists attempt to achieve their aims?**

259

● SOURCE 7.49

260

From *Parliamentary Papers*, 1849.

Committals for seditious offences in 1848.

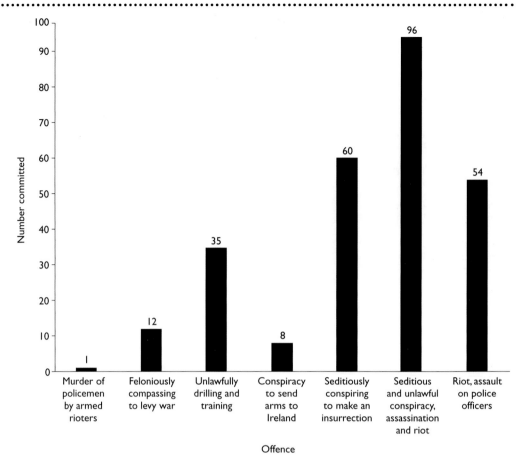

I According to the evidence in Source 7.49, what different forms did seditious activity take in 1848?

2 What were the most serious forms of seditious offence carried out in 1848?

# 7 What was the relationship of Chartism to the other protest movements of the day?

Chartism was not of course the only important protest movement of the day. Others included the anti-Poor-Law agitation movement, the factory reform movement and the Anti-Corn-Law League. Any attempt to explore the relationship between these movements should include an examination of origins and aims, social composition, leadership, methods and their effectiveness. Chartism has been described as a 'snowball of protest movements'. The economic depression and its attendant social ills in the late 1830s and early 1840s channelled the grievances of the 1830s into either the Anti-Corn-Law League or Chartism. Though the movements developed separately and, according to some historians, were on the whole antagonistic to each other, especially between 1838 and 1842, nevertheless they were broadly concerned with similar issues – finding a remedy to the bad times.

● **SOURCE 7.50**

From the Leicester Chartist John Mason to the All Saints Open Chartists in 1840, in which the former Tyneside shoemaker expresses a widely felt suspicion amongst Chartists of the implications of Corn Law repeal for working men.

---

**Corn Law repeal**
abolition of the law restricting imports of foreign corn, which was designed to keep the price of corn high and ensure good profits for landowners.

**free traders**
supporters of the abolition of the Corn Law

**the bill**
the bill for reform of Parliament, which became the Reform Act of 1832, and gave the vote to the middle classes.

**Municipal Reform**
the Municipal Reform Act of 1835, which provided for town councils elected by property owners. In effect it gave control of local government to the middle classes, instead of the local aristocracy.

---

*Not that CORN LAW REPEAL is wrong; when we get the Charter we will repeal the Corn Laws and all the other bad laws. But if you give up your agitation for the Charter to help the FREE TRADERS they will not help you to get the Charter. Don't be deceived by the middle classes again. You helped them to get their votes – you swelled their cry of 'THE BILL, the whole bill and nothing but the bill!' But where are the fine promises they made you? Gone to the winds! They said when they had gotten their votes they would help you to get yours. But they and the rotten Whigs have never remembered you. MUNICIPAL REFORM has been for their benefit – not for yours. All other reforms the Whigs boast to have effected have been for the benefit of the middle classes – not for yours. And now they want to get the Corn Laws repealed – not for your benefit – but for their own. 'Cheap Bread!' they cry. But they mean 'Low Wages'. Do not listen to their cant and humbug. Stick to your Charter. You are veritable slaves without your votes.*

1　In Source 7.50 why does John Mason warn fellow Chartists not to be 'deceived by the middle classes again'?

2　Why were middle-class efforts to secure Corn Law repeal viewed with suspicion by the majority of Chartists?

3　Why does Mason see political reform as being essential before economic reform can take place?

● **SOURCE 7.51**

From the *Manchester Guardian*, 21 December 1839, in which Chartists who gave some support to calls for free trade argue the case for wider reform.

*Let these men know that if it suit them to have a repeal of the Corn Law it will also suit you to have with it that of the malt tax and the excise duties on all the necessaries of life that we may drink as well as eat cheaply. Let us teach them, that we will have these things; and to enable us to keep them once begotten, we will have universal suffrage in local as well as general government.*

1　Why did some Chartists argue (Source 7.51) that the Corn Law should not be repealed by itself?

2　What wider reforms did some Chartists argue should accompany repeal of the Corn Law?

● **SOURCE 7.52**

From *Anti-Bread-Tax Circular*, 21 April 1841, in which a small group of Chartists develop their protectionist view.

*The Corn Laws were not the cause of the evils and sufferings of the labouring classes . . . So long as the working classes had not the power of limiting the use of machinery, and controlling the grasping capitalist in his selfishness after wealth, cheap bread meant low wages, for machinery would multiply in proportion as trade increased, and by its competition with human labour, enable the capitalist to put all the profits of cheap food into his own purse.*

1　What, according to the protectionist Chartists writing in Source 7.52, was the main cause of sufferings amongst workers?

2　What was the basis of the argument of those Chartists who opposed repeal of the Corn Laws?

## SOURCE 7.53

From Charles Pelham Villiers' letter to J. B. Smith, President of the Manchester Chamber of Commerce, and a leading member of the Anti-Corn-Law League, undated (but possibly August 1840). Villiers, MP for Wolverhampton and an opponent of the Corn Laws, explains why the League should secure working-class support.

*We had a meeting of the London association on the night of the Chartist meeting & I thought it not inappropriate to state as strongly as I could my thorough conviction that the working classes are really those most interested in the repeal of the Corn Laws . . . My great object in getting them [i.e. the working classes] to speak out is that I am convinced that until they do the Aristocracy will never yield – I grieve to say that the brickbat argument is the only one that our nobles heed.*

1  What was Villiers' motive for securing working-class support, according to Source 7.53?
2  On what specific grounds would Chartists object to the views expressed by Villiers?

## SOURCE 7.54

From a letter from Edward Watkin to Richard Cobden, *Cobden Papers*, in which the young Leaguer reports on the activities of the free traders and Irish in breaking up a meeting attended by O'Connor in Manchester in March 1842.

**Edward Watkin** was given the task of organising an Operatives Anti-Corn-Law Association in Manchester with the aim of resisting Chartist attempts at obstruction.

**Richard Cobden (1801–65)** was MP for Stockport and a leading member of the Anti-Corn-Law League. He pioneered political propaganda techniques and supported the Liberal Party after 1846.

*The result was a tremendous fight – all the furniture was smashed to atoms; forms, desks, chairs, gas pipes, were used as weapons and the result is something as follows. 'The lion' – the king of Chartism, Feargus O'Connor, knocked down three times – has he says seven wounds – six he can tell the position of – the seventh was I believe inflicted as he was running away – which he did after fighting about two minutes. Christopher Doyle very much hurt – Bailey – confined to his bed – Murray – ditto – four others (Chartists) seriously hurt – Revd Schofield – black eye – loose teeth – cut lip – contusions behind (got in following Feargus) – four of the 'lambs' badly hurt – 2 with their skulls fractured – they however are used to it & will soon be well. The damage is estimated at £40.*

## SOURCE 7.55

From Samuel Smiles, *Autobiography*, in which Richard Cobden describes disruption of League meetings by local Chartists.

*The Chartist leaders attacked us on the platform at the head of their deluded followers. We were nearly the victims of physical force; I lost my hat and all but had my head split open with the leg of a stool.*

## SOURCE 7.56

From a speech by Richard Cobden to the Anti-Corn-Law League, reported in the *Anti-Bread-Tax Circular*, 8 September 1842. Cobden discusses the implications of the disturbances in manufacturing districts for the relationship between employers and workmen.

*I don't deny that the working classes generally have attended our lectures and signed our petitions; but I will admit that so far as the enthusiasm and efficiency of our agitation has gone it has eminently been a middle-class agitation. We have carried it on by those means by which the middle class usually carries on its movements . . . We have had our meetings of dissenting ministers, we have obtained the co-operation of the ladies, we have resorted to tea-parties and taken those peaceful means of carrying out our views, which mark us rather as a middle-class set of agitators. We are no political body; we have refused to be bought by the Tories. We have kept aloof from the Whigs, and we will not join partnership with either Radicals or Chartists, but we hold out our hand ready to give it to all who are willing to advocate the total and immediate repeal of the Corn . . . Law. But Gentlemen the present occasion is a very seasonable one for drawing closer the bonds of union between the*

263

What was the relationship of Chartism to the other protest movements of the day?

*employers and the employed in this district. The present disastrous commotion arises dearly out of a dispute about wages . . . Now our business is first to show the working men that the question of wages is a question depending altogether on principles apart from party politics . . . that if we had the Charter tomorrow the principles which govern the relations between masters and men would be precisely the same as they are now . . .*

Study Sources 7.54–7.56.

1 What was the attitude of the working classes towards the issue of the repeal of the Corn Laws?

2 What was the main obstacle, according to Cobden (Source 7.56), to an alliance between the middle-class-led League and the Chartists?

3 What indirect criticism of the Chartists' methods is made by Cobden?

4 Is it possible to identify Cobden's attitude towards the working classes? Justify your answer by commenting on language and tone.

5 What strategy did Cobden recommend the League to adopt to improve the relationship between employers and employees?

● **SOURCE 7.57**

From the *Manchester Guardian*, 17 December 1845, reporting a change of opinion amongst some of the operatives towards the issue of Corn Law repeal.

*The rapid advance in the price of wheat during the last four months accompanied, not as it had been alleged would be the case by an increase, but by a very evident tendency to a decline in wages, – at once convinced the intelligent working men of this district, that the object of their masters, in seeking the repeal of the Corn Laws, was not to lower wages; and that employers and employed were equally interested in obtaining a plentiful supply of food.*

1 According to Source 7.57, what change of opinion towards Corn Law repeal had taken place by 1845 amongst some workers?

2 Why had there been this change of view?

3 What effect was this likely to have on class relationships?

Study Sources 7.50–7.57.

1 Why did local Chartist leaders hold differing opinions on the issue of Corn Law reform?

2 How useful are these sources to an understanding of the diversity of Chartism?

● **Summary task**

1 Below are a number of questions that might be used for discussion or written answers as a way of testing your understanding of this chapter.

- Did Chartism reflect the fluctuations in the British economy between 1815 and 1850?
- Was Chartism more than a movement for social reform?
- Did Chartism fail because lower-class unrest was basically a 'knife and fork' question?
- Did the Chartists possess a political creed?
- Why was the issue of the Corn Law not entirely an economic issue?
- What were working-class views of the middle class?
- Did Chartism pose a serious threat to public order?
- How effective were the measures taken to avert Chartism's challenge to public order?

2 **Individual activity – an assessment of Chartism**
Those who participated in Chartism felt a deep sense of tragedy – a feeling that the time had been exactly right for a radical change but that by disunity, confused advice and a lack of decisiveness, the opportunity had been missed and might not recur for a generation or more. However, they were also left with a sense of hope and promise. They had gained experience in political affairs and an education in political and social action that led to the establishment of a pattern of local democratic behaviour.

Study Sources 7.58–7.62 on pages 264–5 and then answer the questions that follow.

● **SOURCE 7.58**

From a letter from G. J. Harney to Friedrich Engels, a prominent early socialist, 30 March 1846, in which Harney, a leading Chartist, comments on the future of Chartism and the leadership of O'Connor.

*Your speculations as to the speedy coming of a revolution in England I doubt. Your prediction that we shall get the Charter in the course of the present year and the abolition of private property within three years will certainly not be realised: indeed as regards the latter although it may and I hope will come it is my belief that neither you nor I will see it.*

*As to what O'Connor has been saying lately about 'physical force', I think nothing of it. The English people will not adopt notions about peace and non-resistance but neither would they act upon the opposite doctrine. They applaud it at public meetings but that is all. Notwithstanding the talk in 1839 about 'arming', the people did not arm and they will not arm. A long immunity from the presence of war in their own country and the long suspension of the militia has created a general distaste for arms which year by year is becoming more extensive and more intense. The body of the English people without becoming a slavish people are becoming an eminently pacific people. To attempt a 'physical force' agitation at the present time would be productive of no good but on the contrary of some evil – the evil of exciting suspicion against the agitators. To organise to conspire a revolution in this country would be a vain and foolish project. I must next notice what you say about my 'leadership'. First let me remark that you are too hard upon O'Connor. I must do O'Connor the justice to say that he never interferes with what I write in the paper nor does he know what I write until he sees the paper. You say I am 'international', 'revolutionary', 'energetical' but supposing it to be even as you say it does not follow that I am qualified for 'leadership'. A popular chief should be possessed of a magnificent bodily appearance, an iron frame, eloquence or at least a ready fluency of tongue. I have none of these. O'Connor has them all – at least in degree. A popular leader should possess great animal courage, contempt of pain and death and be not altogether ignorant of arms and military science. In these qualifications I am decidedly deficient. From a knowledge of myself and all the men who live and do figure in the Chartist movement I am convinced that even in this respect was O'Connor thrown overboard we might go further and fare worse.*

● **SOURCE 7.59**

From Ramsden Balmforth, *Some Social and Political Pioneers of the Nineteenth Century*, 1900, in which the author assesses reasons for the failure of Chartism.

**Ramsden Balmforth**
was the son of a Huddersfield Chartist handloom-weaver. He was brought up in a home filled with Chartist and Owenite memories. He gave his final verdict on Chartism in 1900. His views probably reflected those of his father, who lived until 1904.

*The Chartist movement was one to which all social and political reformers look back with a certain amount of pride, mingled with a great amount of sadness. Pride, because it was a movement inspired by great ideals; because it called forth a spirit of devotion and self-sacrifice which is rare in public movements, and caught up on its 'moral force' side some of the finest and most thoughtful working-men of the time. Sadness, because its ideals were either shattered, or passed on, by the natural process of evolution, into other movements and other parties; because its spirit of devotion and self-sacrifice was broken by brutal persecution and imprisonment; and because its 'moral force' was largely neutralised, and its adherents deluded and misled, by one or two inordinately vain and self-seeking agitators. Of these, perhaps the most accountable was Feargus O'Connor. O'Connor was the editor and chief proprietor of the* Northern Star, *the principal working-class newspaper of the time, and, through its pages, wielded great influence. Possessing lungs of brass and a voice like a trumpet, he was the most effective outdoor orator of his time, and the idol of the immense assemblages that were often brought together in those days. Unfortunately, both for the movement and for himself, he was a man of unbounded conceit and egotism, extremely jealous of precedence, and regarding himself as a sort of uncrowned king of the working classes . . . But it would be a great mistake to suppose that the Chartist movement was really fruitless. No movement of its magnitude and intensity can be fruitless. It may have looked too much to outward means, and too little to inward and spiritual reform; but it was an excellent means of political education for the working classes.*

## ● SOURCE 7.60

From D. Jones, *Chartism and the Chartists*, 1975.

**impressment**
the forcible seizure of men for military service, usually in the navy

*The willingness of Chartists to rely on their own strength is the outstanding characteristic of the movement. At the local level, Chartism was often an integral part of the struggle for identity, dignity and improvement . . . 'Am I a man?' is a question which recurs in one form or another in Chartist speeches and poetry. Workmen, who were committed to education and self help, had their own sets of fears, values and objectives. In their support for Chartist schools, halls, churches, newspapers and estates; in their campaigns against capital punishment, army flogging and IMPRESSMENT; and in their belief that science and machinery should ultimately be harnessed to the benefit of all, we catch a glimpse of an alternative society, egalitarian, humane and harmonious . . . Contemporaries were impressed by the initiative and independence shown by working men in the movements of this period. One suspects that some historians have underestimated the power, discretion and class feelings of ordinary Chartist members.*

## ● SOURCE 7.61

From N. Gash, *Aristocracy and People*, 1979.

*Between 1837 and 1843 a large part of the aspirations and discontents of the manufacturing population was drawn into the movement known as Chartism. It was a deceptively simple label. From small and identifiable origins Chartism widened into a mass of activities which make broad generalisations and neat analysis impossible. Chartism floated, as it were, on a conglomeration of working-class movements with different objectives, different philosophies, different grievances and different leaders. The 'Charter' provided nothing new in the way of political thought; and less than was commonly thought in the way of united action. Underneath were still the old complicated phenomena of classes, trades and regions, mass meetings, religious revivalism, the popular press, physical violence and constitutional agitation . . . Regionalism, discordant personalities, local and class rivalries were obvious weaknesses of Chartism. Clashes of policy derived more from these features than from any considered principles of strategy . . . Certainly there was much talk of fighting – too much to offer the likelihood of much action. Speakers, newspapers and handbills called for the people to procure arms and be ready to march when the signal was given . . . In most of the larger manufacturing districts there were reports, duly conveyed to the Home Office, of men drilling secretly at night . . . The more the Chartists exhibited the aggressive proletarian nature of their movement, the more the middle classes doubted their fitness to exercise the parliamentary franchise . . . Though Chartism was in one sense only a continuation under another name of the old radical reform movement and was to last in some shape or other into the 1850s, what gave it contemporary importance was the great industrial depression from 1837 to 1843 . . . Hungry bellies filled the ranks of the Chartists; the return of economic prosperity after 1843 thinned them . . . The inevitable rejection of the Chartist petition in the spring of 1842 marked the end of Chartism as a movement of any real importance.*

## ● SOURCE 7.62

From E. Evans, 'Chartism Revisited', *History Review Journal*, 1999.

*Although students are keen on explaining the rise and fall of Chartism in social and economic terms, it is vital to appreciate two things: it was both a political movement and a genuinely national one . . . Discussions of the reasons why Chartism 'took off' in the late 1830s so often concentrate on 'economic and social' factors: rising food prices, economic depression and reactions to the Poor Law Amendment Act of 1834 . . . Chartism was nourished by a long established radical tradition, stretching back at least to the 1790s and the so called 'artisan radicalism' which took its inspiration from the French Revolution. None of the Chartists' 'Six Points' was new. Most had been widely debated by radical politicians for at least half a century. They were all political. If Chartism was merely a reaction to bad times for working people, why were all the six points political? The Chartist petitions to parliament did not call for a minimum wage, for additional rights for trade unionists or for the abolition of the hated new poor law.*

a)  Why does Harney, in Source 7.58, believe that 'to organise to conspire a revolution in this country would be a vain and foolish project'?
b)  How does Harney assess O'Connor's leadership qualities?
c)  To what extent did another contemporary Chartist, Ramsden Balmforth (Source 7.59), agree with Harney's opinion of O'Connor's leadership of Chartism?
d)  What important role, according to Balmforth, did Chartism play in working-class history?
e)  What were the main strengths and weaknesses of Chartism?
f)  To what extent is it wrong to 'concentrate on "economic and social" factors' (Source 7.62) in explaining the origins and the nature of Chartism?
g)  Why did Chartism fail?

# Examples of examination-type questions

## A  AS questions

1  a)  Who were the Chartists?
   b)  What were their main grievances between 1838 and 1848?

## B  A2 questions

1  Was the collapse of Chartism a sign of the movement's weakness or of the strength of the established social and political system?
2  'The greatest immediate cause of Chartism as a mass movement was economic hardship.' To what extent is this a valid assessment of Chartism?

---

### ● Further reading

A. Briggs (ed.), *Chartist Studies* (Macmillan, 1959); D. Jones, *Chartism and the Chartists* (Allen Lane, 1975); F. C. Mather (ed.), *Chartism and Society: An Anthology of Documents* (Batsford, 1980); E. Royle, *Chartism*, Longman Seminar Studies in History (Longman, 1980); D. K. G. Thompson, *The Chartists* (Temple Smith, 1984); J. T. Ward, *Chartist Studies* (Batsford, 1973)

**Articles**
F. C. Mather, 'Chartism', Historical Association pamphlet, 1965

# To what extent did the status and role of women change by 1914?

## 1836

The Home Colonial Training College is set up to train teachers for the voluntary societies, to the benefit of middle-class women and spinsters.

## 1839

First Custody of Infants Act gives a divorced woman, if of unblemished character, the right to see her children, but the husband retains complete control over them.

## 1842

Mines Act bans employment of women and children underground.

## 1844

Factory Act classifies women in the same way as children and young persons and gives them the twelve-hour day in textile factories.

## 1846

A pupil-teacher scheme provides apprenticeships for young women aged between thirteen and eighteen to work as pupil teachers.

## 1847

Factory Act gives women working in the textile factories the ten-hour day.

## 1850

Factory Act gives women in the textile factories a ten-and-a-half-hour day and no night work.

## 1851

Census records 25.7 per cent of women and girls at work with a 50 per cent fall in the number of women employed in agriculture.

## 1857

Invention of the sewing machine increases the volume of outwork done in the home in the 'sweated trades'.

Matrimonial Causes Act makes divorce possible without the need for a private Act of Parliament. The Act discriminates against women because husbands are given the right to divorce their wives on grounds of adultery but women do not gain this right until 1923.

## 1861

Census records 26.3 per cent of women employed.

## 1864

Endowed Schools Commission transfers funds to provide more endowed schools for girls.

First Contagious Diseases Act lays down that any woman who is a prostitute can be forcibly examined for venereal disease and imprisoned. Men are excluded from being forced to be treated for venereal disease.

268

To what extent did the status and role of women change by 1914?

## 1866

Second Contagious Diseases Act.

## 1867

Agricultural Gangs Act bans the employment of young girls.

London Society for Women's Suffrage is founded to press the case for women to vote in parliamentary elections.

Second Parliamentary Reform Act sees an attempt by John Stuart Mill to have women included in the provisions of the act.

## 1869

Twelve schools open for middle-class girls, the first to be established. A network of training schools opens, associated with the work of Emily Davies.

Girton College becomes the first university college for women students. It transfers to Cambridge in 1872, a year after Newnham College is founded there.

Municipal Franchise Act allows unmarried women ratepayers to vote in local elections.

Third Contagious Diseases Act.

Endowed Schools Act provides the money to found grammar schools such as the Manchester High School for Girls.

## 1870

First Married Woman's Property Act allows women to keep £200 of earnings but her husband continues to own her money, property and clothes.

Elementary Education Act permits women ratepayers to vote for, and serve on, the new school boards.

## 1872

Girls' Public Day School Trust is set up to provide good public day schools of a high academic standard for girls.

## 1873

Second Custody of Infants Act allows a divorced woman to see her children.

## 1874

Factory Act introduces a maximum ten-hour working day/56-hour week for women in factories outside the textile industry. The age up to which children may work only half-time is raised to fourteen.

## 1875

Women make up over 50 per cent of all elementary school teachers.

Women are allowed to serve on Poor Law boards of guardians, an opportunity to gain political influence in municipal politics.

## 1878

Factory and Workshops Act extends protection for women and young people to all industries.

Judicial separation between a husband and wife is formally permitted for the first time.

## 1879

Introduction of the telephone extends the range of clerical work and opens up new opportunities for women to work, for the Post Office, for example.

## 1881

Census records a decline in the percentage of women employed to 25.4 per cent.

## 1882

Second Married Woman's Property Act gives women a right to own all other forms of property as well as their earnings.

Invention of typewriter sees a growth in shorthand and typing jobs for women.

## 1884

A married woman ceases to be regarded in law as her husband's chattel (possession) and women acquire an independent legal status.

## 1887

Women's Liberal Foundation is set up.

## 1888

Local Government Act permits women to vote for new county and county borough councils.

## 1889

Annie Besant helps to organise the first women's strike at the Bryant and May match factory.

The Women's Franchise League takes up the rights of married women and campaigns for equality for women in divorce, inheritance and custody of children.

## 1891

Census records that women make up 59 per cent of the workforce in the clothing trade.

Five Acts of Parliament are introduced to regulate activities in workshops.

The Primrose League records over one million members.

Free and compulsory education is introduced for all working-class children up to the age of twelve.

Legal judgement confirms that a man cannot compel his wife to live in the matrimonial home.

## 1894

Parish Councils Act permits propertied women and ratepayers to serve on urban and parish district councils.

## 1895

Eighty schools for girls are given funds from the Endowed School Commission.

## 1896

Factory Act bans the employment of children under eleven in factories. Women are not to be employed for four weeks after having a child.

## 1897

Non-militant National Union of Women's Suffrage Societies (NUWSS) is formed by well-educated middle-class women frustrated with their lives.

## 1901

Factory Act reduces by one hour the number of hours women work.

## 1903

Militant Women's Social and Political Union (WSPU) is formed. It adopts militant and law-breaking activities to secure votes for women.

## 1905

Suffragettes are imprisoned after disrupting a Liberal rally in Manchester.

## 1906

An inquiry into women's work is carried out by Edward Cadbury. Women themselves believe that it is right for their wages to be much lower than a man's.

## 1906–13

A series of Shops Acts establishes a maximum 64-hour week for shop work.

## 1907

The Mud March is the first NUWSS London procession, held to show politicians and the public the strength of the demand for the vote.

270

To what extent did the status and role of women change by 1914?

### 1908

Industrial Compensation Act compensates matchgirls for industrial injury known as 'phossy jaw'.

### 1909

Trade Boards Act settles the rates of earnings in four trades: box-making, lace-making, chain-making and tailoring.

### 1910

Black Friday. Violence erupts between police and suffragettes after a proposal to give women householders the vote is defeated in Parliament.

### 1911

First Conciliation Bill, which gives the vote to single women with property, is introduced. The Pankhursts suspend militancy while the bill is discussed. Support is given in principle but not enough parliamentary time is given to the bill for it to be passed.

### 1912

Factory Inspectorate recommends abolition of mouth suction shuttles which cause cancer of the mouth in workers.

A further suffrage bill is defeated, leading to a suffrage riot in London and the beginning of a period of extreme militancy.

### 1913

WSPU mounts a violent campaign of arson and bomb outrages.

'Cat and Mouse' Act is passed, whereby women hunger strikers are released from prison, but are re-arrested when fit to continue their sentence.

Emily Davison dies after throwing herself under the King's horse at the Derby.

### 1914

War breaks out and the suffragettes announce a suspension of their political campaign.

# Introduction

A number of images dominate any study of Victorian women. The 'angel in the house' was a term that first appeared in a poem of 1854, at the height of mid-Victorian sentimentality. The image was of the leisured lady living a life of respectability, idleness and frivolity – a domestic idyll. It was an essentially middle-class view, the result of a 'separate sphere' philosophy. Men and women were regarded as having separate aptitudes, which meant that their lives should develop along separate but inter-related lines. A woman's place was in the private world of home and family while a man's world was the wider one of business, public affairs and politics. Marriage and children were to be a woman's sole aim in life. Any woman who attempted to challenge this subservient role faced prejudice and derision.

This notion of a woman's role had little relevance for working-class women, for whom work was an integral part of life. The factory girl or mill hand was the symbol of the new economic order. It was associated with the Lancashire cotton mills and the separation not only of home from work, but of men's work from women's work. Men did the skilled work whilst women's work was unskilled or semi-skilled and paid at much lower rates. Women worked long hours, often in appalling conditions, and were poorly paid. Their situation was a recurring issue in the factory inquiries of the 1830s and 1840s. Concern was expressed at the moral dangers existing for women and girls who worked outside the home and were separated from domestic care and training. There was also concern amongst male reformers at the extent to which the authority of the father might be undermined. However, factory women made up a minority of working women; many continued to work either in the home, where they became part of the 'sweated trades', such as dressmaking, or in workshops.

271

What was the status and role of women in society in the nineteenth century?

The third image of Victorian women was that of the domestic servant, who lived in the world 'below stairs', serving the leisured middle classes or the aristocracy in their great town and country houses. According to the census figures for the second half of the nineteenth century, domestic servants formed the largest single group of women workers. Most worked as general servants in the households of tradesmen, shopkeepers, or artisans, or in the new suburbs. They did domestic work without the company of others and for little pay.

# 1 What was the status and role of women in society in the nineteenth century?

For the majority of women, the only way to rise in the world was through marriage, which could be 'arranged' by, and always had to have the approval of, the male head of the household. Marriage between partners of different rank disrupted social life. Spinsterhood was dreaded, for it led to poverty.

Aristocratic women of the nineteenth century had a realistic view of marriage – they did not expect romance or sexual faithfulness, although this did occur in some cases. Marriage was seen as a business arrangement, designed to protect and increase the wealth of the family. Kinship was of great importance in securing appointments in the Church or in government.

Among the working classes marriage customs varied according to local custom and social group. In contrast with the upper and middle classes, women had more freedom to choose their partners and as the nineteenth century progressed there was a decline in 'common law marriages' as more people married. They married for mutual comfort and support and to take responsibility for raising children, rather than for any reasons of property or social advancement. Birth-control information for working-class women appeared in the 1820s, but abortion and infanticide were not uncommon. Below the level of skilled labourers most men did not earn enough money to keep a family, so women contributed through full-time, part-time or casual work. This made for greater equality between partners, and since money earned was immediately spent on necessities there was little dispute over who legally owned the wages.

Women of the middle classes took marriage more seriously than any other social group. Middle-class wives expected their husbands to maintain them in return for their service as housekeepers and partners. It was amongst this group that the most frustrated women were found, and they had the time and energy to plan action and press for legal reforms.

The average marriage lasted fourteen years before the death of a partner, usually the woman through childbirth. Divorce could only be obtained by a private act of Parliament, which was extremely expensive. There were cases of desertion, wife sales and bigamy among the 'rougher' classes.

● **SOURCE 8.1**

From J. Kitteringham, *Country Girls in Nineteenth Century England*, 1973, in which the author quotes the views of a contemporary moralist, Dr Julian Hunter, writing in 1864 about the impact of work on a girl's character and morals.

*That which seems most to lower the moral or decent tone of the peasant girls is the sensation of independence of society which they acquire when they have remunerative labour in their hands either in the fields or at home as strawplaiters, etc. All gregarious employment gives a slang character to the girls' appearance and habits while dependence on the man for support is the spring of modest and pleasant behaviour.*

1 What fears are expressed by the nineteenth-century writer in Source 8.1 about the effect of outdoor work on girls in a rural community?

2 What evidence is there in the source that the writer believes that a woman's place is in the home?

● **SOURCE 8.2**

From the Petition to the Law Amendment Society, 1856, drawn up by Barbara Leigh Smith, Mrs Jameson and Mrs Howitt, outlining the reasons for the campaign.

This petition was signed by 3000 people and formed the basis of seventy similar petitions, signed by over 24,000 people. It was part of the campaign for a change in the law relating to married women's property rights. A private member's bill was debated in the House of Commons in 1857, but it was opposed by those who feared that it would undermine marriage and lead to a 'corruption of morals'. It was lost in the Divorce Bill debates, to the great disappointment of Barbara Leigh Smith and her fellow female activists. The issue was not revived for years.

*That the manifold evils associated with the present law, by which the property and earnings of the wife are thrown into the absolute power of the husband, become daily more apparent. That the sufferings, thereupon ensuing, extend over all classes of society. That it might have once been deemed for the middle and upper ranks, a comparatively theoretical question, but it is no longer, since married women of education are entering on every side the fields of literature and art, in order to increase the family income by such exertions.*

> **1** What evidence is offered in Source 8.2 that some middle-class women were challenging expectations of their role by the middle of the nineteenth century?

● **SOURCE 8.3**

From George Sturt, *Change in the Village*, 1912, in which the author describes the relationship between men and women in a rural community.

*George Sturt (1863–1927)* was born in Farnham, Surrey, the son of a wheelwright. He wrote a number of books on rural life. He used the pen name 'George Bourne' after the village of Bourne, the subject of *Change in the Village*.

*The main fact is that the two sexes, each engaged daily upon essential duties, stand on a surprising equality the one to the other. And where the men are so well aware of the women's experienced outlook and the women so well aware of the men's affectation of ignorance it might almost be construed as a form of immodesty or at any rate as an impudence. It would indeed be too absurd to pretend that these wives and mothers who have to face every trial of life and death for themselves do not know the things which obviously they cannot help knowing; too absurd to treat them as though they were all innocence, timidity and daintiness. No labouring man would esteem a woman for delicacy of that kind and the women certainly would not like to be esteemed for it. Hence the sexes habitually meet on almost level terms.*

> **1** What does the writer of Source 8.3 regard as the ideal relationship between man and woman?
>
> **2** In what way does Sturt challenge Dr Hunter's view (Source 8.1) of the male–female relationship?
>
> **3** How might you account for this different perspective?

● **SOURCE 8.4**

From J. R. Gillis, *For Better, For Worse: British Marriages 1600 to the Present*, 1985, in which the author describes courtship customs in one area of Dorset, the Isle of Portland, in the early nineteenth century.

*The mode of courtship here is that a young woman never admits of the serious addresses of a young man but on the supposition of a thorough probation. When she becomes with child she tells her mother; the mother tells her father; her father tells his father and he tells his son that it is then proper time to be married . . . If the woman does not prove with child after a competent time of courtship they conclude they are not destined by Providence for each other; they therefore separate.*

> **1** What does the writer of Source 8.4 mean by 'the supposition of a thorough probation'?
>
> **2** Comment on the usefulness of this source for a historian studying courtship patterns.
>
> **3** What was the attitude of a rural community to courtship procedures?

● **SOURCE 8.5**

From Rev. A. Mearns, *The Bitter Cry of Outcast London*, 1883, in which a contemporary comments on the immorality of the lower orders.

*rookeries*
slum dwellings, tenements

'Marriage,' it has been said, 'as an institution, is not fashionable in these districts.' And this is only the bare truth. Ask if the men and women living together in these ROOKERIES are married, and your simplicity will cause a smile. Nobody knows. Nobody cares. Nobody expects that they are. In exceptional cases only could your question be answered in the affirmative. Incest is common; and no form of vice and sensuality causes surprise or attracts attention. Those who appear to be married are often separated by a mere quarrel, and they do not hesitate to form similar companionships immediately. One man was pointed out who for some years had lived with a woman, the mother of his three children. She died and in less than a week he had taken another woman in her place. A man was living with a woman in the low district called 'The Mint'. He went out one morning with another man for the purpose of committing a burglary and by that other man was murdered. The murderer returned saying that his companion had been caught and taken away to prison; and the same night he took the place of the murdered man. The only check upon communism in this regard is jealousy and not virtue. The vilest practices are looked upon with the most matter of fact indifference. The low parts of London are the sink into which the filthy and abominable from all parts of the country seem to flow. Entire courts are filled with thieves, prostitutes, and liberated convicts. In one street are 35 houses, 32 of which are known to be brothels. In another district are 43 of these houses, and 428 fallen women and girls, many of them not more than 12 years of age. A neighbourhood whose population is returned at 10,000, contains 400 who follow this immoral traffic, their ages varying from 13 to 50 . . .

1  What does the Rev. Mearns (Source 8.5) mean by 'marriage, . . . as an institution, is not fashionable in these districts'?

2  In what ways does the Rev. Mearns' account challenge middle-class views of marriage?

3  How does the Rev. Mearns' account illustrate Victorian concern with 'respectability'?

● **SOURCE 8.6**

From Jane Austen, *Pride and Prejudice*, 1813, in which Mr Collins gives his reasons for proposing marriage.

Happiness in marriage is entirely a matter of chance. If the dispositions of the parties are ever so well known to each other or ever so similar beforehand, it does not advance their happiness in the least. They always continue to grow sufficiently unlike afterwards to have their share of irritation; and it is better to know as little as possible of the defects of the person with whom you are to pass your life . . . Almost as soon as I entered the house I singled you out as the companion of my future life. But before I am run away with by my feelings on this subject perhaps it will be advisable for me to state my reasons for marrying – and moreover for coming into Hertfordshire with the design of selecting a wife as I certainly did . . .

My reasons for marrying are first that I think it a right thing for every clergyman in easy circumstances (like myself) to set the example of matrimony in his parish. Secondly, that I am convinced it will add very greatly to my happiness; and thirdly – which perhaps I ought to have mentioned earlier – that it is the particular advice and recommendation of the very noble lady whom I have the honour of calling patroness. Twice has she condescended to give me her opinion (unasked too!) on this subject; and it was but the very Saturday night before I left Hunsford – between our pools at quadrille while Mrs Jenkinson was arranging Miss de Burgh's foot-stool that she said, 'Mr Collins, you must marry. A clergyman like you must marry. Chuse properly, chuse a gentlewoman for my sake; and for your own let her be an active, useful sort of person, not brought up high but able to make a small income go a good way.'

1  From the evidence of Source 8.6, does Jane Austen appear to approve of the institution of marriage?

2  What are Mr Collins' reasons for marrying?

3  What qualities does he consider desirable in his future wife?

4  To what extent do these reflect the middle-class view of the period that wives were housekeepers?

5  What do Sources 8.4–8.6 tell the historian about class differences in courtship patterns?

6  To what extent did relationships within marriage differ between the classes?

274

## ● SOURCE 8.7

From Isabella Beeton, *Beeton's Book of Household Management*, 1861, in which the famous nineteenth-century writer advises middle-class women on running a home.

*As with the Commander of an Army, or the leader of any enterprise, so it is with the mistress of a house. Her spirit will be seen through the whole establishment; and just in proportion as she performs her duties intelligently and thoroughly, so will her domestics follow in her path. Of all those acquirements, which more particularly belong to the feminine character, there are none which take a higher rank, in our estimation, than such as enter into a knowledge of household duties; for on these are perpetually dependent the happiness, comfort, and well-being of a family. Having risen early . . . and having given due attention to the bath, and made a careful toilet, it will be well at once to see that the children have received their proper ablutions, and are in every way clean and comfortable. After breakfast is over, it will be well for the mistress to make a round of the kitchen and other offices, to see that all are in order, and that the morning's work has been properly performed by the various domestics. The orders for the day should then be given. After luncheon visits may be made and received . . . Visits of ceremony, or courtesy . . . are uniformly required after dining at a friend's house, or after a ball . . . The morning calls being paid or received, and their etiquette properly attended to, the next great event of the day in most establishments is 'The Dinner'.*

> 1 From the evidence of Source 8.7, what were the most important responsibilities of a middle-class married woman?
>
> 2 What does Isabella Beeton regard as the most desirable aspects of the feminine character?
>
> 3 How useful is this source for understanding a woman's status and role within marriage?

## ● SOURCE 8.8

From Miss B. L. Hutchins, *The Working Life of Women*, 1911, Fabian Tract, No. 157, in which the author describes the ideology of 'separate spheres'.

*It is still the custom in some quarters to assert that 'the proper sphere for women is the home' and to assume that a degree of Providence or a natural law has marked off and separated the duties of men and women. Man it is said is the economic support and protector of the family, woman is its watchful guardian and nurse; whence it follows that the wife must be maintained by her husband in order to give her time to home and children . . . I am concerned with the actual position of women themselves. Is it the lot of women or even of a large majority of women to have their material needs provided for them so that they can reserve themselves for the duties that tend to conserve the home and family?*

> 1 Does the author of Source 8.8 accept the view that the 'proper sphere for women is the home'?
>
> 2 To what extent does the source suggest continuity in the status and role of women by 1911?

## ● SOURCE 8.9

From Professor Graveson, *Family Law 1857–1957*, in which the author comments on the position of women in the family.

*The English family in the years following Waterloo [1815] differed in many ways from the family of today. The husband was in a very real sense the authoritarian head of the family, with very extensive powers over both person and property of his wife and children. On marriage husband and wife became for many purposes one person in law. On marriage all the wife's personal chattels became the absolute property of the husband, while the husband could dispose of the wife's property during his life and enjoyed for his own benefit her estate during her life . . . the married woman, both physically and economically, was very much in the position of chattel of her husband.*

## ● SOURCE 8.10

From R. Fletcher, *The Family and Marriage in Britain*, 1966, in which the author quotes the views of O. R. McGregor on the status of husband and wife.

*Outside the family, married women had the same legal status as children and lunatics; within it they were their husband's inferiors. By marriage they moved from dependence on fathers or male relatives to dependence on husbands. To the Pauline conclusion that the two shall be one flesh, the Victorians added the explanation: 'and I am he'.*

## ● SOURCE 8.11

From Lord Chancellor Cranworth's speech in the House of Lords, *Hansard*, 1857, in which he explains the reasons for unequal treatment of women in the event of divorce.

*A wife might without any loss of caste and possibly with reference to the interests of her children, or even of her husband, condone an act of adultery on the part of her husband. But a husband could not condone a similar act on the part of a wife. No one would venture to suggest that a husband could possibly do so and for this, among other reasons . . . that the adultery of the wife might be the means of palming spurious offspring upon the husband while the adultery of the husband could have no such effect with regard to the wife.*

## ● SOURCE 8.12

From *The Englishwoman's Journal*, August 1858, in which the author criticises the attitude of the law towards women's property rights.

*As the law now stands protection is afforded to the earnings and property of a wife deserted by her husband but it makes provision for no case where desertion has not taken place thus leaving unprotected a large class of sufferers who are subjected to the daily loss of their property or earnings by the presence of a dissolute or unprincipled husband. It also leaves untouched the anomaly in our law which arises from the different mode in which Courts of Common Law and Courts of Equity deal with questions relating to the property of husband and wife.*

## ● SOURCE 8.13

From the Petition to the Law Amendment Society, 1856, criticising the laws relating to women's property rights (see Source 8.2).

*That it is usual when a daughter marries in these ranks [middle and upper classes] to make if possible some distinct pecuniary provision for her and her children and to secure the money thus set aside by a cumbrous machinery of trusteeship proving that few parents are willing entirely to trust the welfare of their offspring to the irresponsible power of the husband, to the chances of his character, his wisdom and his success in a profession.*

*That another device for the protection of women who can afford to appeal exists in the action of the Courts of Equity that attempt within certain limits to redress the deficiencies of the law . . . That it is proved by well-known cases of hardship suffered by women of station and also by professional women earning large incomes by pursuit of the arts how real is the injury inflicted.*

*That if these laws often bear heavily upon women protected by the forethought of their relations, the social training of their husbands and the refined customs of the rank to which they belong, how much more unequivocal is the injury sustained by women in the lower classes . . . [employed in] multifarious occupations which cannot here be enumerated. Newspapers constantly detail instances of marital oppression, 'wife-beating' being a . . . crime against which English gentlemen have lately enacted stringent regulations . . . But for the robbery of his wife's hard earnings there is no redress.*

*That there are certain portions of the law of husband and wife that bear unjustly on the husband as for instance that of making him responsible for his wife's debts contracted before marriage even although he may have no fortune with her. Her power also after marriage of contracting debts in the name of her husband for which he is responsible is too unlimited and often produces injustice.*

*That in rendering the husband responsible for the entire maintenance of his family the law expresses the necessity of an age when the man was the only money-getting agent. Since the custom of the country has greatly changed in this respect the position of the female sex [then] the law of maintenance no longer meets the whole case.*

*That since modern civilisation in indefinitely extending the sphere of occupation for women has in some measure broken down their pecuniary dependence on men it is time that legal protection be thrown over the produce of their labour.*

*That in entering the state of marriage they no longer pass from freedom into the condition of a slave all whose earnings belong to the master and not to himself.*

Study Sources 8.9–8.13.

1 In what respects were women subservient to men? In your answer comment on each of the following
  a) children
  b) property
  c) legal status.

2 How had families sought to protect the property rights of their women on marriage?

3 What risks were faced by women in relation to their earnings?

4 What financial and legal obligations did husbands have for their wives' actions?

5 What developments had taken place that made necessary a change in the laws relating to property?

6 To what extent had women achieved equality of status within the family and marriage by 1914? You will need to consult the timeline at the beginning of the chapter (pages 267–270). Note the extent to which legislation aimed to redress the balance and emancipate women from male domination. Use a copy of the following table to organise your findings. One example has been completed for you.

| Area of subjection | Legislation | Changes introduced |
| --- | --- | --- |
| Legal custody of children belongs to the father | 1839 Custody of Infants Act | A divorced woman if of 'unblemished' character had rights to see her children but husband retained complete control. |
| | 1873 Second Custody of Infants Act | Divorced women were allowed to see their children. |

● **SOURCE 8.14**

From N. Philip, *Victorian Village Life*, 1973, in which the author quotes Richard Jefferies, the son of a small farmer, who wrote on all aspects of village life.

*Although serious wife beating cases are infrequent, there are few women who escape an occasional blow from their husbands. Most of them get a moderate amount of thrashing in the course of their lives, and take it as much as they take the hardships and poverty of their condition, as a necessity not to be escaped. The labourer is not downright brutal to his wife, but he certainly thinks he has a right to chastise her when she displeases him.*

● **SOURCE 8.15**

From Charlotte Brontë to a friend, Elizabeth Gaskell, *The Life of Charlotte Brontë*, 1857, in which Brontë comments on the presence of violence in marriage.

*You remember Mr and Mrs —? Mrs — came here the other day, with a most melancholy tale of her wretched husband's drunken, extravagant, profligate habits. She asked papa's advice; there was nothing, she said, but ruin before them. They owed debts that they could never pay. She expected Mr —'s instant dismissal from his curacy; she knew, from bitter experience, that his vices were utterly hopeless. He treated her and her child savagely . . . Papa advised her to leave him forever, and go home, if she had a home to go to. She said, this was what she had long resolved to do; and she would leave him directly, as soon as Mr B. dismissed him.*

● **SOURCE 8.16**

From Francis Place, a handbill address *To the Married of both Sexes in Genteel Life*, in which Place campaigns for family planning.

*Among the many sufferings of married women as mothers there are two cases that command the utmost sympathy and commiseration. The first arises from constitutional peculiarities or weaknesses. The second from mal-conformation of the bones of the Pelvis. Besides these two cases there is a third case applicable to both sexes: namely the consequences of having more children than the income of the parents enables them to maintain and educate in a desirable manner. The first named produces miscarriages and brings on a state of existence scarcely endurable . . . The second is always attended with immediate risk of life. Pregnancy never terminates without intense suffering, seldom without the death of the child, frequently with the death of the mother and sometimes with the death of both mother and child. The third case is by far the most common . . . in the middle ranks the most virtuous and praiseworthy of efforts are perpetually made to keep up the respectability of the family but a continual increase of children gradually yet certainly renders every effort to prevent degradation unavailing. It paralyses by rendering hopeless all exertion and the family sinks into poverty and despair.*

Study Sources 8.14–8.16.

1 What do these sources reveal of some of the threats to health faced by women in marriage?

2 To what extent does Source 8.15 challenge the propaganda image of 'the angel in the house'?

3 What were Place's main arguments for birth control (Source 8.16)?

● **SOURCE 8.17**

From P. Bartley, *The Changing Role of Women, 1815–1914*, 1996, in which the author explains why divorce was rare.

| ecclesiastical |
| --- |
| Church |

### (i) Difficulties in obtaining a divorce

Before the Divorce Act of 1857 divorce was extremely rare and only possible for wealthy men. If a couple wished to divorce they had to secure a Private Act of Parliament, which was an expensive (estimated at £475 in the first half of the century) and extremely time-consuming ordeal because it involved three different lawsuits. Before proceedings could take place in Parliament husbands had to obtain a separation order from an ECCLESIASTICAL court and a verdict against their wives for adultery, called 'criminal conversation', in a common law court. Grounds for divorce were tougher for women and without an independent income or family support impossible to enact. Whereas men had to prove adultery women also had to prove gross cruelty, bigamy or incest.

### (ii) Different methods of obtaining an end to marriage

Because of the difficulties in obtaining a divorce, wealthy people took advantage of other legal procedures to end an unhappy marriage. There were three main ways in which this could be achieved (the first two of which could also be used as preparation for a full divorce). The first method was a judicial separation by the ecclesiastical, as opposed to the civil, courts. In cases of sodomy and cruelty, wives were granted legal separation and obtained generous alimony. By contrast, if wives were found guilty of adultery they were left penniless. Ecclesiastical courts could also – and often did – declare marriages null and void: a claim of bigamy or non-consummation could be used to end a marriage even though any children of such a union were declared illegitimate.

Alternatively, husbands were able to sue other men in the civil court for 'criminal conversation'. As wives were considered the property of their husbands, jealous spouses were able to sue other men for trespass. By committing adultery, defendants had used the body of a wife and had thus damaged the property of husbands. It was a particularly vengeful Act as those accused paid high costs: sometimes as much as £20,000. For victorious husbands, a suit of criminal conversation was a lucrative pursuit but for convicted adulterers it meant a huge dent in their income, perhaps penury or life imprisonment if they were unable to pay damages.

Finally, separation by private deed enabled a marriage to be terminated. It benefited women because it evaded the public humiliation of divorce, endowed separated wives with one-third of their husbands' net income, enabled them to live as a single person and even gave them the right to live with another man should they so wish.

Legal divorce, and of course these other devices, was virtually impossible for the working class who sometimes used other methods. Leaving home and working a few miles away enabled husbands to circumvent the courts and sometimes remarry. Husbands who absconded from unhappy marriages often left their deserted wives with dependent children, without alimony or means to survive.

### (iii) Change to the Divorce Law, 1857

By mid century this system changed because of new legislation. The Divorce Act of 1857 is often viewed as a watershed in legal history since it established civil divorce for the first time. However, this reform did not introduce any new principles of divorce but just altered the way in which the law was administered . . . it really only benefited wealthy men and continued to reflect the gender and class inequalities of nineteenth-century England.

### (iv) Obstacles to divorce after 1857

By 1900 only 582 people had obtained a divorce because of a number of weaknesses in the new Act. There was only one divorce court and this was in London, which made it difficult for people living in provincial districts to petition for divorce. Divorce proceedings were expensive and out of the financial reach of most people. In addition there continued to be one law for men and a different law for women. Divorce law is a good example of the sexual double standard of Victorian England for distinctly unequal moral standards applied to each of the sexes. Under the new legislation men were able to divorce their wives for adultery. On the other hand, women's access to divorce was limited. The adulterous husband had to commit either bigamy, rape, bestiality, cruelty or long-term desertion before the long-suffering wife could petition for divorce.

● **SOURCE 8.18**

From J. Perkin, *Women and Marriage in Nineteenth Century England*, 1989.

Number of divorces, 1765–1857.

| Period | Number of divorces |
|--------|--------------------|
| 1765–99 | 95 |
| 1799–1830 | 82 |
| 1830–57 | 99 |

● **SOURCE 8.19**

From J. R. Gillis, *For Better, For Worse: British Marriages 1600 to the Present*, 1985, in which the author quotes the case of George Hitchinson of Burntwood in Staffordshire, who divorced his wife in the Walsall Market in 1837.

It has been estimated that there were 294 cases of wife-sale, called popular divorce, between 1780 and 1880.

*They came into the market between ten and eleven o'clock in the morning, the woman being led by a halter, which was fastened round her neck and the middle of her body. In a few minutes after their arrival she was sold to a man of the name of Thomas Snape, a nailer also of Burntwood. There were not many people in the market at the time. The purchase money was 2s. 6d. [12½p] and all the parties seemed satisfied with the bargain. The husband was glad to get rid of his FRAIL RIB who it seems had been living with Snape three years.*

**frail rib**
wife (a reference to the Biblical story of Eve being made from one of Adam's ribs)

---

Study Sources 8.17–8.19.

1  How could divorce be obtained before 1857?

2  How many people obtained a divorce between 1765 and 1857?

3  How did wealthy couples end their marriages before 1857?

4  What do you understand by 'criminal conversation'?

5  What were the main hazards faced by women who were divorced?

6  Why would women prefer divorce by private deed?

7  What options were available for working-class men who wished to end a marriage?

8  What were the main features of divorce by means of 'wife sale'?

9  To what extent were the interests of the wife involved in the sale ignored?

10  What changes to divorce were introduced by the 1857 Divorce Act?

11  How were women discriminated against by the 1857 Act?

12  Why did divorce remain exceptional after 1857?

---

● **SOURCE 8.20**

From Mona Caird, *The Morality of Marriage*, 1897, in which the author, a feminist, presents a critical view of marriage.

*While marriage remained practically the only means of livelihood for women, there was little danger of their seeing too clearly the seamy side of the arrangement; for to see that would be to see the alternatives of selling themselves for a livelihood, and starvation; or in milder cases, between social failure and a marriage . . . Respectable women therefore buttressed their self-respect by never thinking at all about the conditions of marriage under which they lived, and what would happen if they married a bad man . . .*

*Marry and ask no questions: who are you that you should criticise an institution that has lasted for centuries? Marriage is your natural career, your own highly developed conscience must tell you so. If you do not adopt it, well we fear you will find cause to regret your decision. If you can't secure a husband, we can but regard you as a failure, a supernumerary who has no proper place in the world.*

---

1  To what extent does Source 8.20 indicate the survival of the 'separate spheres' ideology at the end of the nineteenth century?

2  In what respects does Mona Caird present a critical view of marriage? Explain your answer.

3  Is it possible to tell whether Caird was opposed to marriage?

279

What was the status and role of women in society in the nineteenth century?

● **SOURCE 8.21**

From N. Tranter, *Population since the Industrial Revolution*, 1973.

Proportion of the female population married by age, 1871–1911.

| Year | 20–24 | 25–34 | 45–54 |
|------|-------|-------|-------|
| 1871 | 34.8 | 71.1 | 87.9 |
| 1881 | 33.5 | 70.7 | 88.1 |
| 1891 | 29.9 | 67.4 | 87.6 |
| 1901 | 27.4 | 66.0 | 86.6 |
| 1911 | 24.3 | 64.5 | 84.2 |

● **SOURCE 8.22**

From *Papers of the Royal Commission on Population*, Vol. VI, Table 2.

Number of children (live births) per thousand women first married in a) 1870–79 and b) 1900–09.

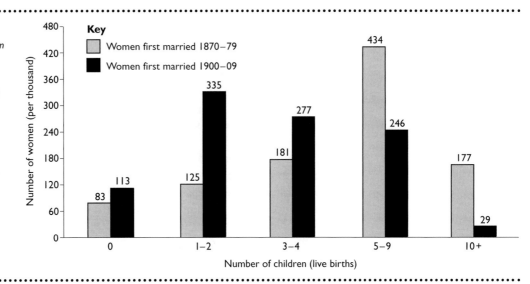

● **SOURCE 8.23**

From Lord Gorell, President of the Probate, Divorce and Admiralty Division, in the divorce case of *Dodd v. Dodd*, 1906, in which he expresses his dissatisfaction with the divorce law.

*That the present state of the English law of divorce and separation is not satisfactory cannot be doubted . . . Whether any and what remedy should be applied raises extremely difficult questions . . . for they touch the basis on which society rests and the principle of marriage being the fundamental basis upon which this and other civilised nations have built up their social systems . . .*

---

Study Sources 8.21–8.23.

1 Comment on the changes in the marriage trends between 1871 and 1911.

2 What changes had occurred in the average number of children per family by 1909?

3 How do you explain the change in the trend for
a) marriage
b) size of family?

4 How far had attitudes towards marriage changed by 1914?

## 2 What was the status and role of women in the economy?

### What changes occurred in the patterns of female employment?

The effect of the Industrial Revolution on women has been a matter of some debate. Reliable statistics do not exist. Most writers accept that women were subordinate to men, both legally and socially, in pre-industrial times. Some have claimed that the rise of industrialisation led to a reduction in status for women. This resulted from the separation of home and work, and women's withdrawal from paid work. Others saw industrial capitalism as possibly 'freeing' women by giving them an opportunity to earn independently, leading to their eventual emancipation. Contemporaries, such as Engels and Shaftesbury, argued that the Industrial Revolution gave women more jobs but at a disastrous cost to themselves, their homes and their families. Other writers claim that although more women worked this was because of their families' great poverty rather than because they wanted greater independence.

Some jobs, such as domestic spinning, were lost, while new ones appeared in carding, weaving, dressmaking, tailoring and domestic service. On the whole, it could be said that the proportion of women at work in the nineteenth century was probably no larger than it had been in an earlier age. Moreover, bearing in mind that in 1861 only 30 per cent of the whole labour force was employed in the new industries associated with the Industrial Revolution, then it is obvious that there were clear continuities in some of the jobs traditionally done by women in their homes and small workshops. In conclusion, industrialisation and urbanisation had little impact on the participation rates of women in the labour force although there was much work that was not counted in the census data. Part-time work, seasonal agricultural work, outwork, casual domestic work, such as washing, and working in family businesses, were not included.

Young women usually did unskilled work, usually for lower wages than men, although some women did skilled work in the potteries and the cotton industry. The workforce in the Lancashire cotton factories was in the main young, single women. Once women left full-time work they rarely returned, unless they were widowed or deserted. Married women factory workers were condemned by observers of the factory system, but mothers of small children were a small proportion of the overall workforce. The married women who worked in the factories did so because their husbands were poorly paid or out of work. Given a choice, married women preferred to work at home.

## ● SOURCE 8.24

From Charles Booth, *Journal of the Royal Historical Society*, 1886.

Women and girls at work, 1851–81.

|      | Women aged 15+ at work (to nearest thousand) | Women workers as % of total female population |
|------|-----------|-----------|
| 1851 | 2,348,200 | 25.7 |
| 1861 | 2,709,900 | 26.3 |
| 1871 | 3,118,200 | 26.8 |
| 1881 | 3,393,600 | 25.4 |

## ● SOURCE 8.25

From A. John (ed.), *Unequal Opportunities: Women's Employment in England, 1800–1918*, 1985.

Main occupations of females of all ages in Great Britain, 1851–1911 (thousands).

| Occupation | 1851 | 1881 | 1911 |
|------------|------|------|------|
| Agriculture, horticulture | 229 | 116 | 117 |
| Textiles | 635 | 745 | 870 |
| Metal manufacture, machines | 36 | 49 | 128 |
| Clothing | 491 | 667 | 825 |
| Food, drink and tobacco | 53 | 98 | 308 |
| Domestic services | 1135 | 1756 | 2127 |
| Professional occupations | 103 | 203 | 383 |
| Commercial operations | 0 | 11 | 157 |
| Public administration | 3 | 9 | 50 |
| Paper, printing | 16 | 53 | 144 |

● **SOURCE 8.26**

Compiled by the author on the basis of data from the 1911 census.

Work opportunities for women in 1911.

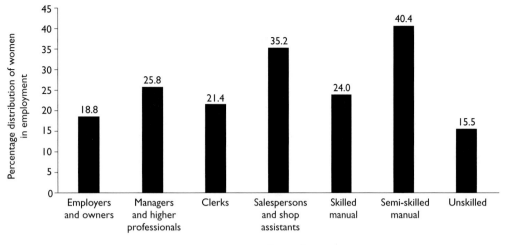

● **SOURCE 8.26** *(chart — Percentage distribution of women in employment by Occupation)*

Employers and owners: 18.8
Managers and higher professionals: 25.8
Clerks: 21.4
Salespersons and shop assistants: 35.2
Skilled manual: 24.0
Semi-skilled manual: 40.4
Unskilled: 15.5

---

Study Sources 8.24–8.26.

1  Comment on changes in the trend of
   a) the percentage
   b) the numbers
   of women in the workforce between 1851 and 1881 (Source 8.24).

2  What was the most important occupation for women in 1851?

3  To what extent had this changed by
   a) 1881
   b) 1911?

4  What were the other most important occupations for women in
   a) 1851
   b) 1911?

5  To what extent had there been a change in importance of these occupations by
   a) 1881
   b) 1911?

6  Which occupation saw the greatest growth in numbers between 1851 and 1911?

7  Which occupation saw the greatest fall in numbers between 1851 and 1911?

8  To what extent does the distribution of occupations indicate segregation on the basis of sex?

## What problems did women face in terms of pay and working conditions?

● **SOURCE 8.27**

From Miss Whyte of the London Bookbinders, 1900, in which she complains to the Trades Union Congress of discrimination in the workplace.

*As to the statement of the Trades Unions that they are willing to admit women, as long as they received equal pay with men, the women knew that such a rule would operate to the entire exclusion of women for if a woman offered herself in competition with a man for the same work the latter would be accepted.*

● **SOURCE 8.28**

From J. Lewis, *Women in England 1870–1950: Sexual Divisions and Social Change*, 1984.

Average earnings of women as a percentage of male earnings, 1906.

| Industry | Female earnings as % of male earnings |
| --- | --- |
| Textiles | 58.5 |
| Clothing | 46.3 |
| Food, drink, tobacco | 41.5 |
| Paper, printing | 36.4 |
| Metal industries | 38.1 |
| **Total (of all industries)** | 43.7 |

● **SOURCE 8.29**

From the Annual Report of the Manchester and Salford Women's Trade Union Council, 1903, in which a trade union secretary reports on low pay for women.

*A man thinks himself badly off if he cannot earn more than 17s. [85p] a week. It is no exaggeration to say that there are thousands of girls in Manchester who think themselves lucky if they bring home 7s. [35p] at the weekend and more older and skilled women who can never hope to earn more than 12s. [60p] to the end of their lives . . . These are surely the wages of the poorest poor. These workers are living very near the subsistence level. Without any industrial or political defence they are fully exposed to the crushing and numbing force of the bare struggle for life.*

● **SOURCE 8.30**

From Frances Ashwell's speech on 'Conditions of Women's Wages in Manchester', given to the Women's Trade Union Council and reported in the *Monthly Herald*, July 1897.

The *Herald* was the local Co-operative paper and was particularly interested because the Women's Co-Operative Guild had taken part in the survey.

*The impact of low wages was made worse by the unreliability of work. A survey organised in the Manchester area in the mid 1890s of conditions in all-women industries, such as shirt making and umbrella covering, showed that out of the hundred and twenty workers questioned only three could always rely on a regular wage. The vast majority were on piecework, and, depending on how fast they worked, could earn anything between 3s. [15p] and 20s. [£1]; in slack periods few earned more than 5s. [25p]. At these starvation rates, commented the organisers of the survey, a woman had 'to use the largest stitch that will stand the inspection of the giver out of work'.*

The climax of such investigations was the exhibition of work in the sweated industries, organised in 1906 by the *Daily News*. The public conscience was sufficiently roused by it for Trade Boards to be introduced in 1909, with the power to fix minimum wage rates in such trades as tailoring, box-making and chain-making (see page 227).

● **SOURCE 8.31**

a) *Needle Money* b) *Pin Money*, cartoons from *Punch*, 15 July 1849.

a)

NEEDLE MONEY.

b)

PIN MONEY.

Study Sources 8.27–8.31.

1  What consequences did Miss Whyte fear would result from equal pay for women?

2  In which industries did wage discrimination based on sex appear to be particularly widespread?

3  What do you understand by 'piecework' (Source 8.30)?

4  What were the main evils associated with piecework?

5  Which industries were 'all-women'?

6  What message is the author of the *Punch* cartoon (Source 8.31) trying to communicate?

7  'Women's work remained low skilled and low paid.' Discuss this conclusion, referring also to the evidence in Source 8.26 (page 281).

● **SOURCE 8.32**

From a speech by Lord Shaftesbury in the House of Commons, on the Ten Hours Bill, 1844, in which the reformer complains of the effect on women of working in the factory (see also pages 66–68).

*Fifty or sixty females married and single form themselves into clubs apparently for protection; but in fact they meet together to drink, sing and smoke; they use, it is stated, the lowest, most brutal and most disgusting language imaginable . . . Why is it that this unnatural change is taking place?*

*Because on women is imposed the duty and burden of supporting their husbands and families, a perversion of nature, which has the effect of introducing into families disorder and conflict. What is the ground on which the woman says she will pay no attention to her domestic duties, nor give the obedience that is owing to her husband? Because on her devolves the labour which ought to fall to his share, and she throws out the taunt, 'If I have the labour, I will also have the amusement.'*

● **SOURCE 8.33**

From the male potters' petition, 1845, which highlighted their fears of a loss of work due to female competition.

*To maidens, mothers and wives, we say machinery is your deadliest enemy . . . It will destroy your natural claims to home and domestic duties and will immure you and your toiling little ones in overheated and dirty shops, there to weep and toil and pine and die.*

● **SOURCE 8.34**

From an address to the Trades Union Congress, 1877, in which Henry Broadhurst, the President of the Congress, supported restrictions on women's work.

*It was their duty as men and husbands to use their utmost efforts to bring about a condition of things where their wives should be in their proper sphere at home, seeing after their house and family, instead of being dragged into the competition for livelihood against the great and strong men of the world.*

Study Sources 8.32–8.34.

1  What criticisms did Shaftesbury make of the effect of factory work on women?

2  What concerns were voiced by male potters about the effect of work on women?

3  To what extent was each of the three authors influenced by the prevailing ideas about the proper roles of men and women?

● **SOURCE 8.35**

From Clementina Black's speech to the Trades Union Congress, 1887, reported in *Women's Suffrage Journal*, November 1887.

**Clementina Black**
was the secretary of the Women's Trade Union League and resisted male attempts to curtail employment opportunities for women, for example, the barring of women as chain-makers in the Black Country.

*. . .[Consider the] sufferings of women employed in trades which no one dreams of forbidding, such as needlework and matchbox-making. But men never proposed to interfere with these trades. Why not? There is no need to ask. Men do not work at these trades and suffer nothing from the competition of women. The real point to be complained of is the low rate of payment earned by the women; and the way to prevent the employment of women in any trade they are unfit for is for men to join in helping them to combine in order that they may receive the same wages for the same work. If employers have to pay women the same prices as men, there would be no temptation to them to employ women to do what they are less fit to do than men. But the women are not represented here to speak for themselves, and I protest against the attempt of one class of workers – especially a class whose interests are concerned – to impose restrictions upon another class of workers.*

284

To what extent did the status and role of women change by 1914?

1 Which trades, according to Source 8.35, failed to attract the attention of reformers?

2 What were men's motives in attempting to ban the employment of women in 'unsuitable trades'?

3 What were Clementina Black's recommendations to prevent exploitation of women in the workplace?

## Case study – domestic service

The largest group of women workers was domestic servants, who worked in the households of the upper and middle classes. By 1881 the percentage change in the number of women employed in domestic service rose by 2.2 per cent compared with 1851 whereas there was a 17.7 per cent fall in the number of men. Domestic service went unregulated and the work was hard, long and poorly paid. There were no labour-saving devices to clean or wash, so it is not surprising that domestics were often known as 'slaveys'. In spite of its extreme exploitation, domestic service was considered very suitable work for girls, since it was a good preparation for the work every woman would have to tackle in the family home. Other jobs were regarded less favourably.

● SOURCE 8.36

From E. Roberts, *Women's Work 1840–1940*, 1988.

Domestic servants of all ages, 1851–1911.

| Year | Total | % of total female population |
|------|-------|------------------------------|
| 1851 | 1,069,865 | 9.8 |
| 1871 | 1,508,888 | 12.8 |
| 1891 | 1,759,555 | 11.6 |
| 1911 | 1,662,511 | 11.1 |

● SOURCE 8.37

From J. D. Milne, *The Industrial and Social Position of Women*, 1857, in which the author discusses the nature of domestic work.

*The situation of a domestic servant . . . is attended with considerable comfort. With abundant work it combines a wonderful degree of liberty, discipline, health, physical comfort, good example, regularity, room for advancement, encouragement to acquire saving habits. The most numerous class of depositors in the Savings Banks is that of domestic servants. The situation frequently involves much responsibility and calls forth the best features of character. Kind attachment in return for honest service is not uncommon with the master or mistress and an honest pride in the relation springs up on both sides and lasts throughout life.*

● SOURCE 8.38

From L. Stanley (ed.), *The Diaries of Hannah Cullwick*, 1871, which describe the work of a domestic servant.

**Hannah Cullwick**
was secretly married to the upper-middle-class barrister and poet Arthur Munby, who liked her to dress up in servant's clothes.

*This is the beginning of another year, & I am still general servant like, to Mrs Henderson at 20 Gloucester Crescent. This month on the 16th I shall o' bin in her service 2 years & a ½, & if I live till the 26th o' May when I shall be 38 year old, I shall o' bin in service 30 years . . . Now there's such a little boy kept here I've a deal more to do of jobs that's hard, like digging coals & carrying 'em up & the boxes, & high windows & the fanlight over the door to clean & anything as wants strength or height I am sent for or call'd up to do it. I clean all the copper scuttles & dig the coals, clean the tins & help to clean the silver & do the washing up if I'm wanted, & carry things up as far as the door for dinner. I clean 4 grates & do the fires & clean the irons, sweep & clean 3 rooms & my attic, the hall & front steps & the flags & area railings & all that in the street. I clean the water closet & privy out & the backyard & the area, the back stairs & the passage, the larder, pantry & boy's room & the kitchen & scullery, all the cupboards downstairs & them in the storeroom.*

● SOURCE 8.39

From Emma Paterson, *The Women's Union Journal*, 1879, in which the middle-class feminist and founder of the Women's Protective and Provident League describes the hard work of being a domestic servant.

*In all but large rich households where there is much idleness and waste, domestic service is incessant hard work at all hours of the day and sometimes of the night also. It is at the best but a kind of slavery and when a girl has a home it is only a human feeling and one that we should respect if she prefers to undertake work in trades because she can return at night and on Sundays to the home circle. At a meeting last year of factory women at Bristol who were earning only 5s. [25p] or 6s. [30p] per week I urged upon them the advisability of going out to service rather than submit to such low wages but without an exception the advice was rejected by all.*

## What changes in attitudes towards women in the workplace had taken place by 1914?

● **SOURCE 8.40**

From E. Roberts, *Women's Work 1840–1940*, 1988.

Percentages of unmarried and married women in full-time work in 1911, based on census returns.

|  | Unmarried | Married |
|---|---|---|
| England and Wales | 54.5 | 13.7 |
| Urban districts | 56.8 | 14.8 |
| Rural districts | 45.8 | 9.3 |

● **SOURCE 8.41**

From E. Roberts, *Women's Work 1840–1940*, 1988, quoting the report of Mrs Bayley to the National Association for the Promotion of Social Science in 1861.

*. . . the wife and mother going abroad for work is a fine example of a waste of time, a waste of property, a waste of morals and a waste of health and life and ought in every way to be prevented.*

# 3 What progress was made in securing women's suffrage by 1914?

The issue of votes for women had first been raised in the 1830s, but it was not until the 1860s that a small suffrage movement was founded in five of the major cities – London, Manchester, Bristol, Birmingham and Edinburgh. Initially, activities were based on peaceful campaigning: collecting petitions, lobbying MPs for support and numerous drawing-room meetings. Membership was mainly female but some men did join in demanding equal citizenship for women.

Writings on the struggle for the vote have investigated the suffrage movement as a middle-class-dominated campaign with well-developed social connections into networks of power. It has been assumed that working-class women were not much affected by the suffrage campaigns or arguments because they had less time to devote to it and were put off by the way it was presented. However, this might only appear to be the case because of the easy availability of middle-class sources. Elizabeth Roberts conducted some interviews in the mid-1980s with women who were young pre-1914 but these seem to bear out the view that the concerns of working women were dominated by the family and domestic management rather than by securing the vote. Current research on local history is needed, but stress on the suffrage campaign as a middle-class movement still remains. Middle-class women played a key role in party politics at constituency level, in arranging transport to the polling booths, raising funds and maintaining the parliamentary register. Upper-class women did not involve themselves in the struggle to acquire the vote because traditionally they had enjoyed a major role as political hostesses presiding over London dinner parties and country house weekends. The following two extracts by an opponent and a supporter of votes for women capture the essence of the Edwardian debate on female suffrage.

● **SOURCE 8.42**

Mrs Creighton, *The Nineteenth Century*, 1889.

*An opponent*

*I do not see why the only way in which women can advance should be along the road to female suffrage. The existing social fabric rests upon the assumption that the family is the unit, and not the individual. It is impossible to deny that an attack upon the existing social fabric must imply an attack upon the family.*

● **SOURCE 8.43**

Ellen Key, *The Woman Movement*, trans. M. B. Borthwick, 1912.

*A supporter*

*The women's movement has now in a word a more universally human, a less one-sided feminine character. It emphasises more and more the fact that the right of woman is a necessity in order that she may fulfil her duties in the small, individual family and exercise her powers in the great, universal human family for the general good. The new woman does not wish to displace man or to abolish society. She wishes to be able to exercise everywhere her most beautiful prerogative to help, to support, to comfort. But she cannot do so, so long as she is not free as a citizen and has not fully developed as a human personality.*

## Arguments for and against women's suffrage

● **SOURCE 8.44**

From the National Union of Women's Suffrage Societies (NUWSS), listing fourteen reasons why women should have the vote.

The NUWSS was a moderate organisation, formed in 1897 (see page 291).

NATIONAL UNION OF WOMEN'S SUFFRAGE SOCIETIES
*14 Gt. Smith Street, Westminster, London, SW.*

*Law-abiding*          *Non-party*

President:—Mrs. HENRY FAWCETT, LLD.

*14 REASONS*
*For Supporting Women's Suffrage.*

1 *Because it is the foundation of all political liberty that those who obey the Law should be able to have a voice in choosing those who make the Law.*
2 *Because Parliament should be the reflection of the wishes of the people.*
3 *Because Parliament cannot fully reflect the wishes of the people when the wishes of women are without any direct representation.*
4 *Because most Laws affect women as much as men, and some Laws affect women especially.*
5 *Because the Laws, which affect women especially, are now passed without consulting those persons whom they are intended to benefit.*
6 *Because Laws affecting children should be regarded from the woman's point of view as well as the man's.*
7 *Because every session questions affecting the home come up for consideration in Parliament.*
8 *Because women have experience which should be helpfully brought to bear on domestic legislation.*

287

What progress was made in securing women's suffrage by 1914?

9 *Because to deprive women of the vote is to lower their position in common estimation.*
10 *Because the possession of the vote would increase the sense of responsibility amongst women towards questions of public importance.*
11 *Because public-spirited mothers make public-spirited Sons.*
12 *Because large numbers of intelligent, thoughtful, hardworking women desire the franchise.*
13 *Because the objections raised against their having the franchise are based on sentiment, not on reason.*
14 *Because – to sum all the reasons up in one – it is for the common good of all.*

● **SOURCE 8.45**

From Christabel Pankhurst, *The Great Scourge and How to Fight It*, in which she gives a moral reason why women should have the vote.

**Christabel Pankhurst (1880–1958)**
trained as a lawyer but was refused permission to practise at Lincoln's Inn because she was a woman. With her mother, Emmeline, she helped to set up the Women's Social and Political Union (WSPU, 1903), a militant organisation that campaigned for women to be given the vote (see page 291). She emigrated to the USA after the First World War.

*. . . the canker of venereal disease is eating away the vitals of the nation, and the only cure is Votes for Women . . . The real cure of the great plague is – Votes for Women, which will give to women more self reliance and a stronger economic position, and chastity for men. Apart from the deplorable moral effect of the fact that women are voteless, there is this to be noticed – that the law of the land, as made and administered by men, protects and encourages the immorality of men, and the sex exploitation of women.*

● **SOURCE 8.46**

From Millicent Fawcett, *Home and Politics*, giving some social reasons for women having the vote.

**Millicent Fawcett (1847–1929)**
campaigned on a number of women's issues, including campaigns for women to be given full property rights, access to university and the vote. She became President of the National Union of Women's Suffrage Societies (see page 291) which was opposed to violence.

**enfranchisement**
acquiring the right to vote

*With regard to the differences between men and women, those who advocate the ENFRANCHISEMENT of women have no wish to disregard them or make little of them. On the contrary, we base our claim to representation to a large extent on them.*
*. . . In proportion as women are good and efficient in what concerns their domestic duties, they will, if they become voters, bring these excellent qualities to bear upon public affairs.*

● **SOURCE 8.47**

*Polling Booth Companions in Disgrace, from the Artists' Suffrage League.*

# POLLING BOOTH.

## COMPANIONS IN DISGRACE.

Convicts and Women kindly note,
Are not allowed to have the vote ;
The difference between the two
I will now indicate to you.

When once the harmful man of crime,
In Wormwood Scrubbs has done his time,
He at the poll can have his say,
The harmless woman *never* may.

C. H.

*Printed and published by the Artists' Suffrage League,
259 King's Road, Chelsea.*

● **SOURCE 8.48**

From E. Roper, 'The Cotton Trade Unions and the enfranchisement of women', in the report of the executive committee of the North of England Society for Women's Suffrage, 1902.

*The Trade Unions have, in one form or another, adopted the principle of the Direct Representation of Labour. They have agreed that Labour Members of Parliament should be paid directly by the Unions to uphold their interests in the House of Commons . . . The women pay, why should their interests not be attended to?*

*If it is necessary, as the men say it is, for men to be directly represented in Parliament, how much more necessary must it be for women, the only entirely unrepresented workers, to have the protection and power of a vote? The women's best chance of winning their own franchise is through the Cotton Trade Unions of the North. Here they have the power because they are more numerous than men . . .*

*The trade unions will become more and more a power in politics. Therefore, let all women having the great power of the Cotton Unions in their hands, help themselves, and the millions of women workers who are poorer and less able to help themselves than they, by making Women's suffrage a Trade Union Question. The Cotton Trade Unions can and must secure the enfranchisement of the women workers.*

● **SOURCE 8.49**

From Mrs Pankhurst, 'The Importance of the Vote', a speech given at Portman Rooms, 24 March 1908, in which the leader of the militant Women's Social and Political Union (WSPU) argues for women's suffrage.

**Emmeline Pankhurst (1858–1928)**
was the daughter of a Manchester cotton manufacturer. She developed an interest in radical politics and joined the Independent Labour party in the 1890s. She was a co-founder of the militant Women's Social and Political Union (see page 291) and as part of a campaign of attacking property attempted to bomb the house of the Chancellor of the Exchequer. While in prison she went on hunger strike. In 1914 she abandoned her campaign and devoted her efforts to nursing.

*. . . it is important that women should have the vote in order that in the government of the country the women's point of view should be put forward . . . Very little has been done by legislation for women for many years – for obvious reasons. More and more of the time of members of Parliament is occupied by the claims which are made on behalf of the people who are organised in various ways in order to promote the interests of their industrial organisations or their political or social organisations. [An MP's] time is fully taken up by attending to the needs of the people who have sent him to Parliament . . . you cannot take up a newspaper, you cannot go to a conference, you cannot even go to church, without hearing a great deal of talk about social reform and a demand for social legislation. Of course, it is obvious that that kind of legislation – and the Liberal Government tell us that if they remain in office long enough we are going to have a great deal of it – is of vital importance to women. We are hearing about legislation to decide what kind of homes people are to live in. That surely is a question for women. Surely every woman, when she seriously thinks about it, will wonder how men by themselves can have the audacity to think that they can say what homes ought to be without consulting women. Then take education. Since 1870 men have been trying to find out how to educate children. I think they have not yet realised that if they are ever to find out how to educate children, they will have to take women into their confidence . . . I assure you that no woman who enters into this agitation need feel that she has got to give up a single one of her woman's duties in the home. She learns to feel that she is attaching a larger meaning to those duties which have been woman's duties since the race began, and will be till the race has ceased to be . . . The home is the home of everybody of the nation. No nation can have a proper home unless women as well as men give their best to its building up and to making it what a home ought to be, a place where every single child born into it shall have a fair chance of growing up to be a fit, and a happy, and a useful member of the community.*

Study Sources 8.44–8.49.

1 What moral, political and social arguments were made for women's suffrage?

2 How would gaining the vote help to improve women's social and economic position?

3 What was the link between the campaign to secure women's suffrage and the cotton trade unions?

4 How did Mrs Pankhurst make use of the 'separate spheres' philosophy to support her arguments for women's suffrage?

5 What reassurances did Mrs Pankhurst give to women who supported the suffrage campaigns?

● **SOURCE 8.50**

From J. Lewis, *Before the Vote was Won*, 1987, quoting the views of Mrs Humphrey Ward in 1889.

**Mrs Ward**
was a famous novelist of the day and the first President of the Anti-Suffrage League.

*. . . the Anti-Suffrage League maintained in 1889 that certain government departments should be the exclusive preserve of men: To men belong the struggle of debate and legislation in Parliament; the hard and exhausting labour implied in the administration of the national resources and powers; the conduct of England's relations towards the external world; the working of the army and navy; all the heavy, laborious, fundamental industries of the State, such as those of mines, metals, and railways; the lead and supervision of English commerce, the management of our vast English finance, the service of that merchant fleet on which our food supply depends. In all these spheres women's direct participation is made impossible either by the disabilities of sex, or by strong formations of custom and habit resting ultimately upon physical difference, against which it is useless to contend . . . Therefore it is not just to give to women direct power of deciding questions of Parliamentary policy, of war, of foreign or colonial affairs, of commerce and finance equal to that possessed by men.*

● **SOURCE 8.51**

From P. Bartley, *Votes for Women 1860–1928*, 1998, quoting the main arguments of an opponent of suffrage in the early twentieth century.

*1 Because women already have the municipal vote, and are eligible for membership of most local authorities. These bodies deal with questions of housing, education, care of children, workhouses and so forth, all of which are peculiarly within a woman's sphere. Parliament, however, has to deal mainly with the administration of a vast Empire, the maintenance of the Army and Navy, and with questions of peace and war, which lie outside the legitimate sphere of woman's influence.*

290

To what extent did the status and role of women change by 1914?

**2** *Because women are not capable of full citizenship, for the simple reason that they are not available for purposes of national and Imperial defence. All government rests ultimately on force, to which women, owing to physical, moral and social reasons, are not capable of contributing.*

**3** *Because there is little doubt that the vast majority of women have no desire for the vote.*

**4** *Because the acquirement of the Parliamentary vote would logically involve admission to Parliament itself and to all Government offices. It is scarcely possible to imagine a woman being Minister for War, and yet the principles of the Suffragettes involve that and many similar absurdities.*

**5** *Because the United Kingdom is not an isolated state, but the administrative and governing centre of a system of colonies and also of dependencies. The effect of introducing a large female element into the Imperial electorate would undoubtedly be to weaken the centre of power in the eyes of these dependent millions.*

**6** *Because past legislation in Parliament shows that the interests of women are perfectly safe in the hands of men.*

**7** *Because Woman Suffrage is based on the idea of the equality of the sexes, and tends to establish those competitive relations which will destroy chivalrous consideration.*

**8** *Because women have at present a vast indirect influence through their menfolk on the politics of this country.*

**9** *Because the physical nature of women unfits them for direct competition with men.*

● **SOURCE 8.52**

From an article by Sir Almroth Wright, *The Times*, 28 March 1912, in which the writer, a doctor, claims that women are liable to hysteria. The article was written at the height of suffragette violence and he attacked the suffragettes as frustrated spinsters.

*These upsettings of her mental equilibrium are the things that a woman has most cause to fear; and no doctor can ever lose sight of the fact that the mind of woman is always threatened with danger from the reverberations of her physiological emergencies.*

● **SOURCE 8.53**

*A Suffragette's Home*, from the National League for Opposing Woman Suffrage, 1912.

Study Sources 8.50–8.53.

1 What part was played by each of the following in the arguments used by those opposed to women's suffrage
   a) 'separate spheres' ideology
   b) women's psychological and physiological make-up
   c) women's physical weakness?

2 How could the scene in the poster (Source 8.53) be used as an argument against women voting?

3 How does it counter the argument used by Mrs Pankhurst in Source 8.49?

## What tactics were employed by the suffrage movement?

In 1897 the National Union of Women's Suffrage Societies (NUWSS) was set up under the presidency of Millicent Garret Fawcett. It was a union of moderate campaigners, whose members, called suffragists, were well-educated, middle-class women who felt frustrated by their lives. It was the oldest and largest national organisation for votes for women and had a democratic structure. Its members decided on policies and voted for the President and a national executive committee. By 1914 it had 600 member societies and 100,000 members, who felt they belonged to a 'sisterhood'.

In the 1890s a group within the NUWSS known as the 'radical suffragists' worked hard to get the vote for working-class women. They gained the support of female cotton workers in the cotton towns of Lancashire and Cheshire. The NUWSS adopted propaganda work based on quiet and peaceful methods. Women were trained as speakers and local women were paid to organise the movement in their area. It had its own paper, the *Women's Suffrage Journal*. It arranged dinner hour meetings amongst cotton workers, held cottage meetings and collected signatures. Radical suffragists toured the country on bikes or in horse-drawn caravans, canvassed from door to door and spoke at local trades union meetings.

### The Women's Social and Political Union

Not all female activists approved of these methods. In 1903 the Women's Social and Political Union (WSPU) was established by Emmeline Pankhurst, her daughters and a group of women in the Independent Labour Party (ILP). Founded in Manchester, it moved to London in 1906. The inspiration for forming the WSPU probably came from a petition signed by women in the textile industry in Lancashire, Cheshire and Yorkshire.

The only working-class woman to get a senior position in the WSPU was Annie Kenney. Other well-known names included Teresa Billington-Greig, a teacher from Blackburn, and Hannah Mitchell, a dressmaker's apprentice from Bolton. Emmeline Pankhurst ruled from the top. The members did not even have a vote in their own movement. Emmeline intended that her members would be single-minded and would concentrate on one political objective – equality with men – rather than on social reforms.

With the slogan 'Votes for Women', they had a very different approach from that of the moderate and law-abiding NUWSS. They were given the name of 'Suffragettes' by the *Daily Mail* newspaper in 1906. From the start, members courted public attention with their loud and often disruptive behaviour at public meetings. The leadership of the WSPU relied on publicity. The movement lurched from sensation to sensation, they packed meetings in the centre of London, they demonstrated, and they attacked property, smashing windows in the West End. Members were frequently arrested and sent to prison for obstruction and disorderly behaviour or for hitting policemen. Liberal MPs were challenged and ridiculed during by-election campaigns. Money was raised to finance a nationwide campaign and deputations were sent to Parliament. The WSPU published a weekly newspaper, *Votes for Women*, and trained women in the art of public speaking and in judo. Suffragettes wore the colours of the union – purple (symbolising dignity), white (purity) and green (hope).

The union enjoyed success in the early years with the motto 'Deeds not Words'. However, not all the members of the WSPU accepted Emmeline Pankhurst's violent methods or her style of leadership.

## The Women's Freedom League

In 1907 some women broke away from the WSPU to form the Women's Freedom League (WFL), led by three senior members of the WSPU, including Teresa Billington-Greig. The WFL developed very quickly. By 1914 it had 4000 members in 60 branches and a newspaper, *The Vote*. It was militant, attacking the government, and also the WSPU for its campaign of vandalism against private and commercial property. Over 100 members went to prison for various offences committed while protesting against government inaction on votes for women. The WFL ran the Women's Tax Resistance League (1909) and they refused to fill in the 1911 census forms. New societies were set up representing specific interest groups, such as working class and professional women (1905), writers and actresses (both 1908) and teachers (1912). They used banners, postcards and posters produced by women artists. Plays on the theme 'How the Vote was won' were performed in private drawing rooms and theatres.

● **SOURCE 8.54**

From Emmeline Pankhurst at Bow Street Magistrates' Court, 21 October 1908, in which the leader of the WSPU publicly defends her methods in court.

*We shall submit to the treatment – the degrading treatment – which we have submitted to before. Although the Government has admitted that we are political offenders we shall be treated as pickpockets and drunkards. We are driven to this . . . We have tried every way. We have presented larger petitions than were ever presented before for any other reform, we have succeeded in holding greater public meetings than men have ever had for any reform. We have faced hostile mobs at street corners because we were told that we could not have that representation for our taxes which men have won unless we converted the whole country to our tide . . .*

*No, sir. I do say deliberately . . . that I come here not as an ordinary law-breaker. I should never be here if I had the same kind of laws that the very meanest and commonest of men have . . . This is the only way we have to get that power which every citizen should have of deciding how the taxes she contributes to should be made . . . That is all I have to say to you. We are not here because we are law-breakers. We are here in our efforts to become law-makers.*

1 What legal methods were employed by the women suffragists in the early stages of the movement?

2 How does Emmeline Pankhurst justify her use of force (Source 8.54)?

3 What is her argument for women having the vote?

4 What evidence is there in her speech that Emmeline Pankhurst was using her court appearance for propaganda purposes?

● **SOURCE 8.55**

From the *Daily Mail*, March 1909, reporting on an outbreak of suffragette militancy.

*From every part of the crowded and brilliantly lighted streets came the crash of splintered glass. People started as windows shattered at their side; suddenly there was another crash in front of them; on the other side of the Street; behind – everywhere. Scared shop assistants came running out to the pavements; traffic stopped; policemen sprang this way and that; five minutes later the streets were a procession of excited groups each surrounding a woman wrecker being led in custody to the nearest police station. Meanwhile the shopping quarter of London had plunged itself into a sudden twilight. Shutters were hurriedly fitted [and] the rattle of iron curtains being drawn came from every side. Guards of commissionaires and shopmen were quickly mounted and any unaccompanied lady in sight, especially if she carried a handbag, became an object of menacing suspicion.*

293

What progress was made in securing women's suffrage by 1914?

## SOURCE 8.56

From 'Outrage in Southampton' (date unknown), a local newspaper article.

*Suffrage militant operations have seemingly extended to Southampton. It was learned on Tuesday that during the previous evening post office officials had detected that some fluid had been placed in a letterbox at the General Post Office. It was understood that several letters were damaged. The police have a clue to the perpetrator of the outrage.*

## SOURCE 8.57

From a speech by Emmeline Pankhurst, at the Albert Hall in October 1912, in which she endorses a shift to a new level of militancy.

*Those of you who can express your militancy by facing Party mobs at Cabinet Ministers' meetings when you remind them of their falseness to principle – do so. Those of you who can express your militancy by joining us in our anti-Government by-election policy – do so. Those of you who can break windows – break them. Those of you who can still further attack the secret idol of property so as to make the Government realise that property is as greatly endangered by Woman Suffrage as it was by the Chartists of old – do so. And my last word to the Government: I cite this meeting to rebellion. You have not dared to take the leaders of Ulster for their incitement to rebellion, take me if you dare.*

Study Sources 8.55–8.57.

1 In what ways had the suffragettes escalated their campaign to secure the vote by 1912?

2 Comment on the language employed in the *Daily Mail*'s report of the demonstration in 1909.

3 On what grounds did Emmeline Pankhurst justify this extension of methods in her Albert Hall speech?

4 What evidence is offered in these sources to indicate that women were challenging the Victorian view of the 'angel in the home'?

5 How fair is the description of the suffragette agitation as a 'campaign of violence'?

## SOURCE 8.58

From Viscount Ullswater, *A Speaker's Commentaries*, 1925, in which the politician comments on the impact of suffragette militancy on attitudes in the House of Commons by 1913.

*The activities of the militant Suffragettes had now [1913] reached the stage at which nothing was safe from their attacks . . . bombs were exploded, the police and individuals were assaulted, meetings broken up and every imaginable device resorted to in order to inconvenience or annoy His Majesty's law officers. The feeling in the House [of Commons] caused by the extravagant and lawless action of the militants hardened the opposition to their demands.*

## SOURCE 8.59

From letters from Edward VII to Home Secretary Herbert Gladstone.

During the previous months, 37 women had been released from prison after hunger striking. It was after this correspondence with King Edward VII that Herbert Gladstone issued orders that the medical officers at Winson Green Jail should use force to feed the hunger-striking suffragette prisoners.

*Marienbad, 13 August 1909*
*Dear Mr Gladstone,*
*The King has signed the enclosed submissions as he feels sure you will have seriously considered the advisability of letting these women out of prison.*
*At the same time His Majesty would be glad to know why the existing methods, which must obviously exist for dealing with prisoners who refuse nourishment, should not be adopted.*
*His Majesty is inclined to think that this short term of martyrdom is more likely to attract than deter women from joining the ranks of the militant Suffragettes.*
*Yours very truly,*
*Ponsonby*

*Rufford Abbey, Ollerton, Notts, 11 September 1909*
*Dear Mr Gladstone,*
*The King is very glad to learn from your Memorandum that more stringent and precautionary measures are to be taken with regard to the Suffragettes whose behaviour of late has, in many cases, been a public scandal.*
*I remain*
*Yours sincerely,*
*Arthur Davidson*

● **SOURCE 8.60**

From a report in the *Daily News*, 29 September 1909, describing the government's defence of its decision to force-feed suffragette hunger strikers.

**Mr Masterman**
a Liberal MP, here speaking on behalf of the Home Secretary

**Mr Keir Hardie's bolts tumble harmless**
criticism of force-feeding by Hardie, first leader of the Independent Labour party and a supporter of women's suffrage, causes the government no difficulties

**Mr Snowden**
another Labour MP and a supporter of reform, although he was opposed to attacks on the state

*This afternoon [Tuesday], before MR MASTERMAN'S courteous replies to questions as to the experiences of the suffragist prisoners in Birmingham, MR KEIR HARDIE'S BOLTS TUMBLE HARMLESS. Even MR SNOWDEN is baffled. Mr Masterman comes forward not to assert a blind authority on the part of the state but to discharge a grave duty to the women themselves. Their lives are sacred, and must be preserved. The officials would be liable for criminal proceedings if these prisoners were to commit suicide by starvation. Yes, they had been induced to take food, and there had been a progressive improvement in their health. No, chains were not necessary to the hospital treatment; female wardresses did what had to be done under the supervision of the doctor. The House cheered; the Ministers had well braved the ordeal.*

● **SOURCE 8.61**

From Keir Hardie's letter to the *Daily News*, 29 September 1909, in which the Independent Labour MP expresses his indignation at the reaction of fellow MPs to debates on the introduction of force-feeding of hunger strikers.

*. . . I was horrified at the flippancy displayed by a large section of the Members of the House when the question [of force-feeding] was being answered. Had I not heard it I could not have believed that a body of gentlemen could have found reason for mirth and applause in a scene that I venture to say has no parallel in the recent history of our country. One of these days we shall learn that Mrs Leigh or some other of her brave fellow-prisoners has succumbed to the 'hospital treatment', as a man did in 1870. I would not envy the position of the Home Secretary or the Government responsible for such a result.*

● **SOURCE 8.62**

A WSPU poster, *The Modern Inquisition – Treatment of Political Prisoners under a Liberal Government.*

Study Sources 8.58–8.62.

I   What was the reaction of the House of Commons to suffragette activities (Source 8.58)?

2   How did Viscount Ullswater justify this reaction?

3   What policies were adopted by the authorities to deal with suffragette activities?

4   What was the significance of the role played by King Edward VII in the adoption of more extreme measures against those suffragettes who went on hunger strike?

5   How did the government justify its policy of force-feeding in the face of criticisms from suffragette supporters such as Keir Hardie?

6   What images are used in the poster (Source 8.62) to embarrass the government?

7   What was the significance of such posters as propaganda?

# 4  How successful were suffragette activities by 1914?

● SOURCE 8.63

From Lady Constance Lytton, 1909, commenting on the ineffectiveness of the methods used by suffragists.

Lady Constance Lytton became a member of the WSPU in January 1909.

*I learnt that before resorting to militancy the women's organisations had for many years past succeeded in obtaining a majority of supporters in the House of Commons and the backing of leading men of both parties. It was startling to realise that the proposed advocacy of such men as Lord Beaconsfield, the late Lord Salisbury and Mr Arthur Balfour had not moved the Conservative Party in any way to assist their cause. When the Liberal Government was returned to power in 1906 under the leadership of Sir Henry Campbell-Bannerman he himself was a declared suffragist as were all but a few of the men of most influence in his Cabinet including Mr Birrell, Mr Buxton, Mr John Morley and Mr John Burns. The women had tried repeatedly and always in vain every peaceable means open to them of influencing successive Governments. Processions and petitions were absolutely useless. I saw the extreme need of their position, the ineffectiveness of every method hitherto adopted to persuade these professed suffragists to put their theories into practice.*

● SOURCE 8.64

From Christabel Pankhurst's letter to the editor of *The Times*, June 1908, in which the WSPU leader expresses her anger at the failure of Asquith's Liberal Government to introduce a suffrage bill.

**obdurate**
obstinate, unwilling to respond

*Sir, The reply of Mr Asquith [leader of the Liberal party] to the deputation of Liberal Members of Parliament confirms the Women's Social and Political Union in their determination to fight against the Government.*

*In the first place, Mr Asquith refuses to deal with the question this session, either on his own initiative or by giving facilities to Mr Stanger's bill. He reverts to the old policy of delay, the fruits of which we have seen so often before.*

*In the second place, he now makes it clear that the Government have no intention themselves at any time during the present Parliament of introducing a measure of woman suffrage, and at the time do intend to introduce a bill dealing with electoral reform for the benefit of men alone. We are not in the least reassured by his reported statement that a woman suffrage amendment, moved by a private Member, to this bill would not, under certain circumstances, be opposed by the Government, as it is of too negative and vague a character to be of any value. Moreover, the Government cannot shirk direct responsibility in this matter. Nothing short of a definite pledge of action this session will satisfy the Women's Social and Political Union, and unless this is given we shall continue to bring effective pressure on the Government. Our policy of opposing their nominees at by-elections, which has proved so successful in the past, will be vigorously pursued. And if, after our demonstration in Hyde Park on Sunday, June 21, the Government is still* OBDURATE, *we shall take it as a signal that further militant action is required to wring from them the necessary reform.*

296

To what extent did the status and role of women change by 1914?

● **SOURCE 8.65**

From D. Marquand, *Ramsey MacDonald*, 1977, in which the future leader of the Labour Party is quoted criticising suffrage militancy.

*I have no objection to revolution, if it is necessary, but I have the very strongest objection to childishness masquerading as revolution, and all I can say of these window-breaking expeditions is that they are simply silly and provocative. I wish the working women of the country who really care for the vote . . . would come to London and tell these pettifogging middle-class damsels who are going out with little hammers in their muffs that if they do not go home they will get their heads broken.*

● **SOURCE 8.66**

From the *Daily Graphic*, 18 October 1912, reporting on the internal disputes in the WSPU, which led to a split between the Pankhursts and the Pethick-Lawrences.

*'The organ of the Women's Social and Political Union in future',* [said Mrs Pankhurst,] *'will be* The Suffragette, *which has come into existence since last Monday. Mr and Mrs Pethick-Lawrence disagreed with what we considered the best policy and we decided it was best that they should take the paper they founded,* Votes for Women, *and run it along their own lines. This is our policy,'* continued Mrs Pankhurst slowly. *'Short of taking human life we shall stop at no step we consider necessary to take . . . Our militant policy is fixed and unalterable.'*

*Mr and Mrs Pethick-Lawrence in an interview with a Daily Graphic representative yesterday emphatically denied that their withdrawal could be construed as a split in the ranks. 'We withdrew',* declared Mrs Pethick-Lawrence, *'so that there should be no split. If we had remained and the . . . opinions of Mrs and Miss Pankhurst and my husband and myself had not coincided as they have in the past it would have meant disruption. That is what we did not desire. We have the cause at heart and we thought it best to work separately. We are as militant at heart as anyone. It was on the question of the expediency of a certain militant policy which was discussed a few days ago that we disagreed. That is all.'*

1 'Militancy remained the obstacle.' To what extent do Sources 8.63–8.65 support this explanation for the lack of progress towards women gaining the vote?

2 To what extent did the issue of women's suffrage divide opinion within the political parties?

3 What was the cause of the internal disputes within the WSPU (Source 8.66)?

● **SOURCE 8.67**

From P. Bartley, *Votes for Women 1860–1928*, 1998.

Failed suffrage bills under the Liberal Government, 1906–13.

| | |
|---|---|
| 1906 | Government refuses to support an amendment to a Plural Voting Bill, which would have enfranchised a number of propertied women. |
| 1907 | Women's Suffrage Bill rejected. |
| 1908 | Women's Suffrage Bill carried. |
| 1909 | Second Reading of Women's Suffrage Bill carried but Asquith fails to give support so the Bill fails. |
| 1910 | First Conciliation Bill, giving women of property the vote, carried but ultimately fails because the Government refuses to grant it parliamentary time. |
| 1911 | Second Conciliation Bill carried but Asquith announces that he prefers to support universal male suffrage, which could also include an amendment for the enfranchisement of women. |
| 1913 | Government Franchise Bill introduces universal male suffrage but an amendment to enfranchise women is declared unconstitutional. |

● SOURCE 8.68

From M. Pugh, 'Votes for Women in Britain, 1867–1928', 1994.

House of Commons votes on women's suffrage bills, 1897–1917.

| | Con | Lib | Lab | Irish | Total |
|---|---|---|---|---|---|
| **1897 F. F. Begg (Con.)** | | | | | |
| For | 138 | 74 | 0 | 18 | 230 |
| Against | 110 | 38 | 0 | 11 | 159 |
| **1908 H. Stanger (Lib.)** | | | | | |
| For | 34 | 185 | 33 | 21 | 273 |
| Against | 30 | 48 | 2 | 14 | 94 |
| **1911 Conciliation Bill** | | | | | |
| For | 53 | 145 | 26 | 31 | 255 |
| Against | 43 | 36 | 0 | 9 | 88 |
| **1912 Conciliation Bill** | | | | | |
| For | 63 | 117 | 25 | 3 | 208 |
| Against | 114 | 73 | 0 | 35 | 222 |
| **1913 W. Dickinson (Lib.)** | | | | | |
| For | 28 | 146 | 34 | 13 | 221 |
| Against | 140 | 74 | 0 | 54 | 268 |
| **1917 Representation of the People Bill** | | | | | |
| For | 140 | 184 | 30 | 33 | 387 |
| Against | 45 | 12 | 0 | 0 | 57 |

Study Sources 8.67 and 8.68.

1 Comment on the trend in Conservative voting.

2 a) Which political party remained consistent in its support of women's suffrage?
   b) How do you account for this consistency?

3 To what extent did Liberal Party support for women's suffrage reflect the views of its leader, Asquith?

4 To what extent do the House of Commons votes on the suffrage bills confirm that the escalation of militancy after 1912 alienated would-be supporters?

5 To what extent does the voting on women's suffrage bills suggest that the principle of women having the vote was won before a programme of militancy was adopted?

● **Summary task**

Below are a number of questions that might be used for discussion or written answers as a way of testing your understanding of this chapter.

• How did the women's suffrage movement emerge?
• Why did the women's suffrage movement emerge?
• What was the basis and strength of the opposition to the women's suffrage movement before 1914?
• What was the social and political impact of the suffrage activists in the campaign for the vote?
• Why did the role of women come to be a controversial issue?
• Why did feminists make so little progress before 1914?

298

To what extent did the status and role of women change by 1914?

# Examples of examination-type questions

## A  AS questions

1  a)  What were the main arguments for women's suffrage?
   b)  Why did the suffrage campaign fail to achieve the vote before 1914?

2  a)  What were the main tactics employed by the various suffrage societies?
   b)  Did militancy do more harm than good to the suffrage campaign?

3  a)  What were the main arguments against women's suffrage?
   b)  To what extent was failure to gain the vote due to the strength of the enemies of women's suffrage?

## B  A2 questions

1  To what extent, if at all, had women been 'emancipated' by 1914?

2  'The condition of women in England steadily improved between 1870 and 1914 except in relation to the franchise.' Examine the truth of this statement.

3  'In practice, the social and economic status of women was little changed from what it had been in 1832.' How far do you agree?

4  'Women's work in the years before 1914 was hard, poorly paid and of low status.' Discuss.

● **Further reading**

P. Bartley, *The Changing Role of Women, 1815–1914* (Hodder & Stoughton, 1996); P. Bartley, *Votes for Women 1860–1928* (Hodder & Stoughton, 1998); B. Caine, *Victorian Feminists* (OUP, 1992); C. Crosby, *The Ends of History: Victorians and the 'Woman Question'* (Routledge, 1991); R. Fulford, *Votes for Women* (Faber & Faber, 1957); J. R. Gillis, *For Better, For Worse: British Marriages 1600 to the Present* (OUP, 1985); B. Harrison, *Separate Spheres: The Opposition to Women's Suffrage in Britain* (Holmes & Meier, 1978); P. Hollis, *Class and Conflict in the Nineteenth Century* (Routledge & Kegan Paul, 1973); P. Hollis, *Women in Public – The Women's Movement 1850–1990* (Allen & Unwin, 1979); S. Holton, *Feminism and Democracy, Women's Suffrage and Reform Politics in Britain 1900–1918* (CUP, 1986); A. John (ed.), *Unequal Opportunities: Women's Employment in England, 1800–1918* (Basil Blackwell, 1985); S. Kingsley Kent, *Sex and Suffrage in Britain 1860–1914* (Routledge, 1990); J. Lewis, *Women in England 1870–1950: Sexual Divisions and Social Change* (Wheatsheaf, 1980); J. Lewis, *Before the Vote was Won* (Routledge & Kegan Paul, 1987); J.Liddington and J. Norris, *One Hand Tied Behind Us* (Virago, 1978); D. Mitchell, *The Fighting Pankhursts* (Jonathan Cape, 1967); J. Perkin, *Women and Marriage in Nineteenth Century England* (Routledge, 1989); M. Ramelson, *The Petticoat Rebellion* (Lawrence & Wishart, 1967); J. Rendall, *Women in an Industrialising Society: England 1750–1880* (Basil Blackwell, 1990); E. Roberts, *Women's Work 1840–1940* (Macmillan, 1988); A. Rosen, *Rise Up, Women* (Gregg Revivals, 1974); L. Stanley (ed.), *The Diaries of Hannah Cullwick* (Methuen, 1871)

**Articles**
B. Harrison, 'Anti-Suffragists', *Modern History Review*, 1990
B. Harrison, 'The First World War and Feminism in Britain', *History Review*, 1993
M. Pugh, 'Votes for Women', *Modern History Review*, 1990
M. Pugh, 'Votes for Women in Britain 1867–1928', *New Appreciations in History*, Historical Association pamphlet, 1994
K. Sayer, 'Feminism and History', *Modern History Review*, 1994
D. Thompson, 'British Woman in the Nineteenth Century', *New Appreciations in History*, Historical Association pamphlet, 1989

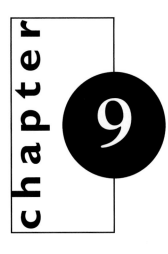
# How literate was society before 1914?

**1807**

Parochial Schools Bill is introduced by Samuel Whitbread to give parish vestries or magistrates the power to raise money for parish schools that would give two years' free schooling to the children of poor parents.

**1810**

British and Foreign School Society is founded by Joseph Lancaster.

**1811**

National Society is founded by Andrew Bell.

**1816**

Parliamentary Select Committee is set up to investigate education in London.

**1820**

Brougham's Parish Schools Bill is withdrawn due to opposition especially from Nonconformists.

**1833**

Factory Act provides for two hours' schooling a day for children aged between nine and thirteen.

The first government grant of £20,000 is divided equally between the two voluntary religious school societies founded by Lancaster and Bell.

**1837**

Select Committee on the Education of the Poorer Classes reports on the state of education in large towns.

**1839**

Committee of the Privy Council on Education is established to check on how the annual government grant is spent.

**1839–49**

Kay-Shuttleworth is the first secretary to the Privy Council on Education.

**1840**

School inspectors are appointed to supervise the spending of the state grant by the two voluntary religious societies.

**1846**

Regulations are issued for pupil-teachers.

**1856**

Education Department replaces the Committee of the Privy Council.

**1861**

Newcastle Commission reports on inadequate provision of education.

**1862–97**

Revised Code introduces 'payment by results' under which the annual grant depends on satisfactory attendance and performance in tests before inspectors in reading, writing and arithmetic – the 3Rs.

**1864**

Manchester Education League is founded to campaign for education for all.

**1869**

Birmingham Education League is founded to campaign for education for all.

**1870**

Forster's Education Act introduces a dual system of education whereby the state intervenes and provides board schools to fill the gaps left by the voluntary sector.

**1876**

Sandon's Act penalises parents who keep their children away from school.

**1880**

Mundella's Act makes education compulsory for children under thirteen.

**1888**

Cross Report supports the continuation of the voluntary system in the face of superior competition from the board schools.

**1891**

Government grant makes education free in elementary schools.

**1893**

School-leaving age is fixed at eleven.

**1899**

School-leaving age is raised to twelve.

**1902**

Balfour's Education Act sets up local education authorities run by county and borough councils to replace the school boards.

**1906**

Free school meals are introduced for poor children.

**1907**

Free medical inspection introduced for poor children.

# Introduction

Most historians measure literacy by the ability to sign one's name on the marriage register. The marriage register was a standard form of marriage certificate, introduced by Lord Hardwick's Marriage Act of 1753. These registers are an important source of information and provide a means of comparing literacy levels over time and between social groups. They indicate that the first two-thirds of the eighteenth century witnessed a rise in literacy levels. This was the result of a slow growth in population along with an expansion in the endowed school or charity school movement with the formation of the Society for the Promotion of Christian Knowledge (SPCK) in 1699. The founding of new endowed schools meant that the number of school places exceeded demand. There was also a strong tradition of self-teaching.

● **SOURCE 9.1**

From M. Sanderson, *Education, Economic Change and Society in England 1780–1870*, 1983.

Male and female literacy by occupation in England, 1700–70.

A female professional at this time would be a person such as a governess; no data are available for female members of the gentry, and husbandmen (agricultural workers) and soldiers were predominantly or entirely male occupations.

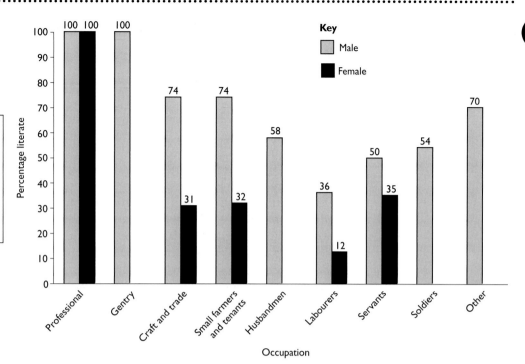

● **SOURCE 9.2**

M. Sanderson, *Education, Economic Change and Society in England, 1780–1870*, 1983.

Regional movement in literacy levels between 1754–62 and 1831–37.

| Region | Number of towns in which literacy rose | Number of towns in which literacy fell |
|---|---|---|
| South West | 4 | – |
| East | 9 | – |
| Midlands | 6 | 1 |
| North | 4 | 10 |

● **SOURCE 9.3**

From R. S. Scofield, 'Dimensions of Literacy 1750–1850', in *Explorations in Economic History*, 1973.

*. . . some occupations were still less literate [in 1814] than they had been in the mid-eighteenth century . . . [figures] suggest the possibility that for many males in a variety of occupations literacy did not become more essential as a cultural skill during this period . . . since many of the new industrial occupations recruited a mainly illiterate workforce.*

Study Sources 9.1–9.3.

1 Identify the social group with
  a) the highest
  b) the lowest.
  levels of literacy.

2 a) Identify the group that saw the widest disparity in literacy levels between men and women.
  b) How do you explain the disparities in literacy levels?

3 a) What disparities are shown in regional literacy levels?
  b) How can this be explained?

The new factories required only a small literate and skilled labour force – clerks, overseers and mechanics. The new machines meant that most of the work could be done by low-skilled and poorly paid women and children. As a result, some regions became more illiterate. By the 1830s barely 30 per cent of the workers in south-east Lancashire could write their names. Literacy levels declined between 1784 and 1814 amongst workers in textiles, coal mining, metal and transport, reaching a low in the 1820s. Thereafter there was a drive for mass literacy, slow at first and with regional variations.

# 1 What were the main features of elementary education at the beginning of the nineteenth century?

For much of the nineteenth century the provision of education reflected the structure of Victorian society. It was not considered necessary to have a literate workforce and most children of the labouring classes did not go to school. Many of the governing classes feared that an educated workforce might spread dangerous notions of republicanism, while employers wanted a cheap and docile workforce. Such education as existed was not universal, free, or compulsory and was provided in inadequate buildings staffed by inefficient teachers. At the 'elementary' level, there were charity, Sunday and private schools.

In contrast, the children of the middle and upper classes were usually educated at home by private tutors during their early years. They subsequently progressed either to one of the old grammar schools, most of which dated from the sixteenth century, or, in the case of the very rich, to one of the nine great public schools. Education for the well to do was based on the study of Latin and Greek, which was considered essential for a gentleman. Girls of wealthy parents had a governess and were taught at home in the pursuits considered essential to fulfil the role of a wife and mother.

● **SOURCE 9.4**

From J. J. Wright, *The Sunday School: Its Origin and Growth*, 1900.

> **Robert Raikes**
> was a well-to-do master printer in Gloucester. His first school had about 80 scholars and four teachers.

*One day, in the year 1780, MR RAIKES chanced to go into the lower part of the town in search of a gardener. The man was not in, and Mr Raikes was waiting about. Nearby, in the street, a swarm of boys were playing 'chuck'. The noise was deafening, the oaths were terrible! Mr Raikes was amazed. Turning to a decent-looking woman in a doorway he expressed his surprise and pain at what he had heard and seen. She replied: 'Ah, sor, that's nothing! We have it so every day. But on Sunday it's worse. Sundays the pin factory yonder isn't working, and so there's more children in the streets, and sir, then it's like hell!' These words to the good Sabbath-keeping heart of Robert Raikes came as a shock and the facts before his eyes were a vivid illustration of the words. 'Something must be done,' said this practical man to himself. But what? Pondering a little he hit upon a new idea – new to him, at any rate; and new to the world at large, as it turned out. The idea was to gather these and such like children into schools on Sundays – on the day when they made 'hell' in the streets.*

● **SOURCE 9.5**

From Hannah More's letters to the Bishop of Bath and Wells and to William Wilberforce, 1801, in which the reformer describes her good works in the Mendip area.

*When I settled in this country thirteen years ago I found the poor in many of the villages sunk in a deplorable state of ignorance and vice. There were I think no Sunday schools in the whole district except one in my own parish which had been established by our own respectable rector and another in the adjoining parish . . . This drew me to the more neglected villages which being distant made it very laborious . . . My plan of instruction is extremely simple and limited . . . I allow of no writing for the poor. My object is not to make fanatics but to train up the lower classes in habits of industry and piety. I know of no way of teaching morals but by teaching principles and of inculcating Christian principles without a good knowledge of scripture.*

## SOURCE 9.6

From the *Report of the Select Committee on the Education of the Poorer Classes*, 1837–38.

Sunday school attendance in the large manufacturing and seaport towns, 1837–38.

By 1832 there were 5463 Sunday schools in England, with 477,225 scholars. In Wales there were 301 schools and 24,408 scholars. The total population in 1831 was 13.9 million.

*With regard to the numbers attending Sunday Schools, Your Committee . . . consider the instruction there given as of great advantage, by implanting feelings of religion and giving habits of order, but as imperfect without daily instruction also.*

| | Children in Sunday schools | | |
|---|---|---|---|
| **Place** | **Established Church (Church of England)** | **Dissenters** | **Catholics** |
| Manchester | 10,284 | 19,932 | 3,812 |
| Salford | 2,741 | 6,250 | 613 |
| Liverpool | 6,318 | 8,350 | 700 |
| Birmingham | 4,500 | 11,830 | 338 |
| Bristol | 2,631 | 8,477 | – |
| Brighton | 870 | 1,820 | – |
| Sheffield | 2,687 | 8,705 | – |
| Leeds | 4,130 | 11,886 | – |
| Reading | 1,000 | 509 | – |
| Westminster | 683 | 872 | – |
| York | 1,708 | 1,655 | – |

Study Sources 9.4–9.6.

1　What were the motives of Robert Raikes and Hannah More in setting up Sunday schools?

2　What type of education was provided by the Sunday school?

3　What contribution did the schools make to the achievement of a literate workforce?

4　How successful was the Sunday school movement?

The Sunday schools were the first schools to try to help the mass of the population. Few of them had suitable buildings; they were often overcrowded and the atmosphere quickly became foul. There was no way to compel children to attend, while teachers were unqualified and unpaid. Despite the schools' limitations they played a part in that they were the first to admit any child who wished to attend. Their very limitations showed that if the children of the poor were to have any proper education then they would have to attend school throughout the week. A variety of schools existed for this purpose. Probably the least instructive were the 'dame schools' for younger children and common day schools for older ones.

## SOURCE 9.7

From reports by the Statistical Societies of Manchester, 1834, and Birmingham, 1838, providing two contrasting views of dame schools.

*1 Manchester*

*Occasionally in some of the more respectable districts there are still to be found one or two of the old primitive dame schools kept by a tidy elderly female whose school has an appearance of neatness and order which strongly distinguishes it from this class of schools . . . [Most were] in the most deplorable condition. The greater part of them are kept by females but some by old men whose only qualification for this employment seems to be their unfitness for any other. Many of these teachers are engaged at the same time in other employments such as shopkeeping, sewing, washing etc., which renders any regular instruction among the scholars almost impossible. Indeed neither parents nor teachers seem to consider this as the principal object in sending them to these schools but generally say that they go there to be taken care of and to be out of the way at home. These schools are generally found in very dirty unwholesome rooms – frequently in close, damp cellars or old, dilapidated garrets.*

**2 Birmingham**

*The physical condition of the Dame Schools of Birmingham is much more satisfactory than could have been anticipated. None of them are kept in cellars, very few in garrets or bedrooms, and they are generally more cleanly and better lighted than schools of the same description in Manchester or Liverpool.*

1 Why were 'dame schools' so-called?

2 According to Source 9.7, what were the limitations of these schools in terms of teaching and accommodation?

3 Why did the reports regard the dame schools of Birmingham to be 'more satisfactory'?

● **SOURCE 9.8**

From a report on the state of education in Manchester, 1834, which comments on the state of the common day schools.

*In the great majority of these schools there seems to be a complete want of order and system. The confusion arising from this defect, added to the very low qualifications of the Master, the number of scholars under the superintendence of one Teacher, the irregularity of attendance, the great deficiency of books and the injudicious plans of instruction, or rather the want of any plan, render them nearly inefficient for any purposes of real education. Religious instruction is seldom attended to. Beyond the rehearsal of a catechism and moral education real cultivation of the mind and improvement of character are totally neglected. 'Morals!' said one Master in answer to the enquiry whether he taught them. 'How am I to teach morals to the like of these?'*

1 What did the report in Source 9.8 identify as the main deficiencies in education?

2 Why did the report pay special attention to 'moral education'?

3 What may be inferred from the report about the methods commonly used at this time to teach working-class children?

The oldest schools for providing education for the poor were the charity schools set up in 1699 by the Society for the Promotion of Christian Knowledge. They were financed by private charity and charged a few pennies a week for each child. These schools tried to do a lot for their children. Classroom teaching was simple; based on reading, religion, writing and arithmetic, as well as practical subjects that would help the children in later life. Girls learned to sew, knit and cook while boys learned weaving, gardening and even ploughing. It was difficult to find a place in a charity school.

● **SOURCE 9.9**

From a charity sermon announcement for the charity school at St Anne's, Westminster, 20 December 1840.

*This School instituted in the year 1699 is entirely supported by voluntary Subscriptions, Donations and Legacies without any assistance from the Parish Rates; and is intended for the benefit of such Inhabitants as are not able to instruct their children in the principles of religion or to give them any education. Any child between the ages of seven and eleven years who has lived in the parish for the last three months and is recommended by a Trustee or subscriber will be received into this school, clothed and educated. There are at present in the school . . . 168 total . . . total clothed 100 . . . 636 boys put out to apprenticeships, 694 boys put out to service, 814 girls put out to service. 2144 educated and provided for by this charity.*

1 According to Source 9.9, what conditions did a potential student at a charity school have to fulfil?

2 How were the schools financed?

3 How did the charity schools help their children?

# The development of British and National Schools

By 1800 many charity schools were in decline but a few did give their children some education. Their role was taken over by voluntary religious societies. Church leaders were concerned at the lack of schools and education amongst poor children and the possible link with crime. They feared that children would grow up unable to read the Bible or earn an honest living, so they set up schools charging the parents a few pennies a week. Two men, Joseph Lancaster and Andrew Bell, took the lead. They gave a lot of thought to the problem of providing full-time education to the children of the poor. Lancaster was a Quaker and Bell was an Anglican clergyman, so while their ideas on education were much the same, they disagreed over religion, and were soon bitter rivals. Nonconformists tended to follow Lancaster, while members of the Established Church (the Church of England) followed Bell.

Lancaster made the first important move in 1803 when he wrote his book *Improvements in Education* and in 1808 his supporters formed the Royal Lancastrian Society to advance his ideas. They shortly afterwards changed their name to the British and Foreign School Society, as Lancaster had proved so difficult for the society's members to get along with that they expelled him. Schools connected with this society called themselves British Schools for short. In 1811 Bell and his friends in the Church of England founded the National Society for Promoting the Education of the Poor in the Principles of the Established Church. Their rivals called these schools *Bellian* Schools, but members of the society, not surprisingly, preferred to call them National Schools.

● **SOURCE 9.10**

From a letter from Lord John Russell to Lord Lansdowne, Whitehall, 4 February 1839, in which he explains the differences between the two societies.

**Churchman**
Anglican

**Dissenters**
members of Protestant Churches that had broken away from the Anglican Church, e.g. Methodists

*The National Society supported by the Established Church contend that the schoolmaster should be invariably a CHURCHMAN; that the Church Catechism should be taught in the school to all the scholars; that all should be required to attend Church on Sundays and that the schools should be in every case under the superintendence of the clergymen of the parish.*

*The British and Foreign School Society on the other hand admit churchmen and DISSENTERS equally as schoolmasters, require that the Bible should be taught in their schools but insist that no Catechism should be admitted.*

I   According to Source 9.10, what were the main differences between the schools provided by each society?

Fierce rivalry broke out between the two societies but, in spite of the competition between them, the societies organised their schools on much the same lines. They had the same problems: a chronic shortage of both money and trained teachers. Each school had only one adult teacher, who it was claimed, was able to control a school of several hundred children. This control was achieved through the help of monitors. The monitors were the older and brighter children who came to school early to have their lessons before the others arrived. Through the day each monitor took a small group of children and taught them what he or she had learned in the morning. This was very like the factory system brought to school, for instead of minding machines the young workers minded small groups of children. The master or mistress was like the overseer who only needed to step in when something went seriously wrong. The idea appealed to the popular imagination: many new schools were founded, financed by subscriptions and managed by clergymen.

● **SOURCE 9.11**

From Joseph Lancaster's *Improvements in Education*, 1803, in which he explains the monitorial system of teaching adopted by the voluntary Nonconformist British and Foreign School Society schools. This method was called the 'Lancastrian' method.

*My school is attended by 300 scholars. The whole system of tuition is almost entirely conducted by boys . . . The school is divided into classes [and] to each of these a lad is appointed as monitor: he is responsible for the moral improvement, good order and cleanliness of the whole class. It is his duty to make a daily, weekly and monthly report of progress specifying the number of lessons performed, boys present, absent, etc., etc. . . . As we naturally expect the boys who teach the other boys to read to leave school when their education is complete and do not wish that they should neglect their own improvement in other studies they are instructed to train other lads as assistants who in future may supply their place and in the meantime leave them to improve in other branches of learning. To be a monitor is coveted by the whole school, it being an office at once honourable and productive of payment.*

● **SOURCE 9.12**

From a *Manual of Teaching*, British and Foreign School Society, 1821, which describes the monitorial system of teaching.

*Writing on paper*

*When the girls have learnt to write freely on slate, they are allowed to write also in copybooks. They are classified according to proficiency – each class occupying a desk. A monitor is appointed to each class. The books just previous to the time of writing are laid by each monitor at the end of her desk. Each writer, in passing up the desk, takes her book, and, holding it up before her, remains standing, until the whole of the writers have taken their stations. The command is then given by the superintending monitor to 'Front – Lay down – books', 'Hands down', 'Look', 'Open books', 'Hands down'. The monitors of the divisions now distribute the copies and pens that have been previously placed before them, at the heads of their desks. At the word 'Begin', the writing commences; they are not allowed to exceed five lines. Each monitor then goes from girl to girl, pointing out defects, by comparing it with the copy slip. At the close of the writing lesson, the general monitor commands, 'Writers', 'Clean pens', 'Show pens', 'Lay down pens', 'Hands down', 'Monitors, gather up pens.' The monitors collect the pens of their respective divisions, and place them at the lower ends of the desks. At the command 'Gather up copies', the monitors return to the upper end, taking each girl's copy-slip on passing her. These being placed at the upper end of the desk, the superintending monitor says, 'Show books' and the mistress inspects. This being done, the monitor commands, 'Lay down books', 'Shut books'; the monitors gather them, tie them together between small wooden boards, and put them in the different departments of a drawer assigned for their reception.*

● **SOURCE 9.13**

From a letter by schoolmaster Frederick Wade in the *National Society Monthly Paper*, 1851, in which he explains his timetable for a National School near Newcastle.

*The boys and girls work together until the hour for sewing arrives; then a separation takes place, the boys working higher rules in arithmetic than we require of the girls. In our mining district the boys go very early to work, and hence it is necessary that at the same age they should be more advanced than the girls . . . After now having had some experience of the working of Mixed Schools for some time, I have no hesitation in stating that for the generality of our villages they have some advantages. They are the cheapest, for you can provide a superior master to superintend the mental training, a seamstress being sufficient for the sewing, etc. The manners of the boys are softened by association with the girls, and the girls' minds strengthened by coming into contact with the stronger intellect of the boys. Separate playgrounds will in all instances be required, and the watchful eye of a vigilant and painstaking teacher.*

Study Sources 9.11–9.13.

1 What was the role of the 'monitor'?

2 What were the advantages of the system to
   a) the children
   b) the society?

3 What were the disadvantages?

4 To what extent did the curriculum reflect society's views of the respective roles of male and female?

5 Why did the schoolmaster in Newcastle favour 'mixed schools'?

In the towns and villages, as with the earlier charity schools, the wealthier people made donations for the building of a school, and agreed to subscribe a certain amount of money each year to help to pay for the running expenses. These subscribers met annually and elected a group of managers, who were responsible for the day-to-day running of the school, the care of the building and the keeping of the accounts. The person who started this was nearly always the local clergyman, who had to do most of the work himself. Subscriptions alone did not meet all the expenses of running the school. Poor parents themselves were expected to pay a few pence each week in school fees. As time went on, subscriptions from the rich dwindled but school fees went up, so that by 1870 in an average school they provided about one-third of its income. This was particularly true of the British Schools, whose managers found that they could attract the children of the better-off parents – skilled workers and shopkeepers – by charging higher fees. The Church of England remained faithful to the idea of helping the very poor, so National Schools kept their fees much lower, and often allowed the children to attend for nothing.

● SOURCE 9.14

From William Cotton on the work of the National Society, *Parliamentary Papers*, 1834.

Progress of the National Schools, run by the National Society, 1813–30.

| Year of enquiry | Number of schools | Number of children |
|---|---|---|
| 1813 | 230 | 40,484 |
| 1817 | 725 | 117,000 |
| 1820 | 1,614 | 200,000 |
| 1830 | 3,670 | 346,000 |

Limited resources were available, so the buildings in which these schools operated were simple. There was usually just one large school room with no separate classrooms, for the teacher could not trust his monitors to take their groups on their own: he had to keep the entire school under his eye. Land was expensive in towns so it was rare for schools to have attractive sites or playgrounds.

As in the Sunday schools, religion was the most important subject taught, since the people who put up the money for the schools hoped, above everything, for a reform in the morals of the working classes. In the National Schools the vicar or the curate often made a point of doing this important teaching himself. After religion it was reading that mattered most, since the children could not use their Bibles and Prayer Books until they were able to read. As the teachers could not afford books, they used to hang reading sheets on the walls of the schoolroom and the children stood round them in their little groups.

These schools faced the same problems as others: the reluctance of parents to have their children attend because it denied them the wage vital to family income. Children rarely attended after the age of nine years. Attendance was best among country girls, because little work was available for them. The schools had a few successes with the very intelligent children but few children who came to the monitorial schools up to the age of eight or nine could have learnt very much. The evidence given by the factory children to various Royal Commissions is disheartening proof of this. Yet the monitorial schools played a vital part in the history of education in this country. Private schools for the poor, charity schools and Sunday schools were all incapable of much useful development. But when monitorial schools had help and guidance from the state, they grew into efficient schools and this started to happen in the second half of the century. The much-needed help and guidance was already on its way before 1850.

307

What were the main features of elementary education at the beginning of the nineteenth century?

● **SOURCE 9.15**

From Joseph Lawson, *Progress in Pudsey*, 1887, in which he recalls the state of education in 1820.

Most children never went to school, some because their parents sent them to work, others because their parents could not afford to pay even 2d. per week. Not until 1880 when attendance was made compulsory did all children go to school.

*There were very few schools, and many of the teachers could not have passed our present Board Schools' Sixth standard. Some taught nothing but reading and spelling, or knitting and sewing; others only reading and writing from printed copies (not being able to write themselves so well). A few taught arithmetic as well, but a grammar, geography, or history were scarcely ever seen in a school . . . A few of the sons of the middle class learnt writing and arithmetic, but very few others learnt anything but reading. Large numbers never entered the door of a schoolhouse – having to work at something when they arrived at school age . . . Writing was looked upon . . . as a luxury for the rich only, and never likely to be wanted by their sons and daughters. A person who was a good reader of the newspaper, and could talk about various wars, battles, and sieges, was looked up to by the people, and said to be a 'great scholar' and 'a far learned man'. There were few schoolbooks, and those were of a poor kind, the tax or duty on paper . . . causing them to be very high in price. Newspapers were scarce and dear; very few could read them. There were no libraries for the people, who had no access even to the few books there were. The house that had a family Bible, hymn book, prayer book, or catechism, the 'Pilgrim's Progress', or 'News from the Invisible World', together with a sheet almanack nailed against the wall, was considered well furnished with literature.*

1  From the evidence of Source 9.15, what were the limitations of the school curriculum in 1820?

2  Why did these limitations exist?

3  What evidence is there of discrimination based on
   a) sex
   b) social class
   in the teaching of subjects?

4  Why did a majority of children not attend school?

5  What abilities were needed in order to be considered a learned man in 1820?

# 2  What were the main arguments for and against an extension of the provision of elementary education?

There were many attempts to improve the quality of education in the late eighteenth and early nineteenth centuries. The Radical wing of the Whig Party took the lead: Whitbread in 1807, Brougham in 1820 and Roebuck in 1833 introduced bills to create a national system of education with funding from the local rates. They all failed, though Brougham's presence in the Whig government of Lord Grey influenced the decision to award a grant of £20,000 to support the proposal in the 1833 Factory Act for two hours a day of schooling for children aged between nine and thirteen. Roebuck was responsible for the series of inquiries into the Education of the Poorer Classes in 1834, 1835 and 1837–38. Lord John Russell continued with this commitment. He was responsible for the steady increase in the state grant and the setting up of administrative machinery to supervise its use. The state's educational policies were influenced by the prevailing belief in self-help, though it had to face opposition from individuals who acted from a range of political, ideological, social and religious motives.

## • SOURCE 9.16

From *Hansard*, July/August 1807, quoting the parliamentary debates on Samuel Whitbread's Parochial Schools Bill, in which two opponents express widely held fears.

**Samuel Whitbread MP**
of the famous brewing family, proposed to give parish vestries or magistrates the power to raise money for parish schools that would give two years' free schooling to children of poor parents.

**factious and refractory**
hostile and disobedient

Davies Giddy: . . . *giving education to the labouring classes of the poor would in effect be found to be prejudicial to their morals and happiness; it would lead them to despise their lot in life instead of making them good servants in agriculture and other laborious employments to which their rank in society had destined them; instead of teaching them subordination it would render them* FACTIOUS AND REFRACTORY *as was evident in the manufacturing counties; it would enable them to read seditious pamphlets, vicious books and publications against Christianity; it would render them insolent to their superiors; . . . Besides if the Bill were to pass into law it would go to burden the country with a most enormous and incalculable expense and to load the industrious orders of society with still heavier imposts.*
Mr Rose: . . . *had no doubt that the poor ought to be taught to read; as to writing he had some doubt because those who had learnt to write well were not willing to abide at the plough but looked to a situation in some counting house.*

1   What, according to Giddy in Source 9.16, would be the effect of education on the character, ambitions and actions of the labouring classes of the poor?
2   Why would this not be in the interests of the property-owning and governing classes?
3   What concerns does Giddy express in regard to the financial implications of Whitbread's bill?
4   Why does Mr Rose express particular objection to the teaching of writing?
5   What can be inferred from these arguments of attitudes towards the structure of society?

Whitbread's bill was defeated in the House of Lords. Henry Brougham took over Radical sponsorship of free education to the masses. In 1816 a Select Committee was set up to investigate educational provision in London.

## • SOURCE 9.17

From *Report of the Select Committee on the Education of the Lower Orders*, 3 June 1818, identifying the gaps in the provision of schooling and recommending two plans to make up this deficiency.

**comprehend the children of sectaries**
include children whose parents belong to Nonconformist churches

**ordinaries of religion**
services or meetings of worship

**interpose**
supply

### (i) Findings of the Select Committee

*Your Committee rejoice in being able to state that since their first appointment in 1818 when they examined the state of the Metropolis there is every reason to believe that the exertions of charitable individuals and public bodies have increased notwithstanding the severe pressure of the times . . . It appears clearly from the returns as well as from other sources that a very great deficiency exists in the means of educating the poor wherever the population is thin and scattered over country districts. The efforts of individuals combined in Societies are almost wholly confined to populous places. Another point to which it is material to direct the attention of Parliament regards the two opposite principles of founding schools for children of all sorts and for those only who belong to the Established Church. Where the means exist of erecting two schools, one upon each principle, education is not checked by the exclusive plan being adopted in one of them because the other may* COMPREHEND THE CHILDREN OF SECTARIES. *In places where only one school can be supported it is manifest that any regulations that exclude Dissenters deprive the poor of that body of all means of education.*

*Your Committee, however, have the greatest satisfaction in observing that in many schools where the* national system *is adopted an increasing degree of liberality prevails and that the Church Catechism is only taught and attendance at an established place of public worship only required of those whose parents belong to the Establishment; due assurance being obtained that the children of sectaries shall learn the principles and attend the* ORDINARIES OF RELIGION *according to the doctrines and forms to which their families are attached.*

### (ii) Recommendations of the Select Committee

*In humbly suggesting what is fit to be done for promoting universal education your Committee do not hesitate to state that two different plans are advisable, adapted to the opposite circumstances of the town and country districts. Wherever the efforts of individuals can support the requisite number of schools, it would be unnecessary and injurious to* INTERPOSE *any Parliamentary assistance. But your Committee has clearly ascertained that in many places private subscriptions could be raised to meet the yearly expenses of a school,* while the original cost of the undertaking, occasioned chiefly by the erection and purchase of the schoolhouse, prevents it from being attempted.

Your Committee conceive that a sum of money might well be employed in supplying the first want, leaving the charity of individuals to furnish the annual school provision requisite for continuing the school, and possibly for repaying the advance . . .

In the numerous districts where no aid from private exertions can be expected, and where the poor are manifestly without adequate means of instruction, your Committee are persuaded that nothing can supply the deficiency but the adoption . . . of the parish school system, so usefully established in the northern part of the island, ever since the latter part of the seventeenth century . . . It may be fair and expedient to assist the parishes where no school-houses are erected, with the means of providing them, so as only to throw upon the inhabitants the burthen of paying the schoolmaster's salary, which ought certainly not to exceed £24 a year. It appears to your Committee that a sufficient supply of schoolmasters may be procured for this sum, allowing them the benefits of taking scholars, who can afford to pay, and permitting them of course of occupying their leisure in other pursuits.

1　Where, according to Source 9.17, did the deficiencies in the provision of schooling exist?

2　Why, according to the report, had this occurred?

3　What impact did the involvement of organisations with different religious traditions have on the provision of education?

4　Why did the Select Committee appear to favour the national system?

5　What were the main features of the two plans recommended by the Committee?

6　In what respect did the Committee support the principle of 'self-help'?

7　What contribution was to be made by the ratepayers?

8　Why did the report recommend that education still should not be free?

9　Identify individuals and groups who would be opposed to the scheme proposed by the report. Justify your answer.

● **SOURCE 9.18**

From *Manual of Teaching*, 1821, which stresses the need to teach the poor.

From their dependent situation the poor are peculiarly the objects of the care and attention of the higher classes of the community: if they are suffered to grow up in ignorance and vice, fearful responsibility will lie upon those who might have prevented it: that vice follows in the train of ignorance will not now be disputed. The cultivation of the mind bestowed in these elementary schools . . . inspires them with sentiments favourable to virtue and habituates them to subordination and control . . . instances are not wanting in which parents have become reformed characters in consequence of their children being admitted to the schools. The middle and upper ranks of society are now more dependent upon the poor than without a little reflection they are yet aware of it: it is to the labour and skill of the poor that we owe our comforts and conveniences.

We indeed have a deep interest in the state of their morals . . . and, what is of still greater importance, the minds of our children may be materially influenced by the good or bad qualities of the servants in whose care they frequently spend so much of their time. The higher ranks of society are then deeply interested in providing a moral and religious education for the whole of the poor.

1　What does the manual (Source 9.18) claim to be the beneficial influence of education on the moral character of the poor?

2　Why does the manual claim that the middle and upper ranks of society have a responsibility to the poor?

3　What practical reasons are given for educating the poor?

4　What type of education does the writer emphasise should be provided for the poor?

5　In what ways does nineteenth-century education appear to concentrate on the social control of the labouring classes?

There was no immediate response to the efforts of reformers or to the Select Committee's recommendations. This was partly due to the strength of the opposition. The ruling classes feared the consequences of educating the poor. There was widespread support for a minimal state role and minimal expenditure, as we have seen in the debates over factory reform and the Poor Law, especially. Rivalry between the two voluntary religious societies also acted as a brake on state intervention because both societies had powerful allies in Parliament. Brougham's Parish Schools Bill was withdrawn in 1820 after opposition, especially from Nonconformists. Another thirteen years passed before any step was taken by Parliament and then it was as a consequence of its concern to regulate the working hours of children. The idea of providing education for all, let alone of compelling parents to send their children to school, continued to be widely disliked at this time.

## ● SOURCE 9.19

From the House of Commons debate on Roebuck's Education Bill, *Hansard*, August 1833. Roebuck, a Radical reformer, proposed to compel children between the ages of six and twelve to attend school regularly.

*A. Roebuck: I propose a Resolution by which this House will acknowledge as a principle of Government that the education of the people is a matter of national concern; that as such it ought to be the object of the most immediate continued and persistent attention on the part of the Legislature . . . One of the most important results from a proper education of the people would be a thorough understanding on their part of the circumstances on which their happiness depended and of the powers by which those circumstances were controlled. They would learn what a government could do and . . . could not do to relieve their distress – they would learn what depended on themselves . . .*

*On the vote of £20,000 for the purposes of education . . . The House divided – Ayes 50; Noes 26; Majority 24.*

## ● SOURCE 9.20

From William Cobbett, *Political Register*, 21 September 1833, in which Cobbett, a Radical, states his reasons for opposing Roebuck's educational proposals.

*In the first place, sir, I have never either spoken or written against the lower classes being educated . . . I have spoken against, written against, and shall speak and write against, laying a tax upon the people, though to the amount of one single farthing a head in twenty years, for the purpose of promoting what is called 'education'. Never shall a vote to the amount of one-penny pass for this purpose, without my dividing the House [of Commons] upon it. What! I lend my hand in taxing the industrious shoemaker, in order to make him pay for the education of the shoemaker who is not industrious, I tax the ploughman, make him pay a tax on his beer, on his sugar, on his tobacco, to compel him to assist in what is called the educating of the children of the shirking slip shod that has just been jostled into matrimony from behind the master's chair; I will do no such thing, even if I had no other objection than this, which is so consonant with justice and with common sense; but I have other and most powerful objections, to any plan of 'national education', which must of necessity create a new and most terrific control in the hands of the Government.*

*I am further of the opinion and I know it to be true, indeed, that such a thing must be most injurious, not only to the morals but to the liberties of the country; and I am ready to maintain these opinions against all the doctrinaires and canters in the world.*

## ● SOURCE 9.21

From the evidence of the Lord Chancellor, Lord Brougham and Vaux, to the Parliamentary Committee on the State of Education, 1834, in which he, a prominent Whig, gives his views on the provision of education.

**individual beneficence**
donations made and efforts put in by individuals

***Do you think that a system of primary education, established by law, would be beneficial?***
*I think that it is wholly inapplicable to the present condition of the country, and the actual state of education. Those who recommend it on account of its successful adoption on the Continent do not reflect upon the funds, which it would require, and upon the exertions already made in this country by* INDIVIDUAL BENEFICENCE *. . . Now, to establish and maintain such a number of schools would be a most heavy expense . . . would cost £2,000,000 a year.*

**public utility or expediency**
benefit to individuals, or in the
national interest

*Do you consider that a compulsory education would be justified, either on*
*principles of PUBLIC UTILITY OR EXPEDIENCY?*
*I am decidedly of the opinion that it is justifiable upon neither; but above all I should regard*
*anything of the kind as utterly destructive of the end it has in view. Suppose the people of*
*England were taught to bear it and to be forced to educate their children by penalties,*
*education would be made absolutely hateful in their eyes and would speedily cease to be*
*endured. They who have argued in favour of such a scheme from the example of a military*
*government like that of Prussia have betrayed in my opinion great ignorance of the nature of*
*Englishmen.*

Study Sources 9.19–9.21.

1   How did Roebuck justify his educational proposals in 1833?

2   What were Cobbett's objections to education being funded out of taxation?

3   Why is Cobbett opposed to the government being the exclusive provider of education?

4   On what grounds of principle were the minority in the 1833 vote likely to have voted as they did?

5   To what extent did Lord Brougham agree with Cobbett's objections?

6   What did he claim would be the reaction of the people to a system of compulsory education?

# 3   What major developments took place in the provision of elementary education between 1833 and 1870?

The government grant of £20,000 (see page 308) was made over to the National
Society and the British and Foreign School Society, with one important condition
attached. Local subscriptions had to pay for at least half the cost of a new building. If
this happened, then government money could be used to pay the remainder. A grant
of £20,000 was not a lot of money for the whole country, but what was important
was the idea behind it. Where local people were willing to make a determined effort
the state would now encourage them. Parliament renewed the grant for education
every year and from time to time increased it. In 1839 a Committee of the Privy
Council was set up to administer the spending of the grant. Its first secretary, till
1849, was Sir James Kay-Shuttleworth. He was a remarkable man, who had started
his career as a doctor amongst the poor of Manchester where he had seen their
suffering (see page 43). Most of their misery, he felt, they could cure for themselves
but they were unable to do so because of their ignorance. He became convinced that
it was only through education that the lot of the poor could be improved so he was
an inspired choice for the post of secretary.

By the 1830s most of the schools were monitorial schools, based on the systems
of Bell and Lancaster. Kay-Shuttleworth knew full well that such schools might
instruct children in elementary reading, writing and arithmetic, but their instruction
was purely mechanical: it would never produce educated people. This criticism was
often to be found in the reports to the Committee of the Privy Council on Education.
In 1846 Jelinger Symon wrote that 'With few exceptions there is no system of
teaching in the schools in my district. The general plan is precisely that of the old-
fashioned village schools. The children sit in rows on forms, and save the master all
sorts of trouble by reading their books; and in order that he may assure himself of
their industry, they all read aloud. Thus a Babel of tongues is kept going on all
subjects, from Leviticus to the alphabet, in which any attempt to correct, or even
distinguish, individual performances would be perfectly hopeless.'

## Teacher training and pupil-teachers

Only good teachers can give a good education and these were in short supply. How was Kay-Shuttleworth to find all the teachers the schools would need? Part of the answer was to have colleges for training teachers. There had been a plan for a state college but, as it had come to nothing, Kay-Shuttleworth and his friend E. C. Tufnell set up their own college in Battersea as a private venture in 1839. By 1842 the government had been persuaded to make a grant of £1000 to the college. Fortunately the British and Foreign School Society and the National Society also realised the need for colleges and built their own. The National Society was especially active, so that by 1845 it had 22 colleges. But where were the new colleges to find their recruits? Kay-Shuttleworth discovered the answer during a visit to the Netherlands, where he saw young people serving as teacher-apprentices in the schools. This was an idea borrowed from industry. A boy or girl aged about fourteen would be apprenticed to a master and, in the same way that the apprentice craftsman did simple jobs in the workshop, the apprentice teacher did simple jobs in the classroom. As the apprentice's skill increased, so he or she did more complicated work and finally qualified as a master or mistress.

Kay-Shuttleworth was so impressed by what he saw in the Netherlands that in 1846 he persuaded the Committee of the Privy Council to accept a scheme for the training of pupil-teachers. These young people were still pupils. They had to carry on their own education, taking such subjects as English, mathematics, history, geography and science. It was the duty of their headteacher to give them seven-and-a-half hours teaching every week, either before or after school. But the apprentices were also teachers and had to work for five-and-a-half hours each day in the classroom. At the end of each year, the pupil-teachers had to sit an examination; and at the end of the fifth year took what was known as the Queen's Scholarship Examination. Those who passed this were given a government grant so that they could go to a training college. To encourage young people to become pupil-teachers, the government paid them a small wage, and to encourage schools to employ them the government paid them a grant, which was usually added to the headteacher's salary. It was a hard life and many failed to reach the required academic standard and abandoned their training. Few were of great value in the classroom.

313

What major developments took place in the provision of elementary education between 1833 and 1870?

● **SOURCE 9.22**

From the *Report of the Select Committee on the Education of the Poorer Classes, 1837–38.*

Daily school attendance in the large manufacturing and seaport towns, 1834–38.

*Your committee now turn to the state of Education in the large manufacturing and seaport towns, where the population has rapidly increased within the present century; they refer . . . to the Evidence taken before them . . . which appears to bear out the following results:*

1st   *That the kind of education given to children of the working classes is lamentably deficient*
2nd   *That it extends to a small proportion of those who ought to receive it*
3rd   *That without some strenuous effort on the part of the government, the greatest evils to all classes may follow from this neglect.*

| Date | Place | Population | Children of working classes at daily schools | | |
|------|-------|-----------|-----------------------------|---------------|-------|
| | | | Day and dame schools, very indifferent | Other, better | Total |
| 1836 | Liverpool | 230,000 | 11,336 | 14,024 | 25,360 |
| 1834 | Manchester | 200,000 | 11,520 | 15,680 | 17,200 |
| 1835 | Salford | 50,810 | 3,340 | 2,015 | 5,355 |
| 1837 | Birmingham | 180,000 | 8,180 | 4,697 | 12,877 |
| 1838 | Sheffield | 96,692 | 3,359 | 5,905 | 9,264 |
| 1836 | York | 25,359 | 1,494 | 2,697 | 4,191 |

● SOURCE 9.23

From M. Sanderson, *Education, Economic Change and Society in England 1780–1870*, 1983.

Amounts allocated by the government to education, 1833–70.

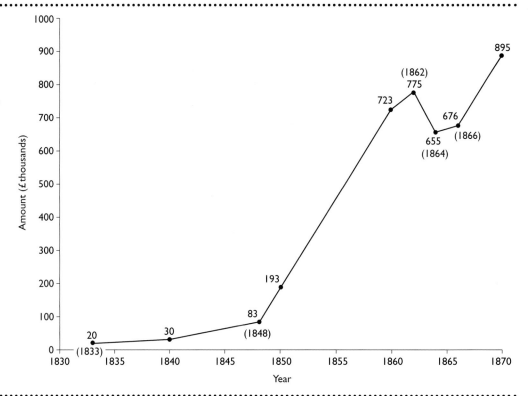

● SOURCE 9.24

From a letter from Lord John Russell, the Whig politician, to Lord Lansdowne, *Parliamentary Papers*, 1839, outlining Whig proposals to set up a Committee of the Privy Council for Education in 1839.

*My Lord, Her Majesty has observed with deep concern the lack of instruction that is to be observed among the poorer classes of her subjects.*

*The reports of prison chaplains show that, to a large number of unfortunate prisoners, knowledge of the fundamental truths of natural and revealed religion has never been taught.*

*It is some consolation to Her Majesty to perceive that of late years the zeal for popular education has increased. Still much remains to be done. I am directed by Her Majesty to desire that your Lordship, with four other of the Queen's Servants, should form a Committee for the consideration of all matters affecting the education of the people. The zeal for popular education has increased, the Established Church has made great efforts to promote the building of schools, and the National and the British and Foreign School Societies have . . . endeavoured to stimulate the liberality of the benevolent . . . friends of general Education.*

*. . . Among the chief defects yet existing may be reckoned the insufficient number of qualified school-masters, the imperfect mode of teaching in . . . the schools . . . and the want of a Model School which might serve for the example of those . . . anxious to improve their own methods of teaching . . .*

*. . . I am directed by Her Majesty to desire . . . that your Lordship, with four others . . . should form a board or Committee, for the consideration of all matters affecting the education of the people.*

*. . . This Board should consist of: the Lord President of the Council; the Lord Privy Seal; the Chancellor of the Exchequer; the Secretary of State for the Home Department; the Master of the Mint.*

*It is proposed that the Board should be entrusted with the application of any sums which may be voted by Parliament for the purposes of education . . .*

*Among the first objects to which any grant may be applied will be the establishment of a Normal [Model] School.*

*In such a school a body of schoolmasters may be formed, competent to assume the management of similar institutions in all parts of the country. In such a school likewise the best modes of teaching may be introduced, and those who wish to improve the schools of their neighbourhood may have an opportunity of observing their results.*

*The Board will consider whether it may not be advisable . . . to apply a sum of money annually in aid of the Normal [Model] Schools of the . . . Societies.*

● **SOURCE 9.25**

From the Minutes of the Committee of Council for Education, Whitehall, August 1840, outlining the instructions issued by the Committee secretary, James Kay-Shuttleworth, to the Rev. John Allan, Inspector of the Church of England schools, and Mr Seymour Tremenheere, Inspector for schools of the British and Foreign School Society.

By 1870 the number of inspectors had risen from two to 73.

2 While an important part of these duties will consist of visiting, from time to time, schools aided by grants of public money made by the authority of the Committee, in order to ascertain that the grant had in each case been duly applied, and to enable you to furnish accurate information as to the discipline, management, and methods of instruction pursued in such schools, your appointment is intended to embrace a more comprehensive sphere of duty . . . local efforts for the improvement and extension of elementary education whether made by voluntary associations or by private individuals [are to be encouraged]. The employment of Inspectors is therefore intended to advance this object, by [indicating through] inspection, what improvements in the apparatus and internal arrangements of schools, in school management and discipline, and in the methods of teaching, have been sanctioned by the most extensive experience . . .

5 . . . it is of the utmost consequence you should bear in mind that this inspection is not intended as a means of exercising control, but of affording assistance; that it is not to be regarded as operating for the restraint of local efforts, but for their encouragement; and that its chief objects will not be attained without the cooperation of the school committees . . .

7 Acting on the principle of assisting local exertions, the Committee of Council has prepared a series of plans of schoolhouses for small parishes, villages, and towns . . . with an explanation of each plan in detail, together with specifications, working drawings, and estimates, and with forms of making contracts with builders . . .

8 their Lordships are strongly of opinion that no plan of education ought to be encouraged in which intellectual instruction is not subordinate to the regulation of the thoughts and habits of the children by the doctrines . . . of religion.

1 Identify the towns listed in the report of 1837 (Source 9.22) where the provision of education appeared to be most deficient in relation to population size.

2 Identify those towns that benefited from better schools.

3 What, according to Lord Russell (Source 9.24), were the chief defects in the provision of education?

4 What policies did Lord Russell propose to overcome these defects?

5 What was the role of the state in the provision of education?

6 What was the impact of these developments on the annual state grant to education (Source 9.23)?

7 What were the duties of the inspectors (Source 9.25)?

8 What limitations were placed on their authority and powers?

9 What was the principle behind inspection?

● **SOURCE 9.26**

Adapted from a speech by Sir James Graham, Home Secretary in Peel's government, in the House of Commons, 28 February 1843, in which he explains the educational clauses of his Factory Bill.

**recent events in the manufacturing districts** Chartist and anti-Poor Law disturbances

It is with particular grief that I say this, but while all the other governments of Europe, warned by the melancholy events which darkened the latter years of the last century, have directed their unceasing attention to the moral training and the religious education of their people, England alone, Protestant Christian England, has neglected this all-important duty of giving her people that training, that education, which so intimately concerns not only their earthly but their eternal welfare.

. . . I must say that I think RECENT EVENTS IN THE MANUFACTURING DISTRICTS are pregnant with solemn warning.

. . . It is time that the seed of sound morality and Christian truth should be sown in the hearts of the people.

. . . I therefore propose that children between the ages of eight and thirteen, employed in factories, shall attend school for at least three hours a day.

. . . I also propose that the schools be grouped in districts managed by trusts containing seven individuals, including a clergyman of the district and two churchwardens, chosen by him.

● **SOURCE 9.27**

Adapted from the Minutes of the Wesleyan Conference, Sheffield, 26 July 1843, in which the dissenters (Methodists) defend their opposition to Sir James Graham's education proposals.

*At the beginning of the present session of Parliament, a measure was introduced to promote the better education of the poor in the manufacturing districts. On a careful examination of this measure, it was found to be based on unjust principles and calculated to inflame those unhappy dissensions that at present exist in our land.*

*The strong and general disapproval that this measure excited has led its proposers to withdraw it. It has been publicly stated that one ground of our strenuous opposition to the measure was its obvious tendency to give the Clergy of the Established Church an unfair and undue control over the religious teaching in the schools it would have established. We agree with this statement.*

● **SOURCE 9.28**

*Who shall educate? Or, Our babes in the wood*, a cartoon from *Punch*, 23 April 1853, showing the duel between Anglicanism and Nonconformity for control of the hearts and minds of young children.

● **SOURCE 9.29**

From *Hansard*, 15 March 1870, quoting a speech by Robert Montague, the Conservative spokesman on education, in the House of Commons, in which he identifies the merits of the voluntary system.

*The late Report on the state of education in four of our great towns had showed that the [Anglican] Church had done nearly everything there. It had established good schools, and carried them on quietly and unostentatiously for years. If anyone desired to know which religious body was the most earnest in the cause of education, let him consult any one of the Reports of the Committee of Council, and he would see how Churchmen had laboured, what large sums they had expended, and how many schools they maintained . . .*

1 To what extent were Graham's proposals in the 1843 Factory Bill (Source 9.26) motivated by concern for an orderly society in a period of rapid social change?

2 Why was there 'strong and general disapproval' of Graham's educational proposals in 1843?

3 What were the implications of the educational clauses of the bill for government financing of education? (Refer back to Source 9.23.)

4 Is it possible to tell whether Montague (Source 9.29) was biased in favour of the National Schools? Explain your answer.

5 What was the effect of religious rivalry on the role of the state in extending the provision of education for the poor?

Despite these developments, the majority of children who attended school left at the age of eleven; only five per cent of children were at school at the age of thirteen. Partly because of the difficulty of paying even small fees, partly because of ill health, attendance of those who went to school was poor. Few poor children attended full time and many did not attend at all. Even so by the late 1850s there was concern at the rising cost of state aid to elementary education, at a time when government policy was directed to reducing expenditure and with it income tax.

In 1856 the Committee of Council was reorganised to become the Education Department with a Vice-President responsible to Parliament. Robert Lowe, an efficient administrator, was appointed and in 1858 it was decided to appoint a new Royal Commission under the chairmanship of the Duke of Newcastle. Its brief was 'to inquire into the present state of popular education in England and to consider and report what measures, if any, are required for the extension of sound and cheap elementary instruction to all classes of the people'. Ten assistant commissioners were appointed to examine in detail, for about six months, the educational provisions of a particular district. The Commission reported on progress that had been achieved but also made many points of criticism. In the words of the report of Carleton Tufnell, 'I assert that it is an impossibility for any inspector to report on the individual qualification of any considerable number of children ... He knows nothing of the individuals ... it would be an intolerable waste of time if he were even to consider making himself acquainted with their names.'

317

What major developments took place in the provision of elementary education between 1833 and 1870?

● **SOURCE 9.30**

From the evidence of Rev. James Fraser, Assistant Commissioner and later bishop of Manchester, to the Newcastle Commission on Education, 1861.

*We must make up our minds to see the last of him ... at ten or eleven ... Whether it would be desirable, with a view to the real interests of the peasant boy, to keep him at school till he was fourteen or fifteen years of age, I doubt ... It is quite possible to teach all that is necessary for him to possess ... by the time that he is ten years old ... He shall be able to spell correctly the words that he will ordinarily have to use; he shall read a common narrative – the paragraph in the newspaper that he cares to read – with sufficient ease to be a pleasure to himself and to convey information to listeners; if gone to live at a distance from home, [a] common shop bill; if he hears talk of foreign countries he has some notions as to the part of the habitable globe in which they lie; ... he has acquaintance enough with the Holy Scriptures to follow ... the arguments of a plain ... sermon, and a ... recollection of the truths taught him in his catechism to know what are the duties required of him.*

1  At what age, according to Fraser (Source 9.30), should children leave school?

2  What did the Assistant Commissioner expect a working-class person to know?

3  To what extent had attitudes towards the education of the lower orders changed by 1860?

4  What can be inferred from the Rev. Fraser's evidence of his view of society?

5  What social role did he consider education should play?

6  To what extent did Fraser's views represent a continuity with those of his predecessors?

● **SOURCE 9.31**

From the *Newcastle Report on Popular Education*, 1861, in assessing the state of elementary education by 1860.

*The whole population of England and Wales in 1858 ... amounted to 19,523,103. The number of children whose names ought to be on the school books ... was 2,655,767 ... the number we found actually to be ... 2,535,462 ... leaving 120,305 without any school instruction whatever. The proportion therefore of scholars in weekday schools of all kinds ... was 1 in 7.7 or 12.99 per cent. ... In 1803 the number of day scholars was estimated at 524,241 or 1 in 17.5 of the whole population at that date. In 1818 the numbers were 674,883 or 1 in 17.25. In 1833 they were 1,276,947 or 1 in 11.2. In 1851 they were 2,144,378 or 1 in 8.6. These statistics prove the great and steady progress that has been made ... both in extent ... and in appreciation of its [education's] worth.*

*While ... we have deemed it to be a matter of the highest importance to leave the religious teaching in schools assisted from public funds to the exclusive decision and control of the managers we feel ourselves compelled to notice a serious evil incident to this arrangement. It sometimes happens that in places too small to allow of the establishment of two schools the only one to which the children of the poor in those places can [go] is ... under regulations which [demand] the teaching of the Church catechism ... and ... attendance ... at Church. In such cases it may result that persons of other denominations are [excluded] unless at the sacrifice of their conscientious convictions from availing themselves of educational advantages for their children furnished in the part by public funds to which as taxpayers they contribute ... We believe that the evil may safely be left to the curative influence of public opinion and will not necessitate a compulsory enactment. Should events prove that we are mistaken it may be the duty of the Committee of Council to consider whether the public fund placed at their disposal in aid of popular education may not be administered in such a manner as will insure to the children of the poor in all places the opportunity of partaking of its benefits without exposing their parents to a violation of their religious convictions.*

## SOURCE 9.32

From M. Sanderson, *Education, Economic Change and Society in England, 1780–1870*, 1983.

Growth in average number of years of schooling for boys, 1805–71.

| Years | Average number of years of schooling for boys |
|---|---|
| 1805 | 2.3 |
| 1846–51 | 5 |
| 1867–71 | 6.6 |

## SOURCE 9.33

From D. Vincent, *Literacy and Popular Culture in England 1750–1914*.

Rise in male literacy rates by social and occupational groups, 1839–69, according to the Registrar General's classification of the census.

| Period | I | II | III | | | | IV | V |
|---|---|---|---|---|---|---|---|---|
| | | | Textile workers | Potters | Metal workers | Miners | | |
| 1839 | 100 | 90 | 63 | 58 | 53 | 21 | 58 | 27 |
| 1844–49 | 96 | 91 | 58 | 50 | 60 | 20 | 62 | 31 |
| 1854–59 | 96 | 91 | 70 | 56 | 61 | 30 | 66 | 41 |
| 1864–69 | 100 | 90 | 85 | 61 | 79 | 47 | 71 | 51 |

Key

I = Upper class – aristocracy, landowners

II = Upper middle class – industrial and commercial property owners, senior military and professional men

III = Middle class – young, professional men, skilled labourers and artisans

IV = Semi-skilled – factory workers, domestic industry workers

V = Unskilled casual labour – agricultural workers, domestic servants, unskilled urban labourers

Study Sources 9.31–9.33.

1 What evidence is there of a steady rise in literacy by 1870 in terms of
   a) the proportion of children of school age actually attending school
   b) the number of years spent at school
   c) social and occupational grouping?

2 Which occupational group showed the biggest rise in literacy?

3 Which social group experienced the biggest rise in literacy?

4 Which social group remained stable in terms of literacy levels?

5 What factors, do you think, made possible this general rise in literacy?

6 Why was the Newcastle Commission (Source 9.31) concerned 'at a serious evil incident' arising from control of education by voluntary organisations?

7 What solutions are proposed by the Commission to prevent this 'evil'?

8 Why did the government feel obliged increasingly to involve itself in education?

Newcastle's report recommended that public money could be saved if payment of the annual grant were made dependent on a school's success in achieving standards of literacy and numeracy in its students. Such success would be tested annually by government-appointed inspectors. Robert Lowe accepted these proposals on the grounds of economy and/or efficiency. In 1862 he introduced the Revised Code for educational grants. The new system became known as 'payment by results' and it lasted until 1897.

## SOURCE 9.34

From Lord Granville's speech in the House of Lords, 13 February 1862, *Hansard,* in which he explains the revised system of funding for elementary education.

*Your lordships are no doubt aware that the State now assists the schools by means of annual grants of various kinds. There is the capitation grant, there are payments to teachers, payment for pupil-teachers, payments for teaching pupil-teachers . . . and capitation grants according to the number of scholars. All these grants will be swept away by the new scheme and the assistance which it is now proposed to give consists of one capitation grant depending* upon certain conditions, such as the state of the school premises and a satisfactory report of the Inspector upon the discipline and the religious instruction of the school; and then the managers of the school [will be able] to claim one penny per scholar for every attendance after the first 100 at the morning or afternoon meetings of the school and after the first twelve of the evening meetings. One-third however of the sum thus claimable is forfeited if the scholar fails to satisfy the Inspector in reading, one-third if in writing and one-third if in arithmetic. For the purposes of examination, the children will be grouped according to age, and their failure in any of these subjects will render the school liable to lose one-third of the allowance, and, if they fail in all, the State will contribute nothing towards the maintenance of the school.

● **SOURCE 9.35**

From Robert Lowe's speech during a debate in the House of Commons, 13 February 1862, in which he explains the basis of the Revised Code.

We propose to give no grant for the attendance of children at school unless they can read [and] write but we do not say that they shall learn no more. We do not object to any amount of learning, the only question is how much of that knowledge ought we to pay for . . . It must never be forgotten that for whom this system is designed are the children of persons who are not able to pay for the teaching. We do not profess to give these children an education that will raise them above their station and business in life; that is not our object but to give them an education that may fit them for that business.

● **SOURCE 9.36**

From Matthew Arnold's Inspector's Report, 1867, in which he criticises the impact of payment by results on teaching methods and the attitude of teachers.

The mode of teaching in the primary schools has certainly fallen off in intelligence, spirit and inventiveness during the four or five years that have elapsed since my last report. It could not well be otherwise. In a country where everyone is prone to rely too much on mechanical processes and too little on intelligence, a change in the Education Department's regulations, which, by making two-thirds of the Government grant depend upon a mechanical examination, inevitably gives a mechanical turn to the teaching, a mechanical turn to the inspection, [which] is and must be trying to the intellectual life of the school . . . In the game of mechanical contrivances the teacher will in the end beat us; and as it is now found possible, by ingenious preparation, to get children through the Revised Code examination in reading, writing and ciphering . . . the question is, not whether this idea, or this or that application of it, suits ordinary public opinion and school managers; the question is whether it really suits the interests of schools and their instruction. I feel sure from my experience of foreign schools as well as of our own, that our present system of grants does harm to schools and their instruction by resting its grants too exclusively, at any rate, upon individual examination, and that we have to relax this exclusive stress rather than to go on adding to it.

● **SOURCE 9.37**

From Joseph Ashby of Tysoe (1859–1919), who describes his experiences in his Warwickshire village school in the 1860s at the time of payment by results.

**lower standards**
younger and/or less able children

You did almost nothing except reading, writing and arithmetic. What a noise there used to be! Several children would be reading aloud, teachers scolding, infants reciting, all waxing louder and louder until the master rang the bell on his desk and the noise slid down to lower note and less volume.

. . . you might wait the whole half-hour of a reading lesson while boys and girls who could not read stuck at every word. If you took your finger from the word that was being read you were punished by staying in when the others went out.

Two inspectors came once a year and carried out a dramatic examination. The schoolmaster came into school in his best suit; all the pupils and teachers would be listening till at ten o'clock a dogcart would be heard on the road even though it was eighty yards away. In would come two gentlemen with a deportment of high authority, with rich voices. Each would sit at a desk and children would be called in turn to one or other. The master hovered round, calling children out as they were needed. The children could see him start with irritation as a good pupil stuck at a word in the reading book he had been using all the year or sat motionless with his sum in front of him. The master's anxiety was deep, for his earnings depended on the children's work. One year the atmosphere so affected the LOWER STANDARDS that, one after another as they were brought to the Inspector, the boys howled and the girls whimpered. It took hours to get through them.

319

What major developments took place in the provision of elementary education between 1833 and 1870?

Study Sources 9.34–9.37.

1 What changes to the system of school funding were to be introduced by the Revised Code?

2 What can be inferred from Granville's speech (Source 9.34) of the main purpose of the change in grant assistance?

3 How effective for that purpose were the changes likely to be?

4 Does the evidence of Source 9.23 (page 314) confirm that the Revised Code had achieved Granville's purpose?

5 To what extent does Lowe (Source 9.35) support Granville's view?

6 Is it possible to infer from Lowe's comments whether he was critical of the voluntary schools? Explain your answer with reference to the source.

7 Would Matthew Arnold (Source 9.36) agree that the Revised Code had achieved Lowe's aim?

8 What are Arnold's main criticisms of the impact of the new system on
a) teaching methods
b) the relationship of the teacher with his pupils and with the inspectors?

9 To what extent would Joseph Ashby have agreed with Arnold's criticisms?

10 Were there any advantages to 'payment by results'?

11 What is the value to a social historian of a study of personal reminiscences, such as those of Joseph Ashby?

# 4 How did state intervention increase between 1870 and 1902?

Disagreements between the Church of England clergy and Nonconformists and Roman Catholics about religious teaching in the schools hampered the growth of education. However, Parliament was slow in coming to the idea that it was the duty of the state to provide education. In 1870 W. E. Forster succeeded in persuading Parliament to pass an Education Act that aimed to provide a school place for every child in the country. It was the granting of the vote to working-class men in the towns in 1867 that finally prompted the government to take a more positive role in education. Robert Lowe, a Liberal politician at the time, said that 'It will be absolutely necessary to educate our masters. I was opposed to centralisation of education: I am now ready to accept [it]. I was opposed to an education rate; I am now ready to accept one. You have placed the government of this country in the hands of the masses.'

The continuing growth in population had put an increasing strain on the resources of the voluntary sector and there were increasing gaps in provision. Moreover, there were groups of deprived children – the very poor, girls, delinquents – who had not qualified for attendance. Ragged schools that had started in 1844 attempted to provide a basic education for the poorest children. Financed by donations from philanthropists, such as Charles Dickens, they numbered 250 in London and 100 in the rest of the country by 1870. Forster proposed that all schools would in future come under the direction of the state.

● **SOURCE 9.38**

From statistics compiled by the author.

Provision of education for children aged six to twelve years by 1868. Total number = 2,486,000.

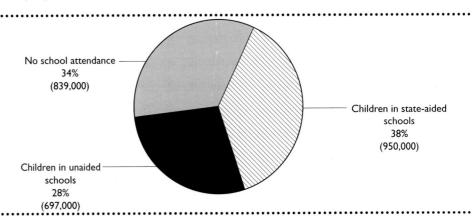

No school attendance
34%
(839,000)

Children in state-aided
schools
38%
(950,000)

Children in unaided
schools
28%
(697,000)

## ● SOURCE 9.39

Adapted from W. E. Forster's speech, 17 February 1870, *Hansard*, introducing the Elementary Education Bill in the House of Commons.

### (i) Forster's criticisms of the existing system

*Last year I moved the Education Estimate . . . I asked for an annual grant of £415,000 for primary schools in England and Wales . . . The number of children upon the registers of those schools was about 1,450,000 and the average attendance about 1,000,000, representing, therefore, the education more or less imperfect of nearly 1,500,000 children. I say the education, according to these returns, is very imperfect, because the attendance is very irregular, nevertheless the figures I have just referred to represent also a great amount of voluntary zeal . . .*

### (ii) The role of the voluntary religious societies

*I think no one could occupy my office without being fully aware of what the country owes to the managers of the schools at present in receipt of government grants . . . particularly ministers of religion of all denominations . . . I know the sacrifices they have made, and not for a moment do I believe it possible that anyone who considers this question will disregard what they have already done, or will wish to do without their aid in the future.*

*. . . though we have done well in assisting the benevolent gentlemen who have established schools, yet the result of the State leaving the initiative to volunteers is, that where State help has been most wanted, State help has been least given, and that where it was desirable that State power should be most felt it was not felt at all . . . Therefore, notwithstanding the large sums of money we have voted, we find a vast number of children badly taught, or utterly untaught, because there are too few schools and too many bad schools . . . Hence comes a demand from all parts of the country for a complete system of national education.*

### (iii) Forster's intentions

*Our object is to complete the present voluntary system, to fill up gaps, sparing the public money where it can be done without. Now I will at once proceed to the main principles . . . They are two in number:*

*1 Legal enactment, that there will be efficient schools everywhere throughout the kingdom.*
*2 Compulsory provision of such schools if and where needed, but not unless proved to be needed.*

### (iv) Defence of his proposals

*We must not delay. Upon the speedy provision of elementary education depends our industrial prosperity. It is of no use trying to give technical teaching to our artisans without elementary education; uneducated labourers – and many of our labourers are uneducated – are, for the most part, unskilled labourers, and if we leave our work folk any longer unskilled, notwithstanding their strong sinews and determined energy, they will become over-matched in the competition of this world. Upon this speedy provision depends also, I fully believe, the good, the safe working of our constitutional system. To its honour, Parliament has lately decided that England shall in future be governed by popular government. I am one of those who would not wait until the people were educated before I would trust them with political power. If we had thus waited we might have waited long for education, but now that we have given them political power we must not wait any longer to give them education.*

---

Study Sources 9.38 and 9.39.

1 On what evidence does Forster claim that education is 'very imperfect'?

2 To what extent is Forster critical of the role played by the voluntary religious societies in the provision of elementary education?

3 Explain fully what Forster means when he says that his aim is to 'complete the present voluntary system'.

4 How does Forster intend to achieve this completion?

5 What are Forster's grounds for urgent state intervention beyond the remedying of existing defects?

6 How far do Forster's recommendations indicate the progress that had been made in contemporary attitudes towards
   a) education of the labouring classes
   b) the role of the state?

● **SOURCE 9.40**

From *Statutes of the Realm*, (the 33rd and 34th Statute of Victoria) summarising some of the main clauses of Forster's Education Act, 1870.

---

*remit*
decide not to charge

---

5 There shall be [in] every school district a sufficient amount of public elementary schools for all the children.

6 Where there is an insufficient amount of accommodation, a school Board shall be formed [to] supply such deficiency.

7 (i) It shall not be required that [any child] shall attend . . . any instruction in religious subjects . . . (ii) the time during which [religious] instruction is given shall be either at the beginning or at the end of [the day] . . .

10 If after six months the Education Department are satisfied that all the accommodation required has not been supplied, the Education Department shall cause a school Board to be formed to supply the same . . .

17 Every child attending a school shall pay . . . fees prescribed by the school Board. The Board may . . . REMIT . . . part of such fee when they are of the opinion that the parent is unable to pay the same [from poverty].

26 If a school Board satisfies the Education Department that, on the ground of poverty, it is expedient to provide a school at which no fees shall be required, the Board may provide such a school.

54 Any sum required to meet any deficiency in the school fund shall be paid out of the local rate.

71 Every school Board . . . may make bye-laws (i) requiring the parents of children of such age, not less than five years nor more than thirteen years, as may be fixed by the bye-laws, to cause such children (unless there is some reasonable excuse) to attend school; (ii) determining the time during which children are . . . to attend school . . .

74 Every Board may make bye-laws for any of the following purposes: (i) requiring parents of children not less than five years nor more than thirteen years, to cause such children to attend school; provided that any such bye-law shall provide for the exemption of a child if one of Her Majesty's Inspectors certifies that such child has reached a standard of education specified in such bye-law.

---

● **SOURCE 9.41**

Quoted in M. Sanderson, *Education, Economic Change and Society in England 1780–1870*, 1983.

Rise in literacy levels, 1841–96, based on census returns.

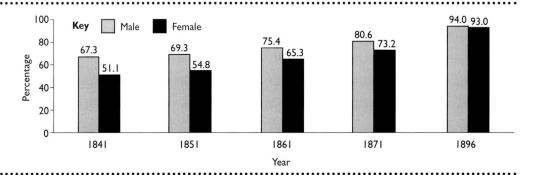

---

Study Sources 9.40 and 9.41.

1 In what circumstances could a school board be set up?

2 When could the central Education Department insist that one be set up?

3 What did the 1870 act say about
   a) attendance at religious instruction
   b) the time at which religious instruction was to be given?

4 What provisions were made by the act to deal with each of the following
   a) school fees
   b) attendance
   c) financing of schools?

5 In what ways did the act support voluntary denominational schools?

6 What new principle was established by the act in terms of the role of the state?

7 What were the strengths and weaknesses of the 1870 Education Act?

8 How far does the evidence of Source 9.41
   a) support Forster's claims that gaps existed in the provision of education
   b) suggest that Forster was achieving his object of 'completing the present voluntary system'?

● **SOURCE 9.42**

From a Cabinet Memorandum by Lord Sandon, Vice-President of the Committee of Council on Education, 1875, in which he warns of the dangers of the 1870 Act.

### Birmingham League
Birmingham Education League, which called for free education for all. Sandon is expressing the suspicion, common among Tory politicians, that giving local town councils control over education would lead to more agitation for reform among the poor.

*School boards (or some such agency) were I believe necessary for the large towns and are productive of no political evil; but in the smaller country towns and villages . . . I am convinced they will produce serious political results. They will become the favourite platform of the dissenting preacher and local agitator and will provide for our rural population by means of their triennial meetings exactly the training in political organisation which the politicians of the BIRMINGHAM LEAGUE desire and which will be mischievous to the state.*

I  What concerns does the Tory Lord Sandon (Source 9.42) express about the implications of the 1870 act on the rural village?

2  To what extent are his concerns motivated by political rather than educational motives?

● **SOURCE 9.43**

*Obstructives*, an etching from *Punch*, 2 July 1870.

"OBSTRUCTIVES."

Mr. Punch (*to* Bull A I). "YES, IT'S ALL VERY WELL TO SAY, 'GO TO SCHOOL!' HOW ARE THEY TO GO TO SCHOOL WITH THOSE PEOPLE QUARRELLING IN THE DOORWAY? WHY DON'T YOU MAKE 'EM 'MOVE ON'?"

I  What can you deduce from the *Punch* cartoon (Source 9.43) of opponents to Forster's act?

The significance of the 1870 act was that the state intervened directly in the provision of education through state-funded, and managed, elementary schools. It did not replace the voluntary schools but introduced a dual system whereby the two providers existed alongside each other. Neither did the act introduce free or compulsory attendance. It did lead to the creation of more school places through both the provision of state-funded schools and the willingness of the voluntary sector to respond to competition from the state by building more schools. Further progress in the drive to increase literacy came first with the introduction of compulsory education in 1880 and then with the advent of free education in 1891. School Attendance Committees were introduced to enforce these new regulations and the school-leaving age was raised to twelve by 1899. These developments promoted an increase in the expenditure for training teachers. The voluntary schools found it increasingly difficult to compete with the state schools in terms of finance, especially after the introduction of the merit grant which was paid to state schools on the basis of an inspection report that assessed the success of a school in training pupils.

● **SOURCE 9.44**

From statistics compiled by the author.

Number of children in state-aided elementary schools, 1868–79.

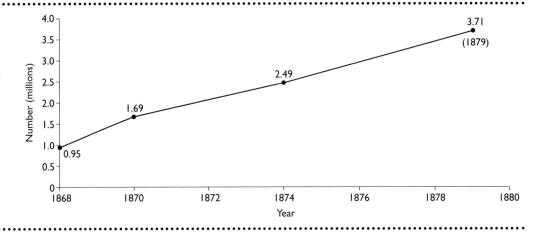

1 Why did the numbers of children in elementary education increase in the 1870s as shown in Source 9.44?

2 Compare Source 9.44 with Source 9.41. To what extent can it be inferred that much of the increase in numbers came from a greater inclusion of females?

● **SOURCE 9.45**

Adapted from *National Education Association Broadsheet*, 1890.

Relative efficiency of voluntary and board schools in 1890.

| Assessment | Infant schools | | Schools for older scholars | |
|---|---|---|---|---|
| | Voluntary | Board | Voluntary | Board |
| Average attendance | 642,339 | 465,466 | 1,635,436 | 997,295 |
| Excellent | 30.8 | 55.8 | 27.2 | 46.7 |
| Good | 53.3 | 37.6 | 54.3 | 45.0 |
| Fair | 14.4 | 6.0 | 16.2 | 7.5 |
| Grant refused | 1.5 | 0.6 | 2.3 | 0.8 |

1 Who provided the most schools – voluntary organisations or the state?

2 Which appeared to be the most successful in terms of the award of good to excellent grades for the provision of
   a) infant education
   b) education for older scholars?

3 To what extent was the voluntary sector justified in feeling it was under threat after the 1870 act?

● **SOURCE 9.46**

From statistics compiled by the author.

Costs of teacher training, 1833–70.

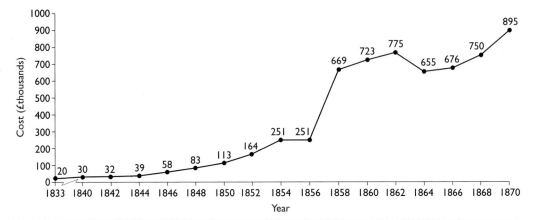

1   What factors help to explain the long-term trend in the cost of training teachers?

By the start of the twentieth century many elementary schools were providing secondary education in what became known as the 'higher elementary schools' or 'higher grade schools'. They were supported by ratepayers' money and came under the control of the school boards. They attracted the attention of a minor official, Robert Morant, who subsequently became Permanent Secretary to the Board of Education. He was in favour of establishing education authorities to replace the various school boards in a local area and regarded the establishment of higher grade schools by the school boards as illegal. His views influenced a government auditor, Cockerton, to surcharge the London School Board with the amount of money that had been spent on higher grade schools, in particular on the North London School of Art. The issue was taken to court and the resulting Cockerton Judgement upheld the auditor's action. As a result, all higher grade schools in the country were in danger of being closed down. The government was forced to act to prevent chaos. After emergency legislation in 1901, the Conservative Prime Minister, Balfour, passed the Education Act of 1902, which established local education authorities with powers to establish and run secondary schools.

● **SOURCE 9.47**

From a speech by A. J. Balfour introducing the Education Bill of 1902, in which the Conservative Prime Minister explains why new education legislation is needed to establish a universal and national system.

*. . . two unforeseen consequences arose [from the 1870 Act] . . . and three considerable omissions made themselves felt as time went on. The first of the two unforeseen consequences was the embarrassment into which the Voluntary Schools were thrown by the rivalry of the rate-aided Board Schools . . . Mr Forster and the Government of that day greatly under-rated the . . . cost. Mr Forster contemplated that a three-penny rate would do all that had to be done . . . There was a wholly unexpected expenditure by School Boards . . . and the voluntary schools were subjected to a competition which, however good for education, was certainly neither anticipated nor desired by the framers of the Act of 1870. The second result was that a strain . . . was put upon local finances . . . through the action of a body responsible indeed to the community so far as regards education, but having no responsibility for general expenditure, which was, of course, in the hands of the local authority . . . Let me just enumerate hurriedly the . . . important omissions . . . In the first place, the Act of 1870 provided no organisation for voluntary schools. Board Schools . . . were organised under the School Boards. But voluntary schools . . . were isolated and unconnected . . . The second omission was . . . that there was no sufficient provision for the education of the great staff of teachers required for our national schools.*

1   What, according to Balfour (Source 9.47), were the two unintended results that emerged from the 1870 act?

2   What areas of education did the 1870 act leave undefined?

3   How had the shortcomings of the Education Act of 1870 necessitated further state intervention by 1902?

● **SOURCE 9.48**

From *Elementary Code*, 1904, which defines the purpose of elementary education.

*The purpose of the Public Elementary School is to form and strengthen the character and to develop the intelligence of the children entrusted to it . . . to fit themselves practically as well as intellectually for the work of life . . . It will be an important though subsidiary object of the School to discover individual children who show promise of exceptional capacity and to develop their special gifts (so far as this can be done without sacrificing the interests of the majority of the children) so that they may be qualified to pass at the proper age into Secondary Schools and be able to derive the maximum of benefit from the education there offered them.*

● **SOURCE 9.49**

From *Regulations for Secondary Schools*, 1904, which defines 'secondary school' and its relationship to elementary education.

*But a definition of the term 'Secondary School' – which has come to have a recognised meaning in English Education – has become indispensable in order to give to Secondary Schools a definite place in the wide and vague scheme of 'education other than elementary' with the provision and organisation of which the Local Education Authorities under the Act of 1902 have been charged and in respect of which they obtain financial aid and administrative regulation from the Board of Education. Secondary schools are of different types, suited to the different requirements of the scholars, to their place in the social organisation, and to the means of the parents [affecting] the age at which the regular education of the scholars is obliged to stop short, as well as the occupations and opportunities of development to which they may or should look forward in later life . . .*

Study Sources 9.48 and 9.49.

1   What did the government regard as the purpose of the public elementary school?

2   How did the government define 'secondary' education?

3   What powers were given to the local education authorities that the school boards had not possessed?

4   What changes had occurred by 1902 in official attitudes, and policy, towards the education of the labouring classes?

● **Summary task**

Below are a number of questions that might be used for discussion or written answers as a way of testing your understanding of this chapter.

• Why were early Victorians opposed to the education of the working classes?
• What facilities existed for the education of the working classes?
• Who were the most literate amongst the working classes?
• Were the voluntary religious societies more of a hindrance than a help to the growth of mass education?
• Why did the literacy rates for women remain below those of men?
• What was the link between industrialisation and education of the masses?
• What were the motives behind Forster's Education Act of 1870?

## Examples of examination-type questions

### A  AS questions

1  a) What were the main defects in the provision of education for the masses in the early nineteenth century?
   b) How far were these defects removed by 1900?

2  a) What were the main objections to education of the working classes?
   b) Why were these objections overcome by 1870?

### B  A2 questions

1  Why did it take so long to achieve a national system of education?

2  To what extent did Forster's Education Act of 1870 represent a major landmark?

● **Further reading**

M. Sanderson, *Education, Economic Change and Society in England 1780–1870* (Macmillan, 1983)

**Articles**
G. Sutherland, 'Elementary Education in the Nineteenth Century', Historical Association pamphlet, 1971

# Acknowledgements to sources

**PREFACE**

**Source 1** S. Smiles, *Self-Help* (Viking Press, 1986)

**Source 2** A. de Tocqueville, *Voyage en Angleterre et en Irlande*, 2 July 1835

**Source 3** S. A. Weaver, *John Fielden and the Politics of Popular Radicalism, 1832–1847* (Oxford University Press, 1987) pp. 5–6

**Source 4** D. Thompson, *The Chartists: Popular Politics in the Industrial Revolution* (Pantheon Books, 1984)

**CHAPTER 1**

**Source 1.1** Performance of the economy – depression and boom, 1830–79, adapted from Poor Law Report, *Parliamentary Papers, 1909/XXXVII*, quoted in G. M. Young and W. D. Handcock (eds), *English Historical Documents, XII (I), 1833–1874* (Eyre & Spottiswoode, 1956), p. 228

**Source 1.2** Growth in the population of England and Wales according to a) size and b) percentage, 1801–1911, from N. Tranter, *Population since the Industrial Revolution* (Croom Helm, 1973), pp. 41–2

**Source 1.3** Changes in the factors affecting population growth: a) births and deaths 1811–1915; b) migration 1841–1915, from B. R. Mitchell and P. Deane, *Abstract of British Historical Statistics* (Cambridge University Press, 1962), p. 6, and N. Tranter, *Population since the Industrial Revolution* (Croom Helm, 1973), p. 53

**Source 1.4** Changes in the proportion of the population married by age and sex, 1871–1911, from B. R. Mitchell and P. Deane, *Abstract of British Historical Statistics* (Cambridge University Press, 1962), p. 6

**Source 1.5** Changes in family size, 1861–1914, from the Registrar General's Statistical Review, 1961, Part III, Commentary, Table XLII, p. 70, quoted in R. Fletcher, *The Family* and *Marriage in Britain* (Penguin/Pelican, 1966), p. 113

**Source 1.6** N. Tranter, *Population since the Industrial Revolution* (Croom Helm, 1973), pp. 68–9

**Source 1.7** N. Tranter, *Population since the Industrial Revolution* (Croom Helm, 1973), pp. 56–7

**Source 1.8** Changes in the distribution of population, 1701–1901, from J. A. Morris, *The Growth of Industrial Britain, 1700 to the present day* (Harrap, 1971), pp. 9, 40, 91

**Source 1.9** Johann Conrad Fischer, *Diary*, 1851, quoted in R. Brown, *Change and Continuity in British Society, 1800–1850* (Cambridge University Press, 1987), p. 84

**Source 1.10** Reverend Sydney Smith, *Collected Works*, 1839, quoted in R. Brown, *Change and Continuity in British Society, 1800–1850* (Cambridge University Press, 1987), pp. 84–5

**Source 1.11** *Factory Commission, Supplementary Report*, 1834, part i, p. 169, quoted in J. L. Hammond and B. Hammond, *The Town Labourer* (Longman Green, 1917; 1966 edn), p. 25

**Source 1.12** Net gain and loss by migration in England, 1841–1911, from A. K. Cairncross, *Home and Foreign Investment 1870–1913* (Cambridge University Press, 1953), p. 70

**Source 1.13** Percentage changes in the urban/rural distribution of the population, 1700–1911, compiled by author on basis of statistics from C. Culpin, *Making Modern Britain* (Collins, 1987), p. 125

**Source 1.14** Destination of emigrants from the UK, 1821–51, from Schools Council History 13–16 Project – *Britain 1815–1851* (Holmes McDougall, 1977), p. 78

**Source 1.15** *Here and There, or, Emigration a remedy*, a cartoon from *Punch*, 15 July 1848

**Source 1.16** *First Report of the Select Committee on Emigration from the United Kingdom*, 1826, quoted in Schools Council History 13–16 Project – *Britain 1815–1851* (Holmes McDougall, 1977), p. 80

**Source 1.17** H. A. Innis and A. R. Lower (eds), *Select Documents in Canadian Economic History 1783–1855* (Toronto, 1933), p. 42

**Source 1.18** *Incentive for Female Migrants*, 1833, quoted in Schools Council History 13–16 Project – *Britain 1815–1851* (Holmes McDougall, 1977), p. 81

**Source 1.19** Estimates of economic growth during given periods between 1700 and 1860, from N. F. R. Crafts, 'The Industrial Revolution: Economic Growth in Britain, 1700–1860' (*Refresh*, York University, no. 4, 1986)

**Source 1.20** Net output of the principal textile industries, 1770–1870 (£ millions), from P. Deane and W. A. Cole, *British Economic Growth 1688–1959* (Cambridge University Press, 2nd edn, 1969), p. 212

**Source 1.21** Estimated output of the coal industry 1800–50 (million tons), from P. Deane and W. A. Cole, *British Economic Growth 1688–1959* (Cambridge University Press, 2nd edn, 1969), p. 216

**Source 1.22** Estimated output of pig iron 1796–1874 (thousand tons) and percentage share of iron industry in national income, 1805–71, from (a) R. M. Reeve, *The Industrial Revolution 1750–1850* (Hodder & Stoughton, 1971), p. 214; (b) P. Deane and W. A. Cole, *British Economic Growth 1688–1959* (Cambridge University Press, 2nd edn, 1969), p. 226

**Source 1.23** a) Changes in the distribution of the labour force, 1811–1914 (as a percentage of the total occupied population), and b) Decline in the percentage of agricultural workers, 1811–1914, from P. Deane and W. A. Cole, *British Economic Growth 1688–1959* (Cambridge University Press, 2nd edn, 1969), pp. 142–3

**Source 1.24** The impact of power-driven looms on the position of the handloom-weavers, from F. Crouzet, *The Victorian Economy* (Methuen, 1981), p. 199

**Source 1.25** Wages of a Bolton handloom-weaver, 1797–1830, from G. R. Porter, *The Progress of the Nation*, 1847 edn, p. 457, quoted in R. Brown and C. Daniels, *Documents and Debates: The Chartists* (Macmillan, 1984), p. 12

**Source 1.26** Course of money wages, 1800–60, and real wages where figures available, from P. Deane and W. A. Cole, *British Economic Growth 1688–1959* (Cambridge University Press, 2nd edn, 1969), p. 23

**Source 1.27** N. Longmate, *Milestones in Working Class History* (BBC Publications, 1975), p. 25

**Source 1.28** P. A. M. Taylor, *The Industrial Revolution in Britain: Triumph or Disaster?* (Heath, 1958), p. x

**Source 1.29** E. P. Thompson, *The Making of the English Working Class* (Victor Gollancz, 1966), p. 230

**Source 1.30** R. M. Hartwell, 'The Standard of Living during the Industrial Revolution: A Discussion' (*Economic History Review*, Vol. 16, August 1963), pp. 135–46

**Source 1.31** P. Mathias, *The First Industrial Nation: Economic History of Britain 1700–1914* (Methuen, 1969), pp. 222–3

**Source 1.32** Average real wages adjusted for unemployment, 1850–1906, from P. Deane and W. A. Cole, *British Economic Growth 1688–1959* (Cambridge University Press, 2nd edn, 1969), p. 25

**Source 1.33** J. Burnett, *A History of the Cost of Living* (Penguin, 1977), pp. 257–8

**Source 1.34** Frequency of riot, 1812–50, based on evidence compiled by the author

**Source 1.35** Number of committals for riotous offences per year by decade, 1839–68 (including riot and sedition), from J. Stevenson, *Popular Disturbances in England, 1700–1870* (Longman, 1979), p. 297

**Source 1.36** *Capital and Labour*, a cartoon from *Punch Volume 2*, 1843

**Source 1.37** Friedrich Engels, *The Condition of the Working Class in England*, 1845 (Penguin edn, 1969), p. 52

**Source 1.38** Benjamin Disraeli, *Sybil, or the Two Nations*, 1845 (Oxford University Press edn,), p. 67

**Source 1.39** Elizabeth Gaskell, *North and South*, 1854 (Penguin edn, 1970), p. 71

**Source 1.40** Joseph Arch, *The Life of Joseph Arch by himself*, 1898 (MacGibbon & Kee edn, 1966), pp. 25–6

**Source 1.41** J. Golby, 'Chartism and Public Order, Popular Politics' (Open University, A401 II), pp. 3–6

## CHAPTER 2

**Source 2.1** Two views of women spinning:
a) women spinning in the cottage, British Museum;
b) *Children in a Cotton Factory*, a painting by T. Onwyn, used as the frontispiece of Frances Trollope, *The Life and Adventures of Michael Armstrong, Factory Boy*, 1840

**Source 2.2** Adapted from Peter Gaskell, *The Manufacturing Population of England*, quoted in K. Dawson and P. Wall, *Society and Industry in the Nineteenth Century*, Vol. 2: *Factory Reform* (Oxford University Press, 1968), pp. 1–2

**Source 2.3** Dr James P. Kay, *The Moral and Physical Condition of the Working Classes Employed in the Cotton Manufacture of Manchester*, 1832, quoted in K. Dawson and P. Wall, *Society and Industry in the Nineteenth Century*, Vol. 2: *Factory Reform* (Oxford University Press, 1968), pp. 5–6

**Source 2.4** William Cobbett, *Political Register*, 20 November 1824, Vol. II, quoted in R. Tames (ed.), *Documents of the Industrial Revolution, 1750–1850* (Hutchinson, 1971), pp. 91–2

**Source 2.5** *Report of Commissioners on the Employment of Children in Factories, Parliamentary Papers, 1833/XX*, quoted in G. M. Young and W. D. Handcock (eds), *English Historical Documents, XII (I), 1833–1874* (Eyre & Spottiswoode, 1956), p. 936

**Source 2.6** J. M. Ludlow and L. Jones, *Progress of the Working Class*, 1867, quoted in E. Royle, *Modern Britain, A Social History, 1750–1985* (Edward Arnold, 1987), p. 237

**Source 2.7** Evidence of R. Cookson, a hosier, before the Committee on the Woollen Manufacture of England, *Parliamentary Papers, 1806*, quoted in R. Tames (ed.), *Documents of the Industrial Revolution, 1750–1850* (Hutchinson, 1971), p. 92

**Source 2.8** Andrew Ure, *The Philosophy of Manufactures*, 1835, p. 474, quoted in R. Tames (ed.), *Documents of the Industrial Revolution, 1750–1850* (Hutchinson, 1971), p. 96

**Source 2.9** Nassau Senior, *Grounds and Objects of the Budget*, quoted in R. Tames (ed.), *Documents of the Industrial Revolution, 1750–1850* (Hutchinson, 1971), p. 90

**Source 2.10** Numbers employed in the cotton industry, 1806–62, adapted from B. R. Mitchell and P. Deane, *Abstract of British Historical Statistics* (Cambridge University Press, 1962)

**Source 2.11** *Enquiry into the Causes of the Increase of the Poor*, 1738, quoted in R. Brown, *Change and Continuity in British Society, 1800–1850* (Cambridge University Press, 1987), p. 92

**Source 2.12** Robert Owen, *A New View of Society and Other Writings*, 1813 (Dent, 1972), pp. 123–5

**Source 2.13** Evidence of a visitor in 1796, published in *Gentleman's Magazine*, LXXIV, pp. 493–4, quoted in P. Mantoux, *The Industrial Revolution in the Eighteenth Century* (Methuen, 1961), p. 467

**Source 2.14** Robert Owen, *A New View of Society and Other Writings*, 1813, quoted in C. McNab and R. Mackenzie, *From Waterloo to the Great Exhibition, Britain 1815–1851* (Oliver & Boyd, 1982), pp. 69–70

**Source 2.15** Robert Southey, *Espriella's Letters from England*, 1807, quoted in K. Dawson and P. Wall, *Society and Industry in the Nineteenth Century*, Vol. 2: *Factory Reform* (Oxford University Press, 1968), pp. 8–9

**Source 2.16** Different methods used by firms to enforce discipline among factory children, 1833, from S. Pollard, *The Genesis of Modern Management* (Penguin, 1968), p. 213

**Source 2.17** Adapted from J. T. Ward, *Popular Movements, c.1830–1850* (Macmillan, 1970), pp. 58–68

**Source 2.18** T. B. Macaulay, *Leeds Mercury*, 16 June 1832, quoted in D. Fraser, *The Evolution of the British Welfare State* (Macmillan, 1973), p. 19

**Source 2.19** Evidence of G. A. Lee of Manchester to the Select Committee on the State of Children Employed in Manufactories, *Parliamentary Papers, 1816*, quoted in K. Dawson and P. Wall, *Society and Industry in the Nineteenth Century*, Vol. 2: *Factory Reform* (Oxford University Press, 1968), pp. 14–15

**Source 2.20** J. R. McCulloch, *Edinburgh Review*, 1835, quoted in V. Brendon, *The Age of Reform 1820–1850* (Hodder & Stoughton, 1994), p. 76

**Source 2.21** Second reading of Michael Sadler's Factory Bill, *Hansard*, 16 March 1832, quoted in M. Willis, *Nineteenth Century Britain, 1815–1914* (Blackwell Education, 1990), p. 27

**Source 2.22** Nassau Senior, *Letters on the Factory Act*, 1837, to the President of the Board of Trade, quoted in P. Lane, *Documents on British Economic and Social History, 1750–1870* (Macmillan, 1968), pp. 82–3

**Source 2.23** Report on the large cotton factories by the Board of Health for Manchester, 1796, in John Aitkin, *A Description of the Country from thirty to forty miles around Manchester*, 1795, *Parliamentary Papers, 1816/III*, pp. 139–40, quoted in J. T. Ward, *Popular Movements c.1830–1850* (Macmillan, 1970), pp. 38–9

**Source 2.24** Sir Robert Peel the Elder's evidence to the Select Committee on the State of Children employed in the Manufactories, 1816, p. 132, quoted in J. L. Hammond and B. Hammond, *The Town Labourer* (Longman & Green, 1917; 1966 edn), pp. 151–2

**Source 2.25** Health and Morals of Apprentices Act, 1802, quoted in K. Dawson and P. Wall, *Society and Industry in the Nineteenth Century*, Vol. 2: *Factory Reform* (Oxford University Press, 1968), pp. 10–11

**Source 2.26** *Report of the Select Committee on Parish Apprentices*, 1815, quoted in K. Dawson and P. Wall, *Society and Industry in the Nineteenth Century*, Vol. 2: *Factory Reform* (Oxford University Press, 1968), pp. 11–12

**Source 2.27** Fate of 2,026 pauper apprentices from London, and some parishes in Middlesex and Surrey, 1802–11, from the *Report of the Select Committee on Parish Apprentices*, 1815, quoted in J. L. Hammond and B. Hammond, *The Town Labourer* (Longman & Green, 1917; 1966 edn), p. 156

**Source 2.28** A propaganda cartoon published to support Sir Robert Peel the Elder's campaign for the 1819 Factory Act, regulating the employment of 'free' apprentices

**Source 2.29** Evidence of Robert Owen to the Select Committee on the State of Children Employed in Manufactories, *Parliamentary Papers, 1816*, quoted in K. Dawson and P. Wall, *Society and Industry in the Nineteenth Century*, Vol. 2: *Factory Reform* (Oxford University Press, 1968), pp. 12–13

**Source 2.30** Factory Act, 1819, quoted in K. Dawson and P. Wall, *Society and Industry in the Nineteenth Century*, Vol. 2: *Factory Reform* (Oxford University Press, 1968), p. 16

**Source 2.31** *Report on the Cotton Mills in the Parish of Bolton*, 1823, quoted in K. Dawson and P. Wall, *Society and Industry in the Nineteenth Century*, Vol. 2: *Factory Reform* (Oxford University Press, 1968), pp. 16–17

**Source 2.32** Richard Oastler's letter on 'Slavery in Yorkshire', *Leeds Mercury*, 16 October 1830, quoted in R. Tames (ed.), *Documents of the Industrial Revolution, 1750–1850* (Hutchinson, 1971), pp. 98–9

**Source 2.33** *Leeds Intelligencer*, 22 September 1831, quoted in R. Tames (ed.), *Documents of the Industrial Revolution, 1750–1850* (Hutchinson, 1971), p. 99

**Source 2.34** *Report of Commissioners on the Employment of Children in Factories, Parliamentary Papers, 1833/XX*, quoted in G. M. Young and W. D. Handcock (eds), *English Historical Documents, XII (I), 1833–1874* (Eyre & Spottiswoode, 1956), pp. 938–9

**Source 2.35** Adapted from the *First Report of the Factory Commissioners, Parliamentary Papers, 1833/XX*, quoted in G. M. Young and W. D. Handcock (eds), *English Historical Documents, XII (I), 1833–1874* (Eyre & Spottiswoode, 1956), pp. 940–1

**Source 2.36** Adapted from Factories Regulation Act, 1833, quoted in G. M. Young and W. D. Handcock (eds), *English Historical Documents, XII (I), 1833–1874* (Eyre & Spottiswoode, 1956), pp. 949–52

**Source 2.37** Adapted from the Report of Leonard Horner, an Inspector of Factories, *Parliamentary Papers, 1837/XXXI*, quoted in G. M. Young and W. D. Handcock (eds), *English Historical Documents, XII (I), 1833–1874* (Eyre & Spottiswoode, 1956), pp. 957–66

**Source 2.38** Number of offences against the 1833 Factory Act brought in Lancashire, 1837, adapted from the Report of Leonard Horner, 18 January 1837, p. 48, *Reports of Inspectors for Half-Year ending 31 December 1836, Parliamentary Papers, 1837/XXXI*, quoted in U. Q. Henriques, *Before the Welfare State* (Longman, 1979), pp. 102–3

**Source 2.39** Report of J. T. Howell, an Inspector of Factories, *Parliamentary Papers, 1841–1842*, quoted in J. Simkin, *The Factory System* (Spartacus Educational, 1988), p. 16

**Source 2.40** Mrs Anna Jameson, *Memoirs and Essays, Illustrative of Arts, Literature, Social Morals*, 1846, quoted in R. Tames (ed.), *Documents of the Industrial Revolution, 1750–1850* (Hutchinson, 1971), pp. 96–9

**Source 2.41** Adapted from the *Report of Commissioners on the Employment of Children in Factories, Parliamentary Papers, 1833/XX*, quoted in G. M. Young and W. D. Handcock (eds), *English Historical Documents, XII (I), 1833–1874* (Eyre & Spottiswoode, 1956)

**Source 2.42** Evidence presented to the Select Committee on Combinations of Workmen, 1837–38, quoted in G. M. Young and W. D. Handcock (eds), *English Historical Documents, XII (I), 1833–1874* (Eyre & Spottiswoode, 1956)

**Source 2.43** Factory Inspectors' Report, *Parliamentary Papers, 1843*, quoted in V. Brendon, *The Age of Reform 1820–1850* (Hodder & Stoughton, 1994), p. 77

**Source 2.44** Speech by Lord Ashley in the House of Commons, 15 March 1844, quoted in V. Brendon, *The Age of Reform 1820–1850* (Hodder & Stoughton, 1994), p. 77

**Source 2.45** Friedrich Engels, *The Condition of the Working Class in England*, 1845 (Penguin edn, 1969)

**Source 2.46** Lord Ashley's introduction of the Ten Hour Bill, 29 January 1846, *Hansard*, quoted in N. Tonge and M. Quincey, *British Social and Economic History, 1800–1900* (Macmillan, 1980), pp. 59–60

**Source 2.47** Adapted from Fielden's Ten Hours Act, 1847, quoted in G. M. Young and W. D. Handcock (eds), *English Historical Documents, XII (I), 1833–1874* (Eyre & Spottiswoode, 1956), pp. 981–2

**Source 2.48** Growth of the cotton industry, 1829–96, from P. Deane and W. A. Cole, *British Economic Growth 1688–1959* (Cambridge University Press, 1969), p. 187

**Source 2.49** Adapted from Factory Inspectors' Report, *Parliamentary Papers, 1850*, quoted in G. M. Young and W. D. Handcock (eds), *English Historical Documents, XII (I), 1833–1874* (Eyre & Spottiswoode, 1956)

**Source 2.50** Report by Leonard Horner, *Parliamentary Papers, 1852–1853/XL*, quoted in G. M. Young and W. D. Handcock (eds), *English Historical Documents, XII (I), 1833–1874* (Eyre & Spottiswoode, 1956), p. 992

**Source 2.51** Age and sex distribution of cotton workers in textile factories, 1835–1901, from G. H. Wood, 'The Statistics of Wages in the Nineteenth Century: The Cotton Industry', *Journal of the Royal Statistical Society*, Vol. LXXIII, June 1910, p. 607

**Source 2.52** Proportion of females, young persons and children to males in the labour force in coal-mining in 1842, from the *First Report of the Commission on the Employment of Women and Children in Mines and Collieries, Parliamentary Papers, 1842/XM*, quoted in G. M. Young and W. D. Handcock (eds), *English Historical Documents, XII (I), 1833–1874* (Eyre & Spottiswoode, 1956), p. 972

**Source 2.53** Drawings accompanying the *First Report of the Commission on the Employment of Women and Children in Mines and Collieries, Parliamentary Papers, 1842*.

**Source 2.54** *Parliamentary Papers, 1842/XV*, p. 72, quoted in C. McNab and R. Mackenzie, *From Waterloo to the Great Exhibition, Britain 1815–1851* (Oliver & Boyd, 1982), p. 78

**Source 2.55** Children's Employment Commission, *Report on the Collieries and Iron Works in the East of Scotland, Parliamentary Papers, 1842/II*, quoted in C. McNab and R. Mackenzie, *From Waterloo to the Great Exhibition, Britain 1815–1851* (Oliver & Boyd, 1982), p. 78

**Source 2.56** *First Report of the Commission on the Employment of Women and Children in Mines and Collieries, Parliamentary Papers, 1842/XIII*, quoted in G. M. Young and W. D. Handcock (eds), *English Historical Documents, XII (I), 1833–1874* (Eyre & Spottiswoode, 1956), pp. 972–7

**Source 2.57** *The Sweater's Furnace: or, the real 'Curse' of labour*, an etching by Linley Sambourne and its accompanying text from *Punch*, 1888

**Source 2.58** *Fifth Report from the Select Committee of the House of Lords on the Sweating System, Parliamentary Papers, 1890/XVII*, quoted in W. H. B. Court, *British Economic History, 1870–1914* (Cambridge University Press, 1965), pp. 388–9

**Source 2.59** Richard Mudie Smith, *Sweated Industries*, a handbook of the *Daily News* Exhibition, 1906, pp. 118–19

**Source 2.60** Report on the Conference arranged by the National Anti-Sweating League, London, *The Times*, 25 October 1906

**Source 2.61** Edward Grey, *Cottage Life in a Hertfordshire Village*, quoted in T. May, *Agriculture and Rural Society in Britain, 1846–1914* (Edward Arnold, 1973), pp. 42–3

**Source 2.62** N. Philip, *Victorian Village Life* (Albion Press, 1973), p. 39

**Source 2.63** N. Philip, *Victorian Village Life* (Albion Press, 1973), p. 39

**Source 2.64** *Sixth Report of the Children's Employment Commission, Parliamentary Papers, 1867*, quoted in T. May, *Agriculture and Rural Society in Britain, 1846–1914* (Edward Arnold, 1973), pp. 42–3

## CHAPTER 3

**Source 3.1** a) Population growth in British towns 1801–61 and b) Percentage growth of population in British towns 1801–61, from D. Fraser, *The Evolution of the British Welfare State* (Macmillan, 1973), p. 52

**Acknowledgements to sources**

**Source 3.2** *Report of the Select Committee on the Health of Towns,* 1840, quoted in P. Lane, *Documents on British Economic and Social History, 1750–1870* (Macmillan, 1968), p. 42

**Source 3.3** Friedrich Engels, *The Condition of the Working Class in England,* 1845 (Penguin edn, 1969)

**Source 3.4** *Report on the Sanitary Condition of the Labouring Population, Lords Sessional Reports,* 1842, Vol. 26, p. 239, quoted in R. Tames (ed.), *Documents of the Industrial Revolution, 1750–1850* (Hutchinson, 1971), p. 135

**Source 3.5** Friedrich Engels, *The Condition of the Working Class in England,* 1845 (Penguin edn, 1969)

**Source 3.6** *A Court for King Cholera,* a cartoon from *Punch,* 25 September 1852

**Source 3.7** Dr James P. Kay, *The Moral and Physical Condition of the Working Classes Employed in the Cotton Manufacture of Manchester,* 1832 (Cass edn 1970, pp. 28–9, 77–82), quoted in E. Evans, *Social Policy 1830–1914, Individualism, Collectivism and the Origins of the Welfare State* (Routledge & Kegan Paul, 1978), pp. 73–4

**Source 3.8** *Leeds Intelligencer,* 21 August 1841, quoted in D. Fraser, *The Evolution of the British Welfare State* (Macmillan, 1973), p. 53

**Source 3.9** *Report of the Leeds Board of Health,* 1833, by Dr Robert Baker, District Surgeon, quoted in M. L. Pearce, *Sources in History, The Nineteenth Century* (Bell & Hyman, 1986), p. 41

**Source 3.10** Adapted from Edwin Chadwick, *Report on the Sanitary Condition of the Labouring Population of Great Britain,* 1842 (Edinburgh University Press edn, 1965), pp. 222–4

**Source 3.11** Average age at death according to region and social class, adapted from Edwin Chadwick, *Report on the Sanitary Condition of the Labouring Population of Great Britain,* 1842 (Edinburgh University Press edn, 1965), pp. 220–4

**Source 3.12** Number of deaths nationally from contagious and respiratory diseases, 1838–39, adapted from Edwin Chadwick, *Report on the Sanitary Condition of the Labouring Population of Great Britain,* 1842 (Edinburgh University Press edn, 1965), pp. 76–7

**Source 3.13** Comparison of the number of deaths from disease between rural and industrial counties, 1838, adapted from Edwin Chadwick, *Report on the Sanitary Condition of the Labouring Population of Great Britain,* 1842 (Edinburgh University Press edn, 1965), pp. 76–7

**Source 3.14** Edwin Chadwick, *Report on the Sanitary Condition of the Labouring Population of Great Britain,* 1842 (Edinburgh University Press edn, 1965), pp. 422–4

**Source 3.15** Edwin Chadwick, *Report on the Sanitary Condition of the Labouring Population of Great Britain,* 1842 (Edinburgh University Press edn, 1965), pp. 422–4

**Source 3.16** D. Fraser, *The Evolution of the British Welfare State* (Macmillan, 1973), p. 52, reproduced with permission of Palgrave

**Source 3.17** Dr Southwood Smith, Appendix C2 to the *Fifth Report of the Poor Law Commissioners, Parliamentary Papers, 1839/XX,* p. 118, quoted in G. M. Young and W. D. Handcock (eds), *English Historical Documents, XII (I), 1833–1874* (Eyre & Spottiswoode, 1956), pp. 768–9

**Source 3.18** Adapted from Edwin Chadwick, *Report on the Sanitary Condition of the Labouring Population of Great Britain,* 1842 (Edinburgh University Press edn, 1965), pp. 266–8

**Source 3.19** Edwin Chadwick, *Report on the Sanitary Condition of the Labouring Population of Great Britain,* 1842 (Edinburgh University Press edn, 1965), p. 147

**Source 3.20** W. A. Guy, 'The Sanitary Question', in *Fraser's Magazine,* Vol. XXXVI, 1847, p. 371, quoted in E. J. Evans, *Social Policy 1830–1914, Individualism, Collectivism and the Origins of the Welfare State* (Routledge & Kegan Paul, 1978), p. 79

**Source 3.21** *The Economist,* 1848, quoted in E. Hopkins, *A Social History of the English Working Classes, 1815–1945* (Arnold, 1979), p. 66

**Source 3.22** Report of the Parliamentary debate on Lord Morpeth's Bill, 1847, quoted in E. Hopkins, *A Social History of the English Working Classes, 1815–1945* (Arnold, 1979), p. 66

**Source 3.23** *The Times,* 22 February 1848, quoted in A. E. Bland, P. A. Brown, R. H. Tawney and G. Bell, *English Economic History: Select Documents* (Longman & Green, 1914)

**Source 3.24** Article in the *Leeds Mercury,* 1848, quoted in E. Hopkins, *A Social History of the English Working Classes, 1815–1945* (Arnold, 1979), p. 66

**Source 3.25** Chartist evidence to the General Board of Health Inquiry into the North Staffordshire Potteries District, *Parliamentary Papers, 1851,* quoted in A. E. Bland, P. A. Brown, R. H. Tawney and G. Bell, *English Economic History: Select Documents* (Longman & Green, 1914)

**Source 3.26** Thoresby Society (Leeds) 22B10, *Projected Leeds Waterworks,* quoted in D. Fraser, *The Evolution of the British Welfare State* (Macmillan, 1973), pp. 61–2

**Source 3.27** *Sanatory Measures. Lord Morpeth Throwing Pearls Before Aldermen,* a cartoon from *Punch,* 1848

**Source 3.28** K. Dawson and P. Wall, *Society and Industry in the Nineteenth Century, Vol. 6: Public Health and Housing* (by permission of Oxford University Press, 1970), p. 19

**Source 3.29** *Fraser's Magazine,* October 1848, quoted in D. Holman (ed.), *Portraits and Documents of the Earlier Nineteenth Century* (Hutchinson Educational)

**Source 3.30** *Report of the Board of Health,* July 1849, *Parliamentary Papers, 1849/XXIV,* quoted in G. M. Young and W. D. Handcock (eds), *English Historical Documents, XII (I), 1833–1874* (Eyre & Spottiswoode, 1956), pp. 794–5

**Source 3.31** *Leeds Intelligencer,* 7 July 1838, quoted in D. Fraser, *The Evolution of the British Welfare State* (Macmillan, 1973), p. 62

**Source 3.32** James Hole, *The Homes of the Working Classes,* 1866, p. 26, quoted in D. Fraser, *The Evolution of the British Welfare State* (Macmillan, 1973), p. 62

**Source 3.33** *The Times,* July 1854, quoted in C. Culpin, *Making Modern Britain* (Collins, 1987), p. 148

**Source 3.34** Letter from Edwin Chadwick to Lord Ashley, April 1844, quoted in R. A. Lewis, *Edwin Chadwick and the Public Health Movement, 1832–1854* (Longman, 1952), p. 27

**Source 3.35** From a journal for engineers and officials, 1856, quoted in R. A. Lewis, *Edwin Chadwick and the Public Health Movement, 1832–1854* (Longman, 1952), p. 396

**Source 3.36** 'Who is to blame for the Condition of the People?', extract from article in *The Economist,* 21 November 1846, quoted in D. Holman (ed.), *Portraits and Documents of the Earlier Nineteenth Century* (Hutchinson Educational)

**Source 3.37** 'Sanitary Consolidation – Centralisation – Local Self-government', *Quarterly Review* Vol. XXXVIII (1850), pp. 436–7, 441–2, quoted in E. Evans, *Social Policy 1830–1914, Individualism, Collectivism and the Origins of the Welfare State* (Routledge & Kegan Paul, 1978), pp. 80–1

**Source 3.38** *Report of the Board of Health on its Work, 1848–1854, Parliamentary Papers, 1854/XXXV,* pp. 48–4, quoted in G. M. Young and W. D. Handcock (eds), *English Historical Documents, XII (I), 1833–1874* (Eyre & Spottiswoode, 1956), pp. 807, 809

**Source 3.39** Movement in death-rate, 1811–75 (per thousand of the population), from B. R. Mitchell and P. Deane, *Abstract of British Historical Statistics* (Cambridge University Press, 1962), p. 6, and N. Tranter, *Population since the Industrial Revolution* (Croom Helm, 1973), p. 53

**Source 3.40** *Father Thames Introducing his Offspring to the Fair City of London,* a cartoon from *Punch,* July 1858

**Source 3.41** Excerpts from the Sanitary Act, 1866, quoted in E. Evans, *Social Policy 1830–1914, Individualism, Collectivism and the Origins of the Welfare State* (Routledge & Kegan Paul, 1978), pp. 85–6

**Source 3.42**  A. Briggs, *Victorian Cities* (Penguin/Pelican, 1968), p. 206

**Source 3.43**  Octavia Hill, *Homes of the London Poor*, 1875, quoted in K. Dawson and P. Wall, *Society and Industry in the Nineteenth Century*, Vol. 6: *Public Health and Housing* (Oxford University Press, 1970), pp. 26–7

**Source 3.44**  An article by the Earl of Shaftesbury in *Fortnightly Review*, 1883, quoted in E. Evans, *Social Policy 1830–1914, Individualism, Collectivism and the Origins of the Welfare State* (Routledge & Kegan Paul, 1978), pp. 180–1

**Source 3.45**  *The Times*, 1 December 1865, quoted in D. Holman (ed.), *Portraits and Documents of the Earlier Nineteenth Century* (Hutchinson Educational)

**Source 3.46**  *The Times*, 25 August 1875, quoted in K. Dawson and P. Wall, *Society and Industry in the Nineteenth Century*, Vol. 6: *Public Health and Housing* (Oxford University Press, 1970), pp. 28–9

**Source 3.47**  Memoirs of Viscount Richard Cross, *A Political History 1868–1900*, privately published 1903, pp. 33–4

**Source 3.48**  Act for Facilitating the Improvement of the Dwellings of the Working Classes in Large Towns, 1875, Part 1, Clause 3, quoted in G. M. Young and W. D. Handcock (eds), *English Historical Documents, XII (II), 1874–1914* (Eyre & Spottiswoode, 1956), p. 615

**Source 3.49**  Report of the Charity Organisation Society, *Dwellings of the Poor*, 1881, p. 17, quoted in M. Willis, *Nineteenth Century Britain, 1815–1914* (Blackwell Education, 1990), p. 66

**Source 3.50**  Fall in death-rates in slum-cleared areas of Birmingham, 1873–80, from the *Report of Birmingham City Improvement Committee*, 1882, quoted in K. Dawson and P. Wall, *Society and Industry in the Nineteenth Century*, Vol. 6: *Public Health and Housing* (Oxford University Press, 1970), p. 33

**Source 3.51**  *Report of the Royal Commission into the Housing Crisis, Parliamentary Papers, 1884–85/XXX*, pp. 23–4, 40, 60, quoted in E. Evans, *Social Policy 1830–1914, Individualism, Collectivism and the Origins of the Welfare State* (Routledge & Kegan Paul, 1978), pp. 182–3

**Source 3.52**  Movement in death-rate, 1846–1915 (per thousand of the population), from B. R. Mitchell and P. Deane, *Abstract of British Historical Statistics* (Cambridge University Press, 1961), p. 6

**Source 3.53**  Movement in death-rate, 1838–1914 (per thousand of the adult and infant population), from E. Hobsbawm, *Industry and Empire* (Penguin/Pelican, 1969), p. 160

**Source 3.54**  Percentage reduction in deaths from diseases by 1901, compared with 1848–54, from T. McKeown, *The Modern Rise of Population* (Edward Arnold, 1976)

## CHAPTER 4

**Source 4.1**  *Parliamentary Papers, 1830–31/VIII*, pp. 26–7, 186, quoted in E. J. Hobsbawm and G. Rudé, *Captain Swing* (Lawrence & Wishart, 1969), p. 43

**Source 4.2**  William Cobbett, *Rural Rides*, 20 October 1825 (1830; Dent edn, 1912), p. 266

**Source 4.3**  Report of the Standing Committee on Poor Laws, 1830–41, pp. 26–7, quoted in E. J. Hobsbawm and G. Rudé, *Captain Swing* (Lawrence & Wishart, 1969), p. 46

**Source 4.4**  Rev. D. Davies, *The Case of the Labourers in Husbandry*, 1795, pp. 55–7, quoted in G. D. H. Cole and A. W. Filson, *British Working Class Movements, Selected Documents 1789–1875*

**Source 4.5**  Arthur Young, *An Inquiry into the Propriety of Applying Wastes to Better Maintenance and Support of the Poor*, Bury, 1801, pp. 21–5, 37ff, quoted in K. Dawson and P. Wall, *Society and Industry in the Nineteenth Century*, Vol. 5: *The Problem of Poverty* (Oxford University Press, 1969), p. 11

**Source 4.6**  William Cobbett, *Rural Rides* (1830; Dent edn, 1912)

**Source 4.7**  *The Agricultural State of England*, 1816, pp. 41, 303, quoted in R. Brown, *Change and Continuity in British Society, 1800–1850* (Cambridge University Press, 1987), p. 66

**Source 4.8**  The decline in migration from south-eastern and eastern counties to London, 1751–1831, from P. Deane and W. A. Cole, *British Economic Growth, 1688–1959* (Cambridge University Press, 1962), quoted in E. J. Hobsbawm and G. Rudé, *Captain Swing* (Lawrence & Wishart, 1969), p. 43

**Source 4.9**  *Report from the Commissioners on the Poor Laws, Report of Alfred Power*, Appendix A, Part 1, pp. 246A–249A, 1834, quoted in R. Brown, *Change and Continuity in British Society, 1800–1850* (Cambridge University Press, 1987), p. 126

**Source 4.10**  A letter from the overseers of Portsea to the overseers of St Peters, Winchester, 16 May 1822, stating the case of John Taylor for relief, from *Poverty Winchester*, Archive Resource Collection, WP19, Hampshire Record Office

**Source 4.11**  William Jackson to the Home Secretary, 1817, *Home Office Papers, 42/160*, quoted in J. L. Hammond and B. Hammond, *The Skilled Labourer* (Longman, 1979), p. 197

**Source 4.12**  Robert Owen, *A New View of Society and Other Writings*, 1813 (Dent edn, 1972), quoted in S. Mason, *Social Problems 1760–1914* (Blackwell History Project, 1986), p. 37

**Source 4.13**  *Report of a Parliamentary Committee*, 1827, quoted in S. Mason, *Social Problems 1760–1914* (Blackwell History Project, 1986), p. 37

**Source 4.14**  William Dodd, *Letters from Leeds*, 18 January 1842, quoted in S. Mason, *Social Problems 1760–1914* (Blackwell History Project, 1986), p. 37

**Source 4.15**  Expenditure on poor relief, 1812–33, in relation to the state of the harvest and the incidence of riot, compiled by the author on the basis of a selection of statistics including those for poor relief from J. D. Marshall, *The Old Poor Law, 1795–1834* (Macmillan, 1968), Table 1, p. 26

**Source 4.16**  Composition of the pauper population by age showing the proportion of elderly, able-bodied and children to the total, 1802–03, adapted by the author from J. D. Marshall, *The Old Poor Law, 1795–1834* (Macmillan, 1968), Table 2, p. 34

**Source 4.17**  Comparison of the composition of the pauper population between agricultural and industrial areas, 1802–03, compiled from *Abstract of Returns relative to the Expense and Maintenance of the Poor, 1802–1803*

**Source 4.18**  Adapted by the author from *Statutes of the Realm, 39 Eliz. I, c.3*; the Elizabethan Poor Law, 1598, modified 1601

**Source 4.19**  *Reading Mercury*, 11 May 1795, quoted in K. Dawson and P. Wall, *Society and Industry in the Nineteenth Century*, Vol. 5: *The Problem of Poverty* (Oxford University Press, 1969), p. 12

**Source 4.20**  Evidence of Rev. Philip Hunt, *Select Committee on Labourers' Wages – Report VI*, 1824, quoted in M. E. Rose, *The English Poor Law, 1780–1930* (David & Charles, 1971), p. 56

**Source 4.21**  Evidence of Thomas Bowyer, *Select Committee on Labourers' Wages – Report VI*, 1824, quoted in M. E. Rose, *The English Poor Law, 1780–1930* (David & Charles, 1971), p. 56

**Source 4.22**  Evidence of Henry Boyce, *Select Committee on the Employment or Relief of Able-Bodied Persons – Report IV*, 1828, quoted in M. E. Rose, *The English Poor Law, 1780–1930* (David & Charles, 1971), p. 60

**Source 4.23**  *Report from the Commissioners on the Poor Laws, Report of J. D. Tweedy*, Appendix A, Part 1, 1834, quoted in M. E. Rose, *The English Poor Law, 1780–1930* (David & Charles, 1971), p. 59

**Source 4.24**  Isaac Wiseman, *Norwich Mercury*, 7 March 1829, quoted in K. Dawson and P. Wall, *Society and Industry in the Nineteenth Century*, Vol. 5: *The Problem of Poverty* (Oxford University Press, 1969), p. 13

**Source 4.25**  Sturges-Bourne Act to amend the laws for the relief of the poor, 31 March 1819, quoted in M. E. Rose, *The English Poor Law, 1780–1930* (David & Charles, 1971), pp. 67–8

**Source 4.26**  Evidence of Lister Ellis, *Select Committee on the Employment or Relief of Able-Bodied Persons – Report IV*, 1828, quoted in M. E. Rose, *The English Poor Law, 1780–1930* (David & Charles, 1971), p. 69

**Source 4.27** Approximate cost of poor relief, 1760–1832, compiled by the author from a range of sources including *Select Committee on Poor Rate Returns – Report V*, Appendix A, 1828, and from J. D. Marshall, *The Old Poor Law, 1795–1834* (Macmillan, 1968), Table 1, p. 26

**Source 4.28** Thomas Robert Malthus, *First Essay on Population*, 1798 (Macmillan edn, 1926), pp. 83–99

**Source 4.29** Patrick Colquhoun, *A Treatise on Indigence*, 1806, quoted in M. E. Rose, *The English Poor Law 1780–1930* (David & Charles, 1971), pp. 47–8

**Source 4.30** Rev. T. Thorp, *Individual Vice, Social Sin*, 1832, p. 14, quoted in Schools Council History 13–16 Project – *Britain 1815–1851* (Holmes McDougall, 1977), p. 104

**Source 4.31** *The Times*, 30 May 1816, quoted in R. Brown, *Change and Continuity in British Society, 1800–1850* (Cambridge University Press, 1987), p. 67

**Source 4.32** *Report from the Commissioners on the Poor Laws*, Appendix A, Part I, p. 682A, 1834, quoted in R. Brown, *Change and Continuity in British Society, 1800–1850* (Cambridge University Press, 1987), p. 124

**Source 4.33** S. G. Checkland and E. O. A. Checkland (eds), *The Poor Law Report of 1834* (Penguin, 1974), p. 355

**Source 4.34** William Cobbett, *Two-Penny Trash*, Vol. 1, no. 6, December 1830, p. 137

**Source 4.35** William Cobbett, *Political Register*, 14 December 1833, quoted in K. Dawson and P. Wall, *Society and Industry in the Nineteenth Century*, Vol. 5: *The Problem of Poverty* (Oxford University Press, 1969), pp. 16–17

**Source 4.36** Adapted from *Main Recommendations of the Poor Law Commissioners of 1834*, Appendix A, HMSO, 1905, quoted in G. M. Young and W. D. Handcock (eds), *English Historical Documents, XII (I), 1833–1874* (Eyre & Spottiswoode, 1956)

**Source 4.37** W. H. Hudson, *A Shepherd's Life*, 1910, quoted in R. Brown, *Change and Continuity in British Society, 1800–1850* (Cambridge University Press, 1987), p. 42

**Source 4.38** Adapted from *Main Recommendations of the Poor Law Commissioners of 1834*, HMSO, 1905, pp. 227–8, 240–1, 257–61, 261–2, 294–7, 306–14, 319–57, quoted in G. M. Young and W. D. Handcock (eds), *English Historical Documents, XII (I), 1833–1874* (Eyre & Spottiswoode, 1956)

**Source 4.39** Causes of the 1830 Swing riots, compiled from Rural Question 53, *Report of the Royal Commission on the Poor Law*, Vol. XXXIV, 1834, HMSO, quoted in E. J. Hobsbawm and G. Rudé, *Captain Swing* (Lawrence & Wishart, 1969), p. 43

**Source 4.40** Adapted from *Main Recommendations of the Poor Law Commissioners of 1834*, HMSO, 1905, pp. 53–4, 64, 78–9, 89–90, 96

**Source 4.41** Adapted from *Main Recommendations of the Poor Law Commissioners of 1834*, HMSO, 1905, pp. 227–8, 240–1, 257–61, 261–2, 294–7, 306–14, 319–57, quoted in G. M. Young and W. D. Handcock (eds), *English Historical Documents, XII (I), 1833–1874* (Eyre & Spottiswoode, 1956), pp. 697–9

**Source 4.42** Adapted from *Main Recommendations of the Poor Law Commissioners of 1834*, HMSO, 1905, pp. 227–8, 240–1, 257–61, 261–2, 294–7, 306–14, 319–57, quoted in G. M. Young and W. D. Handcock (eds), *English Historical Documents, XII (I), 1833–1874* (Eyre & Spottiswoode, 1956), pp. 700, 701–2

**Source 4.43** Adapted from *Main Recommendations of the Poor Law Commissioners of 1834*, HMSO, 1905, pp. 227–8, 240–1, 257–61, 261–2, 294–7, 306–14, 319–57, quoted in G. M. Young and W. D. Handcock (eds), *English Historical Documents, XII (I), 1833–1874* (Eyre & Spottiswoode, 1956), pp. 702–4, 704–5, 705–7

## CHAPTER 5

**Source 5.1** Letter from Nassau Senior to George Villiers, 1 December 1835, in Sir Herbert Maxwell, *Life and Letters of the Fourth Earl of Clarendon*, 1913, quoted in K. Dawson and P. Wall, *Society and Industry in the Nineteenth Century*, Vol. 5: *The Problem of Poverty* (Oxford University Press, 1969), p. 25

**Source 5.2** Letter from Edwin Chadwick to the Clerk of the Poor Law Guardians, St Luke Chelsea, 27 May 1843, quoted in Poor Law Commission, *Ninth Annual Report*, 1843

**Source 5.3** T. M. Loveland, Clerk to the Board of Guardians, St Luke Chelsea, to the Poor Law Commissioners, 15 June 1843, quoted in Poor Law Commission, *Ninth Annual Report*, 1843

**Source 5.4** *Operations of the Poor Law Amendment Act in the County of Sussex*, 1836, pp. 8–11, quoted in M. E. Rose, *The English Poor Law 1780–1930* (David & Charles, 1971), pp. 105–97

**Source 5.5** *Andover Workhouse Papers*, Archive Resource Collection, AW 12, Hampshire Record Office

**Source 5.6** Poor Law Commission, *Second Annual Report*, Appendix B, No. 9, 1836, quoted in M. E. Rose, *The English Poor Law 1780–1930* (David & Charles, 1971), pp. 103–5

**Source 5.7** Cost of poor relief, 1760–1853, compiled by the author on the basis of statistics from the *Select Committee on Poor Law Returns – Report V*, Appendix A, 1828, and from Poor Law Commission, *Fourteenth Annual Report*, Appendix B, No. 2, 1848, quoted in M. E. Rose, *The English Poor Law 1780–1930* (David & Charles, 1971), p. 128.

**Source 5.8** Comparison of the cost of a) poor relief expenditure for England and Wales with b) the expenditure of the Andover Union, compiled by the author on the basis of statistics from *Appendix to the Report from the Select Committee on the Andover Union*, 1846, Andover Workhouse Papers, Archive Resource Collection, AW 32, Hampshire Record Office and from Poor Law Commission, *Fourteenth Annual Report*, Appendix B, No. 2, 1848, quoted in M. E. Rose, *The English Poor Law 1780–1930* (David & Charles, 1971), pp. 128–9

**Source 5.9** Committals for rural 'protest' crimes in England and Wales, from *Returns, Criminal Offenders, Parliamentary Papers, 1835/XLV; 1841/XVIII; 1851/XLVI*, quoted in J. Knott, *Popular Opposition to the 1834 Poor Law* (Croom Helm, 1986), Table 3.1, 1828–50, p. 78

**Source 5.10** From *Appendix to the Report from the Select Committee on the Andover Union*, 1846, Andover Workhouse Papers, Archive Resource Collection, AW 25, Hampshire Record Office

**Source 5.11** *Regulations Governing Life in the Southampton Workhouse*, Archive Resource Collection, Hampshire Record Office

**Source 5.12** Poor Law Commission, *Seventh Annual Report*, 1841, *Parliamentary Papers, 1842/XIX*, pp. 47–53, quoted in G. M. Young and W. D. Handcock (eds), *English Historical Documents, XII (I), 1833–1874* (Eyre & Spottiswoode, 1956), pp. 725–6

**Source 5.13** Andover Workhouse Papers, 1839, Archive Resource Collection, AW 30, Hampshire Record Office

**Source 5.14** Comparison of a typical Tuesday diet in a pre- and post-1834 workhouse, compiled by the author on the basis of evidence from the Poor Law Commission, *Second Annual Report*, *Parliamentary Papers, 1836/XXIX*, pp. 56–9, quoted in G. M. Young & W. D. Handcock (eds), *English Historical Documents, XII (I), 1833–1874* (Eyre & Spottiswoode, 1956), p. 710, and from a *Bill of Fare for the House of Industry in the Isle of Wight, 1804–06*, Archive Resource Collection, Hampshire Records Office

**Source 5.15** A. Dickens, 'The Architect and the Workhouse', *Architectural Review*, No. 160, 1976, p. 347

**Source 5.16** *Interior of an English workhouse under the New Poor Law Act*, 1837, Public Records Office

**Source 5.17**   Poor Law Commission, *Third Annual Report, Parliamentary Papers, 1837/XXXI*, quoted in G. M. Young and W. D. Handcock (eds), *English Historical Documents, XII (I), 1833–1874* (Eyre & Spottiswoode, 1956), pp. 711–14

**Source 5.18**   Employment levels amongst different trades in Bolton, 1836 and 1842, from E. J. Hobsbawm, 'The British Standard of Living, 1790–1850', *Economic History Review*, compiled from H. Ashworth, 'Statistics of the present depression of trade in Bolton', *Journal of the Statistical Society*, Vol. 5, 1842, p. 74, quoted in M. Willis, *Nineteenth Century Britain, 1815–1914* (Blackwell, 1990), p. 17

**Source 5.19**   Richard Oastler, *Damnation! Eternal Damnation to the Fiend-Begotten Coarser Food New Poor Law* (Hetherington, London, 1837)

**Source 5.20**   a) Charles Dickens, *The Adventures of Oliver Twist*, 1838, pp. 8–19, and b) cartoon by George Cruikshank, *Oliver Twist Asking for More*, 1838

**Source 5.21**   *Northern Star*, 10 March 1838, quoted in Schools Council History 13–16 Project – *Britain 1815–1851* (Holmes McDougall, 1977), pp. 74–5

**Source 5.22**   George Tinker, *The State of the Huddersfield Union*, Public Records Office, MH12/15063, quoted in M. E. Rose, *The English Poor Law 1780–1930* (David & Charles, 1971), pp. 119–20

**Source 5.23**   Support for the anti-Poor-Law movement in South Lancashire, 1838, compiled from *The Times*, 7 February 1838, *Northern Star*, 10 February 1838, and D. Jones, *Chartism and the Chartists* (Allen Lane, 1975), p. 87

**Source 5.24**   Poor Law Commission, *Fourth Annual Report, Parliamentary Papers, 1838*, quoted in K. Dawson and P. Wall, *Society and Industry in the Nineteenth Century*, Vol. 5: *The Problem of Poverty* (Oxford University Press, 1969), pp. 34–5

**Source 5.25**   A contemporary drawing from the *Illustrated London News*, August 1842, entitled *An Attack on the Workhouse at Stockport*

**Source 5.26**   Poor Law Commission, *Letter on the Outdoor Labour Test Order, Parliamentary Papers, 1842/XIX*, pp. 105–6, quoted in G. M. Young and W. D. Handcock (eds), *English Historical Documents, XII (I), 1833–1874* (Eyre & Spottiswoode, 1956), pp. 726–8

**Source 5.27**   Poor Law Commission, *Outdoor Relief Regulation Order, Parliamentary Papers, 1844*, pp. 309–12, 317–18, quoted in M. E. Rose, *The English Poor Law 1780–1930* (David & Charles, 1971), p. 143

**Source 5.28**   N. Edsall, *The Anti-Poor-Law Movement, 1834–1844* (Manchester University Press, 1971)

**Source 5.29**   J. Knott, *Popular Opposition to the 1834 Poor Law* (Croom Helm, 1986)

**Source 5.30**   William Day Esq., correspondence with the Poor Law Commissioners, *Parliamentary Papers, 1844*, pp. 23–9, quoted in M. E. Rose, *The English Poor Law 1780–1930* (David & Charles, 1971), pp. 123–4

**Source 5.31**   *Report from the Select Committee on the Andover Union, Parliamentary Papers, 1846/V*, quoted in E. C. Midwinter, *Victorian Social Reform*, Seminar Studies in History (Longman, 1968), pp. 76–7

**Source 5.32**   Cartoon from the *Penny Satirist*, No. 438, 6 September 1845, Vol. 8, Hampshire Record Office

**Source 5.33**   *Report from the Select Committee on the Andover Union, Parliamentary Papers, 1846/V*, quoted in M. E. Rose, *The English Poor Law 1780–1930* (David & Charles, 1971), pp. 127–31

**Source 5.34**   Sir George Grey, Home Secretary, May 1847, *Hansard*, 3rd Series, Vol. XCII, Cols 341–3

**Source 5.35**   Persistence of outdoor relief, 1840–1900, compiled by the author from Poor Law Commission, *Fourteenth Annual Report*, Appendix B, No. 2, *Parliamentary Papers, 1848*, quoted in M. E. Rose, *The English Poor Law, 1780–1930* (David & Charles 1971), pp. 128–9, and Local Government Board, *Thirty-First Annual Report*, 1901–02, Appendix E, p. 312, quoted in M. E. Rose, *The Relief of Poverty, 1834–1914*, Studies in Economic History (Macmillan, 1972), p. 53

**Source 5.36**   a) Number of paupers relieved in England and Wales, 1840–1900, and b) total Poor Law expenditure compared with population growth, 1821–91, compiled by the author on the basis of statistics from K. Williams, *From Pauperism to Poverty* (Routledge & Kegan Paul, 1981), Statistical Appendix, pp. 145–235, and from B. R. Mitchell and P. Deane, *Abstract of British Historical Statistics* (Cambridge University Press, 1962), p. 8

**Source 5.37**   P. Murray, *Poverty and Welfare 1830–1914* (Hodder & Stoughton, 1999), pp. 62–3

**Source 5.38**   J. Walvin, *Victorian Values* (André Deutsch, 1987), p. 99

**Source 5.39**   a) *A Quaker soup kitchen*, from the *Illustrated London News*, 1862 and b) *Refuge for the Destitute* from the *Illustrated London News*, 1843

**Source 5.40**   Charity Organisation Society, *Eighth Annual Report*, Appendix iv, 1876, pp. 24–5, quoted in D. Fraser, *The Evolution of the British Welfare State* (Macmillan, 1973), p. 249

**Source 5.41**   *Report from the Select Committee on Pawnbrokers, Parliamentary Papers, 1879*, quoted in J. H. Treble, *Urban Poverty in Britain, 1830–1914* (Routledge, 1979), p. 132

**Source 5.42**   Thomas Wright, *Our New Masters*, 1873, p. 43, quoted in J. H. Treble, *Urban Poverty in Britain, 1830–1914* (Routledge, 1979), p. 10

**Source 5.43**   Olive C. Malvery, *The Soul Market*, 6th edn, p. 69, quoted in J. H. Treble, *Urban Poverty in Britain, 1830–1914* (Routledge, 1979), p. 134

**Source 5.44**   E. P. Thompson and E. Yeo (eds), *The Unknown Mayhew*, 1973, p. 259, quoted in J. H. Treble, *Urban Poverty in Britain, 1830–1914* (Routledge, 1979), p. 94

**Source 5.45**   L. Lees, *Exiles of Erin* (Manchester University Press, 1979), p. 83, quoted in A. Davin, *Growing up Poor* (Rivers Oram, 1996)

**Source 5.46**   Poor Law Board, *Seventeenth Annual Report*, Appendix No. 3, 1864–65, *Parliamentary Papers, 1865*, quoted in M. E. Rose, *The English Poor Law, 1780–1930* (David & Charles, 1971), pp. 159–60

**Source 5.47**   Charles Booth, *Life and Labour of the People in London*, Third Series, 1902, Vol. 5, pp. 217–18, quoted in K. Dawson and P. Wall, *Society and Industry in the Nineteenth Century*, Vol. 5: *The Problem of Poverty* (Oxford University Press, 1969), p. 42

**Source 5.48**   Report of the *Lancet* Sanitary Commission for Investigating the State of the Infirmaries of Workhouses, 1866, quoted in M. E. Rose, *The English Poor Law, 1780–1930* (David & Charles, 1971), pp. 174–5

**Source 5.49**   Poor Law Board, *Twenty-First Annual Report*, Appendix A, No. 5, 1868–69, *Parliamentary Papers, 1869*, quoted in M. E. Rose, *The English Poor Law, 1780–1930* (David & Charles, 1971), pp. 175–6

**Source 5.50**   *Report of the Royal Commission on the Aged Poor, Parliamentary Papers, 1895*, quoted in K. Dawson and P. Wall, *Society and Industry in the Nineteenth Century*, Vol. 5: *The Problem of Poverty* (Oxford University Press, 1969), p. 40

**Source 5.51**   A photograph of St Pancras Workhouse, London, 1895, Mary Evans Picture Library

**Source 5.52**   Report of a departmental committee, 1894–96, quoted in K. Dawson and P. Wall, *Society and Industry in the Nineteenth Century*, Vol. 5: *The Problem of Poverty* (Oxford University Press, 1969), p. 38

**Source 5.53** Charles Booth, *Life and Labour of the People of London*, 1892, Vol. 2, pp. 20–1, 146–7, quoted in D. Fraser, *The Evolution of the British Welfare State* (Macmillan, 1973), p. 250

**Source 5.54** Charles Booth, *Life and Labour of the People of London*, 1892, Vol. 2, quoted in W. H. Court, *British Economic History, 1870–1914: Commentary and Documents* (Cambridge University Press, 1966), pp. 291, 292–3

**Source 5.55** a) Distribution of the different classes in London, 1892, and b) Causes of poverty in the East End of London, 1892, compiled by author from Charles Booth, *Life and Labour of the People of London*, 1892, Vol. 2

**Source 5.56** B. S. Rowntree, *Poverty: A Study of Town Life*, 1901, pp. 120–1, 136–8, 295–8, 304–5, quoted in M. E. Rose, *The English Poor Law, 1780–1930* (David & Charles, 1971), pp. 242–5

**Source 5.57** Reasons for poverty among the population of York living under the primary poverty line, 1901, compiled by the author on the basis of statistics from B. S. Rowntree, *Poverty: A Study of Town Life*, 1901, pp. 120–1, 136–8, 295–8, 304–5, quoted in M. E. Rose, *The English Poor Law, 1780–1930* (David & Charles, 1971), pp. 242–5

**Source 5.58** Paupers relieved as a percentage of total population, 1840–1900, compiled by author on the basis of statistics from Poor Law Commission, *Fourteenth Annual Report*, Appendix B, No. 2, *Parliamentary Papers, 1848* and from Local Government Board, *Thirty-First Annual Report, 1901–1902*, Appendix E, p. 312

**Source 5.59** B. S. Rowntree, *Poverty: A Study of Town Life*, 1901, p. 167, quoted in D. Read (ed.), *Documents from Edwardian England* (Harrap), p. 203

## CHAPTER 6

**Source 6.1** *Manchester Guardian*, 7 November 1904, quoted in C. Wrigley, *David Lloyd George and the British Labour Movement* (Harvester Press, 1976), p. 26

**Source 6.2** Lloyd George's speech in Cardiff, 11 October 1906, quoted in S. Maccoby, *English Radicalism – the End?* (Allen & Unwin, 1961)

**Source 6.3** Letter to *The Times*, 5 December 1911

**Source 6.4** *Rich Fare*, a cartoon from *Punch*, 28 April 1909

**Source 6.5** W. J. Braithwaite, *Lloyd George's Ambulance Wagon: the Memoirs of William J. Braithwaite* (Methuen, 1957), pp. 62–4

**Source 6.6** A speech by Winston Churchill, reported in *The Times*, 12 October 1906

**Source 6.7** A letter to the *Nation*, 7 March 1908, quoted in K. O. Morgan, *The Age of Lloyd George* (Allen and Unwin, 1971), pp. 146–7

**Source 6.8** T. B. Macaulay, 'Essay on Southey', *Edinburgh Review*, January 1830, quoted in R. D. H. Seaman, *The Liberals and the Welfare State* (Edward Arnold, 1968), p. 9

**Source 6.9** Adapted from an article in the *Economist*, May 1848, quoted in R. D. H. Seaman, *The Liberals and the Welfare State* (Edward Arnold, 1968), p. 9

**Source 6.10** Adapted from J. S. Mill, *Utilitarianism*, 1863, Ch. 2, quoted in R. D. H. Seaman, *The Liberals and the Welfare State* (Edward Arnold, 1968), p. 9

**Source 6.11** Viscount Morley, *Life of Gladstone*, Book V, Ch. 4 (Edward Arnold, 1908)

**Source 6.12** Letter to *The Times*, 3 October 1906

**Source 6.13** Helen Bosanquet, *The Poor Law Report of 1909* (Macmillan, 1909)

**Source 6.14** Adapted from Sidney and Beatrice Webb, *English Poor Law Policy* (Longman, 1910), quoted in W. H. Court, *British Economic History, 1870–1940* (Cambridge University Press, 1966)

**Source 6.15** Adapted from Sidney and Beatrice Webb, *English Poor Law Policy*, 1910, quoted in W. H. Court, *British Economic History, 1870–1940* (Cambridge University Press, 1966)

**Source 6.16** Adapted from A. S. Arkle, *The Condition of the Liverpool School Children*, 1907, quoted in S. Webb and B. Webb, *English Local Government*, Part II, Vol. II (Longman & Green, 1929)

**Source 6.17** Letter by a Surrey rector, *The Times*, 5 October 1906

**Source 6.18** Adapted from the *Report of the Select Committee on Physical Deterioration*, 1904, quoted in R. Pope, B. Hoyle and A. Pratt, *Social Welfare in Britain* (Croom Helm, 1986)

**Source 6.19** A report of the Norwich City Council, *Norwich Mercury*, 22 September 1905

**Source 6.20** Parliamentary speech by Sir H. Clark, MP, in a debate on the School Meals Bill, *The Times*, 7 and 8 December 1906

**Source 6.21** Board of Education Circular 576, 22 November 1907, quoted in R. D. H. Seaman, *The Liberals and the Welfare State* (Edward Arnold, 1968), p. 26

**Source 6.22** Board of Education Circular 596, 17 August 1908, quoted in R. D. H. Seaman, *The Liberals and the Welfare State* (Edward Arnold, 1968), p. 29

**Source 6.23** A speech by the Lord Mayor of London in 1907 on the evils affecting young juveniles, quoted in C. E. Lawrence, *William Purdie Treloar* (Murray, 1925), p. 84

**Source 6.24** Report of the exploitation of children for illegal purposes, *The Times*, 1 October 1906

**Source 6.25** Viscount Samuel, *Memoirs* (Cresset Press, 1945), pp. 53, 54ff

**Source 6.26** Poor Law Board, *Twenty-Second Annual Report*, Appendix A, No. 4, *Parliamentary Papers, 1869–1870*, quoted in M. E. Rose, *The English Poor Law 1780–1930* (David & Charles, 1971), pp. 226–7

**Source 6.27** Adapted from George Lansbury, *My Life*, 1931, quoted in W. H. Court, *British Economic History, 1870–1914* (Cambridge University Press, 1966), p. 377

**Source 6.28** Mrs Barnett, *Canon Barnett*, 1919, Vol. II, p. 282, quoted in R. D. H. Seaman, *The Liberals and the Welfare State* (Edward Arnold, 1968), p. 32

**Source 6.29** Charles Booth, *Pauperism and the Endowment of Old Age* (Macmillan, 1892), p. 133

**Source 6.30** A. G. Gardner, *The Life of George Cadbury* (Cassell, 1923), p. 126

**Source 6.31** A. G. Gardner, *The Life of George Cadbury* (Cassell, 1923), p. 223

**Source 6.32** a) *Hansard*, May 1908, quoted in R. D. H. Seaman, *The Liberals and the Welfare State* (Edward Arnold, 1968), p. 35; b) Old Age Pensions Act, 1908, quoted in L. Butler and H. Jones (eds), *Britain in the Twentieth Century, Vol. 1, 1900–1939* (Heinemann, 1994), p. 21

**Source 6.33** David Lloyd George, *Hansard* (4th series), CXC, Cols 584–6, 15 June 1908, quoted in E. J. Evans, *Social Policy 1830–1914* (Routledge & Kegan Paul, 1978), p. 274

**Source 6.34** A letter by C. H. T. Crosthwaite, *The Times*, 3 July 1908

**Source 6.35** Parliamentary speech by Arthur Balfour, reported in *The Times*, 2 July 1908

**Source 6.36** Criticism of the Liberal decision to introduce a non-contributory pension scheme, *The Times*, 4 July 1908

**Source 6.37** *Diaries of Charles Hobhouse*, Financial Secretary to the Treasury in 1909, published in 1977, quoted in G. M. Young and W. D. Handcock (eds), *English Historical Documents XII* (Eyre & Spottiswoode, 1956)

**Source 6.38** Lloyd George's Budget speech, *Hansard*, 29 April 1909, Series 5, Vol. 4, pp. 474–548, quoted in M. Willis, *Nineteenth Century Britain, 1815–1914* (Blackwell Education, 1990), p. 97

**Source 6.39** *Forced Fellowship*, a cartoon from *Punch*, 27 October 1909

**Source 6.40** A speech by the Leader of the Opposition, Arthur Balfour, *The Times*, 8 May 1909

**Source 6.41** D. Lloyd George MP, *Better Times, Speeches* (Hodder & Stoughton, 1910), pp. 150–1

**Source 6.42** *The Times*, 10 October 1909, quoted in D. Fraser, *The Evolution of the British Welfare State* (Macmillan, 1973), p. 256

**Source 6.43** A speech by Lord Lansdowne in the House of Lords, *Hansard*, 22 November 1909, Series 5, Vol. 4, p. 733, quoted in J. H. Bettey, *English Historical Documents, 1906–1939* (Routledge & Kegan Paul, 1967)

**Source 6.44** Questioning the legality of plans to curb the power of the Lords, *The Times*, 30 November 1909

**Source 6.45** H. H. Asquith in the House of Commons, 2 December 1909, quoted in G. M. Young and W. D. Handcock (eds), *English Historical Documents, XII* (Eyre & Spottiswoode, 1956)

**Source 6.46** General Election results 1900–10, from D. Butler and J. Freeman (eds), *British Political Facts 1900–1960* (Macmillan, 1963), p. 122

**Source 6.47** Parliament Act, 1911 (1 & 2 Geo. V, c. 13), quoted in E. N. Williams, *A Documentary History of England, Vol. 2, 1559–1931* (Penguin/Pelican, 1965), pp. 265–6

**Source 6.48** *Norwich Mercury*, 9 January 1909

**Source 6.49** Describing old age pensions and the aged in workhouses, *The Times*, 11 November 1911

**Source 6.50** Flora Thompson, *Lark Rise to Candleford* (Oxford University Press, 1939), p. 95

**Source 6.51** *The New Year's Gift*, a cartoon from *Punch*, 6 January 1909

**Source 6.52** Pauperism in London, 1908–11, from a report on the Returns of Pauperism in London, *The Times*, 18 October 1911

**Source 6.53** R. Roberts, *The Classic Slum: Salford Life in the First Quarter of the Century* (University of Manchester Press, 1971)

**Source 6.54** G. Haw, *From Workhouse to Westminster: the Life Story of Will Crooks*, 1907, pp. 47–8, 51–2, quoted in W. H. Court, *British Economic History, 1870–1914* (Cambridge University Press, 1963), p. 401

**Source 6.55** Mrs Barnett, *Canon Barnett*, 1919, Vol. II, p. 230, quoted in R. D. H. Seaman, *The Liberals and the Welfare State* (Edward Arnold, 1968), p. 38

**Source 6.56** *Norwich Mercury*, 23 December 1904

**Source 6.57** A speech made by Winston Churchill in the House of Commons, 19 May 1909, quoted in W. H. Court, *British Economic History, 1870–1914* (Cambridge University Press, 1966), pp. 410–12

**Source 6.58** W. Beveridge, *Unemployment: A Problem of Industry*, 1909, pp. 208–9, quoted in D. Fraser, *The Evolution of the British Welfare State* (Macmillan, 1973), pp. 257–8

**Source 6.59** W. Beveridge, *Unemployment: A Problem of Industry*, 1909, pp. 229–30, quoted in D. Fraser, *The Evolution of the British Welfare State* (Macmillan, 1973), p. 259

**Source 6.60** *Law Reports*, 1909, quoted in R. D. H. Seaman, *The Liberals and the Welfare State* (Edward Arnold, 1968), pp. 42–3

**Source 6.61** Part II of the National Insurance Act, 1911, quoted in W. H. Court, *British Economic History, 1870–1914* (Cambridge University Press, 1966), pp. 413–14

**Source 6.62** *Hansard*, 5th Series, Vol. 25, quoted in P. Lane, *Documents on British Economic and Social History, Book Two, 1870–1939* (Macmillan, 1968), p. 74

**Source 6.63** *British Medical Journal*, 1911, I, 1134 (13 May) and 1197 (20 May), quoted in R. D. H. Seaman, *The Liberals and the Welfare State* (Edward Arnold, 1968), p. 53

**Source 6.64** W. J. Braithwaite, *Lloyd George's Ambulance Wagon: the Memoirs of William J. Braithwaite* (Methuen, 1957), pp. 141–2

**Source 6.65** Lloyd George's 'Ambulance Wagon' speech at Birmingham, *The Times*, 12 June 1911, quoted in D. Fraser, *The Evolution of the British Welfare State* (Macmillan, 1973), pp. 256–7

**Source 6.66** Statement by six Labour Party members, *The Times*, 7 December 1911

**Source 6.67** A diary entry for 1 December 1912, Beatrice Webb, *Beatrice Webb's Diaries, 1912–1914* (Longman & Green, 1952)

**Source 6.68** Sir James Barr, President of the British Medical Association, 'Some Reasons why the Public should Oppose the Insurance Act', in *British Medical Journal*, 30 December 1911

**Source 6.69** Report of a parliamentary debate on the Workmen's Compensation for Accidents and Industrial Diseases Bill, *The Times*, 13 December 1906

**Source 6.70** Trade Boards Act, 1909, *Law Reports*, 1909, quoted in R. D. H. Seaman, *The Liberals and the Welfare State* (Edward Arnold, 1968), p. 49

**Source 6.71** Report of a parliamentary debate on the Eight Hours Bill, *The Times*, 7 July 1908

**Source 6.72** *Law Reports*, 1913, quoted in R. D. H. Seaman, *The Liberals and the Welfare State* (Edward Arnold, 1968), p. 47

**Source 6.73** Reduction of pauperism, for England and Wales compared with London, 1915–19, from Ministry of Health statistics, *Parliamentary Papers*, (230), XLII, 1919, II, quoted in M. E. Rose, *The English Poor Law, 1780–1930* (David & Charles, 1971), p. 287

**Source 6.74** R. C. Birch, *The Shaping of the Welfare State* (Longman, 1974), p. 32

**Source 6.75** D. Fraser, *The Evolution of the British Welfare State* (Macmillan, 1973), pp. 162–3, reproduced with permission of Palgrave

## CHAPTER 7

**Source 7.1** G. B. A. M. Finlayson, *England in the 1830s, Decade of Reform* (Edward Arnold, 1969), pp. 90–1, reprinted by permission of the publisher

**Source 7.2** D. Reed, *Chartism in Manchester*, quoted in A. Briggs (ed.), *Chartist Studies* (Macmillan, 1959), p. 31

**Source 7.3** *Manchester Times*, 9 July 1842, quoted in A. Briggs (ed.), *Chartist Studies* (Macmillan, 1959), p. 53

**Source 7.4** Percentage of workers unemployed in Bolton in 1842, from E. J. Hobsbawm, 'The British Standard of Living, 1790–1850', *Economic History Review*, compiled from H. Ashworth, 'Statistics of the present depression of trade in Bolton', *Journal of the Statistical Society*, Vol. 5, 1842, p. 74, quoted in M. Willis, *Nineteenth Century Britain, 1815–1914* (Blackwell, 1990), p. 17

**Source 7.5** *Northern Star*, 29 September 1838, quoted in E. Royle, *Chartism*, Seminar Studies in History (Longman, 1980), p. 89

**Source 7.6** F. Peel, *The Rising of the Luddites, Chartists and Plugdrawers* (Heckmondwike, 2nd edn, 1888), p. 328

**Source 7.7** A petition from Birmingham, 1837, quoted in G. D. H. Cole and A. W. Filson, *British Working Class Movements, Selected Documents, 1789–1875* (Macmillan, 1951), pp. 349–50

**Source 7.8** F. C. Mather (ed.), *Chartism and Society: an Anthology of Documents* (Batsford, 1980), pp. 46–7

**Source 7.9** William Lovett, *Life and Struggles of William Lovett* (Trübner, 1876), pp. 94–5

**Source 7.10** James 'Bronterre' O'Brien's *National Reformer*, 7 January 1837, quoted in R. Brown and C. Daniels, *Documents and Debates: The Chartists* (Macmillan, 1984), p. 27

**Source 7.11** William Lovett, *The Life and Struggles of William Lovett* (Trübner, 1876), pp. 161–2, 208, 238–41, 294–7

**Source 7.12** R. C. Gammage, *History of the Chartist Movement 1837–1854*, (Frank Cass, 2nd edn, 1894), pp. 17–18

**Source 7.13** E. Royle, *Chartism*, Seminar Studies in History (Longman, 1980), pp. 56–61, reprinted by permission of Pearson Education Limited

**Source 7.14** F. C. Mather, *Chartism* (Historical Association, 1965), pp. 10–13

**Source 7.15** Address of the Female Political Union of Newcastle-upon-Tyne to their Fellow-countrywomen, *Northern Star*, 9 February 1839, quoted in E. Royle, *Chartism*, Seminar Studies in History (Longman, 1980), pp. 107–8

**Source 7.16** F. C. Mather, *Chartism* (Historical Association, 1965), pp. 10–13

**Source 7.17** Strength of support for the 1842 National Petition in Lancashire and Cheshire, from *Northern Star*, 23 April 1842, quoted in A. Briggs (ed.), *Chartist Studies* (Macmillan, 1959), p. 52

**Source 7.18** *Hansard*, 1839, quoted in John Wroughton, *Documents on British Political History, 2, 1815–1914* (Macmillan, 1971), p. 32

**Source 7.19** *Parliamentary Representation*, Oxford University Press, p. 22, quoted in N. Tonge and M. Quincey, *British Social and Economic History, 1800–1900* (Macmillan, 1980), p. 26

**Source 7.20** *Northern Star*, 2 May 1840, quoted in A. Briggs (ed.), *Chartist Studies* (Macmillan, 1959), p. 80

**Source 7.21** R. C. Gammage, *History of the Chartist Movement, 1837–1854*, 1854 (Merlin edn, 1969), quoted in J. Stevenson, *Popular Disturbances in England 1700–1870* (Longman, 1979), p. 256

**Source 7.22** The *Operative*, 10 February 1839, quoted in J. Stevenson, *Popular Disturbances in England 1700–1870* (Longman, 1979), pp. 255–6

**Source 7.23** *A Physical Force Chartist Arming For The Fight*, a cartoon from *Punch Volume 15*, 1848

**Source 7.24** Robert Lowery, *Passages in the Life of a Temperance Lecturer*, 1837, quoted in B. Harrison and P. Hollis (eds), *Robert Lowery: Radical and Chartist* (1979), p. 124

**Source 7.25** Weekly sales of the *Northern Star*, 1838–50, based on statistics from H. Martin, *Britain in the Nineteenth Century* (Thomas Nelson, 1996), p. 163

**Source 7.26** Letter from General C. J. Napier to Colonel W. Napier, 3 June 1839, *Life and Opinions of General Sir Charles James Napier*, Vol. II (John Murray, 1857), p. 39

**Source 7.27** William Lovett, *Life and Struggles of William Lovett* (Trübner, 1876), pp. 221–3

**Source 7.28** *Annual Register*, 1839, p. 305, quoted in E. Royle, *Chartism*, Seminar Studies in History (Longman, 1980), p. 94

**Source 7.29** *Bolton Chronicle*, 17 August 1839, quoted in R. Brown and C. Daniels, *Documents and Debates: The Chartists* (Macmillan, 1984), pp. 57–8

**Source 7.30** *Observer*, 18 August 1839, quoted in M. Miliband, *The Observer of the Nineteenth Century* (Observer)

**Source 7.31** *Observer*, 26 August 1839, quoted in M. Miliband, *The Observer of the Nineteenth Century* (Observer)

**Source 7.32** *Report from J. Phillips*, 12 March 1839, quoted in P. Hollis, *Class Conflict in Nineteenth-Century England 1815–1850* (Routledge & Kegan Paul, 1973)

**Source 7.33** *Annual Register*, 1840 (Appendix to the Chronicle, Law Cases, pp. 215–16), quoted in E. Royle, *Chartism*, Seminar Studies in History (Longman, 1980), pp. 96–7

**Source 7.34** 'Reformator', *Charter*, 17 November 1839, quoted in P. Hollis (ed.), *Class and Conflict in Nineteenth Century England 1815–1850* (Routledge & Kegan Paul, 1973), pp. 243–4

**Source 7.35** A letter from the Home Office, 5 November 1839, to the Mayor of Newport, Monmouthshire, Public Record Office, HO 41/15, quoted in E. Royle, *Chartism*, Seminar Studies in History (Longman, 1980), p. 97

**Source 7.36** Eyewitness account of events in Newport by Barnabas Brough, quoted in P. Hollis, *Class Conflict in Nineteenth-Century England 1815–1850* (Routledge & Kegan Paul, 1973)

**Source 7.37** Thomas Dunning, *Reminiscences*, 1894, quoted in D. Vincent, *Testaments of Radicalism; Memoirs of Working Class Politicians 1790–1885* (Europa, 1977), pp. 136–8

**Source 7.38** Lt Colonel Pringle Taylor, *Letters Relative to the Chartists, 1839–1840* (Sunday, 11 January 1840), p. 24, Bodleian Library, Oxford 2288 c. 53

**Source 7.39** Article in *The Times*, 3 May 1842, quoted in R. Brown and C. Daniels, *Documents and Debates: The Chartists* (Macmillan, 1984), p. 70

**Source 7.40** Thomas Cooper, *Life of Thomas Cooper, written by himself* (Hodder & Stoughton, 1873), pp. 190–211

**Source 7.41** John Mayhall, *Annals of Leeds, York and the Surrounding District*, 1865, p. 143, quoted in Schools Council History 13–16 Project – *Britain 1815–1851* (Holmes McDougall, 1977), p. 32

**Source 7.42** *Illustrated London News*, August 1842, quoted in R. Brown and C. Daniels, *Documents and Debates: The Chartists* (Macmillan, 1984), p. 70

**Source 7.43** Total committals for riotous offences, 1838–48, from *Parliamentary Papers, 1850*, pp. 134–5, quoted in J. Stevenson, *Popular Disturbances in England 1700–1870* (Longman, 1979), p. 352

**Source 7.44** Letter from Lord John Russell to Queen Victoria, 2 p.m., 10 April 1848, quoted in A. C. Benson and Viscount Esher (eds), *The Letters of Queen Victoria*, Vol. II, 1908, pp. 168–9

**Source 7.45** *The Chartist procession according to the signatures of the Petition*, a cartoon and its accompanying text from *Punch Volume 14*, April 1848

**Source 7.46** Benjamin Wilson, *The Struggles of an Old Chartist*, 1887, quoted in D. Vincent (ed.), *Testaments of Radicalism: Memoirs of Working Class Radicals* (Europa, 1977), pp. 206, 209–10

**Source 7.47** Committals and convictions for indictable offences of riot, 1835–45, from G. R. Porter, *The Progress of the Nation* (John Murray, 1847), pp. 54–8

**Source 7.48** Committals for indictable riotous offences, 1837–49, as a percentage of all committals from *Parliamentary Papers, 1835–70*, quoted in J. Stevenson, *Popular Disturbances in England 1700–1870* (Longman, 1979), p. 295

**Source 7.49** Committals for seditious offences in 1848, from *Parliamentary Papers, 44 (1849)*, p. 56, quoted in J. Stevenson, *Popular Disturbances in England 1700–1870* (Longman, 1979), p. 353

**Source 7.50** Leicester Chartist John Mason to the All Saints Open Chartists in 1840, quoted in Thomas Cooper, *Life of Thomas Cooper, written by himself* (Hodder & Stoughton, 1873), pp. 136–7

**Source 7.51** *Manchester Guardian*, 21 December 1839, quoted in A. Briggs (ed.), *Chartist Studies* (Macmillan, 1959), p. 36

**Source 7.52** *Anti-Bread-Tax Circular*, 21 April 1841, quoted in A. Briggs (ed.), *Chartist Studies* (Macmillan, 1959), p. 36

**Source 7.53** Charles Pelham Villiers' letter to J. B. Smith, President of the Manchester Chamber of Commerce, quoted in A. Briggs (ed.), *Chartist Studies* (Macmillan, 1959), p. 348

**Source 7.54** A letter from Edward Watkin to Richard Cobden, *Cobden Papers*, quoted in N. McCord, *The Anti-Corn Law League, 1838–1846* (Unwin University Books, 1958), p. 102

**Source 7.55** Samuel Smiles, *Autobiography*, p. 111, quoted in N. McCord, *The Anti-Corn Law League, 1838–1846* (Unwin University Books, 1958), p. 103

**Source 7.56** Speech of Richard Cobden to the Anti-Corn-Law League, reported in the *Anti-Bread-Tax Circular*, 8 September 1842, quoted in A. Briggs (ed.), *Chartist Studies* (Macmillan, 1959), p. 367

**Source 7.57** *Manchester Guardian*, 17 December 1845, quoted in A. Briggs (ed.), *Chartist Studies* (Macmillan, 1959), p. 59

**Source 7.58** A letter from G. J. Harney to Friedrich Engels, 30 March 1846, *The Harney Papers* (Van Gorcum, 1969), quoted in E. Royle, *Chartism*, Seminar Studies in History (Longman, 1980), pp. 115–16

**Source 7.59** Ramsden Balmforth, *Some Social and Political Pioneers of the Nineteenth Century*, London, 1900, pp. 187, 189, 196, quoted in E. Royle, *Chartism*, Seminar Series in History (Longman, 1980), pp. 124–5

**Source 7.60** D. Jones, *Chartism and the Chartists* (Allen Lane, 1975)

**Source 7.61** N. Gash, *Aristocracy and People* (Harvard University Press, 1979), reprinted by permission of the publisher

**Source 7.62** E. Evans, 'Chartism Revisited', *History Review Journal*, 1999

**CHAPTER 8**

**Source 8.1**   J. Kitteringham, *Country Girls in Nineteenth Century England*, History Workshop Pamphlets, No. 11, 1973

**Source 8.2**   Petition to the Law Amendment Society, 1856, drawn up by Barbara Leigh Smith, Mrs Jameson and Mrs Howitt, quoted in J. Perkin, *Women and Marriage in Nineteenth Century England* (Routledge, 1989), p. 294

**Source 8.3**   George Sturt, *Change in the Village*, 1912, quoted in N. Philip, *Victorian Village Life* (Albion Press, 1973), p. 62

**Source 8.4**   J. R. Gillis, *For Better, For Worse: British Marriages 1600 to the Present* (Oxford University Press, 1985), p. 126

**Source 8.5**   Rev. A. Mearns, *The Bitter Cry of Outcast London*, 1883, quoted in R. Fletcher, *The Family and Marriage in Britain* (Penguin, 1966), p. 104

**Source 8.6**   Jane Austen, *Pride and Prejudice*, 1813

**Source 8.7**   Isabella Beeton, *Beeton's Book of Household Management*, 1861, quoted in P. Bartley, *The Changing Role of Women, 1815–1914* (Hodder & Stoughton, 1996), pp. 18–19

**Source 8.8**   Miss B. L. Hutchins, *The Working Life of Women*, 1911, Fabian Tract, No. 157, quoted in P. Hollis, *Woman in Public – The Women's Movement 1850–1900* (Allen & Unwin, 1979)

**Source 8.9**   Professor Graveson, *Family Law, 1857–1957*, quoted in R. Fletcher, *The Family and Marriage in Britain* (Penguin, 1966), p. 94

**Source 8.10**   R. Fletcher, *The Family and Marriage in Britain* (Penguin, 1966), p. 95

**Source 8.11**   Lord Chancellor Cranworth's speech in the House of Lords, 1857, *Hansard*, Vol. 145, 495, quoted in J. Perkin, *Women and Marriage in Nineteenth Century England* (Routledge, 1989), p. 24

**Source 8.12**   *The Englishwoman's Journal*, August 1858, quoted in J. Perkin, *Women and Marriage in Nineteenth Century England* (Routledge, 1989), p. 302

**Source 8.13**   Petition to the Law Amendment Society, 1856, drawn up by Barbara Leigh Smith, Mrs Jameson and Mrs Howitt, quoted in J. Perkin, *Women and Marriage in Nineteenth Century England* (Routledge, 1989), p. 294

**Source 8.14**   N. Philip, *Victorian Village Life* (Albion Press, 1973), p. 70

**Source 8.15**   Charlotte Brontë to a friend, Elizabeth Gaskell, *The Life of Charlotte Brontë*, 1857 (Penguin edn, 1985), p. 208

**Source 8.16**   Francis Place, handbill address *To the Married of both Sexes in Genteel Life*, quoted in J. Perkin, *Women and Marriage in Nineteenth Century England* (Routledge, 1989), p. 284

**Source 8.17**   P. Bartley, *The Changing Role of Women, 1815–1914* (Hodder & Stoughton, 1996), pp. 15–17

**Source 8.18**   Number of divorces, 1765–1857, from J. Perkin, *Women and Marriage in Nineteenth Century England* (Routledge, 1989), p. 303

**Source 8.19**   J. R. Gillis, *For Better, For Worse: British Marriages 1600 to the Present* (Oxford University Press, 1985), p. 213

**Source 8.20**   Mona Caird, *The Morality of Marriage*, 1897, quoted in J. Perkin, *Women and Marriage in Nineteenth Century England* (Routledge, 1989), p. 225

**Source 8.21**   Proportion of the female population married by age, 1871–1911, from N. Tranter, *Population since the Industrial Revolution* (Croom Helm, 1973), p. 102

**Source 8.22**   Number of children (live births) per thousand women first married in a) 1870–79 and b) 1900–09, from *Papers of the Royal Commission on Population*, Vol. VI, table 2, quoted in R. Fletcher, *The Family and Marriage in Britain* (Penguin, 1966), p. 114

**Source 8.23**   Lord Gorell, President of the Probate, Divorce and Admiralty Division, in the divorce case of *Dodd v. Dodd*, 1906, quoted in J. Perkin, *Women and Marriage in Nineteenth Century England* (Routledge, 1989), p. 307

**Source 8.24**   Women and girls at work, 1851–81, from Charles Booth, *Journal of the Royal Historical Society*, xlix, 1886, pp. 321, quoted in G. Best, *Mid-Victorian Britain 1851–1875* (Fontana, 1979), p. 119

**Source 8.25**   Main occupations of females of all ages in Great Britain, 1851–1911, from A. John (ed.), *Unequal Opportunities: Women's Employment in England, 1800–1918* (Basil Blackwell, 1985), p. 37

**Source 8.26**   Work opportunities for women in 1911, compiled by author on basis of 1911 census data

**Source 8.27**   Miss Whyte of the London Bookbinders, quoted in E. Roberts, *Women's Work 1840–1940* (Macmillan, 1988), p. 25

**Source 8.28**   Average earnings of women as a percentage of male earnings, 1906, from J. Lewis, *Women in England 1870–1950: Sexual Divisions and Social Change* (Indiana University Press, 1984), p. 16

**Source 8.29**   Annual report of the Manchester and Salford Women's Trade Union Council, 1903, quoted in J. Liddington and J. Norris, *One Hand Tied Behind Us* (Virago, 1978), p. 36

**Source 8.30**   Frances Ashwell's speech on 'Conditions of Women's Wages in Manchester', given to the Women's Trade Union Council, reported in the *Monthly Herald*, July 1897, and quoted in J. Liddington and J. Norris, *One Hand Tied Behind Us* (Virago, 1978), p. 36

**Source 8.31**   *Needle Money, Pin Money*, cartoons from *Punch*, 15 July 1849

**Source 8.32**   A speech by Lord Shaftesbury in the House of Commons, 1844, on the Ten Hours Bill, quoted in E. Roberts, *Women's Work 1840–1940* (Macmillan, 1988), p. 13

**Source 8.33**   Extract from the male potters' petition, 1845, quoted in E. Roberts, *Women's Work 1840–1940* (Macmillan, 1988), p. 13

**Source 8.34**   Henry Broadhurst, in an address to the Trades Union Congress, 1877, quoted in M. Ramelson, *The Petticoat Rebellion* (Lawrence & Wishart, 1967), p. 103

**Source 8.35**   Extract from Clementina Black's speech to the Trades Union Congress, 1887, reported in *Women's Suffrage Journal*, November 1887, quoted in J. Liddington and J. Norris, *One Hand Tied Behind Us* (Virago, 1978), p. 37

**Source 8.36**   Domestic servants of all ages, 1851–1911, from E. Roberts, *Women's Work 1840–1940* (Macmillan, 1988), p. 31

**Source 8.37**   J. D. Milne, *The Industrial and Social Position of Women*, 1857, quoted in P. Hollis, *Class and Conflict in the Nineteenth Century* (Routledge & Kegan Paul, 1973)

**Source 8.38**   L. Stanley (ed.), *The Diaries of Hannah Cullwick* (Methuen, 1871)

**Source 8.39**   Emma Paterson, *The Women's Union Journal*, 1879, quoted in P. Hollis, *Women in Public, The Women's Movement 1850–1900* (Allen & Unwin, 1979)

**Source 8.40**   Percentages of unmarried and married women in full-time work in 1911, from E. Roberts, *Women's Work 1840–1940* (Macmillan, 1988), p. 45

**Source 8.41**   E. Roberts, *Women's Work 1840–1940* (Macmillan, 1988), p. 44

**Source 8.42**   Mrs Creighton, *The Nineteenth Century*, 1889

**Source 8.43**   Ellen Key, *The Woman Movement*, trans. M. B. Borthwick, 1912

**Source 8.44**   List of reasons why women should have the vote, produced by the NUWSS, Museum of London, Suffragette collection

**Source 8.45**   Christabel Pankhurst, *The Great Scourge and How to Fight It*, quoted in S. Jeffreys, *The Sexuality Debates* (Routledge & Kegan Paul, 1987), p. 318

**Source 8.46**   Millicent Fawcett, *Home and Politics*, quoted in M. Pugh, 'Votes for Women in Britain 1867–1928', *New Appreciations in History* (Historical Association, 1994), p. 9

**Source 8.47**   *Polling Booth Companions in Disgrace*, Artists' Suffrage League, Museum of London

**Source 8.48**   E. Roper, 'The Cotton Trade Unions and the enfranchisement of women', in the report of the executive committee of the North of England Society for Women's Suffrage, Manchester, 1902, pp. 13–14, quoted in A. Rosen, *Rise Up, Women* (Gregg Revivals, 1974), p. 26

**Source 8.49**   Mrs Pankhurst, 'The Importance of the Vote', a speech given at Portman Rooms, 24 March 1908, quoted in M. Willis, *Nineteenth Century Britain, 1815–1914* (Blackwell Education, 1990), p. 11

**Source 8.50**   J. Lewis, *Before the Vote was Won* (Routledge & Kegan Paul, 1987), p. 409

**Source 8.51**   P. Bartley, *Votes for Women 1860–1928* (Hodder & Stoughton, 1998), p. 24

**Source 8.52**   Article by Sir Almroth Wright, *The Times*, 28 March 1912

**Source 8.53**   *A Suffragette's Home*, National League for Opposing Woman Suffrage, 1912

**Source 8.54**   Emmeline Pankhurst at Bow Street Magistrates' Court, 21 October 1908, quoted in M. Mackenzie, *Shoulder to Shoulder* (Alfred A. Knopf, 1975), p. 91

**Source 8.55**   Report of an outbreak of suffragette militancy, *Daily Mail*, March 1909

**Source 8.56**   'Outrage in Southampton' (date unknown), local newspaper article, Hampshire Record Office

**Source 8.57**   Speech by Emmeline Pankhurst at the Albert Hall in October 1912, quoted in P. Bartley, *Votes for Women 1860–1928* (Hodder & Stoughton, 1998), p. 57

**Source 8.58**   Viscount Ullswater, *A Speaker's Commentaries* (Edward Arnold, 1925)

**Source 8.59**   Letters from Edward VII to Home Secretary Herbert Gladstone, quoted in M. Mackenzie, *Shoulder to Shoulder* (Alfred A. Knopf, 1975), p. 130

**Source 8.60**   Report in the *Daily News*, 29 September 1909, quoted in M. Mackenzie, *Shoulder to Shoulder* (Alfred A. Knopf, 1975), p. 131

**Source 8.61**   Keir Hardie's letter to the *Daily News*, 29 September 1909, quoted in M. Mackenzie, *Shoulder to Shoulder* (Alfred A. Knopf, 1975), p. 130

**Source 8.62**   WSPU poster *The Modern Inquisition – Treatment of Political Prisoners under a Liberal Government*, Museum of London

**Source 8.63**   Lady Constance Lytton, 1909, quoted in M. Mackenzie, *Shoulder to Shoulder* (Alfred A. Knopf, 1975), p. 97

**Source 8.64**   Christabel Pankhurst's letter to the editor of *The Times*, June 1908, quoted in M. Mackenzie, *Shoulder to Shoulder* (Alfred A. Knopf, 1975), p. 77

**Source 8.65**   D. Marquand, *Ramsey MacDonald* (Jonathan Cape, 1977), p. 148

**Source 8.66**   *Daily Graphic*, 18 October 1912, quoted in E. Evans, *The Birth of Modern Britain 1780–1914* (Longman, 1997), p. 277

**Source 8.67**   Failed suffrage bills under the Liberal government, 1906–13, P. Bartley, *Votes for Women 1860–1928* (Hodder & Stoughton, 1998), p. 72

**Source 8.68**   House of Commons votes on women's suffrage bills, 1897–1917, from M. Pugh, 'Votes for Women in Britain 1867–1928', *New Appreciations in History* (Historical Association, 1994), p. 23

## CHAPTER 9

**Source 9.1**   Male and female literacy by occupation in England, 1700–70, from M. Sanderson, *Education, Economic Change and Society in England 1780–1870* (Macmillan, 1983), p. 11

**Source 9.2**   Regional movement in literacy levels between 1754–62 and 1831–37, from M. Sanderson, *Education, Economic Change and Society in England 1780–1870* (Macmillan, 1983), p. 17

**Source 9.3**   R. S. Scofield, 'Dimensions of Literacy 1750–1850', in *Explorations in Economic History*, Vol. 10, No. 4, 1973, quoted in M. Sanderson, *Education, Economic Change and Society in England 1780–1870* (Macmillan, 1983), p. 18

**Source 9.4**   J. J. Wright, *The Sunday School: Its Origin and Growth*, 1900

**Source 9.5**   Hannah More's letters to the Bishop of Bath and Wells and to William Wilberforce, 1801, quoted in V. Brendon, *The Age of Reform 1820–1850* (Hodder & Stoughton, 1994), p. 63

**Source 9.6**   Sunday school attendance in the large manufacturing and seaport towns, 1837–38, *Report of the Select Committee on the Education of the Poorer Classes, Parliamentary Papers, 1837–38/VII*, quoted in G. M. Young and W. D. Handcock (eds), *English Historical Documents, XII (I), 1833–1874* (Eyre & Spottiswoode, 1956), p. 849

**Source 9.7**   Reports by the Statistical Societies of Manchester, 1834, and Birmingham, 1838, quoted in M. Sturt, *The Education of the People* (Routledge & Kegan Paul, 1967), p. 38

**Source 9.8**   Report on the state of education in Manchester, 1834, quoted in J. M. Goldstrom, *Elementary Education 1780–1900* (David & Charles)

**Source 9.9**   A charity sermon announcement for the school at St Anne's, Westminster, 20 December 1840, quoted in K. Dawson and P. Wall, *Society and Industry in the Nineteenth Century*, Vol. 4: *Education* (Oxford University Press, 1969), pp. 5–6

**Source 9.10**   Letter from Lord John Russell to Lord Lansdowne, Whitehall, 4 February 1839, *Parliamentary Papers, 1839/XLI*, pp. 255–7, quoted in M. Young and W. D. Handcock (eds), *English Historical Documents, XII (I), 1833–1874* (Eyre & Spottiswoode, 1956), p. 853

**Source 9.11**   Joseph Lancaster's *Improvements in Education*, 1803, quoted in K. Dawson and P. Wall, *Society and Industry in the Nineteenth Century*, Vol. 4: *Education* (Oxford University Press, 1969), pp. 7–8

**Source 9.12**   *Manual of Teaching*, British and Foreign School Society, 1821, quoted in K. Dawson and P. Wall, *Society and Industry in the Nineteenth Century*, Vol. 4: *Education* (Oxford University Press, 1969), p. 9

**Source 9.13**   Letter by Frederick Wade in the *National Society Monthly Paper*, 1851, quoted in V. Brendon, *The Age of Reform 1820–1850* (Hodder & Stoughton, 1994), p. 66

**Source 9.14**   Progress of the National Schools, run by the National Society, 1813–30, from William Cotton on the work of the National Society, *Parliamentary Papers, 1834/LX*, pp. 1876–8, quoted in M. Young and W. D. Handcock (eds), *English Historical Documents, XII (I), 1833–1874* (Eyre & Spottiswoode, 1956), p. 846

**Source 9.15**   Joseph Lawson, *Progress in Pudsey*, 1887, quoted in P. Lane, *Documents on British Economic and Social History, 1750–1870* (Macmillan, 1968), p. 120

**Source 9.16**   Debate on Samuel Whitbread's Parochial Schools Bill, *Hansard*, July/August 1807, quoted in M. Sturt, *The Education of the People* (Routledge & Kegan Paul, 1967), p. 5

**Source 9.17**   *Report of the Select Committee on the Education of the Lower Orders*, 3 June 1818, quoted in K. Dawson and P. Wall, *Society and Industry in the Nineteenth Century*, Vol. 4: *Education* (Oxford University Press, 1969), pp. 11–12

**Source 9.18**   *Manual of Teaching*, 1821, quoted in N. Tonge and M. Quincey, *British Social and Economic History, 1800–1900* (Macmillan, 1980), p. 67

**Source 9.19**   House of Commons Debate on Roebuck's Education Bill, *Hansard*, August 1833, quoted in A. Aspinall and E. A. Smith, *English Historical Documents* (Eyre & Spottiswoode)

**Source 9.20**   William Cobbett, *Political Register*, 21 September 1833, quoted in N. Tonge and M. Quincey, *British Social and Economic History, 1800–1900* (Macmillan, 1980), p. 68

**Source 9.21**   Evidence of the Lord Chancellor, Lord Brougham and Vaux, to the Parliamentary Committee on the State of Education, 1834, quoted in N. Tonge and M. Quincey, *British Social and Economic History, 1800–1900* (Macmillan, 1980), p. 69

**Source 9.22**  Daily school attendance in the large manufacturing and seaport towns, 1834–38, from *Report of the Select Committee on the Education of the Poorer Classes, Parliamentary Papers, 1837–38/VII*, pp. vii–ix, quoted in G. M. Young and W. D. Handcock (eds), *English Historical Documents, XII (I), 1833–1874* (Eyre & Spottiswoode, 1956), pp. 848–9

**Source 9.23**  Amounts allocated by the government to education, 1833–70, from M. Sanderson, *Education, Economic Change and Society in England 1780–1870* (Macmillan, 1983), p. 21

**Source 9.24**  Letter from Lord John Russell, the Whig politician, to Lord Lansdowne, *Parliamentary Papers, 1839/XLI*, pp. 255–7, quoted in G. M. Young and W. D. Handcock (eds), *English Historical Documents, XII (I), 1833–1874* (Eyre & Spottiswoode, 1956), pp. 851–4

**Source 9.25**  Instructions to inspectors, Minutes of the Committee of Council for Education, Whitehall, August 1840, quoted in G. M. Young and W. D. Handcock (eds), *English Historical Documents, XII (I), 1833–1874* (Eyre & Spottiswoode, 1956), pp. 856–8

**Source 9.26**  Adapted from a speech by Sir James Graham, Home Secretary, in Peel's government, in the House of Commons, February 1843, quoted in G. M. Young and W. D. Handcock (eds), *English Historical Documents, XII (I) 1833–1874* (Eyre & Spottiswoode, 1956), pp. 859–63

**Source 9.27**  Adapted from the Minutes of the Wesleyan Conference, Sheffield, on Sir James Graham's education proposals, 26 July 1843, quoted in G. M. Young and W. D. Handcock (eds), *English Historical Documents, XII (I) 1833–1874* (Eyre & Spottiswoode, 1956), pp. 363–4

**Source 9.28**  *Who shall educate? Or, Our babes in the wood*, a cartoon from *Punch*, 23 April 1853

**Source 9.29**  Speech by Robert Montague, the Conservative MP, on education, in the House of Commons, *Hansard*, 1870, Series 3, Vol. 199: 1981, quoted in Michael Willis, *Nineteenth Century Britain, 1815–1914* (Blackwell Education, )

**Source 9.30**  Evidence of Rev. James Fraser, Assistant Commissioner and later bishop of Manchester, to the Newcastle Commission on Education, 1861, *Parliamentary Papers, 1861/XXI*, quoted in G. Sutherland, 'Elementary Education in the Nineteenth Century' (Historical Association, 1971), p. 24

**Source 9.31**  Newcastle Report on Popular Education, *Parliamentary Papers, XXI*, pp. 293–328, quoted in G. M. Young and W. D. Handcock (eds), *English Historical Documents, XII (I) 1833–1874* (Eyre & Spottiswoode, 1956), pp. 891–7

**Source 9.32**  Growth in average number of years of schooling for children, from M. Sanderson, *Education, Economic Change and Society in England 1780–1870* (Macmillan, 1983), p. 18

**Source 9.33**  Rise in male literacy rates by social and occupational class, 1839–69, from D. Vincent, *Literacy and Popular Culture in England 1750–1914*, quoted in M. Sanderson, *Education, Economic Change and Society in England 1780–1870* (Macmillan, 1983), p. 19

**Source 9.34**  Lord Granville's speech in the House of Lords, 1862, *Hansard, 3/CLXV/172–176*, quoted in G. M. Young and W. D. Handcock (eds), *English Historical Documents, XII (I) 1833–1874* (Eyre & Spottiswoode, 1956), p. 897

**Source 9.35**  Robert Lowe's speech during a debate in the House of Commons, 13 February 1862, quoted in E. Evans, *The Birth of Modern Britain 1780–1914* (Longman, 1997), p. 145

**Source 9.36**  Matthew Arnold's Inspector's Report, 1867, quoted in K. Dawson and P. Wall, *Society and Industry in the Nineteenth Century*, Vol. 4: *Education* (Oxford University Press, 1969), p. 26

**Source 9.37**  Joseph Ashby of Tysoe, quoted in G. Sutherland, 'Elementary Education in the Nineteenth Century' (Historical Association, 1971), p. 41

**Source 9.38**  Provision of education for children aged six to twelve by 1868, from statistics compiled by the author

**Source 9.39**  Adapted from W. E. Forster's speech, 17 February 1870, *Hansard, 3/cxcix/440–466*, quoted in G. M. Young and W. D. Handcock (eds), *English Historical Documents, XII (I) 1833–1874* (Eyre & Spottiswoode, 1956), pp. 911–15

**Source 9.40**  *Statutes of the Realm*, 33 & 34 Victoria, c. 75, quoted in P. Lane, *Documents on British Economic and Social History, 1750–1870* (Macmillan, 1968), p. 126

**Source 9.41**  Rise in literacy levels, 1841–96, from *Registrar General's Census Returns*, quoted in M. Sanderson, *Education, Economic Change and Society in England 1780–1870* (Macmillan, 1983), p. 19

**Source 9.42**  Cabinet Memorandum by Lord Sandon, Vice-President of the Committee of Council on Education in 1875, Public Record Office, Carnavon Mss., 30/6/72, pp. 151–65, quoted in G. Sutherland, 'Elementary Education in the Nineteenth Century' (Historical Association, 1971), p. 35

**Source 9.43**  *Obstructives*, an etching from *Punch*, 2 July 1870

**Source 9.44**  Number of children in state-aided elementary schools, 1868–79, from statistics compiled by the author

**Source 9.45**  Relative efficiency of voluntary and board schools in 1890, adapted from *National Education Association Broadsheet*, 1890, quoted in K. Dawson and P. Wall, *Society and Industry in the Nineteenth Century*, Vol. 4: *Education* (Oxford University Press, 1969), p. 33

**Source 9.46**  Costs of teacher training, 1833–70, from statistics compiled by the author

**Source 9.47**  Speech by A. J. Balfour introducing the Education Bill, 1902, quoted in N. Tonge and M. Quincey, *British Social and Economic History, 1800–1900* (Macmillan, 1980), p. 74

**Source 9.48**  *Elementary Code*, 1904, quoted in N. Tonge and M. Quincey, *British Social and Economic History, 1800–1900* (Macmillan, 1980), p. 75

**Source 9.49**  *Regulations for Secondary Schools*, 1904, quoted in N. Tonge and M. Quincey, *British Social and Economic History, 1800–1900* (Macmillan, 1980), p. 75

# Index